Dictionary of Worldwide Gestures

Second Edition

Betty J. Bäuml and Franz H. Bäuml

The Scarecrow Press, Inc.
Lanham, Md., & London

SCARECROW PRESS, INC.

Published in the United States of America
by Scarecrow Press, Inc.
4720 Boston Way
Lanham, Maryland 20706

4 Pleydell Gardens, Folkestone
Kent CT20 2DN, England

British Cataloguing-in-Publication Information Available

Library of Congress Cataloging-in-Publication Data

Bäuml, Betty J.
    Dictionary of worldwide gestures / by Betty J. Bäuml and Franz H.
Bäuml.—2nd ed.
        p.   cm.
    Includes bibliographical references and index.
    ISBN 0-8108-3189-9 (cloth : alk. paper)
        1. Gestures—Dictionaries.   2. Nonverbal communication
(Psychology)—Dictionaries.   I. Bäuml, Franz. H.   II. Title
PN4165.P37   1997
302.2′22—dc20   96-17616
                                                       CIP

ISBN 0-8108-3189-9 (cloth : alk. paper)

♾ ™ The paper used in this publication meets the minimum requirements of
American National Standard for Information Sciences—Permanence of Paper
for Printed Library Materials, ANSI Z39.48–1984.
Manufactured in the United States of America.

IN MEMORY OF
Walter Zeidner
and
Rose Zeidner

Contents

Illustrations

Acknowledgments

For their advice and help with the various aspects of producing this second edition of our dictionary, we are deeply grateful to many more friends and colleagues than we can mention here. We want to express our particular gratitude, however, to the Netherlands Institute for Advanced Study for a Fellowship in 1991–92, which enabled us to complete a large part of the preliminary work in the undisturbed peace of Wassenaar, and to its director at the time, Professor Dr. Dirk van de Kaa. We also want to express our thanks to Dr. Barbara Bopp, Professor Egbert Bakker (University of Montréal), Professor Dr. René J. Devisch (Catholic University, Leuven), Dr. Dorette Egilsson, Professor Dr. W. P. Gerritsen (University of Utrecht), Dr. G. M. Gidley (University of Exeter), Marijke Jalink (Amsterdam), Dr. J. Joosse (Diocesaan Pastoraal Centrum, Rotterdam), Professor Bruce Kapferer (University College, London), Professor Judith L. Kapferer (Flinders University, Adelaide), Dr. Saskia C. Kersenboom (University of Amsterdam), Professor Dr. Lars Olof Larsson (University of Kiel), Dr. Marco Mostert (University of Amsterdam), Professor Dunbar H. Ogden (University of California, Berkeley), Professor David Charles Rubin (Duke University), Professor Dr. Bernard F. Scholz (University of Groningen), Professor D. A. Wells (Queen's University, Belfast). Our special gratitude is due Professor Dr. Ursula Schaefer (Humboldt University, Berlin) for lending a hand, and to the late Professor Archer Taylor (University of California, Berkeley), who urged us to undertake this task in the first place.

We also thank the Los Angeles County Museum of Art for permission to reproduce the Bodhisattva Padmapani, Gift of Henry and Ruth Trubner in honor of the museum's twenty-fifth anniversary and to honor Dr. Pratapaditya Pal; and to the Rijksmuseum Meermanno-Westreenianum, The Hague, for permission to reproduce the miniatures of the marriage of Tobias and Sara (*La Bible Hystorians ou Les Hystoires Escolastres*), of Lamech ridiculed (*Speculum humanae salvationis*), of a blessing gesture used as a pointer (*Collectio canonum*), and of Iniquity gesturing behind her back (St. Augustine, *La Cité de Dieu*). All translations are ours.

Introduction

"Is any text on human affairs so closely read as the faces of the men and women around us? The vocabulary is unmistakable: The pursed lips of distaste, the widened eyes of fear, the wrinkled nose of disgust. To live without the ability to read such facial expressions is to be illiterate in an almost universal, unspoken language of emotion."[1]

Humans act and speak in very specific ways indicated by position or by movement of the body. This presence—or absence—of such positions and movements are semantically equivalent in that both have meaning. Just as a black image on a white page is inseparable from the image of the white page surrounding the black image, an utterance is inseparable from the attitude of the speaker's body at the time it is uttered. If observed, that attitude affects the meaning of what is said. Standing at attention with hands at one's side, eyes straight ahead, and body motionless, is clearly as meaningful as the wildest gesture. To the perceiver a person sitting in a chair, relaxed, with eyes closed, may appear to be dead, asleep, merely resting, or not wanting to be disturbed. Only if dead or asleep could we say that the person is not gesturing—and even then we would be wrong, for the body's position would inevitably tell us something.

Gestures: What Are They?

A gesture does not necessarily require movement, nor must gesturing be a conscious act. How conscious is a shrug of the shoulders accompanying the words "I don't know," a smile while shaking hands with a friend, or the avoidance of eye contact with a stranger? And, for the same reason, a gesture need not be intentional. It follows, therefore, that any distinction between gestures and "body language," between "spontaneous" and "non-spontaneous" gestures, is bound to be artificial: both may be conscious or unconscious, intentional or unintentional, static or moving, and both are potentially meaningful.

Gestures accompany everything we say. A gesture does not always accompany an utterance, nor must we direct it to a perceiver. However,

1

to have meaning, it must be perceived. At whom is one frowning when one speaks on the telephone? At whom is one smiling as one watches the antics of a dog a hundred yards away? The fact that one performs potentially "meaningful" bodily movements in the absence of a perceiver—movements identical to those a perceiver witnesses—illustrates the unity of speech and gesture. Meaning, however, is a social product; a message that is not "received," i.e., seen, heard, imagined, remembered, thought, or dreamt about as meaningful, even in the sense that it means "nothing," cannot have a meaning. This does not mean that the message is not sent; it merely means that the message, under such circumstances, has no meaning. For its very existence, meaning thus depends on reception. The speaker's movements while talking on the telephone have no meaning unless someone, anyone at all, perceives and understands them. Smiling at the dog is meaningless unless someone sees it and assigns a meaning to it. Of course, gestures may be received by the gesturers themselves, and if they are, they mean something to them. But when they do, their meaning comes from the gesture-receiver, not the gesture-originator.

It is a common misconception that a gesture's meaning lies in the intention of the gesturer, rather than in the receiver's understanding of the gesture. Intentions are complex, defining them is problematic, and ascertaining them accurately is usually impossible. Besides, though it cannot be denied that gestures are expressive, they are expressive *to someone*, that is, they are communicative, and their recipients accord them meaning—whether "correctly" or "incorrectly." Communication is a social process, and the meanings given to messages are social products. If meanings were always those intended, there would be no misunderstandings.

For our purpose, therefore, what makes a gesture is its reception, its being understood "rightly" or "wrongly" by a receiver other than the gesturer, or the gesturer as "receiver." In short, a gesture is communication through its reception. We therefore define a gesture as *a posture or movement of the body or any of its members, that is understood to be meaningful.*[2]

Living gestures, gestures actually performed, whether they accompany speech or not, are as ephemeral as the spoken word. They are the visible accompaniment of, or substitute for, heard speech or performed action. Being visible, and therefore observable, gestures can serve as symbols, and thus often represented acts to be witnessed before written records became common. Equally important was—and is—their augmentation of heard speech with visual imagery, with movement in three-dimensional space, which not only increases the vividness of speech for the hearer but also makes speech more easily memorable. This is particularly important in cases of socially significant discourses, such as oral epic performances, liturgical rituals, or political speeches. The relationship of living gestures to their pictorial counterparts is roughly comparable to the relationship between the spoken and the written word.

For present purposes it is pointless, and perhaps even counterproductive, to assign the various kinds of gestures to separate categories, and it is difficult, to say the least, to supply these with precise definitions, though the usefulness of descriptive categories for other purposes is undeniable.[3] It suffices here to distinguish gestures from sign language and to exclude sign language from present consideration. Gesture is nongrammatical; sign language is fully grammatical: Aphasiacs retain the ability to gesture, but the ability to sign is lost, just as the ability to speak is lost. Sign language is thus treated as a language on the neurological level, whereas gesturing is not: Aphasiacs cannot use sign language, but they can be taught the Amerindian gestural code.[4] We shall also exclude specialized codes from consideration, even though such codes may owe much to the cultures surrounding them. Ballet pantomime, for instance, has its own vocabulary that has much in common with demotic gestures, and even the traditional sign vocabulary of the South Indian temple dancer is not totally separable from the gestural vocabulary of the ordinary Tamil speaker.[5] The fact that someone has an occupational reason for using a gestural code does not exclude the influence of the culture in which it is used. Nevertheless, such codes must be considered as systems separate from demotic, i.e., culturally dependent, gestures. First of all, they are systems in themselves, not subject to the variables that affect gestures in general. And second, the execution of gestures during dance or ballet is subject to the timing of the dance steps and the choreography, rather than any aspect of the gestural communication itself. In other words, such systems are, at least in part, subject to constraints different from those governing gestures in general.

Gestures are *seen* as having meanings; they are meaning made visible. They therefore play a significant role in preliterate, traditional cultures, where an act must be witnessed to prove that it took place: For example, a sale or donation of land is signified by the former owner handing a stick or a clump of earth to the new owner; a greeting between two warriors meeting to parley is signified by the raised, open right hand to show that it does not hold a weapon; submission is signified by prostration, bowing or kneeling, making aggressive action visibly impossible or impracticable. Moreover, gestures and body language in general were and are important means of teaching and signalling membership in a given social class. They form a large part of what is considered appropriate, courteous, polite, and proper, by a social class in a given culture, and thus visibly distinguish the members of that class from all others. Such gestures, of course, have survived and still form an important part of daily life in highly literate, Western European cultures. For example, a sale of land is documented in writing, but the verbal agreement prior to the deed may be accompanied by a handshake; the open right hand is still raised in friendly greeting; bowing and curt-sying were still common in the early twentieth century even in nonritual contexts; and a man's rising at the entrance of a woman today marks him as being polite, old-fashioned, or sexist. The use of such gestures as visible symbols of an act, enabling that act to be witnessed, depends on their being readily understood. And the fact that they were readily understood led to their use beyond a special context, entering daily life. The context in which they originated is often difficult, if not impossible, to identify, and it is therefore also difficult to distinguish between kinds of gestures based on their origin. It is the multiplicity of their forms and functions and the pattern of their development and diffusion that are significant, and that this dictionary seeks to begin to document.

Gestures and the Production of Meaning

Gesture, like verbal language, is an integral part of culture. And as with verbal language, the fact that gesture is culture-bound does not mean that there are no influences, no overlaps of the gestural vocabulary of one culture into that of another. When words fail, gestures are well known to be an effective means of communication across cultural boundaries. But does our contention of the cultural boundness of ges-tures not contradict the widespread belief in gesture as some sort of *Ursprache*, some kind of primeval means of human expression, or an outlet for some deep-seated psychic forces? To the extent that this in-cludes a belief in inherent meanings of gestures, it does. No movements or positions of the human body *inherently* have a specific meaning, though no doubt iconic gestures, depicting objects or actions by their form and motion, such as the protective flinch,[6] come closest to having such meanings. But even the flinch can have other meanings in other contexts. It was originally a protective movement; its function as a ges-ture is a secondary development. Meaning, being a social phenomenon, emanates from perceivers who receive, i.e., understand, their percep-tions as being meaningful. Patients with Wernicke's aphasia accompany their "semantically empty" speech with much movement that may well have meaning for them, but is as "semantically empty" to an observer as their speech, and therefore fails to communicate.

The meaning of a body movement or position, being determined by the culture in which it is used, may be completely different in different cultures. When a gesture is adopted by another culture, it may or may not change its meaning, i.e., it may come to be used in different verbal or other contexts, or it may simply be added as a new item in the gestural vocabulary of its adoptive culture. Similarly, a gesture may change its meaning, i.e., the context in which it is used, within the same culture over time. Since it has no innate meaning, but instead has perceived (or misperceived) meanings, the meanings that it is understood to have are dependent on the culture within which it is received, or the culture with which its receiver associates it.

Since gestures are an integral part of language, they contribute to its functions, the most important of which is manipulation. Language obviously cannot communicate in the sense of transmitting a message precisely as it was sent. At best it can serve as a dialectic link between sender and receiver: the sender emits certain verbal, syntactic, vocal, gestural, visual, and contextual signals to a receiver, which are partly conditioned by signals already sent by the receiver to the sender. The receiver interprets the signals as they are received and in terms of the receiver's own vocabulary of meanings as well as that suggested by the sender's signals. Meaning is, therefore, *elicited* from the interaction of the signals of both sender and receiver, rather than simply being transmitted from one to the other. In this dialectic transaction, gestures augment the verbal, syntactic, vocal, and contextual components of the message, and thus increase the "sharpness" of its reception. In short, gestures increase the degree of precision with which the message may be interpreted. The partner in a face-to-face conversation has far less liberty in its interpretation than a reader of a written discourse. But in increasing the precision with which a verbal message is received, gestures alter it by removing ambiguities and by adding "meanings": in short, gestures are not auxiliary to speech; they—along with the entire context of the interaction—provide the parameters within which speech is understood, and are therefore themselves creatively involved in shaping the received "meaning." The function of gestures in *creating* meanings, rather than *modifying* the meaning of purely verbal discourse, can easily be observed in comparing a tape-recorded message with the same message and speaker in a face-to-face situation.

The silently read written text is unaccompanied by such a performative context, and even lacks the modulations of a voice in a tape recording. Silent readers, therefore, supply context themselves. They "hear" what they read with their "inner ears," they see what they read about with their "mind's eyes." Since their understanding of what they read is not guided—as, for instance, in the case of a spoken message transmitted face to face—by the tone of voice, speed of delivery, stance, gestures, facial expressions, and the entire visually and audially perceivable environment, they have much greater liberty to interpret what they read. The same applies to a pictorial message: Theodulf, Bishop of Orléans, remarked in the late eighth century that it is easy to mistake a picture of the Virgin with Child for one of Venus and Aeneas, unless the subject is clearly given in writing—and, one may add, even more clearly by those reading the writing aloud to viewers unable to read. A written label or banderol reduces the possible meanings of the image by identifying the figures; a label or banderol read aloud before an audience characterizes them still more, just as the gestures of the figures in the picture characterize them. By thus shaping possible meanings, gestures play a unique part in creating the meaning understood. On occasion, gestures can be so powerful that they turn the meaning of the verbal message into its opposite: witness, for instance, a verbal expression of sincerity accompanied by a wink at a bystander.

Gestures and Power

Since gestures, as we have defined them, must be perceived as meaningful, they can exist only in social relationships, all of which are marked by manifestations of power. If we define power with Max Weber as the imposition of one's own will in a social relationship,[7] it may be a result of action or the successful resistance to the urge to act. Such resistance may be a display of power by not satisfying the expectations of others.

Language is obviously crucial to the imposition and maintenance of power, particularly if it is rich in imagery, both written and pictorial, which can be controlled and monitored far more easily than communication by word of mouth. Both writing and pictures are permeated by gesture in their imagery of the human body, and gesture itself is deeply embedded in the vocabulary of power. Unlike the gestures accompanying speech, the gestural imagery of pictures and written texts is not ephemeral. The ephemeral nature of the spoken word has particularly grave consequences for the gesture accompanying or substituting for speech. Speech may be quoted; and, though in the quotation its tone, speed and rhythm will inevitably differ from the original, the words can be rendered faithfully. The same applies to sign languages: a South Indian temple dancer may "quote" her teacher, and a "speaker" of American Sign Language can quote as easily as anyone else. Gesture, on the other hand, can only be imitated, and every imitation invites caricature.

Since neither words nor gestures have innate meanings, they must be given meanings and the meanings must be given values. These meanings and values are transmitted by convention and by canons of use, behavior, and belief. Occasionally, one can witness the birth of a new meaning and a new value for an old gesture. Benito Mussolini's use of the fascist salute is one example; Winston Churchill's introduction of the "V-for-Victory" sign is another. Both established a canon, a standard of value or behavior that has changed in the course of time: Mussolini's salute became the standard greeting in the fascist state, a sign of one's overt submission to the standards of the fascist party, and it is now a sign of protest by extreme rightist political parties. Churchill's "Victory" sign, a variant of an obscenity in Victorian England, became a symbol of British, and then generally Allied, confidence in eventual victory in World War II, and is now universally used as a sign of confidence in general.

It is by means of canons that power is imposed and maintained.[8] A canon is a norm, ascribing values to objects and actions, for nothing is inherently good or bad, no object or action possesses inherent value, eternal or otherwise. One needs merely to think of the widespread discomfiture at the discovery that a well-known painting by Rembrandt or a violin concerto by Mozart is not by Rembrandt or Mozart at all, to illustrate the lack of innate value of the objects themselves, as well as the effect of our canons on our values. All value depends on other factors, such as the various and variable individual or collective needs, interests, or resources. Canons direct and manage these constantly fluctuating variables, and thus they manage the culture on which they are imposed. By prescribing and regulating meanings and values, they make possible our relationships to reality, to phenomena regarded as existing independently of our volition.[9] At the same time canons provide the security necessary for individuals, singly and collectively, to maneuver their lives through this reality. For by prescribing meanings and values, canons also make reactions to those meanings and values predictable. For the most part, they are institutionalized in schools, churches, laws, and the news media. Such institutions can subvert old values and inject new ones, literally overnight, into the individual and collective processes of assessing needs, interests and resources, and thus establish new canons. Gestures play a significant role in supporting, controlling, and subverting canons. They can be made publicly and *en masse* as signs of support, they can be observed and thus serve as controls, and they can be made silently or encoded, and thus subvert.

Distinctions among functions and meanings of gestures must, therefore, be made not only synchronically but also diachronically. For instance, certain medieval gestures were symbolic actions in a different sense from modern gestures; they carried a sense of interpersonal binding, which has been replaced in postmedieval culture by the institutionalization of human relationships. Thus, a modern use of medieval gestures, such as in a coronation ceremony, is symbolic of its history and signifies stability; its medieval use is symbolic of actual personal and legal relationships. One need only compare the coronation ceremony of Otto I with modern coronations or the importance of a medieval bow as compared to a modern nod to see the difference. Since the reason for the gesture was to render relationships visible, and therefore witness-able, public and memorable, acts of social significance were commonly described in terms of visual imagery, and interpersonal relations in medieval narratives rendered as images of gestures.[10]

Gestures and Literacy

Such changes in the functions of gestures raise the question of whether canons—and therefore the gestures associated with them—operate in literate societies in the same way as in predominantly nonliterate societies. The processes of evaluation, i.e., the weighing, one against the other, of the needs and interests of members of a nonliterate society, are regulated by oral tradition, which passes on culturally essential information from generation to generation. It thus acts as a cultural "encyclopaedia."[11] The canons of that oral tradition dictate what is tradition and, therefore, sacrosanct. The tradition incorporates the canons, and the needs and interests of the members of such a nonliterate culture are steered accordingly. The difference between the operation of canons in nonliterate and literate societies lies not only in their mode of transmission, oral or written, but also in that the oral tradition is self-controlling and the written transmission is not. A tribal chieftain in a nonliterate culture cannot interfere with its oral tradition. The hero of an oral epic cannot become a coward, nor the villain a hero, no matter how well it may suit the chieftain's political ambitions. In fact, doing so probably would never occur to him, because his culture is dependent on the canons transmitted by the oral tradition. In a nonliterate culture, tradition makes the institutions; in a literate culture, institutions make tradition, thus transforming it into convention. Institutions make and unmake conventions through control of written and pictorial matter—documents, the media, literary production—and, thus, they affect canons. This difference is reflected in a partly different function of gestures in nonliterate cultures, on the one hand, and in a literate society, on the other. In a nonliterate culture or subculture, gestures primarily serve as aids to the memory and, insofar as they are symbolic, as a means of public control. In literate cultures gestures accompanying speech are usually seen as lending the spoken message emphasis or precision, whereas symbolic gestures have retained their preliterate functions in ritualized form. For example, in American courts of law, witnesses still raise their right hand when they are sworn in, and diplomats still take care to be witnessed shaking hands with other diplomats.

In a nonliterate culture, the oral tradition must appeal to memory for the stability of its message. Since that message is an essential part of the information required for the continued cohesion of the culture, its appeal to memory is no trivial matter. The oral performance, therefore, makes use of various mnemonic devices: rhythm, often accompaniment by a musical instrument, rhyme or alliteration, stereotypes of style (formulas) and narrative (patterns of action), parataxis (linear narration), and—not least—gesture.

The use of gestures in an oral performance may be variable or invariable. This is not synonymous with canonical and not canonical; a gesture that is variable for a certain performance must still be canonical in order to be acceptable to the audience. The gestures of a South Indian temple dancer are invariable for every segment of a ritual; to depart from the prescribed gesture is to make a mistake. They are as intricate as the movement of the feet. On the other hand, the gestures of the South Slavic *guslar*, the singer of tales, are variable. They do not "belong" to the narrative in the sense in which the gestures of the South Indian temple dancer are part of the "text." The gestures of the *guslar* are part of the singer's "style," they contribute to the difference between a lively performance and one that may excel in other respects. A lively performance is more memorable than a monotonous one; and, whether the *guslar* thinks of the performances as memorable or not, the gestures are mnemonic devices,[12] as were the gestures of medieval oral performers. The ritual gestures of the South Indian temple dancer, however, just as those of the actors in Sri Lankan rites of exorcism, are—at least in part—communications with a world beyond the human.[13] In this respect, the functions of both differ from those of the *guslar*, as well as from the gestures that usually accompany conversation, and from secular symbols for actions or speech in literate societies. Nevertheless, the ritual communication with gods or demons is performed for human consumption, for it is important for humans to remember how to communicate with gods or demons. The gestures in such rituals, therefore, also serve a mnemonic purpose. Likewise, gestures of emphasis serve the memory. An emphatic gesture in conversation—"No!" accompanied by a fist slammed down on a tabletop—impresses a statement upon the mind of the receiver with a force that "No!" alone would lack. In this respect the function of emphatic gestures is similar to that of symbolic gestures, such as the transference of a staff at a change in the ownership of land, so that witnesses might later remember it. Gestures are signifiers in space, and if they accompany speech, they give it a structure in space. As structures in space, they serve a similar purpose as the architectonic devices suggested by the medieval *ars memorativa* for the retention of knowledge in the memory—both organize the memory by providing a spatial scale of significance.

An act, accompanied by a symbolic gesture, may be rendered public and thereby subjected to public control. If an act is merely documented, the evidence for its performance is left to reading, and, if this reading is private, to private, uncontrolled reception. Hence, symbolic gestures continued—and still continue—to accompany the documentation of legal acts long after their fixation in writing had begun. The medieval canon of reading as a public act also served to control the reception of the written word.[14]

Gestures in Pictures

Gestures in pictures raise other issues.[15] A picture can visually represent a gesture, and it can establish a connection between the representation of an act and a concept, and thus create an emblematic gesture. It may be a snapshot of two persons shaking hands in greeting, or it may represent the ambassadors of two nations performing the same gesture and, thus, visually present the concept *alliance*. "Greeting" here is, of course, a concept, but the handshake in the snapshot is not an emblem; it *is* the greeting. The handshake of the ambassadors, on the other hand, *represents*—is a sign for—*alliance*.

Obviously a picture of a gesture functions in a fundamentally different manner from a "living" gesture or a verbal description of a gesture. A "living" gesture is ephemeral: it disappears while it is being executed, just as the spoken word evaporates as it is spoken. It remains in the receiver's mind merely as a memory. A written description or a picture of a gesture is not ephemeral; it remains a description or a picture which, however, remains open to reinterpretation. A pictorial image is not only not ephemeral; it determines the image that the lines, shapes, and flecks of color stimulate in the viewer's mind far more precisely than written or spoken words, despite the fact that a still picture can only suggest, not portray, movement. This power of determining the mental image of the viewer enables pictorial gestures to assume the functions of emblems.

An emblem is a pictorial rendering of a concept. A picture can create an emblematic gesture from any depicted act. A picture of two hands joined in a handshake is an emblem; it means friendship, alliance, or agreement. This is quite distinct from a picture of two persons shaking hands, which may be emblematic in the sense that it may refer to the friendship, alliance, or agreement of these two persons, or to the alliance or agreement of the groups or nations they represent, but it need not be emblematic at all. It may simply *be* a greeting.

We have noted that any movement or bodily configuration may be understood as meaningful by its perceiver. Similarly, as the perceiver of a bodily movement or configuration interprets a visual perception as a gesture, an artist creates such an interpretation in producing a picture, substituting one visual image for another—the picture for the seen action. If the viewer of the picture is to receive these suggested movements and configurations as meaningful, however, they must be isolated from the entire continuum of movement. The viewer must recognize them as units of movement or stance, distinct from all the other perceptions that the brain registers. In short, they must be "foregrounded." This is exactly what a picture does: it isolates an image from an action. It is, therefore, in an even better position than the perceiver of a living gesture to foreground an act and, thus, to make it into a receptacle for meaning.

Living gestures are foregrounded and received as meaningful by their association with similar movements or configurations recognized by the perceiver as meaningful in a given culture. Pictorial images can be foregrounded in many ways. One is simply by putting a frame around the image serving as a gesture and giving it a title. Another is by using perspective, as in the World War I British "Your Country Needs YOU!" recruiting poster featuring Field Marshal Kitchener pointing directly at the viewer.

It is not necessary to perceive pictorial gestures as living gestures at all. Sir Arthur Conan Doyle, in creating Sherlock Holmes, gifted him with the ability to infer a character's occupation from some small characteristic or movement. Such a talent was not as far-fetched in Doyle's time as it would be in ours, when the human body is often less intimately involved in carrying out occupational tasks, therefore rarely incorporating their effects into its movements. Can such bodily movements or characteristics be considered gestures? They are configurations or movements of the body, and they can certainly be understood as meaningful. Because intention or consciousness of their execution is not part of our definition of gesture, they seem to fit our definition. A customary association of the human body with certain activity can thus be expressed by movements perceived as gestures. Exhaustion, resulting from prolonged physical exertion, is commonly expressed and portrayed by a stooping posture, hanging arms, and slightly bent knees; sailors are often represented as walking with a wide gait, as if steadying themselves on a rolling deck. But such configurations of the body are often habits, personal characteristics, or the result of some physical deformity and are expressed at all times. Thus, they may not be understood as gestures. To determine what they are, it is necessary to rely on evidence external to the apparent gesture. Whether they are understood as gestures, and therefore are gestures according to our definition, depends on the receiver's background information.

The difficulty here is compounded by the fact that a picture not only portrays a person who may or may not be gesturing, it might also *create an image* of the person represented. The two are not identical. In a *representation* of a person, as in a portrait, it is the representation that counts, the background being of lesser importance. The *image* of the represented person consists of the entire pictorial environment, including the person interacting with the surroundings. In a sense it is this image as a whole that creates a gesture by foregrounding it.

Examples of gestures generated by images rather than by representations of persons are not difficult to find. Among other things, they are a common part of the symbolism of power. One of the manifestations of power is superiority over one's physical surroundings. It is, therefore, important that this superiority be made visible. One of the finest literary images of this superiority, this power, are three lines of the celebrated short poem *Die Beiden* by Hugo von Hofmannsthal: "Er saß auf einem jungen Pferde, / Und mit nachlässiger Gebärde / Erzwang er, daß es zitternd stand." [He sat upon a young horse / and with an idle gesture / compelled it to stand, trembling.]

The assertion of power is explicit. An idle gesture effects instant obedience and expresses total confidence in absolute superiority. The importance of this gesture as a social and political emblem of power is evident in its countless appearances as a visual image: statues and pictures of kings and generals on horseback, their bodies and countenances relaxed as if in idle conversation while their mounts cavort wildly. Perhaps one of the best—and certainly one of the most extreme—examples is Velazquez's painting of young Prince Balthasar Carlos, majestically astride a galloping mount, although his little feet required padding to fit the stirrups. Again the message is clear: the prince is not subject to such mere natural laws as those of motion or gravity. The horse is ideal for the construction of this gesture of superiority. It is large and powerful, yet it can be rendered obedient—all qualities familiar and easily recognizable as those of a horse. Of course the same effect can be obtained without a horse.

A particularly clear case in point is that of the well-known photograph of Field Marshal von Rundstedt. The picture portrays von Rundstedt in the midst of a rutted field of stubble and mud. His immaculate uniform, highly polished boots—complete with spurs—and gloved hand negligently holding a cigarette constitute a gesture clearly symbolizing the imperviousness of the very model of a modern Prussian general to the physical effects of war. Whether this was von Rundstedt's intention is beside the point, for the meaning of the gesture as it is understood flows from the reception of the photograph, and not from what its subject thought or did at the time the photograph was taken.

Another illustration of the generative force of an image, rather than a representation, of a person as the source of a gesture is the famous photograph of Winston Churchill by Yousuf Karsh. The image of anger, determination, and strength, which receives its poignancy from a knowledge on the part of the receiver of its physical and historical environment, is not the creation of Churchill, but of Karsh. Ernst Gombrich recounts the story:

"We are told by Yousuf Karsh how unwilling he found the busy Prime Minister to pose for this photograph during a visit to Ottawa in December 1941. All he would allow was two minutes as he passed from the chamber of the House to the anteroom. As he approached with a scowl, Karsh snatched the cigar from his mouth and made him really angry. But that expression, which was in reality no more than a reaction to a trivial incident, was perfectly suited to symbolize the leader's defiance of the enemy. It could be generalized into a monument of Churchill's historic role." [16]

We have observed that a picture arrests motion. The motion we "see" is the projection of our own interpretation of experience onto the picture. If, therefore, we recognize a gesture in a picture, we reconstitute it into a pattern that is already familiar to us. If it is foregrounded, it is given significance. There is little interesting about an immaculate general standing in the mud, and a portly prime minister before a paneled wall, having their pictures taken. In each case what arrests our attention is the artist's selection of a single suggestive aspect of movement. The viewer will receive that aspect as meaningful in terms of his or her own experiences and contexts. Gombrich quotes a professional photographer as having observed that "she searches for the expression which implies all others." [17] The expression that implies the others is foregrounded, and the rest is implied by the viewer. The meaning of the cover photograph (*Life*, Feb. 3, 1941) of Goering and Goebbels in conversation is enriched by the viewer's familiarity, not only with Goering's gesture—arms akimbo and his generous abdomen pushed out toward a defensively gesturing Goebbels—but with the aggressive gesture of pushing out the abdomen in general. The foregrounded stance, therefore, is received as meaningful, despite the fact that it was physically impossible for Goering to face anyone without thrusting his abdomen out. Similarly, a movement that in life may not qualify as a gesture, such as a compulsive tic, might be understood by the viewer of a film or a reader of a text as a representation of "instability" or "madness" and thus constitute a gesture. The same holds true for the creation of emblems. A verbal emblem is a gesture constituted by words as an image. It is neither executed by a subject under directly observable circumstances, nor is it a bodily movement or configuration. The receiver interprets it as meaningful according to the words the author has selected and arranged. Its significance is often specified by the text. Of course, words tend to evoke images of movement more easily than do paintings or still photographs. While it is not possible to depict a handshake in a still picture—one can only depict one hand clasping another—it is simple to describe a handshake as, for example, more or less hearty.

We have observed that living gestures define the meaning of spoken discourse. The same applies to the meaning of the gesture itself. In spoken discourse the living gesture is embedded in a richer array of defining contexts than a gesture in a written text or in a picture. A picture cannot depict movement, words cannot depict shape, and neither of them can render speed, vehemence, or contextual sound except through the means of suggestion open to the medium. Consequently, the meaning of a written or pictured gesture will be less precisely graspable than that of a living gesture. But there is an obverse to this view. None of the three types of discourse—live, written, pictorial—are ever completely available to the receiver. That is, the listener, reader, or viewer can never fully understand everything that constitutes the message at one sitting. If it were possible, the second or third reading of a book or viewing of a picture would be identical to the first. Instead, subsequent readings of a book or viewings of a picture rest on the preceding readings and viewings, and each time items overlooked before are fitted into the pattern made by previous receptions. The result is that our interpretation changes as our previous understanding is augmented or displaced.

This has two consequences for the relative power with which live gestures can give precision to meaning. First, one can reread or review a written text or a picture, but one cannot "replay" a live performance of a gesture or spoken discourse except in the memory. Secondly, each rereading or reviewing will yield an augmentation to prior readings or viewings, leading to continuous reinterpretation. The comparatively low degree of precision provided by written or pictorial messages is accompanied by the possibility of a wide range of interpretation. The comparatively high degree of precision of a live message is linked to a narrow range of possibilities for reinterpretation. In this sense the written or pictorial gesture has the possibility of a more exact reception than does observation of the live gesture itself. The limitation of this dictionary to gestures depicted or described elsewhere is therefore not necessarily a disadvantage. It enables the user to interpret and reinterpret a text or picture in the dictionary or in its source.

Using the Dictionary

The entries in this dictionary are limited primarily to noncodified, nonarbitrary, culturally transmitted gestures. The dictionary does not include sign languages, gestures used in narrative dances, military gestures, Vedic mudras, or such fragmentary sign languages as the occupationally determined gestures of truck drivers, railroad workers, or monks, nor is it concerned with autistic gestures. The reason for these exclusions is that, in function as well as in structure, they differ basically from culturally transmitted gestures.

However, the boundaries between culturally transmitted gestures and codified gesture systems or sign languages, as well as autistic gestures, are fluid. There is considerable overlap in which exchanges between them take place. Rather than sacrifice potentially useful information in the interest of methodological consistency, we have often violated this interest and included material related to culturally transmitted gestures. The use of gestures, unlike that of languages, does not offer natural delimitations. No national, linguistic, or chronological boundaries arise from the material itself that can be applied to delimit or classify it. One can, of course, superimpose boundaries on a chosen set of gestures for practical purposes. But whether the limits chosen are chronological, as in the classic work *Die Gebärden der Griechen und Römer* by Carl Sittl, geographical, as in the *Handbook of Gestures: Colombia and the United States* by Robert L. Saitz and Edward J. Cervenka, or a combination of both, as in *La mimica degli antichi investigata nel gestire napoletano* by Andrea de Jorio, patterns of evolution and distribution remain obscured precisely because forms of gestural communication transcend such limits. By choosing to avoid such delimitations, on the other hand, one surrenders any hope for exhaustiveness. This, in any case, is only achievable by diachronic and/or typologically limited studies such as those of Gerhart B. Ladner on the gestures of prayer in papal iconography of the thirteenth and early fourteenth centuries or of Archer Taylor on the Shanghai gesture.

A dictionary comprising every gesture in existence in the past and present is unthinkable. We have limited our collection to descriptions or depictions of gestures in verifiable sources. No gestures of solely our own observation are included, though we have permitted ourselves an occasional editorial comment. If the description of a gesture in this dictionary is not accompanied by the period of its use, it can be assumed to be current in the twentieth century. Where our source does not give the period or location of its use, we have tried to infer it from the context. If this has been impossible, we have had no choice but to leave its ascertainment up to the reader. In any case, the original description, depiction, or context of a gesture can readily be consulted. The designation *North America* refers here to Canada and the United States, since *Central America*, *South America*, and *Latin America* are separate categories.

Because it would be impossible—as well as pointless—to register every recorded occurrence of any given gesture, we proceed typologically in our selection of entries, by listing variants of types, identifying them geographically and chronologically, and indicating the source. It goes without saying that many of these identifications could be increased endlessly: merely because a gesture is identified as ancient Greek does not imply that it is not also common elsewhere and at other times.

The contents of this dictionary may be approached from two directions. The starting point may be the part(s) of the body primarily involved in the execution of a gesture, or it may be the significance of the gesture. The main alphabetical sequence of the dictionary, i.e., the main entries, are the executing parts of the body. Under these entries are subarranged, likewise alphabetically, the significance(s) of the gesture. An Index of Significances refers the reader to all the parts of the body under which the gestures of a given significance are listed. In addition, we supply an index to the countries and peoples identified with the use of the gestures.

A heading combining two or more parts of the body may signify that all designated parts are involved in executing one gesture, that a cluster of gestures is executed by a number of the parts, or that one part of the body executes the gesture and another receives it (e.g., kissing someone's foot). Since it is often a matter of opinion what part of the body is significant in the execution of a gesture, we give duplicate listings in questionable cases. On the whole, we prefer to err on the side of inclusiveness rather than to adhere to an excessively narrow definition of gesture.

Variations in a gesture sometimes include parts of the body not used in the gesture's basic form. In these cases, the gesture is listed under the body parts used to execute its basic form. The occurrence of apparent synonyms is often due to the necessity of listing gestures under the meaning given them in the source rather than risking possible misinterpretation by listing them under a category of our own devising. Similarly, descriptions of gestures are given under the parts of the body with which the gestures are associated in the source. Occasionally these differ from the parts of the body with which the gesture is most familiarly executed.

Notes

1. From a recent report by Robert Lee Hotz on the discovery of the function of the amygdala in discerning certain human social signals, in the *Los Angeles Times,* Dec. 15, 1994, A1, A32.

2. We owe much of our understanding of the functions of gestures to spirited discussions with Professor Bruce Kapferer of University College, London, and, specifically with reference to our definition of gestures, to thoughtful suggestions by Professor M. Gidley of the University of Exeter, at the Netherlands Institute for Advanced Study, Wassenaar.

3. See, for instance, the categorization and definitions used by (1) David McNeill, *Psycholinguistics. A New Approach* (New York: Harper & Row, 1987), 217–236; (2) "Kendon's Continuum" described by A. Kendon, "How gestures can become like words," *Cross-cultural perspectives in nonverbal communica-*

tion, ed. F. Poyatos (Toronto; Lewiston, N.Y.: Hogrefe, 1988), 131–41, and (3) David McNeill, *Hand and Mind* (Chicago: University of Chicago Press, 1992), 37–40.

4. Oliver Sacks, *Seeing Voices* (New York: 1990), pp. 94–95.

5. We are indebted to Professor Saskia Kersenboom of the University of Amsterdam for her presentations at the Netherlands Institute for Advanced Study (1991–92), and for information on the sign language of South Indian temple dancers.

6. See, for instance, the flinch against bullets in a photograph of the execution of Hungarian police during the uprising in 1956. Jonathan Miller, *The Body in Question* (New York: Random House, 1978), 112.

7. Max Weber, *Wirtschaft und Gesellschaft* (Tübingen: J. C. B. Mohr, 1922), 28, para. 16.

8. For a discussion of the formation and functions of canons, see Barbara Hernstein Smith, "Contingencies of Value," in *Canons,* ed. Robert von Hallberg (Chicago: University of Chicago Press, 1984), 5–39. Her essay heavily influenced the following remarks on canons. For a more detailed consideration of the concepts involved, see *Kanon und Zensur,* ed. Aleida and Jan Assmann (Munich: W. Fink, 1987), particularly the editors' introductory essay, 7–27. Also see *Wertwandel und gesellschaftlicher Wandel,* ed. Helmut Klages and Peter Kmieciak (Frankfurt/Main: Campus, 1981).

9. Peter L. Berger and Thomas Luckmann, *The Social Construction of Reality* (New York: Doubleday, 1966), 1.

10. For the function of gestures in the Middle Ages, see above all Jean-Claude Schmitt, *La raison des gestes dans l'Occident médiéval* (Paris: Gallimard, 1990) and Horst Wenzel, *Hören und Sehen. Schrift und Bild. Kultur und Gedächtnis im Mittelalter* (Munich: C. H. Beck, 1995).

11. Eric Havelock, *Preface to Plato* (Cambridge, Mass.: Harvard University Press, 1963), 61–86.

12. An excellent, if brief, description of a performance of a Serb *guslar* is that by John Miles Foley, "The Traditional Oral Audience," in *Balkan Studies* 18 (1977), 145–52. It makes quite clear that such performances, unlike those of South Indian temple dancers, are participative because the audience does not remain passive but reacts as a "group" in the Neumannian sense, i.e., as a "living unit in which all members are connected with one another . . . as in the tribal group, the family, clan, and the primitive folk group, or . . . as in the totem, sect, and the religious group." See Erich Neumann, *The Origins and History of Consciousness,* trans. R. F. C. Hull (1949; reprinted Princeton, N.J.: Princeton UP, 1973), pp. 421–22. There is evidence that the same applies to the reception of oral narrative texts in the Middle Ages and earlier, which is not surprising, since "traditional songs . . . preserve and celebrate the group values of the membership. Songs, like any ritual, are . . . manifestations of collective values." (Foley, 148). These functions of gestures in oral performances and of such performances as a whole are common in societies in which the performance is that of an oral past, whether that society can be described as at present literate or not. See, for instance, the descriptions of Zuni oral performances in Dennis Tedlock, *The Spoken Word and the Work of Interpretation* (Philadelphia: University of Pennsylvania Press, 1983), particularly 159–77.

13. For information on Sri Lankan demonology, we are indebted to Professor Bruce Kapferer of University College, London.

14. See the pictorial evidence presented by Michael Camille, "Seeing and Reading: Some Visual Implications of Medieval Literacy and Illiteracy," *Art History* 8 (1985), 26–49, particularly 40 and plate 12. For the implications of reading aloud for medieval, specifically Old English literature, see particularly Ursula Schaefer, *Vokalität. Altenglische Dichtung swischen Mündlichkeit und Schriftlichkeit* (ScriptOralia 39) (Tübingen: Narr, 1992).

15. See the important essay by E. H. Gombrich, "Ritualized Gesture and Expression in Art," *Philosophical Transactions of the Royal Society of London* 251 (1966), 393–401; republished with augmented notes in E. H. Gombrich, *The Image and the Eye. Further Studies in the Psychology of Pictorial Representation* (Oxford: Phaidon, 1982), 63–77.

16. E. H. Gombrich, "The Mask and the Face: The Perception of Physiognomic Likeness in Life and in Art," E. H. Gombrich, Julian Hochberg, Max Black, *Art, Perception and Reality,* ed. M. Mandelbaum (Baltimore and London: Johns Hopkins University Press, 1972), 1–46.

17. *The Image and the Eye,* 117.

Abbreviations

Aeschyl.	Aeschylus
Altdt. Ged.	*Altdeutsche Gedichte*
Anc.	Ancient
Annals	*Royal Frankish Annals*
Apol. ad Const.	*Athanasius, Apologia ad Imperatorem Constantium*
Apoll. Rhod.	Apollonius Rhodius
BV	*Bremen und Verden. Die Herzogtümer*
Cath. Encycl.	*Catholic Encyclopedia*
cent.	century
Chron.	*Chronicles*
Claudian.	Claudianus
Cor.	*Corinthians*
Coriol.	*Coriolanus*
Cymb.	*Cymbeline*
Dan.	*Daniel*
DAS	H. Wentworth and S. B. Flexner, *Dictionary of American Slang*
Demosth.	Demosthenes
DEP	*Dictionary of English Proverbs*
Deut.	*Deuteronomy*
DRA	*Deutsche Rechtsaltertümer*
DWb	*Deutsches Wörterbuch*
Eds.	Editors
Encycl. Jud.	*Encyclopedia Judaica*
Eph.	*Ephesians*
Epist.	*Epistolae*
Eurip.	Euripides
Eutrop.	*Eutropius*
Ex.	*Exodus*
Ezek.	*Ezekiel*
Freiberg	*Urkundenbuch der Stadt Freiberg*
Galat.	*Galatians*
GdG	*Gestalt des Gottesdienstes.*

Gen.	*Genesis*
HDA	*Handwörterbuch des deutschen Aberglaubens*
HDM	*Handwörterbuch des deutschen Märchens*
HDV	*Handbuch der deutschen Volkskunde*
Herodot.	Herodotus
Hist.	*Historia(e)*
Hist. eccles.	*Historia ecclesiastica*
Hos.	*Hosea*
Inf.	*Inferno*
Is.	*Isaiah*
JAF	*Journal of American Folklore*
Josh.	*Joshua*
Judg.	*Judges*
Jul. Caes.	*Julius Caesar*
KHM	Jakob and Wilhelm Grimm, *Kinder- und Hausmärchen*
L.A. Times	*Los Angeles Times*
Lat. Am.	Latin America
Lev.	*Leviticus*
Lex Baiuvar.	*Lex Baiuvaria*
Love's Lab. Lost	*Love's Labours Lost*
Lucrece	*The Rape of Lucrece*
Mass	*Treasures of the Mass*
Mathéolus	*Les Lamentations de Mathéolus*
Matth.	*Matthew*
MGH	*Monumenta Germaniae Historica*
Much Ado	*Much Ado about Nothing*
N.Y. Times	*The New York Times*
New Yorker	*The New Yorker*
North Am.	*North America*
NQ	*Notes and Queries*
Num.	*Numbers*
ODP	*The Oxford Dictionary of English Proverbs*
OE	Old English
OED	*Oxford English Dictionary*
Oedip.	*Oedipus*
1001 Nights	*A Thousand and One Nights*
orat.	*orationes*
Par.	*Paradiso*
PG	*Patrologia Graeca*
PL	*Patrologia Latina*
Pet.	*Peter*
Prov.	*Proverbs*

Ps.	*Psalms*
Purg.	*Purgatorio*
Quint. Smyrn.	*Quintus Smyrnaeus*
Rhein. Wb.	*Rheinisches Wörterbuch*
Romeo	*Romeo and Juliet*
Sam.	*Samuel*
Sat.	*Saturnalia*
SAV	*Schweizer Archiv für Volkskunde*
Schwäb. Idiotikon	*Versuch eines schwäbischen Idiotikons*
Schwäb. Wb.	*Schwäbisches Wörterbuch*
Shakesp.	Shakespeare
Sidon. Apoll.	Sidonius Apollinaris
Soester Gerichtsordnung	*Westphalen monumenta inedita*
Temp.	*The Tempest*
Terence	Publius Terentius Afer
Tertull.	Tertullian
Tit. Andr.	*Titus Andronicus*
Troilus	*Troilus and Cressida*
Two Gent.	*Two Gentlemen of Verona*
U.S.	United States
VDM	*Vetus disciplina monastica*
Ven. and Ad.	*Venus and Adonis*
Virgil	Publius Vergilius Maro
vit. Apoll.	Philostratus, Flavius. *Vita Apollonii*
WF	*Western Folklore*
Wint. Tale	*A Winter's Tale*
Wolfr. von Eschenb.	Wolfram von Eschenbach
WW II	World War II
ZDR	*Zeitschrift für deutsches Recht*
Zeph.	*Zephaniah*
ZV	*Zeitschrift für Volkskunde*

The Dictionary

ABDOMEN

Anger   Abdomen pushed out toward someone facing one. If adversary is small, he may be pushed with abdomen. *Portugal.* Basto, p. 7. * "Doing the bump." Doris Jeannette, Times Photo, *U.S. L.A. Times*, Apr. 2, 1979, pt. 3, p. 1. See also Hall, *Hidden Dimension*, Fig. 5.

Mockery   Abdomen forcibly drawn in: "Ventre creux!" ("Hollow belly!). *Central Africa.* Hochegger, p. 208.

ABDOMEN, BUTTOCKS

Sexuality   Abdomen and buttocks of woman moved backward and forward. *Central Africa.* Hochegger, p. 194. * [Editors' note: also commonly observable gesture of rock singers in performance. Predominantly male. *U.S.*]

ABDOMEN, CHEST, HAND

Innocence   (protestation of) Chest and abdomen protruded, hands extended forward. Terence, *Andria* 3, 2. Anc. *Rome.* Baden, p. 450.

ABDOMEN, FINGER

Insult   Tips of right forefinger and thumb touch, forming the equivalent of an anal passage or vagina in front of abdomen; other fingers folded into palm. Obscenity. *Lebanon; Syria.* Barakat, no. 48.

ABDOMEN, HAND

Appreciation   Patting abdomen. Schoolchildren. *U.S.* Seton, p. xxiii; Krout, p. 24. * Circular movement of flat hand on abdomen with happy expression—enjoyment of meal. *Netherlands.* Andrea and de Boer, pp. 42–43. *See also* Satisfaction.

Disbelief   Half-closed hand placed in front of abdomen, then turned slightly—that person addressed is a liar. *Saudi Arabia.* Barakat, no. 215.

Eating   Open hand, palm down, strikes sideways against gesticulator's belt or waist. *Argentina.* Kany, p. 89. * Open hand rubbed back and forth across abdomen. *Colombia; U.S.* Saitz and Cervenka, p. 56. * Open hand moved in circular fashion over abdomen, accompanied by

23

dissatisfied expression—gesturer is hungry. *Netherlands.* Andrea and de Boer, p. 43. * Open hand laid motionless on abdomen, accompanied by hunger—mimicry. *Flanders.* Andrea and de Boer, p. 186. *See also* Satisfaction.

Frustration   Open hand, fingers slightly bent, pressed against abdomen. *Spain; Lat. Am.* Green, p. 45.

Greeting   After elaborate exchange of courtesies, parties slap their sides and pat their stomachs. Uvinza. *Tanganyika.* Cameron, I, p. 226. * Stroke abdomen. *Marianas.* Mallery, p. 4.

Hunger   Tips of joined fingers press abdomen. 19th cent. *Palestine.* Bauer, p. 223. * Right palm pressed on abdomen and moved in circle. *Jordan; Lebanon; Libya; Syria; Saudi Arabia.* Barakat, no. 26. Also *Netherlands.* Andrea and de Boer, p. 43. * Both fists held against abdomen; mouth open. Rural *Colombia.* Saitz and Cervenka, p. 57.

Medico-magical   "grasps the hands of the patient, puts them over his stomach and leads him around the fire, calling out the names of helping demonic animals." Tlingit Indians; Alaska, *U.S.* Danzel, p. 34.

Mockery   Both hands, open, forming contours of large stomach in front of abdomen. *Central Africa.* Hochegger, p. 207. * Both hands half open, palms toward stomach, forming folds of fat. Ibid., p. 208.

Pregnancy   Right hand moved in half circle from lower chest to abdomen—certain woman is pregnant. *Lebanon; Jordan; Syria.* Barakat, no. 195.

Respect   Cross hands over stomach in an attitude of suffering as sign of utmost respect. Kirghiz. *Central Asia.* Louis d'Orléans et Bragance, passim.; see also Cascudo, *História,* p. 62.

Satisfaction   Striking abdomen affectionately with open fingers and palm of one hand. *Spain; Lat. Am.* Green, pp. 31–32. *Colombia; U.S.* Saitz and Cervenka, p. 58. * Tapping stomach, which may be protruded, with flat hand—gastronomic pleasure. Usually men or children. *Russia.* Monahan, pp. 116–17. * Flat hand rubs stomach in circular fashion. *Netherlands.* Andrea and de Boer, p. 42. *See also* Eating.

Saturation   Hands tap stomach lightly: "Je suis saturé!" ("I am stuffed"). *Central Africa.* Hochegger, p. 180. *See also* Satisfaction.

Sick   Hands holding stomach—indigestion. Medieval *Europe.* Miniature of The Angel and the Book in Chapter 10 of the *Apocalypse.* Trinity College MS R. 16.e, fol. 10v (13th cent.). Camille, "The Book of Signs," pp. 133–34. * Hands clasped across abdomen—stomachache. Schoolchildren. *U.S.* Seton, p. xxi. * Hands rubbing abdomen, head inclined forward. Children. *Central Africa.* Hochegger, p. 111.

ARM

Adoration   Arms extended horizontally to side (solar ritual gesture). H. Fischer, "Die kosmurgische Symbolik," p. 91. * Arms extended as for embrace (Venus ritual). Ibid. Arms raised (solar ritual gesture). In Bogomil grave, 13th–14th cent. *Yugoslavia*. Ibid., p.95.

Affection Embrace with one arm if gesticulator wore tunic. Anc. *Greece*. Sittl, p. 31. * Embrace with one arm and shake hands simultaneously. Anc. *Greece* and *Rome*. Sittl, p. 32: also among Roman soldiers. Tacitus, *Hist*., 1, 36. Sittl, ibid; also greeting of parents by their sons. Sittl, ibid. * Two-armed embrace. Anc. *Greece* and *Rome*. Sittl, p. 32. Also Medieval *Germany*: *Kudrun*, st. 1251, 1. Also 16th-17th cent. *England*: Shakesp. *Othello* 4.1.139; and often. Also 18th cent. *England*: Smollett, *Peregrine Pickle*, ch. ci, "clasping him in his arms." Also 19th cent. *England*: he "hugged the old lady with filial cordiality." Dickens, *Pickwick*, I, p. 165. When one refers to the other as "brother," 19th cent. *Greece*. Sittl, p. 31, no. 9. "Love is commonly expressed by an embrace." Boggs, *HDM*, col. 320. "After a silence of some minutes, [my father] pressed me close, kissed my cheek, and adding, 'Persevere, my dearest boy, in the right line and you will be an honour to yourself and me,' dismissed me." 18th cent. *England*. Hickey, p. 62.

Amusement Extended and rigid arm raised from position of rest at side of body to approximately level of shoulder; normally raised to side rather than front. Rare among women. Social context: "¡Os encaprichais del primer hombre en la oficina!" ("You fall for the first man in the office!") *Spain*. Green, pp. 55–56.

Anger Arm raised against someone. "For I may never lift an angry arm against his minister." 16th–17th cent. *England*. Shakesp., *Richard III* 2.40. * Accompanying expression of anger, raising arm vertically from neutral position to near touching the head, then dropping it to original position. *Spain; Lat. Am.* Green, p. 74. * "Her already sufficiently inflamed countenance assumed a deeper tinge, and clapping her arms akimbo, she strutted close up to Mordaunt, vociferating in his face, 'Bitch! Bitch indeed! Not half so much of a bitch as your mother. You a lord indeed! Marry come up! a pretty lord" 18th cent. *England*. Hickey, p. 329.

Apotropy Arms crossed as protection against witches. Ca. 1500. *Germany*. Röhrich, *Gebärde-Metapher-Parodie*, p. 29, and woodcut, pl. 25.

Approach Raising the arm and moving it toward oneself in a wave—waving the person to approach. 19th–20th cent. *Germany*. Grimm and Grimm, *KHM*, nos. 181, 182; Boggs, *HDM*, col. 322. * "Spread her arms" 20th cent. *U.S.* Birdwhistell, *Introduction*, p. 30.

Arrogance Folded arms (*plicatisque brachiis*), Ogier, II, pp. 127–29, on the reaction of the Polish deputies to an address delivered by the Swedish envoy to Poland in 1632—deputies regarded envoy as a boor. 17th cent. *Poland*. See also Bogucka, p. 200.

Assistance   Asking for help and defense. Stretch arms out to comrade in battle. Anc. *Greece* and *Rome*. Sittl, p. 148. *See also* ARM, Plea.

Attention   Extended arm—sign of animation and action. During excitement and discussion it is an understood prelude to speech, implying possession of something that ought to be heard. *Asia*. Hastings, *Dictionary*, I, p. 151. Also general desire for attention. College students. *U.S.* McCord, p. 291.

Authority   Extended arm as sign of power. Biblical. *Middle East*. Hastings, *Dictionary*, I, p. 151. * Arm outstretched with hand in motion; the various movements of the fingers express action commanded, e. g., coming, going. Anc. *Rome,* 19th cent. Naples, southern *Italy*. De Jorio, pp. 86–87. * Arm akimbo—self-possession, authority. In pictorially treated narratives and portraits, lower arm and elbow as aggressive space marker between viewer and subject first used by Albrecht Dürer (*Germany*) in 1498 self-portrait. For perception of arm as symbol of aggressiveness, of lower arm and elbow as means of intrusion in 14th cent. *Netherlands*, see Spicer, p. 88. For pictorial sources and commentary, see Spicer, pp. 84–128. *See also* ARM, Strength.

Baby   Hands and arms across front as if holding infant, rocking from side to side. *Colombia*. Saitz and Cervenka, p. 24. * Same gesture with questioning glance—"Am I going to have a baby?" *Netherlands*. Andrea and de Boer, p. 160. * Arms crossed in front of chest, palms open and up. *Central Africa*. Hochegger, p. 23. * Right hand rests in crook of left elbow. *Central Africa*. Ibid.

Blessing   Arms raised and extended. Biblical. *Middle East*. Ohm, p. 265.

Command   One arm stretched out toward someone. Anc. *Rome*; early Christian. Philostratus, *vit. Apoll.* 1, 29 (37); Gregorius of Nazianzus. *orat.* 45, 1; Sittl, p. 51.

Confession   Spreading of arms during baptism. In Coptic ritual neophyte spreads out arms in form of cross after disrobing. Deacon then takes neophyte's right hand, raises it, and neophyte, turning West, renounces devil and, turning east, confesses faith in Christ. Copts, Anc. *Egypt*. Ohm, p. 257.

Congratulation   Embrace. Anc. *Greece*. Sittl, p. 32.

Death   One arm extended palm down and elbow bent in front of speaker, moving sharply from side to side. *Spain*. Green, p. 317. * Both arms extended, palms down, elbows bent in front of speaker, then arms drawn away from one another sharply, accompanying expressions of death, failure, ruin, or disappearance. *Spain; Lat. Am.* Green, p. 86. * Arms raised and thrown backward while body leans backward—death of an animal. *Central Africa*. Hochegger, p. 123.

Decorum   Arm akimbo. 17th and 18th cent. *Western Europe*. Ripa, pp. 123, 167.

Defiance Arms crossed over chest. Medieval *Germany* and *France*. Lommatzsch, p. 94. Also 19th cent. *Corsica*. Merimée, p. 123. * "She put her arms akimbo, as much to say she defied me." 19th cent. *England*. Gaskell, p. 155. *See also* Authority; ARM, BREAST, Defiance; ARM, HAND, Defiance; ARM, HEAD, Defiance; HAND, HIP, Authority; Challenge.

Despair "It boggled the mind. 'It has all been a series of appalling mistakes!' [The German general] raised his arms and let them fall flat-handed onto the desk." 20th cent. *Germany*. Mulisch, p. 52.

Direction " 'If everybody who bought a foreign car in the last ten years had bought a British one instead, there wouldn't be seventeen per cent unemployment in this area.' He made a sweeping gesture with his arm that took in the wilderness of derelict factories beyond the perimeter fence." 20th cent. *England*. Lodge, *Nice Work*, p. 149.

Disbelief Raising arm vertically from neutral position near side of head, then dropping it to original position. Accompanies expressions of incredulity. *Spain; Lat. Am.* Green, p. 75.

Emphasis " 'Sir,' said Mr. Ben Allen . . . working his right arm vehemently up and down, 'you—you ought to be ashamed of yourself.' " 19th cent. *England*. Dickens, *Pickwick*, II, p. 382.

Encouragement One arm stretched out toward someone. Anc. *Greece*. Sittl, p. 51. * "waving violently towards the postilions, denoted that he was encouraging them to increased exertion." 19th cent. *England*. Dickens, *Pickwick*, I, p. 141.

Enthusiasm Spectators or auditors embrace one another. Anc. *Greece* and *Rome*. Sittl, p. 63.

Etiquette "By 1804 it was customary for a lady and gentleman to link arms when walking. Before that time only the lower classes linked arms." 19th cent. *England*. Rockwood, p. 183. * "Then drawing his arm through that of the obsequious Mr. Cushton, Lord Mutanhed walked away." 19th cent. *England*. Dickens, *Pickwick*, II, p. 122.

Expansiveness "She threw out her arms in an expansive gesture, flushed and excited by her own vision. 'We ought to get rid of the security men and the barriers at the gates and let the people in!' " 20th cent. *England*. Lodge, p. 241.

Farewell Embrace. Biblical. *Middle East. Acts* 20: 1. Only among good acquaintances. Anc. *Greece* and *Rome*. Sittl, p. 31. * Embrace repeatedly. 5th cent. *France*. Sidonius Apollin. *Epist.*, 9, 9, 8. Sittl, p. 36.

Fear Forearms raised diagonally. Anc. *Greece*. Sittl, p. 46. * Lowering of the arms. Anc. *Greece*. Sittl, p. 46.

Flattery Embrace. Anc. *Greece*. Sittl, p. 31.

Friendship Arm in arm. "He marcheth with us arm in arm." 16th–17th cent. *England*. Shakesp., II *Henry IV* 1.1.57. "I was one morning

walking arm in arm with him in St. James's Park" 18th cent. *England.*
Hickey, p. 163. "When, as frequently was the case, I have met him
walking arm in arm with the Prince of Wales" ibid., p. 285. " 'I shall
be very happy, I am sure,' said Mr. Pickwick. 'So shall I,' said Mr.
Alfred Jingle, drawing one arm through Mr. Pickwick's, and another
through Mr. Wardle's, as he whispered confidentially in the ear of the
former gentleman." 19th cent. *England.* Dickens, *Pickwick*, I, p. 113.
* "they were drinking auf Bruderschaft [sic], which is performed by
intertwining arms with one's co-drinker." 19th–20th cent. *Germany.*
Nabokov, p. 180. In walking next to someone, placing arm on his back.
Sometimes mutual. Men. *U.S. AP Photo, L.A. Times,* July 10, 1996, A2.
   Gratitude Embrace. Anc. *Rome.* Sittl, p. 31. 13th cent. *Germany.*
Wolfram v. Eschenbach, iv, 199.
   Greeting Embrace. Biblical. *Middle East. Gen.* 29:13; 33:4; 48:10.
When gods receive dead king (later all the dead) to be one of them, they
take him into their arms. Desire to embrace became polite epistolary
formula. Ancient *Egypt.* Dawson, p. 86. Only close acquaintances or
relatives. Anc. *Greece.* Sittl, p. 31. Only masculine, and only with close
friends, sometimes to seal an agreement. *Spain; Lat. Am.* Green, p. 34.
In Lat. Am. it is often accompanied by one or two hearty slaps on back
of other person. Spanish male equals, relatives or close friends meeting
after prolonged absence, approach each other with extended arms, exclaiming "Hombre, ¿cómo estás? ¡Tanto tiempo sin verte, coño!"
(*"Man, how are you? Haven't seen you in ages, [expletive]!"*) If exclamation is simultaneous with embrace, it is emphasized with pats on
shoulder. Form, duration and intensity of embrace depends on age,
class, social distance, length of absence, nature of meeting—casual, arranged, formal, etc. Male friends who are not close may greet with semi-
embrace: handshake while left hand grips or pats shoulder. Intimates or
relatives may kiss on cheeks while embracing. Female embrace more
restrained than male embrace: hands are placed on shoulders, lips brush
cheeks. *Spain.* Driessen, p. 240–41. "Usually Poles are accustomed to
greet each other with embraces, something which is not the practice in
other countries even among relatives and family members. It is in this
superficial manner that they try to show each other their mutual friendly
affection." 17th cent. *Poland.* H. Starowolski in Bystron, II, pp. 166–68.
See also Bogucka, pp. 194–95. Russians often follow handshake with
powerful embrace; Finns do not. *Russia.* Axtell, *Gestures,* p. 24. El Cid
receives his vassal Martín Antolínez with open arms. *Cid,* i. Medieval
Spain. Also medieval *Germany: Passional,* 165; *Altdt. Ged.,* p. 194, 20.
"Then the Duke came towards me, and embraced me with much kindness." 17th cent. *England.* Evelyn, II, p. 2. Fullest form of embrace, the
hug, is not of wide distribution. *England.* C. P. Snow, p. 263; *Tierra del
Fuego.* Roth, p. 169; *Central Asia; Polynesia; Australia* (aborigines).

Dawson, p. 92. * Silent passing of the person greeted; arms lowered to knees as sign of submission. Anc. *Egypt.* Herodot. 2, 80; Pritzwald, p. 26. * Arm raised in greeting to Krishna. Ca. 1590–1600. *Central India*—Malwa, or Rajasthan, and Mewar. ca. 1590–1600. *Karnata ragini; deux courtisans saluant Krishna chasseur.* Miniature. Fondation Custodia, Coll. F. Lugt, Paris.

Innocence (protestation of): Accompanying disclaimer of blame, arms are raised to the side of the speaker, palms up. *Spain; Lat. Am.* Green, p. 84.

Interrogation Arms raised. *Spain; Lat. Am.* Green, pp. 81–82. * In a hopeless situation, the gesture signals "what do we do now?!" *Netherlands.* Andrea and de Boer, p. 184.

Invitation Arms extended slightly forward, towards a buffet: "Help yourselves!" *Netherlands.* Andrea and de Boer, p. 130.

Joy Embrace. Anc. *Greece* and *Rome.* Sittl, p. 32.

Judgment Judge raises both arms vertically to legitimize a piece of recently acquired land. Fischer, "Heilgebärden," p. 343.

Magnitude Lowering slightly bent arm in front of gesticulator, palm down—shortness. *Spain; Lat. Am.* Green, p. 32–33. * Hand raised, palm down to level referred to verbally—tallness. *Spain, Lat. Am.* Green, ibid. * Outstretched arm moved vertically. 19th cent. *Italy.* Manzoni, ch. xviii; Sittl, p. 111. * Arms extended horizontally on both sides—size. Anc. *Greece* and *Rome.* Sittl, p. 111.

Marriage Bride is carried on arms to the church. Medieval. *Lorraine.* Grimm, *DRA,* I, 598. * Bride is lifted thrice. Ibid.

Medico-magical One arm extended forward, the other drawn back, as if aiming an arrow. *China.* Wallnofer and Rottauscher, p. 147, fig. 64; Fischer, "Heilgebärden," fig. 5, 6; Vogt, p. 119, fig. 91. * With one arm extended horizontally to side, the Asclepiad priest puts patient in incubation. Anc. *Greece.* Völgyesi, p. 20, fig 8; Fischer, "Heilgebärden," p. 334, fig. 16. * Right arm extended vertically upward, left arm extended vertically downward. *Nicobar Islands.* Buschan, p. 208; Fischer, "Heilgebärden," fig. 13. * Left arm extended vertically, right arm bent at right angle, lower arm horizontally across body. *China.* Vogt, p. 119, fig. 91; Fischer, "Heilgebärden," fig. 6. 4. * Both arms raised vertically above the head, fingers of one hand folded over, fingers of the other extended. Dogon, *Sudan.* Leuzinger, p. 70, Fig. 6. Also Celts; and *Austria.* Moser, pp. 144, 740, fig. 2; Fischer, "Heilgebärden," p. 336, fig. 14 and p. 336. * Patient stretches arms out to each side to gain the necessary harmony and basis for improvement of condition. Rosenberg, p. 35 ff.; Fischer, "Heilgebärden," p. 337.

Melancholy Crossed arms. 16th–17th cent. *England.* Shakesp. *Jul. Caes.* 2.1.239.

Mockery Arms form a semicircle in front of stomach: "You are a glutton!" *Central Africa*. Hochegger, p. 82. *See also* ABDOMEN, HAND, Eating; ABDOMEN, HAND, Satisfaction.

Mourning Embracing the grave. Anc. *Greece* and *Rome*. Sittl, p. 74. "at the feet of the statue, embraces the stone knees and weeps" Boggs, p. 319.

Negation With verbal expressions of inability, the bent arms are pushed forward, palms facing one another, then suddenly and sharply the arms are raised behind body. Shoulders are shrugged while executing movement. *Spain; Lat. Am.* Green, pp. 85–86.

Oath Arm raised, calling upon God. After Christianization of Roman Empire. *Anc. Rome*. Athanas., *Apol. ad Const.* p. 674; Sittl, p. 145. * Arms crossed over breast. 19th cent. Naples, southern *Italy*. De Jorio, p. 168. Also anc. *Rome*. Ohm, p. 278.

Pacification Apollo pacifies fighting Lapiths and Centaurs with arm outstretched toward them. West gable of temple of Zeus, Olympia. Anc. *Greece*. Fischer, "Heilgebärden," fig. 15.

Plea Embrace. Only children or close relatives. Anc. *Rome*. Sittl, pp. 31–32. Humbly, in bowed position, embraces the person's arm. Claudian., *Eutrop.* 2, 532; see also Sittl, p. 162. * One arm stretched out toward someone. Anc. *Greece* and *Rome*. Sittl, p. 51. * Crossing arms on breast: "Loosening upon my breast the cross formed by my arms in mortal agony." 13th cent. *Italy*. Dante, *Purg.*, v, 126–27. * "He . . . made a desperate attempt to articulate. It was unavailing—he extended his arm towards them, and made another violent effort." 19th cent. *England*. Dickens, *Pickwick*, I, p. 48. * Extending arms to side of gesticulator, palms up. *Spain; Lat. Am.* Green, p. 83. * Both arms extended in front of body, elbows close to side, palms facing one another. *Spain; Lat. Am.* Green, pp. 82–83.

Pointing "The old gentleman untucked his arm from his side, and having pointed to one of the oaken presses, immediately replaced it in its old position." 19th cent. *England*. Dickens, *Pickwick*, I, p. 231. * " 'Let us take this as a hypothetical case,' said the don, waving in the direction of the naked men." Robinson, p. 229. * Right arm uplifted to demonstrate stars in sky, fingers extended. 16th cent. *Germany*. Brant, woodcut, p. 168.

Praise Swinging one or both arms in applause. Anc. *Greece* and *Rome*. Sittl, p. 62.

Prayer Arms raised. Frequently the patron god stands before deity, holding hand of supplicant, both patron god and supplicant raising arm toward deity. *Babylonia*. Heiler, p. 102. * Arms bared. Requirement in hymnal recitation. *Assyria*. Heiler, p. 104. * Raised arm. Anc. *Egypt*. Heiler, p. 102. Arms spread in front. *India, Persia*, anc. *Egypt, Sumer, Babylon, Assyria, Aegean* region, *Etruria*. Ohm, pp. 253–54. On depictions of sacrifice, extended right arm holds sacrificial bowl, while the left is raised. Anc. *Greece*, Sittl, p. 189; Heiler, p. 102. * Embracing the altar. Anc. *Greece?* and *Rome*. Sittl, p. 179. * Arms extended toward heaven or wherever the deity was thought to reside; the more urgent the prayer, the more energetic the gesture. Anc. *Greece* and *Rome*. Sittl, pp. 174–75, 187–88. Early Christian. Duchesne, p. 107. * A fifth-century Byzantine nobleman twists his arms back before an image of the Virgin. *Byzantine Empire*. Euagrius, *Hist. eccles.* 5, 18, 3; Sittl, p. 175. * Greek Orthodox in church cross their arms. 9th cent. Sittl, p. 175. 15th cent. *France. Très Riches Heures*, pl. 73–74. * The old orans-gesture (arms extended) is still the priest's basic attitude for the Collect, the Secret Prayers, the Preface, the Canon, the Pater Noster. In the late Middle Ages, a crucifix-like extension of arms and hands was used for the Unde et Memores oration. *Western Europe*. Ladner, p. 271. *See also* ARM, HAND, Prayer. * In the Western liturgy, in contrast to Eastern liturgies, prostration (proskynesis) has become rare and is executed only by individuals (cleric and assistants at the beginning of the Good Friday liturgy, candidates for consecration, abbots and abbesses at All Saints' litany), never by the congregation. Roman Catholic. *GdG*, p. 33. * Prostration with arms extended. 12th–13th cent. *Germany: Kudrun*, st. 1170, 2; *Rother*, 376; *Rolandslied*, 6895. "In . . . a mosaic [of Moses at the Battle with the Amalekites] in Sta. Maria Maggiore, Moses stands in an orant position with Aaron and Hur on either side. But by the ninth century Aaron and Hur usually support the outstretched arms of their leader, consistent with the biblical text. Such an illustration alludes to the imagery of the Crucifixion, or the salvation of man through Christ, and numerous literary sources cited by Schapiro mention the particular passage in Exodus as evidence of prayer's efficacy in battle, or the salvation of man through Moses. Visual representations of the emperor with two saints in Ottonian manuscripts clearly recall those of Moses and his two companions, suggesting a further symbological tie between the ruler, Moses and Christ. This typological equation of Moses and Christ is replaced in the Romanesque period by an analogous relation between Moses and the priest at the altar. The coupling of the Moses illustration with an illustration of a priest enacting the mass in . . . Oxford, Bodleyan Library, MS 270b suggests that Moses now fore-symbols the priest" Medieval *Europe*. Hindman, p. 790.

Pregnancy Arms extended, forming circle, fingertips of one hand touching those of the other. 17th cent. Naples, southern *Italy*. De Jorio, p. 172.

Pride Arms extended, father lifts infant over his head. *Spain*. Rare in *U.S.* Green p. 92.

Protection "Upon this, the women . . . flung their arms round them to preserve them from danger." 19th cent. *England*. Dickens, *Pickwick*, II, p. 72.

Refusal   Crossing of arms over breast—refusal of a witness to give evidence. Medieval *Germany*. Amira, "Handgebärden," pp. 230–31; also 16th-17th cent. *England*. Shakesp., *Hamlet* 1.5.174: "with arms encumb'red thus"; and W. Müller, p. 17.

Regret   Arms suddenly dropped at the sides. *Central Africa*. Hochegger, p. 165.

Rejection   Outstretched arms crossed in front of speaker at level of waist. *Spain. Lat. Am.* Green, p. 87.

Resignation   Arms raised and dropped sharply at sides of gesticulator. *Spain*. Green p. 88. * "For answer, Francine went to the chair he had previously drawn out for her, and sat down in it with the air of one who folds her arms." *England*. J. D. Carr, "To Wake the Dead," p. 63. * Arms raised to head level, head suddenly cocked to the right: "Que voulez vous? C'est comme ça!" ("What do you want? That's the way it is!) *France*. Brault, p. 380.

Rest   Arms hanging relaxed, hands clasped or crossed. 14th cent. *Germany*. Oechelhäuser, *Die Miniaturen*, I, p. 57. Medieval *France*. Lommatzsch, pp. 33–34.

Satisfaction   Arms raised. 19th cent. *France*. Zola, p. 259.

Series   Arms extended in front of gesticulator, palms down, one hand above the other; may indicate levels. *Spain; Lat. Am.* Green p. 60.

Silence   Arm stretched forward and moved up and down several times as a command to crowds for silence. Executed by a herald, among Romans, except in military camp, where the emperor did not use an intermediary. The use of both hands made the gesture more emphatic. Greeks used their voice. Anc. *Greece* and *Rome*. Sittl, pp. 214–215.

Sincerity   Arms raised to side to level of shoulders, palms up at conclusion. *Spain; Lat. Am.* Green pp. 78–79.

Sorrow   Arms crossed over breast. 16th–17th cent. *England*. Shakesp., *Lucrece* 1.793; *Titus Andronicus* 3.2.7; *Julius Caesar* 2.1.240, etc.

Stop   Arm extended vertically, palm raised and directed towards the person intended to stop. Anc. *Rome*; 19th cent. Naples, southern *Italy*. De Jorio, p. 152.

Strength   Arm stretched out, clenched fist. Anc. *Rome*. Sittl, p.11. * Arm akimbo. 17th–18th cent. *Europe*. Ripa, pp. 123, 167.

Submission   Arms crossed on chest. *Near East*. Ohm, p. 278.

Surprise   Both arms raised. Anc. *Greece* and *Rome*. Sittl, p. 272. Also Mod. *France*. Mitton p. 146.

Surrender   In surrendering a city, the women and children stretch their arms out toward the victors. Anc. *Rome*. Sittl, p. 148. * Letting gesticulating arms sink. 19th cent. *France*. Doré's illustr. to Rabelais' *Gargantua*, Bk. I, ch. xviii (1854); Röhrich, *Gebärde-Metapher-Parodie*, p. 11 and pl. 2. * The soldier stretches out arms to sides. Anc.

Greece and *Rome* Sittl, pp. 114, 147. * A soldier raises both arms above head to show that he carries no weapons. *Universal.* Axtell, *Gestures,* p. 77.

Time Looking at a slightly raised forearm bent at the wrist, as if looking at a watch: "Quelle heure?" ("What's the time?"). *Central Africa.* Hochegger, p. 87.

Understanding Poking someone in the ribs with the elbow— complicity. *Spain; U.S.* Green, p. 44.

Victory Victor in a fight moves arms up and down and crows (in imitation of cockfight). Anc. *Greece.* Demosth. 54, 9. Sittl, p. 114. * Soccer players raise arms after scoring a goal; boxers raise arms when standing over a defeated opponent. *Universal.* Axtell, *Gestures,* p. 77.

Voting *See* HAND, Voting.

Welcome Embrace. 16th–17th cent. *England.* Shakesp., *Henry VIII* 1.4.63.

ARM, BODY

Greeting Exaggerated submissive greeting, arms crossed over chest, bowing many times. "Zumbáia" from Malay "sembahyang"; etymology attributed to Monseignor Rodolfo Dalgado by Cascudo, *História*, p. 221. *Siam.* Also popular usage, *Brazil.* Cascudo, ibid.

ARM, BODY, HAND

Anger Arms extended slightly to the side, hands open, body inclined toward the object of one's anger. *Central Africa.* Hochegger, p. 3.

Death Extending arms sideways, hands open, palm down, while body moves as if collapsing—a dying vehicle. *Central Africa.* Hochegger, p. 123.

Greeting "Zumbáia" (see ARM, BODY, Greeting above). Bows deeply to knee level, placing the right hand on the ground; repeated three times before approaching the lord; once in front of the lord, places head between the lord's hands, symbolically offering it to him—sign of reverence. *Malaysia.* Morais, *Dicionário*, s.v. "zumbáia." *See also* Cascudo, *História*, p. 221.

Lying-in Arms extended sideways, with elbows somewhat bent; hands flat, palm down; body bent forward a little. *Central Africa.* Hochegger, p. 2.

Ride Sitting position, lower arms extended forward, hands form loose fists, palm down, moving slightly backward and forward—riding horseback. *Netherlands.* Andrea and de Boer, p. 61. * Same position, but hands moved in a circular fashion so that when one hand is up, the other is down—bicycling. *Netherlands.* Ibid., p. 62.

ARM, BREAST

Adoration   Arms crossed on breast. 14th cent. *Italy.* Niccolo di Giacomo, "Annunciation." Ambrosiana, Milan; in Formaggio and Basso, p. 23; also 15th cent. *Italy.* "Coronation of the Virgin," *Missale Fratrum Serv. S. Mariae*, Venice, Marciana, ibid., p. 29; 15th cent. *France. Tres Riches Heures*, pl. 40, 59, 65, 102, 128. *See also* Prayer; BREAST, HAND, Humility; BREAST, HAND, Prayer.

Affection   "Lay his wreathed arms athwart his loving bosom." 16th–17th cent. *England.* Shakesp., *Love's Lab. Lost* 4.3.131.

Alarm   Beating shield against chest, calling "To arms, to arms!" Anc. *Rome.* Statius, 7, 133–4; Sittl, p. 215.

Attention   "When people [fold their] arms in front of their chests, most people . . . interpret this as a sign of resistance. However, this is not a universal interpretation. In her Vietnamese childhood, Thanha had been taught that when someone is talking, she must fold her arms against her body and demonstrate complete attention by displaying inactive hands." *Vietnam.* Dresser, *L. A. Times*, May 4, 1996, B15.

Cold   Arms crossed on chest, body slightly inclined forward. *Central Africa.* Hochegger, p. 77.

Defiance   Arms crossed over chest. 14th cent. *Germany.* Oechelhäuser, *Die Miniaturen*, I, p. 15; Lommatzsch, p. 94. *Corsica.* Merimée, p. 123. *See also* ARM, Defiance.

Disagreement   Arms crossed over chest—a defensive posture or an expression of disagreement. *Europe; North America.* Axtell, *Gestures*, p. 78.

Humility   Arms crossed upon the breast so that hands lie on shoulders while executing a deep bow. *Asia.* Ohm, p. 277. *See also* BREAST, HAND, Greeting; BREAST, HAND, Humility.

Oath   Crossing arms over chest: "Cross cross the Bible, never tell a lie. If I do, my mother will die." Children. Aberystwyth, *Wales.* Opie, p. 123. * Arms crossed on breast. Anc. *Rome.* Ohm, p. 278. *See also* ARM, Oath.

Passion   Arms crossed over breast. In Byzantine religious art in the tenth and eleventh centuries and in western religious art since the thirteenth century. *Byzantine Empire.* Ohm, p. 277; Weise and Otto, pp. 28–47.

Plea   Crossing arms on breast: "loosening upon my breast the cross formed by my arms in mortal agony." 13th–14th cent. *Italy.* Dante, *Purg.* v, 126–27.

Prayer   Arms crossed on chest. Anc. *Egypt*; *Rome*; Buddhists; *Philippines* (Aetas); *Bali.* Ohm, p. 277. Christian: Ceiling carving of the Nativity, Haus Supersax, Sitten, *Switzerland* (after 1500); *Netherlands.* Hendrick Bloemaert, "de Bewening van Christus" (1649). Van der Meulen, p. 19. *See also* ARM, HAND, Prayer.

Refusal Arms crossed on chest—refusal to be impressed or to participate. *Netherlands.* Andrea and de Boer, p. 84. *See* ARM, Refusal.

Smugness " 'Thirty thousand, excluding bonuses,' said Basil, his arms folded smugly across his chest." *England.* Lodge, *Nice Work*, p. 181.

Sorrow Arms crossed over breast. 17th–18th cent. *England.* Shakesp., *Lucr.* 793; *Tit. Andr.* 3.2.7; *Jul. Caes.* 2.1.240.

Submission Crossing arms on breast so that right hand rests on left shoulder and left hand on right shoulder. Anc. *Egypt.* Ohm, p. 277.

ARM, CLOTHING
Threat Rolling up one's sleeve. Vulgar. 16th cent. *Portugal.* Cascudo, *História*, p. 77.

ARM, ELBOW
Avarice Fist closed, forearm raised, elbow thrust forward and struck by palm of other hand; or hitting a tabletop with the elbow when seated at a table. Río de la Plata area of *Uruguay* and *Argentina.* Meo Zilio, p. 99.

Encouragement Encouraging someone to speak by punching him or her with the elbow. Anc. *Greece* and *Rome.* Sittl, p. 222. *See* Warning below.

Insult Closed fist with fingernails facing upward, the forearm is raised brusquely against the upper arm, and the elbow is thrust forward: "¡Embrómese!" Río de la Plata area of *Uruguay* and *Argentina.* Meo Zilio, p. 98.

Warning Warning careless speaker to be careful by punching him or her in the side with the elbow. Anc. *Greece.* Sittl, p. 221. *See* Encouragement above.

ARM, EYE
Surprise "His eyes widened and he spread his arms, palms up, to indicate just how shocked he had been, and just how inevitable it had been that he bounce some expense accounts." *U.S.* Martinez, *L.A. Times*, Feb. 6, 1978, p. 1.

ARM, FACE
Prayer Embracing feet of statue and pressing face upon them. Anc. *Rome.* Sittl, p. 179.

ARM, FINGER
Accusation *See* Guilt below.
Assistance Request for a ride (hitchhiking): Forward swing of the forearm, bent at the elbow and held upright or horizontal with thumb

extended. College students. California, *U.S.* McCord, p. 291. [Editors' note: Generally used by hitchhikers, *U.S.*]

Attention   Student requests teacher's attention and permission to speak. Raising arm with index extended. *France.* Biederman, E11. * Raising arm with index and middle finger extended. *Austria.* Gombrich, p. 67.

Denial   Index shaken from side to side, arm extended forward, palm outward. *Europe; North Am.* Aubert, p. 92, fig. 139. *See* FINGER, Negation.

Depart   Right arm extended forward, index of right hand moved back and forth: "Take it away!" *Central Africa.* Hochegger, p. 61.

Enmity   Little finger of one hand grasps that of the other, arms move in sawing motion from side to side. *Jordan; Saudi Arabia.* Barakat, no. 191.

Enthusiasm   *See* ARM, HAND, Enthusiasm.

Greed   "He put out his good arm and rubbed his fingers together to make the ancient sign of greed for money." *U.S.* Schulberg, p. 83. *See* FINGER, Money; FINGER, Pay.

Guilt   Right arm and forefinger extended in accusation. 16th cent. *Germany.* Brant, woodcut, p. 61.

Hesitation   Lower arm raised, fingers half cupped. Anc. *Greece.* Sittl, p. 273.

Medico-magical   Nosebleed stilled by vertically raising the arm on the side of the bleeding nostril, the other arm extends vertically downward, clenched fists with middle fingers extended. Thuringia, *Germany.* Wuttke, p. 347, no. 518; H. Fischer, "Heilgebärden," p. 324.

Mockery   Left arm extended toward another person, fist closed except for extended index. 16th cent. *Germany.* Brant, woodcut, p. 45. *See* FINGER, Mockery.

Money   Forearm raised, palm forward, fingers repeatedly curled one after another or together. *Colombia.* Saitz and Cervenka, p. 88.

Peace   *See* FINGER, Peace.

Pointing   Arm and index extended. *Germany.* Boggs, col. 322; Grimm and Grimm, *KHM*, nos. 96, 182. *Netherlands.* Andrea and de Boer, p. 179. * Right arm raised to point to stars in sky, fingers extended. 16th cent. *Germany.* Brant, woodcut, p. 168. Elbow is bent and the index about the height of the shoulder—destination is close. Arm is lifted higher and fully extended—destination is distant. Almost *universal.* Axtell, *Gestures,* p. 79. * Driver of an automobile stretches left arm out of the window and points right across the roof of the car: "to the curb." *Netherlands.* Andrea and de Boer, p. 180. * Driver raises lower arm so that the hand is visible through the rear window, extends index upward and moves it in an arc forward: "if you're in such a hurry, fly over me!" *Netherlands.* Ibid., p. 182. * Driver extends arm out of the window and, with flat hand moving backward and forward, motions to other cars to pass. *Netherlands.* Ibid., p. 183.

Pride   Thumbs under armpits, other fingers spread wide, chest thrust out—braggart, or expression of pride. *Saudi Arabia; Bahrain.* Barakat, no. 188. Also *U.S.; Colombia.* Saitz and Cervenka, p. 96.

Threat   Right arm raised, fingers extended upward. 16th cent. *Germany.* Brant, woodcut, p. 32. *See* FINGER, Threat.

ARM, FINGER, HAND

Acclamation   Right arms raised, thumb, index and middle finger extended, two last fingers bent so that thumb touches them. Two figures acclaiming the consul Probianus. Early 5th cent. *Rome.* Delbrück, no. 65.

Affirmation   Right hand clenched, index extended, forearm extended horizontally forward, elbow at waist, forearm waved rapidly vertically. *Spain.* Kaulfers, p. 251.

Anger   Arm extended forward, fingers extended, palm up. Anc. *Greece* and *Rome.* Sittl, pp. 288–89. *See* FINGER, Anger.

Approach   Arm extended, palm down, four fingers extended, then repeatedly folded down to touch palm. *Italy; Balkans; Aegean Islands; Turkey; North Africa; Iraq; Iran; India.* G. Müller, p. 99. *See* HAND, Approach.

Astonishment   Left elbow rests on the right forearm and little finger of the left hand touches the mouth. *Central Africa.* Hochegger, p. 66.

Begin   Forearm raised, hand extended and thumb pointing upward. *Spain.* Flachskampf, p. 226. * Forearm raised, thumb and index extended. In postclassical art the middle finger is added. In painting the index is often raised alone. Anc. *Rome.* Sittl, p. 285.

Blessing   Fingers of right hand extended and joined, moving from forehead to chest and from left to right shoulder. Roman Catholic. Ohm, p. 294. *See* HAND, Blessing.

Bring   Forearm level, extended forward, hand brought back toward body, index curving. Great Plains Native Americans, *U.S.* A. L. Kroeber, p. 6.

Command   Arm energetically extended forward, two or three or all fingers extended. Anc. *Greece* and *Rome.* Sittl, p. 288. * Palm of hand outward, lower arm raised, index extended along same axis as arm or at right angle to it. Frequent in early medieval art, and still in the *Sachsenspiegel.* Medieval *Germany.* Amira, "Handgebärden," pp. 212–13.

Depart   Arm extended sideways, index extended—"out!" *Netherlands.* Andrea and de Boer, pp. 30–31.

Direction   Hand and arm extended, index pointing in specific direction. *Europe; U.S.* Ruesch and Kees, p. 77.

Encouragement   Forearm level, thrust forward, hand brought back toward body. Similar to "Bring" above, except emphasis on thrust forward and less motion of the hand. Gt. Plains Native Americans, *U.S.* A. L. Kroeber, p. 6.

Finished Crossing arms at waist level and extending them in an arc, fingers extended, palms down (specifically used by referee at prize fights). California, *U.S.* King, p. 264.

Homosexuality *See* ARM, HAND, Homosexuality.

Mockery Thumb and index extended, other fingers folded into palm, left arm extended toward object of mockery. 16th cent. *Germany.* Brant, woodcut, p. 106.

Money *See* ARM, HAND, Money.

Negation Right hand clenched, index extended, forearm extended horizontally forward, elbow at waist, forearm waved rapidly back and forth horizontally in an arc of 90 degr. *Spain.* Kaulfers, p. 250.

Often Little jumps executed by fingers on lower arm, in the direction upward from the wrist. Gt. Plains Native Americans, *U.S.* A. L. Kroeber, p. 5.

Pointing A bartender raises arm, hand above head and moving in a circle, index pointing diagonally down, to inquire: "The same round again?" *Netherlands.* Andrea and de Boer, p. 148. * Right arm, hand and index extended energetically forward: "Va t'en!" ("Scram!") *Central Africa.* Hochegger, p. 206.

Prayer Arms extended, fingers spread apart. Anc. *Greece.* Sittl, pp. 189–90.

Pride Thumbs placed under or near armpits as if hooked under suspenders, fingers extended and sometimes wiggling: "Well done, wouldn't you say?" *Netherlands.* Andrea and de Boer, p. 25. [Editors' note: also *U.S.*]

Rejection (of a claim or request): Elbow bent, fist closed, thumb extended downward, the arm is raised to shoulder height, signifying the ironic "Yes, sure!" Children often move the arm up and down. *Netherlands.* Andrea and de Boer, pp. 32–33.

Spotted, striped, tattooed Appropriate movements of fingers made on lower arm, three or four times in the direction of the hand. Gt. Plains Native Americans, *U.S.* A. L. Kroeber, p. 5.

ARM, HAND

Accusation Upper arm low, bent at elbow, forearm raised, hand raised, all fingers except little finger extended. 16th cent. *Germany.* Brant, woodcut, p. 240.

Acknowledgment (of applause) Applauded performer extends one arm upwards and outwards, and slowly moves it toward coperformers, turning the extended hand in the same direction, to indicate they are corecipients of the applause. *Netherlands.* Andrea and de Boer, p. 14. [Editors' note: also *U.S.*]

Admiration Arms akimbo, hands at waist. *Central Africa.* Hochegger, p. 3.

Affection Embrace with one arm and simultaneous handshake. Anc. *Greece* and *Rome.* Sittl, p. 32.

Anger Both arms extended toward the offender, fingers extended, palms parallel, hands shaking vigorously at the side of the listener's face. *Spain; Lat. Am.* Green, p. 75. * Arms akimbo, hands at waist. *Central Africa.* Hochegger, p. 3. * Arms lowered and spread slightly to the side, hands open. *Central Africa.* Ibid.

Apology "Spread his arms with his hands held open . . . raised one hand, turning it slightly outward . . . raised his other hand, and turned it palm-side up . . . dropped both hands and held them, palms forward, to the side and away from his thighs." *U.S.* Birdwhistell, *Introduction*, p. 30. * Lower arms raised sideways so that open hands, palm up, are at height of the shoulders. Head may be tilted sideways simultaneously. *Netherlands.* Andrea and de Boer, p. 176.

Apotropy Arms extended forward, crossed at wrists, hands open or as closed fists. Used predominantly after an unwelcome visit, as a curse on someone not to return; originally. the sign of the cross to protect against the return of the visitor. *Netherlands.* Andrea and de Boer, p. 171.

Assistance Hitchhiking Arm and hand extended, palm facing down. Fingers, hand or arm may be moved up and down. *Colombia.* Saitz and Cervenka, p. 130, see note, p. 70.

Astonishment Arms extended upwards, hands open. In religious art in connection with representations of miracles. Medieval, Renaissance, Baroque. *Europe.* Van der Meulen, p. 18. * Arms akimbo, hands on hips. *Central Africa.* Hochegger, p. 66.

Attention Arm extended, hand raised—students' request for teacher's attention. *U.S.* Biederman, E10. *See* ARM, FINGER, Attention.

Authority Arms at side, bent at elbow, hands (fists) resting on hips. Medieval *France.* Lommatzsch, p. 90. Anc. *Rome*; 19th cent. Naples, southern *Italy*; De Jorio, p. 199. *See* ARM, Authority and Defiance; ARM, HEAD, Defiance; HAND, HIP, Authority; Challenge.

Avarice Arm raised to chest height, fist closed: "¡Éste es de la Virgen del Puño!" ("He belongs to the cult of Our Lady of the Closed Fist!") Río de la Plata region of *Argentina* and *Uruguay*; also *Chile.* Meo Zilio, p. 100.

Baby *See* ARM, Baby.

Calm Arms slightly raised, hands at shoulder height, palms outward, and repeatedly and slowly moved slightly downward: "Calm down." *Netherlands.* Andrea and de Boer, p. 125. Same, hands moved slightly back and forth. *Central Africa.* Hochegger, p. 12. Same, fingers spread, arms slowly pulled back; repeated until excitement subsides. *Russia.* Monahan, pp. 92–93.

Climb Forearms extended forward, hands as if holding a rope that they are rapidly moving upward. *Central Africa.* Hochegger, p. 84.

Cold Each hand grasps opposite upper arm, shoulders hunched. *Colombia; U.S.* Saitz and Cervenka, p. 26.

Complication Right arm reaches over head, right hand scratches left ear—to do everything in a complicated manner. *Russia.* Monahan, pp. 56–57.

Consolation (Maternal) Holding tightly or picking up a child. *Universal.* Ruesch and Kees, p. 85.

Copulation Extended forearms and fists are jerked backward and downward toward the body. *Venezuela.* Kany, p. 187.

Corpulence Arms extended forward and slightly to the sides, hands open, palms facing each other and slightly inward, fingers spread. Vulgar. *Russia.* Monahan, pp. 52–53.

Crowd Forearms raised, hands form teardrop shape, fingers extended: sometimes opened and shut several times, sometimes shaken. *Colombia.* Saitz and Cervenka, p. 30.

Curse Arms extended forward at eye level, hands partly open, shaken energetically in the direction of the person rejected: "Darken my door no more." *France.* Greuze, *Malédiction paternelle* (1765), Paris, Louvre; see also Cascudo, *História,* p. 172.

Defense Arms extended forward, palm facing outward. *Brazil.* Cascudo, *História,* p. 94.

Defiance "She put her arms akimbo, as much to say she defied me." 19th cent. *England.* Gaskell, p. 155. * Left arm raised slowly, right hand passed beneath it simultaneously as body turns slightly. *Jordan; Lebanon.* Barakat, no. 63. See ARM, HEAD, Defiance; HAND, HIP, Challenge.

Delicacy Forearm is raised parallel to the ground with hand extended almost touching chest. *Colombia.* Saitz and Cervenka, p. 26.

Depart Forearm horizontal to waist; fingers held together and extended, palm facing away from body; hand moves out sharply to side. *Colombia.* Saitz and Cervenka, p. 80. * Edge of left hand is brought down smartly over the crook of the right elbow: "Let's get the hell out of here—fast." WW II. *France.* Alsop, p. 29. * Right arm extended forward, palm flat, facing left; left arm bent, so that lower arm extends across chest, palm down; elbow of right arm placed on top of left wrist, making a downward chopping motion: "Let's get out of here, quick!" *Netherlands.* Andrea and de Boer, p. 143.

Disagreement Forearm at right angle to upper arm, fist clenched and moved back and forth several times. Impolite. *Colombia.* Saitz and Cervenka, p. 36.

Disbelief Motion of using a shovel to throw bull manure over one's shoulder. Usually humorous. Male. *U.S.* Saitz and Cervenka, p. 42.

Ease Arms behind the back, hands grasped—sign of ease and control because it exposes the front of the body. Axtell, *Gestures*, p. 79. [Editors' note: Walking with arms behind the back, hands grasped: commonly *Europe* rather than *North America*].

Effeminacy Left forearm rests on the supporting open palm of the right hand. *Lat. Am.* Kany, p. 181.

Encouragement "He squeezed Denis's arm encouragingly." *England.* Huxley, ch. 6. * "Mr. Barbecue-Smith patted his arm several times." *England.* Ibid.

Enthusiasm Vigorous vertical movement of forearm, snapping of middle finger against ball of thumb. *Mexico.* Kaulfers, p. 251. * Arms raised above head, hands agitated. *Central Africa.* Hochegger, p. 64.

Etiquette Two maids or two daughters accompanied Greek woman of good society in public. At least one assisted by supporting her arm. Anc. *Greece.* Sittl, p. 161. Women are led or supported by the lower arm. Hellenistic *Greece.* Sittl, p. 280. * Old men of good society, when walking in public, were supported under the arm by one or two sons. Anc. *Greece.* Nonnos, 14, 100; Heliodorus, 7, 8; Sittl, p. 161. * Men of princely rank appeared in public supported at the arm by distinguished men. *Byzantine Empire*, and also the Greek Voyvods of the *Danubian principalities.* Sittl, p. 162. King Ludwig I of Bavaria was supported under the arm at his arrival on Syra. 19th cent. *Greece.* Sittl, p. 162. * Noblemen walked in public supported under the arm by freedmen. Anc. *Rome.* Sittl, ibid.

Farewell Waving hand up and down. *U.S.* Ruesch and Kees, p. 77. *See* HAND, Farewell.

Fear " 'Don't,' said Tess, clutching her arms, and hunching her shoulders. 'I don't like to think of Daddy dying.' " *England.* Lodge, *Paradise News*, p. 316.

Finished Arms crossed in front of body, palms down; then arms move out to the sides, palms still down. May serve as general negation. *Colombia; U.S.* Saitz and Cervenka, p. 137.

Flat Arm lowered, hand horizontal with palm downward, fingers together. *Europe; North America.* Aubert, p. 82, fig. 121.

Friendship Both arms extended full length at level of shoulders, hands open, palms facing each other. *Europe; North America.* Aubert, p. 85.

Goad Forearm extended parallel to ground; fist makes twisting thrust. *Colombia.* Saitz and Cervenka, p. 42.

Greeting Right arm extended forward, hand half open, or waving parallel extended forearms in greeting of Salus, daughter of Aesculapius: the morning greeting. Anc. *Rome.* Cascudo, *História*, p. 51. * "When greeting each other [in the Tudor period], men approached with both arms extended and simultaneously grasped each other above the elbows. In this way, no hands were free to grab a dagger. By the Tudor period, men were grasping hands just above the wrist, but not shaking them." 16th cent. *England.* Rockwood, p. 162. * Raising the hand with the palm outward and the arm bent at the elbow. Hand occasionally waved from right to left, but fingers not waved. Forearm waved if the person is close by; the whole arm if at a distance. College students. California, *U.S.* McCord, p. 291. * Arm raised, open hand waved backward and forward. *Netherlands.* Andrea and de Boer, p. 117. * Male grasps forearm or upper arm of another male, who grasps upper arm or shoulder of the former, sometimes with patting motion. Women usually grasp one another's forearms; more common among urban women. *Colombia.* Saitz and Cervenka, p. 66. * Closed fist, lower arm raised. Communist salute. *Netherlands.* Andrea and de Boer, p. 63. [Editors' note: *Universal*]. * Arms raised over the level of the head, hands open, palms toward the front. *Central Africa.* Hochegger, p. 179. * Right arm extended forward and slightly upward, hand flat, palm down. Fascist and National Socialist salute. "[Franco] appropriated the ancient term *caudillo*, used by the warrior chiefs who had vanquished the Moors and led Spain to national unity. (Führer, Duce, Caudillo—the parallels were obvious.) Arms outflung, the faithful chanted, '*Una Patria, un estado, un caudillo*,' ('One fatherland, one state, one leader') and the name of Franco was bellowed from every throat." 1938–1976. *Spain.* Steiner, p. 118. [Editors' note: National Socialist salute, performed by an individual under ordinary circumstances, normally took the form of right forearm raised from elbow, palm outward. Hitler's palm often extended backward, facing upward, from raised forearm. Arm was fully extended, palm facing downward, on ceremonial occasions].

Homosexuality Forearm raised, hand limp, palm facing away from body; hand held like this for a moment or moved forward. Head usually inclined to the side. Smile. *Colombia; U.S.* Saitz and Cervenka, p. 119. * Left elbow rests in right palm, raised index of left hand touches left cheek, while head is inclined toward the left. *Spain.* Flachskampf, p. 248. Especially Andalusia, *Spain.* Driessen, p. 247.

Impatience Arm raised to head height, closed fist moves downward pulling an imaginary chain: "¡Déjese de embromar!" ("Quit it!") Vulgar. Río de la Plata region of *Argentina; Uruguay.* Meo Zilio, p. 110.

Innocence Arms raised straight above shoulder height, hands open, as if being searched: "¡A mí que me registren!" ("Let them book me!") Río de la Plata region of *Argentina; Uruguay.* Meo Zilio, p. 111.

Insult Arm (usually the right) bent at elbow and jerked upwards, fist clenched, other hand slapped down on the lower part of the upper arm inside the elbow. Forearm represents a thrusting phallus. Predominantly male gesture, but used by females as a symbol of hostility toward either sex; connotes dominance. The French term "bras d'honneur" clearly equates phallic prowess with honor. Rare in northern Europe; common in southern *Europe* and the *Mediterranean Basin*. Morris et al., pp. 80–92. Also *Russia* ("Up yours!"). Monahan, pp. 158–59. * Bend left arm at the elbow with clenched fist as the edge of the right hand hits inside left elbow—"Sleeve cut," [Spanish "cortes de manga"]. "Cortamanga." 19th cent. *Spain*. Borrow, p. 178. "He made 268 'figs' and 497 'sleeve cuts' at him." *Spain*. Foz, p. 97. Bend left forearm vigorously upward with fist clenched or middle finger extended, and thrusting the extended right hand into the inner bend of the left arm—"Manichetto," or "armas de São Francisco" (Portug.). *Lat. Am.* Kany, pp. 174–75. Also Río de la Plata region of *Argentina* and *Uruguay*. Meo Zilio, p. 99. Also *France*. Mitton, p. 151. Also *U.S.* Saitz and Cervenka, p. 114. * For greater emphasis, left hand slaps right shoulder while right arm, bent at elbow, is thrust upward with clenched fist. *North America; South America; Europe*. Axtell, *Gestures*, p. 36. * Arm bent at elbow, fist (knuckles turned outwards) shaken once. Dubrovnik, *Yugoslavia*. Ibid., p. 36. * Right hand grasps middle of raised left forearm, or both hands grasp a knee. Sometimes made by girls: "Your genitals!" *See also* Magnitude, below. *Central Africa*. Hochegger, p. 64. * Left forearm raised and grasped in the middle by the right hand: "Sexe de ton père!" ("Your father's penis!") *Central Africa*. Hochegger, p. 189. * Forearms raised, open hands some distance from the sides of the head: "Grosse tête!" ("Fathead!") *Central Africa*. Hochegger, p. 203. Forearms raised, flat hands at sides of head, fingertips meeting on top: "Petite tête!" ("Pinhead!"). *Central Africa*. Hochegger, p. 203.

Interrogation Arms raised to the side, palms up. *Spain; Lat. Am.* Green, pp. 81–82.

Invitation Right arm extended toward victim, hand held out limply. 16th cent. *Germany*. Brant, woodcut, p. 258.

Joy Arms extended over head and slightly to the side, hands clenched, head thrown back, face upwards. *U.S.* R. Derk L.A. Times Photo, *L.A. Times*, Feb. 19, 1994, C1. *See also* Plea below.

Large Arm raised and bent at elbow, so that lower arm is vertical, hand horizontally extended, palm down, fingers together. *Europe; North America*. Aubert, p. 82, fig. 122.

Leading Women forcefully led by the upper arm. Anc. *Greece*. Benndorf, pl. 27; Sittl, p. 280.

Little Arm lowered, hand in horizontal position with palm downward, fingers together. *Europe; North America*. Aubert, p. 82, fig. 121.

Magnitude   Thickness indicated by the right hand grasping the middle of the left forearm, or both hands grasping a knee, or the right hand grasping the left upper arm, or the index and thumb of one hand measuring the width of the thumb of the other, or both hands grasping the thigh, or both hands placed on the waist. *Central Africa.* Hochegger, pp. 64–65. * Right hand grasps left forearm: "I've lost weight." *Central Africa.* Ibid., p. 107.

Manipulation   (political): Bent arms moved back and forth horizontally, elbows held close to the body, fingers clenched, thumbs over curled indexes: "Es un hombre que sabe conducirse" ("He's an operator"). Madrid, *Spain.* Green, p. 67. * Both hands slightly closed, at chest level, fingers moved back and forth rapidly so as to intertwine slightly: "Era un hombre que sabía manejar elecciones" ("He knew how to manage elections"). Madrid. *Spain.* Green, p. 67.

Mockery   Upper arm forms right angle with lower arm, hand moves at the level of the head, while lower arm turns back and forth several times around its own axis. 19th cent. Naples, southern *Italy.* De Jorio, p. 127 ff.; *Spain.* Flachskampf, p. 235.

Money   Forearm extended, palm up, thumb and index form almost a complete circle, the remaining three fingers clenched upon palm. *Mexico.* Kany, p. 95.

Mourning   Beating arms. Women. Anc. *Rome.* Sittl, p. 26.

Nothing   Stiff left forearm, hand closed, palm of right hand placed on inside of elbow, performed angrily—gesturer has nothing. *Saudi Arabia.* Barakat, no. 233. * Lower arms extended to side at right angles, hands open, palms up: "I didn't have anything." *Central Africa.* Hochegger, p. 28. * Lower arms extended forward from stomach, open hands turned slightly upward. *Central Africa.* Hochegger, p. 28.

Oath   In swearing an oath, the accused, kneeling, embraces the altar. Anc. *Rome.* Tacitus, *Annales,* 16, 31; Sittl, p. 143. * "The Lord swore by his right hand and by the arm of his power." Biblical. *Middle East. Isaiah* 62:8. * Arms raised and spread. Biblical. *Middle East. Daniel* 12:7; Ohm, p. 265. * Right arm moved from level of waist over right shoulder with palm facing up during movement; head tilted backwards and eyes raised as hand moves up. *Libya; Lebanon; Syria.* Barakat, no. 9. * Right arm extended horizontally forward, hand flat. *Brazil.* Cascudo, *História,* pp. 91–92. * Right arm extended diagonally upwards, hand open. Anc. *Greece* and *Rome, Germanic.* Cascudo, *História,* pp. 91–92. * Right arm extended forward, hand extended, palm down. Ceremonial oath of the governor of Chiapas, *Mexico.* CNN, Dec. 8, 1994. [Editors' comment: The rigid separation of church and state in Mexico prohibits the use of religious symbolism in state affairs. The forward-extended hand, however, appears to have survived the gesture of placing the hand on the Bible.]

Obedience Crossing arms on breast. Monks. 19th cent. *Italy.* Manzoni, ch. 19; Sittl, p. 151. Slave awaits the master's command with arms crossed on chest. Athens. Anc. *Greece.* Sittl, ibid.

Passion Arms crossed over breast. Appears in religious art in the tenth and eleventh centuries and in western religious art since the thirteenth century. *Byzantine Empire.* Ohm, p. 277; Weise and Otto, pp. 28–47.

Patience Right forearm extended forward, open hand, palm out, moves gently up and down. *Central Africa.* Hochegger, p. 142.

Pensiveness Head supported in the palm of the right hand, while the left hand holds the right elbow. *Central Africa.* Hochegger, p. 147.

Plea Arms extended forward, palms upward and slightly cupped. Anc. *Egypt.* Cascudo, *História,* p. 94. * "Hear the voice of my supplications . . . when I lift up my hands" Biblical. *Middle East. Ps.* 28:2. * Extending arms to side of gesticulator, palms up. *Spain; Lat. Am.* Green, p. 83. * Both arms extended in front of body, elbows close to side, palms facing one another. *Spain; Lat. Am.* Green, pp. 82–83. * Arms raised parallel, hands sometimes moving. In the bas-relief of the Death of Aegisthus at the hands of Orestes (Glyptotek, Copenhagen), the first figure on the right raises both hands as supplicant. Also Biblical. *Middle East. Levit.* 9:22; *I Kings* 8:54. *Asia Minor.* Cascudo, *História,* p. 208. Joy at sporting events. *Brazil.* Ibid.

Pointing Arm bent at elbow, palm up, forearm moves back and forth in the direction indicated. *Colombia.* Saitz and Cervenka, p. 34. * Arm raised, hand extended, palm to side; hand makes one or more sharp movements back and forth. *Colombia.* Saitz and Cervenka, p. 35. * " 'Let us take this as a hypothetical case,' said the don, waving in the direction of the naked men." *England.* Robinson p. 229. * More polite to use the entire hand in pointing rather than the index. *Japan; China.* Axtell, *Gestures,* p. 79. * Extended arm with extended pointing hand moved overhead, from back to front: "There he goes!" *Netherlands.* Andrea and de Boer, p. 18.

Possession Adopted child is lifted up by adopter's arms and hands. Anc. *Rome.* Sittl, p. 130. For the gesture of taking a child into one's arms to indicate adoption or responsibility for the child. 12th-13th cent. *Germany.* Hartmann's *Gregorius,* 1110, 1135–36, and Gottfried's *Tristan,* 1961; Wells, pp. 171–72.

Prayer Arms raised, hands holding sacrifice or object of prayer. Anc. *Greece.* Sittl, p. 191. * Hands raised, palms upward. Anc. *Rome.* Sittl, p. 174. * Arms outstretched, hands open and bent back at the wrist. Sittl, p. 291. * Spreading of arms and hands upwards. On Petroglyphs in *Morocco*; the *Sahara.* Frobenius, pp. 129, 131; Weinert, p. 190–91; Ohm, p. 252. * Hands and arms extended toward sides. *Byzantine Empire.* Sittl, p. 175, no. 6. * Hands raised three times. The vestal Quinta

Claudia raises her hands three times before prayer. No Greek evidence; anc. *Rome.* Sittl, p. 190. * Pray to the Olympian gods by spreading arms, hands turned back, palms turned outwards toward heaven. Anc. *Greece.* Seemann, p. 41f. * Lift hands while praying to Jupiter. Late *Roman.* Macrobius, *Saturn.*, III, 9, 12. * Kneeling and raising arms toward heaven once forbidden, but now common during the salat and the du'a'. At the du'a' the palms are turned toward the face. Muslim. Ohm, p. 255. * Spreading of arms, raising of arms. Biblical. *Middle East. Ps.* 143:6; 63:5. *Ex.* 9:29; 9:33; Notscher, p. 348; Ohm, p. 256. The "orantes" of early Christian art are invariably depicted in catacomb frescoes with arms extended or raised. *Cath. Encycl.*, VI, pp. 423–27. * Raised arms, but spread somewhat to the side, approximating figure of the Cross. Early Christian (pre 500 A.D.): Eusebius, Tertullian, Minucius Felix, Ambrose; but also later, cf. Kraus, *Realenzyclopädie* I, pp. 538ff.; Sittl, p. 198. Perhaps also medieval *Germany. Liutprandi leges* 23; 12th cent. *Germany. Visio Tnugdali* p. 44, 16; 13th–14th cent. *Italy.* Dante, *Purg.*, vi, 16. Also women. Bavaria. Mabillon, p. 61. Still seen at shrines to which pilgrimages are undertaken. Sittl, p. 198, n. 7 on p. 199. Still practiced by Dominican nuns. Ohm, p. 266, and pl. 18. See also 13th cent. *Germany. Kudrun,* st. 1170, 1. 2; 12th cent. *Germany. Rother* 376. * Crossing of arms and hands over breast. Carthusians during the "Supplices te rogamus" ("We ask you, almighty God") Roman Catholic. Mass. Ohm, pp. 277–278. A modern example is *Old Peasant Woman Praying* (ca. 1905) by Paula Modersohn-Becker. Detroit Institute of Arts. Harris and Nochlin, p. 280. * Extending arms as symbolic of Trinity: according to the Armenian Ritual, neophyte turns west, spits three times against Satan, then turns east, looks towards heaven and spreads arms in avowal of the Trinity. Conybeare, p. 86; Ohm, p. 264. * Crossing of arms over breast during communion is common, especially among Dominicans. Ohm, p. 278. Prayer with spread arms still common. *Russia.* Ohm, pp. 257–58. Confined to a few orders, particularly Capuchins and Franciscans. Western *Europe.* Ohm, pp. 257–58. * Arms raised. 9th cent. *Germany.* Otfrid von Weissenburg, I, 4, 16. * Cross arms and hands over breast, e. g., Protestants (the officiating pastor) during the silent prayer immediately preceding communion. Ritter, p. 375; Ohm, p. 278. * Arms spread out to the side. Yuin (*Australia*), Sioux (*North America*), Massai (*East Africa*), Kikuyu (*East Africa*). Heiler, p. 101; Ohm, pp. 252–53. * Turn open hands toward the sun to show innocence. Grasslands of *Cameroon.* Vielhauer, p. 150; Ohm, p. 253. * Arms spread out, palms downward. Anc. *Egypt,* and *Rome.* * Prayer to terrestrial and subterrestrial gods. Walk into water with outstretched hands to pray to river and sea deities. Anc. *Greece.* Ohm, pp. 265–66. * Arms extended to the front, hands open, palms up. Samaritan; Christian; Muslim. *Middle East.* Also *Africa; India.* H. Freiberg, p. 12, pl. 2; Ohm, pp.

266–67. Extend arms toward temple. Jews. Biblical. *Middle East. Ps.* 27 (28):2; Sittl, p. 190. *See also* HAND, Prayer.

Pregnancy Arms extended forward and slightly to the sides, hands open, palms facing each other and slightly inward, fingers spread. Vulgar. *Russia.* Monahan, pp. 52–53.

Pride Arms at side, bent at elbows, hands (fists) resting at hips. Medieval *France.* Lommatzsch, p. 92.

Proceed Arm and hand, palm sideways, extended forward and slightly down, moved laterally once or repeatedly, signals "go ahead," or "hurry up." *Netherlands.* Andrea and de Boer, p. 139. * Driver of an automobile extends arm sideways, palm facing forward, as signal to a pedestrian to go ahead. *Netherlands.* Ibid., p. 176.

Refusal Arms crossed at wrist, palms facing forward; then hands move apart. *Colombia.* Saitz and Cervenka, p. 33. * Right hand lightly slaps left forearm, which is raised so that the left hand faces the left shoulder. *Central Africa.* Hochegger, p. 163.

Rejection The right arm moves outward to the right, palm turned outwards. Anc. *Rome.* Sittl, p. 85; Flachskampf, p. 239. Arm moves outward and back, palm turned outwards: "Go away!" *Netherlands.* Andrea and de Boer, p. 104. * Arms extended forward and crossed, hands open, palms vertical, facing outward and waggled laterally as if diffusing an unpleasant odor. Derived from European witchcraft, it signifies "Don't come too close," or "Never again!" *Brazil.* Cascudo, *História,* p. 156.

Rendezvous Right arm and hand, palm down, extended in the direction of sunset: "Le soir!" ("In the evening!") *Central Africa.* Hochegger, p. 167.

Request Right arm raised, right hand open, or index pointing upwards: "I want to speak"; "I know the answer." Both arms raised while snapping fingers of right hand: "May I answer?!" *Central Africa.* Hochegger, p. 48.

Reverence Received Eucharist with arms extended, hands crossed and open. Anc. Christians. Ohm, p. 279.

Rise Arms extended to the sides, elbows slightly bent and palms up, moving slightly upward, signals a crowd, such as an orchestra or an audience, to rise. *Netherlands.* Andrea and de Boer, p. 85.

Series Arms extended in front of gesticulator, palms down, one hand above the other. May indicate levels. *Spain; Lat. Am.* Green, p. 60.

Sit "sit down" Arm and hand, palm down, extended forward and moved once or repeatedly up and down from about shoulder height to waist height. *Netherlands.* Andrea and de Boer, p. 140.

"Slip" Hand flat, palm down, arm gradually slides downward and forward. Invariably denotes sexual misconduct, such as adultery, an affair, etc. *Brazil.* Cascudo, *História,* p. 26.

Slow down   Arm extended, hand, palm down, moved up and down. *Netherlands.* Andrea and de Boer, p. 181.

Sorrow   "and he stood momentarily arrested, one long hand out-stretched, warding off realization. . . . To see him was like glimpsing a flame, an epitome of grief's impact." *England.* Allingham, p. 81. * Head resting in palm of right hand, left hand grasps right elbow. *Central Africa.* Hochegger, p. 147.

Stop   Arm raised, hand upward, palm out. Anc. *Rome*; 19th cent. Naples, southern *Italy.* Sittl, p. 86; De Jorio, pp. 87, 152. Also *Netherlands.* Andrea and de Boer, p. 92. * Both arms extended forward from elbow, hands slightly raised and moving back and forth, palms open toward the receiver. *Central Africa.* Hochegger, p. 12. * Right arm extended, open hand moves up and down. *Central Africa.* Ibid.

Strength   Arm bent at elbow, fist clenched. *Colombia; U.S.* Saitz and Cervenka, p. 133. Also *Netherlands.* Andrea and de Boer, p. 79. * Arm extended, clenched fist. Anc. *Rome.* Sittl, p. 115. Arms raised above head, fists agitated up and down. *Central Africa.* Hochegger, p. 76.

Submission   Subordinates place right hand on left shoulder—peaceful intent. May place left hand on the right shoulder also. Anc. *Egypt.* Ohm, p. 277. * One raised hand grasped by the other at the wrist. *Assyria.* Sybel, no. 6009; Sittl, p. 151. * Arms crossed on the breast. *Byzantine Empire.* Sittl, p. 151.

Surrender   Arms raised, palms facing up. Anc. *Greece* and *Rome.* Sittl, p. 147. * Arms and hands raised as signal that warriors are unarmed. Anc. *Greece* and *Rome.* Sittl, pp. 148, 219. * Arms crossed over chest signify surrender to God. 15th cent. *Spain.* Schmidt-Pauli, p. 50.

Sympathy (false)   Making the motions of playing a fiddle. College students. California, *U.S.* McCord, p. 291. [Editors' note: Derived from silent films' violin accompaniment to scenes calling for pathos.]

Teasing   Palm and back of right hand brushed back and forth over inside of left forearm several times like stropping a razor. *Lebanon.* Barakat, no. 128.

Threat   Arm bent at elbow, palm up, forearm moves back and forth toward person threatened. Used by adult to child. *Colombia.* Saitz and Cervenka, p. 142. * Hand formed into fist, forearm raised and moved back and forth. Vulgar; phallic threat. Originated in Asia Minor, where it had apotropaic value, which has disappeared in modern usage. Imported from Europe into Brazil; currently used among the lower classes. Cascudo, *História,* p. 190. *See also* HAND, Threat.

Victory   Arm of victor raised over his head, or arms raised and hands joined over head. *Spain; Lat. Am.; North Am.* Green, p. 48. *Netherlands.* Andrea and de Boer, p. 24. * Arm raised, index and middle finger spread apart, making a "V." Green, ibid. * Arms raised above

head, fists agitated up and down. *Central Africa.* Hochegger, p. 76. *
Arms raised above the head, open hands, palms facing forwards, agitated from side to side. *Central Africa.* Hochegger, p. 209. *See also* FINGER, Victory.

Volunteer Hand raised. Anc. *Rome.* Sittl, p. 218.

Voting Raised right arm to vote. Anc. *Greece.* Sittl, 217.

Warning Head raised, fingers extended, sometimes waved rapidly. *Colombia; U.S.* Saitz and Cervenka, p. 148.

Welcome Arms extended diagonally forward and to the sides, sometimes accompanied by shifting from one foot to the other. *Netherlands.* Andrea and de Boer, p. 145.

Work Hands joined in front, arms swinging an imaginary hoe: "He's working!" *Central Africa.* Hochegger, p. 90.

ARM, HAND, HEAD

Disbelief Head of gesticulator turned away from the speaker; one arm raised, palm facing speaker; often hand is lowered briskly. *U.S.* Saitz and Cervenka, p. 40.

Pensiveness Head cocked to one side, arms forward, fingers intertwined. *U.S.* Birdwhistell, "Do Gestures Speak Louder than Words?", p. 57.

Perplexity Forearms extended forward at right angles to body, hands horizontal, open palm facing outwards, head cocked to the side, shoulder(s) slightly raised. Or: Arms hanging at side and slightly away from the body, open hands turned with the palm facing forward, head slightly cocked. *Russia.* Monahan, p. 21.

ARM, HAND, MOUTH

Blessing Arm extended to saints on altar, then one kisses one's own hand, in asking for, and receiving a blessing. Came to *Brazil* from *Portugal,* particularly the region between Douro and Minho rivers. Also Galicia, *Spain.* Muslims paid respects to tombs of holy men, kissing back of the hand as it pointed the tombs out. 1938. *Tunisia; Morocco.* Cascudo, *História,* p. 99.

ARM, HAND, SHOULDER

Consolation In friendly conversation one woman puts arm around shoulders of the other. Anc. *Greece* and *Rome.* Sittl, p. 281, fig. 32.

Friendship *See* Consolation above.

Frustration Shoulders shrugged, both arms raised sharply, palms facing upward and fingers spread. Sometimes accompanied with expressions such as "¡Ya estoy harto!" ("I'm fed up!") *Spain; Lat. Am.* Green, p. 88.

Ignorance Palms facing upward, arms bent at elbows, shoulders shrugged. Indicates ignorance of whatever is involved in a case or situation, and therefore a refusal to accept responsibility. *Europe; North America.* Wise and Aldrich, p. 18.

Indifference   Shrugging shoulders, head tilted, arms raised to side of body with elbows close to the body and palms facing up. *Spain; Lat. Am.* Can be exaggerated by arching the arms high above the shoulders with palms down. *Spain.* Green, p. 87.

Oath   Witnesses grasp the arm or shoulder of the person for whose sake they are swearing. Medieval *Germany.* Grimm, *DRA,* II, p. 551.

Submission   *See* ARM, HAND, Submission.

Threat   Right hand, either open or closed, placed on left shoulder, right forearm raised to horizontal. *Mexico.* Kaulfers, p. 252.

ARM, HEAD

Confusion   Head thrown backwards, arms bent so that the waist is visible in the slight bend of the elbow. Anc. *Rome.* Quintilianus xi, 3, 118; Baden p. 451.

Defiance   "And she tossed her head, and put her arms akimbo, with an air of confident defiance" 19th cent. *England.* Trollope, *Barchester Towers*, ch. xxxiii. *See* ARM, Defiance; ARM, HAND, Defiance; HAND, HIP, Authority; Challenge.

Disbelief   Raising an arm vertically from its neutral position to the side of the head, then dropping it to its original position. Accompanies expressions of incredulity. *Spain; Lat. Am.* Green p. 75.

Farewell   Hugging the head of a departing person while he or she was kneeling before parents or guardians. Also outside the immediate family as a sign of special affection of a social superior for an inferior. 16th–17th cent. *Poland.* Bogucka, p. 198.

Shame   Head bowed, forehead covered by arm. *Central Africa.* Hochegger, p. 88.

Sorrow   Head bowed, forehead covered by arm. *Central Africa.* Hochegger, p. 88.

Submission   Head is placed between bound arms. Prostration. *Persia; Egypt.* E. Meyer, p. 313; Sittl, p. 151.

ARM, HEAD, SHOULDER

Modesty   Shrugging shoulders, head tilted to the side, somewhat bent arms raised behind body. *Spain; Lat. Am.* Green, p. 49.

ARM, HIP

Superiority   Arms akimbo, i.e., one or both arms bent at elbow, hand (or fist) placed on the hip(s). *See* HAND, HIP, Authority.

ARM, KNEE

Asylum Embracing knees of the *flamen* carried rights of asylum. 4th–5th cent. *Rome.* Servius, 3, 601; Sittl, p. 163.

Gratitude Touch someone's knees; performed kneeling. Anc. *Greece.* Sittl, p. 164. * Arms extended toward someone's knees without touching them; performed kneeling. Anc. *Greece* and *Rome.* Sittl, ibid.

Oath In swearing an oath, the accused, kneeling, embraces the altar. Anc. *Rome.* Sittl, p. 143.

Plea Embracing someone's knees while kneeling. Anc. *Greece* and *Rome.* Sittl, p. 163. One knee embraced while kneeling. Anc. *Greece.* Sittl, ibid. Poor embrace knees of rich. Anc. *Rome.* Sittl, ibid. By embracing knees, parties plead for mercy in court of law. Anc. *Rome.* Apuleius, *Metamorphoses*, 10, 6; Sittl, ibid. Soldiers embrace knees of their captors after a mutiny. Anc. *Rome.* Tacitus, *Annales*, 1, 21. Sittl, ibid. Soldiers plead with their reluctant commander for continuation of the war by embracing his knees. Anc. *Rome.* Tacitus, ibid; Sittl, ibid. During the late empire, the office-seeker embraced the knees of potential benefactor. Anc. *Rome.* Sittl, ibid. Pleading matron embraces knees of person to whom she pleads. Anc. *Greece.* Sittl, ibid. Sick person embraces physician's knees. Anc. *Rome.* Sittl, ibid. The pleader embraces the knees of the person to whom the plea is directed—thus consecrating the knees to Misericordia. Anc. *Rome.* Servius, 3, 607; Sittl, ibid. * Arms stretched out toward knees without touching them, while kneeling. Anc. *Greece* and *Rome.* Sittl, p. 104.

Prayer Arms bent at right angle at elbow, lower arm extended to side of body. Appears during the twenty-first dynasty and continues to the Coptic period. Anc. *Egypt.* Bonnet, p. 208. * Kneeling, arms spread apart. Anc. *Greece.* Sittl, p. 188. * Kneeling on one knee, arms spread apart. 15th cent. *France. Très Riches Heures*, pl. 88.

ARM, LIP

Affection Embrace and kiss. Biblical. *Middle East.* Gen. 29: 13; 33: 4. 13th cent. *Germany. Kudrun*, 483, 4.

Greeting Embrace and kiss. Kiss either on cheeks or lips, together with embrace—among Germanic warriors of friends or warriors of equal fame. *Germanic.* Stoebe, p. 188. Greeting of husband and wife. Anc. *Greece.* Boggs, p. 320. Also 15th cent. *Greece.* Mazaris, p. 148; Sittl, p. 80. When two men meet, they embrace and kiss. *Saudi Arabia.* Barakat, no. 186. "Our Friend the London lawyer, a man steeped in English reserve, was watching what he called the antics of the frogs from the Fin de Siècle café in Cavaillon . . . 'Look over there,' he said, as a car stopped in the middle of the street while the driver got out to embrace an acquaintance, 'they're always mauling each other. See that? *Men kissing.* Damned unhealthy, if you ask me.' He snorted into his beer, his sense of propriety outraged by such deviant behavior, so alien to the respectable Anglo-Saxon." *France*. Mayle, *A Year in Provençe*, p. 101. After a long absence, men customarily greet each other with the triple kiss: the welcoming male embraces his friend, while the latter kisses him three times, starting at the right. Perhaps related to Russian Orthodox ritual; apparently dying out among the younger generation. *Russia*. Monahan, pp. 72–73. *See also* LIP, Affection; LIP, Greeting.

Seduction   "With kind embracements, tempting kisses." 16th–17th cent. *England*. Shakesp., *Shrew*, Induct. 1, 116.

ARM, MOUTH

Apotropy   " 'You keep out of yur,' Ernie said and backed away from her. 'Don't you go and overlook us'ns.' He actually threw up his forearm as if to protect himself, turned aside and spat noisily." *England*. Marsh, *Death of a Fool*, p. 214.

Pleasure   Arms raised and agitated, mouth open (shouting or crying). Children. *Central Africa*. Hochegger, p. 98.

Vengeance   Pretending to bite one's elbow: "I will do anything to avenge myself—even the impossible, such as biting my elbows." *Italy*. Graham, p. 26.

ARM, NECK

Affection   "So, throwing her arms round his neck and kissing him affectionately. . . ." 19th cent. *England*. Dickens, *Pickwick*, II, p. 417; see also *DWb*, IV/2, cols. 243–4 (*Germany*); 16th–17th cent. *England*. Shakesp., *Shrew* 2.1.300; *Winter's Tale* 5.4.112. "At ovation time, she stretched her pretty arms to her audience" Bernheimer, F1.

Death   Rajah places sword on neck of follower, as if to strike off head, symbolizing execution. Northeast *India*. Frazer, *Golden Bough*, IV, p. 56.

Subjection   Master places arm on the neck of a person accepting unfree status. Medieval *Germany*. Grimm, *DRA*, I, pp. 190, 202; Amira, p. 249. *See also* HAND, NECK, Subjection.

Surrender   Neck is placed under the arm of the victor. Medieval Frankish. *France; Germany*. Aimoinus 3, 4; Grimm, *DRA*, I, 190.

ARM, SHOULDER

Affection   Laying arm on someone's shoulder. 16th cent. *Germany*. *Maximilian's Triumphal Arch*, pl. 20. * "At ovation time, she stretched her pretty arms to her audience—a standing audience, of course— slowly clasped her own slender shoulders, closed her eyes and tilted her head to the left in a perfectly choreographed, much appreciated symbol of universal embrace." *U.S*. Bernheimer, F1. *See also* ARM, HAND, SHOULDER, Friendship.

Mourning   Bare the arm and shoulder; according to the Talmud. Jews. *Palestine. HDA*, II, col. 849.

Negation   With verbal expressions of inability bent arms are pushed forward, palms facing one another, then suddenly and sharply arms raised behind body. Shoulders are shrugged while executing movement. *Spain; Lat. Am.* Green, pp. 85–86.

ARM, WRIST

Contempt   Arm moved downward and to one side away from the body with a flick of the wrist. College students. California. *U.S.* Mc-Cord, p. 291. *See* HAND, Contempt.

BACK

Contempt   Turning one's back toward a person. Anc. *Rome*; 19th cent. Naples, southern *Italy*. De Jorio, p. 132.

Honesty   Straight back. *Germany.* "[Honecker] is not tall, but his back is straight, a symbol of incorruptibility in Germany." "On with the Show." *New Yorker*, Jan. 11, 1993, p. 24.

BACK, BREAST, HAND, HEAD

Respect   "He bows . . . and brings the right hand in a graceful arc first to the ground, then to his chest and forehead." 19th cent. *Palestine.* Bauer, 171.

BACK, HAND

Affection   "and slapped him affectionately on the back." *Germany.* Toland, p. 152.

Congratulation   "Whereupon Mr. Pickwick slapped him on the back several times—with the compliments of the occasion." 19th cent. *England.* Dickens, *Pickwick*, II, p. 322.

Consolation   "With this consolation, old Wardle slapped Mr. Tupman on the back and laughed heartily." 19th cent. *England.* Dickens, *Pickwick*, I, p. 297.

Greeting   Slapping the back of a person. *U.S.* Krout, p. 21.

Prayer   Hands placed or crossed behind back. Bushmen, *South Africa.* Ohm, p. 288.

BEARD

Sorrow   Beard cut off. Biblical. *Middle East. Is.* 15:2.

BEARD, HAND

Admiration   Grasping one's beard in admiration of a pretty woman. Arab. Axtell, *Gestures*, p. 42.

Adoption   Adoptive father touches beard of adopted son. Canisius *lect. ant.* 2, 3 cap. 10: "ut Alaricus barbam tangeret Clodovici effectus patrinus" ("when Alaric touched Chlodwig's beard, he became his father"); Aimoin. 1, 20: "et Alaricus juxta morem antiquorum barbam Clodovei tangens adoptivus ei fiebat Pater" ("and Alaric, according to ancient custom, touching Chlodwig's beard, became his adoptive father"). Early Medieval. Frankish. *France.* * The Goths, Franks and Lombards often cut off the beard as sign of adoption. Medieval *Germany.* Grimm, *DRA*, I, pp. 201–202.

Affection Grasping a person's beard. Anc. *Greece.* Sittl, p. 33. Mullah Kashani, Iranian spiritual leader, stroked the beard of the assassin of Premier Ali Razma to show his affection and approbation. *Iran.* Life Photo. *Life.* Dec. 8, 1952, p. 52.

Anger Grasping beard. Medieval *Germany.* Haseloff, p. 307.

Boredom Stroking an imaginary beard. *Italy.* Graham, p. 26. * Drawing the hand downward from the chin as if stroking a beard: "this comment or story is very old." *Netherlands.* Axtell, *Gestures*, p. 145. [Editors' comment: also common in *Austria*].

Calmness Scratching tip of nose with one hand and the beard with the other. *France.* du Fail, *Rustiques*, I, p. 13. * Stroking beard. 16th–17th cent. *England.* Shakesp., *Much Ado* 5.1.15.

Challenge Twisting the mustache. Manoel de Macedo challenged a bully who had passed by him, arrogantly twisting his mustache. *Brazil.* Cascudo, *Locuções Tradicionais no Brasil*, p. 408, and Cascudo, *História*, p. 229. * A daring boor, who was yelling in the street, challenged anyone to touch his mustache; Natal police shaved it off. 1973. Natal. *Brazil.* Cascudo, *História*, p. 229.

Despair Hands grasp beard. 19th cent. *Albania.* Hahn II, p. 153; Sittl, p. 23.

Disbelief Pulling an imaginary beard. *Argentina.* Kany, p. 70.

Embarrassment Hand strokes chin or beard. Anc. *Greece* and *Rome.* Sittl, p. 47.

Fear Hands grasp beard. 19th cent. *Albania.* Hahn II, p. 153; Sittl, p. 23.

Insult Plucking someone's beard. " 'Never did man born of woman, Moor or Christian, pluck [my beard] as I did yours, o count, at the castle of Cabra! When I took Cabra and plucked your beard, there was no youth but took his share of it.' " Medieval *Spain. Cid*, canto 3. "Takes him by the beard" 16th–17th cent. *England.* Shakesp., *Henry V* 4.6.13; "Camest thou to beard me?" *Hamlet* 2.2.442; "Who calls me villain? breaks my pate across? Plucks off my beard, and blows it in my face? Tweaks me by the nose?" *Hamlet* 2.2.598; "Take our goodly aged men by the beards." *Timon* 5.1.175; "Priest, beware your beard; I mean to tug it and to cuff you soundly." *I Henry IV* 1.3.47; "To pluck me by the beard." *Lear* 3.7.35.

Mockery Plucking someone's beard. Anc. *Rome*. Sittl, p. 105. *
Pulling someone's beard. Lamech ridiculed in *Speculum humanae salvationis*, ca. 1450, Rijksmuseum Meermanno-Westreenianum, The
Hague, Ms. 10 b 34, fol. 21r. *See* Fig. 1. * Cutting someone's beard off:
German soldiers cut off the beard of an aged Jew. July 1941. Western
Ukraine. Photo: Bundesarchiv Koblenz (No. 187/203/8 and 9) *Die Zeit*
(Hamburg, Germany), Nr. 10, March 3, 1995, p. 16. *See also* Insult.

Mourning Letting the beard grow. In 1501 a Ser Cristofal Moro
appeared in Venice wearing a beard because his wife had died on the
way from Cyprus. Middle Eastern tradition. Still (1960) observed in
Crete. Vidossi, "La più antica testimonianza," p. 274. *See also* HAND,
Mourning.

Nervousness Hand strokes chin or beard. Anc. *Greece* and *Rome*.
Sittl, p. 47.

Oath Swearing by the beard. Medieval *France* and *Germany*. Konrad v. Würzb., *Otte,* 6–7; *Rolandslied*, 119 a; Grimm, *DRA*, II, p. 549.
No occurrence of swearing by the beard in legal texts. * Touching or
pulling the beard or hair in swearing an oath. Medieval *Frisian* Islands.
Siccama, *Lex Frisionum* 12, 2: pull hairs out with the left hand, put them
in the right hand and thus swear. The "judge" in the Münsterkirche at
Kastl holds his beard with the right hand, showing that he will keep

Fig. 1. Lamech ridiculed. *Speculum humanae salvationis* (ca. 1450). Rijksmuseum Meermanno-Westreenianum, The Hague, Netherlands. 10 B 34, fol. 21r.

his oath to judge impartially. Palatinate. *Germany.* Röhrich, *Gebärde-Metapher-Parodie*, p. 31, n. 16. Pulling hairs when swearing an oath. *Schwäbisches Idiotikon*, p. 262. Also medieval *Spain.* "Alzó la mano, a la barba se tomó" ("He raised his hand and held his beard"). *Cid*, 2485, 2839, 3196.

Pensiveness   "Si duist sa barbe, afaitat sun germun" ("He stroked his chin, and the hairs of his beard"). Medieval *France. Chanson de Roland*, 215. * Plucking of beard or stroking of chin—thoughtfulness, deliberation, doubt. Ghetto Jews. Eastern *Europe.* Efron, p. 146. * Stroking beard. 16th–17th cent. *England.* Shakesp., *Troilus* 1.3.165. *Germany. Rhein. Wb.*, I, p. 478. * Right hand moves as if gently pulling a beard. *Central Africa.* Hochegger, p. 148.

Plea   Grasping a person's beard. Anc. *Greece.* Sittl, p. 33. * Hand grasps beard and neck, while kneeling, sometimes with both hands. Anc. *Greece.* Sittl, p. 165. * One hand grasps beard, the other the right hand or the knee of the other person, while kneeling. Anc. *Greece.* Sittl, p. 165. Also 13th cent. *Germany. Kudrun*, 386, 2. 3 (chin).

Satisfaction   Stroking beard. "What a great day in the court of the Campeador when he wins the battle and slays King Bucar! My Cid raised his hand and stroked his beard." Medieval *Spain. Cid*, canto 3.

Sorrow   Pulling one's beard. Biblical. *Middle East.* Ohm, p. 230. Anc. *Greece* and *Rome.* Sittl, p. 274. 15th cent. *England.* Malory, II, ch. vii; 16th–17th cent. *England.* Shakesp., *Much Ado* 2.3.153; *Romeo* 3.3.68.

Victory   Victors in battle cut off the beards of the vanquished—victory; vanquished are not virile. *Saudi Arabia.* Barakat, no. 174.

BEARD, LIP
Affection   Kiss on beard. 4th cent. *Rome.* Quint. Smyrn. Sittl, p. 40.

BODY
Acquiescence   During the *supplices et rogamus*, which concludes the prayer of offering, the priest bows deeply; interpreted as a reenactment of the conclusion of Christ's Passion: fulfilling Scripture, Christ bows his head and dies. Barasch, *Giotto*, p. 9. * " 'Can you go through the manual exercise?' 'No, sir.' 'Then you must take care and learn it.' I bowed." 18th cent. *England.* Hickey, p. 92. *See also* BODY, Plea.

Adoration   Squatting: lunar ritual gesture. *Indoeuropean.* H. Fischer, "Kosmurgische Symbolik," p. 91. * Prostration. "Joshua fell to the earth upon his face" Biblical. *Middle East. Josh.* 7:6. Mosaic of Honorius III (1216–27) at St. Paul's, Rome, represents him prostrate at feet of Christ: Bareheaded, on his knees, the upper part of the body thrown forward, extended hands almost touch foot of Christ. 13th cent. *Italy.* Ladner, pp. 249–50. "Devoutly I threw myself at the holy feet."

13th–14th cent. *Italy*. Dante, *Purg.*, c. 9. * Bowing. "He worshipped the Lord, bowing himself to the earth." Biblical *Middle East*. *Gen.* 24:52.
Agreement Moving to the side of the speaker. In Lat. "pedibus sententiam ferre"; Portug. "ficar ao lado" ("to stand shoulder to shoulder"). Those who voted silently in this manner, "pedarios senatores." Anc. *Rome*. Cascudo, *História*, p. 225. [Editors' comment: cf. *U.S.* "voting with one's feet"].
Apology " 'I am exceedingly sorry, Ma'am,' said Mr. Pickwick, bowing very low." 19th cent. *England*. Dickens, *Pickwick*, I, p. 380. "Baxter International Inc. has agreed to settle with 400 Japanese hemophiliacs infected via contaminated blood products with the virus that causes AIDS, . . . The settlement was announced in a dramatic televised news conference in Osaka at which the mother of one victim, dissatisfied with the 'casual apology' offered by the drug executives, approached them and demanded more. With that, several executives silently fell to their knees and slowly brought their foreheads to the floor for several minutes" *Japan*. AP Photo. *L.A. Times*, March 15, 1996, D2.
Apotropy One gets the evil eye if one turns around during communion. Lauenburg, Mecklenburg, *Germany;* similarly in the Languedoc, if one turns around three times while the priest reads the gospel. *France*. Seligmann, I, p. 175.
Applause "After a speech in Russia, Bertrand Wolfe was tossed in the air several times by several men as others stood around and applauded." *Russia*. Hayes, p. 223.
Attention Shaking the body of another. "He gave the child a shake to make him obedient." 19th cent. *England*. Dickens, *Pickwick*, II, p. 43. * Rising while listening to a recitation. Anc. *Greece* and *Rome*. Sittl, p. 61.
Authority In the service for Catechumens in the Russian liturgy, the priest sits upon a raised seat while reading the apostolic epistles. His being seated symbolizes his equality with the apostles. *Russia*. Gogol, p. 25; Ohm, p. 335. Sitting at the side of the king. Medieval *France*. J.-C. Schmitt, pp. 15–16. * Gait marking the gentleman. "I do not think that it is becoming to walk hurriedly. . . . [but] a commendable gait is where there is the appearance of authority, the assurance of weight and the mark of dignity, and one which has a calm, collected bearing." 4th cent. *Italy*. Ambrosius, *De officiis*, 1, 18, 74f., also Bremmer, p. 20. Anc. *Rome,* medieval and early modern *Europe*; see Bremmer, p. 20; Graf, p. 47; P. Burke, p. 77; Roodenburg, p. 159. The Church fathers held that the Christian male had to have a powerful and steadfast gait. Bremmer, p. 21. *See also* Walking below.
Blessing "More than once he bowed toward the road by which the young maid had come" 13th cent. *Germany*. Wolfr. v. Eschenb., Bk. vii, 1136–37. At the *keria*, the blessing pronounced at a Jewish funeral, the

mourners stand in accordance to the Biblical mandate (Job 1:20). Kolatch, p. 60.

Body Distance   North Americans normally stand approx. 30 inches, about an arm's length, apart from one another. Asians prefer a greater distance; Latins and Middle Easterners usually stand much closer. Axtell, *Gestures*, p. 120. (*See also* Hall, *Silent Language*, pp. 180–85). Russian males conversing normally maintain a distance of 6 to 10 inches. In rural areas, this distance is reduced. *Russia.* Monahan, pp. 76–77. Women conversing avoid creating any distance between each other, often touching arms or hands while sitting closely side by side. *Russia.* Monahan, pp. 78–79. Women of all ages customarily stroll arm in arm. *Russia.* Monahan, pp. 80–81.

Brevity   Sitting on one's haunches: "I'll only stay a moment." *Central Africa.* Hochegger, p. 29.

Concentration   The position of the sitting Buddha: legs crossed and lying one above the other, soles resting on thighs, palms up, thumbs toward each other. The "lotus position." Buddhist. Ohm, pp. 332–33. * "Reading the Koran is . . . a spiritual discipline, which Christians may find difficult to understand because they do not have a sacred language in the way that Hebrew, Sanscrit and Arabic are sacred to Jews, Hindus and Muslims. . . . When [Jews] study the first five books of the Bible, they do not simply run their eyes over the page. Frequently they recite the words aloud, savoring the words that God . . . used when he revealed himself to Moses on Sinai. Sometimes they sway backward and forward" Armstrong, pp. 144–45. Swaying of Jews in reading and praying explained by reference to (1) *Prov.* 20:27 ("The spirit of man is the lamp of the Lord"); (2) the necessity of sharing books and alternately bending down to read; (3) reference to *Exodus* 20:18: "And when the people saw [Moses receiving the Law], they moved"; (4) keeping time to rhythm of prayer. Kolatch, pp. 151–52. [Editors' note: this method of reading is similar to the *ruminatio* practiced by medieval monks. See Leclercq, p. 72; Schaefer, pp. 34–38.]

Confidence   "The priest stands erect after his previous humble posture, to signify . . . that both he and the faithful are uplifted and comforted by the firm hope of receiving forgiveness of their sins." Roman Catholic. *Mass*, p. 18.

Copulation   Gestures in brother's seduction of sister; narrator comments that brother is in the correct posture but in the wrong place. 12th cent. *Germany.* Hartmann von Aue, *Gregorius,* 357–92. Condwîrâmur agrees to share a bed with Parzival provided that "you do not tussle with me." 13th cent. *Germany.* Wolfram von Eschenbach, *Parzival*, 194. See also Wells, p. 166.

Dead   Body straight, arms down the side, head slightly inclined backwards. *Central Africa.* Hochegger, p. 29.

Defiance To show an opponent that he is despised, the duellant remains seated at approach. Medieval *France*. Lommatzsch, p. 35; Rajna, p. 322. Cf. Hagen remaining seated, his (formerly Siegfried's) sword across his knees, at Kriemhild's approach. 12th–13th cent. *Germany*. *Nibelungenlied*, st. 1781–86. See Wynne, pp. 104–14.

Despair Throwing oneself on the ground. Anc. *Greece* and *Rome*. Sittl, p. 23.

Destruction Erotic gestures, such as the movements of, or preparatory to, sexual intercourse can signify the destruction of the protector of the female partner(s); 8th cent. *England*. Old English *Genesis*, v. 1969 ff.: Habicht, p. 54.

Disgust "What, dost thou turn away and hide thy face? I am no loathsome leper; look on me." 16th–17th cent. *England*. Shakesp., II *Henry V* 3.2.74. * Whole body turned away from something. Early medieval *Greek*. Sittl, p. 84.

Effeminacy Walking too slowly is mocked in Athenian comedy as effeminate. Anc. *Greece*. Bremmer, p. 19. *See* Impressiveness, Walking below.

Enthusiasm " 'tis he, I ken the manner of his gait; he rises on the toe: that spirit of his in aspiration lifts him from the earth." Shakesp., *Troilus* 4.5.14. * Jumping up during recitation. Arrianus, *Discourses of Epictetus*, 3, 4, 4. Sittl, p. 61.

Etiquette In the Han dynasty, it was expected that, in talking to an official, "one begins by looking him in the face; toward the middle of the interview one looks at his breast, and at the end of the interview one's eyes are again directed to his face. The order is never changed, and is used in all cases. . . . If one is not speaking when the other is standing, one looks at his feet, and, if he sits, at his knees. When bearing a present of silk, one does not walk with great strides but deports himself with an anxious uneasiness. A person carrying jade steps carefully, lifting his toes and dragging his heels." 206 B.C.–220 A.D. *China*. Contemporaneous etiquette manual; see "Retrospective," *Civilization* 1, Nov.-Dec. 1994, p. 26. * Gestures to be avoided are treated by Hugh of St. Victor and numerous etiquette books. Medieval *France*. Hugh of St. Victor, *De Institutione Novitiorum*. *PL* 176, col. 925–52. * "Whoever acts so dishonorably that he turns his back toward someone who deserves respect, displeases anyone with any sense. A peasant who cares nothing for honor can stand and turn anywhere he likes" Medieval *Germany*. Konrad von Haslau, 112–17. * In comparing the gestural canon in the reception scenes of Chrétien de Troyes, Hartmann von Aue and Wolfram von Eschenbach, one can observe—with few exceptions—the same gestures used repeatedly: rising from a sitting position, walking or riding toward the arriving person, holding the bridle or stirrup, bowing, taking off the armor, lending one's clothing to the guest, and leading the guest by the hand. 12th–13th cent. *Germany*; medieval *France*. Peil, p. 70. * "Every man could ride, hunt, shoot, and fish . . . The bearing should be that of an athlete, striding easily from the hips. . . . gentlemen's breeches were padded, making their walk a sort of straddle; and the most comfortable standing position would have been with the feet planted wide apart. Padded breeches make crossing the legs when sitting rather difficult. Besides, . . . crossing them does not display them well. The old term for bowing . . . was 'to make a leg.' . . . The following bow is correct from the fourteenth century onward to men and from the eleventh century onward to women. The hat is swept off and either held close to the hip (inside of hat next to the body) or extended back. A step backward is taken with one foot as though you were going to kneel. A half-bend is executed with both knees, and then you straighten up. If there is no hat, both arms may be swept back to show the flowing sleeves. Another type of bow may be used in the Tudor period. The hat is removed and is held either at the side or across the body. The right foot lunges straight forward and both knees are bent. Keep the head erect. Straighten up by bringing the back foot up to the front one as the hat is replaced. When coming before a lord or a sovereign, kneel on one knee. 'Both knees for God, one for fellow man.' " *Britain*, 1485–1603. Rockwood, pp. 170–72. *See* Greeting, below. "She bow'd her to the people." 16th–17th cent. *England*. Shakesp., *Henry VIII* 4.1.86. * "[Tudor] Women should maintain an erect posture; corsets keep the torso straight and stiff. Turn from the waist, not the hips, and avoid letting the full skirt sway from side to side. The effect, when walking, should be that the entire costume is floating smoothly along. Women were not yet in high heels." 1485–1603. *Britain*. Rockwood, p. 172. * When sitting, Elizabethan "ladies never crossed their legs. Wenches did, . . . since they were less mindful of manners and . . . free of corsets." 1558–1603. *Britain*. Rockwood, p. 175. "In the early seventeenth century a Genoese patrician, a crusader for the vanishing ideal of republican equality, claimed that he was imprisoned unjustly on account of his *gesti del corpo* (for example, his proud way of walking into the room and his failure to stand up straight before the Chancellor), gestures regarded by the government as a form of 'dumb insolence.' " A. Spinola, p. 126. * Royal instruction to diplomats: "Your gestures should be manly and solemn according to the occasion—not womanly, not childish, not fearful, not shameful, not irritable, not frivolous . . . Being received in audience you should stand solidly like a tree, keeping a straight face, looking straight ahead. Look at the person to whom you are sent, without any movement, without looking sideways, without shaking the head. Hands should be quiet, without any trembling, not tugging at the beard. You should abstain from coughing, spitting, blowing the nose, and scratching the head or other parts of the body. Do not pick your nose or teeth or bite your lips." 1601. *Poland.* Bogucka, pp. 200–1. And the royal instruction of 30 May 1667 to Polish diplomats posted to Muscovy required that they "behave according to ancient custom without removing their headgear" and "to bow to the Czar according to Polish habit," i.e., without knocking their heads on the floor in the Russian manner. A long dispute followed in Moscow, which ended when the Poles were permitted to approach the czar with their heads covered, then remove their hats briefly—for to remain bareheaded would be injurious to the Polish King and the Polish-Lithuanian Commonwealth. But the envoy had to kiss the hands of the czar and his son. 1667. *Poland.* Bogucka, ibid. * During the Restoration period, "the lower classes went arm in arm, but a gentleman offered a lady his outstretched hand and she placed her hand on his sleeve. Because of the wide skirt she could not have gotten much closer" 17th cent. *England.* Rockwood, p. 178. "Bows and curtsies were used until 1870, but by 1840 handshaking was seen . . . Ladies shook hands out of doors but continued to curtsy indoors until the crinoline went out of fashion." 19th cent. *England.* Rockwood, p. 183. During the Victorian and Edwardian periods, "servants curtsied and bowed before and after an announcement. The butler bowed from the waist, heels together, hands at the sides with the back of the hands facing front. . . . the bow was used to denote the social standing of the recipient; the bow got deeper as the recipient got more important. Gentlemen bowed to the assembled group when entering a room. During the nineteenth century the bow gradually changed to what we do today. In the early part of the century one foot was placed in front of the other, the front heel slightly raised; the bow was from the waist. Both hands were placed on the heart. A little later, gentlemen bowed while standing in third position (heel of one foot to hollow of the other) with one hand to the heart. During the latter half of the century the heels were put together and eventually the hands were dropped to the sides. . . . As skirts become narrower, the curtsy changes. . . . The skirt is lifted slightly at the sides, and a backward step is taken. The weight is shifted to the back foot, the forward leg being kept straight. . . . Keep the ankle concealed." Ibid., pp. 184–85. * Bowing as an act of courtesy, such as bowing when entering the presence of ladies, or leaving them, or after an introduction. 19th cent. *England.* Dickens, *Pickwick*, I, pp. 23, 266. * As in the maintenance of eye contact, there are cultural variations in the distance maintained between individuals in certain situations; in conversation, this distance is normally about one arm's length in the *United States.* This "comfort zone" is markedly shorter in Arab countries, *Egypt, Iran, Israel, Lebanon, Nigeria, China,* and *Latin America* generally. Axtell, *Gestures,* pp. 157–217. Cf. Hall, *Silent Language,* pp. 180–85; *Hidden Dimension,* pp. 113–66. * An erect posture distinguishes the upper classes from the lower; an example is the Dutch elite: C. van Laar's

Groot ceremonie-boeck der beschaafde zeeden (Amsterdam, 1735), p.
68: Posture should be "without affectation . . . erect, without stiffness
or constraint, free and easy in its natural gestures." Distinct not only
from the postures usually ascribed to the lower classes and German
immigrants, but also from those identified with southern Europeans.
Italians, for instance, "who speak with their head, arms, feet and the
whole body" are viewed as the opposite of the ideal of civility. The
Dutch, in contrast, merely used the eye and "a moderate movement of
the hand" in conversation. 18th cent. *Netherlands.* Roodenburg, p. 160.
In walking (*see* Walking below), one should keep the body "fixed in the
Spanish way, as if not daring to turn one's head"—a standard of solemnity already referred to favorably by the Dutch traveller François Aers-
sen van Sommelsdijck in the 1650s, who commented on the "gravité
naturelle ou affectée" ("natural or affected gravity") that was particularly favored at the Spanish court, but observable in all Spaniards. Previously, this Spanish attribute had been ridiculed as arrogant, as in 1617
by G. A. Bredero, *The Spanish Brabanter,* 17th cent. *Netherlands.* See
also Roodenburg, p. 161. De Courtin (*see* Walking below) mentions
scratching the body, fumbling with hat, buttons, or gloves as "give-
aways," presumably of one's lack of *civilité.* Similarly, the *Groot ceremonie-boeck* warns against crossing one's legs while sitting and conversing (see Frans Hals's portrait of Willem van Heijthuysen [c. 1637–39]),
presumably because it indicates a measure of disrespect toward the other
person, emphasized, perhaps, by the intrusion of the raised knee into the
other's "space" (particularly when combined with a raised elbow, as in
Hals's portrait). Such taboo intrusions are also touching the other person, particularly one of higher rank, grasping buttons, sleeves or coat
while conversing, or kissing a woman of higher rank without her permission. And even if she gives such permission and offers her cheek, one
is expected to fake the gesture without touching her face. If offered a
seat by a person of higher rank, one is to sit opposite him, but without
looking him straight in the eye. Speaking loudly was also seen as violat-
ing the other's "space." 17th cent. *Netherlands.* Roodenburg, pp. 162–
63. The person of higher rank always had precedence, i.e., one had to
walk one step behind and to the left of him. But "right" and "left,"
"hogerhand" and "lagerhand," also were spatial concepts: indoors,
"left" was usually the side on which one had entered the room; on the
street, one was expected to pass a superior on his left, and if the street
had a gutter, the "left" was there, regardless of the superior's location;
if the street was bordered by a wall, the "left" was on the opposite
side, and one had to give the superior "the wall." 17th and 18th cent.
Netherlands. Roodenburg, pp. 166–69. * The function of posture as an
element of class distinction arises clearly from the description of a traveler: "They walk majestically, with a baton in one hand and a sword

hanging from the belt." 17th cent. *Poland.* Bogucka, pp. 191–92; as well as from Mikolaj Rej, *Zwierciado [The Mirror]* (ca. 1650): "You can tell the attitudes and inclinations of people from their comportment. . . . Because when a rustic or cowardly person wants to say something seriously, what do you see? He squirms, picks his fingers, strokes his beard, pulls faces, makes eyes and splits every word in three. A noble man, on the contrary, has a clear mind and a gentle posture; he has nothing to be ashamed of. Therefore, in appearance, in his words, and in comportment he is like an eagle which without any fear looks straight at the sun, or like a commander-in-chief who by his noble posture and proud bearing inspires his soldiers and subordinates to courageous acts." 17th cent. *Poland.* Bogucka, p. 191. This "preference for gravity, even in amusements, resulted in contempt for vigorous sports, especially the ball games popular in Western countries: in Poland only horse riding and hunting were regarded as proper pastimes for the nobility. King Sigismund III Vasa was ridiculed by the gentry because of his fondness for football—judged childish for a man and a ruler." 1587–1632. *Poland.* Bogucka, p. 192.

Farewell Men rise when man or woman leaves room. Women may or may not rise. The more formal the occasion, the more likely everyone is to rise. *Colombia; U.S.* Saitz and Cervenka, p. 69. * Russians of all ages may suggest immediately before the departure of a friend that they sit together in silence for a few minutes. It is customary, at least for the departing friend, to sit on the suitcases. *Russia.* Monahan, pp. 130–31. *See also* Etiquette; Greeting.

Fear Bowing to the ground. Biblical. *Middle East. Num*, 22:31; 1 *Sam.* 28:14; *Isaiah* 21:3; *Luke* 24:5. * Shuddering. *U.S.* Krout, p. 25. * Shaking of the body. *Europe.* Krukenberg, p. 317. * Shrinking, contracting of the body. *Europe.* Krukenberg, ibid. * Women of the Archaic age walking with very small steps "resembled in their steps the timorous doves." Anc. *Greece.* Homer, *Iliad* 5.778, cited by Bremmer, p. 20. * In exorcising the Devil from a woman's body, St. Radegund "commanded the Adversary to prostrate himself with his fear on the pavement." 6th cent. *France.* Venantius Fortunatus, *Vita sanctae Radegundis* 71; see also De Nie, p. 27.

Freedom At Passover the Jews reclined, in order to express and remember that they were no longer slaves, but free since the exodus. Similarly, Christ and the apostles lay at table. Biblical. *Middle East. Mark* 14:18. Ohm, p. 339.

Gratitude Bowing. Biblical. *Middle East.* II *Kings* 4:37; *Gen.* 23:7.12. Anc. *Rome.* Sittl, p. 155. Also 13th cent. *Germany*: "The lady rose and bowed." Wolfram v. Eschenbach, iv, 196. "Thereupon the knights bowed to her." *Kudrun*, st. 64, 1. "She returned the compliment [of a bow] with a curtsey." 18th cent. *England.* Smollett, *Peregrine*

Pickle, I, ch. 36. "with a humble grateful bow to Mr. Pickwick." 19th cent. *England.* Dickens, *Pickwick,* II, p. 425. Bowing as expression of gratitude for applause. *Netherlands.* Andrea and de Boer, p. 45. [Editors' note: *Universal* as a gesture of appreciation by the artist after a performance]. *See* Greeting.

Greeting Bowing. Biblical. *Middle East. Gen.* 18:2; 19:1; 33:3. Beowulf greets the king standing; Siegfried greets Gunther bowing. Pritzwald, p. 42. Medieval *England; Germany.* Bowing as greeting on the part of free men not before the Roman Empire. In the first centuries A.D., it was still considered humiliating. Alexander Severus ridiculed those who greeted him thus. 3rd cent. Anc. *Rome.* Sittl, p. 155. In greeting, the bow can be executed at various angles: the lower the head, the humbler the bower. Medieval *Germanic.* Stoebe, p. 184. The welcome ritual had a large and complicated protocol: several kinds of bowing, handshaking, kissing, kneebending, handkissing, hugging the knees or legs of old people or superiors. First came deep bowings and mutual embraces before entering, then the host led the male visitor, his wife the female visitor into the house. Crossing thresholds and taking seats occasioned more ceding of precedence. Then the host would rise and ask the guest to surrender his sword, which would be done with some teasing." 16th cent. *Poland.* Bogucka, p. 193. " 'and so I humbly take my leave'; which he did with many bows, or at least many attempts at a bow." 18th cent. *England.* Fielding, *Joseph Andrews,* iv, ch. 2. "the supposed stranger made divers awkward bows, and . . . accosted him." 18th cent. *England.* Smollett, *Peregrine Pickle,* I, ch. 14. "he saluted me with a very genteel bow." Ibid., ch. 97. The whole body impulsively flung to the ground. Germanic. Stroebe, pp. 184–85. Bowing in gratitude shows greater intensity of emotion than inclining the head. *Portugal.* Basto, p. 8. Bow of head or upper part of body, standing or walking, is of minimum courtesy. *Colombia.* The male, when he does bow, does so with upper part of body rather than head alone. *U.S.* Saitz and Cervenka, p. 67. "Bows and curtsies were used until 1870, but by 1840 handshaking was seen." 19th cent. *England.* Rockwood, p. 183. Western Europeans and North Americans often view the bow as a sign of subservience; the Japanese view it as a sign of respect and humility. Lower ranking person bows first and deeper to higher ranking person (informally, about 15 degrees, hands at side; formally, about 30 degrees, palms on knees, sometimes bobbing up and down); since Japanese often adopt western ways of greeting outside of Japan, collisions between bows and handshakes may occur. The exchange of business cards (early in the stages of an introduction) is accompanied by a slight bow; the exchange itself is executed by presenting and receiving the cards with both hands, between thumb and index, the lettering facing the recipient. After cards have been studied for a moment, a handshake and a few more bows follow. *Japan.* Axtell, *Gestures*, pp. 26–27. "the stage bow and curtsy, used in almost all professional productions. These are not historically accurate, but they are theatrically effective, and the one bow can be executed with foppish flourishes or with a soldier's curtness. There are, of course, historically correct bows which vary from era to era. . . . [The stage bow] may be used up to the Restoration period. With the weight on the left foot, bend the right knee and sweep the right leg behind the left so that the hollow of the right foot is in line with the left heel. The feet should be at a ninety-degree angle. The distance between heel and hollow should be between fifteen and eighteen inches. As the right foot is swept back, the weight is transferred to it. The right knee remains bent and the left leg is kept perfectly straight. The torso is inclined forward from the waist. As the right leg is being moved back, the hat is swept off with the right hand and either brought to the chest or swung out behind the body so that the right arm is parallel with the ground. The left hand may either grasp the sword belt or the sword hilt or rest on the hip. . . . [The stage curtsy] is excellent for any period in which the actress is wearing a wide skirt which conceals the leg move-ment. The effect is a smooth and graceful sinking and rising . . . the hands are outstretched at the sides, or, if a farthingale is worn, the fin-gers rest lightly on top of the skirt. With the weight on the left foot, slide the right foot well behind and to the left of the left foot. Sink down, gradually transferring the weight to the right foot until you are sitting on the right leg. The thighs will now be crossed, the left on top of the right. Rise by transferring the weight to the left foot and bringing the right foot back in place. During this entire movement the left foot re-mains fixed." 16th-17th century. *England.* Rockwood, pp. 167–69. *See also* Etiquette, above. "For the medieval period the curtsy consists of a bend of both knees, the depth of the dip depending upon the rank of the person being saluted. The skirt is held out and lifted slightly . . . because it gets in the way otherwise. The head may be inclined slightly to one side or slightly forward." Medieval *England.* Rockwood, p. 172. "Eliza-bethan bows and curtsies, thanks to all the starch and padding, are stiff affairs. The man stands with feet straddled (his usual stance), weight on both feet, one foot in front of the other. The hat is removed as both knees are bent. The knees are straightened, and the hat is replaced. . . . [In the curtsy] the arms are outstretched to the sides, the hands resting lightly on the edge of the farthingale. Both knees are bent slightly, and the head is inclined toward the person being greeted. Do not lift the skirt. The curtsy is deeper for the queen; remain down until [she] gives you permission to rise. Curtsy again before leaving the queen." 16th–17th cent. *England.* Rockwood, p. 176. During the Restoration period, "even husbands and wives bowed and curtsied to each other. A gentle-man greeted a lady by bowing and kissing her hand. (When kissing a lady's hand . . . offer her the back of your hand, she will place her fingertips on it, and you gently draw her hand to your lips.) And only dolts allowed their noses to touch the lady's hand. Merchants and innkeepers bowed when receiving honored guests and when given orders. Servants bowed and curtsied when entering and leaving a room. Male servants bowed with heels together." 1660–85. *England*. Rockwood, p. 178. [Editors' note: The bow is executed, in all periods, only by men, the curtsy only by women.] * Prostration, the forehead touching the ground, in greeting a chieftain. *Central Africa*. Hochegger, p. 155. Particular respect or affection is shown by a greeting in which the host approaches the guest. 12th cent. *Germany*. Hartmann von Aue's *Gregorius* (see Wells, p. 183 and Peil, pp. 32–44) or the *Nibelungenlied*, st. 102. * Men rise when a woman or man enters room, women usually remain seated. The more formal the occasion the more likely all are to rise. *Colombia; U.S.* Saitz and Cervenka, p. 69. *See also* BREAST, HAND, Greeting.

Homage Persons of low degree, captives and foreign vassals depicted in ancient Egyptian paintings or reliefs as prostrate. Court officers usually stand up, but incline their heads and bodies slightly. Servants bend forward to a greater degree and place one hand on the knee or kneel and raise both hands before their faces. Anc. *Egypt*. Gardiner, pl. 17, 19, 27, etc. Dawson, p. 86.

Humility Woodsmen prostrate themselves after felling a tree to show humility so spirit will not chastise them as it escapes. Siphnos, *Greece*. Frazer, *Golden Bough*, II, p. 37. * At commencement of Mass, the priest bows at the foot of the altar and presents himself as if laden with the sins of the people before God. Roman Catholic. *Mass*, p. 17.

Impressiveness Paris approaches the battlefield "with long strides in front of the throng." Homer, *Iliad* 3.22. His "gait denotes powerful movement in order to impress the enemy." Bremmer, p. 16. Similarly *Iliad* 7.211–4. Ajax reponds to Hector's challenge with long strides. See also Bremmer, pp. 16–17: "In Homer, then, walking with long strides was the sign of the great commander who wanted to assert himself on the battlefield. In the latter part of the Archaic age (c. 800–500 B.C.), Greek battle tactics were completely transformed by the introduction of the phalanx, a formation in which the troops had to stay together in one line. In this disposition there was no longer room for heroes asserting themselves by striding ahead." Therefore "virtually nothing more" is heard about this gait of males during the Classical period (c. 500–300 B.C.). It reappears in the early Hellenistic period. In 5th cent. Athens, the development of democracy relegated walking with wide strides into the background. Aristocrats now were distinguished by a quiet, unhurried gait. Anc. *Greece*. Ibid., pp. 18–19. *See also* Walking below.

Inferiority In a sitting position before a superior the legs must be apart; it is not permitted to cross one's legs before a superior. *Central Africa.* Hochegger, p. 96.

Insult Women undress before someone whom they want to insult. *Central Africa.* Hochegger, p. 128.

Judgment "Thereupon the chief rabbi rose from his seat (that what he said might not have the force of a judicial decision)" 18th cent. Jewish. *Germany.* Maimon, ch. xxii.

Magical Barren women roll on ground under solitary apple tree in order to obtain offspring. Kara-Kirghiz. *Central Asia.* Frazer, *New Golden Bough*, p. 138. * Upon return from baptism with the infant, the midwife turns infant upside down. Brandenburg, *Germany. HDA*, II, col. 414.

Manliness Erect posture. Medieval *England. Beowulf*, 2092. Also Habicht, p. 22.

Manumission The owner led the slave to be freed into the presence of the Praetor and declared: "Free this man." The Praetor struck the head of the slave with a festuca, repeating: "Be free." Holding him by the shoulders, he then spun him around. Persius, *Sat.*, v, mocked, that a pirouette made a Roman citizen: "quiritem vertigo facit." Anc. *Rome.* Cascudo, *História*, p. 67.

Marriage In the *velatio*, bride and groom kneel under the nuptial veil. Medieval *Western Europe.* See the illustration in Duby, *Private Life*, p. 131 from a 14th cent. copy of the *Decretum* of Gratian. Dijon Library, ms. 341. * Bride circles groom (*Jer.* 31:22) in Jewish wedding, sometimes 3 times, sometimes 7 times. May be apotropaic, to protect from evil spirits, from glances of other women, from temptation. May be symbolic of binding, creating new family circle, shifting primary allegiance from parents to husband and wife. Jews. Diamant, pp. 103–04.

Mockery "As he levelled his gaze he became aware of two figures, a man and a woman, on the illuminated balcony of a neighboring building. . . . They seemed to be amused by Bernard's appearance, giggling and pointing. . . . He didn't know how to respond—whether to wave good-humoredly, or stare stonily. As he hesitated, the woman undid the belt of her robe and, with a theatrical gesture, flung it open. She was quite naked underneath. He could see the crescent shadows under her breasts and the dark triangle of her pubic hair. Then, with a burst of laughter, they turned and went back into their room . . . What did the woman's gesture signify? Mockery? Insult? Invitation?" Hawaii, *U.S.* Lodge, *Paradise News*, pp. 96–97.

Modesty Among the Tupi Indians, it was observed that, though neither men nor women wore clothing, when a man spoke to a woman, he turned his back to her out of a sense of modesty. Cascudo, *História*, p. 211.

Mourning Woman stands next to her husband's grave—she will not remarry. Islamic custom. Rwala Bedouin. *Middle East*. Barakat, no. 211. * Sinking to sitting or kneeling position at a grave. Women. Anc. *Greece* and *Rome*. Sittl, p. 74. * Rolling on the ground. Anc. *Greece*. Bremmer, p. 26. Also Hellenist. *Middle East*. Sittl, p. 68. * Women mourn their husbands by rolling in the dust undressed. *Central Africa*. Hochegger, p. 124. Mourners sit on low stool or hassock for seven days, symbolizing desire to be close to the dead. "Sitting *shivah*." Jews. Kolatch, p. 64. After "sitting *shivah*," mourners walk together for a short distance, symbolizing return to society. Jews. Kolatch, p. 69.

Ostracism Legal requirement to keep distance from a person ostracizes that person by preventing normal social contact, as in the "nidui," part of divorce action of orthodox Jewish wife. Acting through the rabbinate to obtain religious divorce, she won an order forbidding observant Jews to speak to her husband, or come within six yards of him, until he grants her a religious divorce. Orthodox Jewish. *England*. Kampeas, p. 18.

Plea Entire body on the ground, face down. (Not in republican *Greece* and *Rome*). *Persia; Carthage*. Sittl, p. 157. * The priest's low bow in the *supplices te rogamus* ("As supplicants we ask you"), concluding the prayer of offering, has been interpreted as re-enacting Christ's falling on his face in entreaty in Gethsemane. Biblical. *Middle East*. Matth. 26:39. Barasch, *Giotto*, p. 9. "and am enjoin'd by holy Lawrence to fall prostrate here, to beg your pardon" 16th–17th cent. *England*. Shakesp., *Romeo* 4.2.19. To cast oneself at someone's feet, seeking help or protection. Boggs, p. 322. Bowing "this feeble ruin to the earth." 16th–17th cent. *England*. Shakesp., *Tit. Andr.* 3.1.208. Supplicant lies on the ground, supporting himself on one hand. Anc. *Greece*. Sittl, p. 296. * Beggars often sat on the ground. Supplicants sat near places guaranteeing their safety, such as an altar or the hearth of a house or a city. Sitting by the hearth signified an appeal by the supplicant for acceptance in a new group, but this could only be achieved in a manner that "inhibits aggressive reaction by a ritualized act of self-humiliation." Anc. *Greece*. J. Gould, pp. 74–103. In 1772 Tadeusz Rejtan, deputy from Novgorod, protested in the Polish parliament against the first partition of Poland by throwing himself on the floor, baring his chest and asking to be killed first; and in 1791, Jan Suchorzewski, deputy from the Kalisz district and an opponent of the Polish reform, prostrated himself, begging the parliament to postpone voting on the Constitution of 3 May. 18th cent. *Poland*. Bogucka, p. 200.

Pleasure A dainty, light, luxurious way of walking. Anc. *Greece* and *Byzantine Empire*. Bremmer, pp. 20–21. *See also* Walking.

Possession Prostration. Julius Caesar, on disembarking in Africa, prostrated himself, exclaiming: "Teneo te, Africa!" ("Africa, you are mine!"). Anc. *Rome.* Suetonius, *Julius Caesar*, 59.

Prayer Prostration often precedes prayer, which is spoken standing or kneeling. In prostration, the body, the hands and the face touch the ground. Common in *Sumer; Babylon;* anc. *Egypt;* anc. *Rome; India*; and in anc. Judaism. Still customary in Chinese cults. Prescribed in Muslim prayers. Prostration is performed quickly, the actual prayer follows. Heiler, p. 100. Woman lying on ground, face almost touching the ground. Anc. *Egypt.* Papyrus of the 21st dynasty. Bonnet, p. 207. Ancient Egyptian priests' prescribed prayer positions: (1) worshipper must throw himself down, i.e., kneel and bend upper body down; (2) throw self upon the ground so that entire body lies flat; (3) lower the head to the ground, "kiss the earth." Bonnet, p. 206. * After this introductory proskynesis, the worshipper rises and speaks standing to the deity, arms raised, slightly bent, palms open. Prostration. Biblical. *Middle East.* Pritzwald, p. 25, n. 2. In ancient Christianity prostration before graves and relics was common. Heiler, p. 100. * Circular motion of upper body. Celtic; Anc. *Rome;* Yao (Kwantung), *China.* Voullieme, pp. 11–13; Ohm, p. 322. * Inclination of the body or head forwards can precede or accompany prayer. *Sumeria*; *Babylonia*; Jewish; *India*; anc. *Rome;* tribal *German.* Heiler, p. 101. * Prostration during penitential prayers. *Deut.* 9:18. Biblical. *Middle East.* Lack of space in synagogues required change to custom of placing head on left arm. Jews. Kolatch, p. 150. * Turning the body before prayer was common among Celts and in anc. *Rome.* The Romans turned toward the right, the Gauls to the left. Possibly derived from circling a sacred object. Heiler, p. 101. Western Jews face Jerusalem when they pray. Kolatch, p. 149. The priest almost always turns left toward the altar. Roman Catholic. Ohm, p. 322. * Since, to the anc. Romans, standing was a sign of respect, a law of Numa prescribed that a worshipper, having ended his prayer, must sit down. Standing in prayer was usual among early Christians and was perhaps also common in pre-Christian *Egypt.* Sittl, p. 194. Also anc. *Greece* and *Rome.* Cascudo, *História*, p. 49. In 1871 a complaint was lodged against the proposal to install chairs and benches in one of the major churches in Recife, on the grounds that seats were inappropriate in temples in which the Host was exhibited. *Brazil.* Ibid. * In praying during Mass, the priest bows. *Mass*, pp. 18, 36. Also Biblical. *Middle East. Ex.* 4:31; 12:27; *Gen.* 24:26; 24:48; etc. For medieval Christian prayer-gestures, see the references in Knox, p. 29, n. 5 and 7, as well as the discussion and references in Knox, pp. 18 and 34–35, n. 54–56. * Bowing and kneeling were part of ritual in temples in Jerusalem, but when Christians adopted kneeling and prostration, rabbis prohibited them in Jewish worship, except on Yom Kippur during reading of the account of ancient Temple ritual. Orthodox Jews. Kolatch, p. 153. Certain prayers said standing. Jews. Kolatch, p. 154. * At beginning of silent devotion, Jews take three steps forward, at its end three steps backward—as a subject approaches and leaves a king reverently. During *kedusha*-segment of silent devotion, Jews stand with feet together, and when "holy, holy, holy" is pronounced, some stand on tiptoe." Orthodox Jews. Kolatch, p. 156. * Gestures before a statue of the Virgin in Regensburg, *Germany* (1519): prostration, the face touching the ground; kneeling, hands joined palm to palm; kneeling with raised and slightly spread arms; prostration on the back, arms spread to the sides. 16th cent. *Germany*. Beitl, p. 97. * Practices in Polish churches: "Everywhere there was sighing and crying for the Poles are very tender-hearted. When listening to the sermon, they start to groan audibly at the mention of the name of Christ, of the Blessed Virgin or at any other pious word or sentence. During Mass, when the Body of the Lord is elevated, they violently beat their faces, foreheads, cheeks and chests, and bang their heads against the earth." Ogier, p. 74. * In Polish churches worshippers would prostrate themselves to show penitence, lift their swords to show their readiness to defend the faith, stand for hours with arms spread in the form of a cross, or attend Mass in full armor. Bogucka, p. 203. * Mystery cults required nakedness. Anc. *Greece* and *Rome*. Heiler, p. 104. * The ancient Greeks prayed to the chthonic deities half sitting, half kneeling, i.e., squatting. Anc. Roman women were permitted while praying to squat like mourners or supplicants for protection. Anc. *Greece* and *Rome*. Heiler, p. 100. * The men were required to stand during prayer. Anc. *Rome*. Ohm, p. 338. Swaying of the body during prayer is common among Jews and Muslims. *Encycl. Jud.*, VII, p. 130; Bergmann, p. 331. * "About seven in the morning after I came to Amsterdam, where being provided with a lodging, the first thing I went to see was a Synagogue of the Jews (being Saturday) . . . the men, wearing a large calico mantle, yellow coloured, over their hats, all the while waving their bodies, whilst at their devotions." 17th cent. Jewish. *Netherlands*. Evelyn, I, p. 24 (Aug. 19, 1641). * Prostration in the form of a cross ("in kriuzestal"). 13th cent. *Germany*. *Kudrun*, st. 1170, 1. 2; *König Rother*, 376. * Doña Ximena casts herself down on the steps of the altar and prays. Medieval *Spain*. *Cid*, canto 1. * Walking around the altar. Anc. *Rome*. Servius, *Aen*. 4, 62; Sittl, p. 195. * German slave, in manumission, is led around the altar. Anc. *Rome*. Sittl, p. 195, n. 4. * Bride is led around altar. Anc. *India*. Sittl, ibid. * Muslims walk around Kaaba in Mecca. *Saudi Arabia*. Sittl, ibid. * In praying in the open air in Rome, worshippers turned in the direction of the temple of Jupiter. Anc. *Rome*. Sittl, p. 190. * Bowing three times before beating chest four times at the burning of a body. Anc. *Rome*. Sittl, p. 73. * Women were permitted to squat or cower while praying; men only if adoring erotic deities. Anc. *Greece*. Theocritus, *Epigr.* 4 [17], 13–4; Tibull. 1, 3, 30. Sittl, p. 176. *See also* BODY, FACE, Prayer.

Recognition "and knocked gently at the door. It was at once opened by a woman, who dropped a curtsey of recognition" 19th cent. *England.* Dickens, *Pickwick,* I, p. 361.

Respect "And the king [Solomon] rose up to meet her, and bowed down unto her." Biblical. *Middle East.* I *Kings* 2:19. * In a hymn "the great gods bowed in approval and prayer before him [Anu] like sickles." *Assyria.* Ostrup, p. 30; Ohm, pp. 340–41. * The gods arose before Apollo. Anc. *Greece.* Sittl, p. 153. A festive gathering at Olympia rose before Themistocles. Sittl, ibid. Subjects rise when ruler enters. Anc. *Greece.* Sittl, p. 152. According to Suetonius, the father of the emperor Vitellius approached Caligula with covered head, turning before him and prostrating himself. Anc. *Rome.* Ohm, p. 322. Subjects rise when Roman emperor or princes enter the theater. Anc. *Rome.* Sittl, pp. 152–53. Senators rose at entrance of Caesar. Augustus desired them to remain seated at his entrance and exit from the senate. Anc. *Rome.* Sittl, p. 153. Guests rise when an esteemed person enters house or tent. *Saudi Arabia, Syria, Jordan, Lebanon, Kuwait, Iraq.* Barakat, no. 181. One rose in the presence of the highest Roman officials, including the tribunes. Anc. *Rome.* Sittl, ibid. Citizens rose in the presence of professors. Anc. *Rome.* Sittl, p. 154. Everyone, including senators, rose when anyone wearing the citizen's crown entered the theater. Anc. *Rome.* Sittl, p. 153. Someone riding or in a coach had to rise and dismount in the presence of consul or praetor, on the order of the lictor; exception is in the company of a lady. Anc. *Rome.* Sittl, p. 152. Whenever a high personage rose before someone, it was viewed as an extraordinary honor. Anc. *Rome.* Plutarch, *Brut.* 4; Sittl, p. 154. "King Alfonso sees [the Cid] enter and stands and . . . all the others of the court stand also." Medieval *Spain. Cid,* canto 3. * If the emperor was present only symbolically, as when an imperial message was read, one listened to it standing. Anc. *Rome.* Sittl, p. 153. * A knight had to dismount when he met a lady walking. 13th cent. *Germany.* Thomasin v. Circlaria, 419; Schultz, II, p. 181. A layman had to dismount if he met a cleric on foot. Early medieval *France.* Synod of Mâcon (585). *Concilia Galliae* A. 511-A. 695; J.-C. Schmitt, pp. 57–58. * When two men met they sat down at approximately twenty yards distance from one another and looked at each other for a few minutes without speaking. They then rose and walked on together. When a person of importance approached, the other would remain seated while he passed by. Native American. *North America.* Eichler, p. 95. * In the presence of their kings, the Indian tribes of the uplands of Colombia turned their backs as a sign of respect. *Colombia.* Cascudo, *História,* p. 211. The same ritual of turning also obtained among the Indians of colonial Brazil, though it was never transmitted to

Brazilians of European descent or mixed race. *Brazil.* Ibid. * "Unman-ner'd dog! stand thou, when I command." 16th–17th cent. *England.* Shakesp., *Richard III*, 1, 2, 39. * "At ten I got into my chaise, and away I went. As I passed the Cross, the cadies and the chairmen bowed and seemed to say, 'God prosper long our noble Boswell.' I rattled down the High Street . . . I made the chaise stop at the foot of the Canongate; asked pardon of Mr. Stewart for a minute; walked to the Abbey of Ho-lyroodhouse, went round the Piazzas, bowed thrice: once to the Palace itself, once to the crown of Scotland above the gate in front, and once to the venerable old Chapel." 18th cent. *Scotland.* Boswell, *London Journal*, p. 41. * "Observing her at a window, took the liberty of bow-ing to her with great respect." 18th cent. *England.* Smollett, *Peregrine Pickle*, I, ch. 36. * "The old gentleman bowed respectfully." 19th cent. *England.* Dickens, *Oliver Twist*, p. 88. Tribes, believing spirits of ances-tors to be in trees, bow respectfully in passing and excuse themselves for disturbing their repose. *Philippines.* Frazer, *Golden Bough*, II, p. 29ff. * Takes the corner of a stranger's robe and ties it about himself, so as to leave the other almost naked. *Ethiopia.* Eichler, p. 159. * Maburiag boys are instructed to crouch in the presence of old men. *Africa.* Eichler, p. 95. * Uncover the body down to the waist in the presence of a king. *Tahiti.* Eichler, p. 159. * "The Chinese Nationalist government has ruled that any government employee refusing to bow before a portrait of Sun Yat-sen, founder of the Chinese republic, is liable to punishment—presumably dismissal from his government job." Taipei, *Taiwan*, Jan. 27, 1957; Hayes, p. 231. * "some American prisoners of war during World War II were not able to adapt to the deference patterns of their Japanese captors and thus save themselves needless torture. The Japa-nese formal view of life is that there must be order in the relations between men and that this order is expressed by people taking and dem-onstrating their positions in a hierarchy. People of higher status are ad-dressed by certain polite forms; respect is shown by bowing quite low with the upper part of the body held rigid. The Americans who were captured by the Japanese felt it was a violation of their dignity to have to bow. The Japanese thought this showed extreme disrespect and threatened the very foundations of life." Hall, *Silent Language*, p. 81. * Turning one's back to someone. *Japan. Life*, 10 Sept. 1945, p. 33. * Preserving distance as sign of respect: "Perhaps he was actually a gen-eral. He came to a stop, four younger officers remaining a few steps behind him, and asked what was going on." *Germany.* Mulisch, p. 50. * Precedence as sign of respect: at doorways or in entering automobiles, "even a token gesture of yielding the right of way or the seat of honor to a Chinese is appreciated; failure to make the gesture . . . could be interpreted as arrogance." *China.* Axtell, *Gestures,* p. 13. * "On a Mid-dle Eastern guest's arrival at a traditional house, he or she must give a

BODY • 73

formalized greeting and then sit down at the place designated, on the floor. This immediate lowering of the body is a ritual act of deference to the host and his household. Not to do it . . . 'would be sitting on the head of the host.' For the rest of the visit, guests must take care not to rise while the host is sitting. The aim is never to stand higher than the host; if somebody leaves, they bend while exiting, demonstrating a desire to stay lower: physical demeanor is an outward sign of one's will and intent." *United Arab Emirates.* Visser, p. 112. "Sitting, provided that it is on a chair, enhances social stature: people who can arrange to sit while everyone else is obliged to stand are usually eliciting respect. There is only one posture which can beat sitting erect for status, and that is lying down. . . . An Assyrian bas-relief shows us King Assurbanipal lying down to eat in the presence of his respectful, seated wife; and Phoenician ivory couches of the ninth century B.C. have been found together with luxury dinnerware. The Hebrew prophet Amos (ca. 640 B.C.) railed against the inhabitants of Samaria who imitated . . . the Phoenicians and Aramaeans of northern Syria: 'Woe to them . . . that lie upon beds of ivory, and stretch themselves upon their couches.' The custom, perceived at the time as the acme of prestige and luxury, was adopted by upper-class Greek men, except in such isolationist and conservative societies as Sparta and Crete . . . The Romans learned the use of the dining couch from the Greeks and Etruscans in the second century B.C. Lying down remained *de rigueur* at formal banquets in the Roman Empire; it died out as late as the fifth century A.D. In Greek monasteries on Mount Athos, there still exist halls containing couches on which monks may lie down and eat. . . . Women lay down to eat where men were present only in exceptional societies such as that of the Etruscans, or if they were prostitutes. Upper-class women in Imperial Rome appear to have been allowed occasionally to lie down with the men, but for most of the history of the custom, 'proper' women, if they ate with the men at all, sat on chairs with their small tables in front of them." *Assyria; Phoenicia;* anc. Jews; *Syria;* anc. *Greece; Etruria;* anc. *Rome;* Greek Orthodox. Visser, pp. 152–153. * Cessation of all activity in the presence of a superior. *Brazil.* Cascudo, *História,* p. 65. * After a funeral, mourners follow the hearse for a short distance. Orthodox Jews. Kolatch, p. 61.

Revulsion "Professor Penrose's characteristic response to any suggestion that the family should revisit Australia being a shudder." *England.* Lodge, *Nice Work,* p. 42.

Self-discipline "As the well-rehearsed phrases dropped from Thatcher's lips, he observed a change in his companion. Until now Iwamoto had been a robust, outgoing person. His voice had been inflected, his face had mirrored one expression after another, his hands and arms had been in constant play. As he listened to Thatcher, he became Japanese. His hands were stilled, his face was a mask, his brief queries were monotonic. The overall impression was not one of placidity but of great nervous energy under restraint." *Japan.* Lathen, *East is East*, p. 51.

Self-importance "Why, here he comes, swelling like a turkey-cock." 16th–17th cent. *England.* Shakesp., *Henry V* 5.1.15. "Does he not hold up his head, as it were, and strut in his gait?" 16th–17th cent. *England.* Shakesp., *Merry Wives* 1.4.30.

Solemnity "and then with a bow of mock solemnity to Mr. Pickwick, and a wink to Mr. Weller, the audacious slyness of which baffles all description, followed the footsteps of his hopeful master." 19th cent. *England.* Dickens, *Pickwick*, I, p. 434.

Sorrow "Therefore I will wail and howl, go stripped" Biblical. *Middle East. Mic.* 1:8. * "Wallow thyself in ashes" Biblical. *Middle East. Jer.* 6:26. * Sinking to the ground, moaning. Anc. *Greece.* Homer, *Odyss.* iv, 719. * Sitting on a stone. Medieval *England. Beowulf*, 2417; Habicht, p. 17. Criminals sat on a stone before execution. Medieval *Germany.* John Meier, pp. 219–44. See also CHIN, HAND, KNEE, Pensiveness; see Walther von der Vogelweide: "Ich saz ûf einem steine . . ." and the miniature in Heidelberg, Univ.-Bibl. cpg.848, fol. 124r; see Walther, pl. 45.

Space, personal Intimate distance—close phase: distance between individuals while engaged in copulation, contact-sports such as wrestling, and the process of protecting or comforting another: physical contact, possible physical involvement, physical awareness are characteristic. Intimate distance—far phase: distance of 6 to 18 in. between individuals. Considered improper in public by North Americans. If unavoidable, as in crowded subways or elevators, defensive tactics are used to eliminate the intimacy of closeness: immobility, withdrawal whenever possible, hands are kept at the side or used to steady or support the body, eyes avoid those of others and remain fixed on an impersonal object such as the floor or the floor-indicator above the elevator door. Personal distance—close phase: distance of 1½ to 2½ feet. Indicates the relationship between individuals. In North America, it is quite proper for a wife and husband to stay within this distance from one another in public; not so for a man and woman not married to each other. Personal distance—far phase: 2½ to 4 feet: "keeping someone at arm's length." In North America this is the distance at which discussions of personal interest can take place at moderate voice level, and, though halitosis can be perceived at this distance, North Americans usually do not breathe directly at others. The gaze must shift continually so as to avoid staring at the same spot. Social distance—close phase: 4 to 7 feet. In North America, this is the distance at which impersonal business is transacted, and at which people speak to one another at an informal social occasion. North Americans generally shift the gaze from eye to eye or eye to mouth to avoid staring. Looking down at another person at this distance is inappropriate, since it implies dominance. Social distance—far phase: 7 to 12 feet. Conversations conducted at the far end of this scale have a decidedly formal character. If such conversations are conducted for any length of time, it is more important to maintain visual contact than at lesser distances. Public distance—close phase: 12 to 25 feet. At this distance, the voice is loud, though not full volume, the diction is carefully chosen, syntax is planned. Public distance—far phase: 25 feet or more. Shades of meaning imparted by the normal voice and facial expression are lost, and are supplanted by gesture and stance. Tempo of speech is reduced; enunciation is more precise. *North America.* Hall, *Hidden Dimension*, pp. 113–29. For German, English. French, Japanese and Arab views of personal space, see ibid., pp. 131–64. * "Some sociologists maintain that one keeps a distance of 7.5 meters between oneself and prominent people, until they ask one to approach. Some experiments have shown that the distance is least between people of the same status." *Western Europe; North America.* Argyle, p. 289; also Wenzel, pp. 131–32 (transl. by eds.). * "If a squire wants to wash, he should step aside, away from the knights, and wash unobtrusively: that is polite and pleasant to observe." Medieval *Germany.* Thomasin von Circlaria, v. 523–26; also Wenzel, p. 132. * "Whenever a squire is as eager to serve as is proper, he should observe courtly manners. Many a one makes a beeline to put a cup before his master. If he would just stand aside a bit, he could wait until the proper time to serve." 13th cent. *Germany.* Konrad von Haslau, v. 627–34; also Wenzel, ibid. * Wenzel (p. 132–33) observes that the connection between status and distance is supported by the connection between status and height: notable people are placed on a higher level. "A squire should never stand on a bench . . . if he sees a knight sitting on it." 13th cent. *Germany.* Thomasin von Circlaria, v. 413–16; also Wenzel, pp. 132–33. For the legally imposed requirement of space between individuals as a form of ostracism, see Ostracism, above. *See also* Body distance.

Submission Bowing. Biblical. *Middle East.* II *Sam.* 9:8; I *Kings* 1:53; *Gen.* 33:6–7; 43:26. "bowed three times before him" 16th–17th cent. *England.* Shakesp., *Wint. Tale* 3.3.24. * "As low as to thy foot doth Cassius fall." 16th–17th cent. *England.* Shakesp., *Jul. Caes.,* 3.1.56. * Rolling on the ground. Anc. *Greece.* Sittl, p. 161. * Proskynesis: Monks prostrated themselves. 4th–5th century. *Egypt; Palestine.* Sittl, p. 160. Throwing oneself entirely on the ground appears to have occurred only in extreme fear in the Roman empire. Sittl, p. 161. Falling prostrate on the ground. Anc. *Greece* and *Rome.* Sittl, p. 158. Cf. *HDV,* I, p. 318. * In the medieval marriage ceremony, after the hands of bride and groom had been joined and the ring slipped on the bride's finger, the wife (according to two twelfth-century *ordines*) then prostrated herself before her husband. "Later an attempt was made to transform this part of the ritual by having both bride and groom cast themselves at the feet of the priest. But this was too much to ask, and the Church, adept at the use of trial and error in its efforts to absorb the marriage ritual, preferred to eliminate the whole sequence, which was probably only one of many regional peculiarities." Medieval *Europe.* Duby, *Private Life*, p. 130. * Proskynesis was required before the Emperor of Ethiopia, Hailie Selassie, at court. Jalink, 1986. * "Pope Paul, shoeless and without his fisherman's ring, prostrated himself before a cross in the Basilica of St. Mary Major in the Church's mournful Good Friday liturgy." AP Report, UPI Wirephoto. *L. A. Times*, March 28, 1970, pt. 1, p. 8. * After World War II there were cases in which freshmen, before being admitted to a students' organization, were required to prostrate themselves, saying: "I am sinful, I am a Jew and impotent." Amsterdam. *Netherlands.* Jalink, 1986. * Beggars often sat on the ground, and supplicants near a place which guaranteed their safety, such as an altar, the hearth of a house or of a city. Anc. *Greece.* Bremmer, p. 25. * Slaves and brides, in being accepted into a household, were required to sit near the hearth: a rite of passage indicating transition to a new status. Anc. *Greece.* Bremmer, p. 26.

Walking   Children should walk with a steady, not hasty gait. Erasmus, *De civilitate morum puerilium libellus* 1.28. Body should always be kept erect, one should not lean backwards (which is a sign of conceit), nor let one's head hang to one side or another, or gesticulate too widely. One should keep one's feet together when standing; one should not stagger, nor walk too slowly or quickly; nor should one sit with arms akimbo (a military posture), nor hold the knees apart, nor keep the legs crossed, nor play with one's feet. *Het boekje van Erasmus aengaende de beleeftheidt der kinderlijcke zeden* (1678), pp. 17–21 and the discussion in Roodenburg, pp. 158–59. A gait should be "well-ordered, without swaying the body to and fro . . . keeping it fixed in the Spanish way, as if not daring to turn one's head" *Groot ceremonie-boek* (1735), pp. 68, 169, 171, 179 and the discussion by Roodenburg, pp. 160–61, who observes that Erasmus' and De Courtin's recommendations not to walk too slowly or too quickly are very similar to those of Cicero in his *De officiis.* Warned against walking quickly, recommending a senatorial gravity. Paolo Cortese, *De Cardinalatu* (Rome, 1510), pp. xcvi–cxviii and Burke, p. 76. Advises noblemen not to walk too quickly (like a servant), or too slowly (like a woman). Giovanni della Casa, *Il Galateo* (Florence, Italy 1558), ch. 6., and Burke, p. 77. * A well-mannered person had to observe "measure and consonance" in standing, walking or sitting, and recommended a calm and erect posture. 17th cent. *France.* De Courtin, p. 81. * "The general movement for [Restoration] men should be peacocky, which should not be confused with the delicate, mincing movement of the fops in [Restoration comedies]. . . . The Restoration man did not have the same robust, athletic swagger as the Elizabethan, for he was in high heels, which modified his walk; he could not stride or bounce about. Moreover, his costume was very heavy and had to be carried and balanced properly. . . . A good, comfortable stance was with the weight on the back foot, the other foot forward and to the side. This position permitted him to address himself to people scattered over a wide area by simply turning from the waist. 17th cent. *England.* Rockwood, p. 178. * "By 1870 . . . the bustle appeared. The rear thrust of the bustle caused the upper half of the body to be inclined forward to maintain balance. The front of the skirt became tighter and revealed the outline of the leg from the thigh to the knee. . . ; a sway developed to call attention to the hips, and a good forward stride was used to make sure the legs pushed against the skirt and were solidly outlined." Ibid., p. 182. * Balzac, *Théorie,* p. 52, observed that "Le mouvement lent est essentiellement majestueux" ("Slow movement is majestic in its essence") and Nietzsche, II, p. 543, answered the question "Was ist vornehm?" ("What is aristocratic?") with "die langsame Gebaerde, auch der langsame Blick" ("the leisurely gesture, and the slow glance"). 19th cent. *France; Germany.* Roodenburg, p. 159.

BODY, CHEEK, HAND
Sorrow Body on the ground, face down hands, scratching cheeks. Men. Anc. *Rome.* Sittl, p. 25.

BODY, EYE, HAND
Reverence Priest goes to center of the altar, "where raising his eyes to the Crucifix, and immediately lowering them again, he inclines profoundly, keeping his hands joined." Roman Catholic. *Mass,* p. 28.

BODY, FACE
Adoration Romans made a complete turn to the right so that a kiss was thrown toward deity before or after the turn. Not Greek, but Celtic and anc. *Rome.* Athenaeus, 4, 152 d; Sittl, p. 194.

Despair The defeated Darius (in the Middle English *The Wars of Alexander,* 3074 ff.) throws himself face to the ground. 14th cent. *England.* Habicht, p. 52.

Fear Falling or bowing with face to the ground. Biblical. *Middle East.* I *Sam.* 28:14; *Luke* 24:5; *Lev.* 9:24. *See also* BODY, Prayer; BODY, FACE, Prayer.

Gratitude Falling down on one's face at the feet of one's benefactor. Biblical. *Middle East. Luke* 17:16.

Greeting Bowing, face to the ground. Biblical. *Middle East.* I *Sam.* 25:41; 20:41.

Plea Falling down on one's face. Biblical. *Middle East. Num.* 14:5; 16:22; *Luke* 5:12.

Prayer Prostration. Biblical. *Middle East. Josh.* 5:l4; 7:6; *Judg.* 13:20; I *Kings* 18:39; *Ezek.* 1:28; 3:23; *Matth.* 26:39. Early Christian. Tertull. *Iud.* 11; Sittl, p. 199. * Face touches floor. *Portugal.* Basto, p. 12. *See also* Adoration above; BODY, Prayer.

Respect Prostration. 19th cent. *Sandwich Islands.* Eichler, p. 95.

Reverence Prostration. Biblical. *Middle East. Gen.* 48:16; 50:18; I *Sam.* 24:8; II *Sam.* 14:33; 24:20.

Sorrow Prostration. Biblical. *Middle East. Num.* 16:4.

BODY, FINGER
Threat Tips of right thumb, index and middle fingers joined; then this configuration moved rapidly in front of body. *Saudi Arabia; Jordan.* Barakat, no. 28.

BODY, FINGER, HAND
Pensiveness In a squatting position, the right hand drawing on the ground, the left hand, open, holding forehead. *Central Africa.* Hochegger, p. 146.

Respect Tapping with two fingers on table; bowing. "Her waitress returned bearing a white teapot . . . from which she filled Kit's cup. . . . Kit thanked her by tapping twice on the table with two fingers, an act of respect she'd learned . . . in graduate school. In response to this . . . the waitress smiled . . . and bowed more deeply than before . . ." *China.* Donaldson, p. 123.

BODY, FINGER, MOUTH
Pride Blowing on fingernails of one hand, then rubbing them on front of body. Comic. *U.S.* Saitz and Cervenka, p. 96.

BODY, FOOT
Prayer Invoking the dead by sitting (or throwing self) on the ground and beating upon it with either hands or feet. Anc. *Greece.* Sittl, p. 191.

BODY, FOREHEAD
Submission In proskynesis the subjects throw themselves down so that the forehead touched the ground. *Byzantine Empire.* Sittl, p. 160.

BODY, FOREHEAD, MOUTH
Sorrow Vertically furrowed brow, mouth drawn down at corners, bent posture. Depressives. *Europe.* Krukenberg, pp. 258–60; 315.

BODY, HAIR

Prayer In case of danger to the state, the senate ordered a supplication by the matrons, who fell on their knees in the temples or loosened their hair, threw themselves down and kissed the ground. Others tore their hair on the threshold of the temples, beat their shoulders and scratched their cheeks. Anc. *Rome.* Statius, *Thebais* 4, 203. Sittl, p. 185.

BODY, HAND

Etiquette "Here Job Trotter bowed with great politeness and laid his hand upon his heart." 19th cent. *England.* Dickens, *Pickwick*, I, p. 433. * When guests enter the room, the ladies rise and bow, putting the hands together, then they sit down again. Medieval courtly. 13th cent. *Germany.* Schultz, I, p. 529. See also *Kudrun*, st. 334; *Dietrichs Flucht*, 7411; *Biterolf*, 1301.

Finished Cutting across the body with the open hand, fingers extended and palm inward from shoulder of one side to waist of the other. *Spain.* Green, p. 84.

Gratitude Bowing and simultaneously swinging flat right hand, palm up, a little way down and to one side. Schoolchildren. *U.S.* Seton, p. xxiv.

Greeting " 'Moyo pochtenie (My respects),' said both men, bowing to each other over a powerful handshake." *Russia.* Nabokov, p. 126. * "Pnin bowed deeply to them with an 'I am disarmed' spreading of the hands." *Russia.* Nabokov, p. 161. * Man of low social position falls flat on the ground with his hands folded in front. Southern *India.* Thomas, p. 80.

Mourning Body thrown on ground, hands beating ground. Men. Anc. *Greece.* Sittl, p. 26.

Plea Squatting before someone and touching his feet: son pleading for forgiveness from his father. *Central Africa.* Hochegger, p. 93.

Possession Wife expresses her belonging to a man by resting her hand on his knee or leaning against him. Sirionó Indians. *Bolivia.* Key, p. 97.

Prayer Invoking the dead by sitting (or throwing self) on the ground and beating upon it either with the hands or the feet. Anc. *Greece.* Sittl, p. 191.

Quarrel Body leaning slightly forward, hands on hips, scornful expression. *Central Africa.* Hochegger, p. 158.

Refusal Turning silently away while making a gesture of throwing something over one's shoulder. *Flanders.* Andrea and de Boer, p. 185.

Sick Right hand rests on the waist, body inclined forward. *Central Africa.* Hochegger, p. 110.

Strike Cutting across the body with the open hand, fingers extended and palm inward, from the shoulder of one side to the waist of the other. *Spain.* Green, p. 84.

Useless   Crossing the slightly cupped hand sharply across the body. The palm of the hand faces the shoulder at the beginning of the movement; at the conclusion, the palm faces outward. *Spain; Lat. Am.* Green, p. 85.

Virility   "Heavy back pounding after an athletic event often is an attempt to emphasize virility and sometimes reflects inner hostility." *U.S.* Birdwhistell, "Do Gestures Speak Louder than Words?" p. 56.

BODY, HAND, HEAD

Humility   The priest "joins his hands, bows his head and bends low to signify the profound humility of Christ hanging upon the Cross and praying for us, and to signify also his own humility." Roman Catholic. *Mass*, p. 65.

Reverence   Herero bow to omum borum bonga tree and place twigs or grass at its foot as reverence for it as source of life of all four-footed beasts. Southwest *Africa.* Frazer, *Golden Bough*, II, p. 220.

Sorrow   Sinking to the ground, burying the face in the hands, weeping. *Europe.* Boggs, p. 319.

BODY, HAND, NECK

Hanging   Right hand grasps throat, then the body straightens out and assumes the position of a hanged man. *Central Africa.* Hochegger, p. 145.

Refusal   Both hands placed on nape of the neck, body turns brusquely to the side: "Je refuse! Ne me regards pas!" ("I refuse! Don't look at me!") *Central Africa.* Hochegger, p. 161.

BODY, HEAD

Guilt   Shrinking, contracting of the body, bowing of head. *Europe.* Krukenberg, p. 318; cf. also p. 293 and pl. 246.

Pride   Sideways movement of the head or body accompanying expression of affirmation. Arab. George, p. 322.

Shame   Shrinking, contracting of the body, bowing of head. *Europe.* Krukenberg, p. 318.

Submission   Bowing head and entire body. *Portugal.* Basto, p. 21.

BODY, HEAD, LIP

Arrogance   Raising the head, which is drawn slightly to the rear, lips closed, stiff posture. *Europe.* Krukenberg, p. 318.

BODY, OBJECT

Familiarity   "She . . . drew in her skirt with a gesture that indicated he was to sit down beside her." *England.* Huxley, ch. 4.

Mourning Enveloping one's body completely in a cloak. Medieval and Renaissance *Europe*. Barasch, *Gestures of Despair*, pp. 69 ff.

BREAST
Self-importance Throw out chest. Schoolchildren. *U.S.* Seton, p. xxii.

Sorrow As a means of attempting to stop a son from departing, mother opens her clothes to show the breasts that nourished him. Anc. *Greece* and *Rome*. Sittl, p. 173.

BREAST, CHEEK, HAIR, HAND
Mourning Beating breast, tearing hair, scratching cheeks. 16th cent. *Greece*. Sittl, pp. 68–69.

BREAST, EYE, HAIR, HAND
Mourning Beating breast, tearing hair, beating eyes. Men. Anc. *Rome*. Sittl, p. 71.

BREAST, FINGER
Promise Wet finger and make Sign of the Cross on one's heart. Children. Yorkshire, *England*. Opie, p. 124. * With right index make little cross over the heart. *U.S.* schoolchildren. Seton, p. 53.

BREAST, FOOT, HAND, LIP
Applause Audience kisses chest, head, or foot of a rhetor after a speech. Anc. *Greece*. Sittl, p. 166.

BREAST, FOREHEAD, HAND, MOUTH
Apotropy Making a cross over forehead, mouth, and heart, then the "large cross," touching forehead, chest and both sides, kissing a cross, made with thumb and index of right hand. *Spain*. Flachskampf, p. 243.

Greeting Right hand reaches down as if to take dust from the ground, then is raised to chest, mouth, and forehead. Arab. Petermann, I, p. 172; Goldziher, "Über Gebärden," p. 370.

Prayer Right hand touches breast, mouth, forehead in prayer before graves of princes. Anc. *Egypt*. Ohm, p. 288. * "The priest makes the Sign of the Cross on the book at the beginning of the Gospel, then on his forehead, lips, and breast. This is a prayer that the holy Gospel may be, first, on our mind . . . secondly, on our lips . . . thirdly, in our heart." Roman Catholic. *Mass*, p. 29.

BREAST, FOREHEAD, HAND, SHOULDER
Prayer Crossing oneself. With the flat right hand, fingers extended, touch forehead, then the breast, first the left side, then the right. Roman

Catholic. Ohm, p. 294. Same gesture, but from right to left side of breast. Greek Orthodox. Ohm, ibid.

BREAST, FOREHEAD, LIP
Greeting   Only the highest officials were permitted to kiss the chest of the emperor, who in return kissed their foreheads. Diocletian monarchy. *Roman Empire.* Sittl, p. 166.

BREAST, HAIR, HAND
Mourning   One hand beating breast, the other tearing the hair. Idealized. Anc. *Greece.* Schreiber, pp. 86–95; Sittl, p. 75.

BREAST, HAND
Affection   Hand(s) of beloved pressed against one's chest. Anc. *Greece* and *Rome.* Sittl, p. 34.

Affirmation   One hand laid upon the breast, the other extended horizontally and somewhat to the side. Anc. *Greece* and *Rome*, Baroque *Europe.* Ohm, p. 288. *See* Oath below.

Agreement   Conspiratorial poking in the other's chest. Men. 19th cent. *England.* Dickens, *Pickwick*, II, p. 322. *See* Congratulation below.

Alarm   Beating shield against chest, calling "to arms, to arms, to arms!" Anc. *Rome.* Statius, *Thebais*, 7, 133–4; Sittl, p. 215.

Anger   Beating one's breast in anger. 19th cent. *Germany.* Boggs, p. 321.

Apotropy   Hermits beat their breasts with fists to drive out evil thoughts. Early Christian. Sittl, p. 20.

Assistance   Lightly patting one's heart with right palm indicates need for assistance. *Saudi Arabia.* Barakat, no. 187.

Breastfeeding   Left hand as if holding a baby, right hand touches breast. *Central Africa.* Hochegger, p. 5.

Buxom   Both hands pretend to throw pendulous breasts back over shoulders. Men. *Colombia.* Saitz and Cervenka, p. 122. * Tracing form of woman's breasts. *Colombia; U.S.* Saitz and Cervenka, p. 122. Clawlike hands, palms toward chest, moved slightly forward and brought to a sudden stop—ample and firm breasts; movement of hands ends languidly—luxurious, heavy breasts. Men. *Netherlands.* Andrea and de Boer, p. 40.

Congratulation   (familiar) " 'If I were not a married man myself, I should be disposed to envy you, you dog, I should.' Thus expressing himself, the little lawyer gave Mr. Winkle a poke in the chest, which that gentleman reciprocated; after which they both laughed." 19th cent. *England.* Dickens, *Pickwick*, II, p. 322. *See also* Agreement above.

Copulation   Caressing a partner's nipple invites copulation. 15th–16th cent. *Germany.* Dürer. Mellinkoff, *Outcasts*, I, p. 202.

Curse "goes by night in front of the house or on the roof, bares her breast toward the stars and, with the breast toward the heavens." 19th cent. *Palestine.* Bauer, p. 218.

Dedication In connection with the vow, the hand touches the chest whenever the donor is referred to. Anc. *Greece.* Sittl, p. 196.

Despair Beating the breasts. Women. Anc. *Greece* and *Rome.* Sittl, p. 19. Beating breast. Men. Early Christian. Sittl, p. 20.

Determination Right hand beats on breast: "Je le ferai malgré tout!" ("I'll do it in spite of everything!") *Central Africa.* Hochegger, p. 213.

Disappointment Beating the breast. Men. Anc. *Greece* and *Rome.* Sittl, p. 20.

Disgust Hand, palm down, placed horizontally in front of chest. *Colombia; U.S.* Not very common among U.S. young adults. Saitz and Cervenka, p. 43.

Distress "beats her heart." 16th–17th cent. *England.* Shakesp., *Much Ado* 2.3.153; *Hamlet* 4.5.5; *Ven. and Ad.*, 829.

Eating See HAND, Eating.

Emphasis See HAND, Emphasis.

Encouragement "Tradition relates that some lost or losing battles have been restored by the women, by the incessance of their prayers and by the baring of their breasts; for so it is brought home to the men that the slavery, which they dread much more keenly on their women's account, is close at hand" Anc. *Rome.* Tacitus, *Germania* 8.

Enmity See HAND, Enmity.

Excitement See HAND, Excitement.

Gratitude Left hand laid upon chest. *Greece.* Sittl, p. 162. Right palm laid upon chest. *See* Greeting.

Greeting Hands crossed on chest. Obligatory greeting of Byzantine emperors. *Byzantine Empire.* Treitinger, p. 66; Alföldi, p. 64. * Folding hands at chest and bowing down to the ground. High officials to maharajah. *India.* Thomas, p. 80. * Right hand brought to chest twice and head slightly bowed, saying "ram, ram." Among equals in *Hindustan.* Thomas, ibid. * Folding the palms in front of the chest and saying "Namasti." Arya Samjists. *India.* Thomas, ibid. * One hand placed on chest, may be accompanied by a slight bow. Salute of the Civil Service. *Brazil.* Cascudo, *História*, p. 168. * Left hand laid upon chest. 19th cent. *Greece.* Sittl, p. 162. * Right palm pressed upon chest. *Lebanon; Jordan; Syria; Saudi Arabia.* Barakat, no. 25. * Holding each other by the hand, two men bump chest against chest. *Central Africa.* Hochegger, p. 178.

Guilt Flat hand strikes breast: "mea culpa!" "It's my fault!" *Netherlands.* Andrea and de Boer, p. 124.

Humility Arms crossed upon the breast so that hands lie on the shoulders while executing a deep bow. Mandatory for subjects before Byzantine Emperor. Frequent in the East, scarce in the West. *Middle East.* Ohm, p. 277. * Slave awaited commands of master by crossing arms on chest. Athens. Anc. *Greece.* Sittl, p. 151. Coffin shows a child, crossing hands on her breast, one hand holding a lotus flower, the other a cross. Brit. Museum. 3rd cent. A.D. *Egypt.* Joachim Jeremias, pp. 66 ff. Perhaps this is the gesture referred to by Tertullian, *De Anima,* chap. 51, in which he describes a Christian girl laid out in Roman fashion, arms at her sides, who miraculously raised them during the priest's prayer. 2nd-3rd cent. Jacob, p. 19. Possibly it is also the gesture alluded to by the Byzantine author referred to by Gregory of Tours, *De gloria confessorum,* chap. 81, as reproaching a Western European for not burying the dead with their hands crossed. Barasch, however, surmises that he meant the crossing of the hands in the lap. 6th cent. Barasch, *Giotto,* p. 75. The gesture reappears in Romanesque funerary art. Northeastern *Spain;* Provence, *France.* Hands crossed on the breast entered European imagery as a gestural motif in the 13th cent. Barasch, *Giotto,* pp.72–87. In the 9th cent. the gesture was obligatory in the Greek Orthodox Church. The Bulgarians wrote to Pope Nicolaus I that the Greeks maintained that whoever does not cross his arms on his chest in church commits a grave sin, and in 866 received the answer that the gesture signifies: "I have bound my hands and subject myself to God's punishment." Sittl, p. 175.

Insult   Hand is brought to the heart of the gesticulator, feigning offense. *Spain; Lat. Am.; U.S.* Green, p. 81.

Investiture   *See* Oath.

Mockery   Open hands describe spheres on chest—large breasts. Joined hands on the left side of the chest—large breast. Open hands pressed against chest—flat breasts. Open hands, palms up, placed in front of chest as if under breasts—signifying pendulous breasts. Open hands, palms up, placed in front of chest as if under breasts, move as if to support pendulous breasts. *Central Africa.* Hochegger, pp. 184–186.

Mother   Open hands placed on chest, representing breasts; or open hands placed, palm up, low on the chest, indicating heavy breasts; or hands, palms facing each other, placed in form of a triangle in front of chest, indicating first, the left, then the right breast. *Central Africa.* Hochegger, pp. 117–118.

Mourning   Striking chest with hands. Anc. *Egypt,* anc. *Greece* and *Rome,* 2nd–6th cent. Christian. Ohm, p. 281; Quasten p. 217. Gesture prohibited by the third Synod of Toledo (can. 22). Quasten, p. 221, n. 16. * Beating breasts and mouth. Wallpainting in tomb. *Egypt.* Ball, p. 119; Hastings, *Dict. of the Bible,* I, p. 453. * Beating breast. Men. *Asia.* Anc. *Greece* and *Rome.* Aeschyl., *Pers.* 1054; Quint. Smyrn. 7, 33; Sittl, p. 25. Men. Anc. *Rome.* Sittl, ibid. and pp. 19–20; 26. * Beating breast four times at cremation. Anc. *Rome.* Sittl, p. 73. * Beating breast. Men. 4th cent. B.C.–1st cent. A.D. Hellenistic *Near East.* Sittl, p. 67. * Scratching breast. Women. Anc. *Greece* and *Rome,* 2nd–6th cent. Christian. Sittl, p. 27. * Beating breast. 19th cent. *Germany.* Boggs, p. 319. * "When women mourn, they swing or move one hand around the other . . . or they beat their breast alternately with the flat right and left hand." 19th cent. *Palestine.* Bauer, pp. 218–219.

Oath "He struck his hand upon his breast, and kist the fatal knife, to end his vow" 16th–17th cent. *England.* Shakesp., *Lucr.,* 1846. * Women swearing an oath lay the hand upon their breast. *Lex Alamannorum,* 56, 2 (54, 3): "tunc liceat illi mulieri jurare per pectus suum" ("then that woman ought to swear on her breast"). Early medieval *Germany.* Grimm, *DRA,* II, p. 548. * Men likewise swear lesser oaths with hand laid upon chest, particularly princes. In a deed of Bishop Florenz of Münster (1372) (Kindlinger, I, p. 38) the gesture is described "as a bishop customarily swears." Women and clerics, in being invested with a fief, lay hand upon breast. Still common in 19th century. Grimm, *Germany. DRA,* II, 249.

Obedience Left hand placed on chest and held there, slave awaits the command of his master. Anc. *Greece.* Sittl, p. 162.

Penitence Beating one's breast. Anc. Jews. Ohm, p. 281. Taken over by Christians, particularly popular among Catholics. Ohm, ibid. In Christian liturgy it symbolizes confession of guilt and unworthiness, as in the *Confiteor* (once) and before receiving Communion. In the liturgy it is always combined with an appropriate text. *GdG,* p. 35.

Plea Monk lays hand on chest. 18th cent. *France.* Sterne, ch. ii; Sittl, p. 162, n. 4. Left hand placed on breast, right hand raised. Deidamia on a mural. Campania, *Italy.* Anc. *Roman.* Sittl, p. 162, n. 4. "The priest . . . places his left hand on the corporal while he strikes his breast with the right." Roman Catholic. *Mass,* p. 68. "The priest returns to the center of the altar, with his hands joined before his breast and he implores mercy for himself and the people." Roman Catholic. *Mass,* p. 19.

Prayer Hands crossed on breast. 19th cent. *Palestine.* Bauer, p. 192; Also Dominicans; *Russian* liturgy. Ohm, p. 278. * Hands beating upon breast. Bantu. *Central, East and South Africa.* Ohm, p. 281. *See* HAND, Prayer. *See also* BREAST, HAND, Humility.

Pride One hand on chest, pulling up shirt, the other hand, elbow slightly raised, moves up along side of body: "How d'you like the way I did that? Good, eh?" *Netherlands.* Andrea and de Boer, p. 170. * Motion of pinning medal on one's own chest. *Flanders.* Ibid., 191.

Protest "clenched both fists, pulled them with stress against his chest." *U.S.* Birdwhistell, "Background," p. 14; *Introduction,* p. 27.

Regret Smiting breast. Biblical. *Middle East. Luke* 23:48; 18:13.

Relief "she drew her hands, drawn into loose fists, up between her breasts." *U.S.* Birdwhistell, *Introduction*, p. 30.

Remorse Smiting chest. Anc. Jews. Ohm, p. 281. Christians took the gesture from the Jews. Walahfrid Strabo, col. 932. Catholics at Mass beat breast at "Confiteor" ("I confess"), "Domine non sum dignus" ("Lord, I am not worthy"), "Agnus Dei" ("Lamb of God"). Roman Catholic. Ohm, p. 281.

Resignation *See* HAND, Resignation.

Sacrifice Beating chest. Anc. *Egypt.* Ohm, p. 281.

Satisfaction Hands on belt, chest expanded. *U.S.* Birdwhistell, "Do Gestures Speak Louder than Words?" p. 56.

Self-Identification One or both hands, fingers spread, resting on chest. *Colombia; U.S.* Saitz and Cervenka, p. 113. Right hand placed on chest, glance toward the person to whom the gesture is directed; or index of the right hand pointed at one's own chest; or index of the right hand pointed at one's own chest and moved repeatedly back and forth toward the chest. *Central Africa.* Hochegger, p. 118–119.

Shock Right hand on left breast or left hand on right breast, eyes toward heaven. Predominantly women. *Netherlands.* Andrea, de Boor, p. 9.

Sincerity Man puts woman's hand on his heart. Naples, *Italy.* Critchley, p. 89.

Sorrow Beating upon bare chest. Anc. *Egypt.* Ohm, p. 281. Women. Anc. *Greece* and *Rome.* Sittl, p. 19. * Scratching breasts. Women. Anc. *Rome.* Sittl, p. 27. * Beating the breast. Men. Anc. *Persia.* Aeschyl. *Pers.* 1054; *Mysia* (anc. Northwest *Turkey*). Sittl, p. 25. Also anc. *Rome.* Sittl, ibid. The only evidence from anc. *Greece* is Charito 7, 15. 16th-17th cent. *England.* Shakesp., *Richard III*, 2.2.3; Bulwer, pp. 74–75. * Hands (arms crossed) on chest. Medieval *Germany.* Hamburg, *Germany.* Stadtbibl. In scrinio 85, fol. 15a; Haseloff, p. 306.

Strength One or both fists strike chest several times. *Colombia; U.S.* Saitz and Cervenka, p. 133.

Submission The wife of Arminius marched in the Roman victory parade with her hands crossed over her breast: "compressis intra sinum manibus" ("pressing hands together between her breasts"). Anc. *Rome.* Tacitus, *Ann.* i, lvii. It was obligatory to cross the arms of dead Christians over the thorax; thus, according to tradition, Roland arranged the body of Archbishop Turpin: "Sur sa poitrine, entre lex deux clavicules, il a croisé ses blanches mains, les belles, Roland le plaint à la manière de son pays" ("Upon his breast, between his collarbones, Roland crossed Turpin's beautiful white hands; Roland mourned for him according to the custom of his country"). Medieval *France. Chanson de Roland*, Jean de Joinville, on his return from the Seventh Crusade, comments on his discovery of the skeletons of two hermits on Lampedusa: "Et le trouvames dous cors de gens mors, dont la chars etoit tout pourrie: les costes se tenoient encore toutes ensemble, et li os des mains estoient sur leur piz" ("And we found two bodies there; their flesh had rotted away; the ribs were still together and the bones of their hands rested on their breasts"). *Histoire de Saint-Louis*, cxxvi. See also Cascudo, *História*, p. 148.

Teasing   Open hands moved over each other several times on chest. *Lebanon*. Barakat, no. 36.

Truth   "lay hand on heart advise." 16th-17th cent. *England*. Shakesp., *Rom. and Jul.*, 3.5.192.

Woman   Fists placed on chest indicating breasts, or both hands, lightly open, placed over chest. *Central Africa*. Hochegger, p. 71.

BREAST, HAND, HEAD

Affection   Hands moved up the sides of the chest so that thumbs hit undersides of lapels; head is shaken slightly. Unrequited love. Hadhramaut, *Saudi Arabia*. Barakat, no. 203.

Gratitude   Palm of right hand placed on chest, head bowed, eyes closed. *Saudi Arabia*. Barakat, no. 83.

Greeting   Tips of fingers of right hand touched to forehead, then chest and back to forehead while bowing slightly. *Jordan; Saudi Arabia*. Barakat, no. 55.

Humility   In greeting one bows the head and lays the hand upon the chest as sign of humility and gratitude. Arab. Bauer, p. 224.

Mourning   After a death the female relatives uncover their heads, and often throw dust and earth upon them, "scratch their cheeks, tear their hair, blacken their faces with soot and beat their breasts." 19th cent. *Palestine*. Bauer, p. 212.

BREAST, HAND, LIP

Respect   When greeting a dignitary, shake right hand, then the person of lower rank kisses own hand, places it on own chest and bows slightly. *Saudi Arabia*. Barakat, no. 138.

BREAST, LIP

Greeting   At the morning *salutatio* (morning visit), a client kisses the chest of a nobleman upon whom he is waiting. Men. *Roman Empire*. Sittl, p. 166. Kiss on the chest permitted only to high officials who, in turn, were kissed on the forehead by the emperor. Diocletian monarchy. Anc. *Rome*.Sittl, ibid.

Plea   Noblemen kissed the chest of their benefactor. Anc. *Rome*. Sittl, p. 166.

BREAST, LIP, SHOULDER
Affection   Kiss on shoulders and breast. Grandmother to grandson. Anc. *Rome.* Quint. Smyrn., 13, 533–4; Sittl, p. 41.

BUTTOCKS
Apotropy   Vacating against the evil eye. *Phrygia.* Sittl, p. 124. * Buttocks bared against the devil. 19th cent. *Italy.* Kleinpaul, p. 271; Sittl, p. 124. Seamen bare buttocks against unfavorable winds, since winds are ascribed to good or evil supernatural beings. *Italy.* Sittl, ibid. Naked Huzulian sorceresses bare their buttocks toward heaven against hail. Carpathians. Southeastern *Europe. HDA*, IV, col. 63. Baring the buttocks to ward off the evil eye was used primarily to protect children. Jutland, *Denmark.* Meschke, col. 330. Baring the buttocks blunts the enemy's sword. Medieval *Scandinavia.* Seligmann, I, p. 174. The Kafir sorcerer stands on his head, buttocks bared, in order to prevent rain. Non-Moslem Arab. *HDA*, II, col. 847. Belief in the apotropaic powers of the bared buttocks was especially common among seamen, who believed the gesture to be a defence against storms. 18th-19th cent. *France; Italy.* Feilberg, pp. 426ff. *See also* Vidossi, p. 96.

Curse   Having undressed, the person uttering the curse turns his bare buttocks in the direction of the person cursed. *Central Africa.* Hochegger, p. 112.

Disbelief   Baring one's buttocks, or turning one's buttocks, toward someone: "Tell it to my ass!" *Netherlands.* Andrea and de Boer, p. 149.

Effeminacy   Wiggling the buttocks on the part of men. Anc. *Greece.* Bremmer, p. 21. *See* Homosexuality below.

Greeting   Young women greet each other by bumping their buttocks against each other. *Central Africa.* Hochegger, p. 177.

Homosexuality   Wiggling the buttocks ascribed to satyrs, who were sometimes depicted as homosexual; also denotes the passive homosexual. Anc. *Rome.* Bremmer, p. 21.

Insult   Expulsion of intestinal gas. Romans at Jews. Horace, *Sat.* 1, 9, 69–70. Merely ludicrous in anc. *Greece*, serious in mod. *Greece* and *Albania.* Sittl, p. 99. * "Each morning, last January, an entire platoon of Chinese soldiers would march out on the ice, lower their trousers, and aim their buttocks toward the Soviet side of the border. This is the ultimate Chinese insult. This exercise continued until one morning when, just as the Chinese assumed their positions, the Russians set up large portraits of Mao facing in their direction. The Chinese hastily covered themselves and retired. There were no repetitions." *Esquire,* Jan. 1968, p. 55. * "Dun Mihaka [a Maori Rights agitator] . . . succeeded in baring his buttocks in front of the Prince and Princess of Wales during their 1983 tour. . . . The dropping of pants and baring of buttocks is a recognized Maori insult known as *whakapohane*, and has been described by one expert in local customs as 'the ultimate culturally sanctioned Maori way of displaying opprobrium.' Mihaka himself has explained the act as 'a traditional non-violent form of protest.' " Ward, p. 3. * A woman will turn away from the person she intends to offend, bend over and thrust out her buttocks, simultaneously lifting her skirt to a height determined by her vulgarity or desire to offend. *Russia.* Monahan, pp. 150–51. "Annoyed by hecklers who prevented him from giving a speech as he opened an art show, [Colombian National University's President Antanas Mockus] turned his back, dropped his pants and mooned the audience. Thanks to a student who caught the overexposed academic on videotape, the episode showed up on nationwide TV— again and again. . . . Arturo Infante Villarreal, head of Bogotá's University of the Andes, called the act 'despicable,' but *El Tiempo* columnist Poncho Renteria said, 'That he tweaked these toughs who insulted him and his position is something I admire.' " "Talk of the Streets." *Time*, Atlantic Ed., Nov. 15, 1993, p. 12. *See also* Mockery.

Magical Baring the buttocks to call forth a storm. Upper Palatinate, *Germany; Lapland.* Meschke, col. 330. * In Russia one calls up the spirit of the wood on St. John's eve by baring the buttocks. In Norse literature baring the buttocks blunts the enemy's sword. Seligmann, I, p. 174. Baring the buttocks attracts a dragon's treasure. *Lapland.* Meschke, col. 330. Exposure of female buttocks prevents the flight of bees. Pomerania, *Germany.* Meschke, col. 330.

Mockery Expulsion of intestinal gas. Romans at Jews. Anc. *Rome.* Horace, *Sat.* 1, 9, 69–70. Also 19th cent. *Greece; Albania.* Ludicrous in classical *Greece.* Sittl, p. 99. Robert of Cléry, in his chronicle of the Fourth Crusade, states that, when the defenders of Constantinople saw the French and Venetian forces retreating, they climbed the walls, lowered their breeches, and showed them their buttocks. Cascudo, *História*, p. 21. * For the gesture in medieval art, see Mellinkoff, *Outcasts*, I, p. 205. * In the 16th cent., hostilities broke out between the Tenochca and the Tlaltelolco tribes, because the women of the latter showed their buttocks to the angry visitors from the former. *Mexico.* Cascudo, *História*, p. 20. * In Eisleben, Saxony, the devil interrupted the prayers of Martin Luther by lowering his breeches and showing his buttocks to the horrified Reformer. *Germany.* Ibid. "she sticks out her tongue at me whenever she sees me through the curtains, but yesterday she changed her tactics, turned around, lifted up her bathrobe, and showed me her rear end." *France.* Ibid., p. 21. * Patrons of the "Mugs Away" saloon in Mission Viejo "moon" (i.e., bare their buttocks to) commuter trains annually on July 10 "just for fun." California. *U.S.* Los Angeles TV Channel 11 (Fox), July 10, 1994. *See also* Insult.

Sexuality Women wiggling their hips—courtesans and followers of Dionysos. It was also considered the "gait of the rich" and perhaps also describes the waddle of Chinese mandarins. Anc. *Greece*. Bremmer, p. 21. * Buttocks of a woman wiggled from left to right. *Central Africa*. Hochegger, p. 194.

Shame "young and old, naked and barefoot, even with their buttocks uncovered" Biblical. *Middle East*. *Isaiah* 20:4.

BUTTOCKS, HAND

Affluence Men tap their hip-pocket once with the flat hand to indicate that they have plenty of money. *Netherlands*. Andrea and de Boer, p. 75.

Aversion Buttocks turned toward object of aversion and slapped by the right hand. *Central Africa*. Hochegger, p. 18.

Compliment A football player (*U.S.*) or soccer player (*Great Britain*) may pat the buttocks (once) of a teammate who has just performed particularly well. Axtell, *Gestures*, p. 8.

Contempt "In a quarrel, particularly at the end of a quarrel, . . . one participant strike[s] his buttocks with the words 'you are worth that!' " 19th cent. *Palestine*. Bauer, p. 220. Striking one's buttocks. Female gesture, euphemistic for "mooning." *Brazil*. Cascudo, *História*, p. 19.

Encouragement Hand pats another's buttocks once. Only on sports teams. Football players. *U.S.* Saitz and Cervenka, p. 48; Axtell, *Gestures*, p. 8; soccer players, *Great Britain*. Axtell, ibid.

Insult Open right hand moved at right side of buttocks while right side of buttocks is moved. *Lebanon; Syria*. Barakat, no. 49. * Both hands laid over buttocks so that they appear to prolong them downwards. *Central Africa*. Hochegger, p. 72. * Hand on buttocks in medieval art; see Mellinkoff, *Outcasts*, I, p. 200.

Meditation Scratching the buttocks. Medieval *France*. Barb. and Méon, IV, pp. 143; 221.

Prayer Sat on the ground and beat it with hands. Call upon the deities residing in the earth. Anc. *Greece* and *Rome*. Sittl, p. 190.

Refusal Slap one's buttock once. Vulgar. *Netherlands*. Andrea and de Boer, p. 75. * Buttocks pushed out slightly, closed right hand extended backwards and downwards with extended thumb pointing to buttocks: "Kiss my ass!" *Russia*. Vulgar, not widely used. Monahan, pp. 142–43.

BUTTOCKS, HAND, TONGUE

Mockery Baring buttocks while sticking out tongue and making a "fig." 16th cent. *Germany*. Lucas Cranach the Elder, *The Mocking of Christ* (1538), L. A. County Mus. of Art.

CHEEK
Anger Puff up cheeks. Anc. *Rome*. Horace, *Sat.* 1, 1, 20–1. Sittl, p. 14.

Indecision Blowing up cheek. *U.S.* Krout, p. 22.

Submission "He humbly puts his cheek on the ground before one reclining on a silken couch." Medieval Hispano-Arab. *Spain*. Emir Al-Hakam in Nykl, pp. 20–21.

CHEEK, EYE
Embarrassment Blushing and casting eyes down. *Germany*. Boggs, p. 321.

CHEEK, EYE, HAND
Fatigue Eyes closed, head inclined laterally, cheek reposes on back of one hand, which is joined to the other palm to palm. *France*. Mitton, p. 148.

CHEEK, EYE, MOUTH
Disbelief One corner of mouth drawn down, one cheek raised, partly closing an eye. *Europe; North Am.* Aubert, p. 149.

Uncertainty One corner of mouth drawn down, one cheek raised, partly closing an eye. *Europe; North Am.* Aubert, p. 105.

CHEEK, EYEBROW
Surprise Cheeks fill with air and eyebrows are raised. *Colombia*. Saitz and Cervenka, p. 134.

CHEEK, EYEBROW, HEAD, MOUTH
Admiration Head forward, eyebrows raised, slight smile raising cheeks. *Europe; North Am.* Aubert, p. 124.

Affection *See* Admiration above.

Prosperity Head thrown backwards, eyebrows raised, mouth and cheeks expanded. *Europe; North Am.* Aubert, p. 127.

Satisfaction *See* Prosperity above.

CHEEK, FINGER
Admiration Thumb and index touch the cheek, one on each side, and stroke gently down to the chin, suggesting a smile of admiration. Anc. *Greece?* 19th cent. Naples, southern *Italy*. De Jorio, pp. 77–78; Wundt, I, p. 172, Fig. 8; *Spain*. Flachskampf, p. 229. *Greece; Rome*. Morris et al., pp. 178–79. *Greece; Italy; Spain*. Axtell, *Gestures*, p. 70. * Tip of index pressed into cheek while whistling—admiration for a pretty woman. *Italy*. Axtell, *Do's and Taboos*, p. 42. * Stroking one's cheek in admiration for a pretty woman. *Greece*. Axtell, *Do's and*

Fig. 2. Neapolitan gestures. From Wilhelm Wundt, *Völkerpsychologie* (Leipzig, Germany: Engelmann, 1904) I, 172.

Taboos, p. 42. * Tip of right index run down the cheek of a woman—a compliment. *Lebanon; Syria.* Barakat, no. 127. * Twisting tip of forefinger into cheek, when speaking to a beautiful woman. *Libya.* Barakat, no. 126. * Tips of thumb and index joined, other fingers half open, make 45 degree rotary movement against the corresponding cheek, almost always accompanied by a click of the tongue. Río de la Plata region. *Argentina; Uruguay.* Meo Zilio, p. 72. Similar gesture uses only the tip of the index. *Italy.* Ibid. *See* Approval and Effeminacy.

Affection   Cheek of someone (usually a child) is taken between one's fingers. Anc. *Rome.* Sittl, p. 33. * Pinching right cheek of another person with tips of right index and thumb. *Egypt; Lebanon; Jordan; Syria; Saudi Arabia; Libya.* Barakat, no. 11.

Approval   Tips of index and thumb united make twisting movement on cheek, as if curling moustache. Origin is Neapolitan gesture of approval of twirling the tip of moustache. *Italy.* Efron, fig. 42. * Tip of extended index placed against cheek and rotated as if screwing it into cheek. Particularly in approval of taste of food, but by extension also of anything good or beautiful. *Italy.* Morris et al., pp. 62–67; it may be a modified form of the gesture of curling an imaginary moustache with one or both hands, reported by Morris et al. from the vicinity of Naples, *Italy* (p. 64). Rarely seen or understood outside Italy. Axtell, *Gestures*, p. 70.

Attention   Index and thumb of one hand brought to the cheeks to draw attention to whatever expression the face makes. Naples, *Italy.* Wundt, I, p. 172, fig. 29. *See* Fig. 2.

Boredom   Back of the fingers brush up and down over the cheek. Allusion to the tediousness of shaving. *France.* Mitton, p. 150.

Contemplation Thumb and index each stroking down one side of the face. "That's interesting—let me think about that." *U.S.* Axtell, *Gestures*, p. 70.

Cunning Index touches cheekbone; gesture accompanied by slight nod. *Sicily.* Pitrè, p. 355; Flachskampf, p. 236.

Disbelief "Index finger of the right hand is applied to the cheek in a circular motion, while the face is permitted to assume an expression suggesting the recent sucking of a lemon." WW II. *France.* Alsop, p. 27. * Fingers of right hand, loosely cupped, scrub right cheek upwards and downwards; corners of mouth drooping: "La barbe!" ("That's hard to swallow!") *France.* Brault, p. 378.

Effeminacy Raised index touches left cheek. *Lat. Am.* Kany, p. 181. * Tip of extended index is rotated against cheek as if drilling into it. Since it produces dimple in cheek, it may be linked to same gesture of approval, since dimples are often regarded as attractive. But for the same reason it can signify effeminacy or homosexuality, esp. in southern *Spain.* Morris et al., pp. 67. *See* Admiration.

Embarrassment Index placed tip against cheek. Anc. *Rome.* Sittl, p. 273.

Homosexuality *See* Effeminacy.

Illness Thumb and index brought down the cheeks, one on each side, but with some force rather than gently, as in Admiration, see above. *Europe.* Morris et al., pp. 178–79.

Mockery Tips of fingers and thumb joined and hitting on distended cheek, exhaling as fingers strike cheek. Can also signify that a given person is talking nonsense. *Saudi Arabia.* Barakat, no. 232.

Mourning Scratching cheeks. Men. Anc. *Greece.* Sittl, p. 25. Men. Hellenist. *Near East.* Sittl, p. 67. Widows. 19th cent. Epirus, Northwest *Greece.* Sittl, p. 69.

Plea Stroking someone's cheek. Anc. *Greece.* Sittl, p. 33. 13th cent. *Germany: Kudrun*, st. 386, 2.3.

Shyness Index placed with tip against cheek. Anc. *Greece.* Sittl, p. 273.

Sorrow Cheek rested against tips of fingers. Refined. Anc. *Greece.* Sittl, p. 24.

Stupidity Tip of extended index screwed into the cheek; a variant of the index screwed into the temple with the advantage that it is less conspicuous. *Germany.* Morris et al., pp. 67–68; primarily an Italian gesture of admiration for a pretty girl, but in Germany: "That's crazy." Axtell, *Gestures*, p. 70.

Success Thumb and index each stroking down one side of the face. *Yugoslavia.* Axtell, *Gestures*, p. 70.

Surprise Index placed tip against cheek. *Italy.* Sittl, p. 273.

Threat Tips of fingers and thumb joined and hit against cheek:

admonition to a child to behave, or that his mother will deal with child later. *Saudi Arabia.* Barakat, no. 231.
Warning Index touches cheek just below eye, then arm is extended to point in direction of danger. *Colombia.* Saitz and Cervenka, p. 147.

CHEEK, FOREHEAD, MOUTH

Admiration Biting of lower lip, eyebrows raised, lips and cheeks extended as in laugh. *Europe; North Am.* Aubert, p. 131.
Disapproval Cheeks raised, direct stare, brows frowning, corners of mouth drawn down. *Europe; North Am.* Aubert, p. 109.
Joy Biting of lower lip, raising eyebrows, lips and cheeks extended—unexpected joy, as in laugh. *Europe; North Am.* Aubert, p. 131.
* Lips extended in grin pushing up cheeks to form wrinkles under eyes, brows raised, forming lines across forehead. *Europe; North Am.* Aubert, p. 132.
Sensibility Opposing movements of brows and wrinkles on forehead. Contraction of the cheeks. Corners of mouth drawn down. *Europe; North Am.* Aubert, p. 139.
Sorrow *See* Sensibility above.

CHEEK, HAND

Affection " 'You're a sweet pet, my love,' replied Mrs. Colonel Wugsby, tapping her daughter's cheek with her fan" 19th cent. *England.* Dickens, *Pickwick*, II, p. 123. * Pinching cheek of another person. Show of affection or a promise to do something. *Jordan.* Barakat, no. 237. "One night when the household was in the shelter during an air raid, Hermann noticed that Frau Goebbels took her husband's hand and fondly laid it against her cheek." *Germany.* Toland, p. 83.
Amazement Placing the palm on either the cheek or behind the ear. Ghetto Jews. *Eastern Europe.* Efron p. 146.
Anger Hand rubs cheek: "and I rubbed my cheek for vexation." 18th cent. *England.* Richardson, p. 225.
Boredom Hand rubbed against cheek. *France. Life* Photos by David Scherman, *Life*, Sept. 16, 1946; pp. 12–15.
Challenge Slap on the cheek as part of challenge to a duel: "Un grand silence s'etait fait. Puis, tout à coup, un bruit sec claqua dans l'air. Le vicomte avait giflé son adversaire. Tout le monde se leva pour s'interposer. Des cartes furent échangées" ("There was a great silence. Then, suddenly, a crack was heard. The viscount had slapped his adversary. Everyone rose to intervene. Calling cards were exchanged.") 19th cent. *France.* Maupassant; see also Raim, p. 99.
Confirmation Slap on the cheek. Early Christian. Sittl, p. 146.
Despair Hands grasp cheeks. Women. *Albania.* Hahn, II, p. 153; Sittl, p. 23.

Doubt Flat hand taps both cheeks, one after the other. *Brazil.* Cascudo, *História*, p. 226.

Embarrassment Hand scratches cheek under one ear. 3rd. cent. *Greece.* Heliodorus, 2, 8. Sittl, p. 19. One hand placed against cheek. Anc. *Rome.* Sittl, p. 273.

Farewell "Mr. Pickwick . . . patted the rosy cheeks of the female servants in a most patriarchal manner . . ." 19th cent. *England.* Dickens, *Pickwick*, I, p. 165.

Fatigue Hands palm to palm, placed along cheek, head inclined to side, resting on back of hand. Eyes often closed simultaneously. Women. *Colombia; U.S.* Saitz and Cervenka, p. 125. *See* CHEEK, EYE, HAND, Fatigue, and EYE, HAND, HEAD, Fatigue.

Fear Hands grasp cheeks. Women. 19th cent. *Albania.* Hahn, II, p. 153; Sittl, p. 23.

Fever Palm of right hand held against right cheek. *Central Africa.* Hochegger, p. 201.

Greeting Holding each other's hands, women greet by putting cheek against cheek. *Central Africa.* Hochegger, p. 178.

Impatience "He rubbed one side of his face impatiently" 18th cent. *England.* Richardson, iv, p. 154.

Insult Slap on cheek. Anc. *Rome.* Sittl, p. 109. * In Corneille, *Le Cid*, the father of Ximène strikes the father of Rodrigue as catalyst of dramatic action; in the Spanish ballad tradition, the insult is offered by pulling the beard. Cascudo, *História*, p. 96. * Hand makes motion of shaving face with straight razor as indication by one driver to another that the latter is incompetent. Gesture derives from the recognized incompetence of barber-surgeons. *Brazil.* Cascudo, *História*, p. 101.

Kindness " 'I was wrong . . . ' said I, patting her cheek as kindly as a rough old fellow like me could pat it." 19th cent. *England.* Dickens, *Pickwick*, II, p. 437.

Magnitude Cheeks filled with air as hands indicate girth of a fat person. *Colombia; U.S.* Saitz and Cervenka, p. 51. * Right hand passes over cheek: "I've lost weight." *Central Africa.* Hochegger, p. 107.

Mockery Cheeks puffed out, left hand clenched against abdomen, right hand grasps nose, upper part of body doubled over. Customarily a mute gesture. *France.* Brault, p. 379. * Cheeks puffed out, hands raised and at some distance from each other on each side of the face: "Tu es gros comme ça!" ("You are this fat!") *Central Africa.* Hochegger, p. 84. * Cheeks puffed out in imitation of a case of mumps, open hands laid on cheeks. *Central Africa.* Ibid., p. 135.

Mourning Slapping one's cheeks. Women. Arab. Bauer, p. 218. In a manuscript of the *Imperatrix Porcina* (13th cent.) in the Bibl. Nat., Paris (lat. 14463), the Emperor of Rome proclaims his repentance by striking his face with his fists. Cascudo, *História*, p. 96.

Oath Hitting side of face with palm of right hand, then rubbing hand downward on cheek. *Saudi Arabia.* Barakat, no. 109.
Pain Hands scratch cheeks. Women. Anc. *Greece* and *Rome.* Sittl, p. 23. * Holding flat palm against one's cheek. 13th-14th cent. *Italy.* Dante, *Purg.,* c. vii; De Jorio, p. 142.
Pensiveness Cheek in hand. 15th-16th cent. *Spain.* Rojas, 179. See also numerous miniatures in the 14th cent. Heidelberg cod. pal. germ. 848, e.g. that of Walther von der Vogelweide, fol. 124r. Walther, pl. 45. *See also* CHIN, HAND, Pensiveness.
Punishment Slap on cheek. Anc. *Rome.* Sittl, p. 105.
Regret *See* HAND, HEAD, Regret.
Shyness Left hand placed on cheek. Anc. *Greece* and *Rome.* Baumeister, I, p. 589. Hand placed against cheek. Anc. Rom. Sittl, p. 273.
Sorrow Cheek rested in palm of hand. Anc. *Greece* and *Rome*; 13th-14th cent. *Italy:* Dante, *Purg.,* c. vii; 19th cent. *Greece.* Sittl, p. 24. * Scratching cheeks. Men. Anc. *Greece* and *Rome.* Sittl, p. 25. Medieval *Germany.* Haseloff, p. 305. *Sachsenspiegel.* Amira, "Handgebärden," p. 234.
Surprise One hand placed against cheek. Anc. *Rome.* Sittl, p. 273.
Thief Hand, slightly cupped, scrapes cheek lightly. *Colombia.* Saitz and Cervenka, p. 138.

CHEEK, HAND, KNEE
Plea Touching knees and cheek of a women, kneeling. Anc. *Greece.* Sittl, p. 166.

CHEEK, HAND, LIP
Affection While kissing, grasp cheeks of the person being kissed. Anc. *Greece.* Sittl, p. 40.
Greeting When two men meet, they kiss each other on the cheeks—first one cheek, then the other—while placing hands on each other's shoulders. *Lebanon; Syria; Saudi Arabia.* Barakat, no. 139.
Insult Lips form a circle, flat right hand taps left cheek: "Sexe de ta mère!" ("Mother-fucker!") *Central Africa.* Hochegger, p. 192. * Flat hand taps inflated cheek, thus causing expulsion of air through closed lips. *Brazil.* Cascudo, *História,* p. 226.

CHEEK, HEAD, LIP
Complaint Head bowed, brow furrowed, cheeks raised and wrinkled under the eyes, lips pouting. *Europe; North Am.* Aubert, p. 138.
Plea *See* Complaint, above.
Reproach Head bowed, eyes raised, lips pursed, cheeks lowered. *Europe.* Krukenberg, pp. 293, 318, and pl. 247.

CHEEK, HEAD, MOUTH

Humility   Head bowed, eyes raised, mouth smiling, cheeks raised. *Europe.* Krukenberg, p. 318.

Self-importance   Head thrown back, eyebrows raised, expansion of mouth and cheeks. *Europe; North Am.* Aubert, p. 127.

CHEEK, MOUTH

Insult   Cheeks puffed up, mouth pointed forward toward an old person. *Central Africa.* Hochegger, p. 162.

Refusal   Cheeks puffed up, mouth pointed forward. *Central Africa.* Hochegger, p. 162.

CHEEK, NOSE

Affection   Nose laid against cheek of beloved taking a deep breath, eyes closed, then lips make sound of a kiss without touching the cheek. *Mongolia.* Krukenberg, p. 131.

Approach   Man simultaneously wrinkles his nose and one cheek to a woman if he wants her to come to him. *Saudi Arabia.* Barakat, no. 166.

CHEEK, TONGUE

Concentration   Placing tongue in cheek. *Europe; North Am.* Krout, p. 24.

Contempt   "I signified my contempt of him by thrusting my tongue in my cheek." This after the other's assertion of his own valor; therefore, the meaning may instead be disbelief. 18th cent. *England.* Smollett, *Roderick Random,* ch. liv.

CHIN

Affirmation   A short, sharp sideways jerk of the chin, which results in the whole head tipping from side to side once. Usually accompanied by a single grunt—glottal stop followed by long schwa. *Nepal.* Su, LINGUIST 3.1012.

Astonishment   Chin drops, open mouth utters cry. *Central Africa.* Hochegger, p. 68.

Defiance   Chin raised. *England.* Toland, p. 101.

Fear   Chin drops. Anc. *Rome.* Sittl, p. 46.

Greeting   Chin slightly lifted. *Guam.* Dresser, *L.A. Times,* May 17, 1995, p. B7.

Hesitation   Pulling, stroking, or kneading chin. *France.* Mitton, p. 146.

Interrogation   Chin raised in direction of someone and remaining raised. ("What do you want?" "What do you say?") *France.* Mitton p.

141. *Central Africa.* Hochegger, p. 158. *Brazil.* Cascudo, *História*, p. 86.

Pleasure " 'I am glad to have my judgment,' observed Gay, tilting up his chin with shining pleasure, 'confirmed by outside witnesses.' " *England.* J. D. Carr, *To Wake the Dead*, p. 113.

Pointing Pointing with the chin in a direction or toward someone. *Spain; Lat. Am.* Green p. 71. Also Gurkha, *Nepal.* J. Masters, p. 38. Also *Algeria; Morocco; Brazil.* Cascudo, p. 86.

Snobbishness Chin lifted several inches; often eyes are partially closed. *Colombia; U.S.* Saitz and Cervenka, p. 128.

Submission Knocking chin on ground. Anc. *Persia.* Sittl, p. 158.

CHIN, FINGER

Assistance Grasping chin with tips of fingers of right hand—need for assistance. *Saudi Arabia.* Barakat, no. 13.

Boredom *See* FINGER, Boredom.

Challenge Gently grazing another person's chin with tip of right index: threat or challenge. *Lebanon; Saudi Arabia.* Barakat, no. 81.

Contempt Tips of fingers passed rapidly from back to front three or four times under the chin. *France.* Mitton, p. 151. The "chin flick": brushing the fingernails of one hand under the chin and then flicking the fingers outward. *France*; northern *Italy*; *Tunisia*: "Get lost. You annoy me." Insulting in France, northern Italy, Tunisia, merely negative in southern Italy. In France symbolizes a beard; figurative for "throwing of one's masculinity" at someone. Axtell, *Gestures*, p. 76. *See* Negation, Nothing below.

Disappointment Thumb rests between chin and lower lip while fingers, extended, move from side to side. *Colombia.* Saitz and Cervenka, p. 32.

Effeminacy Extended index touches chin, smiling. *Lat. Am.* Kany, p. 182.

Finished (ruined) Point of thumb placed under chin, hand quickly moves forward. *Portugal.* Urtel, p. 15. Also *Spain.* Flachskampf, p. 235. Also 19th cent. Naples, southern *Italy.* De Jorio, p. 224, pl. 21, 2.

Ignorance The "chin flick": fingernails of one hand brush forward under the chin, then fingers flick outward: "I don't know." *Portugal.* Axtell, *Gestures*, p. 148.

Indifference Tips of fingers rub slowly under chin. *Italy.* "The High Price of Silent Insults." *Time*, Apr. 9, 1965, p. 67. * Fingers of one hand close together, palm towards gesticulator, fingertips under chin; then the hand is suddenly flipped outward; originated with flipping the beard. Southern *Italy*, *France.* Efron, p. 156.

Mockery Back of hand, fingers extended, placed beneath chin, fingers wiggling at someone regarded as old. *Saudi Arabia.* Barakat, no.

241. * Tips of thumb, index, and middle finger joined and placed under the chin, indicating a sorcerer. *Central Africa.* Hochegger, p. 197.

Negation Thumb rests between chin and lower lip while fingers, extended, move from side to side. Frequent in public markets: "We don't have any." *Colombia.* Saitz and Cervenka, p. 32. * The "chin flick." *Southern Italy:* "No"; "I can't." Axtell, *Gestures,* p. 76. *See* Disappointment and Nothing.

Nothing The "chin flick": fingernails of one hand brush forward under the chin and then fingers flick outward: "There is nothing." *Southern Italy.* Axtell, *Gestures,* p. 76.

Pensiveness Grasping chin with thumb side of right fist: sign of wisdom or maturity. *Saudi Arabia.* Barakat, no. 78. * Thumb and index grasp chin. *Colombia; U.S.* Saitz and Cervenka, p. 140. Thumb under chin, index along cheek. *Colombia; U.S.* Saitz and Cervenka, ibid. Both gestures accompanied by brow wrinkling and eye narrowing. See FINGER, LIP, Pensiveness.

Respect Stroking chin with fingers of right hand with downward motion. *Saudi Arabia.* Barakat, no. 108. *See* Shame.

Shame Holding extended right thumb near chin with heel of hand out: "shame." *Jordan; Syria.* Barakat, no. 209. Stroking chin with fingers of right hand with downward motion. *Saudi Arabia.* Barakat, no. 108. *See* Respect.

Threat Gently grazing another person's chin with the tip of the right forefinger. *Lebanon; Saudi Arabia.* Barakat, no. 81. *See* Challenge.

Wisdom Grasping chin with thumb side of right fist: sign of wisdom or maturity. *Saudi Arabia.* Barakat, no. 78. *See* Pensiveness.

CHIN, FINGER, HEAD, NOSE

Admiration Extended index of right hand laid alongside the nose; the other fingers clasping chin, head bowed. Arab. 19th cent. *Palestine.* Bauer, p. 224.

Pensiveness *See* Admiration.

CHIN, FOOT, HAND

Contempt When contemplating death, places foot on spear as sign of disdain of death, simultaneously place hand to chin. Anc. *Rome.* Sittl, p. 196.

CHIN, FOREHEAD, HAND, LEG

Pensiveness Wrinkling the forehead, crossing the legs, palm of right hand under chin, elbow resting on left hand. Anc. *Rome.* Baden, p. 453. *See* CHIN, HAND, Pensiveness.

CHIN, HAND

Admiration *See* Pensiveness.

Affection Taking a person's chin between one's fingers. For example: when friends meet on street. Anc. *Rome*. Also 19th cent. *Italy*. Manzoni, c. xv; Sittl, p. 33. Also Children. Anc. *Greece*. Sittl, ibid. Lucas van Leyden's woodcut, *de Verlooren Zoon* (ca. 1520), represents the Prodigal Son being fondled at the chin by the one hand of a young woman, whose other hand is reaching for his purse. 16th cent. *Netherlands*. Van der Meulen, p. 28. Maternal affection: anc. *Greece*. Homer, *Odyss*. xix. Chucking under chin. Erotically affectionate rather than avuncular. Psalter. Ca. 1300. *Flanders*. Oxford, Bodl. Douce 6, fol. 80. Robertson, p. 113. Flicking the underside of a woman's chin with the tip of right index: conciliatory, "cheer up."*Jordan; Syria; Lebanon*. Barakat, no. 32.

Age Fingertips of right hand pull an imaginary beard downwards from the chin: "Father." *Central Africa*. Hochegger, p. 20.

Boredom Backs of fingers of one hand lightly travel up and down over the chin. *France*. Mitton, p. 150. * To indicate that the joke that someone is telling is very old, one puts hand under chin, palm up as if to hold own beard, and then lowers it to indicate that the joke has a long beard. *Netherlands*. Andrea and de Boer, p. 77. * Hand moves repeatedly up and down along the chin: "che barba!" ("What a beard!") *Italy*. Meo Zilio, p. 71. * Flat hand ca. 20 cm below chin, palm down, as if supporting a beard. Río de la Plata region of *Argentina; Uruguay*. Meo Zilio, p. 71.

Concentration Plucking of beard or stroking of chin. 19th cent. Ghetto Jews. *Eastern Europe*. Efron, p. 146. *See* Pensiveness.

Contemplation *See* Pensiveness.

Defeat Flat hand, palm down, passed under chin. Accompanied by the exclamation: "Gagau!" ("I give up!") *Brazil*. Cascudo, *História*, p. 78.

Father The open right hand is placed under the chin, indicating a beard. *Central Africa*. Hochegger, p. 148.

Fatigue Hand holding chin. Medieval *France*. Baudoin de Sebourc, I, p. 72.

Fear Grasping one's beard. Arab. Sachau, p. 189; Goldziher "Über Gebärden," p. 382.

Hesitation Pulling, stroking, or kneading chin. *France*. Mitton, p. 146.

Impatience Flat hand, palm down, placed against or under chin. "Het zit me tot hier!" ("I've got it up to here!") *Netherlands*. Andrea and de Boer, p. 10. Also *U.S.* Hand moved slowly in a cutting motion under the chin; *Flanders*. Andrea and de Boer, p. 187.

Indifference Tips of fingers of one hand (except thumb) touch under the chin and then are flipped forward. Southern *Italy.* Efron, pp. 154, 156. Hand, palm inwards, fingers slightly bent, nails touching underside of chin is quickly whipped out to the front. ("What do I care?") *Italy.* Leone, XX 11. The French name for the gesture, "la barbe," indicates its origin: a symbolic flick of the beard: "I point my masculinity at you," or, more generally, "get lost," or "you bore me;" as in the expressions "quelle barbe!" ("What nonsense!"). *France; Belgium; Italy; Yugoslavia;* southern *Sardinia; Tunisia*; rare or absent in the *British Isles; Scandinavia; Germany.* Morris et al., pp. 170–73.

Insult Pulling someone's chin or imaginary beard downward. *Lat. Am.* Kany, p. 64. * Holding right hand, back of hand forward, under chin then lightly brushing the tips of the fingers beneath the chin several times with forward motion. *Saudi Arabia.* Barakat, no. 137.

Laziness Hand supports chin: "Mão no queixo na janela, nem agulha e nem panela" ("The hand on a chin while looking out the window neither sews nor cooks.") *Brazil.* Cascudo, *História*, p. 24.

Negation Right hand is catapulted out from under the chin. Southern *Italy.* Sittl, p. 86. Backs of the fingers of one hand are flicked out from under the chin, as under Indifference, above. It often accompanies the negative toss of the head, which, by itself, cannot be seen clearly over longer distances. Southern *Italy; Sicily; Malta; Corfu*, northern *Sardinia.* Morris et al., pp. 171–76.

Nothing Fingertips flipped out from under the chin three or four times. Childish. *France.* Mitton, p. 151.

Oath "Stroke your chins, and swear by your beards that I am a knave." 16th-17th cent. *England.* Shakesp., *As You Like It* 1.2.76.

Pensiveness "I had placed into my hand my chin and one cheek." 13th cent. *Germany.* Walther v. d. Vogelweide 8, 5ff., and miniature (c. 1300) in Heidelb. *Codex palatinus germanicus* 848, fol. 124r; see Walther, pl. 45. Medieval English (c. 1270): Initial to Aristotle's *De Memoria et Reminiscentia.* Brit. Lib. Harley MS 3487, fol. 197v; see Camille, "Book of Signs," p. 138. *See* CHEEK, HAND, Pensiveness. See also A. Rodin, *The Thinker.* * "tapping his chin with the cover of the book, in a thoughtful manner." 19th cent. *England.* Dickens, *Oliver Twist*, p. 87. * Plucking of beard or stroking of chin—thoughtfulness, deliberation, doubt. Ghetto Jews. *Eastern Europe.* Efron, p. 146. * "Then rubbing his chin with his hand and looking up to the ceiling as if to recall the circumstances to his memory." 19th cent. *England.* Dickens, *Pickwick*, I, p. 347. * One hand grasps elbow or rests in armpit of the other, other hand against side of chin. *Colombia; U.S.* Saitz and Cervenka, p. 139. * The "chin stroke," i.e., one hand repeatedly stroking the sides of the chin—thumb on one side, other fingers on the other—figurative stroking of the beard: masculine gesture of either contemplation ("I am thinking") or admiration, as of a painting or woman. Axtell, *Gestures,* p. 76.

Perplexity Hand moves repeatedly up and down along the chin, sometimes accompanied by pursed lips. Río de la Plata region of *Argentina; Uruguay.* Meo Zilio, p. 71. The same gesture in Italy indicates Boredom. Ibid. *See* Boredom.

Plea Pleader touches chin of person he is flattering. Anc. *Greece.* Ohm, p. 240; Sittl, p. 282. 13th cent. *Germany: Kudrun,* st. 386, 2.3. * Placing right hand on beard or chin. Polite request. *Saudi Arabia.* Barakat, no. 190.

Prayer Hand covered by toga and laid against chin. Anc. *Rome.* Ohm, p. 290.

Promise Open palm of right hand rubbed down one's face to the chin, then grasping chin with tips of fingers and thumb. *Saudi Arabia.* Barakat, no. 170.

Rejection Thumb is moved forward, tip to underside of chin, and the whole hand catapults forward; or the same movement is made by the back of the right hand. *Sicily.* Pitrè, p. 350. Also *Spain.* Cervantes, *Don Quijote,* II, chap. liv; Flachskampf, p. 234.

Silence Gently grazing chin of another person with right fist: admonition not to argue. *Saudi Arabia; Syria.* Barakat, no. 80.

Sorrow Chin rests on both hands. Anc. *Greece* and *Rome*; one hand: *Italy.* Bresciani, *Edmondo,* chap v. Sittl, p. 24.

Threat Hand, index extended, shaken near someone's chin, back of hand outward. *Europe; North Am.* Aubert, p. 91, fig. 138.

CHIN, HAND, KNEE

Pensiveness "Thereupon [the knee] I placed my elbow; I had placed into my hand the chin and one of my cheeks." 13th cent. *Germany:* Walther v. d. Vogelweide, 8, 5ff. See also the miniature in Heidelberg Universitätsbibl. cpg. 848, fol. 124r; Walther, pl. 45. *See also* CHIN, HAND, Pensiveness and CHIN, FOREHEAD, HAND, LEG, Pensiveness.

Plea One hand grasps knee of another person; the other hand the chin or beard, sometimes repeatedly, kneeling. Anc. *Greece.* Sittl, p. 165. Touching knees and cheek of a woman (kneeling). Anc. *Greece.* Sittl, p. 166.

CHIN, HAND, LIP

Greeting In Oct. 1488, Dom João Bemoim, a prince of Senegal, while visiting the King of Portugal, shocked the court by trying to put his hand on the face of the Queen. When asked for a reason, he explained that the salutation given to royalty in his country was to put a hand on his or her face and kiss the hand. 15th cent. *Senegal.* Cascudo, *História*, pp. 164–65.

CHIN, HAND, MOUTH
Mockery Right hand grasps chin, mouth drawn in malicious smile. *Central Africa.* Hochegger, p. 120.

EAR, EYE, HAND, LIP
Affection Girls kiss one another on the eyes while holding the other's ears. *Greece.* Guys, I, p. 31; Sittl, p. 40.

EAR, FINGER
Approval Signal passage of an attractive woman by pinching the ear. *Portugal.* Birdwhistell, *Introduction*, p. 9. Also *Brazil.* To add emphasis to their appreciation, some Brazilians reach across the top of the head to the opposite ear and grasp the earlobe. Axtell, *Gestures*, pp. 65–66. Pinching earlobe. *Brazil.* Axtell, *Do's and Taboos*, p. 45. Originally a Portuguese gesture, it was used already in the 16th cent. to describe superior wine: "vinho de orelha" ("ear-quality wine"). The gesture is also used in Spanish Galicia. In Brazil, the gesture is being gradually replaced by the "thumbs up" gesture introduced by U.S. aviators during World War II. *Brazil; Spain.* Cascudo, *História*, p. 150.
Attention Fingers of right hand grasp earlobe and shake it. *Central Africa.* Hochegger, p. 60.
Cuckoldry Fourth fingers of both hands placed in ears with the backs of the hands forward and other fingers spread out. *Syria; Saudi Arabia; Lebanon.* Barakat, no. 1.
Effeminacy The ear, usually the earlobe, is pulled downwards slightly a few times by the thumb and index, or it is flicked forward from behind a few times by the index. Morris et al., p. 207, ascribe the gesture with this meaning to "the fact that women wear ear-rings and men do not." Predominantly southern *Italy*; also *Yugoslavia; Greece.* *See* Insult below. Manipulating earlobe. *Flanders.* Andrea and de Boer, p. 191.
Enthusiasm *See* FINGER, Enthusiasm.
Extraordinary *See* Flattery.
Flattery Pulling an earlobe with two fingers signifies that the person indicated is a sycophant. Río de la Plata region of *Argentina; Uruguay.* The same gesture signifies Extraordinariness in *Brazil.* Meo Zilio, p. 76. Ritualistic gesture when a finger is burned. *Poland.* Ibid.
Hearing Tips of indexes put to the ears, then flipped out to each side: "I can't hear!" Or: The right hand, palm forward, is placed behind the ear. *Central Africa.* Hochegger, p. 136.
Homosexuality *See* Effeminacy; Insult.

Influence "describing small circles in the air with the index finger of one hand in the area of the speaker's ear" signifies the exercise of influence by someone close to a high official. Madrid, *Spain*. Green, p. 73.

Insult Index rubs earlobe: "I have no confidence in your masculinity." *Italy*. Graham, p. 26. *See* Effeminacy above. * " 'Shall I lead you out by the ear?' he added, making a step toward the slowly retreating committee-man and lifting his hand with the thumb and forefinger together. The man retired." 19th cent. *U.S.* Thompson, p. 284. * A thumb placed in each ear, flat hands up. Schoolchildren. *U.S.* Seton, p. xxiii. Tips of thumbs placed into ears or on temples, fingers spread, palms to the front, fingers may or may not be waggled back and forth. Children. *U.S.* Perry, Comics. * "every night when they turn on their TV sets they see Saddam Hussein sticking his tongue out at Bush, as well as making wiggly signs with his fingers in his ears." Buchwald, p. 20. * Rotating the index around the ear—someone is crazy. *U.S.* Axtell, *Gestures*, p. 66. May merely indicate that the person at whom the gesture is directed has a telephone call. *Argentina*. Ibid. *See* Telephone below.

Interrogation Earlobe rubbed with tips of right forefinger and thumb: "Do you want me to answer the question for you?" *Saudi Arabia*. Barakat, no. 212.

Pleasure Wiggling ear lobe with thumb and index of right hand. College students. California, *U.S.* King, p. 264. Also *Portugal*. Morris et al., pp. 207; 210–11. Since the gesture is an expression of pleasure, its significance is also praise of that which is perceived as pleasurable.

Praise *See* Pleasure.

Refusal Tips of indexes placed in the ears: "Je refuse d'écouter!" ("I don't want to hear it!") *Central Africa*. Hochegger, p. 160.

Silence To exclude extraneous noise while telephoning, the Lat. Amer. places tip of finger into unencumbered ear; the Spaniard places tip of finger slightly below outer ear and pushes upward. *Lat. Am.; Spain*. Green, pp. 51–52. * Hooking extended index over ear from the back, then moving it slowly over the ear to the front—do not argue with the gesticulator. *Saudi Arabia*. Barakat, no. 224. * Unwillingness to put up with noise is indicated by putting fingers into ears. *Netherlands*. Andrea and de Boer, p. 57.

Teasing Picking the top of the right ear with right thumb and index. *Lebanon*. Barakat, no. 58.

Telephone "She held a hand up to her ear, thumb and little finger extended, the gesture that always accompanies the promise of a phone call in Provence. 'We will talk tomorrow.' " *France*. Mayle, *Hotel Pastis*, p. 235. *See also* Insult.

Threat Making a circular motion around the ear with the index: mother's threat to child to behave or that she will attend to him later.

Saudi Arabia. Barakat, no. 230. * Mother grasps earlobe with index and thumb—admonish the child later and probably punish it. Used in the presence of others. *Saudi Arabia.* Barakat, no. 169. Also *Greece; Turkey.* Morris et al., pp. 207–12.

EAR, FINGER, MOUTH
Debauchery Yawning, scratching behind ears with little finger. Anc. *Rome.* Baden, p. 455.
Magical Priest moistens finger with his saliva and places it upon upper lip and ears of candidate. Early Christian. Duchesne, pp. 304–05. Roman Catholic baptism. Ohm, p. 227.

EAR, HAND
Amazement Palm placed behind ear. Ghetto Jews. *Eastern Europe.* Efron, p. 146.
Anger Both hands, palms at right angles to each other, laid against ear. Anc. *Rome.* Sittl, p. 84. *Spain.* Flachskampf, p. 239. * Hand scratches ear. Anc. *Rome.* Sittl, p. 19.
Concentration "When Mr. Pickwick arrived at this point, Joe Trotter, with facetious gravity, applied his hand to his ear, as if desirous not to lose a syllable he uttered." 19th cent. *England.* Dickens, *Pickwick,* I, p. 433.
Disbelief Scratching ear. 16th cent. *France.* Martial d'Auvergne, p. 320. "The legate scratched himself thoughtfully behind his ear, the single one which remained to him since yesterday." 19th cent. *Europe.* Weissel, p. 99.
Dislike Flicking the ear while referring to someone. *Russia.* E. Bowers, p. 98.
Displeasure Hands placed over ears, so as not to hear. Anc. *Greece* and *Rome.* Sittl, p. 85. Also *U.S.* Seton, p. 119.
Enjoyment The enjoyment of a meal, a film, a book, is indicated by swinging the open hand past the ear. *Netherlands.* Andrea and de Boer, p. 46.
Film Fist makes cranking motion near ear to signify making a film. *Netherlands.* Andrea and de Boer, p. 53.
Foolishness Hands, open palms forward, flapped from temples to earlobes: "Birdbrain! Shake the dust out of your ears!" *Russia.* Monahan, pp. 64–65.
Gossip Left ear cocked in direction of gossip, right arm extended downward, holding garment out from body. 16th cent. *Germany.* Brant, woodcut, p. 276. * Hand, palm forward, placed behind an ear, signifies that the person referred to is a gossip. *Russia.* Monahan, pp. 104–5.
Greeting The Gond pull one another's ears in salutation. Central *India.* Dawson, p. 94.

Incomprehension Hand, palm forward, placed behind an ear. *Central Africa.* Hochegger, p. 94. "I can't hear." *Russia.* Monahan, pp. 104–5. * Both hands, palm forward, placed behind ears: "I am trying very hard to hear." *Russia.* Ibid., pp. 106–7.

Indecision Half-open right hand makes a downward and upward movement at the back of the ear, suggesting a semicircle formed downward. *Spain.* Flachskampf, p. 215.

Insult Slap on ear. Anc. *Greece.* Sittl, p. 109. Hands, palm forward, lifted to head, thumbs in ears. Anc. *Rome,* not class. *Greece.* Sittl, pp. 109–10. * Monk scratches ear ("like a dog") to request books written by pre-Christian Roman authors. Performed during silent hour in medieval Cluniac library. Medieval *France. VDM,* p. 172. * Right thumb placed in right ear, remaining fingers wave, suggesting donkey's ears. 19th cent. southern *Italy.* De Jorio, p. 304; Sittl, p. 109. * Ears are twisted, or thumbs placed in ears and fingers fluttered. Children. *England.* Opie, p. 319. Universal children's gesture. Axtell, *Gestures,* pp. 37–38. * Tugging at one's ear questions the virility of the person at whom the gesture is directed. *Italy. Time,* Apr. 9, 1965, p. 68. *See* EAR, FINGER, Insult.

Louder "the constable put his hand behind his ear, to catch the reply." 19th cent. *England.* Dickens, *Oliver Twist,* p. 270. Hand held cupped behind one ear. *U.S.* Ruesch and Kees, p. 77. *Netherlands.* Andrea and de Boer, p. 93.

Memory Those present in the Roman senate were reminded to give their opinions by being pulled by the earlobe. Seneca, *Apocol.* 9, 17; traceable to the 8th cent.: *Lex Baiuvar.,* 15, 2 (16, 6). Anc. *Rome.* Sittl, p. 146. * Frequent in Bavarian law between the 8th and 12th centuries as reminder to witnesses. 8th–12th cent. *Bavaria.* Grimm, *DRA,* I, p. 199; see also the *Lex Ribuaria*; with reference to the slap on the cheek. 13th cent. *Germany. Ortnit,* vv. 285,2 ff., 286,1. In general the pulling of the ear, or slapping of someone's ear, is ancient Germanic and still in the 18th century boys' ears were pulled or slapped on important occasions so that they might always remember what they witnessed. 18th cent. *Germany.* Grimm, *DRA,* I, p. 198. * Plaintiff grasps witness by the earlobe to refresh his memory. Also in use generally, since the earlobe was considered the seat of memory. Anc. *Rome.* Sittl, p. 146. Possibly the slap as a device to stimulate the memory has its analogy in the *alapa militaris* as practiced in the ceremony of bestowing knighthood; see also Wenzel, p. 63.

Mockery Hands, palm forward, lifted to head, thumbs in ears. Anc. *Rome,* not class. *Greece.* Sittl, pp. 109–10. * Hands placed to ears make waving movements, suggesting donkey's ears. Children. *Germany. HDV,* I, p. 323. * Hands, palms open and forwards, are placed behind ears, appearing to elongate them. Or: Each hand pulls each ear upwards.

Or: Hands placed to ears like wings. *Central Africa.* Hochegger, p. 133–34.

Pederasty   Fondling the back of one's ear alludes to the pederasty of the person at whom the gesture is directed. *Italy. Time,* Apr. 9, 1965, p. 68.

Pensiveness   Pulling one's ear. *U.S.* Krout, p. 24.

Poverty   Right thumb placed in right ear, remaining fingers wiggle—lacks money. *Portugal.* Flachskampf, p. 231; Urtel, p. 18.

Punishment   Slap on ear. Anc. *Greece.* Sittl, p. 109. * Pulling one's own ear (e. g., in anticipation of punishment). *Colombia.* Saitz and Cervenka, p. 98. * "Upon hearing this I instantly ran into school, where Mr. Hinchliff, (afterwards Bishop of Peterborough) was the only usher then present, and I roared out, 'The King is dead'; whereupon Mr. Hinchliff came up to me, and taking hold of my ear, said, 'What's that you say, young man? Do you know you are liable to be hanged for treason?' " 18th cent. *England.* Hickey, p. 28.

Refusal   Grasping one's earlobes signifies one's remorse. *India.* Axtell, *Gestures,* p. 178. *See* HAND, Refusal.

Silence   Unwillingness to put up with noise is indicated by placing flat hands over ears. *Netherlands.* Andrea and de Boer, p. 57.

Sincerity   "Grasping one's ears is a sign of repentance or sincerity in India." Axtell, *Do's and Taboos,* p. 45.

Telephone   Fist rotates at side of ear, as if turning a handle. *Colombia.* * Hand closed, as if holding French telephone receiver, held near ear. *Colombia; U.S.* Saitz and Cervenka, p. 136. Rio de la Plata region, *Argentina; Uruguay.* Meo Zilio, p. 107. * Hand loosely closed, makes cranking motion near the ear. *Netherlands.* Andrea and de Boer, p. 52.

Warning   Touching, pulling earlobe or pushing it forward slightly as if eavesdropping, is a warning of the presence of secret police. *Lat. Am.* Kany, p. 121.

EAR, HAND, LEG

Adoration   "He crosses the hands, lets them hang, puts them flat against the ears, kneels, stands up, throws himself to the ground several times, arises again" Muslim. Bauer, p. 13.

EAR, HAND, LIP

Affection   While kissing, each person grasps the ears of the other. Anc. *Greece* and *Rome.* Sittl, p. 40. * "The worthy old gentleman pulled Arabella's ear, kissed her without the smallest scruple, kissed his daughter also with great affection." 19th cent. *England.* Dickens, *Pickwick,* II, p. 452.

EAR, HAND, TONGUE
Mockery Hands raised to level of head, palms forward, fingers extended, thumbs placed in ears; tongue extruded. *Netherlands.* Andrea and de Boer, p. 76.

ELBOW
Attention Elbow gives a neighboring person a blow in the side: "Pay attention!" *Central Africa.* Hochegger, p. 16.

Authority *See* ARM, Authority.

Avarice Touching table with the elbow, saying "es codo" or "suda antes por el codo que gastar un peso" ("he's tight" or "he sweats through his elbow rather than spend a cent"). *Lat. Am.* Kany, p. 70.

Finished Elbows spread to the sides and vigorously brought back to the sides. *Central Africa.* Hochegger, p. 74.

Plea The Scythians applied the Egyptian surrender stance of putting elbows together behind the back to other instances of pleading. Anc. *Rome.* Lucian, *Toxaris*, 48. Sittl, p. 152.

Reconciliation Women nudge their husbands with their elbows after a dispute, urging them to talk and reconcile. Rural *Brazil.* Cascudo, *História*, p. 122.

Silence Elbow gives a neighboring person a blow in the side: "Shut up!" *Central Africa.* Hochegger, p. 16.

Submission The Egyptian surrender stance of elbows together behind back formed part of Persian proskynesis. Lucian, *Ploion, 30.* Sittl, p. 152.

Surrender Since the elbows of captives in anc. Egypt were often tied together behind the back, the Egyptians assumed the position of putting their elbows together behind the back when surrendering. Anc. *Egypt.* Heliodorus, 9, 5. Sittl, p. 151–52.

ELBOW, EYE
Sorrow " 'And what's become of the others, sir?'. . . The old gentleman applied his elbow to his eye as he replied, 'Gone, Tom, gone . . .' " 19th cent. *England.* Dickens, *Pickwick*, I, p. 230.

ELBOW, FINGER
Foolishness Fingertips of one hand joined and held at elbow of the other arm, fingertips of the other hand also joined, hand waving back and forth. Southern *Italy.* Efron, p. 157.

ELBOW, HAND
Anticipation Flat right hand slaps bottom of bent left elbow: "We're going to have fun!" *Central Africa.* Hochegger, p. 7.

Avarice In many regions of Lat. Amer. the left forearm is held up with fist clenched, the right palm strikes the left elbow, or the left elbow strikes any surface, and the clenched fist opens. *Lat. Am.* Kany, p. 70. * Metaphoric: "Well, you see, we Mexicans are very nosy, and we gossip a lot. We do it because we do not want anyone to say *que somos bien codos*, that we're stingy." *Mexico.* E. Carr, p. 54; Indian. *Mexico.* Key, p. 94. * Cupped hand, or fist, strikes elbow several times in succession. *Colombia.* Saitz and Cervenka, p. 129. * Tapping an elbow with the other hand: "he's cheap," "he's stingy." *Colombia.* "He's unreliable." *Netherlands.* Axtell, *Gestures*, p. 79. Lifting forearm vertically and hitting bottom of elbow with palm of other hand is an insult. *Mexico.* Axtell, ibid.

Emphasis " 'With a 10-power lens, you can see no flaws. With a 12-power, you see it,' he said, squeezing the reporter's elbow for emphasis, like a rabbi making some Talmudic point or a salesman closing in on a deal." Jews. *U.S.* Behrens, p. 3.

Foolishness Fingertips of one hand are held together at the elbow of the other arm, fingertips of other hand are also held together while hand is waved back and forth. Southern *Italy.* Efron, p. 157.

Obviousness "At this point Robyn, with elbows tucked into her sides, would spread her hands outward from the wrist, as if to imply that there is no need to say more." *England.* Lodge, *Nice Work*, p. 40.

Threat Elbow half bent, right forearm is moved diagonally, so that the right hand arrives near the shoulder, the hand remains there for a moment and then falls again. ("Will you shut up?" "You deserve a slap." "Aren't you ashamed of yourself?" "If I didn't restrain myself") *France.* Mitton, p. 145.

Unreliability Arm bent at elbow, other hand taps underside of elbow to indicate that another person is unreliable or underhanded. *Netherlands.* Axtell, *Gestures*, p. 145; Andrea and de Boer, p. 33.

ELBOW, HIP

Virility Elbows placed on hips, abdomen moved back and forth rapidly in *cachondeo*, an imitation of a type of foreplay, i.e., playful, though aggressive suggestion of sexual intercourse. Andalusia, southern *Spain.* Driessen, p. 248.

ELBOW, MOUTH (*See* ARM, MOUTH)

ELBOW, RIB

Attention Neighbor is nudged with elbow. Proper only with close friends. *Colombia; U.S,* Saitz and Cervenka, p. 23.

Emphasis " 'She's a Miss, she is; and yet she ain't a Miss—eh, Sir—eh?' And the stout gentleman playfully inserted his elbow between the ribs of Mr. Pickwick, and laughed very heartily." 19th cent. *England.* Dickens, *Pickwick*, I, p. 61.

Reminder   Poking someone in the ribs with the elbow. *Spain; Lat. Am.* Green, p. 44.

EYE

Amazement   Rolling the eyes. *Universal.* Axtell, *Gestures*, p. 64.

Amusement   "His delivery was so melodramatic that he seemed to have acquired his rhetorical manner by overcoming a speech defect, like Demosthenes training with the pebbles in his mouth. He made Sandra look up and wink with amusement at her father." *Netherlands.* Mulisch, p. 102.

Anger   Rolling the eyes. 16th-17th cent. *Poland.* Bogucka, p. 196.

Apotropy   Bride must weep on the way to church, for someone who weeps is not envied and is therefore safe from the evil eye. Poznan, *Poland.* Seligmann, II, p. 207. * Whoever is involuntarily the center of interest must look at his nose (Syria), at his nails (South Slavic), before looking at his relatives and friends. Seligmann, II, p. 287–88. * It is believed that staring at someone who is eating absorbs the nutriment of the food being eaten. The black kings of the Slave Coast could not be looked at while they ate. *Africa.* Cascudo, *História*, p. 212. * Admiring a child and expressing this admiration in a compliment is regarded as giving the child the evil eye. The threat is nullified if the child is touched by the person admiring it. Some believe that such admiration arouses envy, which poses a danger to the child. Admiring a child in a photograph can also be considered potentially dangerous to the child. *Lat. Am.* Dresser, *L.A. Times*, Sept. 16, 1995, B17.

Approval   Winking eye. Usually performed by men. *Colombia; U.S.* Saitz and Cervenka, p. 20. * "The suit she wore was pale gray and might have been made out of silk. Whatever it was made of it reminded Chee that Janet Pete had a very nice shape. It also reminded him that his town jeans, leather jacket, and bolo tie did not put him in the mainstream of fashion in Washington, D.C., as they did in Farmington or Flagstaff. . . His eyes shifted back to Janet, studying her. 'Nobody ever looks at anyone,' Chee said, who had been caught by Janet staring at her." *U.S.* Hillerman, *Talking God*, p. 71.

Attention   Looking at a person while closing one eye. *France.* Mitton, p. 145.

Awaken   "The clerk repeated the question thrice, and receiving no answer, prepared to shut the door, when the boy suddenly opened his eyes, winked several times," 19th cent. *England.* Dickens, *Pickwick*, II, p. 433.

Complicity   Winking with one eyelid. *North America; Europe.* Impolite in Hong Kong. Axtell, *Gestures*, p. 64. *Netherlands.* Andrea and

de Boer, p. 29. Río de la Plata region, *Argentina; Uruguay*. Meo Zilio, p. 101–02.
Concentration   Gaze directed at the sun while praying. Amaterasu cult of Shinto. Gaze directed at the shrine in the ancestor cult of Shinto. *Japan*. Ohm, p. 183. * Gaze directed at point of nose during prayer. Yogi. Ohm, p. 184. * Gaze fixed on navel. Hesychasts; Palamites; Hindu. Ohm, pp. 184–85. * Fixing one's eyes in the distance without perceiving any object. Buddhist; Christian during prayer. Ohm, pp. 180–81. * Narrowing the eyes. *Russia*. Monahan, p. 27.
Contempt   Closing of eyes during prayer not only aids concentration, but signifies contempt of surroundings. Buddhist; Christian. Ohm, p. 187. * In the monastery of Tulasidas, the monks sit in a corner and turn their backs to the world in order to separate themselves from it. Benares, *India*. Schjelderup, p. 149.
Conviviality   A quick wink of one eye. *U.S*. Saitz and Cervenka, p. 55.
Depart   The Yorubas wink at their children if they want them to leave the room. *Nigeria*. Axtell, *Gestures*, p. 165.
Despair   Rolling the eyes. Anc. *Greece*. Bremmer, p. 23. "Madame sat us down and gave us a drink, and we asked how the truffles were. She rolled her eyes and an expression close to pain crossed her face. For a moment we thought they had all gone, but it was simply her reaction to one of life's many unfairnesses" *France*. Mayle, *A Year in Provençe*, p. 61.
Detachment   " 'Morning,' said Hildebrand, in his country English voice, and 'Morning' they replied, in the same tone. Nobody met anyone else's eye; it was very English" *England*. Byatt, p. 532. " 'Nobody ever looks at any one [in Washington, D.C.],' Chee said . . . 'You notice that?' 'Avoid eye contact,' Janet said. 'That's the first rule of survival in an urban society. I hear it's even worse in Tokyo and Hong Kong and places like that. And for the same reason. Too damn many people crowded together.' " *U.S*. Hillerman, *Talking God*, pp. 71–72. * "The more the men whistled, the more ribald their remarks, the faster she walked; but the faster she walked, the more of a sexual object, or sexual quarry, she became . . . her cheeks as red as her hair, the wings of her nostrils white, her eyes steadfastly ahead, refusing to meet the gaze of her tormentors." *England*. Lodge, *Nice Work*, pp. 145–46. * "Here the workers were fewer than in the machine shop, and shyer—perhaps because they were mostly Asian. They avoided her glance, and turned away at her approach." *England*. Lodge, *Nice Work*, p. 145.
Direction   "The priest raises his eyes to heaven when he elevates the host to denote that the oblation is made to God." Roman Catholic. *Mass*, p. 35.
Disapproval   Eyes opened wide and turned upwards: "Regarde! Où

sont tes yeux?" ("Pay attention! Where are your eyes?") Or: Eyes opened wide and turned toward the person at fault. *Central Africa.* Hochegger, pp. 169–170.

Disbelief Winking. *Lat. Am.* Kany, p. 70. Also *U.S.* Saitz and Cervenka, p. 40.

Discretion Looking at someone and slowly closing one eye: "Pay attention, but don't act as if anything had happened." *France.* Mitton, p. 145, no. 33.

Dislike Eyes closed. Late *Rome.* Sittl, p. 84.

Embarrassment Wandering of the eyes. Anc. *Greece.* Sittl, p. 48. " 'Mamma!'. . . Georgiana protested . . . and dropped her eyes." *England.* Huxley, ch. xix.

Emphasis Winking an eye to hint at emphasis. *Portugal.* Basto, p. 56.

Enmity Eyes fixed on ground. 17th cent. Naples, *Italy.* De Jorio, p. 188.

Etiquette In public, Spartan youths were required to look only to the ground; Diogenes the Cynic prohibited the sons of his master from looking about them in the streets. Anc. *Greece.* Bremmer, p. 22. * "Because—as I have learnt at court—a woman is to lower her eyes, one speaks of "wild looks" if her eyes look hither and yon, as if she were extremely fickle. Therefore I advise you to control your eyes all the better, my daughter" Medieval *Germany. Winsbecke,* 7, 1–9. * "A woman who casts her eyes up, down and sideways like a ball, laughing all the while, is no adornment to the house of virtue" Medieval *Germany. Winsbecke,* 8, 7–10. Women are to be seen, but should not actively look around. After all, they might "regale their eyes with the thing that the men have" 14th cent. *Germany.* Heinr. d. Teichner, 722, 29–30, who also complains (672, 24–28) that "nowadays women walk uncovered and erect, as was the custom only for men, so that one can see what they've got. Some have a *décolleté* that one could drive a plow through." "A lady should not look behind her, it seems to me. In walking, she should cast her eyes down and not look around much. If she hears a noise, let her think of her upbringing." 13th cent. *Germany.* Thomasin v. Circlaria 459–464. * The medieval stress on discipline of the eyes is supported by the Christian prohibition of the *vana curiositas,* empty curiosity; thus monastic rules require the same governance of the eyes as courtly etiquette: "When the blessed Mother went to table, she sat the young novices at a separate table opposite her, so that she could see clearly how they observed all the spiritual rules, how they ate . . . demurely and modestly. She did not permit a novice to let her eyes roam back and forth; she could look as far as her bread and plate, but no further without sufficient reason." Cited from the chronicle of the Bickenkloster at Villingen (1238–64) by Wenzel, p. 141. In the monastery of Frenswegen, the Prior Hendrik Loeder (1420; 1430) is said to have required monks who let their eyes roam about to ask forgiveness on their knees and kiss the floor. Medieval *Germany*. Wenzel, ibid., who cites the following from the *Codex germanicus monacensis*, Cgm 829: "First of all, dear child, you should take care that your eyes are steady and do not roam, and do not look up higher than the eyes of the turtledove; that your ears are closed and not tempted to hear new and useless tales or gossip. If, however, you hear something said against someone close to you, you should not believe it immediately and tell others. You should guard your mouth and your words well, and speak little" (p. 142).

Eye contact   Dutch etiquette books warn against looking a higher-ranking person straight in the eye after being invited to sit down in his presence. This, as an intrusion of his "space," was regarded as a serious lack of respect. Sitting sideways, with slightly tilted head, one's gaze was expected to be modest and humble. 17th-18th cent. *Netherlands*. Roodenburg, pp. 162–63. During the Victorian and Edwardian period, "young girls were thought to be forward if they looked anyone straight in the eye, and so they sat with eyes downcast and head lowered. They perfected a knack of raising the eyes to a gentleman while keeping the head drooped." 19th-early 20th cent. *England*. Rockwood, p. 184. "Face-to-face" relationships are generally favored in *North America, Great Britain, Europe*, and by Jews. This does not necessarily mean eye contact (*see* Detachment above). Hispanic women, apart from Puerto Ricans, may hold eye contact, even with strange men, longer than others; Asians, West Indians, African-Americans avoid it. Among Native Americans it is considered impolite to look an older person in the eye; in *Japan, Korea, Thailand* it is impolite to maintain prolonged eye contact. Strong eye contact is favored in *Saudi Arabia*. Axtell, *Gestures*, pp. 62–63. In conversation, eye contact is important. *Finland; the Netherlands; Argentina; Australia* (in business meetings); *Chile; El Salvador; Nicaragua; Venezuela; Canada; U.S.* Ibid. pp. 135 et passim. But esp. with reference to the U.S., *see* Detachment. Long, direct eye contact is important among Arab men. Axtell, *Gestures*, p. 158. Eye contact is important in toasting, both in raising and in lowering the glass. *Norway; Sweden*. Axtell, *Gestures*, pp. 147, 151. Children are trained not to maintain eye contact with adults, since it is regarded as disrespectful. *Ghana*. Axtell, *Gestures*, p. 160. Direct eye contact between sexes suggests romantic interest. *Zambia*. Axtell, *Gestures*, p. 169. Prolonged eye contact is considered rude. *Zimbabwe*. Axtell, ibid. In combination with the handshake, eye contact is not normally made in Japan, since it is considered a sign of disrespect. Eye contact must always be made in the Arab world when greeting someone, "due to the Arab belief that the eyes are the windows of the soul and to avert them is to expose a lack of sincerity." Baggott, p. 4. Observed eye contact may lead to defensive behavior: in flirting, a "woman will hold a man's glance and cross her leg. However, if another man looks, she will pull her skirt down." Moody, p. 9.

Facetiousness "Here Mr. Weller winked the eye . . . with such exquisite facetiousness, that two boys went into spontaneous convulsions" 19th cent. *England*. Dickens, *Pickwick*, I, p. 314.

Fatigue Blinking eyelids. *U.S.* Krout, p. 22. * Drooping eyes. Ibid. * Rubbing eyes. *U.S.* Krout, p. 25. * Eyes closed, head inclined laterally, cheek reposes on the back of one hand which is joined to the other, palm to palm. *France*. Mitton, p. 148. *See* EYE, HAND, HEAD, Fatigue.

Flirting "This involved the necessity of looking up at the windows also; and as the young lady was still there, it was an act of common politeness to wink again, and to drink to her good health in dumb show." 19th cent. *England*. Dickens, *Pickwick*, II, p. 279. * "Mr. Samuel Weller had been staring up at the old red brick houses . . . bestowing a wink upon some healthy-looking servant girl as she drew up a blind . . ." 19th cent. *England*. Dickens, *Pickwick*, I, p. 386. * Rolling eyes. *U.S.* Krout, p. 24. * Winking eye. *Colombia; U.S.* Saitz and Cervenka, pp. 20, 55. A "rather bold" flirtatious gesture in the *U.S.*, improper in *Australia*. Axtell, *Gestures*, p. 64. * Narrowing the eyes denotes apprehension or the challenging invitation to flirtation in women. *Russia*. Wilson, p. 198.

Gratitude "Mr. Bumble raised his eyes piously to the ceiling in thankfulness." 19th cent. *England*. Dickens, *Oliver Twist*, p. 241. *See* also Mourning.

Greeting "Good friends who pass close to each other may wink in greeting." College students. California, *U.S.* McCord, p. 291. * Weeping for joy. Biblical. *Middle East. Gen.* 43:30ff.; 45:2;14ff.; I *Sam.* 20: 41, etc. Ainu women weep when they meet after parting. *Japan*. Batchelor, pp. 101–106. Men and women observe the same custom in the *Andaman Islands, India*. Man, pp. 147–148, pl. ix, fig. 2; Dawson, p. 95.

Homosexuality Looking around indicates the passive homosexual. Anc. *Greece*. Bremmer, p. 23.

Humility "He [the priest] again lowers his eyes in token of his own unworthiness." Roman Catholic. *Mass*, p. 35.

Incredulity *See* Amazement.

Joy Weeping. *Germany*. Boggs, p. 320. In the 16th-17th centuries it was common for Polish men to weep openly both in joy and grief. In 1570 Stanislaw Czarnkowski wrote, surely sarcastically, to the Duchess of Braunschweig, that King Sigismund August had managed to weep at the death of his exiled wife Catharina of Habsburg, thus weeping openly on such occasions was expected. 16th cent. *Poland.* Bogucka, p. 199. *See* Greeting above.

Madness Rolling the eyes. Anc. *Greece.* Bremmer, p. 23.

Mockery Crossing the eyes. College students. California, *U.S.* Mc-Cord, p. 291.

Mourning "She had one eye declined for the loss of her husband, another elevated that the oracle was fulfilled." 16th-17th cent. *England.* Shakesp., *Winter's Tale* 2. 2. 81.

Passion "The poet's eye, in a fine frenzy rolling." 16th-17th cent. *England.* Shakesp., *Midsummer Night's Dream* 5. 1. 12.

Plea Raising one's eyes to heaven as if seeking support or confirmation of what one is saying. Madrid, *Spain.* Green, p. 80. " 'I hope you are not angry with me, sir!' said Oliver, raising his eyes beseechingly." 19th cent. *England.* Dickens, *Oliver Twist*, p. 102.

Poverty Closing both eyes and holding them closed while saying "estoy así" or "ando ciego" or "estoy seco" or "ando pato" ("I'm flat broke"). *Argentina.* Kany, p. 89.

Prayer Whoever calls upon the *manes* turns the glance toward the ground. Anc. *Rome.* Seneca, *Oedip.* 580. Sittl, p. 193. * In praying to the Olympians, one glances toward heaven. Anc. *Greece* and *Rome.* Sittl, ibid. * Achilles looks toward the sea while praying. *Iliad.* Psi 143. Sittl, ibid. * Eyes directed toward the sky. Anc. *Germanic*; anc. *Greece*; Muslim; early Christian, northern *Italy.* Ohm, pp. 163ff. * Eyes directed toward East or rising sun. Anc. *Egypt; Babylonia; Rome.* Ohm, pp. 168ff. * Monks pray lying down on their backs, contemplating the sky and sun. *Tibet.* Ohm, p. 186. * Weeping during prayer. Anc. *Germanic.* Ohm, p. 200. Also anc. *Greece.* Chryses praying to Apollo. *Iliad.* Muslim. Wensinck, p. 110; Goldziher, "Entblössung," p. 304f.; Ohm, p. 201. Particularly among the Sufi. Lammens, p. 138; Smith, pp. 155–57. Also *India.* Worship of Krishna. Grönbech, pp. 150ff. and *Japan,* Ohm, p. 201. Early Christian, northern *Italy* and Biblical. Ohm, p. 202. Not modern Christian. Ohm, p. 208. * Lowering of eyes. Particularly Old Testament, but also Christian. Ohm, pp. 177–78. Kikuyus worshipping Nja are not allowed to look up during thunderstorm. Nairobi. Kenyatta, p. 310; Ohm, p. 178.

Prohibition Eyes closed. Late *Rome.* Sittl, p. 84.

Recognition One eye, looking in direction of referent, closes slowly. "Creo que lo conozco" ("I think I know him"). *Colombia.* Saitz and Cervenka, p. 99.

Reproach Eyes staring severely at person reproached, eyebrows and eyelids motionless. Río de la Plata region of *Argentina; Uruguay.* Meo Zilio, p. 101. [Editors' comment: The *U.S.* equivalent is "a dirty look."]

Respect "Moses hid his face, for he was afraid to look upon God."

Biblical. *Middle East. Exodus* 3:6. * After the Tablets of the Law had been given to Moses and he had proven his loyalty to God and his leadership of his people, "the Lord spoke unto Moses face to face as a man speaketh unto his friend." Biblical. *Middle East. Exodus* 33:11. * Cascudo (*História* p. 210) suggests that Moses' gesture may have been a mechanical repetition of an anc. Egyptian ritual, and points out that looking at someone fixedly is almost universally felt to be a challenge. A survival of lowering the eyes in respect or submission is the ritual of bowing the head when the Host is elevated in Roman Catholic liturgy. [Editors' comment: The same ritual accompanies the opening of the Ark and exposure of the Torah in Jewish liturgy]. As late as the first two decades of the 20th cent., a ritual of respect in the back-country of north-eastern *Brazil* was an avoidance of looking at a superior while speaking to him. Cascudo, *História*, p. 209. * Karl von den Steinen noted in 1884, that among the Juruna Indians, who are descended from the Xingu tribe, it was customary not to look at one another when they spoke. Cascudo, *História*, p. 211, cites the observation, in 1909, of a similar ritual by Dr. Emilia Snethlage among the Xingu and the Tapajós. * Lowering eyes during prayer. Northern *Italy*. Ohm, p. 10. * Listeners to someone speaking are expected to lower their eyes as sign of respect. *Vietnam.* Dresser, *L. A. Times*, May 4, 1996, B15.

Rudeness Winking an eye at anyone is considered impolite. *Hong Kong.* Greenberg, L4. Winking at a woman, even in a friendly manner, considered improper. *Australia.* Axtell, *Do's and Taboos*, p. 45.

Secrecy Winking any eye to imply having some secret knowledge, unknown to others, or inferring the understanding of some particular action, puzzling to others. 19th cent. *England*. Dickens, *Pickwick*, I, pp. 190, 143, 262, 372, etc. *See* Understanding, Complicity.

Shame Lowering of the eyes. Biblical. *Middle East. Ezra* 9:5f.; *Luke* 18:13. Also common later. *Middle East.* Heiler, p. 327; Ohm, p. 179. Anc. *Greece.* Bremmer, p. 23.

Sincerity "Eye contact is a large part of the Thai culture. As long as you look into a person's eyes, your look probably will be returned with a smile. But don't stare." *Thailand.* Greenberg, L4.

Sorrow Eye directed at the ground. *Universal.* Ohm, p. 166. Implications of the common gesture of weeping in sorrow are pointed out by Wells, pp. 167–68 on the basis of Hartmann's *Gregorius* 465–549: "So great is his grief that his sister's looks and words bid him behave in a more manly fashion (465–67), and the recourse to reason, indicated by motions of the heart (483–84) and silence (485) is so successful that her words 'gehabe dich als ein man' ['act like a man'] (466) are now paralleled by his 'gehabe dich baz' ['behave better'] (486) to her, so that finally she ceases to weep (508). Further weeping, however, accompanies their prostration at the feet of the counsellor (534–35) who, not yet privy to their secret, does not recognize the gesture as one of repentance and, assuming it is an excessive mark of supplication or deferential greeting, bids the boy stand up (536–39); on learning the truth, he joins them in weeping (548–49)." 12th cent. *Germany*. Hartmann v. Aue, *Gregorius*, 465–549.

Submission   The modest maiden is to keep her gaze lowered (Anc. *Greece*); young are (were?) required to look no higher than the breast-bone of the elder. *Japan*. Bremmer, pp. 22–23. * On marriage portraits of the 17th cent., the woman usually looks at the man; if she looks at the viewer, she focuses the viewer's attention upon the man by some gesture. *Netherlands*. Van der Meulen, p. 36. *See also* Etiquette and Shame.

Surprise   "Opening her eyes very wide, she then closed them slowly and held them closed for several words." *U.S.* Birdwhistell, *Introduction*, p. 30. * "The meeting looked at each other with raised eyelids, and a murmur of astonishment ran through the room." 19th cent. *England*. Dickens, *Pickwick*, II, p. 72. * Surprise is indicated by raising the eyes or opening them wide. *Germany*. Boggs, p. 321.

Sympathy   "It is conjectured that his unwillingness to hurt a fellow-creature intentionally was the cause of his shutting his eyes." 19th cent. *England*. Dickens, *Pickwick*, I, p. 35.

Treachery   Squinting eyes denoted the treacherous person. Anc. *Greece*. Bremmer, p. 23.

Understanding   Winking one eye indicates complicity. *Spain; Lat. Am.* Green, p. 44. Schoolchildren. *U.S.* Seton, p. xxi. Shakesp., *Midsummer Night's Dream* 3.2.238. " 'You wouldn't think to find such a room as this in the Farringdon Hotel, would you?' said Mr. Roker, with a complacent smile. To this Mr. Weller replied with an easy and unstudied closing of one eye; which might be considered to mean, either that he would have thought it, or that he would not have thought it, or that he had never thought anything at all about it: as the observer's imagination suggested." 19th cent. *England*. Dickens, *Pickwick*, II, 214. Winking at another person suggests that there is a secret between them or that one is putting the other on. Arab. Barakat, no. 162. *See* Secrecy above. * "Fearing their conversation in Agnew's office—adjacent to the White House—would be overheard or taped, Green said he referred to the payment as a political contribution. He said he raised his eyes to the high ceiling in the room so that Agnew would understand the reference." *U.S.* Ostrow, p. 1.

EYE, EYEBROW
   Affirmation   Eyebrows lowered, eyes blinking. *Germany*. *HDV,* I, 23.

Disagreement Eyes fixing the person with whom the gesturer disagrees, eyebrows drawn together. *Central Africa.* Hochegger, p. 52.
Mistake Eyebrows raised, eyes looking upward. *Colombia; U.S.* Saitz and Cervenka, p. 52.
Sanctimoniousness Glance downward, eyelids lowered, eyebrows raised. *Germany.* Krukenberg, p. 175.

EYE, EYEBROW, FIST
Anger Fists clenched in front, eyes staring, eyebrows drawn down. *Europe; North Am.* Aubert, p. 121.

EYE, EYEBROW, HEAD
Annoyance Eyes rolled upwards, while head and eyebrows are slowly raised: "¡Bajá Manolo!" ("Come off it!"). Río de la Plata region, *Argentina; Uruguay.* Meo Zilio, p. 102.
Attention Eyes directed at the person whose attention is sought, eyebrows raised, head rapidly raised. Río de la Plata region, *Argentina; Uruguay.* Meo Zilio, p. 102.

EYE, EYEBROW, HEAD, JAW
Ecstasy Eyebrows raised, eyes turned toward heaven, head thrown back, lower jaw dropped. *Europe; North Am.* Aubert, p. 144.

EYE, EYEBROW, HEAD, LIP
Pain Raising eyebrows, dilated eyes, grinning, open lips, contraction of all facial muscles. *Europe; North Am.* Aubert, p. 141.
Suffering Eyebrows drawn down, fixed look, facial muscles relaxed, head bowed, line of lips drawn low. *Europe; North Am.* Aubert, p. 116, Fig. 162.

EYE, EYEBROW, JAW
Concentration *See* Deception.
Deception Lowering of brows, gaze directly ahead, jaws tightly closed. *Europe; North Am.* Aubert, p. 114, fig. 160.
Determination *See* Deception.

EYE, EYEBROW, LIP
Brooding Eyebrows drawn together, eyes staring into distance, lips closed and pushed forward. *Germany.* Krukenberg, p. 316.

EYE, EYEBROW, MOUTH
Surprise Eyes opened wide, eyebrows raised, often with mouth wide open. *Europe; U.S.* Krukenberg, p. 316, and pl. 237.

EYE, FINGER

Admiration Index pulls down lower eyelid, while the other hand indicates object of admiration. *Italy.* Leone, XX 11. *See* FINGER, Admiration.

Alertness Extended index placed below eye, pulling down the skin, can be an expression of alertness on the part of the gesturer or a request for the alertness of someone else. In the latter sense, it may be a warning. Western *Europe*, but primarily Southern *Europe*. Morris et al., pp. 70–78. Also *Netherlands.* Andrea and de Boer, p. 152. Also *France; Spain; Portugal; Brazil.* Cascudo, *História*, p. 167. *See* Warning; Complicity; Awareness.

Anger Right index extended from fist, pointing upwards, eyes looking upwards: anger or swearing an oath. *Saudi Arabia; Syria.* Barakat, no. 72.

Apotropy Tip of right index on right eyelid, rubbing lightly: bad luck to person to whom the gesture is directed or as prevention of the evil eye. *Saudi Arabia.* Barakat, no. 73.

Approval Index touches skin below eye. Used frequently to refer to members of opposite sex. *Colombia.* Saitz and Cervenka, p. 19.

Assurance Tips of index and middle finger placed on closed eyelids, accompanied by an expression such as: "May I go blind if this isn't true"; "By the light of my eyes." Jews. *Netherlands.* Andrea and de Boer, p. 161.

Attention Index pointed to eye, then to object to which attention is to be directed. If no such object, the index is merely pointed at the eye. *Colombia.* Saitz and Cervenka, p. 21.

Awareness Awareness of a secret: Index touches lower lid of the right eye, sometimes pulls it down a little. Accompanying an "¡ojo!" ("Take care!" [to keep it between us]). *Spain.* Flachskampf, p. 236. Also 19th cent. Naples, southern *Italy.* De Jorio, p. 174. Also *Rome; France.* Meschke, p. 337. Awareness of an attempt to outwit: "You can't fool me." *England; France.* Axtell, *Gestures,* p. 64.

Beckoning "and therefore shutting one eye, with a jerk of his thumb towards his left shoulder, and a most significant twist of his countenance, he beckoned the young lady." 18th cent. *England.* Smollett, *Roderick Random,* I, ch. 19.

Censure *See* EYE, HAND, Censure.

Chinese Tips of indexes draw outer corners of the eyes upward, indicating that someone is Chinese. *Netherlands.* Andrea and de Boer, p. 121.

Cleverness Index draws down the outer corner of the eye. Naples, *Italy.* Critchley, p. 89. * Index draws down lower lid of the eye: "I am clever"; "I am keeping my eye on it, you too?" *Netherlands; Flanders.* Andrea and de Boer, pp. 16, 190. * Right index pulls down right lower eyelid: indicates that someone is clever, or that one is clever enough to see through someone else's intentions. Andalusia, *Spain*. Driessen, p. 245. * For the gesture in medieval art, see Mellinkoff, *Outcasts*, I, pp. 202–03. *See* Distrust.

Complicity "When Schäfer saw him, he placed his middle finger on his left eyelid and pulled it down, whereupon Martin raised his thumb." *Germany*. Schwanitz, p. 340; transl. by editors.

Disbelief Index pulls down lower eyelid. *France*. Life Photos by David Scherman, *Life*, Sept. 16, 1946, pp. 12–15. Brault, p. 377: " 'Et mon oeil?' The American expression 'In a pig's eye!' is a rough equivalent, but no such gesture is ever used." * Index pulls down lower lid of left eye. *Near East*. Critchley, p. 91. * A figure at the foot of the Cross in the *Wiltener Crucifixion* (1420/30), Lower Belvedere, Vienna, touches the closed left eye with the tip of the index. Disbelief or Complicity? * Exposing white of eye with finger. Schoolchildren. *U.S.* Seton, p. xxi. * One eye sometimes half closed, fist clenched, thumb points to speaker. *U.S.* Saitz and Cervenka, p. 41.

Distrust Finger pulls down lower eyelid. Southern *Italy*. Röhrich, *Gebärde-Metapher-Parodie*, p. 28 and pl. 12. Also soldiers, WW II. *German*. Ibid., p. 28. Karel Dujardin's *De Morraspelers* represents one soldier speaking, and another smiling at the viewer while putting his index below his right eye, thus commenting ironically on the remarks of the former and putting them in doubt. 17th cent. *Netherlands*. Van der Meulen, p. 27. * The gesture may also be a warning to someone against someone else. *Netherlands*. Andrea and de Boer, p. 16. *See* Cleverness.

Embarrassment Shutting eye with fingers drawn together and one hand behind the back. Anc. *Rome*. Baden, p. 453.

Fatigue Forefinger in vicinity of right eye. 16th cent. *Germany*. Brant, p. 114.

Greeting Forefinger pointed, thumb raised, then brought down in imitation oi the hammer of a pistol. A wink often accompanies this gesture. Informal, slightly patronizing. California, *U.S.* King, p. 264.

Insult Tip of right index placed on lower lid of right eye implies that the person to whom the gesture is made is stupid. *Saudi Arabia*. Barakat, no. 34.

Jealousy Shutting eye with fingers drawn together. Terentian masks. Anc. *Rome*. Baden, p. 452. Same, with one hand behind back. Ibid.

Leniency Looking with one eye through spread fingers of one hand placed vertically upon the face. *Germany*. Röhrich, *Gebärde-Metapher-Parodie*, p. 34, pl. 37. *See* FINGER, Understanding.

Magical Finger pulls down lower eyelid—the evil eye. Röhrich, *Gebärde-Metapher-Parodie*, pp. 27–28. "In my neighborhood, a double whammy is put on someone by pointing at them with index fingers of each hand and staring intensely as that person tries to put the eight ball in the side pocket. When the player fails, it proves the true effect of the whammy . . . .the double whammy was described by Dr. H. Ferrer in 1928 in the American Journal of Ophthalmology, when he described a patient's ability to voluntarily propel and retract the eyeballs." Bruckheim, p. 18.

Nothing Finger pulls down lower eyelid. Insolent; vulgar. *France.* Mitton, p. 150.

Readiness Index tugs loose skin below lower eyelid. *Spain; Lat. Am.* Green, p. 77. * Pointing to the eye with the index. *Spain.* Green, p. 77.

Refusal Index of right hand pulls down lower lid of right eye: "Je refuse!" "Pas d'accord!" "C'est ton affaire!" ("I refuse!" "I don't agree!" "That's your problem!"). *Central Africa.* Hochegger, p. 160.

Reliability Right index pulls down right lower eyelid: indicates that someone is a reliable person. Andalusia, southern *Spain.* Driessen, p. 245.

Sorrow With index at each eye, trace course of tears. Mock sorrow. Schoolchildren. *U.S.* Seton, pp. xxi, 54. Common at farewells. *Netherlands.* Andrea and de Boer, p. 94. * One index: *Yugoslavia.* Axtell, *Gestures,* p. 64. * Index traces the flow of tears from the eye along the cheek. *Central Africa.* Ibid., p. 151. * Fingers of right hand gently rub left eye. *Central Africa.* Hochegger, p. 33.

Surprise Shutting eye with fingers drawn together, one hand behind the back. Anc. *Rome.* Baden, p. 453.

Suspicion Tip of index placed below one eye, to indicate the advisability of keeping one's eyes open. 19th cent. Naples, southern *Italy.* Wundt, I, p. 184. See Fig. 3. *See* Surprise above.

Warning Index touches lower eyelid of right eye, sometimes pulls it down a little. *Portugal; Spain; Morocco; France.* Flachskampf, p. 236. Andalusia, southern *Spain.* Driessen, p. 245. "Be careful. Pay attention." *Italy.* Axtell, *Gestures,* p. 64. *Honduras.* Ibid., pp. 209–10. Río de la Plata region, *Argentina; Uruguay.* Meo Zilio, p. 77.

EYE, FINGER, LIP

Complicity " 'If there's anything else you remember, just have a chat with me, eh? And remember, mum's the word.' He placed a stumpy finger across his lips and winked ludicrously." *U.S.* Hill, p. 147.

EYE, FINGER, MOUTH, TONGUE

Mockery Sticking out tongue and at same time pulling down lower eyelids with indexes of both hands, while middle fingers stretch corners

Fig. 3. Neapolitan gestures. From Wilhem Wundt, *Völkerpsychologie* (Leipzig, Germany: Engelmann, 1904) I, 184.

of mouth. *Germany*. Hans Maler, *Christ bearing Cross*. Chicago Art Inst.

EYE, FOREHEAD

Fear Forehead furrowed in pain, eyes opened wide. Insane. *Germany*. Krukenberg, p. 285, Fig. 235.

EYE, HAND

Admiration Hand slightly extended, palm up, slightly cupped and jerked slightly upwards while one eye winks at a male companion. A vulgar male gesture of erotic admiration for a female body. *Netherlands*. Andrea and de Boer, p. 129. * Placing an imaginary telescope to one's eye in admiration of a pretty woman. *Brazil*. Axtell, *Do's and Taboos*, p. 42.

Affection Hands of beloved pressed against one's eyes. Anc. *Greece* and *Rome*. Sittl, p. 34.

Amazement "signified his amazement on the whole, by lifting up his eyes and hands . . ." 18th cent. *England*. Smollett, *Roderick Random*, ch. xliv. "There was casting up of eyes, holding up of hands." 16th-17th cent. *England*. Shakesp., *Winter's Tale*, 5, 2, 51.

Anger Lift hands and eyes, strike three times on stomach. 17th cent. *England*. Butler, I, ii; *Russia*. R. H. Bowers, p. 271.

Blessing "The priest looking up to God, raises his hands, folds them reverently, and makes the Sign of the Cross over the oblation." Roman Catholic. *Mass*, p. 37.

Censure Pulling down the skin of the lower eyelid. Partic. to children eyeing toys. Arab. 19th cent. *Palestine*. Bauer, p. 222.

Concentration "As Tom was gazing at a chair, it seemed to change and assume the features and expression of an old shrivelled human face, so he rubbed his eyes as though to wipe away the illusion." 19th cent. *England.* Dickens, *Pickwick,* I, p. 226. * Thumbs placed along nose, other fingers curled around eyes in imitation of binoculars indicates reflection or concentration on something; perhaps symbolic of focussing on a single point or bringing the subject-matter closer, as an object is brought closer by binoculars. *Netherlands.* Andrea and de Boer, p. 73. Worshippers close their eyes and cover them with palm of one hand to block out distractions while reciting the *Schema* (*Deut.* 6:4). Jews. Kolatch, p. 155.

Confidence Eyes steady and directly forward, one hand in pocket, the other forward and holding paper. *U.S.* Birdwhistell, "Do Gestures Speak Louder than Words?" p. 57.

Despair Eyes raised, hands, palms up, spread diagonally in front: "Haven't I had enough already?!" *Netherlands.* Andrea and de Boer, p. 34. * Eyes closed, one hand covering eyes. *Netherlands.* Ibid., p. 90. * Two hands covering eyes: "Oh no! How stupid!" *Netherlands.* Ibid., p. 111.

Disbelief Rubbing eyes. 19th cent. *Greece* and *Italy.* Bresciani, *Don Giovanni,* c. viii; Sittl, p. 47.

Displeasure Hands and eyes raised. "Such aggravating looks; such lifting up of hands and eyes; such a furrowed forehead, in my sister!" 18th cent. *England.* Richardson, I, p. 148.

Distress "Messrs. Dodson and Fogg intreated the plaintiff to compose herself. Sergeant Buzfuz rubbed his eyes very hard with a large white handkerchief . . ." 19th cent. *England.* Dickens, *Pickwick,* II, p. 79.

Fatigue Fist placed in each eye. Schoolchildren. *U.S.* Seton, p. xxi. * Hand, palm to face, moves slowly across brow or eyes. *Colombia; U.S.* Saitz and Cervenka, p. 144.

Greeting Son greets father with handshake, but does not look into his eyes; instead, he looks slightly to the left. *Central Africa.* Hochegger, p. 173.

Helplessness "He looks at him with a pitiful expression. Closes his eyes and wrings his hand in a gesture of helplessness." *Argentina.* Weyland, p. 19.

Horror *See* HAND, Horror.

Insult Hands cupped over eyes: "Gros yeux!" ("Big eyes!") *Central Africa.* Hochegger, p. 214.

Magnitude (amount of money): Hitting or patting of the flat hand against the pocket, simultaneously looking alternatively at the person one is talking to and at one's pocket. Arab. Bauer, p. 221.

Medico-magical Flame of *havdala*-candle is doused with overflow of wine from goblet. Dabbing the eyes with this wine is believed to cure weak eyes. Jews. Kolatch, p. 179.

Mourning Holding cloak before one's eyes. Anc. *Greece.* Homer, *Odyss.*, Bk. iv.

Oath Hand laid on eyes. *Samoa.* Röhrich, p. 12.

Prayer Arms bent at elbow, forearms lifted skyward, fingers closed, palms pressed together, eyes skyward. 16th cent. *Germany.* Brant, woodcut, p. 72.

Recognition "He began to gaze in the same direction, at the same time shading his eyes with his hand, as if he partially recognized the object . . . and wished to make quite sure of its identity." 19th cent. *England.* Dickens, *Pickwick*, I, p. 330.

Refusal *See* HAND, Refusal.

Rejection "At this inquiry, Mrs. Weller raised her hands and turned up her eyes, as if the subject were too painful to be alluded to." 19th cent. *England.* Dickens, *Pickwick*, I, p. 449.

Self-gratitude "And after such feasts, upon meeting gruff Pnin, Serafima and Oleg (she raising her eyes to heaven, he covering his with one hand) would murmur in awed selfgratitude: 'Gospodi, skol'ko mi im dayom!' ('My, what a lot we give them!')—'them' being the benighted American people." *Russia.* Nabokov, p. 71.

Shame Both hands cover eyes. *Central Africa.* Hochegger, p. 88.

Sorrow " 'Where,' said Mr. Tupman, with an effort—'where is— she, Sir?' and he turned away his head, and covered his eyes with his hand." 19th cent. *England.* Dickens, *Pickwick*, I, p. 297. * "At the conclusion of this address . . . Mr. Jingle applied to his eyes the remnant of a handkerchief" 19th cent. *England.* Dickens, *Pickwick*, I, p. 128. * Drying one's tears is a common gesture denoting sorrow in art from the anc. Roman period onward; *Europe.* Sittl, pp. 173–75; Bloemaert (16th-17th cent. *Netherlands*), *Bewening.* Van der Meulen, p. 19. * Both hands cover eyes. *Central Africa.* Hochegger, p. 88.

Surprise *See* Amazement above.

Time Glance at wrist. *Colombia; U.S.* Saitz and Cervenka, p. 143.

Understanding Index of right hand pulls down the lower eyelid. Anc. *Rome.* Meschke, col. 337.

Warning Index pointed at the eye means "look out for that fellow!" Southern *Italy.* Efron, p. 154.

EYE, HAND, HEAD

Curiosity Blinking one eye, head turned slightly to side and moved forward, hand moved forward and to the side, fingers somewhat apart. Accompanied by "What's up?" Arab. 19th cent. *Palestine.* Bauer, p. 223.

Fatigue Putting head sideways with eyes closed, resting it upon the right hand. *Spain*. Flachskampf, p. 230. *Central Africa*. Hochegger, p. 70. * Eyes closed, head inclined to one side, cheek leaning against two hands placed palm to palm. *France*. Mitton, p. 148. *See* CHEEK, HAND, Fatigue; EYE, Fatigue.

EYE, HAND, MOUTH
Disbelief Eyes fixed and straight ahead, hands folded in front of mouth. *U.S.* Birdwhistell, "Do Gestures Speak Louder than Words?" p. 57.

EYE, HEAD
Attention Head to one side, gaze directly forward, eyebrows raised, smile. *Europe; North America*. Aubert, p. 130. * Head to one side, eyes turned to the side. Listening. *Europe; North America*. Aubert, p. 104. * Eyes closed, head nodding slightly shows attentiveness. *Japan*. Axtell, *Gestures*, p. 13.
Concentration Fixed look, head forward. *Europe; North America*. Aubert, p. 98.
Curiosity *See* Concentration above.
Devotion Glance directed into the distance, eyes and head upward, forehead and eyebrows completely smooth. *Germany*. Krukenberg, p. 317.
Disapproval Head raised, angry glance. Anc. *Greece* and *Rome*. Sittl, p. 93.
Greeting Head inclined forward, eyelids droop. *Europe; North America*. Aubert, p. 97, fig. 141.
Interrogation Look, nod, brows raised. *U.S.* Seton, p. xxiii.
Mockery Nodding head or winking at someone who is a stranger. Anc. *Rome*. Plutarch, cf. Bresciani, *Edmondo*, ch. vii; Sittl, p. 94.
Modesty Bending head forward, drooping eyelids. *Europe; North Am.* Aubert, p. 97, fig. 141. Head bowed, glance downward. *Europe*. Krukenberg, p. 318.
Pointing Nod of head and movement of eyes indicating location. Sirionó Indians, Chama Indians. *Bolivia*. Key, p. 94.
Reproach Head turned aside while the eye fixes the person reproached: "Comment, je te connais!" ("Oh, sure, I've got your number!") Women's gesture. *Central Africa*. Hochegger, p. 170.
Surprise Head raised, astonished glance. Anc. *Greece*. Sittl, p. 93.
Uncertainty Head to one side, eyes turned to the side. *Europe; North Am.* Aubert, p. 104.
Understanding " 'That 'ere young lady,' replied Sam. 'She knows wat's wot, she does. Ah, I see.' Mr. Weller closed one eye and shook his head from side to side" 19th cent. *England*. Dickens, *Pickwick*, II, p. 140.

EYE, HEAD, LIP, TOOTH
Pleasure   Head back, eyes cast upward. Upper eyelids drooping. Eyebrows raised, line of lips stretched taut to disclose upper teeth. *Europe; North America.* Aubert, p. 134.

EYE, HEAD, MOUTH
Attention   One eye rapidly closed, mouth twisted to the side, head slightly inclined. *Central Africa.* Hochegger, p. 15.

Disagreement   One eye rapidly closed, mouth twisted to the side, head slightly inclinded: "I don't agree!" *Central Africa.* Hochegger, p. 15.

EYE, HEAD, MOUTH, NOSE
Discouragement   Head drawn backwards, frown, eyes squinting, raised nose, corners of mouth drawn down. *Europe; North Am.* Aubert, pp. 111–12.

Disgust   *See* Discouragement above.

Distrust   *See* Discouragement above.

EYE, JAW
Depravity   Eyebrows raised, drooping of upper eyelids, jaw, and all the muscles of the lower part of the face. *Europe; North Am.* Aubert, p. 135.

Exclamation   Glance upward, dropping of jaw. *Europe; North Am.* Aubert, p. 110.

Horror   Frown, eyes wide open, dropping lower jaw. *Europe; North Am.* Aubert, p. 118.

EYE, LIP
Disapproval   Lips pursed and pointed at the person at fault, accompanied by a fixed stare: "Tiens-toi comme il faut!" ("Behave yourself!") Or: Eyes opened wide, lower lip pushed forward in the direction of the person at fault: "Attention, toi!" ("Hey, you!") *Central Africa.* Hochegger, pp. 168–169.

Relief   "Peyrol did not take his eyes off Catherine's straight back till the door had closed after her. Only then he relieved himself by letting the air escape through his pursed lips and rolling his eyes freely about." *U.S.* Conrad, p. 179.

EYE, LIP, NOSE
Disgust   Lips turned outward and pulled apart, upper lip raised, mouth assumes rectangular form, nostrils flare, eyes closed. *Europe.* Krukenberg, p. 319.

EYE, LIP, TOOTH
Frustration "One turned up his eyes to heaven, and bit his nether lip." 18th cent. *England*. Smollett, *Peregrine Pickle*, ch. lxix.
Silence Biting lips, eyes lowered. Anc. *Greece*. Sittl, p. 54. Biting lips, winking. Arab. Bauer, p. 222.

EYE, MOUTH
Affection Kiss on eyes. Among men. Anc. *Rome*. Sittl, p. 40. In general. Anc. *Greece* and *Rome*. Sittl, ibid.
Anger Eyes wide open, clenched teeth, lips pulled back so that teeth are visible. *Europe*. Krukenberg, p. 317.
Cunning Lowered eyelids, raised eyebrows, face muscles tense, lips tightly closed. *Europe*. Krukenberg, p. 314.
Magnitude Lips pursed, as in speaking of something small. *Europe*. Krukenberg, p. 247. * Mouth is opened wide in relating something large or important. *Europe*. Krukenberg, ibid.
Sorrow Deep and irregular breathing and raising of the eyes. *Universal*. Boggs p. 319.
Warning One eye closed, the other wide open, face drawn down, lips pursed. *Europe; North Am*. Aubert, p. 106.

EYE, NAVEL
Prayer Staring at one's navel. Hindu; Hesychasts. Ohm, pp. 184–85.

EYE, NOSE
Prayer Staring at tip of one's nose. Yoga. Ohm, p. 184.

EYE, TONGUE
Contempt Alternately winking with left and right eye, lips stretched laterally, tip of tongue protruded. *Spain*. Alas, p. 6.

EYEBROW (See also FOREHEAD)
Admiration Lifting eyebrows in admiration of a pretty girl. *U.S.* Axtell, *Do's and Taboos*, p. 42.
Affirmation Eyebrows pulled down. Anc. *Greece* and *Rome*; mod. *Greece;* 19th cent. Naples, southern *Italy*. de Jorio, p. 40; Sittl, p. 92. * Eyebrows raised. *Philippines*. Su, LINGUIST 3.1012. *Tonga*. Axtell *Do's and Taboos*, p. 45. *Micronesia*. Dresser, *L.A. Times*, May 17, 1995, B7.
Agreement Eyebrows rapidly raised and lowered. *Central Africa*. Hochegger, p. 1. *Tonga*. Axtell, *Do's and Taboos*, p. 45. Raising eyebrow, usually accompanied by nod documented by Darwin. Dyak,

Borneo. Raising eyebrow and throwing head back. *Ethiopia; Samoa.* Kelleher, E3.

Anger "How eagerly I taught my brow to frown." 16th-17th cent. *England.* Shakesp., *Two Gent.* 1.2.62; *Hamlet* 1.2.231.

Anticipation "and elevating his eyebrows in a rapture of anticipation." 19th cent. *England.* Dickens, *Oliver Twist*, p. 170.

Arrogance Raised eyebrows. Anc. *Greece* and *Rome.* Sittl, pp. 93–94. 18th cent. *Spain.* Cadalso, p. lxxxii.

Concentration "See how the ugly witch doth bend her brows, as if, with Circe, she would change my shape!" 16th-17th cent. *England.* Shakesp., *Henry VI* 5.3.34.

Disapproval "Why do you bend such solemn brows on me? Think you I bear the shears of destiny?" 16th-17th cent. *England.* Shakesp., *King John* 4.2.90. "And I confess that my conduct in the City, as the Wodehouse story puts it, would have caused raised eyebrows in the fo'c's'le of a pirate sloop." J. D. Carr, *To Wake the Dead*, p. 87. Raised eyebrows. *Europe; North Am.* Kelleher, E3.

Disbelief "slowly raised and lowered one eyebrow." *U.S.* Birdwhistell, *Introduction*, p. 33.

Disdain Forehead wrinkled, eyes together, moving from side to side, head moves from side to side at irregular intervals, cheeks distend. Pretending to know more than one is saying. *Spain.* Feijoo, in del Rio, II, 6a.

Disengagement "And by the time Marilyn had hobbled into the elevator, apparently without offering any clear explanation of what had been done to her, there were shrugs, raised eyebrows, other signs of disengagement." *U.S.* Logan, p. 53.

Displeasure "And many good young people considered it a treat and an honor to see Pnin pull out a catalogue drawer from the . . . card cabinet and take it . . . to a secluded corner and there make a quiet mental meal of it, now moving his lips in soundless comment, critical, satisfied, perplexed, and now lifting his rudimentary eyebrows and forgetting them there, left high upon his spacious brow where they remained long after all trace of displeasure or doubt had gone." *Russia.* Nabokov, p. 76.

Fear " 'The form [deeply arched brows], rhythm [jerking sharply up] or what the action does [pulls the face back and upward] resembles the message it stands for.' . . . In cases of fear or surprise, the eyebrow flash is part of a facial recoiling." *Universal.* Kelleher, E3.

Flirting Eyebrows moving up and down rapidly. *Lebanon; Saudi Arabia.* Barakat, no. 101. * The "eyebrow flash," perhaps popularized by Groucho Marx, usually combined with a smile. *U.S.* Axtell, *Gestures*, pp. 63–64. " 'The flirting girl at first smiles at her partner and lifts her eyebrows with a quick, jerky movement upward so that the eye slit is briefly enlarged. . . . Flirting men show the same movement . . . after this most initial, obvious turning-toward the person in the flirt there follows a turning-away.' The raised eyebrow in American culture 'breaks the taboo of the sustained eye contact' and 'is used in everyday flirting to signal interest in a person and is also used as a tactic in prostitution. If a woman returns a stare and her eyebrows are raised, it means she is interested in you or she is a lady of the evening.' " U.S. Kelleher, E3.

Greeting   Raising eyebrows. *Guam.* Dresser, *L. A. Times*, May 17, 1995, B7.

Ignorance   "One curious, patient gesture which never entirely left Ishi was characteristic of him in those days—a raising high of his mobile, arched eyebrows. It was an expression of wonder, but also of ignorance, of incomprehension, like our shrugging of the shoulders." Native American. California, *U.S.* Kroeber, p. 124.

Impatience   Frowning. *Portugal.* Basto, p. 45.

Interrogation   "Luke's glance turned to the man in the horn-rimmed spectacles and his brows rose enquiringly." *England.* Allingham, p. 78. " 'It's almost certain, isn't it, that in writing down that he did take out an insurance policy he'll make some reference to why he did it?' She paused, raising her eyebrows." *England.* J. D. Carr, *Constant Suicides*, p. 155.

Money   Eyesbrows raised: "Pay me." *Peru.* Axtell, *Do's and Taboos*, p. 45.

Negation   Eyebrows raised. Anc. *Greece* and *Rome.* Sittl, p. 93. *Lebanon; Turkey.* Su, LINGUIST 3.1012.

Prohibition   Eyebrows raised. Anc. *Greece.* Sittl, p. 93.

Skepticism   *See* Birdwhistell under Surprise below.

Surprise   Eyebrows raised. *Universal.* Krout, p. 24. "Lawyer is often a master of the raised eyebrow." *U.S.* Birdwhistell, "Do Gestures Speak Louder than Words?" p. 56. " 'Still here?' he said, lifting an eyebrow." *England.* Lodge, *Nice Work*, p. 148.

Teasing   Eyebrows moved up and down rapidly. *Saudi Arabia; Syria.* Barakat, no. 194.

Threat   Frowning. *Portugal.* Basto, p. 45.

EYEBROW, FINGER

Command   Looking directly at someone, eyebrows raised, index pointing at him, signals: "You! Come here!" *Netherlands.* Andrea and de Boer, p. 103.

Homosexuality   Wetting tip of right little finger, it is then rubbed along right eyebrow: indicates that person spoken to or about is homosexual. *Lebanon.* Barakat, no. 39. *U.S.* Axtell, *Gestures*, p. 64.

Question   Looking directly at someone, eyebrows raised, index pointing at him, signals: "Wasn't it your turn?" *Netherlands.* Andrea and de Boer, p. 103.

Shame Tip of right index placed between eyebrows. May also be an admission of inability to do something. *Saudi Arabia.* Barakat, no. 229.

EYEBROW, FINGER, NOSE

Disapproval "Nostrils are pinched between the thumb and forefinger with fingers 3, 4, and 5 remaining lax and with the brows bilaterally and minimally raised." *U.S.* Birdwhistell, *Introduction*, p. 9.

EYEBROW, FOOT, HEAD, MOUTH

Confusion Head bowed, crosswise and double movement of the eyebrows, lips taut, weight of body on backward foot. *Europe; North America.* Aubert, p. 137.

EYEBROW, HAND, HEAD

Negation Raising hand, throwing head back, rolling eyes, raising eyebrows. *Greece.* Kelleher, E3.

Perplexity Head is scratched, eyebrows raised, lips often pursed. *Colombia*; more frequent in *U.S.* Saitz and Cervenka, p. 135.

Remorse *See* EYEBROW, FOOT, HEAD, MOUTH, Confusion.

EYEBROW, HAND, MOUTH

Dismay Eyebrows raised, hand placed over mouth. *Netherlands.* Andrea and de Boer, p. 114.

Surprise Eyebrows raised, mouth open, hands placed on cheeks. *U.S.* Saitz and Cervenka, p. 135.

EYEBROW, HEAD

Affirmation Throwing the head back, eyebrows raised. *Ethiopia.* Su, <LINGUIST 3.1012>.

Attention *See* EYE, HEAD, Attention.

Despair Eyebrows drawn down, fixed look, facial muscles relaxed, head bowed low. *Europe; North Am.* Aubert, p. 117.

Dignity Head raised, brows lowered. *Europe; North Am.* Aubert, p. 113.

Greeting Nodding and then flicking the eyebrows upward. *Fiji.* Axtell, *Gestures*, p. 175.

Interrogation Eyebrows raised, head jerked backwards signals a silent inquiry (over a distance). *Netherlands.* Andrea and de Boer, p. 132. *See* EYE, HEAD, Interrogation.

Surprise Eyebrows raised, head tilted or turned. *Colombia*; *U.S.* Saitz and Cervenka, p. 134.

EYEBROW, HEAD, JAW
Interest   Head forward, lower jaw relaxed, eyebrows raised. *Europe; North America.* Aubert, p. 123.

EYEBROW, HEAD, LIP
Appetite   Head advanced and tilted backward, eyebrows raised, slightly contracted, lips pursed. *Europe; North Am.* Aubert, p. 125.
Attention   *See* EYE, HEAD, Attention.
Desire   *See* Appetite.
Discouragement   Eyebrows drawn down, fixed glance, facial muscles relaxed, head bowed, lips drawn down. *Europe; North Am.* Aubert, p. 116, fig. 162.
Flirting   Head leaning to side, eyebrows raised, lips smiling and slightly pursed. *Europe; North Am.* Aubert, p. 126.
Greeting   Eyebrows raised and lowered quickly, often with nod or smile. Casual, across distance. *Colombia; U.S.* Saitz and Cervenka, p. 69.
Perplexity   *See* Discouragement.

EYEBROW, HEAD, SHOULDER
Agreement   Eyebrows raised, head nodding, shoulders raised. 18th cent. *Spain.* Cadalso, ch. lxxx.

EYEBROW, JAW
Boredom   Lowering and drawing together of the eyebrows, jaws contracted, corners of mouth drawn down. *Europe; North Am.* Aubert, p. 115, fig. 161.
Concentration   *See* Boredom.
Depravity   Eyebrows raised, drooping of upper eyelids, jaw, and all the muscles of the lower part of the face. *Europe; North Am.* Aubert, p. 135.
Desperation   *See* Boredom.
Disappointment   Raised and frowning brows, jaw lowered, corners of mouth drawn down. *Europe; North Am.* Aubert, p. 136.
Regret   (esp. after being punished) *See* Disappointment.
Weakmindedness   Eyebrows raised, drooping of eyelids, jaw, and all muscles of lower part of face. *Europe; North Am.* Aubert, p. 135.

EYEBROW, LIP
Disbelief   *See* EYEBROW, MOUTH, Disbelief.
Sorrow   Eyebrows drawn down, corners of mouth pulled down. *Europe; North Am.* Krukenberg, p. 315.

EYEBROW, MOUTH
Disbelief   Eyebrows raised, corners of mouth drawn down. Can also indicate disparagement. *U.S.* Saitz and Cervenka, p. 41.

Sorrow   *See* EYEBROW, LIP, Sorrow.

Surprise   Eyebrows raised, eyes fully open, mouth open. *U.S.* Saitz and Cervenka, p. 135.

EYEBROW, MOUTH, SHOULDER

Amazement   Eyebrows raised, mouth open, shoulder raised. *Europe; North Am.* Aubert, p. 143.

Ignorance   Shoulders hunched, eyebrows raised, corners of mouth drawn down. *Europe; North Am.* Aubert, p. 128.

Uncertainty   *See* Ignorance.

EYELID (*See* EYE)

Command   At a meal, the order for wine is given by looking at the wine steward and lowering the left and right eyelids alternately. *Anc. Rome.* Sittl, p. 220.

Hypocrisy   Glancing through nearly closed eyelids. *Europe; North America.* Aubert, p. 101.

EYELID, FINGER (*See* EYE, FINGER)

Oath   Right index placed on right upper eyelid. *Saudi Arabia.* Barakat, no. 157.

Proxy   Touching lower eyelid with right index indicates one's readiness to act as proxy. Moving the finger from right to left while on the eyelid is a variant. *Saudi Arabia.* Barakat, no. 192.

FACE (*See* HEAD)

Affection   Blush. Medieval *France.* Lommatzsch, p. 73. Also 12th-13th cent. *Germany: Nibelungenlied*, st. 285, 4; 292, 2.

Anger   Red face, contraction of cheek, mouth, chin, or brow muscles. *Universal.* Boggs, col. 321. Twisting one side of face. *Syria.* Barakat, no. 193.

Apotropy   Contorting face against the evil eye. *Bothnia; India.* Seligmann, II, p. 287.

Contempt   "Turn away her face." 16th-17th cent. *England.* Shakesp., *Love's Lab. Lost*, 5.2.148.

Disapproval   "a dead-pan look." *U.S.* Birdwhistell, "Do Gestures Speak Louder than Words?" p. 56.

Mockery   "laughing . . . grinning contemptuously." *Germany.* Boggs; col. 321. Laughing into a person's face, sometimes accompanied by pointing a finger at the person laughed at, is a common motif in representations of the Mocking of Christ; see van der Meulen, pp. 23–24.

Mourning   Face turned away from funeral pyre while lighting it.

Anc. *Rome.* Vergil, *Aen.* 6, 224. Sittl, p. 73. * Covering face. Biblical. *Middle East.* II *Sam.* 19:4.

Rejection   "The Lord will not turn away his face from you." Biblical. *Middle East.* II *Chron.* 30:9.

Shame   Blush. 15th-16th cent. *Italy.* Ariosto, 20, 130–31. Med. *France.* Lommatzsch, p. 71. "Ah, now thou turnst away thy face for shame!" 16th-17th cent. *England.* Shakesp., *Titus Andr.*, 2.4.28.

Sorrow   Cloak drawn over face. Anc. *Greece* and *Rome.* Sittl, p. 275. "For when the noble Caesar saw him stab ingratitude . . . quite vanquish'd him. Then burst his mighty heart, and in his mantle, muffling up his face." 16th-17th cent. *England.* Shakesp., *Jul. Caes.*, 3.2.192.

Submission   "fell before the throne on their faces." Biblical. *Middle East. Luke* 24:5. Also I *Sam.* 5:3 and 28:14.

FACE, HAND (*See also* HAND, HEAD)

Anger   Beating the face. Anc. *Greece* and *Rome.* Sittl, p. 20.

Apotropy   Crossing the face. Medieval *Spain. Cid,* 20, 411. Crossing oneself to ward off the devil or for luck, as when a field is sown or a new loaf of bread is cut. Early Christian. Meschke, col. 335.

Concentration   Supporting face with hands. *U.S.* Krout, p. 26.

Confusion   Hiding face in hands. *Portugal.* Basto, p. 24.

Curse   Priests and priestesses turn towards the West and shake purple cloths. Anc. *Greece.* Sittl, p. 197.

Despair   "and covering his face with his hands, threw himself upon the grass." 19th cent. *England.* Dickens, *Pickwick,* I, p. 98. " 'William, I lament that you should once more have deceived and disappointed me.' Then, pausing and covering his face with both hands for some moments, he continued" 18th cent. *England.* Hickey, p. 88. * Beating the face. Anc. *Greece* and *Rome.* Sittl, p. 20.

Disgust   Face hidden behind hands. Anc. *Greece* and *Rome.* Sittl, p. 84.

Dishonor   A man's face indicates his morality: if he has a good face, he is said to have *vergüenza*—a sense of shame (honorable behavior); if he has a hard face (*cara dura*), he is insensitive, immoral. In order to point out that someone present has a hard face, one slaps one's right cheek two or three times with the right hand, while the corners of the mouth are lowered. A jocular version consists of pinching a man's cheek, implying that he has a hard face. Andalusia, southern *Spain.* Driessen, p. 245.

Dislike   *See* Disgust above.

Disregard   Open hand raised to side of face, then moved across in front of the face, closing as it is lowered: "Never mind him!" "Never mind!" *Netherlands.* Andrea and de Boer, p. 89. Hand must be closed at end of motion. *Flanders.* Ibid., p. 188.

Embarrassment   Rubbing face with hand. Anc. *Greece* and *Rome*. Sittl, p. 47. " 'Well, young sir, what do you learn at school?' was a standing question with uncle Pullet; whereupon Tom always looked sheepish, rubbed his hand across his face, and answered, 'I don't know.' " 19th cent. *England*. Eliot, p. 460.

Fatigue   Supporting face with hands. *U.S.* Krout, p. 26.

Fear   Hiding the face. Biblical. *Middle East. Exod.* 3:6.

Horror   *See* HAND, Horror.

Ignorance   (pretended) Hand held over face, fingers extended to permit vision. 16th cent. *Germany*. Brant, woodcut, p. 89.

Insult   *See* HAND, Insult.

Jail   Spread fingers cover face as one says "¡Qué pena!" ("What a pity!") *Lat. Am.* Kany, p. 117.

Mockery   Flat hands, palms against cheeks, so that the hands form a triangle under the chin: "What a drag!" *Central Africa*. Hochegger, p. 20.

Mourning   "Men and women were beating their faces and uttering loud cries, as it is the custom to do in the East when someone is dead." Frazer, *Golden Bough*, IV, p. 8. Hands beating face. Men. Anc. *Greece* and *Rome*. Sittl, p. 24. * Scratching face. Women. Anc. *Greece* and *Rome*. Sittl, p. 27.

Nervousness   Rubbing face with hand. Anc. *Greece* and *Rome*. Sittl, p. 49.

Prayer   One or both hands held in front of face. African blacks; *Egypt*; Hittites; anc. *Crete*; Germanic tribes. Ohm, p. 289.

Shame   Motion of pulling blanket over face. Gt. Plains Indians. *U.S.* A. L. Kroeber, 10. Cf. anc. *Greece*. Homer, *Odyssey*, Bk. viii. * Hiding face in hands. *Portugal*. Basto, p. 24. Also Schoolchildren. *U.S.* Seton, p. xxii.

Shock   Face hidden behind hands when suddenly seeing corpse. Anc. *Rome*. Sittl, p. 84.

Sick   Grimace accompanied by limp dropping of hands. Schoolchildren. *U.S.* Seton, p. xxii.

Sorrow   Scratching face. Women. (*See* Mourning.) Sittl, p. 27. * Covering face. Biblical. *Middle East.* II *Sam.* 19:4. Hands placed vertically over face. Anc. *Greece* and *Rome*. Sittl, p. 275. Hands over face. Medieval *Germany*. Haseloff, p. 306. * Hands beating face. Men. Anc. *Greece* and *Rome*. Sittl, p. 24.

FACE, HAND, KNEE

Adoration   Right hand touches knees of adored, left hand reaches up to touch face. Performed kneeling. Permitted as form of adoration during later *Roman Empire*. Sittl, p. 165.

Affection   *See* Adoration above.

Sorrow   Face placed on knees of a friend. Women. Anc. *Greece* and *Rome*. Sittl, p. 34.

FINGER (*See also* FINGER, HAND)

Acceptance   "During Islamic conquest, a raised forefinger of the right hand signified acceptance of Islam." *Encycl. Mensuelle d'Outre-Mer*, p. 10.

Accusation   "Leaf laughed. 'I'm glad to see you all getting along so famously. It wasn't long ago, you know, that you were pointing fingers every-which-way.' He folded his arms across his chest, index fingers extended, pointing to both sides at once." *U.S.* Carkeet, p. 238.

Admiration   Index and thumb of right hand are placed respectively above and below the eye as if to make the eye larger. *Spain*. Flachskampf, p. 98. *See* EYE, FINGER, Admiration. * Placing thumb and index together to form a circle. *France*. WW II. Alsop, p. 28. * Mouth firm, somewhat drooped, thumb of right hand erect and pushed forward as if pushing thumbtack, signifying "first class." *France*. Brault, p. 379. "I recently observed a French student using an amusing variant of this gesture to describe admiringly a pretty girl's figure: the thumb is moved downwards in a configuration approximating a large 'S,' delineating in profile a form which an American would outline frontally with both hands as a figure 8." Brault, ibid. * Thumb extended from right fist, but not moving it: item referred to is best. *Libya*. Barakat, no. 86.

Admonition   Wagging the index. Western culture. Austin, pp. 594–95. Extended index, usually of the right hand. Painting of Camillus and Brennus by Perino del Vaga (c. 1525) in Elworthy, *Horns*, p. 40, fig. 20; cf. also n. 171 in Taylor, p. 53.

Affection   Touching finger of beloved. Anc. *Greece*. Sittl, p. 34. * "Anton was pinched on the cheek by index and middle finger; then the sergeant led him out of the office." *Germany*. Mulisch, p. 46.

Affirmation   Thumb and forefinger of raised hand form a circle—o.k. *France; U.S.* UPI Telephoto, *L.A. Times*, June 13, 1964, p. 1. * Index and thumb of left hand form right angle; index of right hand curls around left thumb, middle finger and thumb of right hand are snapped. ("You guessed.") *Spain*. Flachskampf, p. 223. Holding up the thumb. *Russia*. F. Bowers, p. 98. Raised index lowered. Native American, *U.S.*; Sittl, p. 92.

Agreement   The two indexes, palm of hands down, are rubbed together. *Middle East*. Critchley, p. 91. * Touching or pushing someone with a finger or thumb. Medieval and post-medieval *Germany*. *DRA*, II, pp. 147–48. * Linking little fingers of right hands and shaking them up and down, occasionally repeating a warning—making a bargain. Schoolchildren. *England*. Opie, p. 130. * Indexes of both hands extended, other fingers lightly closed. Tips of indexes touch and separate repeatedly. Southern *Italy*. Efron, p. 59. *Israel*. *The Economist*. Sept. 4–10, 1993, coverphoto. * " 'We didn't come through here, Jesus,' said Concha. Jesus grinned broadly and made an expressive gesture of thumb and middle finger. 'Hokay, Señorita Pelayo.' " *Mexico*. Boucher, p. 206. * Thumb extended upward: "Martin raised his thumb as if in confirmation that one could rely on him" *Germany*. Schwanitz, p. 188; "Martin raised his thumb in confirmation. This was supposed to mean 'It shall be done!' " (Transl. by ed.) *Germany*. Schwanitz, p. 197.

Ahead   Index extended at level of chest and perpendicular to it, describes one or two counterclockwise circles in the air. Río de la Plata region, *Argentina; Uruguay*. Meo Zilio, p. 95. *See* Behind.

Anger   Fingers of both hands are extended to threaten the eyes of one who has extended the fingers of one hand to threaten the eyes of the former. 19th cent. *Greece*. Sittl, p. 46. * Fingers of one hand are pushed toward the eyes of another. Bresciani, *L'ebreo*, ch. xxxxix. Index and little finger stretched out as threat toward someone's eyes. 19th cent. Naples, southern *Italy*. de Jorio, p. 94. Extended index or all fingers pointed to the eyes of another. Anc. *Greece*. * Sittl, p. 45. In saying "están de punta" or "están así" the tips of the fingers are struck together. *Lat. Am*. Kany, p. 64. In this gesture the fingers may be reinforced by the extended small fingers. Variation: Nails and knuckles of the two thumbs may be struck together. Kany, ibid. * The little fingers are hooked together and then released. This is repeated two or three times. *Middle East*. Critchley, p. 91.

Apology   After someone has said something pejorative about someone else, he asks God's forgiveness and simultaneously grasps his coat at his chest with two fingers and shakes it, as if he wanted to shake dust off. Arab. 19th cent. *Palestine*. Bauer, p. 222.

Apotropy   *See* HAND, Apotropy. Thumb of right hand placed into left hand, thumb of left hand into right. 6th cent. b.c.-5th cent. a.d. *Babylonia; Palestine*. Talmud. Seligmann, II, p. 183. * Superstitious "Africans" held the left thumb with the right hand against hiccups. 4th-5th cent. North *Africa*. Augustin. *De doctrin. Christ*. 2, 20. Sittl, pp. 125–126. * The thumb of an epileptic is forced out of his fist, in order to break the power of the evil spirit. Anc. *Rome*. Sittl, p. 125. Raising index, middle and ringfinger in protection against evil spirits and illnesses. Early Christian. Sittl, p. 329. * The "fig" (clenched fist, thumb protruded between middle and ringfinger) in form of amulet against barrenness. Southern *Germany*. Röhrich, *Gebärde-Metapher-Parodie*, p. 20. Amulet thumbs worn around neck against the evil eye. Rio de Janeiro, *Brazil*. Seligmann, II, p. 183. The "fig" as talisman against witchcraft. Temple of Isis in Pompeii, *Italy*. Chevalier, p. 283. Against demons during the witching-hour. Ovid. Sittl, p. 123. * The middle finger is extended (palm upwards?) toward demons. Anc. *Greece*. Sittl, ibid. The "fig" is made to raise the spell of an evil oath. *Germany.* Meschke, col. 334. The "fig" is made to someone whom one praises, to protect him from evil. *Yugoslavia.* Röhrich, *Gebärde-Metapher-Parodie*, p. 20. The "fig" is made by a child while clothing which he is wearing is being repaired "so that his sense is not sewn up." *Germany.* Röhrich, ibid. p. 20. The "fig" can be made secretly: Ferdinand I of Naples, when in public, often made the fig in his pocket against the evil eye. *Italy.* Röhrich, p. 20. *See also* Meschke, col. 334. Fist clenched, middle finger extended. ("Mönch stechen.") *Germany.* Meschke, col. 331; ("digitus infamis") *HDA*, II, col. 1492–93. and Seligmann, II, p. 183. See Mockery for "einen Mönch stechen" [i.e. to stab a monk]. *See* FINGER, HAND, Oath. "Present [the "fig"] towards the person of whom you are afraid, but do it unobserved, and you are safe." Martial, *Ep.* 28. *NQ*, Oct. 5, 1867, p. 261. Making the "fig" toward crucifixes and sacred images was prohibited by statute in medieval Italy. Its first mention in Germany appears to be in the Chronicle of Heinrich v. Erfurt (before 1355) to the year 1178. See Sittl, pp. 102–03. The "fig" is most common as antidote to magic. *Spain.* Sittl, p. 123. Made when someone stares at a child. 19th cent. *Greece.* Sittl, ibid. The apotropaic use of the "fig" is an alternative to the "horns." *Sicily; Portugal,* less common in mainland *Italy.* Morris et al., p. 156. On the "fig," see generally A. Cook, p. 134; Seligmann, pp. 184; 188, et passim; Potter, p. 452 et passim; Cascudo, *História*, p. 311; in medieval art, Mellinkoff, *Outcasts*, I, p. 199. *See also* HAND, Apotropy. In distribution the use of the "fig" includes *Portugal* (Hildburgh [1906], p. 458; [1908], pp. 214–22; [1913], pp. 65–66; Hastings, *Encycl.* vol. 6, p. 495; Seligmann, p. 187; [1927], p. 255); *Spain* (Hastings, ibid.; L.L.K. p. 32; Kunz, p. 367; Seligmann [1910], p. 187; [1927], p. 255; Hildburgh [1908], p. 215; [1906], p. 454–61; [1913], p. 63–66; [1914], p. 206–10); *France* (Leach, p. 378; L.L.K. p. 32); *Italy* (Hastings, *Encycl.* vol. 6, p. 495; Leach, p. 378; A. Cook, p. 135; Ashby pp. 145–146; Elworthy, *Horns*, pp. 151, 152, 255–257; Seligmann, pp. 185, 186, 308, 203, 376; [1927], p. 255; Cascudo, *História*, p. 311; Gifford, p. 76; Hildburgh [1906], p. 455; Günther, p. 140); *Greece* (Clarke, p. 365; A. Cook, p. 134; Seligmann [1910], p. 186); *Serbia* (Seligmann [1910], p. 186); *England* (Leach, p. 378; Elworthy, *Horns*, pp. 255–56; Seligmann [1910], p. 186); the *Netherlands* (Leach, p. 378); *Bohemia* (A. Cook, p. 134); *Poland* (A. Cook, p. 134); *Germany* (Leach, p. 378; Seligmann [1910], p. 188; Hildburgh [1914], p. 210; *Austria* (Hastings, *Encycl.* vol. 6, p. 495; Seligmann [1910], pp. 186, 188; Hildburgh [1914], p. 210); unknown in Scandinavia, at least at the beginning of this century (Seligmann [1910], p. 186); "fig" amulets have been found in *Armenia* (Clarke, p. 365); Kertsch (A. Cook, p. 134; Elworthy, *Horns*, p. 136); *Olbia* (Marshall, p. 353); and *Russia* (Seligmann [1910], p. 187, as well as *India* (Hastings, *Encycl.* vol. 6, p. 495); *Cambodia* (Seligmann [1910], p. 166), *Java* (Elworthy, *Horns*, p. 177); *China* (Seligmann [1910], p. 203). Not in *Africa.* Common throughout *South America* (Cascudo, *História*, p. 313; Seligmann [1910], p. 187; Gifford, p. 97). * The "horns": middle finger extended, or index and little finger extended, the other fingers clenched into palm. Against the evil eye and cats. Southern *Italy.* Sittl, p. 124. The "horns" (index and little finger extended, other fingers folded down): " 'Oh, sure. But give her the sign once in a while and you'll have no trouble.' He sat beside his wife and pointed at her with extended first and little fingers." *U.S.* MacDonald, p. 73. "Then [the mortician] decided to expand his business and established a second funeral parlor on the other side of [the butchershop]. And with that, the signore and the housemaids suddenly began to avoid the butchershop like the plague. 'The customers,' said [the butcher], 'thought that the dead bodies were casting an evil eye on my veal chops . . .' This left him no choice but to transform his shop into one giant amulet 'to beat the whammy once and for all.' Since many Italians believe that horns can jab away the evil spirits of death, the embattled butcher ordered an 'arena of horns' from Rome's abattoir." "Meat and Mortality," *Newsweek*, Feb. 28, 1966, p. 42. The statement that the "horns" jabbed with index and little fingers toward the ground are used apotropaically, if the fingers point upward, the gesture implies cuckoldry (*Italy. Time*, Apr. 9, 1965, p. 68) reflects the older literature on the subject. In current use, both the horizontal and vertical "horns" are used with the predominant meaning of cuckoldry; though the horizontal "horns" have an apotropaic meaning more often than the vertical "horns." Morris et al., pp. 140–41. In some African countries, the apotropaic significance of the "horns" pointed at someone is reversed to function as a curse. Axtell, *Gestures*, p. 54. Its apotropaic use is also implied in a mosaic of St. Luke in the church of San Vitale, Ravenna. Additional instances in Elworthy, *Horns*, pp. 149, 174–75. "Horns," with fingers aimed at photographer. Mexico City, *Mexico.* Photo, Dan Williams, *L.A. Times*, March 23, 1987, pt. 1, p. 10. The "horns" were used in antiquity to chase away evil spirits by virtue of the divinity of bulls' horns. *France.* Mitton, p. 149. The use of horns as symbolic defense against evil can be traced back to the Neolithic period. "Horns" against the evil eye. *Spain.* Flachskampf, p. 249; Sittl, p. 124; not observed in Andalusia. Driessen, p. 248. *See also* HAND, Apotropy. * "We cannot even remark on our good health without touching wood or crossing our fingers or otherwise averting the gods' anger at mortal well-being." *England.* Tey, p. 144. Crossing fingers (middle and index) against demons. Anc. *Rome.* Ohm, p. 274. Used while lying, to ward off evil that lying might cause. *U.S.* Saitz and Cervenka, p. 82. Archer, p. 6, Morris et al., pp. 16–18, accept the view that the crossed fingers used apotropaically was originally 'a cryptic version of making the sign of the Christian Cross.' However, they mention three other views: that it is a special form of the *mano pantea*, i.e., thumb, index and middle finger erect, other fingers bent; that it originates in a 'belief in magic that can tie things together'; and that it is a childlike attempt to 'cross something out.' "The sound of the ambulance siren recedes. 'Cross my fingers, cross my toes, Hope I don't go in one of those,' Amanda chants under her breath, crossing her toes inside her sandals." *England*. Lodge, *Paradise News*, p. 107. * Cracking one's fingers to frighten off evil spirits. Meschke, col. 336. "I thought of that scene in *Kidnapped* where David Balfour meets the old crone in front of his wicked uncle's large and gloomy house. 'Blood built it and blood shall bring it down,' she tells him. 'And I crack my thumb at it.' The image had seemed so wonderfully powerful . . . that for days afterward I had gone around muttering these words and cracking my thumb at anything that displeased me." *Britain*. Llewellyn, p. 41. * When someone yawns, South Asians snap their fingers (middle finger against thumb) in order to prevent the soul from leaving the body. *HDA*, II, col. 1489. Snapping the fingers (index or middle finger against thumb) in front of one's ear as a defense against demons which make the ears ring. *Germany*. *HDA*, I, col. 322. Snapping fingers three times close to one's ringing ear. 19th cent. *Greece*. Sittl, p. 121. * Fingers pressed together (tip of index to tip of thumb?) against evil encounters, such as with pigs. Anc. *Rome*. Sittl, p. 125. *Germany*. *DWb*, II, col. 849. * Tip of thumb joined to tip of index, as in the gesture of Approval, representing here a bodily orifice. Anc. and mod. *Greece*. Morris et al., pp. 105, 115–18. * Waving index of left hand three times after a witch. East *Prussia*. Meschke, col. 336. Snapping fingers against ghosts. *HDA*, II, col. 1489. A miniature in Getty MS 88, f. 2b shows Thomas à Becket riding away from Kings Henry II and Louis VII, his right hand raised, back of hand outward and index extended, in answer to the accusatory and threatening gestures of the kings and their followers. * Folding thumb under fingers against evil eye. *Spain; Ireland; Brittany*, partic. Noirmoutier, *France*. Seligmann, II, p. 178. Thumb of each hand tucked inside closed fist protects the health of one's parents while walking past a cemetery. *Japan*. * Archer, p. 6. Middle finger of old woman touches someone who is bewitched or strokes him, in order to free him from the spell. Persius, Petronius. Anc. *Rome*. Sittl, p. 123. * Five fingers spread and extended as plea against being cast under a spell. 19th cent. *Greece*. Sittl, p. 123, n. 7.

Applause Thumbnails tapping against one another, one hand held above the other. *Colombia*. Ironic applause. *Panama*. Saitz and Cervenka, p. 111.

Approach The master snaps his fingers as signal for servant to approach. At table this meant that the matella is necessary. Anc. *Rome*.

Sittl, pp. 222–23. Snapping middle finger against thumb to call a servant. Anc. *Rome*. Baden, p. 450. Calling animals, one snaps middle finger against thumb, palm facing down. *Spain*. Flachskampf, p. 226. Snapping index and thumb: call for someone to approach. *Saudi Arabia*. Barakat, no. 182. Rhetor calls his students together by snapping his fingers. Early Christian. Sittl, p. 223. * Index crooked, moving repeatedly toward gesturer. Familiar. *France*. Mitton, p. 143. Predominantly to children, subordinates or intimates. *Netherlands*. Andrea and de Boer, p. 59. * Palm down, fingers closed, index repeatedly straightened and bent. Southern *Italy*, southern *Balkans, Near East, North Africa*. Röhrich, *Gebärde-Metapher-Parodie*, p. 13 and pl. 7. * Also palm down, all fingers repeatedly straightened and bent. *Spain; Portugal; Morocco; Turkey; Arab* countries; southern *Italy; Greece*. Flachskampf, p. 225. Palm up, fingers repeatedly straightened and bent: northern and central *Europe*, the Po-plain and Toscana, northern *Italy*. Both forms (palm up and palm down) in Naples, southern *Italy*. Flachskampf, ibid. * "He beckoned to him slightly." 19th cent. *England*. Dickens, *Oliver Twist*, p. 229. " 'Oliver,' cried Fagin, beckoning to him" ibid., p. 503. "beckoning furiously to his confederate." ibid., p. 248. "Holding up one finger and shouting" to summon a taxi. College students. California, *U.S.* McCord, 291. One finger is used to beckon to animals, four fingers to beckon to people. *Vietnam*. Prelutsky, p. 7. * Palm up, index extended and repeatedly bent. *U.S.* Used only for calling animals. *Hong Kong; Indonesia; Australia; Yugoslavia*. Axtell, *Gestures*, pp. 85, 155.

Approval Thumb and index join to form a circle, palm facing outward. As the hand is raised and the fingers assume their position, it is briefly jerked forward and held still for a moment before being lowered. UPI Telephoto, *L.A. Times*, June 13, 1964, pt. 1, p. 1. First appearance was in the *Boston Morning Post* of March 23, 1839. Read, pp. 5–27. Morris et al. p. 103, trace it to a baton gesture, i.e., a gesture of emphasis, referred to by Quintilian in his *Institutio Oratoria*, Bk. XI, III, 104: "If the first finger touch the middle of the right-hand edge of the thumbnail with its extremity, the other fingers being relaxed, we shall have a graceful gesture well suited to express approval." "The top of the forefinger moved to join with the nail of the thumb that is next unto it, the other fingers in remitter, is opportune for those who relate distinguish, or approve." 1644. *England*. Bulwer, p. 199. For other instances, see Morris et al., pp. 100–04, and for its distribution, pp. 108–18. Generally *Europe*, incl. the Medit. basin, except *Tunisia*. It is also generally understood in *North Am*. College Students. California, *U.S.* King, p. 264. Also, "Wahre Begebenheit am Stuttgarter Marktbrunnen." 19th cent. *Germany*. See Fig. 4. *U.S.* Archer, p. 5. *Netherlands*. Andrea and de Boer, p. 44. *Russia*. Monahan, pp. 166–67. Raising the thumb. Called "premere pollicem," and meant applause in the circus, as well as a ges-

Fig. 4. "A True Occurrence at the Marketfountain in Stuttgart." Postcard. Stuttgart, Germany: Zobel, n.d.

ture of mercy for the wounded gladiator. Anc. *Rome*. Cascudo, *História*, p. 191. [Editors' comment: Cascudo here, however, interprets *premere pollicem*, the closing down of the thumb, to mean its "closing down" by the tip of the index, and thus associates it with the common "approval"-gesture of the joined tips of index and thumb. This is a misunderstanding: *premere pollicem* refers to the enclosure of the thumb by the other fingers: the gesture signifying "mercy"]. *See* Mercy, below. Tips of thumb and index joined as "A-OK" sign. Obscene. *Greece; Turkey; Malta; N. Sardinia.* Morris et al., p. 114. Threatening. *Tunisia.* Ibid., p. 115. Rude. *Paraguay.* Axtell, *Gestures*, p. 213. * Thumb erect, corners of mouth drooping. *France. Life*, Sept. 16, 1949, p. 12. Hand closed, thumb erect. College Students. California. *U.S.* King, p. 264; 17th cent. *England.* Bulwer, p. 201, 213; *U.S.* UPI Wirephoto, *L.A. Times*, Nov. 20, 1969, pt. 1, p. 28; "Bay Buchanan recalls that Bush aides were 'all smiles' after they looked over the speech. 'They gave us double thumbs-up after they read it,' she said." Braun, A18. *England.* UPI Telephoto, (San Fernando, Calif.) *Valley News*, Nov. 26, 1977, sec. 1, p. 3. *Netherlands*, common since 1945, through its use by Brit. and

Amer. troops. Andrea and de Boer, p. 14. *Russia*. Monahan, pp. 166–67.
* The closed hand with thumb erect, signifying "O.K." is often viewed
as descended from the anc. Roman gesture said to have been performed
by the emperor or the spectators at gladiatorial contests in the Colos-
seum to signify that a gladiator should be spared; the same gesture, but
with the thumb pointing downwards is said to have meant "kill him."
This is incorrect. The closed fist with thumb erect was the signal meaning "kill him," whereas the thumb folded away, compressed under the
other fingers, meant "spare him." For the development of these misin-
terpretations, see Morris et al., pp. 186–93. * "When French youths are
thrilled, they say 'super.' They also thrust out an upturned thumb."
France. Biederman, E10. The gesture is common in Northern and Central *Europe* and *Spain*, less so in *Italy*, where it is sometimes regarded
as having been imported by *U.S.* soldiers in WW II. Morris et al., pp.
193–95. * The down-turned thumb signifying disapproval was not part
of the Soviet kinesic system (Leningrad, Moscow, Ukraine) as late as
1983. Monahan, pp. 166–67. * The upturned thumb is an insult in *Nigeria* and, if given a slight jerk, in *Australia*. Axtell, *Gestures*, p. 50. Putting three fingers together. *Syria; Egypt*. Goldziher, "Über Gebärden,"
p. 386. * Hand raised, palm outward, fingers slowly bent under the
thumb in a grasping motion, indicates that the gesturer approves of
something. *Turkey*. Axtell, *Gestures*, p. 153. * Thumb extended upward
from closed fist, fingers of other hand held above tip of extended thumb
and rubbing tips together. The configuration resembles an icon of a former letter of the cyrillic alphabet, combined with the notion of sprinkling poppyseed, a delicacy. It signifies very strong approval. *Russia*.
Monahan, pp. 168–69.

Assistance   Index of one hand raised upward in a series of spirals
alongside the body and head, together with references to divine wisdom
or intervention. *Spain; Lat. Am.* Green, pp. 79–80.

Attention   Snapping thumb against middle finger or ringfinger. Familiar. *France*. Mitton, p. 146. *Spain; Lat. Am.* Green, p. 96. *Central
Africa*. Hochegger, p. 59. *U.S.* Krout, p. 25. Snapping the fourth finger
and thumb of the right hand. *Russia*. Distinct from the *U.S.* equivalent,
which is a snap of thumb and middle finger. The Russian finger snap is
used also by animal trainers in circuses as a signal that his animals are
ready to perform. Monahan, pp. 108–09. * At auctions one raised a
finger to draw attention of the auctioneer. Anc. *Rome*. Sittl, p. 218.
" 'And now attend to this,' and he raised his finger." 13th-14th cent.
Italy. Dante, *Inf.*, c. x. Extended index shaken back and forth: 'You
listen to me!' *Netherlands*. Andrea and de Boer, p. 86. "The instrument
of warning and argument is the index finger, in one of its three opera-
tional positions. Thrust up, rigid and unmoving, beneath your conversa-
tional partner's nose, it signals caution—watch out, *attention*, all is not

what it seems. Held just below face level and shaken rapidly from side to side like an agitated metronome, it indicates that the other person is woefully ill informed and totally wrong in what he has just said. The correct opinion is then delivered, and the finger changes from its sideways motion into a series of jabs and prods, either tapping the chest if the unenlightened one is a man or remaining a few discreet centimeters from the bosom in the case of a woman." *France*. Mayle, *A Year in Provençe*, pp. 103–04. " 'Mais attention.' ['Pay attention.'] The General wagged a warning finger." *France*. Mayle, *Hotel Pastis*, p. 45. Index extended forward and slowly moved up and down. *Central Africa*. Hochegger, p. 14. Hand raised and index extended upward. *Central Africa*. Ibid.

Avarice   Tips of thumb and index of the right hand joined, accompanied by the exclamation "Ni tanto así!" ("Not even this much!") *Spain*. Flachskampf, p. 232. Rubbing the thumb over the tips of the first two fingers. College students. California, *U.S.* McCord, p. 291.

Begging   "Dearest, dearest Miss, concluded she, clasping her fingers, with the most condescending earnestness, let me beg of you" 18th cent. *England*. Richardson, ii, 2. * Forming a circle with thumb and forefinger signifies begging for money. *Japan*. Greenberg, L4.

Behind   Extended index at chest level and perpendicular to it, makes one or two counter-clockwise circles in the air. Río de la Plata region of *Argentina; Uruguay*. Meo Zilio, p. 95. *See* Ahead.

Betting   Two people lick their thumbs, say "Bets," and press their thumbs together to signify that they accept a bet. If one person does not lick the thumb or touch the other's, it signifies that a proposed bet is not accepted. Children, *Scotland*. Opie, p. 129. Licking thumb and pressing it against the thumb of a disbeliever who has also licked his thumb signifies "you want to bet?" Children. Ibid. Wetting thumb and holding it up, shouting "I bet you." Children. Ibid. Bettors link little fingers of one hand. Sometimes one strikes linked fingers with free hand. *Colombia*. Saitz and Cervenka, p. 24. (See HAND, Agreement.)

Blessing   *See* HAND, Blessing; FINGER, HAND, Blessing. One distinguishes between the *benedictio latina* of the Roman Catholic Church and the *benedictio graeca* of the Greek Orthodox Church as well as some Protestant sects. Cabrol and Leclerq, s. v. 'bénir' and 'bénediction grecque'; Eitrem, pp. 35 ff.; Barasch, *Giotto*, pp. 18–20. In the *benedictio latina* the thumb, index and middle finger are extended, the other two fingers curled against the palm of the hand. The thumb often touches the ring finger. * The *benedictio graeca* is similar to the *benedictio latina*, except for a raised little finger. * Possibly both gestures have common origin. Used in early medieval art as a speaking gesture. Quintilian (*Inst.* XI.3.92) regards most common speaking gesture as that 'in which the middle finger is drawn in towards the thumb, the other three fingers being open.' Barasch, *Giotto*, p. 19. * Index and little finger extended, middle and ring finger bent (sometimes middle finger extended). *Byzantine Empire*, partic. mosaics in *Sicily*. Haseloff, p. 301. Also medieval *Serbian*: Sta. Sophia, Ohrid; St. John the Baptist, Gracanica; Christ with angels at Lesnovo. *Yugoslavia*; *Medieval Frescoes*, pp. 6, 16, 23. * Thumb and index extended, the other fingers separately bent, third and fourth fingers cross index, little finger curled toward thumb. Psalter of the landgrave Hermann of Thuringia. Medieval *Germany*. Stuttg. Bibl. fol. 24; Haseloff, p. 301. * Third finger crosses index. Master of Vysebrod, *Resurrection*. ca. 1350. Prague. *Czech Republic*. Duby, *Foundations*, p. 75. * St. John's right hand has middle finger crossed over ringfinger. Medieval *France*. Villeneuve *Pietà*. Louvre. Paris. * Thumb, index and little finger extended, middle and ringfingers bent toward palm. Medieval *Germany*. Psalt. of Hermann of Thuringia.; also Hamburg, Stadtbibl. In scrinio 85, fol. 11b; Haseloff, p. 301. * Thumb, index, middle finger extended, ring finger and little finger bent, ring finger touching thumb. Medieval *Germany*. Donaueschingen, Bibl. 309; Kupferstichkab., Berlin, Hamilton-Erw. 545; Haseloff, ibid. Also medieval *Serbia*: *Prophet Ezekiel* at Resava. *Medieval Frescoes*, p. 25. * Three first fingers extended, ring and little finger bent. Medieval *Germany*. Wolfenbüttel, Cod. Helmst. 568 (521); Haseloff, ibid. * Thumb and index extended, middle finger bent, little finger extended. Hamburg, Stadtbibl. In scrinio 85, fol. 12a; Haseloff, ibid. * Thumb touches bent ring and little finger, index straight, middle finger crosses over index. *Greece*. Hamburg, ibid., fol. 14b; Haseloff, p. 300; W. G. A. Otto, I, p. 466. * Thumb, index and middle fingers extended, ring and little finger bent in toward palm. Haseloff, pp. 299–300. * First three fingers extended, last two bent against thumb or thumb against the two bent fingers. Medieval *Germany*. Psalter of Hermann of Thuringia, fol. 3b; Breviary of St. Elizabeth, Cividale Museum, p. 17; Cod. Helmst. 568 (521), fol. 29b; in scrinio, Hamburg, Stadtbibl., fol. 12a; Munich, cod. lat. 23094, fol. 91a; Haseloff, p. 300. * Christ makes the blessing gesture by making the "horns," middle and ring finger not clasped by thumb, but loosely bent inward. Medieval Catalonia, *Spain*. Mural from church of Tosas, Rm. 14, Museu d'art de Catalunya, Barcelona. * Three first fingers extended, last two bent inward is the gesture of priestly blessing. *Germany*. *HDA*, II, col. 663. * Making sign of the cross with finger or fingers to oneself or another person. Roman Catholic. Ohm, p. 293. * Index, middle and little fingers extended, ringfinger bent in toward palm. 12th cent. *Byzantine Empire*. Marciana lib., Ms lat. I, 100. Venice; Formaggio and Basso, p. 13; 15th cent. *France*. *Très Riches Heures*, pl. 126. * Thumb holding down bent ringfinger. Fresco at Mount Athos. *Greece*. Didron, I, fig. 21. * Index extended and crossing middle finger, little finger extended, ring finger folded in, its tip touching thumb. Fresco from Convent of Kaicariani, Mount Hymettus. *Greece.* Didron, I, Fig. 24; cf. also ibid., fig. 49. * Index and middle finger extended, thumb bent inward. Master Bertram (ca. 1340–1414/ 15). Germany. *Creation of the Animals.* See also Johannes Schermann, *Christus* (Fig. 5).

Boredom　　Backs of fingers of one hand lightly travel up and down over the chin. *France.* Mitton, p. 150. * Fingers drum rhythmically on a surface, usually beginning with the little finger and moving to thumb. *U.S.* Saitz and Cervenka, p. 74. * "Father Pirrone had transformed himself . . . into [a] Moslem sage and, with four fingers of his right hand crossed in four fingers of his left, was rotating his thumbs around each other, turning and changing their direction with a great display of choreographic fantasy." *Italy.* Lampedusa, p. 130. * Rotating thumbs

Fig. 5. *Christus*, by Joh. Schermann. Graz, Austria. Wood carving.

around each other ("twiddling thumbs") indicates boredom or tranquility. *France; Brazil.* Cascudo, *História,* p. 172. *See also* HAND, Boredom.

Bravery Touching together the thumbs and forming a W with thumbs and indexes. Children. *England.* Opie, p. 231.

Bribery Thumb and index rubbed together. Modern *Greece.* Sittl, p. 115.

Caution *See* Attention, above.

Censure "and others thought he acted so in order to point his third finger at the candidates for the doctorate and thereby censure their folly." *U.S.* Mencken, p. 100.

Challenge Little finger held up. Anc. *Rome.* Sittl, p. 97. * Bending the middle finger. Boys. Zürich. *Switzerland. Schweizerisches Idiotikon,* I, 862. * The "fig" (fingers form fist, thumb protruded between middle and ring fingers). 16th-17th cent. *England.* Shakesp., II *Henry VI* 5.3.123.

Christ The ringfinger is the symbol of the soul, logos; the thumb is the symbol of love. Tip of bent ringfinger touching tip of thumb is symbolic of Christ. Early Christian; Greek Orthodox. Sittl, pp. 304–05; H. Fischer, "Heilgebärden," p. 323.

Clarification Fingers of one hand stretched out and united in one point. The hand in this position is lifted towards the face of the gesticulator and is then moved several times towards the other person and back. 19th cent. Naples; southern *Italy.* De Jorio, p. 85. * Thumb and index united at the tip, the other fingers separately opened. The hand is moved several times towards the other person and back again towards the gesticulator's face. Anc. *Rome.* de Jorio, pp. 85–86.

Cleansing Priest rubs along each finger, repeating a different formula over each, symbolizing the driving out of impurities through the fingertips. *India.* Critchley, p. 71.

Command Index raised. Breviary of St. Elizabeth, Cividale, Museum, fol. 173. Medieval *Germany.* Haseloff, p. 302. Index extended. 17th cent. *England.* Bulwer, pp.124–27. * Snap of fingers to command dogs to attack or to drive on the horses. Anc. *Greece.* Metope of Seliunte; Sittl, p. 223. "The farmer snapped his fingers, as one might to recall a dog, and pointed toward the path . . ." *France.* Simenon, *Maigret Abroad,* p. 50.

Concentration Putting together tips of five fingers to one point. *France.* Life Photos by David Scherman, *Life,* Sept. 16, 1946, p. 12.

Confidence Snapping index or middle finger. Anc. *Greece.* Sittl, p. 95.

Consolation Wiggling one's thumb in front of the eyes of someone who is glum or sad, usually accompanied by "Lach's om me duimpje" ("Laugh around my thumb.") *Netherlands.* Andrea and de Boer, p. 47.

Contempt Little finger held up. Anc. *Rome.* Sittl, p. 97. * Tips of fingers passed rapidly from back to front three or four times under the chin. *France.* Mitton, p. 151. * Tips of fingers rubbed together. *Italy.* Sittl, 97. * Index, extended, is raised once or twice. *Italy.* Sittl, p. 98. * Thumb and index tip to tip, forming a circle. 19th cent. Naples, southern *Italy.* De Jorio, p. 134. * "Miss Jenny, snapping her fingers, told him, she did not value his resentment a louse." 18th cent. *England.* Smollett, *Roderick Random,* ch. xi. "snapping his fingers contemptuously." "snapping his fingers in his face." 18th cent. *England.* Smollett, *Peregrine Pickle,* I, ch. 45. 19th cent. *England.* Dickens, *Oliver Twist,* p. 30. * The "fig" (thumb protruded between clenched index and middle or middle and ring fingers). *Germany. HDA,* II, col. 1306. * "thrusting out the middle finger." College students. California, *U.S.* King, p. 263. Middle finger of either hand extended, fist clenched, or at least the other fingers bent. UP Wirephoto, *L.A. Times,* Dec. 31, 1968, p. 3; Times Photos by John Barr, *L.A. Times,* June 2, 1978, pt. 3, p. 1; and Chriss, ibid., Feb. 17, 1977, pt. 2, p. 7. * The "fig": "A fico for the phrase." 16th-17th cent. *England.* Shakesp., *Merry Wives* 1.3.32. Also *Portugal.* Urtel, p. 35. Sittl, p. 103: brought by foreign mercenaries from *Italy* to *Germany* and Slavic countries. Flachskampf, p. 246: in *Spain* the "fig" is used only apotropaically. (For the "fig," see also FINGER, Apotropy; HAND, Apotropy.) * Francis I of Naples, on the occasion of a popular demonstration, showed the people his disdain by pressing the tips of his fingers together and moving the hand repeatedly forward. *Italy.* Sittl, p. 97. * Snapping fingers toward person disdained. Schoolchildren. *U.S.* Seton, p. xxi. "Mr. Blandors snapped his finger and thumb again, with one loud contemptuous snap." 19th cent. *England.* Dickens, *Little Dorrit,* II, p. 148. *See* HAND, Contempt.

Copulation Bringing both indexes together or the index and middle finger of one hand. *Lat. Am.* Kany, p. 166. * Extended indexes rubbed together. *Brazil.* Cascudo, *História,* p. 237. * Thumb and index form circle, other fingers curl back slightly; circle held parallel to ground, hand near waist. *Colombia.* Saitz and Cervenka, p. 119. * Right thumb extended from right fist and moved in circular motion: obscenity or proposition of man to woman. *Saudi Arabia.* Barakat, no. 85. * Right index placed in hole formed by joining tips of left thumb and index; right index is then moved in and out of the opening. *Lebanon; Libya.* Barakat, no. 102. * Index moved in and out of the opening formed by joining tips of index and thumb of other hand. *Netherlands.* Andrea and de Boer, pp. 106–09. * The 'fig': thumb protruded between index and middle finger of closed fist. *Netherlands.* Andrea and de Boer, p. 48. Mocking gesture of Flemish drivers. Ibid., p. 189. Index and middle finger extended vertically in "V for Victory" gesture used by Russian male adolescents as a gesture of sexual braggadocio. Monahan cites

Morris et al., p. 231, as quoting an informant that he means by it "one penis for her vagina and one for her anus." Never used about accomplished sexual conquest; appears to combine both its significations of imagined victory and sexual obscenity. *Russia*. Monahan, pp. 156–57. * The space between index and middle finger, making a "V", is inserted into the same space of the other hand, one hand making a riding motion. *Brazil*. Cascudo, *História*, p. 236. * Index and middle finger of one hand form a "V", index of the other hand laid through the base. Symbolic of firing a rifle or gun. *Europe; Brazil*. Ibid. * Fingers of both hands intertwined, middle finger of one hand extended and moving. *Brazil*. Ibid. * Extended index and middle finger walking on a table, thumb protruded between them—a male "on the make." *Brazil*. Ibid. (Fig. 6). * Extended index and middle fingers of one hand crossed over those of the other, forming a grill, tip of thumb protruding through it, is an invitation to copulation. If the invitation is accepted, a finger of the other party is inserted in the grill, and pinching the protruding thumbnail confirms the acceptance. *Brazil*. Ibid., p. 237. * Fingers of one hand extended and joined, make a fanning gesture at the level of the lips, but without touching them. *Brazil*; originally *Portugal*. Ibid., p. 214. Cascudo derives eating as synonymous with copulation from classical mythology: Juno conceived Hebe by eating wild lettuce; Menéndez Pelayo cites a late 16th-cent. ballad of Tristan and Isolde, in which the lovers kiss, weep,

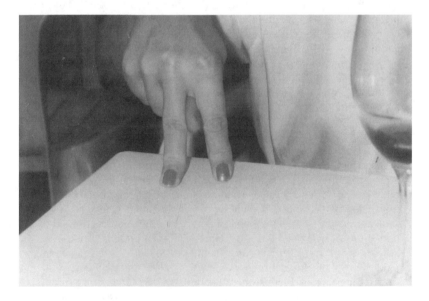

Fig. 6. A Brazilian woman's gesture signifying a "man on the make."

and from their tears a flower is born: "Allí nace un arboledo,/ que azucena se llamaba,/ Cualquier mujer que la come / luego se siente preñada" ("There was born a plant called lily, / Any woman who eats it / immediately becomes pregnant"). Cascudo also cites Mme. de Sevigné: "Pauline est une petite fille à manger" ("Pauline is a tasty morsel"). * Index extended from hand held at head height rotates, then the thumb indicates a direction. *Brazil.* Ibid., p. 237.

Counting Both hands used in counting, beginning the count with the small finger and separating each finger from the others. *Spain.* Green, pp. 64–65. * Thumb and fingers of one hand raised as they simultaneously utter the numbers. *Lat. Am.* Green, pp. 64–65. * Thumb, index, middle finger of left hand are successively grasped by right. *France.* Mitton, p. 148. * Thumb extended—"one." *Europe; North Am.* Aubert, p. 80. * Right hand raised to the height of the face, clenched fist, thumb raised—"one." *France.* Mitton, ibid.; Brault, p. 379. *Germany.* Axtell, *Gestures*, p. 51. * Index raised—one. *Japan.* Ibid. * Thumb raised—five. *Japan.* Ibid. * Thumb and little finger extended—six. *Japan.* Ibid., p. 88. * Right hand raised to height of face, clenched fist, thumb and index extended—two. *France.* Mitton, p. 148. * Index of one hand points to the middle of the index of the other hand—one half. *Europe; North Am.* Aubert, p. 80, fig. 118. * Both hands raised to the height of the face, fingers extended, then both hands closed to fists and the right thumb extended—eleven. *France.* Mitton, p. 148. * Both hands raised to height of face, all fingers extended—ten. *France.* Mitton, ibid. * Right hand raised to the height of the face, fingers extended, left hand raised, thumb and index extended—seven. *France.* Mitton, ibid. * Right hand raised to height of face, fingers extended, left fist raised, thumb extended—six. *France.* Mitton, ibid. * Right hand raised to height of face, thumb, index, and middle finger extended—three. *France.* Mitton, ibid. * Tip of index of left hand touches thumb of right hand—first. ("Ticking off.") Schreiber and Heitz, pl. 1. See figs. 2, 3, 5, 6 in Schreiber and Heitz for process of "ticking off." * "Kennedy held up a hand, all fingers extended. He bent down one. 'One. You'll want some sort of latent fingerprint check on the luggage.' He bent down another. 'Two. You'll want identification of the eighty-two people who have handled it since the owner.' He bent down a third. 'Three. You'll want a rundown on everybody who was on that particular Amtrak trip.' Kennedy bent down the surviving finger. 'Four. You'll want interviews with the train crews. Five—' Kennedy had exhausted his supply of fingers. He extended his thumb. 'In summation, you'll want the same sort of stuff we'd do if the Emperor of the Earth had been kidnapped by the Martians.' " U.S. Hillerman, *Talking God*, p. 67. * Adolescents: "Crossing one index finger over the other to indicate one-half. Alternatively, chopping at a wrist . . . youths . . . count on their hands differently than most Americans. 'They start with the thumb, . . . and they thought we were rather stupid for starting with a finger, usually the index finger, that is not the first.' [Teens] can keep the little finger pressed tight against the palm until it is extended to represent the number 5, a tough maneuver for most Americans." *France.* Biederman, E10–11. * " 'There are two little inconveniences.' He held up a stubby finger. 'The first is that . . . there is a security check . . . ' . . . The General raised two fingers. '*Voilà le deuxième problème* ("And here is the second problem"). Because . . . the door is wired.' " Provençe, *France.* Mayle, *Hotel Pastis,* p. 44. * Thumb of left hand raised, then the tip of the right index ticks off in succession the left thumb, index, etc.: first, second, etc. Fingers of left hand extended and raised, index of right hand ticks off in succession the little finger of the left, then the ring finger, etc.: one, two, etc. *Central Africa.* Hochegger, p. 129. * Count beginning with the little finger, which is bent on the count of one. Successive fingers are bent as one counts, the thumb remaining upright until the count of five. The position of the thumb is distinguished from the gesture of approval by holding it upright, but extended outward when counting. The left hand may hold the right while counting. *Russia.* Monahan, pp. 174–75. *See also* FINGER, HAND Counting.

Cuckoldry Index and little finger raised ("the horns"). Anc. *Greece* and *Rome*; *Italy.* Sittl, p. 103. 17th cent. *France.* Taylor, pp. 36–37. *Colombia; U.S.* Saitz and Cervenka, p. 121. Index and little finger raised vertically, or extended horizontally forward. Andalusia, southern *Spain.* Among men frequently used in jest. In *cachondeo* (following foreplay), i.e., aggressive, but playful joking, the gesture is made behind the victim's head. Andalusia, southern *Spain.* Driessen, p. 247. For theories of the origins of this gesture, see Morris et al, pp. 120–129. Since adultery is no longer regarded as crime reflecting upon his virility, the cuckolded husband is no longer considered ridiculous; therefore use of the gesture in Europe is currently declining, and largely limited to areas strongly Catholic, where divorce is frowned upon; e.g., *Portugal; Spain; Italy.* Ibid., pp. 129–31. * Index and middle finger extended and placed at the back of a man's head so that they suggest horns. The gesture may be a serious comment, but usually is made in jest. *Russia.* Monahan, pp. 148–49. * Setting both thumbs against the temples and waving the fingers. 19th cent. *England.* Sittl regards this gesture as of modern origin. Taylor, p. 39. * Index and little finger extended, the other fingers bent over, the hand in this position placed to the forehead. * 19th cent. Naples, southern *Italy.* De Jorio, p. 93. *See* FINGER, FORE-HEAD, Cuckoldry. For variants of this gesture, see Morris et al., p. 133. * Index and little finger extended horizontally, other fingers held down by the thumb. *Etruria*; ca. 500 b.c. East Central *Italy*; 300 b.c. Apulia, *Italy*; 6th cent. Ravenna, *Italy.*; Morris et al., pp. 136–37; Herculaneum, anc. *Rome*. Sittl, p. 104. This is the apotropaic gesture in its form (see Apotropy, and HAND, Apotropy), but it has come to be used predominantly as signifying cuckoldry. Primarily *Portugal; Spain; Italy*. Morris et al., pp. 140–41. The "horns"—"good luck." *Brazil; Venezuela*. Axtell, *Gestures*, p. 54. * Index and thumb extended. Arab. Barakat, no. 110.

Cunning "Horns" (fist clenched, index and little finger extended) used to indicate slyness, cunning, maliciousness, perverseness. In such a case the hand is not held near the forehead. *Mexico*. Kany, p. 191.

Curse Forking thumb and index. *Italy*. Hovorka and Kronfeld, I, p. 22. The "horns" (index and little finger extended) pointing at someone places a curse in parts of *Africa*. Axtell, *Gestures*, p. 54.

Cut Index and middle finger repeatedly spread apart, then closed, imitating the action of a pair of scissors. *Netherlands*. Andre and de Boer, p. 164.

Dance Index pointed downwards, making a circle. *Colombia*. Saitz and Cervenka, p. 30.

Deafness Finger placed in one ear. *Greece*. Sittl, p. 115.

Death Placing thumb and index together at tip as if snuffing a candle. *Lat. Am.* Kany, p. 28. * Index placed under chin. Critchley, p. 53.

Deception Fingers placed between cravat and neck, rubbing the neck slowly with the back of the hand. Critchley, p. 89.

Decision Man shuts eyes and holds out both hands with fingers pointed towards each other slowly so that fingertips touch; if he succeeds, a trip may be taken, if not, it must be cancelled. Rwala Bedouin, *Kuwait; Iraq; Syria; Saudi Arabia*. Barakat, no. 133.

Defiance The "fig" (clenched fist, thumb protruding between middle and ringfinger) toward the heavens. *Italy*. Ulloa, Bk. iv, p. 65. * "He had learned to snap his fingers at all enemies." *England*. Simms, p. 24. * Left index and middle finger form an inverted V, right index placed between the V and moved back and forth rapidly. *Jordan; Lebanon*. Barakat, no. 64. *See also* HAND, Defiance and Contempt above.

Depart Finger extended in direction of desired departure signifies a request to someone to depart. *Colombia; U.S.* Saitz and Cervenka, p. 80. * Fingers held in pear-shaped configuration so that they point forward, then opened quickly: "go away!" *Egypt*. Barakat, no. 151. * Tips of index and thumb joined, index snapped away from thumb so that its tip hits first joint of ring finger: "scram!" Río de la Plata region of *Argentina; Uruguay*. Meo Zilio, p. 73.

Derangement Tapping forehead with index, then describing a circle with it. Schoolchildren. *U.S.* Seton, p. xxi. *See* FINGER, FOREHEAD, Foolishness.

Desperation *See* HAND, Desperation.

Destruction *See* HAND, Destruction.

Direction Index raised or extended. Breviary of St. Elisabeth, Cividale, Biblioteca del Museo Archeologico Nazionale, fol. 206, 262, 313; Haseloff, p. 302. * Index pointed, the other fingers in any other position, usually turned back. *France*. Mitton, p. 143. * As a rule, extension of the index, other fingers folded in; occasionally both index and middle finger are extended. Medieval *Germany*. Amira, "Handgebärden," p. 208. Witnesses point at the accused. Medieval *Germany*. Ibid. p. 209. An injured person must point to his injury in accusing another of inflicting it. Medieval *Germany*. Ibid., p. 210. See FINGER, HAND, Direction.

Disagreement Hooking one's little finger into that of another person, then suddenly pulling them apart. Arab. 19th cent. *Palestine*. Bauer, p. 220. * Linking thumbs, shaking them up and down, accompanied by a verbal formula. Children. *England*. Opie, p. 324. * Indexes pointed at each other and moved repeatedly apart and together. *Colombia*. Saitz and Cervenka, p. 36. "one finger wagging from side to side in the Provençal shorthand that expresses violent disagreement." Provençe, *France*. Mayle, *A Year in Provençe*, p. 152.

Disappearance Snapping the fingers accompanied by verbal indication of disappearance or absence. *Spain*. Green, p. 87.

Disapproval "Allied to the *digitus impudicus* ["shameless finger"] in both form and meaning is the classical Latin gesture of the *pollex infestus* ["threatening thumb"] or extended thumb. Both an erect thumb and a thumb turned down were signs of disapprobation. Juvenal writes 'Et verso pollice vulgi quemlibet occidunt populariter' (*Sat*. 3, 36–37), which Dryden (1693) translated 'Where . . . with Thumbs bent back they popularly kill.' Dryden understands that the thumb is erect and is bent backward, but the quotation need not necessarily be read in this way. A thumb turned down is now generally regarded as a gesture of condemnation. There is, however, evidence to show that raising a member of the body, and especially the thumb, was an unfavorable gesture. A thumb turned back, up, and away shows hostility to the suppliant." Anc. *Rome*. Taylor, p. 53. Cf. refusal to shake hands in greeting by extending right hand, then suddenly raising right thumb and jerking hand upward as if pointing to something behind one with the thumb. U.S. Life Photo. *Life*, Sept. 3, 1945, p. 25.

Disbelief "this story seemed so outlandish that she asked the manager of the hotel about it. The manager crossed his fingers and confirmed the fat man's tale." I.e. he refused to commit himself to the truth which he asseverated. *U.S.* Randolph, p. 3. * Index and little finger extended (the "horns"). College students. California, *U.S.* King, p. 263. * Lightly hitting thumbnails of both hands together. *Saudi Arabia*. Barakat, no. 173.

Discord Indexes of both hands placed tip to tip to one another in a straight line. Each is then alternately bent, while the other continues to touch its tip. *France.* Mitton, p. 147.

Discouragement   Extended index pointing down. *Brazil.* Cascudo, *História*, p. 218.

Disdain   "she snapt her fingers, in testimony of disdain." 18th cent. *England.* Smollett, *Peregrine Pickle*, ch. 87.

Dishonest gain   Five fingers bent (palm down?). Anc. *Rome*; 19th cent. Naples, southern *Italy.* De Jorio, p. 63; 19th cent. *Italy.* Bresciani, *Edmondo*, c. 7. Sittl, p. 111.

Dislike   Thumb extended and turned down. Grimm and Grimm, *DWb*, II, col. 849.

Dissociation   "The female homicide cop at my favorite Downtown lunch counter shudders whenever somebody mentions Fuhrman's name. 'He's a good cop,' she'll say when pressed, 'but he's an incredible creep.' That's probably the nicest thing I've heard anybody say about the guy. Something about it all bothers me, and it's not just that almost everyone I know flashes that funny two-handed, two-finger sign whenever a news reader refers to McKinny as a 'screenwriter.' The signal—implied quotation marks—is meant to separate her from screenwriters who have written something that actually made it to the screen." U.S. Gold, p. 8.

Drink   Thumb raised repeatedly to the mouth. Anc. *Rome; Southern Europe.* Sittl, p. 115. * Extended thumb (other fingers clenched) directed towards a glass or cup may mean "pour"—a gesture seen in coffeehouses when someone wishes the waiter to pour him a cup of coffee. *Lat. Am.* Kany, p. 82. * A thumb jabbed at the mouth: "Waiter, bring some wine." *Italy.* "The High Price of Silent Insults," *Time*, April 9, 1965, p. 67. * Making a "C" or "T" with the index or indexes signifies a request for coffee or tea or an invitation to the taproom. College Students. California, *U.S.* McCord, p. 290. * Space between extended index and thumb indicates size of drink desired. *Colombia; U.S.* Saitz and Cervenka, p. 44. * Space between extended index and little finger indicates size of drink desired. *Colombia.* Saitz and Cervenka, p. 45. * Hand held in front of stomach, index and middle finger extended to the side: invitation to share the cost of a bottle of vodka. Male. *Russia.* Monahan, p. 34–35. * Same gesture, index, middle and ring finger extended to the side: two males looking for a third to share the cost of a bottle of vodka. *Russia.* Monahan, p. 36–37. * Hand raised toward mouth, thumb and little finger extended: "Let's down a few." *Russia.* Typical of Muscovites. Hand raised to the level of the eyes, index and thumb extended about one inch apart: "Just a few." Prevalent in the *Ukraine.* Monahan, p. 38–39.

Dropping   Points of index and thumb are tightly joined and turned down, as if holding an imaginary object. Then the points are moved apart from one another, as if dropping the object held. *France.* Familiar, seldom used. Mitton, p. 150.

Embarrassment Tip of index vertically placed to lips. Anc. *Greece* and *Rome.* Sittl, pp. 272–73.

Emphasis "He leaned forward and jabbed at Denis with his finger." *England.* Huxley, ch. 6. "with a raised forefinger marked his points as he made them, beating time, as it were, to his discourse." Ibid. * Hand raised, index and middle fingers extended, forming a "V." U.S. UPI Telephoto, *Austin* (Texas) *Statesman*, Oct. 15, 1962, p. 13. * Lowering joined thumb and index of one hand, palm down, directly in front of gesticulator's face to a position in which fingers are spread apart widely. Executed sharply, ending at waist level. Suggests ultimatum. Essentially feminine. *Spain; Lat. Am.* Green, p. 39. * " 'But we didn't.' Ashmore tapped his finger on the arm of his chair. *'Christelow* succeeded.' " *England.* Robinson, p. 233. * Thumb in contact with tip of middle or index finger, forming a ring. *France.* Mitton, p. 151. * Bunched fingers of one hand pushed toward imaginary point in the air. Madrid, *Spain; Lat. Am.* Green, p. 29. * Raising the slightly clenched fingers of one hand, palm up, to or above the speaker's chest. Occasionally both hands. When performed with one hand, the fingers may be rotated back and forth with the wrist serving as an axis. Accompanies expressions indicating a nucleus of an entity or survey or synopsis. Madrid, *Spain; Lat. Am.* Green, p. 31. * "He leaned forward and jabbed at Denis with his finger. 'That's my secret.' " *England.* Huxley, ch. vi. *See* Attention.

Encouragement Thumb extended and turned up signifies encouraging verification, i.e., "See, I told you so." *India.* Simple encouragement. College students. California; *U.S.* King, p. 264.

Engagement "Here, take my ring; my house, mine honour, yea, my life, be thine, and I'll be bid by thee." 16th-17th cent. *England.* Shakesp., *All's Well* 4.2.52,54. 13th cent. *Germany. Kudrun*, st. 1649–50; *Wigamur*, 4633; Heinr. v. Freiberg, *Tristan*, 654.

Enmity Tips of indexes of each hand moved repeatedly toward each other until they touch. 19th cent. *Spain.* Pérez Galdós, pt. IV, iii, vi. *France.* Mitton, p. 147. Indexes extended, one diametrically opposed to the other, the other fingers closed. 19th cent. Naples, southern *Italy.* De Jorio, p. 188. *See also* Disagreement. * Middle fingers horizontally extended, covering the extended index and then suddenly detaching itself from it. Covering the index with middle finger indicates friendship, separating them indicates broken friendship. 19th cent. Naples, southern *Italy.* De Jorio, p. 186. Southeastern *Europe.* Morris et al., pp. 19–24. * Index and thumb, touching each other at the tips, are separated by the index of the other hand. 19th cent. Naples, southern *Italy.* De Jorio, p. 184. * Fists clenched, nails and knuckles of thumbs beaten together.

Spain. Kaulfers, p. 257. * Little fingers of right hands joined. Children. *Lebanon; Saudi Arabia. See* Friendship. Barakat, nos. 37, 38. * Little fingers of right hand moistened and linked, shaking them up and down. Children. Croydon, *England.* Opie, p. 324.

Enthusiasm Wiggling lobe of ear with thumb and index of right-hand. Extreme: right hand is passed behind head and lobe of left ear is wiggled. São Paulo, *Brazil.* King, p. 264. * Thumb(s) of one or both hands pointed up, fist clenched. Popular during WW II. *Britain; U.S.* Hayes, p. 308. *See also* Good Luck.

Equality Indexes extended, outer side up, horizontally moved away from and towards gesticulator as if over an imaginary surface. 19th cent. Naples, southern *Italy.* De Jorio, p. 88.

Etiquette "Her little finger, elegantly crooked, stood apart from the rest of her hand" while holding a drumstick of chicken. *England.* Huxley, ch. xix.

Exchange Hooking little fingers and shaking them while chanting "Touch teeth, touch leather, no backsies for ever and ever." Children. Swansea, *Wales.* Opie, p. 132.

Facility *See* HAND, Facility.

Farewell Arm raised, all fingers except thumb flapped, palm facing gesticulator. *Spain.* Kaulfers, p. 260.

Fatigue Thumb of one hand extended upwards, stroking the forehead slowly from side to side. 17th cent. Naples, *Italy.* de Jorio, p. 151. * Extended index pointing down. *Brazil.* Cascudo, *História*, p. 218.

Fear Hands folded, fingers pressed until joints crack. Anc. *Rome.* de Jorio, p. 265; Sittl, p. 23. * Hand purse, i.e., fingers joined at the tips, palm upward. *Belgium*; northern *France.* Morris et al., pp. 53–54, cite a striking contrast in familiarity with the gesture between Flemish-speaking Belgians and the Dutch: 77% : 0%. The same gesture, but opening and closing of the fingers, is cited as a plebeian and vulgar gesture. Río de la Plata region of *Argentina; Uruguay* by Meo Zilio, p. 66.

Finished Extended index raised once or twice. *Italy.* Sittl, pp. 97–98; *England. Spectator*, April, 6, 1712, cited by Taylor, p. 17.

Flattery Turning of the thumb. *Germany.* Meschke, p. 331.

Friendship Linking little fingers of right hands, shaking them up and down. Schoolchildren. *England.* Opie, p. 324. * Two indexes extended and placed parallel with each other. *Morocco.* Flachskampf, p. 230. * Holding up two fingers close together. College students. California, *U.S.* McCord, p. 291. * Middle finger crosses index of same hand. *U.S.* Saitz and Cervenka, p. 57. * Index and middle finger together, other fingers pressed tightly into palm under the thumb. *Saudi Arabia.* Barakat, no. 77. * Indexes of right hands joined. Children. *Lebanon.*

Barakat, no. 38. *See* Enmity. Little fingers of right hands joined. Children. *Lebanon*. Barakat, no. 37. *See* Enmity above.

Frustration   Fist bangs slowly and repeatedly on table. Lips usually tight. *Colombia; U.S.* Saitz and Cervenka, p. 58.

Future   Extended index at level of face and perpendicular to it, describes one or two clockwise circles. Río de la Plata region of *Argentina; Uruguay*. Meo Zilio, p. 94. (See Past).

Gossip   Thumb and middle finger opening and closing while moving the hand away from the body as if cutting with scissors. Southern *Italy*. Efron, p. 66.

Greeting   Cascudo, *História*, p. 18, cites Pohl (1820) as having observed fashionably dressed ladies greeting one another with a curtsy followed by a mutual pinch on the left thigh. *Brazil*. Cf.: "I set my eyes on that chick, and since I thought that she was now old enough to lay eggs, I gave her a pinch one day, as hard as my love for her was great." *El Pícaro Estebanillo* (1640), cited by Cascudo, ibid. * Squeezing nostrils with index and thumb of left hand, and pointing to navel with index of right hand. Friendly greeting. Astrolabe Bay, *New Guinea*. Comrie, p. 108. * "Mr. Smauker dovetailed the top joint of his right hand little finger into that of the gentleman with the cocked hat, and said he was charmed to see him looking so well." 19th cent. *England*. Dickens, *Pickwick*, II, p. 144. * Index extended on raised hand, as children signify their readiness to answer the teacher and vassals report to their lord. Therefore the finger is called salutaris. Medieval *Europe*. Martianus Capella 1, 90; Isid. Hisp. 11, 1, 70. * Rapping the edge of a table with the knuckles is the customary greeting and farewell of German university students for their professors. On arriving or leaving a communal dining table, one may rap the table lightly in greeting and thus avoid having to interrupt the others by shaking hands. *Germany*. Axtell, *Gestures*, pp. 98–99. *See* HAND, Greeting.

Gunshot   Right index is placed into the juncture of left thumb and index. *France*. Mitton, p. 148.

Health   Little finger is symbolic of the body. Christ as apothecary holds scales in hand and raises little finger. *Austria*. Ganzinger, p. 14; H. Fischer, "Heilgebärden," fig. 9.

Homosexuality   Extended middle finger, Seligmann, II, p. 183. * Tips of thumb and index joined, forming a circle. *Ethiopia*. Arnold, p. 7. Río de la Plata region of *Argentina; Uruguay*. Meo Zilio, p. 80. * Fist, thumb extended (the U.S. hitchhiking gesture): homosexual invitation. *Turkey*. Axtell, *Gestures*, p. 95. * Left index extended and screwed into left cheek. Andalusia, southern *Spain*. Driessen, p. 247.

Hot   Middle finger wetted in mouth, extended forward and jerked back. Schoolchildren. *U.S.* Seton, p. xxiii.

Humility   "and then, touching his fur cap in token of humility" 19th century *England*. Dickens, *Oliver Twist*, p. 19.

Hurry up   Snapping fourth finger and thumb as a signal to hasten a response. *Russia*. Monahan, pp. 108–09.

Idea   Thumb extended, other fingers loosely closed. Hand swings down and up again, thumb forward, as if to dig out something with the thumb. Ghetto Jews. Eastern *Europe*. Efron, table 32.

Idealism   Raising index to the side of the head and describing small circles in the air. *Spain; Lat. Am*. Green, p. 48.

Identification   Snap of fingers used among conspirators as signal of identification. Anc. *Rome*. Sittl, p. 223. * Index points at chest. ("I," "Me.") *U.S*. Saitz and Cervenka, p. 113. Left thumb and index form a ring around right extended index. Father and son are then tapped on the shoulder, while saying "son." Indicates paternity. Nhambiquara Indians, *Brazil*. Cascudo, *História*, p. 107. *See also* HAND, Identification.

Idleness   Four fingers of one hand interlaced with the four fingers of the other, thumbs turn around each other. Twiddling thumbs. *France*. Mitton, p. 151.

Ignorance   Jerking the fingers—"I don't know." *Europe; India*. Rose, p. 312.

Impatience   Fingers drumming on an object. *U.S*. Krout, p. 23. * Fingers drum on a surface rhythmically, usually beginning with little finger and moving to thumb. "The stranger . . . drummed with his fingers on the counter until he was attended to." 19th cent. *England*. Gaskell, II, 36. "though he did not reply, he drummed with his fingers, which action she felt and resented as very disparaging to Dr. Johnson." Ibid., II, 17. Also may signify boredom. *U.S*. Saitz and Cervenka, p. 74. * Snapping thumb against middle or ring finger. Impatience while trying to think of something. *France*. Mitton, p. 146. * Fingers of one hand raised in succession, starting with the thumb, as if counting to five, five being the limit one can bear with patience. *Central Africa*. Hochegger, p. 44.

Impotence   Hand held palm down, fingers closed to a loose fist, index slightly extended but curled down. *Russia*. Monahan, pp. 140–41. * Extended index pointing down. *Brazil*. Cascudo, *História*, p. 218. * Fingers partially open, as though gently brushing a surface. *Brazil*. Ibid., p. 237.

Indecision   Putting finger against tongue and shaking it as if it had been burnt. Arab. 19th cent. *Palestine*. Bauer, p. 223.

Indifference   Middle finger snapped against thumb. *Spain*. Kaulfers, p. 253. "Well, let him forfeit the estate, then! Do you think any of us would care a snap of our fingers . . ." *England*. J. D. Carr, *Hag's Nook*, p. 49. * Extended fingers slowly rubbing the underchin. ("I couldn't care less.") *Italy.* "The High Price of Silent Insults." *Time,* Apr. 9, 1965, p. 67.

Infidel Index raised, then bent to touch its lowest joint—non-Moslem. *Saudi Arabia.* Barakat, no. 93.

Insult *See also* Mockery. The "pistola": the extended right index briskly thrust between extended or circled left thumb and index. *Lat. Am.* Kany, p. 175. * The "fig": thumb thrust between index and middle fingers of the same hand. *Lat. Am.* Kany, ibid. *Central Africa.* Hochegger, p. 191. * The quadruple fig: thumbs of both hands thrust between indexes and middle fingers, and ring and little fingers of both hands crossed. *Russia.* Monahan, pp. 170–71. The inhabitants of Pistoia, Italy, placed on a high tower of Carmignano two large marble arms ending in "figs" pointing toward Florence. This aggressive gesture brought about a war, and the two Figs of Pistoia were destroyed by the Florentines in 1228. *Italy.* Vanni Fucci, from Pistoia, making the "fig" to God: "Togli, Dio ch'a te le squadro!" 13th-14th cent. *Italy.* Dante, *Inferno* xxv, 1–2. For the "fig" in medieval art, see Mellinkoff, *Outcasts,* I, p. 199. "Virtue? A fig 'tis in our selves." 16th-17th cent. *England.* Shakesp., *Othello* 1.3. Sancho Panza, finding Don Quijote, "marrido, triste, pensativo y malacondicionado" ("bruised, sad, brooding and in a bad mood") gives him the advice: "alce vuesa merced la cabeza . . . , dé una higa al médico, pues no le ha menester para que le cure en esta enfermedad" ("raise your head, your Worship, make a fig at the doctor, for you don't need him to cure you in this illness"). 17th cent. *Spain.* Cervantes, *Don Quijote,* II, lxv. By the 16th cent., the "fig" acquired sacrilegious overtones in Brazil. Note the following denunciation to the Holy Office: Alvaro Lopes Antunes, in 1586, repeatedly made the "fig" toward the Crucifix; Salvador de Maia, whenever presented with a salver for alms, made the "fig" instead of depositing coins; Filipe de Guillem, Knight of the Order of Christ, in 1571, while pretending to have a thumb that was too long, crossed himself with a "fig." 16th cent. *Brazil.* Cascudo, *História,* pp. 151–52. * Middle finger extended erect as phallic symbol, the other fingers folded into palm. *Lat. Am.* Kany, p. 175. *Colombia; U.S.* Saitz and Cervenka, p. 114. Anc. *Greece* and *Rome.* Sittl, pp. 101–2. * Extended right thumb. *Lebanon; Syria; Saudi Arabia.* Barakat, nos. 44, 87. * Little finger held up. Anc. *Rome.* Sittl, p. 97. * Tips of right middle finger and thumb touch, forming a circle, other fingers extended. *Lebanon; Syria.* Barakat, no. 47. * Tip of index joined to tip of thumb. Since the gesture is symbolic of a zero, it can be used to signify 'worthless.' Primarily southern *France; Tunisia.* Morris et al., pp. 105–6, 113, 115. *Brazil,* from *Portugal.* In Brazil, as well as in Portugal, it refers to the anus. Cascudo, *História,* p. 191. * Stiff middle finger extended, other fingers pressed into palm, back of hand forward. *Lebanon; Syria.* Barakat, no. 43. The extended middle finger, or *digitus*

impudicus, "is an ancient opprobrious gesture that often has obscene implications. Diogenes insulted Demosthenes with it. Although the identification is not certain, Caligula may have used this gesture when he aroused scandal by his manner of holding out his hand to be kissed. Sittl believes that the hostile attitude of the Roman church explains the disappearance of this gesture in the West, while it remained in use in Byzantium and has survived in modern Greece. However, the gesture has not disappeared as completely in the West as Sittl seems to imply." Taylor, pp. 52–53. [Editors' note: It has, in fact, not disappeared in the West at all, but is extremely common, particularly in the *U.S.*; see Los Angeles Strings (tennis) coach Ilie Nastase; John Burr, Times Photo, *L.A. Times,* June 2, 1978, pt. 3, p. 1; Chriss, p. 7, and a letter from a teacher in Los Angeles to the *L.A. Times,* Dec. 17, 1994, B18, in which she claims that she "encouraged parents not to stop in the middle of the street, push their car doors open and yell for their kids to run into the street. At least weekly, I would be given the middle finger by parents, even told to 'F——— mind my own business.' "] For some legal consequences of "shooting the finger," see Chriss, p. 7. Stiff middle or index finger extended from the right fist, back of the hand turned toward the object of the gesture, and forearm jerked quickly upward. The *corte de mangas.* Andalusia, southern *Spain.* Driessen, p. 248. For the index extended vertically in insult or mockery, see the miniature of Thomas à Becket parting company from Henry II and Louis VII in the Becket Leaves, The British Library, Loan MS (from J. Paul Getty) 88, f. 2b. *See* FINGER, Apotropy. The extended middle finger as an insulting gesture is unknown in Russia. Monahan, p. 158. "Hughie yelled back at the other driver, which of course resulted in a few more hurled insults, and then the two of them were out of their cabs, doors flung open amidst the porters and the bags, the arrivals and departures, the two of them going at it hammer and tongs: 'Fuck you!' 'Fuck you!' 'Well, fuck *you,* man!' 'Fuck *you,* dude!' . . . and on and on that litany born of the city streets, repeated over and over, *fuckyoufuckyoufuckyou,* accompanied by gestures, two fingers poked into a shoulder, another poked into the air, poke poke poke, in such a way that it was clear no one was really going to fight, but that they were merely engaged in a ritual of insult, a steady rain of invective as necessary and appropriate for this occasion as the telling of beads in church." *U.S.* Grimes, pp. 328–29. "To counter anti-abortion protesters, one Democrat marched around them, wearing a huge mock-up of a human hand with the middle finger prominently extended." U.S. Pederson, p. 13. "Behind his back stood two grinning construction workers, and one of them pointed the middle finger upward from his fist in an unmistakable gesture." *Germany.* Schwanitz, p. 228.
* Left middle finger extended and bent back by right index: "Shove it!" Very vulgar. *Russia.* Monahan, pp. 152–53. Tip of right thumb on sec-

ond joint of middle finger of right hand with other fingers extended. *Lebanon; Syria; Saudi Arabia.* Variation: thumb between index and middle finger of right fist, i.e. "the fig." Barakat, no. 45. "with the thumb between the index finger and second finger, though the thumb between the index and third finger is not unknown. Often the wrist of the fist making the gesture is caught in the other hand, and the fist is then shaken. In variations of this one grabs the inside of the elbow, the biceps and even the shoulder with the other hand." Italian-American. *U.S.* King p. 263. * Left index extended, inverted "V"-configuration formed with right index and thumb and placed over the lower part of the left index near thumb. ("I'll ride you like a donkey.") *Saudi Arabia.* Barakat, no. 227. * "Horns": index and little finger extended, other fingers folded into palm. *Germany.* Röhrich, *Gebärde-Metapher-Parodie,* p. 23, pl. 18. Index and middle finger extended, slightly parted and jerked upwards, the back of the hand facing outward. Schoolchildren. *England.* Opie, p. 319. This is the obscene form of the V-for-Victory gesture, the difference being that here the palm faces inward, toward the gesturer, whereas in the V-for-Victory gesture in its canonical form the palm faces outward, away from the gesturer—though on some early occasions of its use, Churchill made the sign with the palm turned inward. The insulting V-gesture is mentioned by Rabelais in the 16th century, by Chapman in the early 17th century, and was well-known in the 19th cent. The obscene V-gesture with the palm turned to the gesturer is exclusively British and Maltese. Elsewhere it is usually mistaken for the V-for-Victory gesture. It is not well known in the U.S., nevertheless, it is possible that the insulting V-gesture with the palm toward the gesturer developed here independently, though it seems to have had a short history: Morris et al., pp. 232–33, cite G. Legman to the effect that during the 1960's the hippies reversed the generally used V-for-Victory gesture, turning the palm inward, as an insulting gesture toward the police, in order to avoid using the common *digitus impudicus*-gesture and the mayhem it would inevitably occasion. For the history of the insulting V-gesture and its relationship to the V-for-Victory gesture, see Morris et al., pp. 226–40; for instances of confusion, see UPI Telephoto, *Austin* (Texas) *Statesman,* Nov. 8, 1962, p. 7 and Times Photo, *L.A. Times,* May 30, 1963, p. 1; *see also* Victory, below. * Raised index and middle finger, palm facing the gesturer, hand pumped up and down several times. *Lebanon; Syria; Saudi Arabia.* Barakat, no. 130. A variation consists of placing the "V"-configuration of index and middle finger beneath the nose and pumping it up and down. Barakat, ibid. * Tips of left fingers and thumb placed together so that hand faces right, then the tip of right index is placed on left fingertips. Insult directed at one's birth or parentage: "You have five fathers." *Saudi Arabia.* Barakat, no. 234. * Palm of right hand placed on back of left hand with fingers slightly interlocked, thumbs rotated several times. *Lebanon; Saudi Arabia*. Barakat, no. 60. * Thumb and index rubbed together at tip. *Lebanon; Syria*. Barakat, no. 66. * Right hand extended, palm down, index pointing down, other fingers extended stiffly. *Lebanon; Syria; Saudi Arabia; Jordan*. Barakat, no. 59; Axtell, *Gestures*, p. 34. * Thrusting four extended fingers into someone's face. ("Animal" to Koreans in Japan.) Osaka, *Japan*. Frayn, pt. 1A, p. 6. * "made the hitchhiking gesture, thumb over his shoulder, which proclaimed to all the world 'What a rotter that one is!' " *Italy*. Graham, p. 26. * Thumb jerked over left shoulder, implying illegitimate birth. London. Post-middle 18th cent. *England*. Thomas Burke, p. 94. * Two fingers jerked upwards. London. 20th cent. Burke, ibid. *See also* FINGER, Victory. * Tips of thumb and index joined, forming a circle. Obscene. *Brazil*. Archer, p. 7. * Thumb extended upwards from closed fist means "sit on this." *Sardinia*. "Screw you." *Iran*. Archer, p. 7. Also obscene insult in *Sardinia; Greece; Nigeria;* with slight jerk, *Australia*. Morris et al., pp. 195–96. Axtell, *Gestures*, pp. 50, 95. * The *puñeta* (masturbation): fingers slightly bent toward the palm, hand pumped vigorously up and down several times. The gesture signifies a gross rejection toward outsiders, and it can imply a reduction of the object of the gesture to an inferior sexual position. Andalusia, southern *Spain*. Driessen, p. 248. *See* FINGER, HAND, Insult; HAND, Insult.

Intimacy Index and middle finger crossed: "they are just like that." The position of the fingers indicates closeness, unity. In reference to a sexual relationship, the fingers represent copulating lovers. The index on top of the middle finger means "the woman on top of the man," i.e., it indicates a domineering woman; similarly the gesturer can identify himself with the uppermost finger, indicating "I'm on top." Morris et al., pp. 18–19.

Invitation The "fig" (thumb thrust between middle and ring fingers of fist) as invitation to sexual intercourse. Röhrich, *Gebärde-Metapher-Parodie,* p. 21. Gerard Terborch's *The Suitor's Visit* (c. 1658) depicts a young man entering a room, bowing to a young lady in front of him, who is making the "fig." 17th cent. *Netherlands*. Mauritshuis, The Hague. * Pointing at another person may signify an invitation to join in going somewhere. College students. California, *U.S.* McCord, p. 291.

Jail Index and middle finger of one hand crossed over those of the other (may also indicate a "Julia," i.e. a policewagon). *Mexico*. Kany, p. 118. * Fingers of the right hand crossed over extended fingers of the left, forming a grating suggesting prison bars. *Lat. Am.* Kany, p. 117. * Two fingers of one hand laid across two fingers of the other. *Russia*. F. Bowers, p. 98.

Joy Cracking one's knuckles. *Brazil*. Cascudo, *História*, p. 239, who also cites Dmitri Merejkowski as maintaining that the gesture was popular in 4th cent. *Byzantium.*

Judgment   In outlawing someone, judge and people raise a finger. Medieval *Germany. Sachsenspiegel,* II, 4, para. 1; Ermisch, xxi, para. 2. * The *Zwickauer Rechtsbuch* prescribed the raising of two fingers. *AGA,* IX, p. 128; His, I, p. 445. In Eastphalian territory the proscription was lifted by the pronouncement of a formula while raising the finger. Medieval *Germany. Zwickauer Rechtsb.,* III, 2, 23, para. 2. * "Point up or down, to signify good or bad." Edwin Booth's promptbook to Shakesp., *Othello* 1.3.328. * The presiding judge of the *collegium agrimensorum,* in rendering judgment, placed the tip of the ring finger (signifying the word) to the tip of the thumb (signifying love). Anc. *Rome.* H. Fischer, "Heilgebärden," p. 343.

Kill   Thumb down, right hand closed, thumb outside fist, pressed close as in grasping a knife, and jerked, thumb edge down, sharply. Austin, p. 596. *See* Mercy below.

Life   Middle finger (symbolic of life) bent inward, all other fingers of left hand (signifying the past) extended. Viennese woodcut of *Janus bifrons,* early 16th cent. *Austria.* Fischer, "Leben und Tod," pl. 2.

Light   (for cigarette): Fist held forward, thumb on top and flicked upwards, imitating the action of a cigarette lighter. *Netherlands.* Andrea and de Boer, p. 164.

Limits   Describing one or more small circles in the air with extended index of one hand pointing downward. Madrid, *Spain; Lat. Am.* Green, pp. 59–60.

Luck   Thumb of one or both hands extended upwards from fist(s). Popularized in the 1940's. *U.S.* Archer, p. 6. *See* Enthusiasm. * Index and middle finger of one hand crossed. *U.S.* Crossed fingers can be considered offensive. *Paraguay.* Axtell, *Gestures,* pp. 104, 213. Crossing index and middle finger while looking at the person on behalf of whom the gesture is made. College students. California. *U.S.* McCord, p. 291. * Middle finger of one or both hands crossed over index. Advertisement. *U.S. News and World Report,* March 27, 1961, p. 117. *Colombia.* U. S. Saitz and Cervenka, p. 82. "She was calm and collected as her victory was announced, in marked contrast to her husband, . . . who sat in the audience, fingers crossed for good luck, . . ." [Unidentified] Times Staff Writer, "L.A. Mother Wins $1,251,388," *L.A. Times,* April 6, 1983, pt. 1, p. 3. "She glanced at Pascoe under lowered eyelids. 'This is confidential, is it? I wouldn't like . . .' 'Absolutely,' said Pascoe. A policeman's fingers are always crossed, he thought." *U.S.* Hill, p. 152. * Fingers of both hands crossed. *France.* Reuters Photo of Lt. Gen. Philippe Marillon in *N. Y. Times International,* March 20, 1993, p. 5. * Index and little finger extended ("Horns") pointing down, arm vertical. *Italy. N. Y. Times,* March 1, 1959. * Thumb enclosed by fingers of same hand. Anc. *Rome.* Sittl, p. 125. Pressing the thumb with the rest of the fingers—the person for whom thumb is pressed will have success. Anc. *Rome; Italy; Germany.* Meschke, p. 331. Thumb of one or both hands tucked into fist. *Germany.* Axtell, *Gestures*, pp. 98, 104. * Thumb erect, fist closed for luck. West *Germany.* Sartori, I, p. 87; II, p. 187; Meschke, p. 331. * "The Spanish movement associated with spilled wine is performed by dipping the finger or fingers into the spilled wine and touching the forehead of those present or seated at the table . . . The movement is no longer common, but . . . may be observed occasionally . . . Olga Bauer enjoins etiquette conscious Spaniards from executing this gesture, and she holds a similar view with respect to the act of throwing spilled salt over the shoulder." *Spain.* Green, pp. 93–94. * Index, middle, and ring finger extended touch the ground. *Brazil*, imported by African slaves, influenced by North African Muslims, who in turn received the gesture from anc. *Rome.* Cascudo, *História*, p. 139.

Magical Crossing of fingers prevents births. Anc. *Rome.* Röhrich, *Gebärde-Metapher-Parodie*, p. 29. * Hooking of little or middle fingers into one another prevents an animal from giving birth. *Germany.* *HDA*, II, col. 1487. * If two people pronounce the same word simultaneously, they hook their little fingers of their right hand into one another, in order to bring about whatever they are thinking at the time. Silesia, *Germany.* *HDA*, II, col. 1491. * Interlacing of fingers often serves magical purposes. Ohm, p. 176. * In looking through the three fingers with which one makes the Sign of the Cross, one can recognize demons. *Germany.* Eisel, no. 207, cited in *HDA*, col. 1489.

Magnanimity Showing ring finger of left hand to emphasize statement or willingness to give someone everything. Anc. *Rome.* Sittl, p. 114.

Magnitude Smallness: Joining tips of index and thumb. Palm facing either up or down. Or palm up, thumb on first joint of the index of same hand. Or snapping fingernails of index and thumb of same hand. *Spain.* Green, pp. 33–34. * Index extended, thumb rests against first joint of index. *Colombia.* Saitz and Cervenka, p. 126. * Index of one hand points at tip of index of the other. *Europe*; *North Am.* Aubert, p. 81, fig. 119. * Index extended from fist, tip of thumb placed on lower joint. *Lebanon; Syria.* Barakat, no. 148. * Index extended, about 2 inches above extended thumb: informal, familiar way of ordering a glass of jenever. *Netherlands.* Andrea and de Boer, p. 17. * Index even closer to thumb—"a tiny bit." Ibid., p. 173. * Index and thumb of the right hand measure the thickness of the little finger of the left hand: "I've lost weight." *Central Africa.* Hochegger, p. 108. * Index extended parallel to thumb, the distance between them indicating the size of the drink. *Brazil.* Cascudo, *História*, p. 130. Also used to indicate a small quantity or something of little importance. *Portugal; Brazil; France.* Ibid., p.

173. * Raising bunched fingers of one hand to the level of the chest with palm facing speaker indicates "nothing." *Spain; Lat. Am.* Green, p. 30. * With expressions suggesting a limited scope or range, small circles are described in the air with the spread fingers of one hand, palm down, at level of waist. Madrid, *Spain.* Green, p. 31. * Tips of thumb and index joined, forming a circle. *France.* Archer, p. 7. * "Many people": indexes hooked one into the other. Arab. 19th cent. *Palestine.* Bauer, p. 221. * Expressions suggesting emergence or growth can be accompanied by raising bunched fingers of one hand, fingers upward, from the waist to approx. the level of the chest. *Spain; Lat. Am.* Or: drawing the bunched fingers of each hand, waist high, palms facing inward, gradually apart. Madrid. *Spain.* Green, pp. 65–66. * "Large crowd": rapid and repeated opening and closing of the bunched fingers of one or both hands in front of gesticulator. *Spain; Lat. Am.* Green, p. 69. * "Small": index of right hand separated slightly from index of left hand. *Spain.* Flachskampf, p. 233. * Specifically mocking someone's thinness: little finger raised, accompanied by: "Es así" ("He/She's like this"). *Lat. Am.* Kany, p. 41.

Marriage Bridegroom's presentation of ring to bride sanctioned by Talmudic authority. Hastings, *Dictionary*, p. 271. Bridal ring is put on the fourth finger, from which the veins go to the heart. Anc. *Rome.* Pliny, Nat. hist., xxx, 34, I; xxii, 59, I; medieval *Germany.* Grimm, *DRA*, pp. 244–45. In medieval marriage ceremony, after joining of hands, the man slipped onto three of his wife's fingers, in succession, the blessed ring which signified marriage, and which was supposed to protect her from demons. "According to ecclesiastical theory, it was given for love and as a token of fidelity; the reciprocal gesture, the giving of a ring to the groom by the bride, did not appear before the sixteenth century. Duby, *A History of Private Life*, p. 130; see also the illustration, ibid., p. 249, from a Veronese Master, *A Marriage: The Exchange of Rings* (1490–1500), in Staatl. Museen Preuss. Kulturbesitz, Berlin. In this instance, as often in Italy, no priest and only a few Witnesses are present; more pomp is displayed on Sano di Pietro, *Marriage of Nobles: The Exchange of Rings* (15th cent.), ibid., p. 250, in Siena, State Archives. Also *Germany.* HDA, II, col. 1494. * Index finger taps ring finger. *Colombia* (ring finger of right hand); *U.S.* (ring finger of left hand). Saitz and Cervenka, p. 84. * Indexes of both hands linked. *Colombia.* Ibid. * The little finger of the right hand holds the little finger of the left hand as on a hook. The woman (left hand) is attached to the man (right hand); or: Both indexes placed parallel to each other. *Central Africa.* Hochegger, p. 113.

Medico-magical In order to still a nosebleed, the arm on the bleeding side is raised with middle finger extended, the other arm points downwards, also with middle finger extended. Thuringia, *Germany.*

Wuttke, p. 347, para. 518; *HDA*, II, col. 1493. * According to Sir Thomas Browne, ancient physicians mixed their medicines with the third finger, the *digitus medicinalis*. Anc. *Rome*. *HDA*, II, col. 1494. * Dirt and spittle laid on with the middle finger heals the effects of the evil eye. Anc. *Rome*. Petron., *Sat.* 131; Persius 2, 32; Sittl, p. 123. * The medico-magical and apotropaic use of the middle finger is widespread; hence the *digitus impudicus* becomes the *digitus medicinalis*. The ring finger is also sometimes regarded as *digitus medicinalis*. *Germany*. *HDA*, II, col. 1495. If one's leg falls asleep, one should wet the middle finger with spittle and make the sign of the Cross over it. *Belgium*. Wolff, p. 225, no. 290; *HDA*, II, col. 1491. * Ringfinger bent, all others straight: stops hiccups and bleeding. Fischer, "Heilgebärden," p. 323. * Thumb and little finger touch at tip to regulate sexual relations. Indian relief in Kamrisch, pl. 69 (ca. 740); Fischer, "Heilgebärden," fig. 10. * Middle finger crosses over index of same hand. Gesture made by kings in healing by laying on of hand. Schroeder, p. 157; Fischer, "Heilgebär-den," fig. 1 (see Fig. 7); see also Miller, p. 59. *See* HAND, Authority. * Little fingers of both hands hooked into one another prevents diar-rhoea. Rural *Europe*. Fischer, "Heilgebärden," p. 333. * Thumb and little finger touch at tip. Through the ring thus formed, he who would be cured of impotence must urinate. 19th cent. and before. Swabia, *Ger-many*. Buck, p. 25; Fischer, "Heilgebärden," p. 322. * In medieval sym-bolism the middle finger symbolized life. In being bled a woman ex-tends the middle finger. Schultze, p. 186; Fischer, "Heilgebärden," fig. 8 and p. 341.

Mercy The common notion is that raising a finger was a plea for mercy by a gladiator (Anc. *Rome*. Otto, p. 117); that if the patron of a gladiatorial combat wished a surrendering gladiator to be spared, he raised his thumb; if not, he turned his hand over, thumb downwards;

Fig. 7. "The King's Touch." From H. R. P. Schroeder, *Geschichte des Lebens-magnetismus und des Hypnostismus* (Leipzig: A. Strauch, 1899), 157.

that the spectators as a whole expressed their wishes in this respect in the same manner. Among the sources adduced are Horace, Juvenal, Prudentius. Sittl, pp. 218–219. This is wrong: the phrase *pollice verso*, usually interpreted as meaning the thumb reversed, "down," means merely a turned thumb, without implying any particular direction in which it is turned. The gesture of mercy, of those wishing to spare the gladiator, was *pollice compresso*, thumb folded under, compressed. The extended thumb signified "kill," the thumb folded under the other fingers signified "mercy." For the history of this misunderstanding, see Morris et al., pp. 186–93.

Minimization of difficulties Snapping index or middle finger against thumb. Anc. *Rome*. Sittl, p. 95.

Mockery Thumb put to the lips and fingers spread. 18th cent. *England*. *Gulliveriana* (1728), cited by Taylor, p. 18. * Palm vertical, fingers extended and parted, thumb placed at tip of nose; thumb of other hand placed against tip of little finger of first hand—"to thumb the nose." *France*. Mitton, p. 149, no. 61. [Editors' comment: for the classical form of the gesture, see the AP Photo of German Chancellor Helmut Schmidt, *L.A. Times*, Oct. 3, 1982, pt. 4, p. 2.] "We cannot safely identify the Shanghai Gesture [thumb tip to nose, fingers spread] with the classical Sign of the Stork (ciconiam facere, curvare), although both gestures involve use of the fingers and have a derisive sense. According to both a scholiast on Persius and St. Jerome, this classical gesture consisted in interlacing the index and middle fingers to resemble a stork's bill [Sittl, pp. 109–10]. Since the verb 'curvare' is ordinarily used in describing the gesture, we can probably infer that the interlaced fingers are bent [Urtel, p. 12, n. 2 . . .]. The bending of the fingers . . . is not altogether appropriate to a stork, which has a straight bill. The reference to a stork seems, moreover, to imply a horizontal position of the fingers. This opprobrious use of the stork is curious because the bird has no characteristically unpleasant associations in either classical or modern times. In the modern German 'Storch stechen' or 'Storchschnabel stechen' the fingers are said to be interlaced and raised, although . . . 'stechen' might suggest a thrusting forward [Meschke, col. 332, n. 61: 'to raise the index like the neck of a stork and to bend it.']. Rudolf Kleinpaul regards (p. 265) this gesture as obsolescent and only partially intelligible. The allied German gesture known in Carinthia as 'den Guler stechen (zeigen)' that consists in thrusting forward the two index fingers laid over each other is used in mockery [Meschke, col. 332, no. 51; Kleinpaul, pp. 265–66, 374; *DWb*, IV, 1a, col. 1121; *Schweizerisches Idiotikon*, II, cols. 57–59, 65]. In identifying this with the Swiss 'einem ein Gabeli machen,' i.e. to mock with the fingers thrust out like a fork [*DWb*, IV, 1a, col. 1121], the editors of the *DWb* seem to have a confusion with another gesture of similar meaning [i.e. they may be referring to the horizontal 'horns' used as simple mockery without overtones of apotropy or cuckoldry. See Morris et al., p. 141 and the distribution map on p. 142.] Since forks originally had only two tines, they were very much like two fingers thrust out. [For the 'horns' signifying mockery in medieval art, see Mellinkoff, *Outcasts*, I, p. 200.] Leopold Schmidt discusses a gesture with interlaced fingers, . . . citing it from children's games without mention of classical or other parallels [pp. 243–44]. De Jorio suggests that the Sign of the Stork is the Digitus Impudicus, . . . [pp. 136–37]." Taylor, pp. 51–52. * "Some cried, some swore, and the tropes and figures of Billingsgate were used without reserve in all their native zest and flavour; nor were those flowers of rhetoric unattended with significant gesticulations. Some snapped their fingers, some forked them out, some clapped their hands, and some their backside; at length they fairly proceded to pulling caps, and everything seemed to presage a general battle." 18th cent. *England*. Smollett, *Humphrey Clinker*, letter of Melford, April 30; Taylor, p. 18 and notes 32–35. * German "Eselbohren," i. e. index and little finger or middle finger extended in imitation of mule ears. Meschke, col. 332. The "fig" (thumb thrust through clenched fingers between middle and ring or index and middle fingers). Anc. *Rome*. Meschke, col. 331. 14th and 15th cent. songs. *Germany*. Röhrich, *Gebärde-Metapher-Parodie*, p. 21. Also used by Luther, Sachs, Grimmelshausen, Abraham a Santa Clara. *Germany. HDA*, II, 1309. North Korean photograph of captured crew of USS Pueblo. *U.S.* UPI Wirephoto, *L.A. Times*, Dec. 31, 1968, p. 1. * Fool points to other figures with left hand, index and middle finger extended, fourth and fifth fingers folded into palm, thumb extended, tongue sticking out, right hand holding branch. 16th cent. *Germany*. Brant, woodcut, p. 79. * The "fig": a young woman, riding a hen, makes the "fig," mocking husband whose sexual performance is inadequate. Engraving from 1650. *Germany*. Bolte p. 78–9. Cf. also the "fig" in Dürer's drawing of hands, Röhrich,*Gebärde-Metapher-Parodie*, p. 20 and pl. 14. On the "fig" see also Mellinkoff, *Outcasts*, I, p. 199, who observes that Italian artists generally avoided vulgar gestures in portrayals of Christ's Passion; ibid., p. 201. * Rubbing of one index on the other (German "Rübenschaben," or "Schabab"). *Germany. HDV*, I, col. 324. (*Italy*: "far pepe.") *HDA*, II col. 1487. Urban Görtschacher, *Ecce Homo* (1508). Lower Belvedere, Vienna. Also "Rübenschaben" with sticks. Ibid. Left index pointed at person, all other fingers closed, right index rubs on back of left from middle to tip and beyond. Seton, p. 180. "Rübenschaben" on altarpiece of Hans Holbein the Elder. 16th cent. *Germany*. Röhrich, *Gebärde-Metapher-Parodie*, pl. 27; medieval depictions of Christ's Passion. Röhrich, ibid., pl. 28, and in Abraham a Santa Clara. Röhrich, ibid., pp. 28–29. *Netherlands*: "Sliep-uit, sliep-uit!"; *Flanders*: "scharesliep-scharesliep!" Andrea and de Boer, p. 10. [Editors' note: *Austria*:

"Etsch, etsch!"] * Extended middle finger signifies homosexuality. Seligmann, II, p. 183. * "Horns" (index and little finger extended, other fingers folded over). Children. *France.* Mitton, p. 149. * Snapping of fingers. Drunken faun of Herculaneum. Naples Museum. Sardanapaulus is said to have been represented on his tomb as snapping his fingers. Anc. *Rome.* Kleinpaul, p. 269. *Denmark.* Klitgaard, p. 89. "Then you'll cross over into Illinois and you can . . . snap your fingers under the nose of them that ordered you around . . ." *U.S.* Kroll, p. 194. "To snap one's fingers as a gesture signifying delight or contempt from 1742 to the present . . . The former use is rare, and the latter use is recent and frequent. Compare also the idiom 'Not to care (give) a snap of one's fingers for . . . ' which is also classical Greek and is known in Latin use of uncertain date . . . *NED* (Snap, 12b)." *Britain; U.S.* Taylor, pp. 65–66, n. 33. "When Frederick the Wise gave an audience to Dr. Luther, he received him most graciously . . . Only when the good man had left, he snapped his fingers at him ('schlug ihm ein Schnippchen') in his pocket or 'stach ihm einen Mönch,' " which, according to Adelung, means that he made the sign of the "fig" at him. *Germany.* Thümmel, II, p. 293. According to Meschke, col. 331, however, the meaning of the German phrase "einen Mönch stechen" (i.e. to "stab a monk") refers to the extension of the middle finger as apotropaic or mocking gesture. * One finger of right hand extended and moved up and down as if playing a guitar. Children. *Mexico.* Lomas, p. 35. * Index of right hand slides between angle of thumb and index of left hand, moving slowly as if playing a violin. *Mexico.* Lomas, p. 35. * Thumb and index of left hand rub the tip of the right index, referring to a boy who is not yet circumcised. *Central Africa.* Hochegger, p. 153. *See* FINGER, Insult; FINGER, HAND, Mockery; FINGER, NOSE, Mockery; HAND, Mockery.

Money Accompanying expressions suggesting either possession or lack of money, thumb is rubbed over fingertips of same hand. *Spain; Lat. Am.* Green, p. 32. *Russia.* Monahan, pp. 176–77. *Brazil*, from Portugal. Cascudo, *História*, p. 195. * Movement of dropping money piece by piece between thumb and index. Familiar. *France.* Mitton, p. 147. * An open circle made with thumb and index, the other fingers bent in on palm. *Lat. Am.* Kany, p. 182. * Rubbing tips of thumb and index together. 19th cent. Naples, southern *Italy.* De Jorio, p. 126. *Brazil.* Cascudo, *História*, p. 130. Indicates wealth. *Italy.* Graham, p. 26. Can also signify "to pay." *U.S.* Saitz and Cervenka, p. 90. * Fist closed very loosely and the four fingertips then brush the palm inward several times. *Lat. Am.* Kany, p. 95. * Rubbing back of the thumb against the ball of the index. *Lat. Am.* Kany, p. 94. * Palm facing person addressed, fingers move back and forth either together or one after the other. *Colombia.* Saitz and Cervenka, p. 88. "The informant 'asked James Barnett what his motives were and James Barnett rubbed his thumb and three fingers together,' which the informant took to indicate money, . . ." *L. A. Times*, July 12, 1985. * " ' . . . If the owner installs an alarm system, the *patron* gets an envelope.' Jojo rubbed his thumb and index finger together." Provençe, *France*. Mayle, *Hotel Pastis*, p. 37. * Tips of thumb and index joined, forming a circle. *Japan*. Archer, p. 7.

Mourning Women digging up the earth on grave mound with their fingers. Anc. *Rome*. Petronius, 74. Sittl, p. 74. * Fingers interlaced. Anc. *Rome*. Ammian. 29, 2, 15. Sittl, p. 72.

Nagging Fingers of both hands pointing down and moving as if sprinkling grain denote a nagging woman. The movement suggests constant drizzle. Biblical. *Middle East*. Prov. 27:15. *Brazil*. Cascudo, *História*, p. 31.

Negation Tip of middle finger placed under the thumb and catapulted forward. Benedictine monks. Critchley, p. 53. * Right arm at full length, fingers closed, thumb extended and pointing downward. Anc. *Rome*. Seton, p. 211. * Tip of thumb, hand open, placed against throat, then catapulted forward. Or the same with all fingers. 19th cent. Southern *Italy*. De Jorio, p. 224; Sittl, p. 95. * Index extended, moving from side to side. *Colombia*. Saitz and Cervenka, p. 151. *Central Africa*. Hochegger, p. 125. * "that peculiar backhanded shake of the right forefinger which is the most expressive negative in the Italian language." 19th cent. *England*. Dickens, *Little Dorrit*, I, p. 10. * Index extended, other fingers closed (palm forward), and wagged from side to side. *Netherlands*. Andrea and de Boer, p. 141. *Brazil*. Cascudo, *História*, p. 218. * Show all fingers except the thumb. Trappist monks. Critchley, p. 53. "Now he stretches finger and thumb and turns his hand, to say, 'No money, nothing doing!' " *Italy*. Graham, p. 26. * Arm bent, fingers closed, thumb extended and pointing downward. *U.S.* Archer, p. 6. *See also* Attention.

Nervousness Twiddling thumbs. *Colombia; U.S.* Saitz and Cervenka, p. 92.

Nothing Point of index is catapulted off the underside of the thumbnail. Anc. *Greece*. Sittl, p. 95. * Upper incisor scratched with thumbnail signifies "nothing" or "nothing for you." Familiar. *France*. Mitton, p. 149. * " 'The girls he went out with didn't even mean that to Mel.' He snapped his fingers." *U.S.* Kemelman, p. 113. " 'you won't wonder I wouldn't vally a feller like that—no, not that much!' and her ladyship snapped her little fingers." 19th cent. *England*. Thackeray, II, ch. xxv. * Thumb placed under the upper incisor and rapidly flicked forwards. Southern *France*. Critchley, p. 91. *Spain*. Blasco Ibañez, p. 29. The gesture may be identical with that of biting the thumb as insult. *See* Insult and FINGER, TOOTH, Nothing. *France; Spain; Tunisia; Yugoslavia*. Morris et al., pp. 198–204. * Lower eyelid is pulled down with the finger. ("My eye!"). Insolent, vulgar. *France*. Mitton, p. 150. "and [he] marked the black of the fingernail of his little finger." *Spain*. Pereda, ch. xii. *See* FINGER, Contempt. * Thumb inserted between index and middle finger of a fist: the "fig." *Yugoslavia*. Axtell, *Gestures*, p. 87. * Tips of index and thumb joined, forming a zero. *Central Africa*. Hochegger, p. 215.

Oath "Wet my thumb, wipe it dry, cut my throat if I tell a lie." Children. Farnham, Surrey, *England*. Opie, p. 127. * Raising of thumb or laying thumb upon table of justice. Medieval *Germany*. Grimm, *DRA*, 1, p. 196. * Three fingers extended. "The first is the thumb, signifying God the Father, the next signifies God the Son, the third God the Holy Ghost." 1585. Appenzell, *Switzerland*. *HDA*, II, col. 663. * Crossed middle and index fingers make an oath invalid. Rural *Balkans*. Hellwig, p. 58. * Link little fingers and spit, saying "spit your death." Children. Liverpool, *England*. Opie, p. 126. * Linking little fingers of the right hand and shaking the hands up and down. 19th cent. *Asia Minor*. Opie, p. 131. * Spit and cross the throat, or spit over wrist or little finger, saying "spit your mother's death." Children. Cumberland, *England*. Opie, p. 126. * Crossing two forefingers, saying "Cross God's honor." *England*. Children. Opie, p. 122. * One finger extended. Medieval *Germany*. Grimm, *DRA*, I, p. 195. * Fingers raised. Anc. *Persia*. Niebuhr, II, tab. 33; Grimm, *DRA*, I, p. 196. * Raising two fingers. Medieval *Germany*. Wolfr. v. Eschenbach, *Parzival*, Bk. I, 902–03; * Touching a reliquary with index or middle finger. Medieval *Germany*. Amira, "Handgebärden," p. 227; or holding the fingers in the direction of the reliquary, or holding them out, even though no reliquary is there. Amira, ibid., pp. 228–29. Hartmann v. Aue, 7923; Grimm, *DRA*, 1, p. 195. * "All of them repeated it with three fingers raised." Stage direction, 18th-19th cent. *Germany*. Schiller, *Tell*, ii, ii. * "He swore to me, interlacing his fingers, by the crosses thus formed." 19th cent. *Spain*. Pereda, *Peñas arriba*, p. 397. * "By the life of my father I swear, . . . and by this sign of the cross [making the cross with two fingers] which I kiss with my dirty mouth." 17th cent. *Spain*. Cervantes, *Novelas ejemplares*, p. 136. * Child making oath crosses fingers, and the other child puts his fingers through them, snapping them apart. "Breaking the cross." Hertfordshire, *England*. Opie, p. 125. * Holding right index down with thumb and extending other fingers. *Saudi Arabia*. Barakat, no. 79.

Obedience Index extended on raised hand, as children signify their readiness to answer the teacher and vassals report to their lord. Therefore the index is called "salutaris." Early medieval *Europe*. Martianus Capella, 1, 90; Isidor. Hisp., *Etym.* 11, 1, 70; Sittl, p. 162. Index, extended on raised hand, is held up by vassal before his lord. Medieval *Europe*. Prutz, I, pp. 487, 682. * Index raised, the hand makes four or five spiraling motions, gradually rising above the head of the gesturer: "This will be decided at the top." *Russia*. Monahan, pp. 180–81.

Oppression   Describing a circle with right thumb and index around left index. "I wind him around my finger." Schoolchildren. *U.S.* Seton, p. xxii. * Pressing firmly down with tip of right thumb. "I have him under my thumb." Schoolchildren. *U.S.* Seton, p. xxii.

Ordering   (wine): The classic "horns" (index and little finger extended, other fingers folded into palm). When the hand is held vertically rather than horizontally in gesturing toward a glass, it may mean facetiously "dos dedos de vino" ("two fingers of wine"). *Lat. Am.* Kany, p. 191. *See also* FINGER, MOUTH, Drink.

Pain   Index taps on middle finger of same hand, thumb touches middle finger. Other fingers folded over into palm. 19th cent. Naples, southern *Italy.* De Jorio, p. 141.

Past   Verbal expression suggesting the past accompanied by pushing the fingers of the cupped hand away from the side of the gesticulator's head. Madrid, *Spain*; *Lat. Am.* Green, p. 65. * Snap index and thumb, then thrust out hand with index extended. *Saudi Arabia.* Barakat, no. 213. * Index extended horizontally from fist at level of face, describing one or two counter-clockwise circles in the air. Río de la Plata region of *Argentina; Uruguay.* Meo Zilio, p. 94; *See* Future; for a more common gesture, *see* HAND, Past.

Pay   Thumb and index of same hand rubbed together. 19th cent. *Crete*; 19th cent. *Greece*; 19th cent. *Germany.* Sittl, p. 115, n. 4. *France.* Mitton, p. 147. * Index rubbed against ball of thumb, hand clenched, forearm extended at right angles to body. *Spain.* Kaulfers, p. 256.

Peace   Tips of indexes pressed together, arms raised, accompanied by the formula "Friedauf bis ins Himmeli ouf." *Switzerland. SAV,* XXI, p. 76; *HDA,* II, col. 1486. * Middle finger crosses index. Truce, "King's X," "King's Cross," "Fins," "Bar up," "Pax." Claim to exemption. Schoolchildren. *U.S.* Seton, pp. xix, xxii: "This is a very ancient sign and seems to refer to the right of sanctuary. The name 'King's Cross,' used occasionally in England, means probably the sanctuary in the King's palace." * Crossing index and middle finger of one hand, sometimes of both, signifies wish to drop out of a game. Children. *England; Wales.* Opie, p. 143. * Thumbs extended upwards, sometimes licking them first, expresses a wish to withdraw from a game. Children. *Scotland.* Opie, p. 143. * The "V for Victory" gesture of index and middle finger extended to form a "V," palm facing outward, has come to be used to signify "Peace"; see Photo David Crane, *Daily News,* April 11, 1993, p. 1. *See also* Victory, below.

Pensiveness   Drumming with fingers. *U.S.* Krout, p. 23. "Tall and slightly stooped, his fingertips pressed together like a banker considering a loan" Brownstein, p. 1.

Perfection   Thumb and index joined at tips, forming circle held at right angle to ground at eye level. Hand sometimes moves back and forth slightly. *Colombia; U.S.* Saitz and Cervenka, p. 95. * Thumb and index or middle finger joined at tip, brought to the lips, then suddenly removed from lips, which are left pursed. The fingers remain some distance from the face for a moment, slightly parted. *France.* Mitton, p. 151. * Thumb slowly traces a descending vertical line. Accompanies a statement of praise, e.g.: "She was educated in Paris, but she makes a Brazilian *feijoada* [black beans and smoked meats] which is perfect." The gesture represents a geographical coordinate. Cascudo, *História*, p. 217. *See also* Praise; FINGER, LIP, Admiration and Superlative.

Pleasure Index and thumb joined at tip. *France; U.S. L.A. Times,* Nov. 20, 1969, pt. 1, p. 27.

Plenty "Preguntóle a ella si tenía galanes o pretendientes. -Si tiene?, respondió la abuela; así, así. Y meneaba los dedos levantando la mano" ("He asked her if she had boyfriends or suitors. -Does she have them?, answered the grandmother; a fair number. And raising her hand she waggled her fingers"). *Spain.* Foz, p. 192.

Pointing Pointing at object of conversation. Anc. *Greece* and *Rome.* Sittl, pp. 51–52. In speaking of someone, index is pointed at him. Anc. *Rome.* Sittl, p. 49. * Someone claiming to have purchased something from an unknown person at an open market clears himself of the accusation of theft, if he points in the direction in which the place of purchase lies and swears to have made the purchase there. Medieval *Germany.* Amira, "Handgebärden," p. 203. * A fief, at the time of being given, receives the required definition by being pointed to. This, as a gloss indicates, is done with hand and with mouth, i.e. *patenter ostendere, oculariter demonstrare*; thus also in connection with transfers of land ownership. Medieval *Germany.* Amira, "Handgebärden," p. 203. See also Old Icelandic *merkjaganga* and *merkjasyning.* Amira, *Obligationenrecht,* II, 688 ff. "Monstrache des fiés" ("to point out fiefs"). Medieval *France.* Du Cange, s. v. monstrare. Pointing to an object that is to be placed under lien was reserved for the debtor in Upper German law; in the laws of Meissen, under some circumstances, the plaintiff could point to property of the debtor. Referees in determining the boundaries of property had to point to the boundary signs. Freiberg municipal law required that one pointed at a thief carrying the stolen goods on his back if one wanted to bring him to justice; similarly in respect to already arrested robbers and counterfeiters. Physically abused women were required to indicate their injuries. Medieval *Germany* and *England. Sachsenspiegel,* II, 64, para. 1; Bracton, *De legib. angl.,* II, 28, para. 1. 13th–14th cent. *Italy.* Dante, *Inf.,* c. v; *Purg.,* c. vi. Pointing finger. 16th cent. *Germany.* Dürer, woodcut of Last Supper (1523). "The good lady pointed, distractedly, to the cupboard." 19th cent. *England.* Dickens, *Oliver Twist,* p. 241. * "He leaned forward, and with a raised forefinger marked his points as he made them." Huxley, ch. vi. *

Whoever points at a mourner with his finger will die or someone in his family will die. Erzgebirge, *Germany*. *HDA*, II, col. 1485. * Pointing with all fingers of one hand, particularly with the palm upwards. Anc. *Greece*. Baumeister, 1293, 1985; Sittl, pp. 289–90. * It is impolite to point at someone; if one points at someone one stabs an angel. 17th cent. *Germany*. Weise, *Ertznarren*, p. 226. If one points toward heaven, one kills an angel or deprives him of his eyesight; whoever points at a thunderstorm will be struck by lightning; pointing at a witch will draw the evil eye to oneself. *Germany*. Röhrich, *Gebärde-Metapher-Parodie*, p. 30. * Thumb protrudes from fist and points backward. *U.S.* (rude); *Colombia* (acceptable). Saitz and Cervenka, p. 34. Use of thumb to identify or point out someone or something, since it is considered impolite to point with the finger. *Spain; Lat. Am.* Green, pp. 70–71. The thumb is used to point. *Malaysia*. Axtell, *Gestures*, p. 79. * Index pointing at oneself, accompanied by a questioning expression ("Me?"), may indicate defensiveness. *Netherlands*. Andrea and de Boer, p. 102. Pointing at something with the index. *Central Africa*. Hochegger, p. 55. * Index at chest height, pointing down, hand moved down once or twice: "Here!" "Now!" Río de la Plata region of *Argentina; Uruguay; also Italy*. Meo Zilio, p. 94.

Poverty Index and middle finger of the right hand take nose between them and, closing, slide downward—"broke." *Spain*. Flachskampf, p. 232. * Thumb is raised quickly while other fingers are extended, index first—"broke." *Italy*. Efron, p. 148. * Index drawn across throat and snapping relaxed index and middle fingers. *Venezuela*. Kany, p. 88.

Praise Holding up both thumbs. 17th cent. *England*. Bulwer, pp. 161–62. Fingers pressed together (tip of index to tip of thumb?). Anc. *Rome*. Sittl, p. 125. Also *Germany*, see *DWb*, II, col. 849.

Prayer Interlacing fingers of one hand with those of the other. Protestant. Ohm, p. 273. First mention in Christianity in the account of Santa Scholastica. 6th cent. Gregory the Great, *Dial.*, 33; Heiler, p. 103. Also anc. *Roman*. Heiler, p. 103. Sarcophagus (5th cent.) from a catacomb at Syracuse: woman with fingers intertwined squats before Virgin Mary. Sittl, p. 176; Heiler, p. 103; Liell, p. 344.

Precision Lowering and raising index and thumb joined at tip, palm down, directly in front of the speaker, or at the side of his head; or drawing joined thumb and index across the body from shoulder to shoulder. Madrid, *Spain; Lat. Am.* Green, p. 70. * Tips of fingers and thumb of right hand joined and agitated gently; eyes often squint: "Comment dit-on déjà? . . . voyons voir un petit peu" ("How does one say? . . . let's consider a bit"). *France*. Brault, p. 380. Morris et al., pp. 44–60, refer to de Jorio as defining the characteristic Italian gesture of the hand purse, i.e. fingertips joined, palm facing up, as a request for precision, and conclude that irritation on the part of the gesturer frequently accompanies the gesture. 19th cent. southern *Italy*. Since it indicates precision, the gesture can also be used in a positive sense elsewhere, e.g. *Corfu; Greece; Turkey*. But this positive sense, as "this has class," can also be turned into an ironical use, and therefore a negative sense. *Malta.*

"Probably"   One finger raised. *Italy*. "The High Price of Silent Insults," *Time*, April 9, 1965, p. 67.

Promise   Wet finger and make sign of the cross on one's heart. Children. Yorkshire, *England*. Opie, p. 124. With right index make little cross over the heart. Schoolchildren. *U.S.* Seton, p. 53.

Prophecy   Eyes closed, arms spread to the side, indexes pointing at each other and moved towards each other; if they meet tip to tip, the hoped-for event will occur. *Russia*. Monahan, pp. 126–27.

Prostitute   Indexes and thumbs of both hands joined at tips to form diamond shape. *Colombia*. Saitz and Cervenka, p. 118.

Quantity   The hand purse, i.e. fingertips of one hand joined at tips, palm facing up, indicates "a lot," particularly "a lot of people." *Spain; Yugoslavia*. Morris et al., pp. 54–55.

Question   The "hand purse": fingers of one hand joined at the tips, palm facing up. The gesture can accompany or substitute for a verbal question. *Italy*. Morris et al., pp. 48–51.

Quickly   Snapping fingers. *U.S.* Saitz and Cervenka, p. 99.

Reconciliation   Little fingers of right hand linked, then separated, saying "We'll never break any more." Children. South Molton, *England*. Opie, p. 325. Hooking indexes one into the other. 19th cent. *Palestine*. Bauer, p. 220.

Redemption   Thumb (symbolic of Love in the Middle Ages) and middle finger (symbolic of Life) touch at tip (the so-called "Mittelfingerbrücke"). The Virgin as portrayed by the Master of the late medieval *Garden of Paradise*. Fischer, "Leben und Tod," pl. iv.

Refusal   Holding up of the thumb as sign of contemptuous refusal. *India*. Rose, p. 313. * Five fingers bent (palm down?) indicates refusal to give. Anc. *Greece* and *Rome*. Sittl, p. 111.

Reminder   Index or middle finger snapped on thumb—forgot something. Arab. Barakat, no. 112. * Snapping fingers in an effort to remember something, or in the moment of remembering. *Colombia; U.S.* Saitz and Cervenka, p. 86. * If one has overlooked or forgotten something, one should put the index into one's mouth, say "fff! ai! ai!," and make the sign of the cross. *Germany*. HDA, II, col. 1483.

Repetition   Circling motion with index pointed down on extended hand. *Colombia*. Saitz and Cervenka, p. 102.

Reproach   Middle finger placed tip to thumb, the other fingers extended. Leonardo da Vinci, *Modesty and Vanity*. 15th–16th cent. *Italy*. Baden, p. 454. * Index of right hand is wagged vigorously to left and right, hand at chest level or belt level: "Non, non: pas de ça!" ("No, no, not that!") *France*. Brault, pp. 379–80.

Result   Snapping fingers in association with expressions suggesting revelation or the solution of a problem. *Spain; Lat. Am.* Green, p. 64.

Retreat   Snapping the thumb against the middle or index finger with forearm usually raised upward and outward. *Lat. Am.* Kany, p. 111.

Royalty   Middle finger crosses index of same hand. Symbolic of kingship, perhaps as symbolic of the power to heal by touch. *See* Medico-magical; Peace. Seal of Waimar II of Salerno (*See* Fig. 8). 11th cent. *Sicily*. Mabillon, p. 115. Also *Christ*, woodcarving. 1959. Graz, *Austria*. Johannes Schermann.

Rudeness   Finger pointing. Rude. *Thailand*. Greenberg, L4.

Sadism   "The Friar's Pinch": index and middle finger bent, forming a pair of tongs—reference to sexual torture by means of hot tongs practiced by the Dominican friars of the Holy Office. *Portugal; Brazil*. Cascudo, *História*, p. 69.

Sanctuary   *See* Peace.

Scorn   The *corte de mangas* ("sleeve cut"): stiff middle or index finger extended from right fist, back of hand outward, forearm jerked quickly upward. Andalusia, *Spain*. Driessen, p. 248.

Secrecy   Index of right hand placed over middle finger, imitating a closed eye: "Gardez cela secret!" ("Keep that a secret!") *Central Africa*. Hochegger, p. 182.

Seeking   Looking about and pointing finger in same directions as those in which one glances. Schoolchildren. *U.S.* Seton, p. xxiii.

Separation   Fingers extended, moved from position of hands palm

Fig. 8. Seal of Waimar of Salerno. From J. Mabillon, *De re diplomatica* Supplementum. (Paris: C. Robustel, 1709) II, 115.

to palm with fingers touching lightly at tips, to a position in which fingers are still extended but separated slightly and palms have separated and turned slightly toward gesticulator. Madrid, *Spain; Lat. Am.* Green, p. 69. * Holding an imaginary object between thumb and index and pretending to drop it. Familiar, seldom used. *France.* Mitton, p.150. * Accompanying expressions of dissociation, fingers of both hands rapidly raised and lowered, chest-high, palm down. Madrid, *Spain; Lat. Am.* Green, p. 41.

Servant Index raised on statues or vase-paintings indicates that the gesturer is a servant. Anc. *Greece.* Sittl, p. 179.

Sexual intercourse (homosexual, invitation to) "González says if he wants to engage the man for sex, he simply taps his brake lights a couple of times or gives a casual two-fingered wave." Los Angeles, *U.S.* Japenga, E10.

Shame Fingers closed into fist, index and little finger raised and extended. ("Horns.") Children. *France.* Mitton, p. 149. First mentioned in Germany by Heinrich of Erfurt (1178) as *signum probrosum.* Sittl, p. 103; *HDA*, II, col. 1308. * Indexes extended from fists, one index crossing the other, rubbing it several times. Children. *U.S.* Saitz and Cervenka, p. 123. *See* Mockery above.

Shoot Index of left hand pointed at something or someone, while right thumb is placed above the left thumb, pulling it back by the tip. *Central Africa.* Hochegger, p. 79.

Shyness Tip of index, vertical, placed to lips. Anc. *Greece* and *Rome.* Sittl, pp. 272–273.

Silence Placing index over closed mouth. *France.* Mitton, p. 145. "Still your finger on your lips, I pray." 16th–17th cent. *England.* Shakesp., *Hamlet*, 1.5.188; *Troil.*, 1.3.240. * Ringfinger bent, all others straight. Anc. *Greece* and *Rome.* Fischer, "Heilgebärden," II, p. 323. * Thumb and middle finger in an open and closed motion while moving the hand away from the body, "as if cutting with scissors . . . cutting off yards of gossip." Southern *Italy.* Efron, p. 157. * Pointing vigorously at floor or ceiling ("Be quiet, the landlady is an ogre"). College students. California, *U.S.* McCord, p. 291. *See* FINGER, LIP, Silence and FINGER, MOUTH, Silence.

Sorrow Hands folded, fingers pressed until joints crack. Anc. *Greece* and *Rome*, 17th cent. Naples, southern *Italy.* De Jorio, p. 265; Sittl, p. 23. * Index traces course of tears from each eye—mock sorrow. Schoolchildren. *U.S.* Seton, pp. xxi, 54.

Speech *See* FINGER, HAND, Speech.

Stealing Thumb and index, or index and middle finger, extended toward a vest pocket or an inner coat pocket, closing the fingers and withdrawing them. *Lat. Am.* Kany, p. 106. * Fingers extended like claws, then first and second joints bent inward as if scratching something, or hand thus formed is drawn down cheek as if scratching it. *Lat. Am.* Kany, p. 107. * Scratching empty space with fingers—an accusation of being a thief. *Mexico.* Lomas, p. 36.

Stop Putting thumbs up, or licking them—desire to drop out of a game. Children. *Scotland.* Opie, p. 143. * Fingers, sometimes index and middle finger of one hand, crossed; usually fingers of both hands must be crossed and raised. Children. *England; Wales.* Opie, p. 143. * Crossing one's fingers and uttering a truce formula. Children. *England.* Opie, p. 142. *See* Peace.

Suicide *See* HAND, Suicide.

Superiority Hands raised to level of chest, palms facing one another, tips of fingers of one hand lightly touching tips of fingers of the other. Righteous superiority. *U.S.* Birdwhistell, *Time,* July 15, 1957, p. 68. "Steepled fingers indicate a feeling of superiority." Birdwhistell, "Do Gestures Speak Louder than Words?," p. 56.

Superlative Thumb and index or middle finger touch and placed on lips, then pulled away abruptly. Simultaneously lips produce sound of kiss. Hand remains for a moment, fingers half open, palm towards face at some distance from it. *France.* Mitton, p. 151. * Snapping the fingers. *Spain; Lat. Am.* Green, p. 72. * Bunched fingers of one hand raised to level of chest, palm facing speaker. Madrid, *Spain; Lat. Am.* Green, p. 30. * Bunched fingers of one hand, palm up, raised to approximately the level of the speaker's chest, then spread abruptly. Madrid, *Spain; Lat. Am.* Green, p. 71–72. *See* FINGER, LIP, Admiration.

Surprise Tip of index, vertical, placed to lips. Anc. *Greece* and *Rome.* Sittl, pp. 272–73.

Surrender In Athenian boxing the defeated signals surrender by raising his index. Anc. *Greece.* Sittl, p. 219. *See* Mercy.

Talk Fingers of one hand or both hands extended, thumb below, and fingertips repeatedly and rapidly brought together with tip(s) of thumb(s). "Babble-babble-babble" or "yackety-yackety-yack." [Editors' note: common in *U.S.*] "Kwek-kwek". *Netherlands.* Andrea and de Boer, p. 20.

Taste Finger laid on tongue. Schoolchildren. *U.S.* Seton, p. xxi.

Teasing Thumb nails of both hands struck together lightly. *Saudi Arabia.* Barakat, no. 173. * Tips of index and thumb touch, then point at someone. *Saudi Arabia.* Barakat, no. 217. * Tip of right thumb placed on middle joint of extended index, other fingers pressed into palm, then index makes pecking motion several times. *Saudi Arabia.* Barakat, no. 168. * Both indexes rubbed together several times while fingers extend forward. *Saudi Arabia.* Barakat, no. 77a. * Tips of thumb and index rubbed together. *Saudi Arabia.* Barakat, no. 172.

Thin Index extended vertically, accompanied by an expression indicating that someone is very skinny. Río de la Plata region of *Argentina; Uruguay*. Meo Zilio, p. 68.

Threat Right index held down with thumb, other fingers extended; rapidly executed. *Saudi Arabia*. Barakat, no. 79. * Right index firmly held down by the right thumb, other fingers extended like a fan, hand is then moved several times. *Lebanon; Saudi Arabia; Syria*. Barakat, no. 46. * Forming a circle with thumb and index is a threat: "I'll kill you." *Tunisia*. Greenberg, L4. * Since the joined tips of thumb and index symbolize zero, the gesture can be used in the meaning 'you are a zero,' i.e. as an insult (*see* Insult), and, with the other fingers stiffly extended and the hand repeatedly chopped in the air, it can be used aggressively, as a threat. The connection between the gesture as a symbol of zero and the gesture as a threat is supported by the frequency of the former in *France* and the limitation of the latter to *Tunisia*, a former French colony. Morris et al., pp. 106–07, 115. * Fingers of one hand pushed toward the eyes of another. *Italy*. Bresciani, *L'ebreo*, c. xxxxix; Sittl, p. 45. * Shaking clenched fist in the direction of offender. Or index extended accompanies verbal threat. Or crossing one's arms. *Spain; Lat. Am*. Green, p. 40. * Index raised and extended stiffly, other fingers clenched. *Germany*. Boggs, col. 321. Holding up index. *England*. Bulwer, pp. 202. * Right index extended from fist, then shaken at someone. *Jordan; Lebanon; Libya; Syria; Saudi Arabia*. Barakat, no. 21. *Brazil*. Cascudo, *História*, p. 77. * Right index extended and pointed directly at someone without moving it. *Jordan; Syria; Lebanon; Saudi Arabia*. Barakat, no. 22. * Index and middle finger extended from fist with back of hand up, then hand is moved forward once or twice toward another person's eyes. *Saudi Arabia*. Barakat, no. 201. * Fingers of both hands are extended to threaten the eyes of one who has extended the fingers of one hand to threaten the eyes of the former. Anc. *Greece*. Sittl, p. 46. * Index and little finger ("horns") extended toward someone's eyes. 19th cent. Naples, southern *Italy*. de Jorio, p. 94; Sittl, p. 46. * Index pointed at someone and violently agitated up and down from the wrist. *France*. Mitton, p. 144. * Extended index or all fingers as threat to the eyes of another. Anc. *Greece*. Sittl, p. 45. * "but wag his finger at thee." 16th–17th cent. *England*. Shakesp., *Henry VIII*, 5.3.130. Hitting table with index while making verbal threat. *Argentina*. Weyland, p. 36. *See* HAND, Threat.

Time Index points to watch: "It's time!" "Look at the time!" [Editors' comment: frequent in *U.S.*] * Fingertips of right hand placed on forehead as one looks at the sun, or pointing to the sun and indicating its position. *Central Africa*. Hochegger, p. 86–87.

Tomorrow Index extended, starting close to the chest, describes half circle forward, curving up. 19th cent. Naples, southern *Italy*. de Jorio, p. 142. * Semicircle drawn in the air with the index, from below upward. Naples, *Italy*. Critchley, p. 89. * Extended index held about waist-level, then moved up in circular motion to its original position— "see you the day after tomorrow." *Jordan; Lebanon; Saudi Arabia; Syria*. Barakat, no. 92.

Tortuousness   Little fingers of both hands are hooked together, both hands moved forwards in zigzag fashion. Naples, *Italy*. Critchley, p. 89.

Truth   Right index moved forward emphatically from corner of mouth. Native American. *U.S.* Austin, p. 594. * Wagging index. *U.S.* Austin, p. 595. * Index pointing straight forward under the chin, then moving forward with an upward curve. *U.S.* Seton, p. 210. * Middle finger (symbolic of Truth and Justice in the Middle Ages) extended. Sculpture at minster of Freiburg. Late medieval *Germany*; also Hans Holbein, *The Dead Christ* (1521) in the Kunstmuseum, Basel, Switzerland; Fischer, "Mittelfingersymbolik," fig. 1.

Understanding   "using the forefinger as an imaginary chalk to mark a board (the finger is occasionally dampened on the tongue at the start) . . ." College students. California, *U.S.* McCord, p. 290. * Tip of index tapped against forehead. 19th cent. *Italy*. Manzoni, c. xiv; Sittl, p. 115. * Indexes on the table, zigzagging back and forth (away and then together again). Southern *Italy*. Efron, p. 154. * Fingers held up in front of the eyes, squinting through them. *Germany*. *DWb*, III, col. 1654, 10; *Schwäbisches Wb.*, II, col. 1506. *See* EYE, FINGER, Leniency.

Undetermined (future)   Index draws as many semicircles as one's arm's length will permit, starting at the chest. The semicircles increase in shape and in the end the index is raised. 19th cent. Naples, southern *Italy*. De Jorio, p. 143. * Thumb (symbolic of Love in the Middle Ages) and index (symbolic of the Spirit) of right hand (symbolic of that which is yet to be manifested, the future) form circle by touching at the tip. Viennese woodcut of a *Janus bifrons* (early 16th cent.) in Fischer, "Mittelfingersymbolik," Fig. 2.

Union   Intertwining rigidly held fingers of each hand in front of gesticulator may accompany verbal expression of fusion. Madrid, *Spain; Lat. Am.* Green, pp. 68–69. * The two indexes united. *Europe; North Am.* Aubert, p. 92. * Interlacing fingers. Islam. Goldziher, "Gebärden und Zeichensprache," p. 376.

Useless   Index is passed horizontally under the nose of someone or under one's own nose. "No go!" "Nothing doing!" Familiar, uncommon. *France*. Mitton, p. 149.

Vengeance   Thumbnails touch each other repeatedly, hands one above the other. ("I told you so.") *Colombia*. Saitz and Cervenka, p. 111.

Victory   Index and middle finger extended, forming a "V," other fingers folded toward palm, hand raised. In connection with politics, Times Photo, *L. A. Times*, May 30, 1963, p. 1. Invented in January 1941 by the Belgian lawyer Victor De Lavelaye as an anti-German graffito to be used by the Resistance, taken up by the BBC in a successful propaganda campaign, it became the characteristic gesture (palm facing outward) of Winston Churchill during WW II. For a detailed history of the gesture, see Morris et al., pp. 226–33. For additional, and probably apocryphal historical notes, see Axtell, *Gestures*, pp. 51–53. The gesture is used and recognized universally. *Lebanon; Syria.* Barakat, no. 129. *Netherlands.* Andrea and de Boer, p. 50. "On his Pacific Rim tour in January [1992], President Bush greeted a large crowd of Australians with a gesture he *assumed* was Churchill's famous 'V' (for victory) gesture. Unfortunately, the President had the gesture backwards, inadvertently flashing the crowd the British Commonwealth equivalent of the American 'finger' (or 'screw you') gesture. The Australians were more dumbfounded than angry; many could not quite believe that a head of state would stoop to obscene gestures." Archer, p. 4. "Former Prime Minister . . . Margaret Thatcher repeatedly and enthusiastically flashed the British obscene gesture to large crowds of puzzled admirers. Again, this was the incorrect use of the palm-facing-in 'V' instead of the palm-facing-out 'V' for 'Victory.' Critics immediately charged that only someone light years distant from England's working classes could fail to recognize one of their most common expressions." Archer, p. 6. Both the correct and incorrect versions of the gesture are featured in *L. A. Times*, May 30, 1963, p. 1. The *Austin Statesman* features President Kennedy (Oct. 15, 1962) and Senator Lister Hill (Nov. 8, 1962) making the gesture incorrectly. The gesture (made correctly) has come to signify "Peace"; see Photo David Crane, *Daily News*, April 11, 1993, p. 1 and Bagott, p. 4.

Virility   The *puñeta* (masturbation): fingers of one hand slightly bent toward the palm, the hand is vigorously pumped up and down several times. If the gesture is made among friends, it connotes praise of the other's sexual prowess. Andalusia, southern *Spain.* Driessen, p. 248.

Warning   "giving Oliver a sly pinch, to intimate that he had better not say he didn't." 19th cent. *England.* Dickens, *Oliver Twist*, p. 24. * "And in conclusion, very slowly, Pnin showed how, in the international 'shaking the finger' gesture, a half turn, as delicate as the switch of the wrist in fencing, metamorphosed the Russian solemn symbol of pointing up, 'the Judge in Heaven sees you!' into a German air picture of the stick—'something is coming to you!' " *Russia.* Nabokov, pp. 41–42. Index and middle fingers extended, forming a "V." * Right index raised, other fingers closed, hand turned so as to have right eye, index and the whole person in line, simultaneously head is shaken a little. *U.S.* Seton, p. 221. Index raised. Schoolchildren. *U.S.* Seton, p. xxi. * Index shaken. *U.S.* Saitz and Cervenka, p. 149; also *Argentina.* Weyland, p. 160. * Index extended and moving from side to side. *Colombia.* Saitz and Cervenka, p. 148. * Holding fingers in pear-shaped configuration with tips pointing up at about waist level, hand is moved slightly up and down ("Wait until later," "Enough," "Be careful"). *Lebanon; Saudi Arabia.* Barakat, no. 152. * Indexes and middle fingers of both hands extended and apart, forming two V's, are crossed and held before the right eye in a metaphor for prison bars: "Careful!" *Russia.* Monahan, pp. 88–89.

Wish   Little fingers of right hand interlocked with those of another, then unlocked simultaneously. Children. Illinois, *U.S.* Opie, p. 312. * Linking fingers and pressing thumbs together. Children. Glasgow, *Scotland.* Opie, p. 311. * Thumbs pressed together. Children. Iowa, *U.S.* Opie, p. 312.

Work   Rubbing the forehead with the thumb from side to side— hard work. Naples, *Italy.* Critchley, p. 89.

FINGER, FOREHEAD

Cleverness   Pointing to the forehead with the index of one hand or tapping forehead with fingers of one hand. *Spain; Lat. Am.* Green, p. 75–76.

Cuckoldry   The "horns" (index and little finger extended, other fingers folded into palm), hand held near or over forehead. *Lat. Am.* Kany, p. 190. *See* FINGER, Cuckoldry. * Indexes extended vertically at side of forehead merely signify an animal with horns, and not cuckoldry. *Central Africa.* Hochegger, p. 39.

Decisiveness   Verbal suggestion of clarity of thought can be accompanied by raising the fingertips of each hand, palms inward, to the forehead. Hands are withdrawn suddenly and held in front of speaker, palms inward. Madrid, *Spain.* Green, p. 79.

Enlightenment   Tip of index touching forehead, then quickly pointing outward, palm facing in. *Europe; North Am.* Aubert, p. 92.

Fatigue   Thumb of one hand extended upwards, stroking the forehead slowly from side to side. Anc. *Rome*; 19th cent. Naples, southern *Italy.* De Jorio, p. 151. * Curved index of right hand drawn across forehead as if to wipe off perspiration, then flicked outward to throw it off: "Quel travail!" ("What a job!") *Central Africa.* Hochegger, p. 204. [Editors' note: also *North America* and *Europe.*]

Foolishness   Placing the index at the temple, making the movement of drilling it into the head. *France.* Mitton, p. 147. * Tapping one's forehead with the index slightly curved. *France.* Mitton, ibid. *Italy. N. Y. Times*, March 1, 1959. *Spain.* Kaulfers, p. 258. * Tapping the center of the forehead: "Do you think I'm stupid?" *Italy. Time*, April 9, 1965, p. 67. * Relentless tapping of forehead with tip of index: "You're crazy." *Netherlands.* Andrea and de Boer, p. 27. If a third party is indicated by pointing or movement of the head before this gesture—"He's got a screw loose." Andrea and de Boer, ibid. * Raising index and middle finger to forehead. *Lat. Am.* Kany, p. 59. " 'He must be a little touched here,' my lord said, tapping his own tall placid forehead." 19th cent. *England.* Thackeray, II, ch. xxiv. * Finger pointing at forehead. *Portugal.* Flachskampf, p. 231. * Tips of all fingers of one hand together touch forehead. 19th cent. *Palestine.* Bauer, p. 223. * Raising index of one hand to temple and twisting it back and forth slowly or simply raising index to temple. *Spain; Lat. Am.* Green, pp. 53–54. *See* FINGER, Derangement.

Gratitude   While one's cigarette is being lighted, back of hand of person who is lighting it is touched with tips of one's fingers of right hand, then placed on one's forehead, while bowing head slightly. *Syria; Jordan; Saudi Arabia.* Barakat, no. 6.

Luck   *See* FINGER, Luck.

Mockery   "The gesture of the Ass's Ears consists in placing the thumbs of one or both hands at the temples and waving the fingers. [In] an example cited by Kleinpaul (p. 265) . . . the identification of the gesture as the Ass's Ears is probable but not certain. On the occasion of a shooting match at Coburg in 1614, a figure of a man was placed on the target. It waved a flag for a hit and made the sign of the Ass's Ears for a miss. Kleinpaul, who does not quote the exact words of his source, goes on to say that the master of ceremonies at other shooting matches presumably of the same period called up the marksman who had missed the target and, after mocking him in a short speech, asked the musicians to strike up a tune and suggested that if the audience wished to mock him with the 'Eselsohren,' this might be decently done behind his back. Hermann Schrader calls 'den Esel bohren' [to 'drill the ass(es ears)'] an unfamiliar idiom in northern Germany. Borchard-Wustmann cites the idiom from a glossary of 1735 with the definition 'asininis auribus manu effictis illudere' ['to mock by imitating asses' ears with the hand']." Taylor, p. 37. "The gesture . . . is, however, much older. . . . For example, an allusion in verses . . . that were published in 1537 . . . shows the identification of ass's ears and frustration: 'si truogen alle esel orn: ir gang und mueje heten s' verlorn. ['They all wore asses' ears: their walk and labor was in vain.'] . . . At the end of the thirteenth century Meister Stolle . . . implies a similar idea: 'Er welte ouch louwen sprunge pflegen:/do erkos an im sin meister esels oren, /er strakte in (al)so mit slegen.' ['He (the ass) also wanted to leap like a lion: thereupon his master recognized that he wore ass's ears, he therefore beat him thoroughly']. Meister Stolle's mention of the ass's ears is altogether literal, but their significance appears in his comment. By an easy development gestures arise from such allusions. The gesture implies that the one who mocks observes that the persons mocked have ass's ears, that is, have been disappointed or have exhibited their folly, or he expresses his wish that they may have them. Somewhat later Der Teichner . . . puts ideas of this sort into the concrete form of a gesture: 'Als ir secht [seht] ma zaichent torn / Mit eim wunderleichn snit, Das man sew [sie] Erkenn damit / Einem macht man esel orn.' ['As you see one designates fools in a curious manner, so that one can recognize them by it, one makes them ass's ears.]" Medieval *Germany*. Taylor, p. 39. "Nor mocked by a hand nimble at mimicking white donkey's ears." Anc. *Rome*. Persius, *Sat.* I, 59; Sittl, p. 109–10. "A modern Portuguese variation shows some difference in form and use. It consists in putting the thumbs between the neck and collar and waving the extended fingers up and down. It accompanies the colloquial phrase 'andar a voar' [to go flying, i. e., to have no money]." Taylor, p. 39. *See* FINGER, HAND, TONGUE, Mockery.

Perplexity   Fingertips of one hand, palm inward, raised to the forehead. Fingers are withdrawn immediately and hand dropped, palm down. Madrid, *Spain; Lat. Am.* Green, p. 78.

Plea   All fingers and thumb of right hand joined, the united tips pressed against forehead. Naples, *Italy*. Critchley, p. 89.

Promise   Moisten index and make sign of the cross on the forehead or neck. Children. Liverpool, *England*. Opie, p. 124.

Reminder   Tip of index touching forehead, then slowly pointed outward, palm facing in. *U.S.* Aubert, p. 92, fig. 140.

Sorrow   Raising cupped fingers of one hand to the forehead, palm facing outward. Predominantly women. *Spain; Lat. Am.* Green, p. 80

Threat   Tip of index placed against forehead. *Spain*. Sittl, p. 115, n. 1.

Understanding   Tip of index tapped against forehead. 19th cent. *Italy*. Manzoni, c. xiv; Sittl, p. 115.

Work   *See* FINGER, Work.

FINGER, HAND

Accusation   Right hand extended, index pointing at the accused. *Central Africa*. Hochegger, p. 2.

Anger   Middle finger held down with thumb, other fingers extended, hand shaken at someone. *Saudi Arabia*. Barakat, no. 71. * Both fists clenched at waist level, thumbs extended in opposite directions. *Lebanon; Syria*. Barakat, no. 16.

Apotropy   The "fig" (thumb protruded between clenched index and middle, or middle and ring fingers) accompanies the formula "my angel guards me." Vicinity of Lorient and Bearn. *France*. Seligmann, II, p. 186. Mother carrying an infant in her arms forms the child's hand into a "fig" at a suspicious person. Andalusia, southern *Spain*. 19th cent. Custine, I, p. 173. The "fig" is protection against witchcraft. Somerset and Yorkshire, *England*. A. Cook, p. 135. The "fig" not only serves to protect from the evil eye, but also to bring misfortune on the person against whom it is directed. *Asia Minor.* Clarke, p. 365. The "fig" used against witches with the formula "witch, retreat from me." Basques. Seligmann, p. 186. Plaster and terracotta "figs" are placed on doorposts and shopwindows to protect the building against misfortune. Naples, *Italy.* Seligmann, II, p. 308. The loss of a "fig" amulet is feared, since it is believed that the wearer is now susceptible to all adversities of life. *Brazil.* Cascudo, *Dicionario*, p. 311. "Fig" amulet an object of devout worship, esp. by childless women. *Java.* Elworthy, p. 177. An Italian physician recommended that a coral "fica" be tied around the neck of a child with a "crick" in its neck, and believed that the little girl had been "overlooked." A. p. 118. For the use of the "fig" as amulet against the evil eye, see Marques-Riviere, p. 78; Hastings, *Encyclopaedia*, VI, p. 495; Hildburgh, p. 214. When King Ferdinand of Naples appeared in public, he made the "fig" from time to time in his pocket, to avert the evil eye that someone on the street may have cast on him. *Southern Italy.* F.S. p. 325. Seligmann, II, p. 186. Neapolitans make a "fig" under their coat or in their pocket in order to avoid obviously insulting a person as a witch or, in general, at a social gathering. Naples, *Italy.* Seligmann, II, p. 185–86. "Everybody knows to double your thumb in your right hand averts danger." Elworthy, *Evil Eye*, p. 256. If one sees someone who may bewitch one, one should hold some garlic and make the sign of the "fig" with the left hand to avert the evil eye. *Portugal.* Vasconcellos, p. 35. The "fig" as protection against ghosts. Anc. *Rome.* Seligmann, II, p. 185. The double "fig" (thumb of one hand between index and middle finger of the other) against the evil eye and the demonic influence of even numbers. 6th cent. B.C.–5th cent. A.D. *Middle East. Talmud.* Bischoff, II, p. 181; *HDA*, II, col. 1307. In the neighborhood of Hennebont, ropemakers, coopers and tailors are considered uncanny. To guard against their evil influence, the gesture of the "fig" is recommended together with the formula "Ar garet" ("Stay back"). Early 19th cent. *France.* Michel, I, p. 171. For the preservation of their hair, Madrid women are said to carry jet figas on any part of the body, but Toledo women place them in the hair itself, so that the effect may be more immediate. *Spain.* Kunz, p. 368. The "fig" as protection against ghosts. Anc. *Rome.* Ovid, *Fasti*, 5, 433f. The "fig" was used against snakes, according to the hieroglyphics of Pyramid 672. Anc. *Egypt.* Riviere, p. 78. The "fig" made when a witch is in a whirlwind. Guarda, *Portugal.* Vasconcellos, p. 37. The "fig" against sinister people, especially the deformed and witches. *Portugal.* Leite de Vasconcellos, ibid. King Victor Emmanuel continually made the sign of the fig during the battle of Solferino (1859) to protect his army. *Italy.* Seligmann, II, p. 186. * Index and little finger extended ("horns"), and rotating from side to side several times while the gesturer says "lagarto" (lizard) to counteract the possible effect of an utterance of the taboo word "culebra" (snake). *Colombia.* Saitz and Cervenka, p. 83. *See* Oath. In western Christian iconography, Lucifer is portrayed on his seal with his right claw raised in the form of the horns pointing outward. 15th cent. *France.* Fig. 10. Didron, II, p. 147. *See* FINGER, Apotropy.

Approach Hand raised, palm outwards, fingers moved downwards and toward palm. Beckoning. Muslim tribes. *India.* Rose, p. 313. * Hand raised, palm inwards at level of face, arm half bent, tips of fingers moved inward. *Europe; North Am.* Aubert, p. 84. Beckoning with fingertips bent down. Anc. *Greece* and *Rome*; *Greece; Italy.* Sittl, p. 216. * Index pointing downward, hand moved forward from shoulder-height to the level of the waist: 'Come!' 'Come here!' *Netherlands.* Andrea and de Boer, p. 38. * Beckoning with the index is only used to call animals; it is considered insulting if used to people. *Indonesia.* Bagott, p. 4. * Hand raised, index extended—calling taxi. New York, *U.S.* Michael Crawford, cartoon, *New Yorker*, Aug. 19, 1996, p. 55. *See also* FINGER, Approach.

Approval Hand raised, thumb and index forming a circle. *U.S.* Ruesch and Kees, p. 77. *Premere pollicem* (to press, lower the thumb) meant approval, applause in the circus, as well as a gesture of mercy for the wounded gladiator. Cascudo, *História*, p. 191; but *see also* FINGER, Approval; FINGER, Mercy. * Tips of all fingers of the right hand joined at tip of thumb, tips directed upward, hand moved up and down a few times. *Near East.* Critchley, p. 91. * Extended index pointed at referent, then hand placed on chest. *Colombia.* Saitz and Cervenka, p. 20. * Hand raised to level of face, fingers curled in, thumb extended vertically. *Central Africa.* Hochegger, p. 9. * The "thumbs up" gesture of approval is insulting in Australia. Bagott, p. 1.

Arrogance Open hands, held in front of stomach, joined by interlaced fingers, palms facing up, thumbs rotating around each other ("twiddling thumbs"). Used almost exclusively by adults to indicate that someone is arrogant or conceited. *Russia.* Monahan, pp. 68–69.

Assurance All fingers spread out, thumb curled up. Diagram of the "Abhaya mudra." *India.* Rose, p. 314. * Hand raised to shoulder level, tips of index and thumb joined, forming a circle; other fingers extended. *Central Africa.* Hochegger, p. 14.

Attention Snapping fingers (either middle or ringfinger against thumb). Familiar. *France.* Mitton, p. 146. * Hand extended with fingers together. *Colombia; U.S.* Saitz and Cervenka, p. 22. * Hand raised, finger extended. Common in classrooms. *Colombia; U.S.* Saitz and Cervenka, p. 22. *Netherlands*—"Listen!" Andrea and de Boer, pp. 155, 166. See also the Neapolitan gesture in fig. 31 b. Wundt, I, p. 186, Fig. 10. * Hand about shoulder-level, index and middle finger extended vertically as in blessing gesture and the medieval speaking gesture—"it may be described as a gesture of unambiguous non-action, the hand is immobilized and can neither grip nor push. We still used this conventional speaking gesture of 'aufzeigen' at school in Vienna, to signify that we wished to speak." Gombrich, pp. 66–67. * Student eager to speak waves raised hand from side to side. *U.S.*, and thrusts it forward repeatedly. *Colombia.* Saitz and Cervenka, p. 22. * Hand raised, palm outward, index extended, other fingers folded in. In early medieval art it could accompany any kind of emphatic speech, as when Joseph says to his brothers: "Vos cogitastis de me malum, sed vobis convertitur in bonum" ("You thought evil against me; but God meant it unto good") Biblical. *Middle East. Gen.* 50:20, or when the Bridegroom said to the Foolish Maidens: "Amen dico vobis, nescio vos" ("Truly, I say to you, I do not know you"). Biblical. *Middle East. Matth.* 25:12. It can also accompany a curse or a blessing, a plea or a question. Medieval *Germany.* Amira, "Handgebärden," p. 213. It is also executed in connection with numerous legal transactions; see Amira, ibid., pp. 214–16. Raised hand or the finger pointed heavenwards, a preachers' gesture frequent in Italian painting. Medieval and Renaissance *Italy.* Van der Meulen, p. 10. * Right index pointing upward and moving back and forth, while left hand is pointed in the direction of danger. *Central Africa.* Hochegger, p. 15. *See also* Blessing.

Betting Little finger of right hand hooked into little finger of partner's right hand; or: each partner raises right hand above his head and clicks his fingers. *Central Africa.* Hochegger, p. 138.

Black (ethnic) Extended right index moves once or twice across the back of the left hand—"color of skin: negro." *Lat. Am.* Kany, p. 31.

Blessing The "small cross" in form of a cross or "T" made with one or several fingers, is used for crossing oneself or other objects, and is used liturgically as well as privately. Appears to be the oldest of the forms of the sign of the cross and is mentioned by Tertullian. It was first made over the forehead and mouth, then it was applied to other parts of the body also, as well as to objects. An early development was the signing of mouth and breast or heart, or forehead, mouth, and heart. Gaudentius, col. 890. Double cross is still used in baptism: "accipe signum sanctae crucis tam in fronte quam in corde" ("Receive the Sign of the Holy Cross on your brow as in your heart"). Roman Catholic. Ohm p. 292–93. * Right hand raised, palm outwards, thumb, index, middle finger extended, last two fingers turned down. Early Christian and still current blessing gesture. Sittl, p. 286; Amira, "Handgebärden," p. 202. * In pronouncing Priestly Benediction, the Priest extends arms and hands forward, separating little and ring finger from the other fingers. The rabbis of the *Talmud* interpreted the "lattice" of the *Song of Solomon* 2:9 as the priestly fingers in blessing. Represented on tombstones of members of Priestly Family. Jews. Kolatch, p. 158. Blessing gesture used as pointer to the beginning of the text, combined with raised hand as attention gesture. *Collectio canonum.* 8th cent. Rijksmuseum Meermanno-Westreenianum. The Hague. Ms. 10 B 4, fol. 1v. See Fig. 9. *See also* FINGER, Blessing; HAND, Blessing.

Book (request for) "According to Bernard of Cluny's Customary, in the scriptorium [of the monastery of Cluny] where silence was the rule, the monk who wanted to ask for a book written by a pagan author made the sign that indicated a book (open hands, palms upward), but in addition, touched a finger to his ear to imitate a dog scratching his ear,

Fig. 9. Blessing gesture as pointer, combined with attention gesture. *Collectio canonum* (8th cent.) Rijksmuseum Meermanno-Westreenianum, The Hague, Netherlands. 10 B 4, fol. 1v.

for, as the text says, a pagan may rightly be compared to a dog." Medieval *France*. Cited by Leclercq, pp. 156–57.

Boredom   Open hands, held in front of stomach, joined by interlacing fingers, palms facing upward, thumbs turning around each other ("twiddling thumbs"). *Russia*. Monahan, pp. 68–69.

Bravery   "Fig" as amulet was worn as an ornate, vulgar part of the costume to show gallantry and display bravery. 18th cent. *Portugal*. Bras, p. 626. * Fist raised to level of chest, thumb on top. *Central Africa*. Hochegger, p. 19.

Calmness   Thumbs of both hands hooked over belt, hands at rest. 15th cent. *France*. Lacroix, p. 399. * See also the Neapolitan gesture for calmness or silence in Wundt, I, p. 186, fig. 31 a. See Fig. 10.

Cat   Hands raised to level of mouth, fingertips joined to thumbtips, hands moving laterally back and forth at both sides of mouth, simulating whiskers. *Central Africa*. Hochegger, p. 35.

Challenge   Fist, thumb on top, raised to height of chest. *Central Africa*. Hochegger, p. 19.

Cheating   One hand crossed over the other, the little finger of one hooked into that of the other. 19th cent. Naples, southern *Italy*. De Jorio, pl. 20; see Fig. 10; Fischer, "Heilgebärden," p. 333.

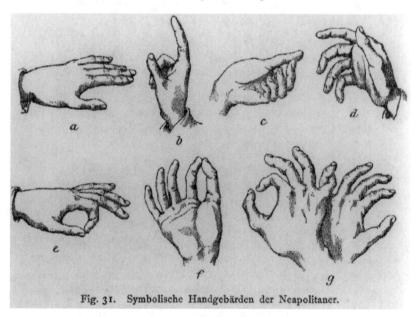

Fig. 31. Symbolische Handgebärden der Neapolitaner.

Fig. 10. Neapolitan gestures. From Wilhelm Wundt, *Völkerpsychologie* (Leipzig, Germany: Engelmann, 1904) I, 186.

Choice   In the choice of a guardian, the person making the selection must lay the fingers of his right hand upon the left shoulder of the person chosen. Medieval *Germany*. Amira (1909), p. 219.

Cigarette   Index and middle fingers form "V" in front of lips. *Colombia; U.S.* May also mean "Your car is smoking, burning." *Colombia*. Saitz and Cervenka, p. 25.

Command   Hand raised, palm outward, index extended, other fingers folded in. Frequent in early medieval art in depictions of God commanding Adam and Eve to refrain from eating of the Forbidden Fruit, of Isaac sending Esau hunting, of Joseph ordering the arrest of Simeon and the sale of the grain, of David ordering the census, of Christ awakening the dead and healing the sick, and of countless rulers. Medieval *Germany*. See Amira, "Handgebärden," pp. 212–13 and the references in n. 5.

Contempt   The "fig": "El fe le fiche a Dio 'l superto vermo" ("the . . . serpent made a 'fig' at God"). 18th cent. *Italy*. Frezzi, II, 19. Over the gates of the fortress of Comora there is a stone image of a maiden showing the "fig" to the enemy: an allusion to the impregnability of the stronghold. *Italy*. L.L.K., p. 32. In 1228 the Florentines defeated the inhabitants of Carmignano, the latter having erected an ivory statue of a "fig" on a cliff facing in the direction of Florence. 13th cent. *Italy*. Seligmann, II, p. 185. "Poi facea con le man le fiche al cielo" ("Then he made a "fig" at Heaven with his hand"). 18th cent. *Italy*. Trissino, c. xii. See also Frezzi, iii, 10; 13th–14th cent. *Italy*. Dante, *Inf.*, c. xxv. Caligula used the 'fig' to greet his guard tribune Cassius Chaerea, to show he thought he was effeminate. Anc. *Rome*. Seligmann, II, p. 184. * Hand extended, fingers in shape of claws, moved back and forth several times. *Saudi Arabia*. Barakat, no. 177. * Francis I of Naples expressed his opinion of the populace at a riot by joining the fingertips of one hand and moving it forward repeatedly. 19th cent. Southern *Italy*. Sittl, p. 97, n. 4.

Copulation   Tip of right index placed into left palm and twisted. *Egypt*. Barakat, no. 150. * Tips of index and thumb held together with other fingers pressed into palm, hand moved rapidly up and down in pecking motion. *Lebanon; Libya*. Barakat, no. 105. * Right index tip ground into left palm. *Lebanon; Syria*. Barakat, no. 118. * Palms together so that fingers are in contact, then all fingers moved back into palm except the two middle fingers which remain extended. Men, implying that they have slept with the woman to whom the gesture is made. *Saudi Arabia*. Barakat, no. 235. * Scratching woman's palm with middle finger when shaking hands. Adolescent. *Colombia; U.S.* Scratching someone's palm. *Brazil*. Cascudo, *História*, p. 236. Saitz and Cervenka, p. 116. * Right index brought down sharply upon the left thumb holding down folded left middle finger. As right index hits left thumb, its tip slides off and hits palm of left hand with suggestive slap, then it is inserted in the circle of left thumb and middle finger. Invitation. *Russia.* Monahan, pp. 144–45. * Extended middle finger of one hand moves in and out of circle made by index and thumb of the other hand. Pederasty. *Brazil.* Cascudo, *História*, p. 236. * One flat hand, palm down, on the back of the other, fingers together, thumbs extended and moving up and down. *Brazil.* Ibid., p. 236.

Counting Two hands at level of face, palms turned outward, fingers curved. Right thumb extended = 1, thumb and index extended = 2, etc. Fingers of right hand and thumb of left hand extended = 6. Both hands, fingers extended = 10. Fingers of both hands extended, then both hands make fist, then right thumb extended = 11, etc. The gesture serves mostly to announce hour of a rendezvous. For each ten the two fists are quickly opened and closed. *France.* Mitton, p. 148. * Clasping successively with the right hand the thumb, the index, and the middle finger of the left hand. *France.* Mitton, p. 148. * Fingers bent, thumb extended upward = 30. Islam. Goldziher, "Über Gebärden und Zeichensprache," p. 385. * Hand raised, index extended = 1. *U.S.* Aubert p. 80, fig. 114. *See* FINGER, Counting. * For the medieval use of the fingers and the hand to enumerate for mnemonic purposes, see Wenzel, pp. 72–84: "The preference of the left hand is explained by the organic relationship of the index of the right hand to the topography of the left" (p. 78, transl. by ed.), a cooperation of the hands which is reflected in the "speaking gesture" in medieval pictures.

Criticize Index and middle finger of one hand extended and moving forward like scissors. Río de la Plata region of *Argentina; Uruguay.* Meo Zilio, p. 112.

Cuckoldry The "fig" exhibited to someone intimates that he is a cuckold. Potter, I, p. 452.

Danger Index of right hand points upward and moves back and forth while left hand indicates direction of the danger. *Central Africa.* Hochegger, p. 15.

Deception *See* HAND, Deception.

Defiance Both fists clenched at waist level, thumbs extended in opposite directions. *Lebanon; Syria.* Barakat, no. 16. * "Strictly speaking, Webb raised her fist at the senator with the middle digit extended, then stormed out. Colloquially put, Webb gave Feinstein the finger. Flipped her the bird. . . . But Webb's flamboyant defiance embarrassed her fellow council members." U.S. Martinez, *L. A. Times*, March 29th, 1996, B10. "Let's get this straight. Sandi Webb did not jump up and give Dianne Feinstein the finger in a vicious, hostile, in-her-face manner as the media would have you believe. It was done in a more casual, over-the-shoulder way. . . . You might even say it was performed in a humorous, if not whimsical, manner. Perhaps even joyfully." Martinez, B10.

Depart   Hand, thumb extended, moves back and forth indicating direction of desired departure. Male. Impolite. *U.S.* Saitz and Cervenka, p. 80. * Index of right hand points at wrist of left hand as if at a watch: "It's time to go." *Russia.* Monahan, pp. 110–11. * Hand is shaken energetically, as though shaking a thermometer, so that the fingers snap: "Scram!" Río de la Plata region of *Argentina; Uruguay.* Meo Zilio, p. 75.

Desperation   *See* HAND, Desperation.

Direction   Judge points to personified wind: in absence of opponent, combatant in judicial combat must make two blows and one thrust in direction of the wind; similarly, the king points to reliquary, because possessions are freed from the ban under oath; minstrel points to shadow of a man (minstrels are said to lack shadows, which symbolically excludes them from humanity). Medieval *Germany.* Amira, "Handgebärden," p. 206. * Jerking thumb over shoulder indicates a backward direction. Schoolchildren. *U.S.* Seton, p. xx. * Left hand held out flat, palm down, right index run across it, signifies "across." Schoolchildren. *U.S.* Seton, p. xx. * Pointing up—upward. Schoolchildren. *U.S.* Seton, ibid. * Index swung forward and down in a curve—"forward." Schoolchildren. *U.S.* Seton, ibid. * For direction in various contexts in medieval *Germany*, see Amira, "Handgebärden," pp. 204–212.

Disbelief   Fingers of right hand scratch top of head. *Central Africa.* Hochegger, p. 159. * Half-closed fist at chest height, curved index extended slightly forward, hand moves toward person addressed as though offering first joint of index: "¡Tomá, chupate el dedo!" ("Here, suck my finger!") Popular, ironic. Río de la Plata region of *Argentina; Uruguay.* Meo Zilio, p. 81, who comments that the same gesture, when accompanied instead by a prolonged "prrrr," as though imitating a parrot, signifies an ugly woman. In Río de la Plata region, "Loro"—"ugly woman." Limited to men.

Drink   Closed fist, thumb extended and moved toward mouth until tip of thumb touches lips. Vulgar. *France.* Mitton, p. 147, no. 51. * Hand raised in front of body, thumb and little finger extended, knuckles outward: "Would you like a drink?" *Mexico.* Axtell, *Gestures*, p. 88.

Drunkenness   *See* Drink.

Emphasis   Inserting hand or finger into clenched fingers of other hand. *U.S.* Krout, p. 23. * Poking with index on palm of other hand. Ghetto Jews. *Eastern Europe.* Efron, p. 146. * Fingers of each hand joined at tips, tap chest. Men. *Colombia.* Saitz and Cervenka p. 47. * Hand raised to approx. shoulder level, index extended toward person or people addressed. Matthias Grünewald, figure of St. John the Baptist, Isenheim altarpiece, c. 1515, central panel, closed position. Colmar, Musée d'Unterlinden. 16th cent. *Germany.* Mellinkoff, *The Devil*, p. 4, fig. 2. Anonymous poster, *Lenin.* Ca. 1920. *Russia.*

Encouragement   Spit on fingertips or palms and rub hands together. Children. *England.* Opie, p. 231.

Enforce   Fist raised to level of chest, thumb on top. *Central Africa.* Hochegger, p. 19.

Etiquette   Hand slightly cupped and rapidly moved back and forth from table to mouth—uncouth eating habits. *Netherlands.* Andrea and de Boer, p. 167.

Failure   Fingertips of one hand joined and pointed upwards, then suddenly released and spread in shape of tulip blossom. Accompanied by bilabial retroflex occlusive: "disappeared, gone up in smoke." Río de la Plata region, *Argentina; Uruguay.* Meo Zilio, p. 67.

Fairness   Holding hand and fingers in position that would not disturb free movement of hand-held scale; see the Neapolitan gesture in Fig. 10 e. Naples; southern *Italy.* Wundt, I, p. 186, fig. 31, and p. 189.

Falseness   Little finger of one hand hooked into that of the other. Naples; southern *Italy.* See Fig. 10 g. Wundt, I, p. 186, fig. 31, and p. 189.

Fear   Fingertips of one or both hands joined and pointed upwards, hands move back and forth while the fingers open and close. Vulgar reference to contractions of sphincter. Plebeian, men only. Infrequent. Río de la Plata region of *Argentina; Uruguay.* Meo Zilio, p. 66.

Finish   Fingertips of one or both hands joined point upwards, hands move back and forth in request to finish, to get it over with: "Finíshela!" Río de la Plata region of *Argentina; Uruguay.* Meo Zilio, p. 66.

Friendship   Index of left hand curls around extended little finger of right hand—"We are friends." *Central Africa.* Hochegger, p. 6.

Gossip   *See* HAND, Gossip.

Greeting   While walking, hands at side, index extended—sign of recognition and greeting to fellow hipsters, cool way of shaking hands; if thumb is extended, invitation to women to copulation. *DAS*, p. 470. * Hand raised to level of head, index and middle finger extended, held together tightly, pointing upwards. Casual. *Colombia.* Saitz and Cervenka, p. 65.

Hitchhiking   Hand extended, thumb up and in direction the gesturer wishes to go. *U.S.* Saitz and Cervenka, p. 70. *Netherlands.* Andrea and de Boer, p. 13. * Closed fist at shoulder level, thumb extended, pointing in the direction in which the hitchhiker wants to go; fist moves back and forth horizontally in that direction. *Central Africa.* Hochegger, p. 12.

Homage   Hand vertical, palm inward, held at the level of the face, arm half bent, moving of the fingertips from the heart. *Europe; North Am.* Aubert, p. 84.

Homosexuality   Fingers of one hand pat the back of the other—"he or she is a homosexual." *Netherlands.* Axtell, *Gestures*, p. 145.

Hunger Hand is moved to the mouth, fingers joined—"I am hungry." Vulgar. *France*. Mitton, p. 148, no. 52.

Hunt Left hand extended forward, index extended, extended index of right hand placed behind it at level of eyes, which sight along it. *Central Africa*. Hochegger, p. 34.

Idea Sudden idea or sudden solution to problem is indicated by raising hand to face level and extending index vertically. *Netherlands*. Andrea and de Boer, p. 70.

Impossibility Index poked on the open palm of other hand—"this will happen when grass grows on my palm." Can also signify hammering in of an idea. Ghetto Jews. *Eastern Europe*. Efron, p. 146.

Impotence Hand hangs down, fingers relaxed, moving gently. *Brazil*. Cascudo, *História*, p. 237. * Flat palm of one hand facing the ground, the index is bent several times. *Brazil*. Ibid.

Inferiority Fingers of right hand scratch top of head in the presence of a superior. *Central Africa*. Hochegger, p. 159.

Insult Index inserted in loose fist of other hand and moved back and forth several times. *Colombia; U.S.* Saitz and Cervenka, p. 116. * Ragamuffins make four "violins" (index and middle finger of one hand placed on either side of nose and moved downward as if bow were being drawn over violin strings) at once with quadrupled force of insult: little finger is placed below the mouth, the tongue extruded, ring finger placed below nose, middle finger below eye, thumb behind ear. *Mexico*. Kany, p. 175. * Hand outstretched for handshake, withdrawn just before contact with other person's hand, fingers closed to a fist with thumb raised, hand jerked upward so that thumb points to back of gesturer. *Life*, Sept. 3, 1945, p. 25. * The "fig." Insult to prostitutes, particularly southern *France*. Mitton, p. 151. *Colombia*. Saitz and Cervenka, p. 115. Río de la Plata region of *Argentina; Uruguay*. ("Hand of Fathma"). Meo Zilio, p. 69. * Thumb extended from fist, which is jerked up and down several times. Vulgar. Men. *U.S.* Saitz and Cervenka, p. 78. * Right index extended from fist, which is slapped into palm of left hand so that index goes between thumb and index of left hand. *Colombia*. Saitz and Cervenka, p. 115. * Thumb placed in mouth, rubbed down on tongue, hand then dropped to waist level, heel of hand outward, and jerked forward once or twice. *Lebanon*. Barakat, no. 246. * Hands placed back to back, interlocking fingers, then twisted in opposite directions until thumb protrudes from opening made by hands. *Saudi Arabia; Syria*. Barakat, no. 74. * Hand raised, tips of index and thumb meet, making a circle; or: tips of index and thumb of right hand grasp middle of the little finger of the left, indicating its thickness: "Petit sexe!" ("Little prick!") *Central Africa*. Hochegger, p. 190. * Fingers of right hand scratch top of head in the presence of an old person. *Central Africa*. Hochegger, p. 159. * Thumb extended upward from fist ("thumbs-up" gesture). *Australia*.

Bagott, p. 1. * On one of the first stops of a good-will tour of Latin America, President Nixon emerged from his aircraft and gave the "A-O.K." sign, his thumb and index forming a circle. "The next day, splashed across front pages from Mexico City to Buenos Aires, was a picture of Nixon making the gesture, which throughout Latin America means 'Up yours!' " Bagott, p. 4. *See also* FINGER, Insult; HAND, Insult.

Interrogation   Both hands held half cupped, palm up, fingertips pointing toward speaker, thumb pressed against index. "What do you want?" *Italy.* Efron, p. 149. * Fingertips of each hand are united, pointing up, both hands held in front of body, palms turned in, hands moved slightly up and down. *Italy.* Efron, p. 149, Fig. 45.

Invitation   Right hand extended, palm down, fingers pointing down: *Spain; Portugal; Morocco; Asia Minor;* Arabs. Flachskampf, p. 225. * Hand extended with palm raised, fingers fanned slightly downwards. 15th-16th cent. *Italy.* Botticelli, *A young man received by the Liberal Arts*; also *Primavera*; and Jacobus de Cessolis, *Liber scaccorum*; see Knox, p. 13; see also Baxandall, p. 68. *See also* FINGER, Approach.

Judgment (negative)   Flat hand strikes thumb and index of closed fist: "¡Te embromaste!" ("You screwed it up!") Río de la Plata region of *Argentina; Uruguay.* Meo Zilio, p. 70.

Kill   Both closed hands held at waist level, palm down, thumbs extended and pointing horizontally toward each other as their tips are repeatedly brought together. *Netherlands.* Andrea and de Boer, p. 118. Unknown among Flemish speakers. Ibid., p. 188.

Listen   Hand raised to level of face, index extended upward— "Listen!" *Netherlands.* Andrea and de Boer, p. 66.

Love   Tips of index and thumb joined. Naples; southern *Italy.* See Fig. 10 f. Wundt, I, p. 186, fig. 31 and p. 189.

Magical   Left thumb held in right hand when hiccoughing. 4th–5th cent. *North Africa.* Augustin. *Doctrin. christ.*, 2, 20. * If one dislikes someone, one makes the sign of the "fig" with both hands, accompanied by the formula "Viloa, viloa, danada, / Quando Deus veio ao mundo, / tu não eras nada" ("Damned bitch, when God came to the world, you were nothing"). As a result the person is disoriented and unable to move until after one has left. *Portugal.* Vasconcellos, p. 35.

Magnitude   To indicate height of child: the fingers held one above the other so that little finger is nearest to ground. Improper to indicate height of child by holding hand so palm is turned to ground—used for animals and objects only. Medellín, *Colombia.* Ades, p. 325. * Fingertips of one hand joined and pointing up, accompanied by upward glance; can be reinforced by a back-and-forth movement of wrist: "¡Así!"— "this big!". Río de la Plata region of *Argentina; Uruguay.* Meo Zilio,

p. 65. *Brazil.* Reyes, p. 92. *See* HAND, Magnitude. * A small quantity is indicated by the gesture in Fig. 10 c. Wundt, I, p. 186, fig. 31.

Marriage   *See* Love.

Masculinity   Fist, thumb resting on index, moves up and down sharply and repeatedly. *Colombia.* Saitz and Cervenka, p. 85.

Medico-magical   The Italian physician recommended that a coral "fica" be tied around the neck of a child with a "crick" in its neck, and believed that the little girl had been "overlooked." A., p. 118. * Hands crossed, thumbs bent into closed fist, stops bleeding. Hovorka and Kronfeld, II, p. 563. *See also* FINGER, Medico-magical.

Mockery   *See* Fig. 11 a, b, c for Neapolitan gestures indicating asses' ears. Naples; southern *Italy.* Wundt, I, p. 164, fig. 26. * Fingers of one hand boring into the palm of the other. *Switzerland.* Meschke, p. 337. * One index pointed at the person mocked, the other drawn along it several times in the same direction. Schoolchildren. *U.S.* Seton, p. xxi. *See* FINGER, Mockery "Rübenschaben." * Right hand raised, index folded under thumb: "You've got a cut-off finger!" *Central Africa.* Hochegger, p. 56. * Hands in front of chest, indexes pointing outward and upward, signifying small breasts. *Central Africa.* Hochegger, p. 184. Hand raised, claws making "horns" in mockery of blessing gesture. Seal of Lucifer. 15th cent.? *France.* Didron, II, fig. 193. See Fig. 12. *See also* Disbelief; FINGER, Mockery; HAND, Mockery.

Money   Extended fingertips of right hand (sometimes only of index) brush up into the open left palm. May also mean "pay." *Lat. Am.* Kany, pp. 94–95; *Colombia.* Saitz and Cervenka, p. 89. * Tips of right index and thumb rub together, other fingers pressed into palm. *Egypt; Lebanon; Jordan; Syria, Saudi Arabia.* Barakat, no. 7.

Mourning   *See* HAND, Mourning.

Negation   Hand pointing upwards, palm out, or the first three fingers, or the index is moved from the wrist as pivot from side to side.

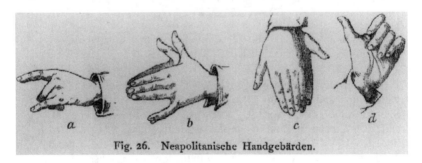

Fig. 26.   Neapolitanische Handgebärden.

Fig. 11. Asses' ears. From Wilhelm Wundt, *Völkerpsychologie* (Leipzig, Germany: Engelmann, 1904) I, 164.

Fig. 12. Seal of Lucifer. From Adolphe Napoleon Didron, *Christian Iconography*, transl. E. J. Millington (London: G. Bell, 1886) II, 147.

19th cent. *Italy*; Native American, *U.S.* Sittl, p. 86. * Semi-rotating hand with thumb and index up ("No can do.") *Italy*. "The High Price of Silent Insults," *Time*, April 9, 1965, p. 67. * Hand raised to height of, and several inches in front of, speaker's mouth, fingers waggled. *Brazil*. Su, LINGUIST, 3.1012. * Index extended upwards from fist, palm outward, and waggled from side to side with the forearm or wrist as fulcrum of the waggle. The waggled finger is at head height, but often to the side of the speaker's face. *Venezuela*. Ibid.

Nothing Fist raised and pointed at someone, thumb protruding between index and middle finger (the "fig") is not necessarily obscene or mocking in Russia. Used frequently by children and adults—"Nothing will come of this." *Russia.* Monahan, pp. 86–87.

Oath Three fingers extended. Künssberg believes this gesture is derived from the ancient apotropaic gesture of extending three fingers as protection against the evil eye and demons. Ohm, p. 251. *See also* FINGER, Oath. Temporal and eternal punishments for swearing a false oath prompted the development of protective formulas and gestures, e.g. the so-called lightning-rod: while right hand was raised with three fingers extended in swearing an oath, left hand with similarly extended fingers was extended downwards, thus causing the dangerous oath to go to ground like lightning. Künssberg, *Volkskunde*, p. 74. * Raised hand, index and middle finger extended, thumb parallel to index. *Germany.* Käthe Kollwitz, *Nie wieder Krieg!* ("No more war!"), poster (1924): "the gesture of the hand with two outstretched fingers which conventionally accompanies the swearing of an oath in central Europe." Gombrich, p. 64. Also *Netherlands.* Andrea and de Boer, p. 27. *See also* the Bayeux Tapestry (Harold swearing fealty to William on two reliquaries). Medieval Normandy, *France.* The Dresden MS (14th cent.) of the *Sachsenspiegel*, where fingers touch relic. Medieval *Germany.* Amira, "Handgebärden," p. 217. * Hand raised, palm inward, index extended, other fingers folded in. Required in giving a guarantee *digito et lingua* "with finger and tongue." A writ of Henry the Illustrious for Altenburg (1256) requires that a writ of compensation (*emenda*) be executed in the usual manner by *digitum levare infra quatuor scampna*. 13th cent. *Germany.* Amira, "Handgebärden," p. 217. Distinct from this is the gesture accompanying an oath, which requires the raising of two fingers. In the 13th–14th centuries, however, the distinction between the gestures accompanying a guarantee and an oath seems to have been in flux. Ibid., p. 218. * The "fig," accompanied by a kiss on the cross formed by thumb and index. Child's oath. Río de la Plata region of *Argentina; Uruguay.* Meo Zilio, p. 69.

Obedience *See* FINGER, Obedience.

Overcoming obstacles Fingers pointing to the front, palm vertical to the side, hand undulating: (1) To thread oneself through a maze of obstacles; (2) To overcome obstacles by going around them. *France.* Mitton, p. 147.

Past *See* FINGER, Past.

Patience "Hanna held up one hand, palm inward, thumb touching index finger. Signaling *savlanut*. Patience." *Israel.* Kellerman, p. 54.

Pay Closed hand extended, palm up, thumb and index rub tips together. Schoolchildren. *U.S.* Seton, p. xxii. * Patron simulates writing on palm in asking for the check in a restaurant. *Colombia; U.S.* Saitz and Cervenka, p. 109. * Hand held so that thumb is on top, rubbing lightly against curved index, other fingers closed against palm. *Netherlands*. Andrea and de Boer, p. 39. * One hand flat, palm up, while thumb of other hand is repeatedly drawn forward over it. May be preceded by licking the thumb. *Netherlands*. Ibid., p. 142. * Both hands raised to shoulder height (elbow bent), fingers closed, knuckles facing out, thumbs rub against indexes. *Central Africa*. Hochegger, p. 11. * Knuckles of one hand, fist almost closed, strike open palm of other hand two or three times, accompanied by "Taca-taca" ("I'm paying right now"). Río de la Plata region of *Argentina; Uruguay*. Meo Zilio, p. 110.

Pensiveness   Hands out to sides, fingers and thumbs of each hand rubbing together. *Colombia*. Saitz and Cervenka, p. 139.

Photograph   Hands before face, index and thumb of each hand spread apart, index of one hand closing toward thumb as if tripping the shutter of a camera. *Netherlands*. Andrea and de Boer, p. 162.

Plea   Hands clasped in front of body, fingers tightly interlocked, then hands moved several times from the wrists: plea for mercy. *Saudi Arabia; Lebanon*. Barakat, no. 167. * Hands clasped, fingers tightly interlocked, arms extended forward, kneeling. *Netherlands*. Andrea and de Boer, pp. 153, 161.

Plenty   Both hands raised, fingertips pointing up, bending fingers a few times quickly to the thumbs. *Spain*. Flachskampf, p. 222.

Praise   Bending four fingers, thumb turned up and pointing at person whom one applauds. Arab. Goldziher, "Über Gebärden," p. 385.

Prayer   Hands palm to palm, thumbs crossed, right over left. Mestre do Retabulo de S. Bento, *A Adoração dos Reis Magos*. Early 16th cent. Museo Nacional de Arte Antiga, Lisbon. *Portugal*.

Question   Fingertips of one or both hands joined, pointing upwards, hands moved back and forth in an ample movement. Frequently, but not necessarily, a hostile or mocking manner of putting the question "y?" Italian in origin. In Argentina it is deliberately used ironically to imitate Italians. Río de la Plata region of *Argentina; Uruguay*. Meo Zilio, p. 65.

Reconciliation   Hooking little fingers, touch thumbs and then turn hands over and clap. Children. Radnorshire. *England*. Opie, p. 325.

Reflection   Fingers of right hand scratch top of head. *Central Africa*. Hochegger, p. 159.

Regret   *See* HAND, Regret.

Rejection   Thumb and index of the right hand joined at tips and thus lengthening the pointed lips. Rejection of an importunate gossip. *Spain*. Flachskampf, p. 230.

Relax   Hand raised to head height, thumb and little finger extended: "Hang loose"; "stay cool." *Hawaii*. Axtell, *Gestures*, pp. 87–88.

Remembering   Hand raised, index extended upward: "Voici, je me rappelle!" ("I remember now!") *Central Africa*. Hochegger, p. 115.

Rendezvous Right hand, closed, in front of forehead, thumb extended downward: "Chez moi!" ("At my place!") Same gesture, thumb extended upward: "À midi!" ("At noon!") *Central Africa.* Hochegger, pp. 166–67.

Renunciation All or some fingers curved "abnegationem facere incurvatis digitis" ("to indicate rejection with curved fingers"), possibly resembling the Cistercian sign for negation as described by William of Hirsau, I, 23, by putting thumb under other fingers and snapping it up, or the medieval Holstein gesture for renunciation or transfer of ownership: thumb under the ring and little finger, palm forward. Medieval *Germany.* Amira, "Handgebärden," p. 219.

Request Hand extended, palm up, fingers (except thumb) rapidly moving back and forth. *Colombia; U.S.* Saitz and Cervenka, p. 104. * Index pointing up or down is rotated to ask for another round of drinks. *U.S.* Saitz and Cervenka, p. 110.

Resignation Hand held out horizontally with palm upwards, fingers in disarray. Rose, p. 314.

Result Cupped hand pushed outward in an arc from the chest, index extended. At conclusion of movement the palm faces up. Madrid, *Spain.* Green, p. 65.

Rise Fist clenched, thumb pointing upwards, fist suddenly raised. Used only in addressing a group of people. *France.* Mitton, p. 145.

Self-irony One hand on top of the other, backs of the hands upward, extended thumbs move like fins: "I was as dumb as a fish; I didn't know a thing in the exam." *Spain.* Flachskampf, p. 232.

Shame Tip of index of right hand placed between teeth, left hand covers eyes. *Central Africa.* Hochegger, p. 89.

Sorrow Wiping tears from eyes with back of hand, index or thumb. Anc. *Rome.* Sittl, p. 275.

Speech Arm raised, all fingers extended, thumb uppermost; or only thumb and index extended; or thumb, index and middle finger extended (particularly common in post-classical "decadence"; or index alone raised, as in German threatening gesture, which Greeks and Italians still lack. Anc. *Greece* and *Rome.* Sittl, pp. 285–86. * Hand extended forward, sometimes three fingers curled inward; arm extended diagonally downward, all fingers, or only the first two, extended. Anc. *Greece* and *Rome.* Sittl, pp. 285–87. For the "speaking"-gesture in the Middle Ages, see Barasch, *Giotto,* pp. 15–39, and Counting, above. *See also* FINGER, Blessing; FINGER, HAND, Blessing; HAND, Blessing. * Fingers of right hand placed before slightly open mouth, imitating a speaking mouth. *Central Africa.* Hochegger, p. 139. * Thumb and index of right hand placed on mouth, holding lips shut as if between pincers: "Arrêtez votre discours!" ("Shut up!") *Central Africa.* Hochegger, p. 140.

Stealing   Extending open hand, palm down, then gradually folding fingers, one after another, to the right downward and inward upon the palm, beginning with the little finger, with fanlike motion, imitating seizure of some object and holding it in the fist. *Lat. Am.* Kany, p. 106. Similarly, the Neapolitan gesture in Fig. 10. Southern *Italy*. Wundt, I, p. 186, fig. 31 d and p. 190.

Stop   Fist raised, thumb extended upwards. "Pax." Children. *France*. Mitton, p. 149.

Strength   Fists agitated vigorously back and forth in front of chest: "I'm strong, I can take care of myself." *Central Africa*. Hochegger, p. 75. * One fist beating against one's chest. *Central Africa*. Ibid., p. 76.

Stupidity   Hand, palm up, the fingers separated. *Chile*. Greenberg, L4.

Surrender   Gladiator wanting to surrender lowers weapon and raises hand that had carried the shield, index extended. Anc. *Rome*. Sittl, p. 218.

Teasing   Tip of right index placed into left palm and twisted. *Egypt*. Barakat, no. 150.

Thin   Little finger extended vertically from fist, moved in spiral upwards to the level of the hair. Río de la Plata region of *Argentina; Uruguay*. Meo Zilio, p. 111.

Thirst   *See* Drink, above.

Threat   Hand raised vertically, index extended, pointing upward and turned repeatedly. Eastern frieze of the Parthenon. Anc. *Greece*. Sittl, pp. 288–89. * Middle finger held down with thumb, other fingers extended toward someone as hand is shaken. *Saudi Arabia*. Barakat, no. 71.

Time   Index taps wrist. *Colombia*. Saitz and Cervenka, p. 143. *Netherlands*. Andrea and de Boer, p. 127. * Index of right hand pointed repeatedly at wrist. *Central Africa*. Hochegger, p. 202.

Truth   Hand raised, index bent, accompanied by "Hookey, Hookey Walter" or "With a hook," indicates that what is said is to be taken as a lie. Ca. 1810. *Britain*. Taylor, Note, p. 114. *See* HAND, NOSE, Truth,

Union   "[The priest] takes the Host between the thumb and forefinger of his right hand, and makes the sign of the cross with it three times over the chalice" Roman Catholic. *Mass*, p. 69.

Vengeance   *See* HAND, Vengeance.

Victory   Index extended upward, hand closed and moved energetically once up and down, accompanied by: "Y ahora se sienta(n) acá" or vulgar Ital. "glielo ho messo in c . . ." Men. Río de la Plata region of *Argentina; Uruguay*. Meo Zilio, p. 67.

Wish   Scratching the palm of one hand with the fingers of the other indicates the desire to possess an object. 19th cent. Naples, southern *Italy*. De Jorio, p. 172.

Withdraw   Holding up one hand, three fingers extended, indicates desire to withdraw from game. Children. Bradford-on-Avon. *England.* Opie, p. 143.

FINGER, HAND, LIP

Homosexuality   Raised right index kissed, then placed into opening of left fist and moved in and out. Andalusia, southern *Spain.* Driessen, p. 247.

FINGER, HAND, MOUTH

Apotropy   "The Mass was long and solemn: the mayor . . . crossed himself by bringing the thumb of his right hand to his mouth according to the time-honored custom of the Isnello women at the approach of thunder to avert a storm." *Italy.* Levi, p. 46.

Drink   Thumb extended, pointing toward lips, fingers closed. WW II. *France.* Alsop, p. 29. * Index and little finger extended from closed hand and brought to mouth while head is tilted back a little. Arab. Barakat, no. 198. * Holding thumb side of right fist on mouth. *Saudi Arabia.* Barakat, no. 199.

Eating   Hand moved to mouth, all fingers united at tips. Vulgar. *France.* Mitton, p. 148. * Tips of right index and thumb touching and brought to slightly open mouth, head tilted back a little. Arab. Barakat, no. 197.

Gratitude   Modest kiss of the hand, limited to kiss of the fingers. Anc. *Greece* and *Rome.* Sittl, p. 168.

Greeting   Both hands stretched out, united at fingertips, touching other person's hand in same position, then leading them to lips. Muslim. Women. Goldziher, "Über Gebärden," p. 379.

Medico-magical   "Put thy hand upon me, sign me with thy thumb, / could I but kiss thy hand, / I would be healed of all this affliction." 13th cent. *Spain.* Berceo, 340–42.

Pensiveness   "Biting the thumb, thumbnail, fingers, or hands may be a selfregarding act that indicates doubt, hesitation, or annoyance and is, in such uses, not a gesture directed toward another person. It is allied to the gesture of putting the thumb into the mouth to signify that one is giving thought to a matter. An early instance of this is . . . the figure of a young Egyptian god with his left thumb in his mouth as represented on a wooden coffin of the twenty-first dynasty. Sittl regards (pp. 17–18) the act of biting the thumb in this sense as characteristically Roman in origin. Persius mentions it as a symbol of vexation . . . Horace knew it . . . (*Sat.* 1, 10, 70). In this use the act becomes a topos with a long history. Persius imitated Horace, when he wrote 'nec emorsos sapit ungues' (*Sat.* 1, 106)" Anc. *Egypt;* anc. *Rome.* Taylor, p. 56.

Plea   Kiss of the fingers. Anc. *Greece* and *Rome.* Sittl, p. 168.

Silence Index or hand laid vertically across lips. Anc. *Greece* and *Rome*. Sittl, p. 54. * Pressing mouth with fingers and right hand. Anc. *Rome*. Sittl, p. 215, n. 4.

FINGER, HAND, NOSE
Mockery "Silently he placed both outstretched hands before his nose and wiggled the fingers. Even this derisive action drew no comment." *U.S.* Boucher, p. 115. *See* FINGER, NOSE, Mockery.

FINGER, HAND, TONGUE
Disgust Hand, palm down, at shoulder level, fingers apart and slightly bent, tongue extruded: "Wlôh!" ("Yuck!") *Netherlands*. Andrea and de Boer, p. 156.

Insult Thumbs to ears, fingers of both hands extended and moving backwards and forwards, tongue stuck out. Children. *Colombia; U.S.* Saitz and Cervenka, p. 76. *See* also FINGER, FOREHEAD, Mockery.

FINGER, HEAD
Apotropy Extended indexes placed on top of head against evil eye, and against cats. Southern *Italy*. Against dogs. *Germany*. Meschke, col. 332.

Approval Right index taps right temple: "Thank God, all is well up here!" *Russia*. Monahan, pp. 44–45.

Concentration "Then lays his finger on his temple" 16th–17th cent. *England*. Shakesp., *Henry VIII*, 3.2.112. * Extended index placed with tip against temple. Masculine only; for feminine, *see* FINGER, NOSE, Concentration. Río de la Plata region, *Argentina; Uruguay*. Meo Zilio, p. 113. * Tip of right or left index scratches back of one's head: concentration or possibly indicating veracity of someone's statement. *Egypt; Jordan; Lebanon; Kuwait; Saudi Arabia; Syria*. Barakat, no. 3.

Cuckoldry The "horns." Anc. *Greece* and *Rome*. Sittl, p. 103, who interprets the two fingers as referring to the two men. *Spain*. Flachskampf, p. 248. The gesture already appears on Etruscan tombs of the 6th cent. B.C. *Etruria*. Meschke, col. 31; Sittl, p. 103. *Colombia*. Saitz and Cervenka, p. 121. * Tips of thumbs placed on both temples, palms facing forward, fingers spread widely and moved back and forth. *Syria*. Barakat, no. 19.

Disbelief Indexes of both hands extended and placed along temples, pointing upward. College students. California. *U.S.* King, p. 263.

Dissatisfaction Index extended and placed with the tip against the temple in imitation of the barrel of a gun: jocular or ironic dissatisfaction with oneself or someone else. *Russia*. Monahan, p. 23.

Embarrassment Scratching the head. Anc. *Rome*. Sittl, p. 48.

Foolishness Thumb against temple, hand open. Naples, southern

Italy. Critchley, p. 89. * Suggestion in Booth's Prompt-Book in connection with *Othello*, 1.3.308 "If thou do'st, I shall never love thee after. Why thou silly gentleman" is "Tapping him playfully on the forehead." *England.* * Tapping center of forehead. ("Do you think I'm stupid?") *Italy.* "The High Price of Silent Insults," *Time*, Apr. 9, 1965, p. 67. Index points to temple and makes circular motion. *Colombia; U.S.* Saitz and Cervenka, p. 75. *Netherlands.* Andrea and de Boer, p. 80. * Tip of extended index placed at temple and rotated clockwise. *Russia.* Monahan, pp. 58–59. * Index taps temple. *Colombia; U.S.* Ibid. *Russia.* Monahan, pp. 44–45. * Right index makes circular motion near right temple, head tilted slightly. Arab. Barakat, no. 61. * Right index taps right temple, then is thrown out to side of head as head is tilted slightly to one side and brows are wrinkled. Arab. Barakat, no. 62. * Index pointed at temple. *Central Africa.* Hochegger, p. 75. * Tip of thumb pressed to right temple, palm open, facing forward and pivoting up and down on the thumb: "He's an idiot!" *Russia.* Predominantly children. Monahan, pp. 60–61.

Gratitude   Tip of extended index placed at the bill of an imaginary cap, then moved quickly upward and outward. *Netherlands.* Andrea and de Boer, p. 86.

Greeting   Tip of extended index placed at the bill of an imaginary cap, then moved quickly upward and outward. Accompanies a greeting. *Flanders.* Andrea and de Boer, p. 185. *See also* Respect.

Hesitation   Head is scratched with one or more fingers of one hand. *France.* Mitton, p. 146.

Idealism   Raising index to the side of the head and describing small circles in the air. *Spain; Lat. Am.* Green, p. 48.

Insult   Ragamuffins make four "violins" (index and middle finger of one hand placed on either side of the nose and moved downward as if bow were being drawn over violin strings) at once with quadrupled force of the insult: the little finger is placed below the mouth, the tongue extruded, ring finger placed below nose, middle finger below eye, thumb behind ear. *Mexico.* Kany, p. 175. * Index, with tip against temple, is twirled, indicating stupidity. *U.S.;* same position of index, but rotated with tip against temple. *Germany.* Axtell, *Gestures*, p. 39. * Index tapped against forehead. *Netherlands* (but see Intelligence, below). Axtell, ibid.

Intelligence   Index taps lightly against temple or forehead; or it is simply placed against temple. *Colombia; U.S.* Saitz and Cervenka, p. 78. Archer, p. 4. Index tapping the temple. *Netherlands* (but see Insult, above). Axtell, *Gestures*, p. 39.

Meditation   "J'ai beau frotter mon front, j'ai beau mordre mes doigts" ("I can rub my brow, bite my fingers in vain"). 17th–18th cent. *France.* Boileau, *Sat.* 7.

Mistake   Index extended, tip at temple, thumb extended or bent. *Colombia; U.S.* Saitz and Cervenka, p. 52.

Negro   Touching the head with the curled index to indicate kinky hair. *Lat. Am.* Kany, p. 31.

Oath   Finger moistened, shown, wiped—usually in the armpit—head tilted back, finger drawn across throat. Children. *Englamd.* Opie, p. 126.

Perplexity   Index scratches head just above and to the side of the forehead. *Netherlands.* Andrea and de Boer, p. 82. * Fingertips of one hand joined scratch the head—perplexity of others. Río de la Plata region of *Argentina; Uruguay.* Meo Zilio, p. 72.

Respect   Right fingertips touched to forehead while bowing head slightly. *Jordan; Kuwait; Saudi Arabia.* Barakat, no. 54.

Warning   Right index raised, other fingers closed, hand turned so as to have right eye, index, and the whole person in line, simultaneously shaking the head a little. *U.S.* Seton, p. 221.

FINGER, HEAD, MOUTH

Pointing   "jerked his thumb, cocked his head, and gestured with the corner of his mouth toward him." *U.S.* Birdwhistell, *Introduction*, p. 33.

FINGER, HEAD, NOSE

Disbelief   Nose held with index and thumb, head ducked as if to say "me hundo para que pase" ("I'm going under so that it passes me by"). *Lat. Am,.* Kany, p. 70.

FINGER, KNEE

Impatience   Fingers of one hand drum on a knee. *Netherlands.* Andrea and de Boer, pp. 100–01.

Oath   The swearer of an oath laid down arms, helmet or hat before kneeling and raising two fingers. Medieval Wendic, Rugian. Medieval *Germany.* Rugians also northern *Italy.* Grimm, *DRA*, II, p. 556.

FINGER, LIP

Admiration   Tips of right index, middle finger and thumb held in pear-shaped configuration and kissed while bowing slightly forward, whereupon the head is flicked up. *Jordan; Lebanon; Syria.* Barakat, no. 89. * Tips of fingers of one hand joined in pear-shaped configuration touch lips gently, quickly move away while lips make kissing sound: "Chic!" ("Beautiful!") *Uruguay.* Meo Zilio, p. 72. * Kissing fingertips in admiration of a pretty woman. *France.* Axtell, *Do's and Taboos*, p. 42.

Adoration   Tips of fingers and thumb of right hand held together and kissed lightly, then the hand tossed forward as the fingers open outward. Biblical. Anc. *Middle East*. *Job* 31:27; *Deuteron*. 4:19; also anc. *Greece* and *Rome*. Sittl, pp. 181–84; Morris et al., pp. 2–5, who refer to Giovanni della Casa, *Galateo* (1774), as describing the gesture as being used by clerics toward the altar and during divine service, but criticizing its secular use. *See also* Greeting and Perfection.

Affection Fingertips of right hand kissed and thrown forward. Schoolchildren. *U.S.* Seton, p. xxii. * Palm toward body, tips of fingers against lips, then hand extended toward someone (throwing a kiss). *France*. Mitton, p. 147; *Europe; North Am.* Aubert, p. 84. *Colombia; U.S.* Saitz and Cervenka, p. 79. *Netherlands*. Andrea and de Boer, pp. 88, 99. Palm toward body, tips of fingers against lips, then palm moved to horizontal position at level of mouth, and lips "blow the kiss" toward someone. *Netherlands*. Ibid., p. 174.

Amusement (ironic) Index of each hand placed on corners of mouth, pulling lips in imitation of a smile, indicates that one is not amused. *Netherlands*. Andrea and de Boer, p. 65.

Anxiety "While he did so, Troy went out to the balcony and Alleyn, seeing her there, her fingers against her lips in the classic gesture of the anxious woman, joined her and put his arm about her shoulders." *England*. Marsh, *Spinsters*, p. 113.

Approval Fingers of one hand joined at tips and pressed against lips, then opened quickly and spread. Used more frequently by men. Can refer to a person or an object. *Colombia*. Saitz and Cervenka, p. 19. * Kissing the side of an index finger, then pinching an earlobe between the index and thumb compliments the hostess for her dinner. *Portugal*. Axtell, *Gestures*, p. 148. * Tips of index and thumb joined, placed to the lips and kissed; other fingers extended. *Netherlands*. Andrea and de Boer, p. 138.

Astonishment With a thoughtful expression, the thumb and index pinch the lower lip. *Central Africa*. Hochegger, p. 67.

Attention "I in order that the leader should attend, put my finger upward from my chin to my nose. 13th–14th cent. *Italy*. Dante, *Inf.*, c. 25.

Cigarette Index and middle finger placed vertically across lips. *Central Africa*. Hochegger, p. 36.

Drink Touching lips with the tip of the extended thumb, other fingers closed. Vulgar. *France*. Mitton, p. 147. * Extended thumb (from clenched fist) jerked toward mouth. Eyebrows raised "On va boire un coup?" ("Should we have a drink?") Brault, p. 378.

Drunkenness *See* HAND, Drunkenness.

Eating *See* the Neapolitan gesture in Fig. 2 c. Wundt, I, p. 172, fig. 29, and p. 173.

Embarrassment Tip of index placed vertically to lips. Anc. *Greece* and *Rome*. Sittl, pp. 272–273.

Etiquette Fingertips of right hand joined together and led toward the lips. "You must always pull off your glove, and kiss your hand when you take from or present anything to, a person of quality, or when you return anything to them." By the late 17th cent., the gesture had become reduced to a circular flourish of the hand toward the mouth and forwards. 16th–17th cent. *England*. Morris et al., pp. 5–7, who add that "it was important not to keep them waiting, so the correct form was to hand over the object first and then afterwards not to forget to kiss your hand." By the 18th cent., the gesture had become reduced to a circular motion of the hand and arm in being extended forward, and by the early 19th century the gesture had begun to disappear. Ibid.

Exquisiteness *See* HAND, Exquisiteness.

Farewell Fingertips to lips, then thrown forward. Intimate and casual. *Colombia; U.S.* Saitz and Cervenka, p. 63.

Foolishness Extending lower lip, or pulling the lower lip downward with the index. *Lat. Am.* Kany, p. 49.

Greeting Fingertips of right hand joined and led to lips. According to F. Caroso's *Della Nobiltà di Dame* (1600), cited by Morris, et al., pp. 4–5, the right hand should not touch the lips, but be kept "somewhat distant, and bending it a little." The gesture was to be accompanied by a bow or curtsy. "It was clearly not employed by the general population," though it was used in court circles. Elizabethan *England*. Morris et al., p. 5. By the Restoration, the gesture had become a mere flourish of the hand toward the lips, combined with a bow; and by the 18th cent. it had become a circular motion of the hand toward the body and forward, combined with a bow. By the 19th cent. the gesture was going out of use. Morris et al., p. 7, cite a 1774 edition of della Casa's *Galateo*, in which the gesture is described as a "ridiculous custom," and they ascribe its survival in modern Europe to its shift from the formal to the informal: "it is used in a light hearted way towards a loved one, or in an exuberant moment of praise . . . for something tasty or beautiful." *See* Etiquette. In the 17th cent., kissing one's fingers and throwing the kiss in the air was a very popular greeting among social equals. The gesture allowed a show of affection without touching. Bonifatius Vanozzi, who visited Jan Zamoyski in 1596, recalls his introduction to Zamoyski's wife and other ladies. The Chancellor's wife shook hands with him, the other ladies curtseyed and kissed their fingers. Vanozzi himself used such gestures in greeting Zamoyski's courtiers. 17th cent. *Poland*. Bogucka, p. 195. *See* Adoration, above, and Perfection, below.

Mockery Tips of fingers of one hand are serially passed over lips, producing a bubbling sound. French: "faire babu." "Panurge luy feist la babou, en signe de dérision" ("Panurge made the 'babu' at him as a sign of derision"). 16th cent. *France*. Rabelais, *Le Quarte Livre*, LVI. Cascudo, *História*, p. 86. *See also* FINGER, Mockery.

Mysterious   "He laid his finger on his lips mysteriously, walked in, and closed the door. 19th cent. *England*. Dickens, *Pickwick*, I, p. 127.

Oath   Thumb and index form a cross and are led to the lips. *Spain*. Flachskampf, p. 242; Green, pp. 91–92. Variant: forming a cross with the indexes of both hands and kissing the point at which the fingers bisect. *Spain*. Green, ibid.

Pensiveness   Index or index and middle finger touch lower lip. Sometimes all fingers rest against lower lip. *U.S.* Saitz and Cervenka, p. 141. * Tips of fingers touch in front of or at lips or chin. *Colombia; U.S.* Saitz and Cervenka, p. 142. See also Rembrandt's drawing of two soldiers playing cards, one frowning, his index at his lower lip, the other impatiently leaning forward. 17th cent. *Netherlands*. van der Meulen, p. 28.

Perfection   Thumb and index or middle finger joined at tip, brought to the lips, then suddenly removed from the lips, which are left pursed. The fingers remain some distance from the face for a moment, fingers slightly parted. *France*. Mitton, p. 151. * Tips of fingers of right hand joined and brought toward the lips. Light-hearted praise. *France*. Morris et al., p. 7. *See also* Adoration and Greeting.

Regret   One or more fingers inserted between lips and teeth. *Colombia; U.S.* Saitz and Cervenka, p. 102.

Respect   Tips of right index touch mouth, second finger and thumb to mouth, bowing slightly. Variation: touching mouth, then forehead as body is bowed. *Jordan; Lebanon; Saudi Arabia; Syria*. Barakat, no. 24.

Silence   Lips pressed together with index and thumb of one hand. *Mexico*. Jimenez, p. 34; *Spain*. Nieto, p. 32; Flachskampf, p. 226; 19th cent. Naples, southern *Italy*. De Jorio, p. 293; Sittl, p. 54. *Central Africa*. Hochegger, p. 195. * Index of one hand brought to the lips. 17th cent. *Spain*. Cervantes, *Don Quijote*, II, xxxiii. 16th–17th cent. *England*. Shakesp., *Troilus* 1.3.240. Cf. also Green, p. 43. *Central Africa*. Hochegger, p. 195. * Shutting lips with finger. *U.S.* Krout, p. 25. * Head advanced, index laid on pursed lips, eyebrows raised. *Europe; North Am.* Aubert, p. 148. * Index or hand laid vertically across lips. Anc. *Greece* and *Rome*; *Byzantine Empire*. Sittl, p. 54. See the Neapolitan gesture in Fig. 2 a. Wundt, I, p. 172, fig. 29. "laying his finger on his lip, drew his companions back again, with the greatest caution and circumspection." 19th cent. *England*. Dickens, *Oliver Twist*, p. 81. * Touching lower lip of a child with tip of right index. *Jordan; Kuwait; Lebanon; Libya; Saudi Arabia; Syria*. Barakat, no. 27. * Laying index vertically on lips. *Colombia; U.S.* Saitz and Cervenka, p. 123. *Netherlands*. Andrea and de Boer, p. 56. *Russia*. Almost exclusively feminine. Monahan, pp. 92–93. * Thumb extended moves from one corner of closed lips to the other. May also mean "keep it secret." *Colombia; U.S.* Saitz and Cervenka, p. 123. * Fingers move as if sewing lips closed.

Reminiscence of European medieval witchcraft. *Brazil.* Cascudo, *História*, p. 116.

Superlative Fingers of one hand bunched, hand is brought to the lips and fingertips are kissed before the fingers are opened. Reserved "for expressing the more subtle and refined emotions (e.g. describing a fine wine) and for this reason usually execute[d] . . . very gently. In its ultimate form, only the thumb and forefinger are pressed together, placed parallel to the face and . . . softly brushed with the corner of the lips." *Spain; Lat. Am.* Green, p. 72. *France.* Brault, p. 377.

Surprise Tip of index vertically placed to lips. Anc. *Greece* and *Rome.* Sittl, pp. 272–73. * Expressions of feigned shock may be accompanied by bringing the fingertips of one hand, palm inward, to the lips. *Spain; Lat; Am.* Green, pp. 80–81.

Teasing Tip of index placed below lower lip, then flipped up so that it barely grazes the underside of the lip. *Saudi Arabia.* Barakat, no. 223.

FINGER, MOUTH
Admiration Tips of bunched fingers taken to the mouth. 19th cent. *Spain.* Pérez Galdós, pt. 2, iv, vii.

Affection Index put in mouth, then joined to middle finger and placed between breasts. 10th cent. *Persia? 1001 Nights,* II, p. 302–303.

Childishness Sucking thumb. *Flanders.* Andrea and de Boer, p. 186.

Copulation Pulling the mouth apart with the fingers, sometimes with the tongue stuck out, has sexual connotations. Mellinkoff, *Outcasts,* I, p. 199. * Placing a finger in the partner's mouth (Dürer), is an invitation to copulate. 16th cent. *Germany.* Mellinkoff, ibid., I, p. 202.

Deception Holding the right index and middle finger a little in front and to the right of the mouth, pointing to the left, moving the hand to the left, past the mouth and downward. *U.S.* Seton, p. 119.

Disagreement Tip of index placed on mouth by pointing at it from the front. *Central Africa.* Hochegger, p. 52.

Disappointment Thumb at corner of mouth, fingers extended, palm facing away from the body. *Colombia.* Saitz and Cervenka, p. 37.

Disbelief Brushing fingers outward from the mouth, meaning "de dientes para afuera" or "de labios afuera," that is, what has been said is "idle talk." *Lat. Am.* Kany, p. 70.

Drink Thumb raised repeatedly to the mouth. Anc. *Rome* and throughout 19th cent. southern *Europe.* Sittl, p. 115. * Putting thumb into mouth. 19th cent. *Palestine.* Bauer, p. 223. 19th–20th cent. *Spain.* Pardo Bazan, p. 27. * Thumb jabbed at the mouth ("Waiter, bring some wine"). *Italy.* "The High Price of Silent Insults," *Time,* Apr. 9, 1965, p. 67. * Thumb extended, pointing to mouth, little finger raised; hand rocks back and forth. *Colombia.* Saitz and Cervenka, p. 44. Can also indicate intoxication. Ibid., p. 45. *See* FINGER, Ordering [wine]; HAND, Drunkenness.

Eating   Thumb is repeatedly waved vertically before mouth. Anc. *Rome.* Sittl, p. 115. * Tips of thumb and index applied around the mouth with rapid alternations in a vertical and horizontal direction. Naples; *Italy.* Critchley, p. 89. * Cupped fingers of one hand move back and forth in front of open mouth. Women often move one finger after another. *Colombia.* Saitz and Cervenka, p. 56. * Mouth wide open, fingers of one hand bunched at tips and brought to the mouth. *France.* Life Photos by David Scherman, *Life*, Sept. 16, 1946, p. 12. * Chin raised, fingers and thumb of the right hand pinched together, curved and jerked two or three times toward the open mouth; eyebrows raised: "On va bouffer?" ("Are we going to eat?") *France.* Brault, pp. 378–79. * Mouth open, index pointing into it: "Mealtime, are you coming?" Or: Closed hand (not a fist: nails remain visible), thumb sticking up; move from wrist toward mouth. Or: With the hollow hand make spooning movement toward mouth (peasants?). *Netherlands.* Andrea and de Boer, p. 20. * Tips of index and thumb of right hand joined and alternately moved toward and away from the mouth. It can also signify that "all the talk has led to nothing." *Central Africa.* Hochegger, p. 128.

Embarrassment   Hand raised to mouth, covering mouth with fingers. *Spain; Lat. Am.* Green, p. 81.

Encouragement   Spitting on fingertips or palms and rubbing hands together. Children. *England.* Opie, p. 231.

Fasting   Making the sign of the cross on the mouth. Derived from the use of the mark of the cross in commercial documents, indicating payment or forgiveness of a debt. The penance of fasting as symbolized by the gesture of the cross is believed to serve as heavenly credit against one's sins. *Brazil.* Cascudo *História*, p. 195.

Insult   Fingers in mouth. 16th cent. *Germany.* Dürer, *Christ at the Pillar.* Tip of right middle finger placed in mouth, lips pursed around it, then removed and held out with back of hand forward, other fingers pressed into palm: obscenity directed at female members of family of person to whom gesture is made. *Saudi Arabia.* Barakat, no. 165.

Lying   Sucking the thumb indicates that someone is lying. *Netherlands.* Axtell, *Gestures*, p. 145; Andrea and de Boer, p. 23.

Mockery   Indexes of each hand pull corners of mouth apart. 16th–17th cent. *Netherlands.* Brueghel, *Pride*, in Gowing, p. 12. See also Röhrich, figs. 20, 23, 26. * Index and middle finger of both hands pull mouth apart at the corners, thumbs at temples. Variant: same with one hand. 16th cent. *Germany.* Lucas Cranach the Elder, *The Mocking of Christ* (1538), L. A. County Museum of Art. * One or more fingers in the mouth as a mocking gesture in medieval art. Mellinkoff, *Outcasts*, I, p. 199. * Thumbs inserted at corners of mouth and tugging sideways, while indexes pull skin down from underneath the eyes. Children. *England*. Opie, p. 320.

Negation   Clicking of tongue, index of right hand raised and moved from right to left at level of chest, head slightly raised. 19th cent. Naples, southern *Italy*. De Jorio, p. 224. Also *Spain*. Flachskampf, p. 237.

Oath   Link little fingers and spit, saying "spit your death." Children. Liverpool, *England*. Opie, p. 126. * Spit and cross the throat, or spit over wrist or little finger, saying "spit your mother's death." Children. Cumberland, *England*. Opie, p. 126.

Pensiveness   Index of left hand raised to mouth, lips pursed. 16th cent. *Germany*. Brant, woodcut, p. 3. * Placing finger in mouth and sucking or gnawing it. 17th cent. *England*. Bulwer, pp. 158–60.

Poverty   Putting index into mouth as if sucking it. 19th cent. *Palestine*. Bauer, p. 221.

Refusal   Tip of thumb placed in mouth, cheeks inflated: "Forget it!" "Go screw yourself!" *Netherlands*. Andrea and de Boer, p. 133.

Reminder   If one has overlooked or forgotten something, one should put the index into one's mouth, say "fff! ai! ai!," and make the sign of the cross. *Germany*. *HDA*, II, col. 1483.

Silence   Tip of finger placed over closed mouth, index vertical. *France*. Mitton, p. 145. Also anc. *Rome* and early medieval *Europe*. Pliny, *Nat. hist.* 33, 1; Juvenal 1, 160; Apuleius, *Met.* 1, 8; Martianus Capella 1, 90; Jerome, *Epist.* 27, 2. Sittl, p. 213. 17th cent. *England*. Bulwer, pp. 128–29, 143. 19th cent. *Palestine*. Bauer, p. 223. Placing extended right index in front of mouth and blowing on it. *Saudi Arabia*. Barakat, no. 75. *See* FINGER, Silence; FINGER, LIP, Silence.

Speech   Finger curved and put to the mouth. Trappist monks. Critchley, p. 53. * Raising the bunched fingers of one hand to the mouth. *Spain*. Green, p. 81.

Surrender   Thumbs of both hands placed in mouth, other fingers pointing directly at someone. Rwala Bedouin of *Kuwait*; *Iraq; Saudi Arabia; Syria*. Barakat, no. 131.

Useless   Fingers of one hand joined at tips, pointing to mouth: "Il ne sait que parler!" ("All he can do is talk!") *Central Africa*. Hochegger, p. 207.

FINGER, MOUTH, TONGUE

Mockery   Two fingers spread mouth at corners, tongue stuck out. Rabelais, Bk. I, ch. xviii. Numerous gargoyles on European buildings, occurrences in German masques of the 15th and 16th centuries, the Schembartlauf of Nürnberg of 1539 and depictions of the mocking of Christ. Medieval *Europe*. Röhrich, *Gebärde-Metapher-Parodie*, p. 26 and pl. 20, 23, 24, 26. * Thumb of one hand drawn forward under chin, tongue extruded. *Netherlands*. Andrea and de Boer, p. 135.

FINGER, NAVEL

Mockery Fingers of one hand held over the navel, pointing to it, then turned outward and opened: "Tu as un nombril gros comme une aubergine!" ("Your navel is the size of an eggplant!") *Central Africa.* Hochegger, p. 127.

FINGER, NECK

Danger Index and middle finger spread apart, forming a "V," and held with tips against the throat at the Adam's apple: metaphor for having a pitchfork held at one's throat. "I'm in danger!" *Russia.* Monahan, pp. 96–97.

Death Drawing the index, or index and middle fingers, representing a knife, quickly across the throat. *Lat. Am.* Kany, p. 27. "He looked at the sentry . . . and, pointing with one finger, drew the other across his throat." *Spain.* Hemingway, pp. 36–37.

Drink Tip of thumb touching tip of middle finger and one of these snapped against throat. 19th cent. *Palestine.* Bauer, p. 223. Flicking a finger against the neck invites a close friend to join the gesturer in a drink. *Poland.* Axtell, *Gestures*, p. 147. * Tips of thumb and index joined, held against neck just below jaw line under the ear, then snapped open against neck. If the gesturer is male, the gesture is an invitation to go drinking or to buy vodka and drink in someone's apartment or outdoors. Used by both men and women to indicate they went on a spree. A variant consists in holding the index lightly pressed against the neck, and bringing thumb and fourth finger down after the snap. *Russia.* Monahan, pp. 40–41.

Hanging Moving index across throat. *Lat. Am.* Kany, p. 107.

Homosexuality Tickling one's neck, accompanied by a mocking expression, indicates that someone is a homosexual. *Flanders.* Andrea and de Boer, p. 191.

Insult Moving the fingers between collar and neck as if brushing back hair behind the ear, with annoyed facial expression, or moving index and thumb back and forth on the neck. Women. *Lat. Am.* Kany, p. 176.

Mistake Index horizontally extended and moved across throat. *Colombia; U.S.* Saitz and Cervenka, p. 51.

Mockery *See* FINGER, FOREHEAD, Mockery.

Mourning Scratching neck. Women. Anc. *Greece.* Sittl, p. 27.

Negation Tip of thumb, hand open, placed against throat, then catapulted forward. Or the same with all fingers. 19th cent. Southern *Italy.* De Jorio, p. 224; Sittl, p. 95.

Oath Licking tip of index and making sign of the cross on the throat. Children. *England.* Opie, p. 122. *See* also HAND, Neck.

Perplexity Fingers of one hand scratch the back of the neck. Typical of Muscovites. *Russia.* Monahan, p. 25.

Poverty Drawing index across throat and snapping relaxed index and middle finger. *Venezuela.* Kany, p. 88. * Thumb on throat, fingers up. Cervantes *Don Quijote*, II, liv. * Putting thumbs between the neck and collar and waving the extended fingers up and down, accompanied by the colloquial phrase "andar a voar," "to go flying," i.e. to have no money. *Portugal.* Taylor, p. 39.

FINGER, NOSE

Amazement "To express amused amazement, it is only necessary to place the index finger along the nose and assume an expression of amazed amusement." WW II. *France.* Alsop, p. 27. Index of right hand placed alongside of nose, mouth slightly open, eyes wide open: "Pas possible!" ("Impossible!") or "Non, sans blague!" ("No kidding!") *France.* Brault, p. 376.

Attention "I, in order that the leader should attend, put my finger upward from my chin to my nose." 13th–14th cent. *Italy.* Dante, *Inf.*, c. xxv. As a warning to be alert, also mod. *Italy.* *See* Cleverness.

Cheap Index rubs nose from the bridge downward to indicate that someone is stingy. *Netherlands.* Axtell, *Gestures,* p. 145.

Cleverness " 'Why, one need be sharp in this town, my dear,' replied the Jew, sinking his voice to a confidential whisper; 'and that's the truth.' Fagin followed up this remark by striking the side of his nose with his right forefinger." 19th cent. *England.* Dickens, *Oliver Twist*, ch. xlii. " 'Pay attention to the reply, constable, will you?' said the doctor, shaking his forefinger with great solemnity of manner, and tapping the bridge of his nose with it, to bespeak the exercise of that worthy's utmost acuteness." Dickens, ibid., ch. xxx. * Thumb and bent index placed to nose (as if blowing the nose). Anc. *Rome.* Sittl, p. 111–12; 19th cent. Naples, southern *Italy.* De Jorio, pp. 55–56; see Fig. 3 f; Wundt, I, p. 184, fig. 30. As a friendly warning to be alert, *Italy*, partic. Rome and Naples. Morris et al., pp. 217–22. As a gesture in praise of cleverness it has some slight currency in southern *Italy; Sicily.* Ibid., pp. 218, 221, 224. * "He smiled and tapped the side of his nose with a finger and then, as though it was a small matter hardly worth mentioning, he asked if we would like 250 asparagus plants put in while we still had the use of the tractor and the men. It was done the next day. So much for our theory that nothing happens fast in Provençe." Southern *France.* Mayle, *A Year in Provençe,* p. 49. " 'You think so?' Jojo winked, and tapped the side of his nose. 'Maybe not. That's why I called you. *Allez.* Let's go and have that drink.' " Southern *France.* Mayle, *Hotel Pastis,* p. 36. " 'It's all old stones and old tiles. Heaven knows where Monsieur

Blanc gets them. When I asked him, he just tapped his nose.' " Ibid., p. 201.
Complicity "and laying a finger aside of his nose" *U.S.* Clement C. Moore, *A Visit from St. Nicholas.* "When he turned round he found two students solemnly staring at him through the large open window. They nodded approvingly, each tapped the side of his nose with the forefinger, and they went on their way." *U.S.* Hill, p. 25. "Uncle Carl flashed a look at him which might have been a warning. Lance tapped the side of his nose exaggeratedly to show that the point was taken." *U.S.* P. Carr, p. 50. * Index placed along the nose, sometimes tapping it gently several times, or the tip of the index taps the side of the nose. Origin may be a "sniffing out" signal, signifying either that the gesturer and accomplices can sniff out something, or that they can be sniffed out: "Keep it a secret." *Great Britain; Italy*; particularly *Scotland; Sardinia.* Morris et al., pp. 216–22. The nose tap in England "probably means . . . 'Let's keep this between us only.' On the other hand, in Italy it is more of a friendly warning: 'Watch out. Take care.' " Axtell, *Gestures*, p. 67. "Massot stopped his explosions and tapped the side of his nose, sly and conspiratorial." Provence, *France.* Mayle, *A Year in Provençe*, p. 119. *See* Secrecy. By extension, the gesture also signifies a necessity for alertness or cleverness. "The detective tapped the side of his nose. 'This is France, monsieur. Journalists know their place.' " Provençe, *France.* Mayle. *Hotel Pastis*, p. 353. *See* Cleverness; Secrecy.

Concentration Tip of extended index placed against tip of nose, pushing it up slightly. Women and children. Río de la Plata region of *Argentina; Uruguay.* Meo Zilio, p. 113.

Contempt Thumbing the nose. 16th–17th cent. *Poland.* Bogucka, p. 196. *See also* Mockery above.

Copulation Rubbing side of index over bridge of nose: proposition to a woman. *Jordan.* Barakat, no. 239.

Cunning " 'J'y ai souvent pensé, Milor,' ['I've often thought so'] says the little Baron, placing his finger to his nose very knowingly, 'that Baroness is capable of anything.' " 19th cent. *England.* Thackeray, I, chap. xxv. "If Gastone moved his forefinger and thumb up and down each side of the bridge of his nose, his verdict on my new landlord was 'A smart one!' But if, instead, he tapped one side of his nose, he was telling me, 'Watch out! He's a fishy chap, he stinks.' " *Italy.* Graham, p. 26. " 'Swallow has a bit of a weakness where women are concerned. Forewarned is forearmed.' Sutcliffe tapped the side of his long nose with his index finger as he uttered these words." *England.* Lodge, *Nice Work*, p. 63. "Robert tilted his head and laid a stubby finger along the side of his nose. It is not quite as *décontracté* as it appears, he said." Provençe, *France.* Mayle, *Toujours Provençe*, p. 155. * Tip of index placed against side of nose, closing one nostril, while sniffing through the other, signifies discovery or understanding of something concealed. Río de la Plata region of *Argentina; Uruguay*. Meo Zilio, p. 78.

Defiance   Right index hooked over tip of nose. "I'll do it in spite of you." *Saudi Arabia*. Barakat, no. 153.

Disappointment   Left thumb placed against nose. 19th cent. *Italy*. Manzoni, ch. xvi, 198; Sittl, p. 116.

Disbelief   "The Shanghai Gesture [tip of thumb to nose, other fingers extended] is in current use in Greece . . . Persons born in the Peloponnesus have informed A. R. Nykl that it is ordinarily accompanied by the expletive 'Na!' and implies 'If you believe this story, you are a d—— fool.' " Taylor, p. 49. * "So the burgess of Preston who has charged a married woman with unchastity must proclaim himself a liar holding his nose with his fingers." Medieval *England*. Pollock and Maitland, II, xv. * "He wears his forefinger perpetually upon the side of his nose. He is not to be amused with fancies and chimeras." 19th cent. *England*. Simms, p. 31. "I could see the critter [the seacaptain] had heard on him afore, by the way he twisted his mouth around the long nine [cigar]; but when I told him about the carriage and the rooster and so on, he jest took and give the long nine a fling clapped his thumb again the side of his nose, and winking one eye, made his finger twinkle up and down for as much as a minit without saying a word." 19th cent. *U.S.* Slick, I, p. 144; Taylor, p. 22.

Dissatisfaction   Holding nose with thumb and index. College students. California, *U.S.* McCord, p. 291. *Russia*. Monahan, pp. 182–183.

Drink   Touching nose with tip of index. Trappist monks. Critchley, p. 53.

Drunkenness   Index and thumb, forming a circle, placed around nose and twisted to signify that the person is drunk. *France*. Axtell, *Gestures*, p. 68. "He curled an index finger around the end of his nose and twisted, the gesture for drunkenness." Provençe, *France*. Mayle, *A Year in Provençe*, p. 142.

Emphasis   " 'What do you think them women does t'other day,' continued Mr. Weller, after a short pause, during which he had significantly struck the side of his nose with his forefinger, some half-dozen times . . . 'Goes and gets up a grand te drinkin' for feller they calls their shepheard.' " 19th cent. *England*. Dickens, *Pickwick*, I, p. 363.

Etiquette   Index extended and placed below the nose, exerting mild pressure inward and upward to stifle a sneeze. *Spain; Lat. Am.* Regarded as mildly offensive in Lat. Am. Green, p. 94.

Facetiousness   "Mr. Jackson's fingers wandered playfully round his nose at this portion of his discourse, to warn his hearers that he was speaking ironically" 19th cent. *England*. Dickens, *Pickwick*, II, p. 310.

Familiarity   "as he remarked afterward to Pen, winking knowingly, and laying a finger on his nose." 19th cent. *England.* Thackeray, *Pendennis*, ch. v.

Frustration Index passed under someone else's nose indicates an unexpected failure. Derived from the gesture used to indicate that hunting dogs lost the scent. *Europe; Brazil.* Cascudo, *História*, p. 171.

Greeting Squeezing nostrils with index and thumb of left hand, and pointing to the navel with the index of the right. Friendly greeting. Astrolabe Bay, *New Guinea.* Comrie, p. 108.

Homosexuality Index and thumb form a circle and place it around the nose as a sign that the person referred to is homosexual. *Colombia.* Axtell, *Gestures*, p. 67.

Humiliation Thumb to nose, fingers extended: "tanto di naso." Late 16th cent. Naples, southern *Italy.* Taylor, p. 45.

Ignorance "Mr. Jackson struck his forefinger several times against the left side of his nose, to intimate that he was not there to disclose the secrets of the prison-house, and playfully rejoined: 'Not knowin', can't say.' " 19th cent. *England.* Dickens, *Pickwick*, II, p. 28. *See also* Secrecy.

Insult The so-called "violin" (Mexico) in which index and middle fingers of one hand are placed on either side of the nose and moved downward as if a bow were being drawn over violin strings. *Lat. Am.* Kany, p. 175. Index and middle finger form a "V," the other two fingers are held down by the thumb. Hand is then raised to nose, so that the "V" formed by the fingers surrounds nose. *Mexico.* Jiménez, p. 37. *Saudi Arabia.* Axtell, *Gestures*, p. 67. * Index taps one side of the nose ("I have no confidence in your masculinity.") *Italy.* Graham, p. 26. * Thumb to nose, fingers extended, moving from side to side. Children. *U.S.*; Adults. *Colombia.* Saitz and Cervenka, p. 77. Universal children's gesture. Axtell, pp. 37–38. * Thumb of one hand to tip of nose, thumb of other hand to little finger of the first hand, fingers extended and moving from side to side. *Colombia.* Saitz and Cervenka, p. 77. * Picking nostrils with right index and thumb ("Go to hell"). *Syria.* Barakat, no. 33. * Pushing tip of nose in with right index (implies that the person to whom the gesture is made is a Black). *Saudi Arabia.* Barakat, no. 103. * Flicking tip of nose with tip of right index (implies that the person to whom the gesture is made is a homosexual). *Lebanon; Syria.* Barakat, no. 18. * Picking nostrils with tips of right index and thumb, then thrusting out middle finger stiffly. *Libya; Syria.* Barakat, no. 12. *See also* Contempt, Mockery.

Jew Index moves in an arc above the nose, indicating a large, bent nose. *Netherlands.* Andrea and de Boer, p. 19.

Joke Index rubs side of nose. Schoolchildren. *U.S.* Seton, p. xxi.

Mockery Index and thumb of one hand pull down lower lip, index and thumb of the other pull up tip of nose. 15th cent. *Netherlands.* Mock-

ing of Christ, Hours of Catherine of Cleves, Guennol Coll., N. Y., f. 53. Cf. *The Hours of C. of C.*, N. Y., n. d., pl. 19. For the gesture in medieval art, see Mellinkoff, *Outcasts*, I, pp. 202–203. * Thumb or index presses tip of nose upwards, fingers extended. *Spain*. Flachskampf, p. 231; *Portugal*. Urtel, p. 29. [Editors' comment: The classic form of the gesture is exhibited by German Chancellor Helmut Schmidt. *Germany*. AP Photo, *L.A. Times*, Oct. 3, 1982, pt. 4, p. 2.] * Fingers of both hands spread wide open, one thumb applied to tip of nose, the other to the tip of the little finger of the other hand. *Britain*. Taylor, Note, p. 114. *See* HAND, NOSE, Truth. Thumb to tip of nose, fingers extended ("The long nose"). *Germany*. *HDV,* I, p. 323. *See* FINGER, Mockery. Placing the thumb of the left hand on the tip of the nose, joining the thumb of the right hand to the little finger of the left and spreading the fingers to the fullest extent. 19th cent. *England*. Hone, Jan. 1831; Opie, p. 318. "The seventeenth century satirist Scarron is an altogether appropriate person to show knowledge of the [Shanghai] gesture (tip of thumb to nose, other fingers extended). In Book III of *Le Virgile travesti* (1651), Celaeno, one of the harpies, complains that Aeneas and his companions are trespassers. The narrator of the scene concludes 'Elle nous fit un pied de nez; / Et nous laissant bien étonnez, / La mal-plaisante prophetesse / S'envola de grande vitesse.' And in Book DX the gesture is used again in the same sense" ("She made a Shanghai gesture at us; and leaving us quite astonished, the unpleasant sorceress flew quickly away"). 17th cent. *France*. Taylor, *Shanghai Gesture*, pp. 15–16. "The earliest illustration of the Shanghai Gesture that has come to my knowledge is a print of 1560 entitled "La Fete des fous" by Peter Brueghel. Here a fool makes the tandem (thumb of one hand to nose, fingers extended, thumb of other hand to little finger of first hand) gesture with the thumb of his left hand placed just beneath his nose and not, as is usually the case, at the tip of the nose. This minor variation in form does not appear to be significant." 16th cent. *Netherlands*. Taylor, pp. 11–12. Mellinkoff, *Outcasts,* I, pp. 202–203, has found the gesture in a parchment roll (c. 1230) from Soest, *Germany*, which has one of Ham's descendants thumbing his nose. The significance here is unclear. She has also found it in the Kremsmünster *Speculum humanae salvationis* (14th cent.), clearly signifying mockery. " 'Panurge suddenly lifted up in the air his right hand, and put the thumb thereof to the nostril of the same side, holding his four fingers straight out closed and orderly in a parallel line to the point of his nose, shutting the left eye wholly and making the other wink with a profound depression of the eyebrow and eyelids. Then he lifted up his left hand, with hand wringing and stretching forth his four fingers and elevating his thumb, which he held in a line directly correspondent to the situation of his right hand, with the distance of a cubit and a half between them. This done, in the same form he abased toward the ground both the one and the other hand. Lastly, he held them in the midst, as aiming right at the Englishman's nose.' . . . The Englishman responded to Panurge suitably enough with a modification of the tandem gesture: 'Then made the Englishman this sign: his left hand all open he lifted up into the air, then instantly shut into his fist the four fingers thereof, and his thumb extended at length he placed upon the gristle of his nose. Presently after, he lifted up his right hand all open, and abased and bent it downwards, putting the thumb thereof in the very place where the little finger of the left had been and did close in the fist, and the four right-hand fingers he softly moved in the air. Then contrarily he did with the right hand what he had done with the left, and with the left what he had done with the right.' " 16th cent. *France*. Taylor, *Shanghai Gesture*, pp. 9–10. *Gargantua and Pantagruel*, Book II, chap. 19. "Like Rabelais' use of the gesture, the association with a fool in both [Brueghel's] example and the following sketch by Bernardo Passeri that was made in Rome and engraved in Antwerp seems important. It will be noted that this association is characteristic of the earliest uses of the gesture and occurs in widely separated places." *Italy*. Taylor, *Shanghai Gesture*, pp. 11–12. "A superb example of the tandem gesture occurs in 'a design illustrating a passage in the parable of the Prodigal Son' as found in 'Wierix's Bible 1594' . . . 'Wierix's Bible, 1594' that Hone cites in the Year Book . . . never existed. What Hone means is a series of engravings of scenes in the New Testament planned by Hieronymus Natalis (Jerome Nadal, 1507–1580) at the suggestion of Ignatius Loyola." 16th cent. *England*. Taylor, p. 12. " 'Truth stripping a fine lady of her false decorations, with one hand removes a painted mask, and with the other pulls away her 'borrowed' hair and headdress, showing an ugly face, and a head as round and smooth as a bullet. Below there are four little satyrs, one of whom is taking a single sight, or making a 'nose' at the lady; whilst a second is taking a double sight, or 'long nose,' towards the spectator.' " Quoted by Taylor, *Shanghai Gesture*, p. 17, from a description (1875) of a depiction of 1702. William Hone refers to it as "a ludicrous practice . . . , which suddenly arose as a novelty within the last twenty years [after 1812] among the boys of the metropolis." 19th cent. *England*. Hone, col. 65. "In 1845 Benjamin Disraeli refers to 'putting his thumb to his nose.' " 19th cent. *England*. Taylor, *Shanghai Gesture*, pp. 21–22. "But the varmint didn't wink, but stood still as a post, with the thumb of his right paw on the end of his smeller, an wigglin' his t'other finger thus (and Mike went through with the gyration)." 19th cent. *England*. Taylor, ibid., p. 24. Ezra Pound alludes to the gesture in 1917 in his *Lustra*. *U.S.* Taylor, ibid., pp. 25–26. " 'I've been naughty, have I?' 'You know best about that, old boy. No, I don't feel you quite get my drift. I happen to think Bill Evans is rather a good chap, you see. And if you don't mind my saying so, I'm not very much of the same opinion about you. Quite the contrary, in fact. Sorry to have to mention it.' Barking excitedly, I gave him the English snooks (left hand to nose with fingers extended, right hand subjoined with fingers extended), then the German snooks as Jean had demonstrated them (left hand as before, but right hand curled up and rotated as if cranking a movie camera), then the donkey's-ears treatment with raspberry or Bronx cheer obbligato. This completed, I moved off once more, feeling a little toned up for the moment." *England*. Amis, p. 232, quoted from the English ed. by Taylor, *Shanghai Gesture*, p. 27. "the definition in Maller's dictionary of 1561, which equates 'einem eine Nase machen' and 'uncis naribus indulgere,' concerns a phrase which often means the Shanghai Gesture in later use and is apparently accepted in that sense by the editors of the *Deutsches Wörterbuch* . . . However, the Latin definition has been obviously suggested by Persius, *Sat.* 1. 40–41: 'Rides,' ait, 'et nimis uncis naribus indulges' ('You are scoffing,' he says, 'and use your turned-up nose too freely'), and this does not mean the Shanghai Gesture." Taylor, ibid., p. 35. "Especially curious are the figures of a devil cocking a snook that Elworthy describes and illustrates [pp. 111–12]. Crouching forward with his bovine tail flying up over his back, and with horns on his head, he cocks a double snook with his left hand at his nose. Elworthy found figures of this sort on the back of a cab horse in Naples, in oxidized silver in Rome, and also in silver in Florence, and yet again . . . in shops in Paris and London around 1900. Presumably such figures had originally an apotropaic use and became articles of commerce. Elworthy comments, 'This is the attitude of vulgar mockery among all people. Neapolitans call this Beseggiare. . . . Hence it may be assumed that the devil is looked upon generally as a contemptuous mocking personage, with a dash of vulgar humour.' His word 'Beseggiare' is an error . . . for 'fefeggiare,' i.e. to mock, and has no exclusive reference to the Shanghai Gesture." 19th cent. *France*; 19th cent. *Italy*. Taylor, ibid., p. 46. "References to the use of the Shanghai Gesture in Spain, Portugal, and Latin America are rare, but friends assure me of its current use in all these lands. The Spanish idiom 'hacer un pito catalán' ('to make a Catalan fife [horn, whistle]') is significant for the use of the same metaphor . . . in Servian and French names for the gesture." *France; Lat. Am.; Portugal; Spain; Serbia*. Taylor, p. 46. "Urtel [p. 17] reports a Portuguese idiom 'achetar o beque' ('to buy the prow of a ship')." *Portugal*. Taylor, p. 47. Extended fingers with thumb to nose. 19th cent. *Palestine*. Bauer, p. 224. Thumb to nose, other fingers extended; sometimes the other hand is added, thumb to little finger of the first hand; children sometimes add a foot to the two hands. In the use of one hand, one sometimes waggles the fingers, closed to form a flag. *Netherlands*. In the use of one hand, one sometimes waggles the separated fingers.

Flanders. Andrea and de Boer, pp. 64, 185. Río de la Plata region of *Argentina; Uruguay; Italy.* Meo Zilio, p. 93. "Here Mr. Jackson smiled once more upon the company, and, applying his left thumb to the tip of his nose, worked a visionary coffee-mill with his right hand, thereby performing a very graceful piece of pantomime, (then [1828] much in vogue, but now, unhappily, almost obsolete) which was familiarly denominated 'taking a grinder.' " 19th cent. *England.* Dickens, *Pickwick*, II, pp. 28–29. "Mr. Jackson's fingers wandered playfully round his nose, at this portion of his discourse, to warn his hearers that he was speaking ironically." 19th cent. *England.* Dickens, *Pickwick*, II, p. 280. "Hacer un pito catalán"—extended and waving fingers resembling those of a fife player. *Lat. Am.* Kany, p. 145. *See* Insult. Right thumb to nose, left thumb to tip of little finger of right hand, fingers waggled rapidly. Usually a children's gesture. *Russia.* Monahan, pp. 54–55. Morris et al., p. 27, cite Godefroy's *Dictionnaire de l'ancienne langue française. IXième-XVième siècle* (1884) as referring to the oldest instance of the gesture known to them, as 'un nez de cire.' The expression 'to make a wax nose,' they suggest, may derive from the practice of making wax figures of people, which represented them as having long noses, hence also the name for the gesture in English, French, Italian, Dutch, and German. For illustrations and variants of the gesture, see pp. 26–39. Schoolchildren. Use rapidly decreasing. *Europe. See* p. 41. * Extended index raised to the nose, pointed forward in prolongation of the nose; its opposite is indicated by the thumb and index pinching the tip of the nose: small nose; the fingers of one hand may be held over the tip of the nose, pointing toward the face, and thus indicate a lump of a nose. *Central Africa.* Hochegger, pp. 126–27. * Tip of extended index pushes up tip of nose. Predominantly children. Signifies mockery of someone who has a high opinion of himself or deems himself too good to do something. *Russia.* Monahan, pp. 62–63.

Odor Index of right hand moves up and down, pointing at a nostril: "Quel parfum!" ("Some perfume!") *Central Africa.* Hochegger, p. 131. * Nose pinched shut by thumb and index of right hand and moved left and right: "Quelle [mauvaise] odeur!" ("What a stench!") Ibid., pp. 132–33. * Nostrils are blocked by tips of indexes, or nostrils are squeezed shut by index and thumb. Ibid., pp. 132–33.

Pensiveness Tip of index placed at the side of the nose. *Netherlands.* Andrea and de Boer, p. 164–65.

Poverty Placing right index and middle finger on either side of one's nose and (optional) drawing fingers downward. *Spain.* Flachskampf, p. 232; Kany, p. 89. * Placing slightly curved index on the nose. *Guatemala.* Kany, ibid.

Prayer The Phrygian sect of the Kataphryges put finger to nose (sign of submission to God's will, as an animal submits to being led by its driver). *Phrygia.* Sittl, p. 186.

Promise Touching tip of nose with tip of right index, accompanied by the formula "on my nose," indicates promise to do something. *Libya; Saudi Arabia; Syria.* Barakat, no. 96.

Refusal Passing the index horizontally under the nose of another person, or one's own nose. Familiar, seldom used. *France.* Mitton, p. 149.

Retraction The person guilty of slander, in retracting his statements, had to pull himself by the nose. Medieval Normandy, France. Grimm, *DRA*, I, p. 198.

Revulsion Nostrils held shut briefly by thumb and index—unpleasant smell, revulsion in general. *Colombia.* U. S. Saitz and Cervenka, p. 127. *Netherlands.* Andrea and de Boer, p. 49. * Index, extended horizontally, moves up and down between upper lip and nose. Men sometimes spit in presence of unpleasant smell. *Colombia.* Saitz and Cervenka, p. 127.

Secrecy "Mr. Jackson struck his fore-finger several times against the left side of his nose, to intimate that he was not there to disclose the secrets of the prison-house." 19th cent. *England.* Dickens, *Pickwick*, II, p. 19. " 'Ah,' said the coot profoundly, 'that's telling.' He looked out of the corners of his eyes at Fabian, leered, and with a ridiculously Victorian gesture laid his finger alongside his nose." *England.* Marsh, p. 157. "[he] clapped his finger on the side of his nose, thereby recommending secrecy and discretion." 18th cent. *England.* Smollett, *Peregrine Pickle*, I, ch. xix. *See also* Cleverness, Complicity, Understanding.

Silence Putting index to nose. *Portugal.* Flachskampf, p. 226.

Solemnity "shaking his finger with great solemnity of manner, and tapping the bridge of his nose with it." 19th cent. *England.* Dickens, *Oliver Twist*, p. 270.

Suspicion Index placed alongside nose. Naples, *Italy.* Critchley, p. 89. Index laid tip to side of nose. *Italy.* Leone, XX 11.

Threat Pushing tip of nose in with index. *Saudi Arabia.* Barakat, no. 95.

Understanding "laying a finger beside the nose to indicate full awareness of a situation . . . occurs in J. J. Hooper's description, written in 1845, of a man who 'chuckled longer than before, at the wit of calling corn-whisky 'spring water,' and put his fingers by the side of his old cut-water of a nose!' " 19th cent. *U.S. Simon Sugg's Adventures*, p. 120. "In an aquatint of 1818 dealing with counterfeit claims to public benefits, 'The lame sailor approaches the begging-can with a finger to his nose, but holding a coin in his left hand; his face is twisted to show that he is not deceived.' In an engraving that has reference to a scandal connected with the Derby of 1826, 'A man stands beside [the wife of a man accused of trickery] with a pair of top-boots under his arm; he puts a finger to his nose, grinning, and says: 'I'll bet my Awl! I'm up to snuff, Mum.' In a lithograph of the same year, 'A John Bullish fellow grins knowingly at Heath, his finger pressed against his nose and thus indicating his full understanding of the situation.' A vignette, also of the same year, is much to the same effect. . . . Heath himself, who published the last two scenes in his Northern Looking Glass, meant the reader to consider him to be a knowing spectator. Such examples as these suggest that J. J. Hooper, and Mrs. Stephens [Jonathan Slick] have consciously or unconsciously mingled two gestures." 19th cent. *England*. Taylor, p. 23. "Upon which Mr. Weller struck three distinct blows upon his nose in token of intelligence, smiled, winked, and proceeded to put the steps [of a coach] up, with a countenance expressive of lively satisfaction." 19th cent. *England*. Dickens, *Pickwick*, II, p. 177.

Useless Index is pressed horizontally under the nose of some one or one's own nose. ("No go!" "Nothing doing!") Familiar, uncommon. *France*. Mitton, p. 149.

Warning Tapping side of nose with index as a friendly warning. Peer, p. 71. *See* Cleverness.

FINGER, NOSE, TONGUE

Hurry Tip of right index placed on tongue, then on tip of nose: sign for person to hurry. *Saudi Arabia*. Barakat, no. 228.

Mockery Nose pressed upwards with thumb, tongue extruded. Children. *England*. Opie, p. 319. * "A child holds his hands with the palms together and both thumbs against the nose. Another child that does not know the trick is asked to pull the little finger of one hand. Thus, one hand slips over the other, the fingers spread, and the Shanghai Gesture is made. The tongue is often stuck out as an accompaniment to it." Taylor, *Shanghai Gesture*, p. 7.

Teasing Extended index placed sideways over nose, then moved across nose several times with tongue extended. *Egypt*. Barakat, no. 216.

FINGER, OBJECT

Apotropy Knocking on unpainted wood with the knuckles in order to ward off bad luck. *Netherlands*. * Tapping on unpainted wood with fingertips. *Flanders*. Andrea and de Boer, p. 185.

Warning Tapping the face of one's wristwatch with the index— "it's almost 12 o'clock and all Sikhs go mad at 12 o'clock." A Sikh warning: "Watch your step. It may be close to noon." *India*. Axtell, *Gestures*, p. 106.

FINGER, SHOULDER

Danger Index and middle finger of right hand extended and placed on left shoulder. Metaphoric for epaulettes. "I'm in danger of being arrested by the militia." *Russia*. Monahan, pp. 96–97.

Insult   *See* FINGER, HAND, Insult.

Mockery   "At this inquiry Mr. Martin looked, with a countenance of excessive surprise, at his two friends, and then each gentleman pointed with his right thumb over his left shoulder. This action, imperfectly described in words by the very feeble term of 'over the left,' when performed by any number of ladies or gentlemen who are accustomed to act in unison, has a very graceful and airy effect; its expression is one of light and playful sarcasm." 19th cent. *England*. Dickens, II, p. 214.

Pointing   Right thumb held out from fist and moved back and forth over right shoulder: indicates where someone has gone. *Jordan; Lebanon; Saudi Arabia; Syria*. Barakat, no. 88. *See also* FINGER, Direction; FINGER, Pointing.

FINGER, TEMPLE (*See also*) FINGER, FOREHEAD, and FINGER, HEAD

Cuckoldry   *See* FINGER, Cuckoldry.

Derangement   Index placed with tip against temple and given the motion of a drill. Familiar. *France*. Mitton, p. 147. *Spain*. Flachskampf, p. 231. * Drivers, having passed those at whom the gesture is directed, will tap their temple repeatedly with the index; an adaptation of the Dutch gesture meaning 'intelligence' to serve as its opposite. *Netherlands*. Andrea and de Boer, p. 26. *See also* FINGER, FOREHEAD, Foolishness; FINGER, HEAD, Intelligence.

Disbelief   Pointing the indexes of both hands, placing them along the temples, pointing upward. College students. California, *U.S.* King, p. 263.

Intelligence   Tip of index placed against temple. *Netherlands*. Andrea and de Boer, p. 36.

Understanding   Tip of index placed against temple. Anc. *Greece*. Sittl, p. 115.

FINGER, TESTICLES

Apotropy   "[Mussolini] would touch his testicles to ward off a curse when he thought someone in a crowd had fixed the evil eye on him." *Italy*. Review of Christopher Hibbert, "*Il Duce*," *Time*, May 4, 1962, p. 96.

FINGER, THROAT

Finished   " 'So more money is borrowed, and then more . . . *Bref*, he runs out of money.' She pulled a finger across her throat. 'He goes bankrupt' " Provençe, *France*. Mayle, *Hotel Pastis*, pp. 67–68.

Poverty   "Putting a thumb to his throat and extending his hand upward he gave them to understand that he had not a coin of any kind on him." 17th cent. *Spain*. Cervantes, *Don Quijote*, II, liv.

FINGER, TONGUE

Betting *See* FINGER, Betting.

Disgust Thumb and index placed on slightly extruded tongue. *U.S.* Archer, p. 5.

Gossip Index touches tip of tongue. *Spain.* Flachskampf, p. 230. *Colombia.* Saitz and Cervenka, p. 64.

Greeting Customary Tibetan greeting to a fellow traveller: thrusting up thumb of right hand and thrusting out tongue. Hayes, p. 223.

Indecision Placing finger against the tongue and shaking it as if it had been burnt. 19th cent. *Palestine.* Bauer, p. 223.

Medico-magical *See* FINGER, Medico-magical.

Success Tip of index touches tongue and then makes an imaginary figure "1" in the air. Indicates that speaker has said something particularly effective, clever, witty. *Colombia; U.S.* Saitz and Cervenka, p. 134.

Taste Laying finger on tongue. Schoolchildren. *U.S.* Seton, p. xxii.

FINGER, TOOTH

Anger Biting one's thumb. *England. DEP*, p. 46. Biting fingers. 13th–14th cent. *Italy.* Dante, *Inf.*, c. xxxiii, lviii. 19th cent. Naples, southern *Italy.* De Jorio, p. 265; Bresciani, *L'ebreo* c. li. 19th cent. *Spain.* Sittl, p. 18, n. 10. Biting fingertips. *Brazil.* Muslims. *Koran*, Surata of the Family of Imram 3, 115. Cascudo, *História*, p. 105. *See* Chagrin.

Apology Biting middle joint of right index with heel of hand pointing forward, hand closed. *Saudi Arabia.* Barakat, no. 155.

Assurance Tip of thumb placed at the edge of the upper front teeth and flicked out: "Pull out my tooth if I'm lying!" Sometimes combined with the Russian throat-cutting gesture. *See* FINGER, NECK, Hanging. Teeth crowned with gold were once a sign of affluence; hence the sacrifice of a tooth was tantamount to offering payment for a lie. *Russia.* Monahan, pp. 178–79.

Chagrin Moving the index laterally between the upper and lower rows of teeth while biting it lightly. 19th cent. *Palestine.* Bauer, p. 219.

Contempt "First, you place the nail of the right thumb inside the upper front teeth, . . . You then bring the thumb and enclosed fist forward in a sharp, throwing motion. While making this gesture it is permissible . . . to make a hissing noise, which can be roughly transliterated as 'Pssssst.' " *France.* Alsop, p. 27. Right thumbnail placed under tip of upper front teeth, then withdrawn rapidly, creating a noise. Arab. Goldziher, "Über Gebärden," p. 370. Fist of right hand is clenched, thumbnail inserted under upper front teeth, then snapped forward, face scornful: "Celui-là, je ne lui donnerais seulement pas ça!" ("I wouldn't give him only that!") *France.* Brault, p. 381, who quotes Randle Cotgrave (1611): "Nique, faire la: To mocke by nodding or lifting the chinne; or more properly, to threaten or defie, by putting the thumb naile into the mouth, and with a jerke (from th'upper teeth) make it to knacke." Always vulgar. *See* FINGER, Nothing. Also Anc. *Greece*. Sittl, p. 96, who draws attention to the German "nicht was schwarz unterm Nagel ist" ("not even what's black under the nail").

Embarrassment   Biting the bent index. 19th cent. *Palestine*. Bauer, p. 219.

Flirting   Thumb placed in mouth sideways and bitten, then removed and shaken. *Syria*. Barakat, no. 206.

Frustration   "But don't fret your pretty self, Mrs. Jones, for dinner passed and tea-time came, but no Jones. Mrs. Jones began to get snappish, and by ten o'clock she had bitten all the ends from her taper finger, besides dreadfully scolding the servants, all round." *U.S.* Kelly, p. 189; Taylor, p. 57.

Insult   Biting one's thumbs. *England. DEP,* p. 46. "The very offensive gesture of biting the thumb has a meaning somewhat related to that of the Shanghai Gesture, but appears never to be understood whimsically. It also differs from the Shanghai Gesture because the fingers are very rarely said to be spread. . . . In a Danish gesture described as 'pege Fingre' [to point the fingers], one thrusts the thumb into the mouth and spreads the fingers in the direction of the person to whom the gesture is addressed. Klitgaard cites this along with gestures excerpted from sixteenth- and seventeenth-century legal records, but seems to imply that 'pege Fingre' is more recent than these. However this may be, biting the thumb is an old and very famous insult, best known perhaps from the quarrel of Mercutio and Tybalt in *Romeo and Juliet*, i, i: 'Do you bite your thumb at us, sir?' 'I do bite my thumb, sir.' Sittl traces the gesture back to classical times. . . . The form of the gesture varies. It may consist in merely biting the thumb, in putting the thumb in the mouth or against the front teeth and withdrawing it with emphatic motion, or, as in the Danish example, in biting the thumb with the accompaniment of spread fingers. Urtel cites (pp. 13–14) two forms, one in which the thumb with an open perpendicular hand is drawn emphatically forward from under the chin and another in which a finger with the palm of the hand upward is similarly drawn forward. This means that the person to whom the gesture is addressed is ruined or done for. This variation of the gesture is current in Portugal, Spain, and with some modification in Italy. According to Urtel (p. 16), a gesture in which the thumb is placed against the upper teeth is widely known. He cites it from Portugal, Spain (the thumb is placed against the upper lip rather than the teeth), France, Italy, Greece and the North American Indians. . . . Biting the thumb may degenerate into meaning 'Nothing!' [see below], which may, according to the situation, be more or less insulting or may be merely a comment on a situation." *Portugal; Spain; Italy;*

France; Greece; England; Denmark; Native Americans. Taylor, *Shanghai Gesture*, pp. 54–55. Serious insult. *Italy*. Graham, p. 25. Morris et al., p. 199, cite "a seventeenth-century etiquette book, *The Rules of Civility*," which indicates that biting the thumb and flicking it out from the upper incisors may be the same gesture " 'Tis no less disrespectful to bite the nail of your thumb, by way of scorn and disdain.' " Biting the knuckle of the index. *Yugoslavia*. Axtell, *Gestures*, p. 75. * In showing the teeth, the fingers are passed over them several times: "Your teeth are rotten." *Central Africa*. Hochegger, p. 50. * The indexes of both hands are extended diagonally upward and placed over the lower lip, suggesting two long teeth sticking out. Or: Thumb and index placed on mouth and suddenly pulled upwards, suggesting extraction of a tooth. *Central Africa*. Hochegger, p. 51. *See* also FINGER, Contempt.

Luck   Placing index sideways in mouth and biting it, then removing it, shaking it vigorously: reference to luck of another person. *Lebanon; Saudi Arabia; Syria*. Barakat, no. 67.

Medico-magical   Letting the ringfinger glide over the teeth at the daily ablutions protects against toothache. *Germany*. *HDA*, II, col. 1495.

Mourning   Putting the index of one hand between the rows of teeth and letting the head sink into the palm of the other. 19th cent. *Palestine*. Bauer, p. 219.

Negation   Thumbnail against front teeth, then catapulted forward. 19th cent. *Greece; Italy*. Sittl, p. 95.

Nothing   Thumbnail placed against front teeth, then catapulted forward. 19th cent. *Greece* and *Italy*. Sittl, p. 95. * Fist raised, thumb extended, pointing with the tip to the upper teeth. *Europe; North Am*. Aubert, p. 81. * Scraping upper incisor with the thumbnail. Familiar. *France*. Mitton, p. 149. * Thumb snaps from teeth, meaning "absolutely nothing doing." *France*. Life Photos by David Scherman, *Life,* Sept. 16, 1946, p. 12. Thumb placed under the upper incisor, then rapidly flicked forwards. Southern *France*. Critchley, p. 91. *Spain*. Blasco Ibáñez, p. 29. Putting tip of nail of the right thumb to the upper teeth and flicking thumb forward. Arab. Goldziher, "Über Gebärden," p. 370. *See* Insult, and FINGER, Nothing.

Oath   "And they [the Saracens] put their fingers to their teeth—cut them to pieces after that and they would not lie." Medieval Muslims. *Chevalerie Vivien*, Ms. B, 1. 215–216.

Pain   Biting fingers. 13th–14th cent. *Italy*. Dante, *Inf.*, c. xxxiii; 19th cent. Naples; southern *Italy*. De Jorio, p. 265; 19th cent. *Italy*. Bresciani, *L'ebreo*, c. li. 19th cent. *Spain*. Sittl, p. 18 n. 10.

Pensiveness   Biting fingernails. 16th cent. *France*. Rabelais, Bk. v, ch. 20; Cascudo, *História*, p. 105.

Poverty   Putting thumbnail against one of the upper teeth and catapulting the hand forward. 19th cent. *Palestine*. Bauer, p. 221.

Regret   Index of the right hand lightly grasped by the teeth. *Central Africa*. Hochegger, p. 164. *See* also FINGER, LIP, Regret.

Reminder   If one has forgotten or overlooked something one should bite one's finger three times, so that one sees the traces on it. Bohemia, *Czech Republic*. *HDA*, II, col. 1485.

Secrecy   Biting the index. *Russia*. F. Bowers, p. 98.

Threat   Biting the thumb. *Germany*. *HDA*, col. 331–32; Kleinpaul, p. 176. * Biting right index placed sideways into mouth. *Egypt; Saudi Arabia*. Barakat, no. 125. *See* Insult.

Warning   To indicate to another driver that a traffic policeman is following, one may bite the ends of the three middle fingers. *Mexico*. Kany, p. 121. * Tip of index placed between upper and lower teeth; thumb slightly bent under the index, other fingers closed in a loose fist. The gesture assumes complicity: it signals awareness of another person's knowledge of a criminal act committed by the gesturer, who thus silently commands that person to "bite his tongue." Prevalent only among criminals. *Russia*. Monahan, pp. 98–99.

FINGER, WRIST

Greeting   "The salutation between Mr. Weller and his friends was strictly confined to the freemasonry of the craft [coachmen], consisting of a jerking round of the right wrist, and a tossing of the little finger into the air at the same time." 19th cent. *England*. Dickens, *Pickwick*, II, p. 247.

FINGERNAIL

Desperation   "She, desperate, with her nails her flesh doth tear." 16th–17th cent. *England*. Shakesp., *Lucr.*, 739.

Displeasure   Tapping thumbnails together as if applauding with the thumbnails is a form of ironical applause indicating displeasure. *Netherlands*. Axtell, *Gestures*, p. 145.

Disbelief   *See* FINGER, Disbelief.

Evasiveness   " 'What you mean,' said Vic bitterly, 'is that by selling off Pringle's now, you can show a profit on this year's accounts at the next AGM.' Stuart Baxter examined his nails, and said nothing." *England*. Lodge, *Nice Work*, 365.

Insult   Rubbing or pressing thumbnails together. *Spain*. Flachskampf, p. 234.

Nothing   *See* FINGER, Nothing.

Obstinacy   Thumbnails rubbed together as though squashing fleas indicates that someone is obstinate. The origin appears to be a European tale of a woman with a flea, whose obstinacy became proverbial in the 13th century. *Portugal*. Cascudo, *História*, p. 103.

Self-satisfaction   "The fingernails are first breathed upon and then rubbed against the right coat lapel—I congratulate myself." *Italy*. Graham, p. 26.

Vengeance   *See* FINGER, Vengeance.

FINGERNAIL, HAND

Blessing   Cupping hands and scanning fingernails while reciting benediction over lighted *havdala*-candle symbolic of pleasure from light, or of distinction between light and darkness reflected from fingernails to palm, and thus the end of the Sabbath. Jews. Kolatch, p. 180.

Ignorance   Fingernails of the closed fingers of one hand rub the heel of the hand as they move repeatedly and energetically outward. Río de la Plata region of *Argentina; Uruguay*. Meo Zilio, p. 76. Implies Indifference. *Italy*. Ibid.

Indifference   *See* Ignorance.

FINGERNAIL, LIP

Blessing   On completing the Sign of the Cross, kissing thumbnail. Rome, *Italy; Portugal; Brazil* after 17th cent. Cascudo, *História*, p. 75.

Resignation   Licking one's fingernails, Portuguese (Brazilian) "lamba as unhas," is derived from a popular exorcism formula of the 16th cent. Isabel Davila, accusing Mecia Roiz to the Holy Office in Salvador in Nov. 1591, stated: "I frequently saw Mecia Roiz habitually lick the fingers of both her hands whenever she heard of someone having had a miscarriage; upon asking her why she did this, she never answered." Cited from *Denunciações da Bahia*, São Paulo 1925, by Cascudo, *História*, p. 229. The gesture is no longer current; the allusion to it is part of Brazilian oral tradition. It is probably related to the Roman gesture of kissing the thumbnail after the Lord's Prayer, which is customary among Christian matrons and was current among the Roman aristocracy of the 16th cent. Cascudo, ibid.

FINGERNAIL, TOOTH (*See also*) also FINGER, TOOTH

Admiration   Thumbnail rapidly bitten by incisors indicates admiration for a culinary performance. "Delicious!" *Brazil*. Cascudo, *História*, p. 169.

Anger   Biting nails. Anc. *Rome*; 19th cent. *Italy*. Sittl, pp. 17–18.

Anxiety   Biting nails. *Germany*. Photo argus/Mike Schröder, *Die Zeit*, No. 22, May 22, 1992, p. 84.

Chagrin   "another gnawed his fingers, as he stalked across the room." 18th cent. *England*. Smollett, *Peregrine Pickle*, ch. lxix.

Concentration (nervous)   Biting nails. Anc. *Rome*. Sittl, p. 18.

Contempt   *See* FINGER, TOOTH, Contempt.

Desire   Biting nails. Anc. *Rome*. Sittl, p. 18.

Embarrassment   Biting nails. Anc. *Rome*. Sittl, p. 18.

Forgetfulness   *See* Embarrassment.
Frustration   *See* FINGER, TOOTH, Frustration.
Insult   *See* FINGER, TOOTH, Insult.
Jealousy   Biting nails. Anc. *Rome.* Sittl, p. 18.
Negation   *See* also FINGER, TOOTH, Negation. Biting nail of right thumb, then quickly protruding the hand. Women. Aleppo, *Syria.* Goldziher, "Über Gebärden," p. 379.
Nothing   Nail of right thumb catapulted off the upper incisor. *Spain.* Flachskampf, p. 233. 19th cent. southern *Italy.* De Jorio, p. 231. Arab. Goldziher, "Über Gebärden," p. 370. *Portugal.* Urtel, p. 15. Anc. *Greece* and *Rome.* Sittl, pp. 95ff. *See* also FINGER, TOOTH, Nothing.
Oath   Saracens swore by tapping fingernail against teeth. Medieval Islam. Grimm, *DRA*, II, p. 550.
Poverty   Flick right thumbnail on front teeth: "I have no money" or "I have only a little." *Jordan; Lebanon; Saudi Arabia; Syria.* Barakat, no. 97. *See* also FINGER, TOOTH, Poverty.
Sorrow   Biting nails. Anc. *Rome.* Sittl, p. 18.
Tension   Biting fingernails. *Germany.* Photo argus/Mike Schröder, *Die Zeit*, No. 22, May 22, 1992, p. 84.

FOOT
Adoration   Taking off shoes in entering sacred place. 19th cent. *Palestine.* Bauer, p. 192.
Anger   "The girl stamped her foot violently on the floor as she vented this threat." 19th cent. *England.* Dickens, *Oliver Twist*, p. 142. Stamping the feet. Anc. *Rome.* Sittl, pp. 14–16. "Let go my hand!—stamping with her pretty foot: How dare you, Sir!" Richardson, iv. "Stamp, rave, and fret." 16th–17th cent. *England.* Shakesp., III *Henry VI* 1.4.91. " 'Damn you,' Gombauld repeated, and stamped his foot again." *England.* Huxley, ch. 21. * "Mr. Weller—quite transfixed at his presumption, led him by the collar to the corner and dismissed him with a harmless but ceremonious kick." 19th cent. *England.* Dickens, *Pickwick*, II, p. 483. Kicking. *U.S.* Krout, p. 23. * Trample. Biblical. *Middle East.* Isa., 63:3. * Tapping floor with the foot. *Lat. Am.* Kany, p. 64. * Standing up. *Portugal.* ("cresce"—"he grows" i.e. he attacks). Basto, p. 6. * Stamping the right foot—"I'm annoyed!" "I refuse!" *Central Africa.* Hochegger, p. 78.
Apotropy   In some villages of Brandenburg, the newly married couple must step over an axe or a horseshoe on the way home. *Germany.* Beitl, p. 163.
Approval   Stamping feet at basketball game. College students. California, *U.S.* McCord, p. 292.
Attention   "I sat down before [the bench] and knock'd with my

foot, a boy came presently, and I bad him fetch me a pint of warm ale."
17th cent. *England.* Defoe, II, p. 13.

Blessing   Gods as well as priests bless with the lotus-anointed foot.
Hindu. Ohm, p. 321.

Contempt   Kicking with heels. Anc. *Rome.* Sittl, pp. 106–07.
Stroking the ground with one's foot several times as if to trample some-
thing that one has thrown away. 19th cent. Naples, southern *Italy.* De
Jorio, p. 131. * Moving the foot as if administering kicks. Used particularly in speaking of someone absent. 19th cent. Naples, southern *Italy.*
De Jorio, ibid. * Treading on an imperial coin was prohibited in ancient
Rome. Vita Beati Stephani; Sittl, pp. 107–08. Treading on sacred
ground. The Greeks complained that the Turks trod on the ground of
Sta. Sophia at the conquest of Constantinople. *Byzantine Empire.* Also
anc. *Rome.* Sittl, p. 108. Treading the cross. It was prohibited to portray
a cross among decorations on the floor. Early Christian. *Cod. Justin.* I,
8; Sittl, p. 108. The Huguenots trod upon crosses and sacred images.
17th cent. *France.* Holzwarth, p. 167. In Prud., *Peristephanon* 3, 74
Eulalia threatens: "Idola protero sub pedibus" ("I tread the idols with
my feet"). Early Christian. Sittl, p. 108. Treading on someone or something by jumping, e.g., a grave. Anc. *Greece.* Eurip., *El.* 327f.; Sittl, p.
108. Treading on recumbent person, living or dead. Anc. *Rome.* Sittl, p.
107. 17th cent. *Spain.* Cervantes *Don Quijote*, I, ch. xvi. Victor sets foot
or knee on the body of the vanquished. 18th cent. *Austria.* Balthasar
Permoser, *Apotheosis of Prince Eugene of Savoy* (1718–21). Lower Belvedere, Vienna. Trampling on defeated enemy. *Mesopotamia. Stele of
Naram Sin.* 23rd cent. B.C. Paris, Louvre. 15th cent. *Italy.* Filippino
Lippi, Thomas Aquinas trampling on Averroes in *St. Thomas confound-
ing the Heretics* (1489–93). Rome, Sta. Maria sopra Minerva. Detail in
Gombrich, p. 70, fig. 50.

Denial   The Portuguese expression "negar de pés juntos" ("to deny
with feet together," i.e., to deny in no uncertain terms) is derived from
an older gesture of putting the feet together, heels touching, in order to
swear an oath to legitimate authority. The expression now implies the
stubborn denial of an evident truth. Cascudo, *História*, p. 223.

Depart   Kicking as if kicking a ball is a command to someone to
leave. Men. Rude, often comic. *Colombia; U.S.* Saitz and Cervenka, p.
81. Particularly toward dogs. *Netherlands.* Andrea and de Boer, p. 119.

Determination   "and beating his foot upon the ground, as a man
who is determined to deny everything." 19th cent. *England.* Dickens,
Oliver Twist, p. 460.

Displeasure   Kicking seats in theater with heels. Anc. *Rome.* Sittl,
p. 65. * Deputies to parliament sometimes trampled on or chopped up
unpopular bills. 17th cent. *Poland.* Bogucka, p. 200. * Stamping on the
floor in a theater. *Brazil.* Cascudo, *História*, p. 242.

Embarrassment Shuffling the feet. *U.S.* Birdwhistell, *Introduction*, pp. 30, 34. Also Anc. *Greece* and *Rome*. Sittl, p. 48. "Everyone muttered disclaimers and shifted from one foot to the other." *U.S.* Carkeet, p. 238.

Emphasis In classical antiquity it was common to patter with the feet during religious song. Early Christian. Paulus Energeticos. Ohm, p. 321.

Engagement Bridegroom brings bride a shoe; as soon as she has put it on, she is considered to be subject to his authority. 6th cent. *France*. Gregory of Tours, xvi. Medieval *Iceland. Vilkinasaga,* c. 61.

Etiquette Men rise from a sitting position in the presence of a lady. 13th cent. *Germany. Kudrun,* st. 342, 1. Messengers rise when delivering a message. 13th cent. *Germany. Kudrun,* st. 768, 1–2. * Clicking the heels together, accompanied by a slight bow [Editors' note: this was the rule for middle and upper class men before World War II to signify "at your service" and in greeting ladies and superiors]. *Germany; Austria*. It is no longer common, except in parody of Prussian manners. Axtell, *Gestures*, p. 109. In general, standing with heels together and toes pointing out at a slight angle suggests the military stance of attention and therefore suggests attentiveness and respect. Axtell, ibid.

Fatigue Dragging the feet. *U.S.* Krout, p. 22.

Fear Stepping back. *U.S.* Krout, p. 22. Jumping up from sitting position. Anc. *Greece* and *Rome*. Sittl, p. 14.

Femininity Standing with feet close together and one toe pointed inward. Narrow stances are regarded universally as feminine. Axtell, *Gestures*, p. 109. *See* Masculinity.

Finished Termination of affair: kick (not made in presence of former partner). *Colombia*. Saitz and Cervenka, p. 137.

Greeting Removing a slipper when greeting ceremoniously. *Japan.* Eichler, p. 159. * Islanders take a person's hand or foot and rub it over their face as greeting. *Philippines*. Eichler, p. 162. "In the straits of the Sound . . . it is customary to raise the left foot of the person greeted, pass it gently over the right leg, and then over the face." *Philippines*. Eichler, ibid. * Natives bend very low, raising one foot in the air with the knee bent. (They also place their hands on their cheeks in saluting a friend.) *Philippines*. Eichler, ibid. * Among the people of Arakan it is still the custom to remove the sandals in the street and the stockings in the house as sign of greeting. *Burma (Myanmar)*. Eichler, p. 159.

Impatience "I even stamped with impatience!" 18th cent. *England*. Richardson, II, p. 277. " 'Do you hear me?' cried Nancy, stamping her foot on the ground." 19th cent. *England*. Dickens, *Oliver Twist*, p. 417. " 'Come in!' he cried impatiently, stamping his foot upon the ground." 19th cent. *England*. Dickens, ibid., p. 344. * Both feet alternating stamping on the ground. *Central Africa*. Hochegger, p. 91. * Tapping foot several times on ground. Arms may be akimbo or folded across chest. *Colombia; U.S.* Saitz and Cervenka, p. 73.

Insult "To keep on one's shoes on entering a friend's home or the temple was bad manners." Anc. *Middle East.* Bouquet, p. 144. * Showing the sole of one's foot is an insult, therefore one should not cross one's legs. *Japan.* Prelutsky p. 7. Showing the sole of one's foot to another person. *Thailand.* Axtell, *Gestures*, p. 11; *Saudi Arabia; Egypt; Singapore.* Axtell, ibid., p. 106. * Pointing one's feet in the direction of another person is a serious insult. *Middle East; Thailand.* Greenberg, L4; Axtell, *Gestures*, p. 107. * It is advisable not to sit cross-legged, since it would show the sole of one's shoe to another person, which is an insult. *Egypt.* Axtell, *Gestures*, p. 160.

Investiture In some ecclesiastical courts-leet the lord, on the occasion of an investiture, stepped with his right foot upon that of the vassal. Medieval *Germany.* Grimm, *DRA*, I, p. 196. *See also* Submission and FOOT, HAND, Submission.

Joy Stamping with the feet. Biblical. *Middle East. Ezek.*, 25:6.

Luck Entering a building, right foot first. Anc. *Rome; Brazil.* Cascudo, *História*, p. 143.

Magical On St. Andrews' night one is to turn around barefoot upon the threshold, thereafter one will see one's future beloved. Thuringia, *Germany. ZV,* V (1895), p. 97. * Stepping on one's foot, looking over the shoulder to see spirits. *Germany.* Bolte and Polivka, II, p. 320, n. 1 and p. 518, n. 1. * The temporary king must stand on one foot during a ceremony in order to win a victory over evil spirits. *Siam.* Frazer, *Golden Bough*, IV, p. 150. * The *Pontificale Romanum* prescribes that the candidate for confirmation is to place his foot upon the right foot of the sponsor. Roman Catholic. *HDA*, III, col. 246. The custom of stepping upon someone's foot in order to obtain his supernatural powers such as seeing spirits, flying, hearing over great distances, also occurs in *Denmark; France; Corsica; Greece*, southern Slavs; Celtic belief. *HDA*, III, col. 244–45. The oldest (German) mention of this gesture occurs in a poem of the Stricker. 13th cent. *Germany. HDA*, III, col. 243.

Masculinity Standing with feet apart. In general, a wide stance is universally regarded as masculine. Axtell, *Gestures*, p. 109. *See* Femininity.

Medico-magical A strong man should place his bare foot upon a person suffering a stroke and remain in this position for some time. *Germany. HDA*, III, col. 850. In a charm of the 11th to 12th century it is advised that one step on the right foot of a horse suffering from stiffness of the limbs. *Germany. HDA*, III, col. 245. "Dextro pede" ("with the right foot") was used by Juvenal (10, 5) almost in the sense of "feliciter" ("lucky"). Anc. *Rome.* Boehm, p. 27f. King Sancho of Castile set his foot on the throat of a patient. Medieval *Spain*. Bloch, pp. 151–52, 155. Pyrrhus "could cure the spleen by sacrificing a white cock and gently pressing with his right foot on the spleen of the persons as they lay down on their backs." Anc. *Rome*. Plutarch, *Pyrrh*. 468–69.

Mourning Go barefooted and bareheaded. Biblical. *Middle East. Ezek*. 24:16.17; *Mic*. 3:7. Bare feet were part of the Roman mourning ritual. Anc. *Rome*. *HDA*, II, col. 850.

Oath Stepping on a cut up sacrificial animal when taking oath. Anc. *Greek*. Sittl, p. 143. * A cross made with the foot on the ground is an oath not to return to a certain place. 19th cent. Naples, southern *Italy*. De Jorio, p. 170. * The Saxons of Siebenbürgen swore in cases of boundary disputes with bare feet, loosened belt, and a lump of earth upon their heads. 14th cent. *Hungary*. Kahle, p. 116.

Pain Stamping foot on ground. 19th cent. *Italy*. Bresciani, *L'ebreo*, c. xlviii.

Possession In claiming a plot of land, the right foot must be placed upon it. Medieval *Germany*. Grimm, *DRA*, I, p. 197.

Prayer Standing in prayer. Ethiopian Hosannah liturgy. *Ethiopia*. Löfgren, p. 81. In general standing is the prayer posture in oriental Christian liturgy. Ohm, p. 326. * The Romans ascended to the temple by starting with the right foot; a remnant of this is probably the custom that the priest in the Roman liturgy ascends to the altar with the right foot first. Anc. *Rome*. Ohm, p. 304. Stepping up to pray. Awesta. 4th cent. B.C. Northwestern *Iran*. Bartholmae, p. 102; Biblical. *Middle East. Ex*. 24:1f.; 3 *Cor*. 19:11; Ohm, p. 304. * Kneeling as symbolic of original sin is inappropriate during Easter in the Roman liturgy, therefore one stands; similarly during the reading of the Gospel at Mass. Roman Catholic. Ohm, pp. 326–27. Standing as prayer posture. *Sumer*. Also Brahmins, *India*; anc. Jews. Ohm, p. 324. * Taking off shoes before praying or entering a mosque. Muslim. Wächter, pp. 23f. Greek temple inscriptions require the taking off of shoes. Anc. *Greece*. Anrich, pp. 200f. At the offering of sacrifice Greeks and Romans went unshod; Roman women prayed "nudis pedibus" for rain. Anc. *Greece* and *Rome*. Wächter, p. 23f.; Petron., *Sat*. 44. Taking off shoes while praying to the sun. *Peru*. Heiler, p. 104.

Refusal Relinquishment of property is symbolized by taking off a shoe. Medieval *Germany*. Grimm, *DRA*, I, p. 215. Also Biblical. *Middle East. Ruth* 4:7; *Deut*. 25:9.

Rejection In baptism of a former heathen, after the formula for rejection of heathen deities has been pronounced, the neophyte places his foot upon that of his godfather (see also Magical). Medieval *Germany*. Grimm, *DRA*, I, p. 197.

Respect "The taking off of shoes is a very practical gesture, but it also means to a Middle Eastern guest that he is disarming himself, showing respect, and making himself similar to the host, who himself is shoeless. A milder version of this takes place when guests arrive at our houses and wipe their shoes on a mat . . ." *Middle East.* Visser, 111. Everyone who approaches the royal presence bares his feet. *Persia.* Eichler, p. 159. Considered courteous to take the sandals off before entering the house of a stranger. Damaras, *South Africa.* Anderson, p. 231. Similarly *Morocco.* Dawson, p. 97.

Submission Falling before a person's feet. 16th–17th cent. *England.* Shakesp., *Love's Lab. Lost* 4.1.92; *Richard II* 1.1.165; *King John* 5.4.13. * Bride mounts ram representing husband over whom she asserts superiority. She hangs on it a necklace to make him weak, and when ram has been killed she puts her right foot on its stomach. *Morocco.* James, pp. 60–61. * "I had read in a Hebrew book of an approved plan by which one spouse might secure lordship over the other for life. One was to tread on the other's foot at the marriage ceremony; and if both hit on the stratagem, the first to succeed would retain the upper hand. Jews. 18th cent. *Poland.* Maimon, ch. x. Also 13th cent. *Germany.* Bastow, pp. 318–19. Shoes sent by one king to another, less powerful king, had to be put on the latter's feet as sign of submission. Medieval *Norway.* Du Cange, s.v. calceamenta; Grimm, *DRA*, I, p. 215. *See* FOOT, HAND, Submission.

Vanity Looking at one's feet. Medieval *France. Chevaliers as deus espees*, 2726. 13th cent. *Germany.* Thomas von Circlaria, 433.

Victory Setting foot upon the vanquished. Medieval *Germany.* Grimm, *DRA*, I, p. 196. St. Radegund, having exorcised the Devil from a woman's body, "had trampled his head underfoot." 6th cent. *France.* Venantius Fortunatus, *Vita sanctae Radegundis* 71; see also De Nie, p. 27. St. Radegund, having exorcised the Devil from a woman's body, it came out in form of a worm, and "she related that she had been liberated by [the saint's] grinding that very worm underfoot." Ibid., p. 30. A coin from the reign of Valentinian III (425–455) commemorates Aetius' victory over Attila on the Catalaunian (correctly the Mauriacan) Fields between Troyes and Châlons-sur-Marne (451) by showing Aetius with one foot raised over the head of Attila. 5th cent. Western *Roman Empire.* Wolfram, p. 20, plate 15. Shakesp., *Cor.* 1.3.49; *Cymb.* 3.2.92. *See also* Magical, Rejection, Submission. * In touching the neck, one says: "Aqui não se bota o pé!" ("No one puts a foot here!") *Brazil.* Cascudo, *História*, p. 93, who also refers to the Old Testament.

FOOT, HAND

Blessing Girl stands on one foot, cakes in lap and a cup of brandy in right hand for blessing flax crop. *Prussia.* Frazer, *Golden Bough*, IV, p. 156.

Contempt Foot placed on spear as sign of disdain of death. Simultaneously, hand placed to chin. Anc. *Rome*. Livy. Sittl, p. 196.

Forgetfulness Right hand placed on forehead: "I forgot!" *Central Africa*. Hochegger, p. 114.

Impatience Open hands shaken in front of chest or above the head, while feet stamp on the ground: "Combien de temps encore?" ("How much longer?") *Central Africa*. Hochegger, p. 91.

Joy "then there was a great clapping of hands, and stamping of feet, and flourishing of handkerchiefs; to all of which manifestations of delight" 19th cent. *England*. Dickens, *Pickwick*, II, p. 71.

Medico-magical "A gesture . . . restricted to women . . . is performed when one or both legs have become numb . . . [It] consists of wetting the thumb of one hand with saliva and drawing a sign of the cross on the instep of the foot. . . . In urban Spain, the gesture is performed in the privacy of one's home; in rural areas, the movement is doubtless more publicly observable." *Spain*. Green, p. 93.

Submission "A 'polluting' stranger in one's house needs to be incorporated and . . . 'made to feel at home.' . . . Guests must do everything to reassure their hosts that they bear nothing but good will, and a determination to subordinate themselves to them while they are under their roof. . . . In Japan or the Middle East, one takes off one's shoes. Outside the house is dirt, and leaving shoes at the door not only respects cleanliness, but also ritually recognizes the sacrality of 'inside.' In the past, when people usually walked to where they were going. . . . guests had their feet washed by the host or the host's servant on arrival." *Japan; Middle East*. Visser, p. 110. * If the bride is to rule the household, when her hands are joined to those of the groom, hers must lie on top, her left foot must be on top of his, and she must rise first after kneeling at the altar. *Germany*. Beitl, p. 163. *See also* FOOT, Submission. * Hands of the vassal are folded before his standing lord, vassal kneels before his sitting lord. In the latter case the vassal laid his hands upon the feet of his lord. Medieval *Germany*. Grimm, *DRA*, I, p. 193.

FOOT, HAND, HEAD

Greeting Bowing, touching feet and raising hand to head. Son to parents, pupils to teachers, laymen to religious heads. Hindu. *India*. Thomas, p. 80.

FOOT, HAND, LIP

Homage Kissing feet and hands of dead emperors and bishops. Anc. *Rome*; early Christian. Sittl, p. 170. * Soldiers and common people voluntarily kiss Otho's hand at his election as well as after his death, whereas the upper classes objected to being required to kiss hands or feet of Caligula or Domitian. Anc. *Rome*. Suetonius, *Caligula* 56; *Domitian*. 12; Tacitus, *Hist*. 1, 45. 2, 49. Sittl, p. 167.

FOOT, LEG
Determination Kicking oneself on the shins. Boys. *England*. Opie, p. 230.
Flirting "When a woman sits with legs crossed, one foot curled, it often indicates she's interested in a nearby man." *U.S*. Birdwhistell, "Do Gestures Speak Louder than Words?", p. 56.
Joy Stamping on the ground with joy. Anc. *Greece* and *Rome*. Sittl, p. 12.
Nervousness "young girl changes stance and exhibits restless behavior when a breeze ruffles a lock of her hair." *U.S*. Birdwhistell, *Introduction*, p. 8.
Prayer Legs folded under body with right foot on left thigh, left on right thigh. "Lotus position." Buddhist. Critchley, p. 68. * Stamping on the ground accompanies address to powers of the nether world. Anc. *Greece* and *Rome*. Sittl, p. 191.

FOOT, LIP
Adoration As modest request Phaedra wishes to kiss the foot of Hippolyte. Anc. *Rome*. Sittl, p. 166. Kissing of feet. Lienhard Scherhauff, *Adoration of the Magi* (1450/60). Lower Belvedere, Vienna.
Gratitude Kissing the foot of a person. Anc. *Rome*. Sittl, p. 170, n. 1. Kissing the foot of the Ethiopian king. Sittl, ibid.
Greeting Diocletian required senators and other dignitaries to kiss his foot at their reception and their departure. Anc. *Rome*. Sittl, p. 170. Relatives of emperors had to kiss the imperial foot. *Roman Empire*. Sittl, p. 170, n. 1. At the end of the Empire, arrivals were heartily greeted by kissing their feet. *Roman Empire*. Sittl, p. 170. Kissing the feet of their parents was expected of children during the 17th cent. when leaving or returning home. *Poland*. Bogucka, p. 198. *See also* LIP, Greeting.
Homage The younger Maximinus had his feet kissed. *Roman Empire*. Sittl, p. 169. Emperor Tiberius II kissed the foot of Pope Constantinus. *Roman Empire*. Sittl, p. 170. Since the Germanic invasions of the Roman empire, the kissing of the foot obtains only if a cross sanctifies the shoe. *Roman Empire*. Sittl, p. 170. Kissing the foot. Anc. *Persia* since Cyrus; Punic; Biblical. *Middle East. Isaiah*, 49, 23; *Luke*, 7, 38. Sittl, p. 169. Caligula and Domitian had their feet kissed (see Greeting above). *Roman Empire*. Sittl, ibid.
Plea Slaves and clients kiss the feet of their masters. Anc. *Rome*. Sittl, p. 169. Lover kisses foot of beloved. Anc. *Rome*. Sittl, ibid.
Respect Kissing feet and hands of dead emperors and bishops. *Roman Empire*. Sueton. *Otho*, 12; *Vita S. Hucberti, c. 13, p. 66*. Early

Christian. Sittl, p. 170. Kissing feet of a dignitary. *Saudi Arabia*. Barakat, no. 121. *See also* LIP, Humility.

Submission "I will kiss thy foot." 16th–17th cent. *England*. Shakesp., *Tempest* 2.2.153; *Love's Lab. Lost* 4.1.86. *See also* LIP, Submission.

FOREHEAD *See also* EYEBROW

Concentration "Contract and purse thy brow together, as if thou then hadst shut up in thy brain some horrible conceit." 16th–17th cent. *England*. Shakesp., *Othello* 3.3.13. * Scratching forehead. *U.S.* Krout, p. 25.

Disapproval Frown. Biblical. *Middle East*. I *Sam*. 3:13. 14th cent.-present. *England*. *OED*, p. 572.

Homage Falling to earth and striking forehead to the ground. *Egypt*. Eichler, p. 95.

Submission Greek orthodox secular clergy touch forehead to the ground three times before the metropolitan. Eastern *Europe*. Sittl, p. 160, n. 4.

FOREHEAD, HAND

Affection Stroking children's forehead. 19th cent. *Japan*. Sittl, p. 33, n. 11.

Anger "I recollect, as I passed by one of the pierglasses, that I saw in it his clenched hand offered in wrath to his forehead." 18th cent. *England*. Richardson, IV, p. 173.

Awareness Palm of hand struck against forehead. ("Oh! I forgot!") *France*. Mitton, p. 146. * Fingers of both hands on both sides of forehead. *France*. Life Photos by David Scherman, *Life*, Sept. 16, 1946, p. 12.

Concentration Thumb edge of hand placed to eyebrows or forehead. Anc. *Rome*. Baumeister, I, p. 589. * Hand rubs forehead. 19th cent. *Italy*. Bresciani, *Edmondo*, ch. v. Sittl, p. 47. *See also* HAND, Concentration.

Confusion "[Miriam] seemed bewildered, and pressed her hand upon her brow." 19th cent. *U.S.* Hawthorne, ch. xiii.

Crazy Palm of hand placed on someone's forehead—"you're crazy." *Netherlands*. Andrea and de Boer, p. 47.

Despair Beating the forehead. Anc. *Greece* and *Rome*; *Italy*. Bresciani, *L'ebreo*, ch. xlix; Sittl, p. 21.

Dismay "She gave herself a great slap on the forehead, like one who hears a dreadful piece of news." 15th cent. *Spain*. Rojas, vi.

Emphasis Fingers extended, heel of palm strikes forehead. "El es / esta el mas" ("It's the most"). *Colombia*. Saitz and Cervenka, p. 46.

Fever   Flat right hand placed on forehead. *Central Africa.* Hochegger, p. 201.

Greeting   A careless salute as greeting. College students. California, *U.S.* McCord, p. 290.

Hot   Hand, fingers extended, palm to forehead, moves across forehead, then is shaken out once. Hot weather or discomfort. *U.S.* Saitz and Cervenka, p. 72.

Intelligence   "If he placed his forefinger to his forehead, he was saying 'That's a bright girl, quite intelligent.' But if he struck his forehead with the side of his outstretched hand, the message changed to 'She's pazza! Crazy!' " *Italy.* Graham, p. 26.

Pain   Hand (palm) placed on forehead. Anc. *Greece* and *Rome.* Baumeister, I, p. 588.

Plea   A supplicant for protection, sitting, puts forehead on his hands, which are on his knees. Anc. *Greece.* Sittl, p. 173.

Reconciliation   "a khaki-shirted man suddenly stepped forward and fired three pistol shots into Gandhi's chest and abdomen. 'Ram! Ram!' ('God! God!') the Mahatma whispered, touching his palm to his forehead in a gesture of forgiveness to his assassin. Then he crumpled to the ground." *India.* Review of S. Wolpert, *Nine Hours to Rama.* In *Newsweek*, March 19, 1962, p. 121.

Relief   Mopping the brow. ("The exam was difficult.") College students. California, *U.S.* McCord, p. 291.

Reminder   " 'Ah' said the invalid, passing his hand across his forehead; 'Hutley—Hutley—let me see.' He seemed endeavoring to collect his thoughts" Dickens, Pickwick, I, p. 44. * Slapping forehead with extended fingers of right hand. *Argentina.* Kaulfers, p. 253. * Placing extended fingers of one hand on forehead in effort to remember. *Colombia; U.S.* Saitz and Cervenka, p. 87. * Slapping the forehead with the fingers of one hand or with the base of the palm of the open hand. *Spain; Lat. Am.* Green, pp. 63–64; *U.S.* Saitz and Cervenka, p. 46. "Snapping the fingers—the standard American gesture associated with recall—is rarely observed in this social context in Spain." Green, ibid. * Sudden intuition or recall is expressed by fingertips of both hands slapping forehead sharply. *France.* The corresponding American gesture is snapping one's fingers. *North America.* Brault, p. 380.

Surprise   Striking the forehead. Anc. *Rome.* Sittl, p. 21. 15th cent. *Spain.* Rojas, vi; 17th cent. *Spain.* Cervantes, *Don Quijote*, I, prol. * Striking forehead with palm of right hand, head moving back as hand makes contact: expression of surprise or one's own stupidity. *Jordan; Lebanon; Saudi Arabia; Syria.*

Barakat, no. 29.

FOREHEAD, HAND, NECK, NOSE

Insult   "When low city rascals meet a superior on the road and wish to insult him with a pretence of respect they do not salam in the ordinary way but bring the hand up to the nose, then to the forehead and then to the neck, rubbing these parts of the body as if they felt itchy." 19th cent. *India*. Chauvé, p. 125; Taylor, p. 33.

FOREHEAD, HEAD

Assurance   Head raised, brows lowered, firm glance. *Europe; North America*. Aubert, p. 113.

FOREHEAD, KNEE

Prayer   Pure proskynesis with forehead touched to the ground. Anc. Roman territories in *Middle East*. Sittl, p. 179. Biblical. *Middle East*. Matth. 26:39.

FOREHEAD, LIP

Affection   Kiss on forehead. Anc. *Greece* and *Rome*. Sittl, p. 40.

Anger   "His mouth was drawn down and his upper face was pulled into a tight frown." *U.S.* Birdwhistell, "Background," p. 14.

Greeting   Man kisses woman on forehead; son kisses mother on lips or forehead, girls kiss older woman on forehead. *Saudi Arabia*. Barakat, no. 141.

Respect   Kissing a person's forehead, nose, feet or right hand. *Saudi Arabia*. Barakat, no. 115.

FOREHEAD, MOUTH

Dislike   Mouth closed, corners of the mouth drawn down, forehead wrinkled. *Central Africa*. Hochegger, p. 8.

GENITALS

Apotropy   Touching one's genitals through the holes in one's pockets. *Germany*. *HDA*, II, col. 334. Touching one's genitals against the evil eye. *Italy; Greece; Russia*. *HDA*, III, col. 731. Phallus gestures do not seem to appear in Germany. Meschke, col. 330. * Baring the cunnus of a menstruating woman against hail and storm. Anc. *Rome*. Pliny, *Nat. hist.*, 28, 7, 23. * Baring male or female genitalia against the evil eye, transferred to phallic amulets. Anc. *Rome*. Jahn, pp. 66ff., 72ff.; Sittl, p. 122; Seligmann, II, p. 200–07. See Fig. 13. Seligmann, II, p. 276, fig. 192. A phallus was suspended under the chariot of a triumphant general. Anc. *Rome*. Pliny, *Nat hist.*, 28, 7. On an Etruscan lamp in the Würzburg collection are two phalli. Sittl, p. 128, n. 1. (Cf. making the Sign of the Cross when lamps are lit).

Contempt   "They must not be sent away without a cup of good Christmas ale, for fear they should p-ss behind the door." 17th cent. *England*. Swift, p. 148.

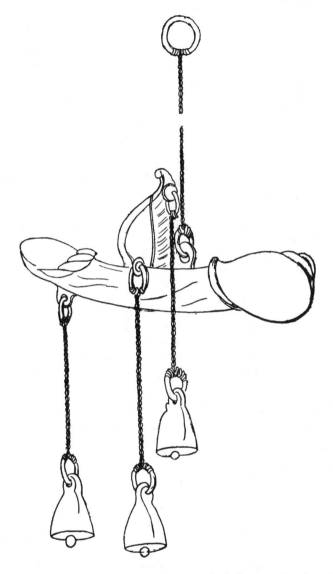

Fig. 13. Apotropaic phallus with bells. From S. Seligmann, *Der böse Blick* (Berlin: H. Barsdorf, 1910) II, 277.

Insult   Showing phallus to women. Anc. *Greece*. Sittl, p. 100. *See also* Mockery.

Medico-magical   Pressing the left testicle against stomach ache. South Slavic. *HDA*, III, col. 731. * Urinating on the ground or on a grave. Originated in *Middle East* (*Mardrus* vi), became common in anc. *Rome*, where it was prohibited in cemeteries. Persius, in his first Satire, recalls the prohibition against urinating in sacred precincts by an altar inscription. Statues showed a similar prohibition: "Damnati sunt eo tempore qui urinam eo loco facerunt" ("Henceforth those who urinate here are damned").

Mockery   Persian and Spartan women bared their genitalia to fleeing warriors, asking them if they wanted to take refuge in their bodies. Anc. *Greece; Persia*. Sittl, p. 104. Women travelling on the Nile mocked those on the shore similarly. Anc. *Egypt*. Sittl, ibid. For the gesture of exposing genitals in mockery in medieval art, see Mellinkoff, *Outcasts*, I, pp. 205–08. * "When the crowd hooted at a bullfighter . . . because of unsatisfactory performance, he insulted them by touching his trousers at the crotch." *Mexico*. Hayes, p. 309. Teofilo Braga (1843–1924), future president of the Portuguese Republic, was observed urinating at the journalist Antoniô Rodrigues Sampaio, who was at that time a government minister. Common throughout *Brazil*. Cascudo, *História*, p. 163. " 'Stop the car,' Churchill said. 'Let's get out.' He walked across the bridge and climbed down the bank toward the river to a long row of 'dragon's teeth,' the German tank defense system. There he waited until Montgomery, Brooke, Simpson and several other generals joined him. . . . 'Gentlemen,' Churchill said sonorously, 'I'd like to ask you to join me. Let us all urinate on the great West Wall of Germany.' " *England*. Toland, p. 176. *See also* Insult.

Threat   Showing of phallus. Priapus' threat to thieves. Anc. *Greece* and *Rome*. Sittl, pp. 100–1.

GENITALS, HAND

Cleverness   Right hand, loosely open, palm up, held just below the waist, then swings to the genital area and away to the right: "You won't put one over on me!" Male. *Russia*. Monahan, pp. 154–55.

Refusal   Hand, palm down, is moved toward penis as if to hold it: "Go screw yourself!" "Count me out!" Male. *Netherlands*. Andrea and de Boer, p. 105.

Rejection   Right hand close to the genital area, a male "strums the strings of his guitar" by making short downward motions from the wrist: "Go play with yourself." Male. *Russia*. Monahan, pp. 138–139.

GLOVE (GAUNTLET)

Agreement   Like a handshake, transmission of a glove signified agreement of debtor to claims of creditor. Medieval *German*. ("Wadiation"). Schwineköper, pp. 92–94. As agreement of two participants in judicial process to carry process through—an agreement either between participants or of participants with the judge—earliest evidence for use of glove is English; see "The Song of Dermont and the Earl" (13th cent.) and MS Egerton 656, fol. 188 b of the British Library: "he shall wage his law with his folded glove (de sun gaunt plyée)." 13th cent. *England.* Schwineköper, pp. 102–3. *See also* Challenge below. Late medieval evidence from *Germany* and the *Netherlands*: A plaintiff in Liège in 1348 must appear before the court holding gloves in his hands. Hüttebreuker, p. 267. In Westphalia, lay assessor who is to swear before the court is to appear with appropriate document, folded hands, a green cowl, two white gloves and a royal guilder. Wiegand, p. 433; Schwineköper, p. 103. In agreement [1219] on customs, Worms and Nürnberg sent one another pepper and gloves, and in 1264 it was agreed between Nürnberg and Mainz that the first merchant from Nürnberg to enter Mainz after a similar agreement had been in force for a year is to present the archbishop with a pound of pepper and a pair of white gloves in recognition of the customs freedom between the two cities. Sometimes a staff, a sword, or a package of needles was also used. Medieval *Germany.* Schwineköper, pp. 115–16. As sign of agreement of the authority of a guild, artisans entering a guild present it with gloves. 15th and 16th cent. *Germany.* Schwineköper, pp. 117–18.

Authority Messengers carry glove (and staff) as symbol of their mission and authority. Oldest evidence is in the *chansons de geste*, particularly the *Chanson de Roland* and the *Rolandslied.* Medieval *France; Germany; Netherlands.* Schwineköper, pp. 60–62. In order to grant a settlement for the special protection of markets, the king sends his glove, i.e. he grants in the form of the covering the shape of his hand, and henceforth it is displayed hanging on the market-cross. 13th cent. *Germany.* Amira, "Handgebärden," pp. 198–99. See also the legend of the origin of the municipal laws of Magdeburg, cited by Amira, ibid., p. 199. Anglo-Saxon law distinguishes between *pax data manu regis* (*peace by the hand of the king*) and *pax per breve data* (*peace by writ*). Medieval *England.* See R. Schmid, p. 584.

Calmness Playing with gloves in hand. Medieval *France. Pèl. de vie hum.*, 1893.

Challenge Throwing a glove (gauntlet). Medieval *Europe.* Gottfr. v. Strassburg, 6458; *Reinke de vos.*, 4, 5; Ms. Harl. 4380, fol. 141 in Coulton, p 94. Du Cange III, p. 977; Grimm, *DRA*, I, p. 212; *DWb*, IV, 2, col. 417. * In case of an ordeal by combat, i.e. single combat before a judge, the "wadium"—a glove or a staff—was handed to the judge by both parties. If not, the "wadium" was thrown to the ground by one combatant, and the other picked it up as sign of acceptance of the challenge. Medieval *England; France; Germany.* Schwineköper, pp. 95–98.

The son of King Wratislaus threw a glove into the face of a faithless steward. Medieval *Bohemia*. Schwineköper, p. 96, n. 114, interprets this not as renunciation of friendship, nor as challenge, but as insult. Matthew Paris reports a challenge in 1243 "in the French manner," in which a glove was cast at feet of person challenged. Symbol of glove is specifically referred to as "wadium duelli," indicating its function as "wadium" was still remembered. Schwineköper, p. 98. Glove as "gage de bataille" in the *Chanson de Roland*, v. 3845. In an ordinance of Philip the Handsome (1306) the judge of an ordeal by combat is to hurl the "gage" into the ring, shouting "Laissez les aller" ("Let them go to it") as a sign for the fight to begin. Medieval *France*. Schwineköper, ibid. See also a very early (1098) reference to a similar gesture in *Italy*, which may, however also be seen as insult; Muratori, p. 648; Schwineköper, p. 99, n. 129. * In the *Chronicon Estense* (1344), a captain begins a battle by sending his opponent a glove. Medieval *Italy*. Schwineköper, ibid. and n. 132. Fiorentino and Boccaccio mention the gesture, and in the Papal States a challenge was issued as late as in the 16th century by handing over a glove. 14th cent. *Italy*. See Schwineköper, pp. 99–100. In *Germany* and the *Netherlands* the usage is mentioned first in literary texts dependent on French models; e.g. 13th cent. *Germany; Netherlands*. *Lancelot*, Gottfried v. Straßburg's *Tristan*, the Middle-Dutch *Aiol*, the beast-epics *Ysengrimus* and *Vos Reinaerde*. Usage continues into late Middle Ages. References in C. Justinger's *Berner Chronik* (p. 65). 14th cent. *Switzerland*. Heinrich Wittenweiler's *Ring* (45 d), as well as in 16th cent. *Germany*. *Zimmernsche Chronik* (I, p. 368). 17th cent. *Germany*. Grimmelshausen, pp. 214–216. Earliest English evidence at the first mention (1327) of the "Champion of the King," who, following the coronation ceremony, was to appear in full armor before the portal of Westminster Abbey (later in Westminster Hall before the royal table) and cast down a glove, challenging all doubters to an ordeal by combat, to prove that the king is the legitimate king of England. Throwing of a glove is first mentioned in 1377 in connection with the coronation of Richard II. George IV's coronation was the last at which the champion appeared. Other English instances of the use of the glove in a challenge are transmitted from 1571, 1631, 1638 and 1818. Medieval to 19th cent. *England*. Schwineköper, p. 102.

Engagement Glove as symbol of the right of possession is handed by father of the bride to the groom, who immediately returns it. 11th century. Northern *Italy*. Schwineköper, pp. 90–91. See *Possession* below.

Etiquette It is polite for a gentleman to wear gloves when dancing with a lady. Hugo von Trimberg satirizes peasants aping this courtly custom. 13th cent. *Germany*. Hugo von Trimberg, v. 1617–18. In the 18th cent. it was polite for gentlemen to wear gloves only when riding and to remove them when dismounting. If this was not done, they became the property of the jockey or huntsman. Required to enter stables of a prince only after removing one's gloves, otherwise they became property of the stableboys. 18th cent. *Germany*. Custom survives in requirement that whoever raises gloved hand at the "Halali" ("Tally-ho") must pay for a claret-cup. 1938. *Germany*. Schwineköper, p. 129.

Gift Giving a *retrodonum* ("return gift"), the so-called *Launegild*, in return for a gift. Originally this had to equal the value of the gift. *Edictus Rothari*, c. 175. The *Launegild* became symbolic; after the middle of the 8th century the glove began to serve this function. Medieval *Germany*. Schwineköper, pp. 68–71. A charter of Lothar III for St. George's at Bamberg mentions that the king had given the Market of Staffelstein to the altar of St. George's "per manum comitis Reginbodonis" ("by the hand [glove] of count Reginbod"). The act itself is mentioned in a charter of Frederick I, which describes it as having been accomplished publicly "in accordance with custom" by means of a glove. Medieval *German*. Bresslau, vol. II, p. 67. A Swiss law (Fischental nr. Zürich) of 1511 requires that if one summons another to the annual assize, one is to give the judge five shillings or a pair of gloves. 16th cent. *Switzerland*. Schwineköper, 104. In the Rhineland, officiating priest received gloves from newly married couple. 15th and 16th cent. *Germany*. Schwineköper, ibid. *Arnold's Chronicle* (1521) requires "among the artycles upon whiche is to inquyre in the visitecyons of ordynaries of churches . . . Item wether the curat refuse to do the solemnysacyon of lawfull matrymonye before he have gyfte of money, hoses or gloves." 16th cent. *England*. Schwineköper, p. 117.

Greeting Politeness requires removal of gloves before shaking hands. A record of 1398 relates a case in which two enemies met, one removed his glove as sign of peace and friendship, the other took his hand without removing his gloves as sign of his unwillingness to accept the offer. 14th cent. *France*. Schwineköper, p. 127.

Insult In *Heimskringla*, Olaf Tryggvisson slaps his bride with a glove. 13th cent. *Iceland*. Schwineköper, pp. 53, n. 155 and 96, n. 114. Similarly the Old French chronicle of the dukes of Normandy, 12th cent., *Coll. d. Doc. inéd.*, v. 33397, and the *Zimmernsche Chronik*, 2nd ed., III, p. 536, which reports that the Emperor Charles V dubbed a person of bad repute a knight with a perfumed glove. 12th cent. *France*; 16th cent. *Germany*. See Challenge.

Laziness Leisurely playing with gloves. Medieval *France*. Montaiglon, I, p. 307.

Magical Liturgical use of the glove in early Middle Ages in western Europe stems from "rite of the hidden hands" of oriental origin, which reached Europe in the Hellenistic period. It consisted in protecting oneself from unknown magical effects to which one is exposed in touching

244 • GLOVE (GAUNTLET)

a deity by covering one's hands. Schwineköper, p. 24. In sacrificing to a deity or receiving gifts from a deity gloves are worn. 5th cent. *Persia*; early medieval *Europe*. Schwineköper, pp. 25–26. Remnants of this usage today. *HDA*, 3, pp. 1387 ff. Bearers of reliquaries in processions. Medieval Angers, *France*. Assistants at the altar. Besançon, *France*. St. Charles Borromaeus prohibited the priests of his diocese of Milan, *Italy*, from putting their gloves on the altar during mass. Lower clergy buried with gloves. Du Saussay (17th cent.) reports of a case of such a burial in which the deceased holds the chalice in gloved hands. Schwineköper, p. 38. In the 12th century opposition arose against use of gloves by the clergy. The Rule of Fontevrould, *France*, prohibits their use; so does the *Reformatio nigri ordinis*. But there is evidence that in the late Middle Ages the monks in some monasteries still wore gloves. In 1580 Pope Gregory XIII granted the right of wearing violet gloves to the Order of the Holy Cross. Roman Catholics. Schwineköper, p. 39. The coronation order of 1365 for the King of France requires that, if the king does not wish to put on the gloves at his coronation, his hands should be rubbed and washed, in order to protect the unction from being profaned. 14th cent. *France*. Ibid., p. 45.

Permission "And the king should justly send his glove along, to show that it is his will." Medieval *Germany*. *Sachsenspiegel*, 2, 26, 4.

Pledge As part of a pledge to marry, a Swabian freeman must give his intended seven gloves. Medieval *Germany*. Müllenhoff and Scherer, p. 239; *DWb*, IV, col. 417.

Possession Transference of land was accompanied by a glove handed over or thrown down. Medieval *Germany*. Grimm, *DRA*, I, p. 209; Medieval *Brittany; England; Netherlands; Germany;* and Gothic. Schwineköper, pp. 73–92. A vassal transferring part of his fief to another had to pay his lord a special contribution and give him a pair of gloves. Chartres (1100); 13th cent. Central and northern *France*. Later the beneficiary of the transference is required to give the lord *vente et gants*. Schwineköper, p. 107. Similarly in 14th cent. *Germany*. Schwineköper, p. 111. Annual gifts of gloves to the lord or his representative was required of vassals in 13th cent., but soon payment of money took the place of gloves and remained in effect until the 18th century, though the requirement was still referred to as the *droit des gants*. 13th cent. *France*. Schwineköper, pp. 107–8. The custom was probably imported to England by the Normans; the earliest evidence is from 1200, and in November 1937, when the King, as Duke of Cornwall, visited Launceston, his tenant Gerald Curgenven presented him with a pair of white gloves. 1937. *England. Germany* (since the early 13th cent.); *Switzerland* (14th cent.) have the same custom. Schwineköper, pp. 109–10. As part of the installation ceremony of a new bishop, the *Ordo Romano-Germanicum*, composed by monks of St. Alban's of Mainz ca. 960, prescribes the transference of gloves to the new bishop with a special prayer. Medieval *Germany.* Schwineköper, pp. 29–30. After the 10th century it became general practice in the Church of Rome. Roman Catholics. Schwineköper, pp. 30 ff. Similarly, gloves were handed to new abbots at their installation. Ibid., pp. 35–37. Although gloves were recognized by the Salian period as insignia of German kings, they were not considered part of coronation orders until Henry VI. Medieval *Germany.* Ibid., pp. 42–43. In France the glove was handed to the king at the coronation in the same liturgical form as at the consecration of a new bishop. Medieval *France.* Ibid., pp. 45. Gloves were given to the lord at the marriage of a serf as symbol of his recognition of the lord's ownership. 15th and 16th cent. *Germany; Switzerland.* Schwineköper, p. 112. A judge of the lower courts, elected by serfs, had to present gloves to the lord when seeking installment in his office. 14th and 16th cent. Franconia, *Germany;* 17th cent. *Switzerland.* The mayor of Erfurt received a pair of gloves from the council on St. Mark's Day (1482); the dukes of Bavaria received gloves from the city of Regensburg annually from 1294 when they moved their customs administration there; the alderman of the Hanseatics in London received gloves from them annually (1383) in recognition of the city's jurisdiction; in the case of a "maiden assize," i.e. if in a given jurisdiction no sentence of death had been pronounced during the preceding year, the sheriff sent the judge gloves. The auditor of the convent Eschenbach is to be given white gloves (*Schweiz. Idiotikon,* 8, p. 466), and if a beadle comes to the estate at Weinzierl (Austria, 1455), he is to be given wine right away, and if he is well behaved, he is to receive sword, gloves and a jacket in addition. Medieval *Austria; Germany; Switzerland.* Schwineköper, pp. 113–14.

Prohibition The king or judge threw down the glove as sign of proscription about to be pronounced. Medieval *Germany.* Grimm, *DRA,* I, p. 211. Also medieval *Italy* by *missi* of German kings. Schwineköper, pp. 54–57. The royal proscription of acts of violence in connection with the foundation of markets required the glove as symbol of royal justice. Medieval *Germany.* Gradually this symbolic function of the glove lost its precision: in 1218 the glove is regarded as transmitting, from the king, the right to establish a market; and soon thereafter the *Sachsenspiegel* (as well as the *Schwabenspiegel* and *Deutschenspiegel*) maintain that the king must send a glove for the establishment of markets "to prove that it is his will." The illustrations of the *Sachsenspiegel* show that the glove was hung up on the market cross. Medieval *Germany.* Schwineköper, pp. 54–58.

Surrender A probable development from the use of the glove as "wadium" (*see* Challenge, above) was its use as a symbol for surrendering oneself into the power of an opponent. In the battle of Poitiers (1356) King Jean II handed his glove to Denis de Morbec and thus surrendered; an English statute of 1385 requires a prisoner to surrender his glove, which is here explicitly referred to as "gage"—"wadium"; see W. Knorr, p. 36; and the same is reported of Antoine of Luxembourg in 1499, and of Francis I in the battle of Pavia (1525); two German sources of 1462 refer to the same custom. 14th–16th cent. *France;* 15th cent. *Germany.* See Schwineköper, p. 105.

HAIR, HAND

Admiration   Hands gently touch one's hair several times in admiration of someone's coiffure. *Central Africa.* Hochegger, p. 37.

Adoption   "Boso, King of Provençe (879–889), is said to have cut off his hair and given it to Pope John VIII (872–882) as a sign that the latter had adopted him." 9th cent. Provençe, *France.* Brewer, p. 11.

Affection   Stroking someone's hair. To animals. Anc. *Greece* and *Rome.* Sittl, p. 33. To children, slaves, and to the grown man by his mother. Anc. *Greece* and *Rome.* Sittl, pp. 33–34. Teachers to pupils. Anc. *Greece* and *Rome.* Sittl, p. 33.

Age   "Expressions suggesting aging may be accompanied by . . . running the fingers of one hand through the hair, as if to draw attention to the gray hairs on the head." *Spain; Lat. Am.* Green, p. 64.

Approval   Patting the hair. *U.S.* Birdwhistell, "Do Gestures Speak Louder than Words?", p. 56.

Bargain   Pulling a hair from the head, blowing on it and saying "Pelillos a la mar" ("Hairs fly away to the sea") seals a bargain. Children. *Spain.* Hayes, p. 300.

Despair   Tearing hair. Ohm, p. 230. 19th cent. *Italy.* Bresciani, *L'ebreo,* c. xxxxix. Men: Anc. *Greece* and *Rome.* Sittl, p. 22. Women: Anc. *Greece* and *Rome.* Sittl, p. 22. 10th–11th cent. *England.* Old English *Judith* 280 ff. Habicht, p. 50. 12th cent. *Germany. Orendel,* 680. 16th–17th cent. *England.* Shakesp., *Troil.* 4.2.113. 18th cent. *Germany.* Wieland, p. 232. Schoolchildren. *U.S.* Seton, p. xxi. In the Old Testament, it was a protest against iniquity, injustice, and sacrilege. Biblical. *Middle East.* Cascudo, *História,* p. 93.

Emphasis   "adding force to his declamation by striding to and fro, pulling his hair." 19th cent. *England.* Dickens, *Pickwick,* I, p. 400.

Frustration   "the expression 'Estoy hasta la punta del pelo' ["I've had it up to here"] is a female movement and expression. The mover raises a single hair in the rear of the head." Student, Univ. of Madrid, *Spain.* Also *Lat. Am.* Green, p. 89.

Gratitude   "pulling at the forelock of his shock head of hair in honour of the steward's clemency, and giving another double pull at it in honour of the farmer's kindness." 19th cent. *England.* Trollope, *Barchester Towers,* II, p. 138.

Mourning   Women cut off bits of their hair. 19th cent. *Palestine.*

Bauer, p. 211. * Tearing hair. 19th cent. *Italy.* Bresciani, *L'ebreo,* c. xxxxix; Sittl, p. 22. Men: Hellenistic *Near East*; Sittl, p. 67. * Tearing hair out and strewing it over the corpse, perhaps as proof of sorrow. 19th cent. *Greece.* Also anc. *Greece* and *Rome.* Sittl, p. 71. Ca. 500 B.C. *India. Mahabharata* IX; Cascudo, *História,* p. 93. Only men in the heroic age: Sittl, p. 25. Customary, esp. for women, to scratch face and shave off hair. *Arab.* Similarly among Israelites, despite Deuteronomic prohibitions. Biblical. *Middle East.* Hastings, *Dictionary,* III, p. 454. Tearing out one's hair in mourning was prohibited by the city council of Lisbon in 1385. 14th cent. *Portugal.* Cascudo, *História,* p. 93.

Oath Men swore by touching their hair. Medieval *Frisian Islands.* Grimm, *DRA,* II, p. 549. * Touching chest and the hair hanging over the shoulder. Medieval *Bavaria; Swabia; Germany.* Grimm, *DRA,* II, p. 548. * Grasping another man's moustache with fingers of right hand. *Saudi Arabia.* Barakat, no. 183.

Prayer Shaking and pulling hair. Cybele cult. Women loosen hair. Anc. *Rome.* Ohm, p. 230. Anc. *Rome.* Brissonius, I, c. lxiv; Sittl, p. 185.

Respect "the rather broad-set but active figure, perhaps two years older than himself, that looked at him with a pair of blue eyes set in a disc of freckles, and pulled some curly red locks with a strong intention of respect." 19th cent. *England.* Eliot, p. 571.

Shame Cut off a man's plait of hair. Variations: cutting off a man's right hand or cutting off a man's beard. Rwala Bedouin, *Kuwait; Iraq, Saudi Arabia; Syria.* Barakat, no. 161.

Sorrow Pulling beard. Biblical. *Middle East.* Ohm, p. 230. Anc. *Greece* and *Rome.* Sittl, p. 274; Early 16th cent. *Europe.* Röhrich, *Gebärde-Metapher-Parodie,* pl. 35; see also Röhrich, ibid., p. 34 and pl. 36. 15th cent. *England.* Malory, II, ch. vii. 16th–17th cent. *England.* Shakesp., *Much Ado* 2.3.153; *Romeo* 3.3.68. * Violent gestures such as tearing the hair and other forms of selfmutilation rare in the 17th cent.; but see the two studies by Rembrandt. 17th cent. *Netherlands.* Van der Meulen, p. 20. *See* also Mourning. "if they [women] are pressed by sorrow, they are to tear their veils, browbands, caps or whatever else they may have, off their heads and tear their hair and wring their hands. Gloss to the *Sächsisches Landrecht,* II, 64. Medieval *Germany.* Amira, "Handgebärden," p. 234.

Surrender Hair is drawn through dust. Anc. *Rome.* Sittl, p. 161. * At capitulations Gallic women showed their disordered hair. *Gaul.* Sittl, ibid.

HAIR, HAND, MOUTH

Sorrow Biting the thumb and tearing the hair. *Germany.* Boggs, p. 319.

HAIR, LIP
Affection   Kissing the hair. Anc. *Rome*. Sittl, p. 41.

HAND
Absence   Right hand held in front of face, back of hand facing forward, then flipped so that palm is up: person asked for is not present. *Saudi Arabia*. Barakat, no. 200.

Acceptance   The newly born child lies on the floor until the father declares whether he wants it to live or not. If he accepts it he lifts it up or has it lifted up. Then it is sprinkled with water and given a name. Medieval *Scandinavia*. Grimm, *DRA*, I, pp. 627–28.

Accolade   After the sword belt has been put on, there follows the blow with the sword, the *alapa militaris*. This blow, administered by the knight accepting the squire into knighthood, is directed against the neck and accompanied by formal admonitions. Medieval *Europe*. Schultz, II, p. 185.

Accompaniment   Man takes woman by the hand or the wrist in walking. Anc. *Greece*. Sittl, p. 81.

Acknowledgement   "She still had the curious trick—shared by two or three other small-town young women within Pnin's limited ken—of giving you a delayed little tap on the sleeve in acknowledgment of, rather than in retaliation for, any remark reminding her of some minor lapse." *U.S.* Nabokov, p. 152. * "stuck out his hand as though to shake hands" in acknowledgment of an introduction. *U.S.* Birdwhistell, *Introduction*, p. 34. * "With an infectious gurgle of laughter, she threw up her hand in the classic gesture of one duelist acknowledging a tricky touch by the other." *U.S.* Lathen, *East Is East*, p. 165.

Address (passionate)   Both hands extended toward someone. Anc. *Greece* and *Rome*. Sittl, p. 50. * The Vestal Quinta Claudia precedes her prayer by raising her hands three times, in addition to washing her head three times. Anc. *Rome*. Sittl, p. 190.

Admiration   Hand shaken as if burnt. Particularly signifies admiration of feminine beauty. *Italy*. Leone, p. XX 11. " *'Elle est magnifique, non?'* ("She's beautiful, isn't she?") He shook one hand vigorously from the wrist. *'Un bonne paquet'* " ("What a dish"). Provençe, *France*. Mayle, *Hotel Pastis*, p. 232. * With palms facing each other, hands move downward from ca. shoulder-level to hip-level, exaggerating an attractive female figure. *Colombia; U.S.* Saitz and Cervenka, p. 54. *Netherlands*. Andrea and de Boer, p. 128. *See also* FINGER, Admiration. " 'That good-looking lawyer.' Dashee created curves in the air with his hands." *U.S.* Hillerman, *Talking God*, p. 33. * Clapping hands. *Germany*. DWb, IV/2, col. 414. * "advancing with extended hand, 'I honour your gallantry. Permit me to say, Sir, that I highly admire your conduct' " 19th cent. *England*. Dickens, *Pickwick*. I, p. 37. * Both hands pass gently over the face and follow the contours of the face of a beautiful young woman. *Central Africa*. Hochegger, p. 22.

Admonition Right hand oscillates obliquely or semi-vertically in front of nose. *Spain*. Kaulfers, p. 252. "slapped him across the anterior portion of his upper leg." *U.S.* Birdwhistell, "Background," p. 14.

Adoption Lifting the adopted child up. Slav. Eastern *Europe*. Grimm, *DRA*, I, p. 640. *See* Acceptance. Accompanying an act of adoption or suggesting parentage. 12th–13th cent. *Germany*. Hartmann v. Aue, *Gregorius* 1135–36; Gottfried v. Straßburg, *Tristan* 1961; Wells, pp. 171–172.

Adoration Raising the hand. *Middle East*. Ebert, V, p. 93. Holding or carrying an object in a cloth or on a cloak signifies respect for that object. Medieval *Europe*. Haseloff, pp. 304–05. * "holding the Host over the Chalice with his right hand, and holding the Chalice with his left [the priest] elevates it a little together with the Host, saying the words 'omnis honor et gloria.' " Roman Catholic. *Mass*, p. 69. * "St. Thomas tells us that after the Consecration the priest does not make the Sign of the Cross for the purpose of blessing or consecrating, but to commemorate the virtue and power of the Cross and the manner of Christ's death." Roman Catholic. *Mass*, p. 63. "The priest makes the Sign of the Cross three times—once over the Host, once over the Chalice and once on himself; by which is represented that the torments which Christ endured in His Flesh and which He suffered in the effusion of His Blood, profit and always will benefit both priest and people to eternal salvation." Roman Catholic. *Mass*, p. 66. * Both hands raised, palms toward the object of adoration. Anc. *Egypt*. Heiler, p. 101. * Clapping hands in adoration of spirits. Ohm, p. 285.

Affection Hand(s) of beloved pressed against one's eyes. Anc. *Greece* and *Rome*. Sittl, p. 34. * Pressing a person's hand. 18th cent. *Germany*. *DWb*, IV/2, col. 367. Woman pressing a man's hand. *DWb*, ibid. Man pressing woman's hand. 16th cent. *Germany*. *Grobianus* (1552); *DWb*, IV/2, col. 331. Paternal pressing of someone's hand. 18th cent. *Germany*. *DWb*, ibid. Man and woman pressing each other's hand. 13th cent. *Germany*. *Nibelungenlied*, st. 294. "The sick man drew a hand of his old fellow prisoner towards him, and pressing it affectionately between both his own, retained it in his grasp." 19th cent. *England*. Dickens, *Pickwick*, II, p. 277. Hand(s) of one person grasped by hand(s) of another. Anc. *Greece* and *Rome*. Stephani, pp. 69–113. "and pressing her son's hand, affectionately" 19th cent. *England*. Dickens, *Oliver Twist*, p. 310. Taking someone's hand. 16th–17th cent. *England*. Shakesp., *Tempest* 1.2.377; *Mids. Night's Dream* 4.1.90. Also Maupassant. 19th cent. *France*; see Raim, p. 97. * Touching or tapping someone lightly for whom affection is felt. Sirionó Indians, *Bolivia*. Key, p. 97. * Handshake while conversing. Anc. *Greece* and *Rome*. Sittl, pp. 28–29.

Handshake not a matter of etiquette, but an expression of emotion; if context of handshake is insignificant, performer of handshake is regarded as flatterer. Anc. *Rome.* Sittl, p. 28. * Love to animals manifests itself in stroking them. 19th cent. *Palestine.* Bauer, p. 321. * "Slaps of affection can be observed striking the back of the head, the back of the neck, the stomach, and the chest of the listener." *Spain; Lat. Am.* Green, pp. 36–37. * Stroking someone's cheek. 16th–17th cent. *England.* Shakesp., *Troil.* 5.2.51. * "Preston, who kept the house, instantly came up to me and, kindly taking me by the hand, in the most feeling manner, said, 'Good God, my dear Mr. Hickey, what ails you, what is the matter?' " 18th cent. *England.* Hickey, p. 172. " 'You're such a good man, Mr. Farragan!' the old one shrieked. She had taken both his hands fiercely into her own and immediately knocked over his glass of beer." *U.S.* McHale, p. 160. * Hand held with palm downward, fingers flicking away from the body: "I love you." *Ethiopia.* Axtell, *Gestures,* p. 93.

Affirmation   Palm upward, hand is moved in a slight curve upward and to the side. Assimilated Eastern Jews. Eastern *Europe.* Efron, p. 117. * Hands raised to level of head and clasped vigorously. *Colombia.* Saitz and Cervenka, p. 15. * Hands repeatedly moved downward from height of throat. Ainu. *Japan.* Cascudo, *História,* p. 166. * "At a signal from the Principal the pupils, in ordered ranks, hands to the side, face the Flag . . . Standing thus, all repeat together, slowly: 'I pledge allegiance to my Flag and the Republic for which it stands; . . .' At the words 'to my Flag,' the right hand is extended gracefully, palm upward, towards the Flag, and remains in this gesture till the end of the affirmation; whereupon all hands immediately drop to the side." U.S. "National School Celebration," *The Youth's Companion,* Sept. 8, 1892, p. 446. [Editors' note: This gesture, as well as the Fascist and National Socialist version (palms down) may be a distant descendant of the extended hand on Hellenistic votive reliefs, and of the placement of the hand on the shoulder or arm of someone whom the gesturer sees as representing him or with whom he agrees, or whom he sends forth with a message.] See also Anc. *Greece* and *Rome.* Sittl, pp. 291–95; medieval *Germany.* Sachsenspiegel. Amira, "Handgebärden," p. 247; medieval *Italy.* Barasch, *Giotto,* p. l67. * The handshake is "a masculine ritual of recognition and affirmation" serving "to perpetuate male clubbiness and to exclude women from the club." *Universal.* Henley, p. 10.

Age (of a female)   Right hand indicates state of development of breasts: right hand raised to shoulder level, fingers closed and extended forward, palm down, thumb parallel to, and under, index, tip touching index: pre-puberty; right hand raised to shoulder level, fingers closed and pointing forward, palm down, thumb extended under and away from fingers: puberty; hand open at shoulder level, palm outward, fingers vertical, thumb horizontal: nubile; hand open at shoulder level, palm outward, fingers vertical, thumb bent downward as far as possible: mature. *Central Africa*. Hochegger, p. 4.

Aggressiveness Right hand raised, palm out, fingers curved so as to form a claw. *Central Africa*. Hochegger, p. 83.

Agreement "And when James, Cephas and John . . . perceived the grace that was given unto me, they gave to me and Barnabas the right hands of fellowship." Biblical. *Middle East. Galat.* 2:9. "And they gave their hands that they would put away their wives." Biblical. *Middle East. Ezra* 10:19. "Seeing he despised the oath by breaking the covenant, when lo, he had given his hand, and hath done all these things, he shall not escape." Biblical. *Middle East. Ezek.* 17:18. The people declared their agreement with the election of Henry I in 919 and Otto I in 936 *cum clamore valido* (by acclamation) and *dextris in coelum levatis*, by raising their right hand. Medieval *Germany*. Widukind of Corvey I, 26 and II, 1. In connection with coronation of the King of France. Medieval *France*. Montfaucon, III, pl. 1. Medieval *Germany. Sachsenspiegel*. Amira, "Handgebärden," pp. 201, 239–40. * Palm of right hand is touched to the palm of the right hand of the partner, then the right hand is presented to be touched by the palm of the partner's right hand. Mutual agreement concerning a transaction. *France*. Mitton, p. 142. * Handshake, i.e. German "Handschlag." Regarded as purely Germanic by Sittl, p. 13. *Colombia; U.S.* Saitz and Cervenka, p. 24. Common in all Germanic laws. Many variations. *Sachsenspiegel*. Amira, "Handgebärden," pp. 239–42. * Right hand of one person grasps right hand of another so that thumbs touch. German, possibly anc. *Greece*. Sittl, pp. 136–37. * Right hand raised, palm laid in the palm of the raised right hand of the partner. [Editors' note: similar to the contemporary *U.S.* "high five" gesture.] *See* Approval. *Sachsenspiegel* manuscripts as well as others from the 12th–14th centuries. Medieval *Germany*. Amira, "Handgebärden," pp. 239–41. * Raising the hand. *Germany. DWb*, IV/ 2, col. 331; "A man striketh hands and becometh surety." Biblical. *Middle East. Prov.* 17:18. Sealing agreement with handshake. Biblical. *Middle East.* II *Kings* 10:15. Handclasp accompanying marriage in church, between father of the bride and the groom. Medieval northern *England; Scotland*. Vinogradoff, p. 246; Ebert, V, 95. Right hand of one person clasps that of another in confirmation of a treaty. Insufficient in actuality, used as poetic license. Anc. *Rome*. Sittl, p. 137. "Take hands, a bargain!" 16th–17th cent. *England*. Shakesp., *Winter's Tale* 4.4.394. * At a sale of animals the right hands of seller and buyer grasp thrice. 19th cent. *Palestine*. Bauer, p. 167. * One party strikes the palm of the other. 17th cent. *England*. Butler, II, 1, 540. " 'I have said so my dear friend. I have said so already,' replied Mr. Wardle, shaking the right hand of his friend." 19th cent. *England*. Dickens, *Pickwick*, I, p. 276. * Joining hands, grasp broken by a blow from the hand of a third party.

South Molton, *England.* Children. Opie, p. 130. Handclasp, a bystander separates the hands by bringing the edge of his right hand down upon the clasped hands, signifying the conclusion of a bargain. *Germany.* Röhrich, *Gebärde-Metapher-Parodie,* p. 31. * In reaching agreement, handshake is covered by coattail while whinnying. 18th cent. *Estonia.* Hupel, II, pp. 149–50. * "He let everything go for a sum so contemptible that Gouy at first opened his eyes wide, and exclaiming 'Agreed!' slapped his palm." 19th cent. *France.* Flaubert, ch. ii. * For the political significance of the handshake of agreement, see Blumenthal, pp. 74–76. "In the latest issue of Rolling Stone, Jann Wenner asks Bill Clinton what's the biggest laugh he has had since being president: 'When I was practicing shaking hands with (Yasser) Arafat before I shook hands with (Yitzhak) Rabin,' said the president. 'We had an understanding that there would be no Arab embrace.' 'Yeah,' Rabin said. 'OK, I'll shake hands, but no kissing.' So there could be no Arab embrace. '[National Security Adviser] Tony Lake was pretending to be Arafat, and we finally worked out that the way to stop someone from embracing you—without seeming like a bad guy—is to embrace the biceps. If you hold his biceps (with your left hand, while shaking his right hand with your right), he can't move up and embrace you. I thought, 'I got elected president to do this?' " U.S. "Peacekeeping Has Its Limits," *Daily News,* Nov. 23, 1993, p. 18. * The palm of the right hand slaps against the palm of the person spoken to, followed by an energetic handshake. *Europe; Brazil.* Cascudo, *História,* p. 117.

Ahead   Open hand at level of chest and perpendicular to it, describes a 270 degree (clockwise?) arc in the air. Río de la Plata region of *Argentina; Uruguay.* Meo Zilio, p. 95.

Alarm   "all shall clap the hands over thee." Biblical. *Middle East. Nahum* 3:19.

Amazement   "The ring was answered by a very smart and pretty-faced servant-girl, who, after holding up her hands in astonishment at the rebellious appearance of the prisoners" 19th cent. *England.* Dickens, *Pickwick,* I, p. 413. * Palm on cheek or behind ear. Ghetto Jews. *Eastern Europe.* Efron, p. 146. * Shaking loosely held fingers of slightly cupped hand in front of the speaker or at the side at waist-level. *Spain; Lat. Am.* Green, p. 56.

Anger   Hands beaten together. Anc. *Greece* and *Rome.* Sittl, p. 19. * Fist moved from left to right several times at approx. chin level. *Colombia.* Saitz and Cervenka, p. 54. * Striking the open palm of one hand with the closed fist of the other hand. *Spain; Lat. Am.,* but particularly frequent in Spain. Green, pp. 74–75. * Twitching hands. Schiller, *Tell,* iii, iii. * Hands beaten together. Biblical. *Middle East.* IV *Moses* 24:10; 17th cent. *Austria.* Abraham a Santa Clara, p. 139. Anc. *Greece* and *Rome.* Sittl, p. 19. * Quivering hands. 17th cent. *Germany.* Zigler und

Klipphausen, p. 98; Immermann, II, p. 13. * Knuckles of both hands rubbed together. *Lat. Am.* Kany, p. 64. "clenched his fist and shook it expressively at the object of his indignation." 19th cent. *England.* Dickens, *Pickwick*, I, p. 142. "shook his fist in the countenance of the Honourable Samuel Slumkey." 19th cent. *England.* Dickens, *Pickwick*, I, p. 213; also *Roman Empire.* Tacitus, *Annales*, xiii. Bulwer, pp. 57–59. * Clenching fists. *U.S.* Krout, p. 22. " 'They had better not!' said Mr. Bumble, clenching his fist." 19th cent. *England.* Dickens, *Oliver Twist*, p. 244. Also *Colombia; U.S.* Saitz and Cervenka, p. 16. * Striking left hand with right, or fist into palm. Biblical. *Middle East. Ezek.* 21:14; anc. *Rome.* Bulwer, pp. 32–34. Striking fist into palm. *Netherlands.* Andrea and de Boer, p. 110. " 'She would assure me, if ever again'—And there she stopped, with a twirl of her hand. When we meet, I will, in her presence, tipping thee a wink, show thee the motion, for it was a very pretty one. Quite new." 18th cent. *England.* Richardson, IV, p. 45. * Right fist rubbed on the extended left palm. *Lat. Am.* Kany, p. 64. * Fists held together and twisted as if wringing cloth. *Colombia; U.S.* Saitz and Cervenka, p. 17. *Netherlands.* Andrea and de Boer, p. 147. * Hands hanging at side and clenched. *Europe; North Am.* Aubert, p. 83. * " 'I tell you,' said the man, clenching his hands, and stamping furiously on the floor." 19th cent. *England.* Dickens, *Oliver Twist*, p. 43. * Clenched hands crossed behind back. 18th cent. *Germany.* DWb, IV/2, col. 334. * Hands vertically extended, palms facing out, fingers separated and hooked. *Europe; North Am.* Aubert, p. 87. * Clenched fists held so that knuckles face downward, forearms extended in front parallel to ground; fists make short, sharp downward and upward motion. *Colombia; U.S.* Saitz and Cervenka, p. 16. * When angry person feels superior to the other, he will approach, staring, grab the other by lapel or arm, or touch his face and fingers. Equal adversaries grab each other. *Portugal.* Basto, p. 7. * "whereupon Grant jumped up from his chair and, putting his fist close to Mordaunt's face, told him his own house alone protected him from that chastisement he was disposed to give him." 18th cent. *England.* Hickey, p. 323.

Anticipation   Right palm rubbed rapidly over horizontally extended left palm; joyful face; shoulders sometimes hunched. *France.* Brault, p. 377. *Colombia; U.S.* Saitz and Cervenka, p. 17. Hands palm to palm or clasped in front of body. Women. *U.S.* Saitz and Cervenka, p.18.

Antipathy   Hands extended, palms facing outward. Ohm, p. 44. * Same, palms facing down. Yuki Indians. California coast, *U.S.* Ohm, ibid.

Anxiety   "The Fat Man's hands twisted together at the thought, anxiously." U.S. Hillerman, *Talking God*, p. 41.

Apology   One hand, palm outward, raised to the side of the speaker's face, suggesting the warding off of anticipated criticism. *Spain; Lat. Am.* Green, p. 83.

Apotropy Passing hand over mouth to ward off evil eye. *Germany.* Meschke, col. 336. * Touching wall of house to pass on evil influence of witch that one has just met, or touching witch's right hand. *England.* Meschke, ibid. * Meeting a witch calls for touching her shoulder. Tirol, *Austria*; Messina, *Sicily*; Cambray, *France.* Meschke, ibid. * Making sign of the cross with oil over animals at time of epidemic protects animal. 6th cent. *France.* Sittl, p. 127. * Making sign of the cross over open mouth while yawning. Early Christian. Sittl, p. 127. *Germany.* Meschke, col. 335. Tirol, *Austria.* Zingerle, p. 58. *Russia.* Monahan, pp. 128–29. * Extending index and small finger, preferably of left hand, middle fingers bent inward on palm and thumb holding them in place ("horns"). *Lat. Am.* Kany, p. 190. * One thumb crossed by the other against evil eye. Noirmoutier; Poitou, *France.* Seligmann, II, p. 183. * "Fig" as protection against evil spell. 19th cent. Naples, southern *Italy.* De Jorio, p. 155. * Making sign of the cross. *Spain.* Flachskampf, p. 243. *Colombia.* Saitz and Cervenka, p. 29. * Image of hand on walls, or amulet in metal or glass against evil eye. Muslim. Seligmann, II, p. 168. * Making sign of the cross protexts against magic and demons. Early Christian. Sittl, p. 127. * Crossing oneself against devils. Medieval *German.* Kaufringer, no. 2, 187–95. * Upon entering house where butter is being made, one must lay one's hand on butterkeg as proof of lack of evil intentions and willingness to drive off influences of the evil eye. Northeastern *Scotland.* Seligmann, II, pp. 185–86. The "fig": Tip of thumb projects from between index and middle finger of fist—or both fists. Esp. Neapolitan. F. Liebrecht (1846), p. 186. Morris et al., p. 156 and the map on p. 158, find centers of this usage to be *Portugal* and *Sicily*, rather than mainland Italy. *See* FINGER, Apotropy. The "fig" against the evil eye, made under cloak to avoid insulting person with whom one is speaking. Naples, *Italy.* Seligmann, II, ibid. * Making the sign of the cross when entering public baths, which were sometimes considered as evil. Early Christian. Sittl, pp. 127–28. Making sign of the cross when lights were lit, to protect against demons wandering about. Early Christian. Sittl, p. 128. * Washing hands by wedding guests prevents dangerous contacts. *Yugoslavia.* Ebert, V, col. 94. Washing hands before begiming work in garden or field, to prevent infection of plants by touch of hand which may have been cursed by touching certain trees, leaves, etc. Ewe, *West Africa.* Ebert, V, col. 93. * To protect someone from evil influence of spell, sign of the horns is made against several parts of a person's body. 19th cent. Naples, southern *Italy.* De Jorio, p. 99. The sign of the horns is made to the eyes of the person against whose spell one wants to protect oneself, for eyes are regarded as source of the spell. 19th cent. Naples, southern *Italy.* De Jorio, p. 98. In protecting oneself against evil spirits, the hand, making the sign of the horns, is moved around in the air aimlessly, since it is presumed that evil spirits roam in the air. Ibid., p. 97. One hand extended, making a blessing-gesture with thumb, index and middle finger extended toward another figure, the other hand makes the "horns" in the same direction. *Noli me tangere.* Ivory panel, late 11th cent. *Spain.* Metropolitan Museum, N. Y., in de Palol and Hirmer, pl. 79. For gestures and stances associated with 'Noli me tangere'-representations in medieval art, see Barasch, *Giotto*, pp. 169–82. * Thumb bent under the other fingers of one hand against evil eye. *Spain; Ireland;* Bretagne, *France;* Noirmoutier, *France.* Selig-mann, II, p. 178. * Clapping hands to frighten witches away from chil-dren. 16th cent. *Greece.* Sittl, p. 117. * Index extended and bent three times while silently stepping behind old women protects against their evil eye. East Prussia, *Germany.* Seligmann, II, p. 183; Meschke, col. 336. * Amulet of hand of which the tip of the thumb touches the tip of the index, or hand with extended index against the evil eye. Seligmann, II, p. 182. * Extending thumb, index and middle finger simultaneously to ward off evil spirits. Early Christian. Meschke, col. 335. * Tip of index placed to tip of little finger against the "Hacker." *Germany. HDA,* II, col. 1496. * Middle finger laid across index against the "Letzten." Ratzeburg, *Germany.* Ibid. * Old women make the sign of the cross over the open mouth of yawning children and say "Heiligs Kreuz" simulta-neously. Bavaria, *Germany.* Sittl, p. 127. * Clapping hands when some-one sneezes, to frighten demons away. *Turkey.* Sittl, p. 117. * The hand extended, fingers spread. "Hand of Fatima." *North Africa; Sicily; Spain.* Taylor, *Shanghai Gesture,* pp. 53–54 and n. 74. *See also* Insult below. "Mrs. Beumer made the sign of the cross. 'It's always the best ones,' she said softly, 'that God calls to him first.' " *Netherlands.* Mulisch, p. 71. *See* FINGER, Apotropy.

Appeasement Hands horizontal, arms straight, palms down, arms folded slowly, moving from above downwards. Aubert, p. 89.

Applause Clapping hands. *Germany. DWb,* IV/2, col. 368. It was a Spartan custom to elect its senators by applause. Plutarch, *Lycurgus* xxxviii. Striking palms of the hands together was the anc. Roman ges-ture of applause; striking the center of the palm of the left hand with the extended joined fingers of the right was the anc. Greek custom. Ap-plause was a religious gesture to attract the presence of the gods in order to protect those making the gesture. Applause was unknown to Africans and indigenous Americans before the European presence. Anc. *Greece* and *Rome;* Native Americans. Cascudo, *História* p. 50. Objectionable as expression of joy. Anc. *Rome.* Sittl, p. 10. Limited to barbarians, sailors, children, and characters in Petronius. Anc. *Rome.* Similarly in anc. *Greece.* Sittl, p. 11. Women did not clap in the theater. *Portugal.* Urtel, pp. 12–13. Similarly early 19th cent. *Germany;* and anc. *Greece* and *Rome*. Sittl, p. 56. Likewise to speeches of the emperor, both in the *Roman Empire* and the *Byzantine Empire*, whence it was taken over by the Franks. High officials were received with applause. Anc. *Rome*. The Emperor Julian was applauded in visiting the temples. Anc. *Rome*. Sittl, pp. 55–59. Clapping of hands at a wedding. 19th cent. *Greece*; *Sardinia*. Sittl, p. 59. Clapping of hands repeated three times on a birthday. Anc. *Rome*. Sittl, ibid. Clapping of hands in applause. 6th cent. *France*. Sittl, p. 58. *Byzantine Empire*. Sittl, ibid. No applause in the theater when the king was present. 18th cent. *France*. Rousseau, *Confessions*, Bk. viii. Right-handers applaud by clapping the right hand onto the left, left-handers by clapping the left onto the right. To indicate special appreciation, a seated audience will rise to applaud. In Central and Eastern Europe it is common for audiences to clap rhythmically; in N. America it signifies impatience. Axtell, *Gestures*, p. 82. [Editors' note: Drumming knuckles of fist on table top. Traditional academic applause. *Germany; Austria*.] *See also* Praise below.

Appreciation Two hands curved in the air to suggest an attractive female shape may express appreciation or sensuousness. *U.S.* Ruesch and Kees, p. 82; Axtell, *Gestures*, p. 82. *See* Admiration. "In many cultures, accepting [a gift] in both hands means appreciation of the generosity of the donor: the idea is that one hand would not be sufficient to hold the symbolic value of the gift. Stretching out only one hand to receive shows lack of gratitude, and might be interpreted as contemptuous behavior." *Malawi*. Visser, p. 50.

Approach "Writing in the air with an imaginary pen or pencil—intended to simulate the act of computing the check—is a movement observed frequently in Spanish restaurants. The movement often replaces verbal behavior of any kind, but it may accompany expressions such as '¡La cuenta, por favor!' ['The check, please!'] . . . This movement is socially acceptable in any environment. Voiced gestures, such as '¡Chist!,' simply raising the hand, or snapping the fingers are all movements which can be observed in Spanish restaurants. [Snapping fingers. Superiors to inferiors, or equals informally. *Colombia*. Saitz and Cervenka, p. 28.] Clapping the hands . . . is acceptable only in mesones or tascas. . . . As a general rule, American movers consciously avoid movements and gestures which tend to attract attention." Green, p. 57. Raising hand with index extended, or the open hand, waved slightly laterally, about head high. *U.S.* Extended index is considered rude in *Japan*; open hand waved laterally could be considered signalling 'no' in *Europe*. Axtell, *Gestures*, p. 31. Arm and hand extended in front of chest, palm down, fingers lowered and raised repeatedly. *Spain*. Rare in urban social contexts and "probably largely confined to rural areas. . . . The movement can be observed . . . performed by recent arrivals to more densely populated areas and by somewhat older madrileños. Young children in the care of middle-aged nannies can also be observed performing this movement. The gesture most frequently observed today in association with expressions of beckoning is performed exactly as it is in many parts of the United States, that is, by bending the index finger of one hand toward the gesticulator . . . The movement can also be performed using all of the fingers of one hand . . . When beckoning toward . . . taxi drivers, Spanish movers tend to extend one arm directly to their front and lower and raise the rigid arm repeatedly and brusquely." *Spain.* Green, pp. 37–38. Index finger bent repeatedly toward gesticulator, palm up. *Colombia; U.S.* Saitz and Cervenka, p. 28. * Same, palm down, other fingers folded in and held by the thumb. *Colombia.* Saitz and Cervenka, ibid. To request something to be brought to one. *Central Africa.* Hochegger, p. 10. Beckoning by repeatedly bending the index, palm up, is used only for calling animals. *Yugoslavia; Malaysia.* To beckon streetwalkers. *Indonesia; Australia.* Axtell, *Gestures*, p. 32. Beckoning with curled index considered insulting. *Philippines; Singapore.* Axtell, *Gestures*, pp. 193, 195. Similarly in *Central Africa.* Hochegger, p. 9. * Clap hands once or twice: signal for waiter to come. *Saudi Arabia; Lebanon.* Barakat, no. 219. * "He beckons with his hand and smiles on me." 16th–17th cent. *England.* Shakesp., I *Henry VI* 1.4.92. "He beckoned to him that he should come to shore." 13th–14th cent. *Italy.* Dante, *Inf.* c. xvii. "produce from the breast-pocket of his coat, a short truncheon surmounted by a brazen crown, with which he beckoned to Mr. Pickwick with a grave and ghost-like air." 19th cent. *England.* Dickens, *Pickwick*, I, p. 406. Peter beckoning to them with the hand. Biblical. *Middle East. Acts* 12:17. In beckoning with the hand, the palm is held vertically. Anc. *Greece; Etruria.* Sittl, p. 216. "The officer evinced his consciousness of their presence by slightly beckoning with his hand; and the two friends followed him at a little distance." 19th cent. *England.* Dickens, *Pickwick*, I, p. 34. * Drawing in flat of hand, palm toward gesturer. Schoolchildren. *U.S.* Seton, p. xx. * Hand flapped, palm down. Southern *Italy.* Efron, p. 156. Palm down, fingers repeatedly straightened and bent. Southern *Italy*; southern *Balkans; Near East; North Africa.* Röhrich, *Gebärde-Metapher-Parodie*, p. 13 and pl. 7; (respectful) *Zaire.* Hochegger, p. 8. Fingers together or moving separately, usually beginning with the smallest; the latter primarily by women. *Colombia.* Saitz and Cervenka, p. 27 In some European countries, e.g. *Italy* and *Greece*, palm-down beckoning gesture can be confused with palm-down farewell gesture in which the fingers are waggled up and down, whereas in the beckoning gesture, they make a scratching motion. Axtell, *Gestures*, p. 32. * Fingers repeatedly straightened and bent, palm up. Eastern *Mediterranean*, p. 45. Often used to call people at short distances. *Colombia; U.S.* Saitz and Cervenka, p. 27. * Clapping hands. *Asia; Spain.* Röhrich, *Gebärde-Metapher-Parodie*, p.

13. *Mongolia*. Ohm, p. 285. *Japan*. Ohm, p. 286; anc. *Greece*. Sittl, p. 222. Common people. *Colombia*. Axtell, *Gestures*, p. 33. * Waving hand, palm inwards in direction of gesturer. Anc. *Greece*. Sittl, pp. 215–16. Also a signal to the enemy to approach for a conference. Anc. *Rome*. Polybius, 1, 78. Sittl, p. 216. Signal to attack. Anc. *Rome*. Sittl, p. 216. * Right hand held up, palm down, then moved several times in slightly clawing motion. *Jordan; Lebanon; Bahrein; Saudi Arabia; Syria*. Barakat, no. 189. * There are two basic European beckoning gestures: palm-up and palm-down, finger movements may be idiosyncratic. Beckoning with the palm up is common in *Britain; Scandinavia; Netherlands; Germany; Austria; Belgium; France; Yugoslavia*; palm-down beckoning is common in *Spain; Malta; Tunisia;* southern *Greece; Turkey; Corfu; Italy; Sicily; Sardinia*. Northern *Greece* and *Portugal* have no preference for one form of beckon over the other. These patterns are linked to patterns of waving: palm-up beckon to palm-out wave, the palm-down beckon to palm-out wave, with the exception of *Italy, Sicily, Sardinia*, where the preferred wave is palm-in. Northern *Greece* and *Portugal* show strong preference for the palm-out wave, whereas *Corfu* showed no preference for one form of wave over the other. Morris et al., pp. 241–46; for differences in beckoning to a waiter and in beckoning generally, see Axtell, *Gestures*, pp. 128–20: beckoning generally takes the form of holding the hand palm down and curling the fingers in a scratching motion in *Iran; Lebanon; China; Fiji; India; Japan; Philippines; Singapore; Taiwan; Thailand; Argentina; Bolivia; Colombia; Guatemala; Mexico; Puerto Rico*. See FINGER, Approach.

Approval Shaking hands. 19th cent. *England*. Dickens, *Pickwick*, I, p. 456; II, pp. 155, 168. "Your conduct is most noble, Sir"—as he grasped hand. Dickens, *Pickwick*, I, p. 199. 19th cent. *France*. Raim, p. 97. * Stroking chest downwards with right hand two or three times, accompanied by ironical exclamation "och! och!" *Near East*. Critchley, p. 91. * All five fingers of one hand joined at tips, held to mouth, then suddenly spread out. *France*. Life Photos by David Scherman, *Life*, Sept. 16, 1946, p. 12. The Israelites clapped their hands when Joash was anointed king. Biblical. *Middle East*. II *Kings* 11:12. * "The ladies waved a choice collection of pocket-handkerchiefs at this proposition." 19th cent. *England*. Dickens, *Pickwick*, II, p. 67. * Pretending to curl tip of imaginary moustache. Southern *Italy*. Efron, p. 148. * Slapping another man's palm with open palm—sign that that person has done something good. *Jordan*. Barakat, no. 240. * Hand raised above head height, flat palm outward, slaps into flat palm of hand similarly held by another person: the "high five" gesture popular in the *U.S.* Axtell, *Gestures*, pp. 88–89. * Open hands raised above the head. *Central Africa*. Hochegger, p. 10. * A person seeking approval or appreciation extends the open right hand, palm up. If approval is granted the other person strokes the extended hand with his palm. *Caucasus; Central Asia.* Monahan, pp. 164–65.

Approximation Palm down, fingers spread, hand moves sideways in the fashion of a see-saw: "Más o menos" ("More or less"). Río de la Plata region of *Argentina; Uruguay.* Meo Zilio, p. 97.

Arrest Hand laid on shoulder of captive. Medieval *Germany. Sachsenspiegel* as well as other Germanic laws. Amira, "Handgebärden," pp. 246–47; Fruin, II, p. 315. * Grasping the hand of a malefactor in the process of passing counterfeit money renders him "manufestus" (arrested). Medieval *Germany.* Amira, "Handgebärden," p. 251.

Arrogance (of another) Indicate a swelled head. Schoolchildren. *U.S.* Seton, p. xxi. The sign of the "horns." 19th cent. Naples, southern *Italy.* De Jorio, p. 95. *See* FINGER, Mockery.

Assistance King, before ascending throne, stopped before the statue of Bel and took his hands. *Assyria.* Winkler, p. 20. King took the hands of the Marduk idol at New Year's festival. *Babylonia.* Frazer, *The Golden Bough*, IX, p. 356. *See* HAND, Legitimation. * The *restitutio*-motif in Roman art and coinage consists of showing the emperor raising a kneeling figure personifying *Libertas* or *Roma* or some other personification by holding it by the hand. Anc. *Rome.* Sittl, p. 347; Brilliant, pp. 189 ff. and passim. Christ holds St. Peter's hand in Giotto's *Navicella* (St. Peter's, Rome) as symbolic gesture indicating the salvation of his disciple from drowning. Medieval *Italy.* Barasch, *Giotto*, pp. 129–32. Medieval representations, particularly of Byzantine origin, usually show Christ grasping St. Peter's wrist or the arm above the wrist. Barasch, *Giotto*, p. 131. *See* HAND, Leading. Hartmann von Aue, *Gregorius* 135–37, "alsus huop in bî sîner hant / diu gotes gnâde als sî in vant / ûf ir miltes ahselbein," adapts "the secular courtly gesture of lifting a defeated opponent by the hand, often accompanied in the chivalrous sphere by tending wounds." 12th cent. *Germany.* Wells, p. 164; Peil, p. 155–56.

Assurance Person giving assurance of something to another, gives him the right hand. Anc. *Greece* and *Rome.* Sittl, p. 135. " 'I assure you, Ma'am,' said Mr. Pickwick, grasping the old lady's hand" 19th cent. *England.* Dickens, *Pickwick*, I, p. 82.

Astonishment " 'for to the best of my knowledge, I was never here before.' 'Never in Bath, Mr. Pickwick!' exclaimed the Grand Master, letting his hand fall in astonishment." 19th cent. *England.* Dickens, *Pickwick*, II, p. 114. * Crossing oneself. 15th–16th cent. *Spain.* Rojas, v, ix.

Attention "He gave the child a shake to make him obedient." 19th cent. *England.* Dickens, *Pickwick*, II, p. 43. * "He raised himself in bed, and extended his hand, as if he were about to say something more." 19th cent. *England.* Dickens, *Pickwick*, I, p. 382. * Clapping hands to call attention of spirits, awaken and call souls of ancestors during worship. *Japan*. Ohm, p. 286. * Hand cupped behind ear, indicating that one is giving attention. Schoolchildren. *U.S.* Seton, p. xxi. * Gently pulling the skirts of someone's coat to get his attention. 19th cent. *England*. Dickens, *Pickwick*, I, p. 462; II, p. 231. * Hand extended forward, palm down, fingers together. Hand is lowered several times. Used only when addressing a group of people. *France*. Mitton, p. 145. * Clapping hands, as used in ancient *Rome*, spread in France during the 18th cent. and is used only when a great number of people are to be brought to attention. *France*. Mitton, p. 146. Clapping to call waiter. *Colombia*. Saitz and Cervenka, p. 106. *See* Approach above. * "It was at the end of the chorus to the first verse, that Mr. Pickwick held up his hand in a listening attitude." 19th cent. *England*. Dickens, *Pickwick*, II, p. 50. * "leaned toward his mother and . . . grasped her upper arm tightly." Ibid. * Raising hand to get waiter's attention. *U.S.* Saitz and Cervenka, p. 107. Hand extended to get teacher's attention. *Colombia; U.S.* Saitz and Cervenka, p. 22. (U.S. student eager for attention waves hand from side to side, Colombian student thrusts it forward repeatedly.) Hand raised, finger extended. Common in classrooms. *Colombia; U.S.* Saitz and Cervenka, p. 22. * "Anne . . . laid her hand on Mr. Wimbush's shoulder." *England*. Huxley, ch. 10. * "Mr. Scogan, like a policeman arresting the flow of traffic, held up his hand." Ibid., ch. 15. * Open right hand raised to level of mouth, threatening to slap someone. *Central Africa*. Hochegger, p. 16. * Listener holds both hands relaxed in front of his body, one hand grasping the wrist of the other. See the miniatures in Heidelberg, Univ.-Bibl. cpg 848 (*Germany*, 14th cent.) of König Tyro von Schotten (8r), the margrave of Hohenburg (29r) and Der Winsbeke (213r) in Walther, pl. 3, 15, 70. *See also* ARM, BREAST, Attention; FINGER, HAND, Attention; HAND, Speech.

Authority The hand as symbol of power. Anc. *Egypt*; *Babylonia*. Ebert, V, col. 95. Anc. *Rome; Phoenicia; Libya; Carthaginia; Ireland;* Celtic; *Central America;* pre-Columbian *America*. Seligmann, II, p. 165. Medieval *Europe*. "dextera dei." Ibid. On seals, coins, crosses, fence-posts and staves as well as in the form of sanctuary-granting objects, there is to be found the flat hand (before its transformation into a swearing hand) as symbol of justice and protective power. Medieval *German*. Amira, "Handgebärden," pp. 198–99. * Hand on hip, chest out, head high. Typical in portrayals of kings, generals and heroes. *Europe*. See, e.g., van Dyck's *Charles I*. See particularly Spicer, pp. 84–128; also 19th cent. Naples, southern *Italy*. De Jorio, p. 199. "Pilar stood with her hands on her hips looking at the boy mockingly now." *Spain*. Hemingway, p. 140. * Hand, or image of raised right (or left) hand, middle finger crossed over index, seal of Waimar of Salerno. Southern *Italy*. 11th cent. *See* Fig. 8.

Avarice   Clenched fist. *Persia.* Rose, p. 312. *Lat. Am.* Kany, p. 70. 19th cent. *Spain.* Pérez Galdós, II, vi, p. 246. * Hands extended horizontally, fingers separated and hooked. *Europe; North Am.* Aubert, p. 86, Fig. 129. * Left fist raised, right hits under left elbow, simultaneously the fingers of the left fist open. *Spain.* Flachskampf, p. 231. * Right hand slightly extended forward, palm up, fingers closed on palm. *Central Africa.* Hochegger, p. 17.

Aversion   Open right hand, palm backwards, is moved abruptly backwards past the head. *Central Africa.* Hochegger, p. 18.

Awe   *See* HAND, Submission.

Begging   Holding out the cupped hand, palm up. Anc. *Rome.* Suetonius, II, xci, 2. Bulwer, pp. 53–55. * Holding out two cupped hands abutting at the edge of their palms. *South Africa.* Axtell, *Gestures,* p. 95. * Beggars throw dust on themselves while standing. 19th cent. *Poland.* Sittl, p. 158. Rubbing hands on earth, indicating readiness to throw dust on oneself. Anc. *Persia.* Sittl, ibid.

Behind   Open hand at level of chest and perpendicular to it, describes a 270 degree arc in the air. Río de la Plata region of *Argentina; Uruguay.* Meo Zilio, p. 95.

Betting   Handclasp. *Germany. DWb,* IV/2, col. 414.

Blessing   Raising hand toward those to be blessed. Biblical. *Middle East. Lev.* 9:22; *Luke* 24:50. * Placing hand on the head of person to be blessed. Biblical. *Middle East. Gen.* 48:14. * Laying on of hands also served to transfer sins to sacrificial animals. Biblical. *Middle East. Lev.* 4:4,24, etc., Ohm, pp. 290 ff. Laying on of hands symbolizes sympathy and identification with another. In baptism, confirmation, ordination, unction it plays a central role. Symbolically related to touching of hands and embrace, which can augment it and enrich liturgical movement (see *Mark* 1:16). Roman Catholic. *GdG,* p. 34. * Sacred Judaic blessing gesture consists of holding palms down, thumb nails touching, index and middle fingers touching but held separated from the ring and little fingers which touch each other. Gesture is covered by a cloth. If an ordinary person sees the gesture he will go blind. It may only be given by high priests, descendants of Aaron. Judaism. Hayes, p. 229. * Sophocles has Oedipus put his hands upon his children to bless them before his death. Frequent non- and pre-Christian form of blessing. Ohm, p. 290. Also Christian. Biblical. *Middle East. Mark* 10:16; "And Israel stretched out his right hand and laid it on Ephraim's head, who was the younger, and his left hand on Manasseh's head, crossing his hands—for Manasseh was the first-born." *Gen.* 48:14. "Hold up thy hand." 16th–17th cent. *England.* Shakesp., II *Henry IV,* 3.3.28. "And hold your hand in benediction o'er me." 16th–17th cent. *England.* Shakesp., *Lear,* 4.7.57. 19th cent. *Germany.* Immermann, p. 40. On the imposition of hands in medieval art, see Barasch, *Giotto,* pp. 117–27. * "The sign of the cross is made either upon others or upon one's self; in the first it is an action of benediction, in the second an individual act. God is the source of all benediction . . . The delegated representatives of God on earth, Popes and Bishops more especially, are also divinely commissioned to bestow benedictions on mankind. Angels, although the ministers of the Deity, are not his representatives by the same title as the Pope, or Bishops, who are his vicars by virtue of their apostolical descent. The functions of the priesthood can be exercised by men only; angels are not, and cannot be represented blessing." Roman Catholic. Didron, I, p. 406. Making the sign of the cross with or without accompanying formula. Christian. Since the 2nd century. Ohm, p. 296. After exorcism the bishop makes the sign of the cross over the neophyte's forehead, ears and nose according to the Aegyptian liturgy. Ohm, p. 298. Cross is to be made over the neophyte before baptism according to St. Augustine. Roman Catholic. Ohm, p. 298. Luther advised use of the sign of the cross upon arising in the morning, but rejected its use in the liturgy. Protestant. Ohm, pp. 299–301. Making the sign of the cross over saddles of horses before mounting to enter judicial combat. Medieval *Spain*. *Cid*, c. iii. For variations of the sign of the cross, see Ohm, pp. 292–93 and particularly Baumer, cols. 1135–41; and *GdG*, pp. 34–35. The right hand is regarded as the blessing hand. Ohm, p. 249. Elderly Russian Orthodox women often make the cross when leaving their house, and in the Soviet Union, even Party members sometimes crossed themselves at the beginning of the day. The index, middle finger and thumb are joined lightly at the tips, touching first the forehead, then the breast, then the right and left shoulders. *Russia*. Monahan, pp. 128. The sign of the cross is made either with the hand or with a sacred object. A distinction is made between the "Roman" and the "Greek" cross: in making the latter, the hand is moved from forehead to the breast vertically and then from the right to the left shoulder, the former is made by moving the hand from forehead to breast and then from the left to the right shoulder. The first positive evidence for this "Roman" major cross dates from the 11th century. Endres and Ebner, p. 302. As late as the 13th century the form of the major cross was still not settled in Roman liturgy. Ohm, pp. 293–95. "Some persons sign themselves from the head even to the feet, to signify mystically that God, having bowed the heavens, descended upon earth . . . They next sign from right to left; first, to show that they prefer things eternal, signified by the right hand, to things temporal signified by the left; secondly to remind us that Christ passed from the Jews to the Gentiles; and, thirdly, because Christ, coming from the right hand, that is to say, from the Father, conquered on the cross the Devil, typified by the left, whence the words, 'I came forth from the Father and am come into the world' (*John* 16:28). But others signing themselves from left to right justify that formula by the text, 'He came from the Father, he descended into hell, and returned to the throne of God.' In fact, they commence by making the sign in the upper part, which designates the Father; then they descend below, meaning the earth; then they go to the left, which marks hell, and so re-ascend to the right, signifying to heaven . . . Secondly, by doing thus they intimate that we must pass from misery to glory, and from vice, signified by the left, to virtue, whose place is on the right, . . . Thirdly, because Christ raises us, through faith in his cross from things which pass away, to things which endure for ever. In the present day, however, an individual making on his body the sign of the cross employs the right hand entirely open, instead of the three fingers only; but, on the contrary, he uses one finger only, the thumb, to trace the sign of the cross on the forehead, the mouth, and the heart, when (before reading the Gospel, and as a response to the deacon who prepares to chant it,) homage is rendered to God by inclining the body and saying '*Gloria tibi, Domine!*' " ("The glory is Thine, o Lord"). Didron, I, pp. 410–11. But see also Suntrup, pp. 256 ff., and Barasch, *Giotto*, pp. 10, 19. * In Greek liturgy the gesture of blessing is the raised index, middle, and little finger (symbolic of the Trinity); the thumb and ringfinger (symbolic of the two natures of Christ) are folded toward the palm. Seligmann, II, p. 179. Didron, I, pp. 407–8 cites a Byzantine "Guide for Painting": "When you desire to represent a hand in the act of blessing, you must not join the three fingers together, but let the thumb be crossed on the third finger, so that the first called the index, may remain open, and the second finger be slightly bent. Those two fingers form the name of Christ Ιησους, I.C. In fact, the first finger remaining open signifies an I (iôta), and the curvature of the second forms a C (sigma). The thumb is placed across the third finger, and the fourth, or little finger, is slightly bent, thus indicating the word Χριστος, X.C. The union of the thumb with the third finger makes a X (chi), and the curvature of the little finger forms a C (sigma), and these two letters form the 'sigle,' or abridgment of Christos." *See* Fig. 14, Didron I. fig. 49. * Roman blessing gesture is the extended thumb, index, and middle finger, with the ring and little finger folded toward the palm. Seligmann, ibid. "The Latin benediction is given with the thumb and two first fingers open; the third and the little finger remaining closed. [*See* Fig. 15.] This arrangement of the fingers appears to be symbolic. Gulielmus Durandus [*Rat. Div. Off.*, lib. 5, cap. 2] and Jean Beleth [*Explic. Divin. Off.*, cap. 39] affirm that that manner of blessing symbolizes the Trinity, and that the three open fingers signify the three Divine persons." Roman Catholic. Didron, I, p. 408. "It appears that in former times priests as well as bishops gave the benediction with three fingers extended; but at a later period, when it was thought desirable to establish a more marked difference between the episcopal benediction and that of a simple priest, bishops reserved to themselves

Fig. 14. Greek blessing gesture. From Adolphe Napoleon Didron, *Christian Iconography*, transl. E. J. Millington (London: G. Bell, 1886) I, p. 176.

the right of blessing with three fingers; and priests no longer gave the benediction except with the hand entirely open. In addition to this, bishops gave their blessing as it were full face, priests only in profile, with the hand held sideways. Lastly, during the performance of ecclesiastical offices and prayers, in which bishops give three successive benedictions, and three times make the sign of the cross, priests give one blessing only, and make one single sign. The episcopal benediction is then the same as that of the priest, but in its fullest amplification." Roman Catholic. Didron, I, pp. 408–9. "The hand [of God] is either in the act of blessing, with two or three fingers only extended or it is bestowing (*Donatrice*), that is to say, entirely open, and shedding from each finger rays of light, signifying favor and acceptance." Roman Catholic. Didron I, p. 205. *See also* FINGER, Blessing; FINGER, HAND, Blessing; HAND,

Fig. 15. Roman blessing gesture. Adolphe Napoleon Didron, *Christian Iconography*, transl. E. J. Millington (London: G. Bell, 1886) I, p. 24.

Speech). The priest sprinkles holy water in four directions. Roman Catholic. Beitl, p. 260. *See also* FINGER, Blessing; FINGER, HAND, Blessing.

Boredom Fingers of one hand are interlaced with those of the other, and the two thumbs continuously turn around each other. *France.* Mitton, p. 151. Hands raised to chest height, palm down, fingers slightly curved, are suddenly moved forward: "Go away, you annoy us!" *Central Africa.* Hochegger, p. 63. *See also* FINGER, Boredom.

Bribery Hollow hand, palm up, held behind back of gesticulator. Schoolchildren. *U.S.* Seton, p. xxiii.

Calmness Outstretched hands, palms down, pushed toward the floor, indicate request for calmness. *Spain; Lat. Am.* Green, p. 43. * Folding of hands indicates calmness. *Universal.* Ohm, p. 269. * Infant on left arm is lightly tapped by right hand. *Central Africa.* Hochegger, p. 30.

Carelessness Twisting the open hand back and forth, fingers together, palm may face down. Madrid, *Spain.* Green, p. 90.

Challenge Offering one's gauntlet to the enemy. 13th cent. *Ger-*

many. Gottfr. v. Strassb., 6453–4. * Throwing down the gauntlet to one's enemy. Challenge is accepted if it is picked up. 16th–17th cent. *England*. Shakesp., *Richard II* 4.1.46; also 1.1.146; 1.1.69. *See* GLOVE [GAUNTLET], Challenge. * "that unaccountable person flung the money on the pavement, and requested in figurative terms to be allowed the pleasure of fighting him (Mr. Pickwick) for the amount!" 19th cent. *England*. Dickens, *Pickwick*, I, p. 8. * " 'Come on,' said the cab-driver, sparring away like clockwork. 'Come on—all four of you.' " 19th cent. *England*. Dickens, *Pickwick*, I, p. 9. * The inner side of the right fist beats against the top of the outer side of the left fist, accompanied by a formula of challenge. Children. *Turkey*. Critchley, p. 91.

Change "Verbal behavior suggestive of a change . . . may be accompanied by a movement performed by rotating both hands—one after the other and with the palms facing the speaker—in a circular motion at the level of the mover's chest." Madrid, *Spain; Lat. Am.* Green, p. 68.

Claim Seizure of a goblet and inverting a torch (as though to set fire to a field) represent seizure of territory. Medieval *German*. Wolfr. v. Eschenbach, iii, 146.

Cleansing Brushing hands. *U.S.* Krout, p. 22.

Cold Rubbing hands together vigorously. *Spain*. Green, pp. 90–91. *Colombia; U.S.* Saitz and Cervenka, p. 26. * Fists placed near shoulder and shaking. Schoolchildren. *U.S.* Seton, p. xxiii.

Collect "The priest joins his hands as if to collect the hearts of all those present." Roman Catholic. *Mass*, p. 42.

Command Open hand raised, palm outward, so that lower arm forms an approximate right angle with upper arm, index extended, other fingers closed; the hand may extend in the same line as the lower arm, or it may form a slight angle with it. In pronouncing a ban over someone (*missio in bassum*) the judge had to raise his hand. Medieval *Germany* and *Italy*. Amira, "Handgebärden," pp. 196–97; J. Ficker, III, p. 33, 35; IV, no. 2, 47. * In a miniature of Cgm 63, fol. 91 (ca. 1300) of *Wilhelm v. Orlens* King Amelot places Savine under his protection, holding the scepter in his right hand and raising the left. * In Heidelberg, Univ.-Bibl. cgm 848, fol. 219b, Landgrave Hermann, holding the sword in his extended left, raises his right hand in judgment as Heinrich von Ofterdingen is defeated in the poetic contest of the *Wartburgkrieg*. Extremely common in European medieval art; early medieval Christian art appears to prefer the ancient, so-called blessing-gesture, with index and middle finger raised. Medieval *Germany*. Amira, "Handgebärden," pp. 212–13. *See* HAND, STAFF, Command. * In a picture of the Palatinate "Nequambook" (1300–1325) the seated judge gives commands to a beadle, on another to the executioner, with the "speech-gesture" of the raised hand. Similarly the French Berlin Beaumanoir-manuscript (Hamilt. 193), chap. 67, in Bibl. Nat. ms. lat. 18437, fol. 2, of 1331 and in the digest of clm. 14022 (14th cent.) referred to by Amira, ibid., p. 195, show the judge with raised hand. In the latter, he holds a lily in his hand in reference to the book *de integrum restitutionibus*, a sword in reference to the book *de condiccione furtiva*. Amira, "Handgebärden," p. 198. In Ms O 30b of the *Sachsenspiegel* the mayor is "finding" precedents for the count and is shown raising the left index (recte: the right index; see Amira, ibid., pp. 169–70); the count questions the five jurymen with the command-gesture, and four of them raise a hand; Ms D 17b, in the corresponding illustration, has all five raise the right index. Medieval *Germany; France.* Amira, ibid., p. 200. See also Gombrich, p. 67 on "the pointing hand, which indicates a degree of emphasis that can be unbecoming." *See also* HAND, Speech.

Commendation The bride emerges from the house of her parents holding a bare sword vertically before her face; in the house of the groom she surrenders the sword. 19th cent. *Palestine.* Bauer, p. 94. * Vassals extend hands toward the lord at enfeoffment. 13th cent. *Germany. Kudrun,* st. 190, 1. 2. *See* Investiture below. In Hartmann's *Gregorius,* "the father employs a legal, feudal gesture of commendation to carry out his intention of committing his children to the protection of his counsellors (196–99), taking their hands and placing them in the hands of their protectors (221–22), a ward being legally in the role of one who has commended himself to a guardian." 12th cent. *Germany.* Wells, p. 165; Amira, "Handgebärden," pp. 242–46.

Complication Fingers loose, hands rotate over each other. *Colombia.* Saitz and Cervenka, p. 29. * Hands open and extended forward, palm down, are crossed left to right and right to left and back again: "It's a complicated matter." *Central Africa.* Hochegger, p. 38.

Compliment *See* Confusion.

Concentration "Then goes he to the length of all his arm and with his other hand thus o'er his brow." 16th–17th cent. *England.* Shakesp., *Hamlet* 2.1.88. * Index laid on brow, head lowered. Schoolchildren. *U.S.* Seton, p. xxii. *See also* FOREHEAD, HAND, Concentration.

Confidence Arms raised to level of head, hands clasped. *U.S.* Photo, *Berkeley (California) Daily Gazette,* June 2, 1964, p. 1. * "On their small balconies older men and women were using both hands to make the victory sign, remembered from the War." *Netherlands.* Mulisch, p. 171.

Confirmation Laying on of hands as sign of transmission of spirit or official duties. Anc. *Greece*; anc. Jewish; Christian. Ohm, p. 291. * In one of the sanctuaries of the Ziggurat stood the image of Bel-Merodach, the annual touching of which by the kings at the New Year's festival confirmed their title. *Babylonia.* Hastings, *Dictionary,* I, p. 213.

Confusion Open hand raised vertically to approx. eye level, then moved past the face and downwards, gradually closing as it moves. The gesture indicates that the gesturer thinks someone is temporarily confused or has a screw loose. The gesture can also be a compliment: "He's hilarious!" *Netherlands.* Andrea and de Boer, p. 89.

Congratulation Handshake. Anc. *Greece* and *Rome.* Sittl, p. 30. *Netherlands.* Andrea and de Boer, p. 74. " 'When this programme wins an award for investigative journalism,' I said to him in Hank's cutting room, 'I am going to be the one whose hand gets shaken.' 'Fine by me,' said Dan. 'My own wrist will be limp from hours of handshakings and congratulations on my Wagner film.' " *England.* Marrin, p. 60. * One can also shake one's own hand while looking pointedly at the person one is congratulating. *Netherlands.* Andrea and de Boer, p. 74. * Clapping of hands. Sittl, p. 54. * Clapping raised hands. 17th cent. *England.* Bulwer, pp. 34–35. * Grasping someone by the hand. 19th cent. *England.* Dickens, *Pickwick,* I, p. 310. * Hand extended to someone. Anc. *Greece* and *Rome*; early Christian. Sittl, p. 50. * Slapping someone on the shoulder. Men. *Netherlands.* Andrea and de Boer, p. 146. * Clinking glasses or milk cartons in drinking a toast. College Students. California, *U.S.* McCord, p. 291. *See* HAND, OBJECT, Toast.

Consecration Laying on of hands. *Num.* 27:18; *Acts* 8:18. Bishop elect is presented by two bishops to the archbishop of the province. After litany is said, while two bishops hold Gospels over neck of the elect, all other bishops touching his head, the consecrator begins "veni creator" ("Come, o Creator"). Head and hands of elect are consecrated with chrism and oil. *England.* Swete, p. 207. At ordination of a bishop, a consecrator, chosen from the bishops, lays his hand on the head of the elect. Early Christian. Canons of Hippolytus. 3rd cent. Swete, p. 200. At ordination in the English church of the 8th cent., the imposition of hands followed the Gallic rule: deacons received it from bishops, the priests from the bishops and priests present, the bishop from the bishops present while the open gospels were held over his neck. Medieval *England.* Swete, p. 203. Ordination and consecration with visible laying on of hands. Biblical. *Middle East. Num.* 8:10; *Acts* 6:6; 13:3; I *Tim.* 4:14. Bulwer, pp. 107–119. *See also* HAND, HEAD, Consecration.

Consolation Placing the hand on someone's shoulder may signify moral support or comfort. *U.S.* Ruesch and Kees, p. 85. * Deity clasps hand of mortal. Anc. *Greece.* Sittl, p. 276.

Contempt The "fig" (clenched fist, thumb protruding between index and middle, or middle and ring fingers). Anc. *Greece.* A. Cook, p. 134. * Middle finger extended, rest of hand clenched into a fist. 17th cent. *England.* Bulwer, pp. 143, 203. * Clapping of hands. 15th–16th cent. *Italy.* Ariosto, xvii, 91. * An imaginary pinch of sand thrown at person. Schoolchildren. *U.S.* Seton, p. xxi. * Open palm, fingers radiating from it and bent slightly back. Southern *India.* Rose, p. 314. * Fingers of one hand united at their extremities, taking saliva from under the tongue and making the gesture of throwing it towards a person. 19th cent. Naples, southern *Italy*. De Jorio, p. 131. * Both hands form a circle, 10–30 cm in diameter, indicating the size of the anus of the person despised. *Mexico*. Jiménez, p. 37. * Slight wave of right hand by moving it from the wrist outward in a rapid movement. Anc. *Greece* and *Rome*. Sittl, p. 98. * Thrusting out the closed hand and opening it, palm down. *Europe; North Am.* Aubert, p. 83. "thrust his hands beneath his coat tails." 19th cent. *England*. Dickens, *Pickwick*, II; p. 429. * Holding out left hand, palm forward, in front of face, then hitting the back of it lightly with palm of right hand. *Saudi Arabia*. Barakat, no. 176. *See also* ARM, WRIST, Contempt; FINGER, Contempt; FINGER, HAND, Contempt.

Contentment "he smiled to himself and rubbed his large white hands together." *England*. Huxley, ch. 6.

Copulation Extended left fist is jerked downward or to the side from a loose wrist two or three times, either in the air or against a surface. *Lat. Am.* Kany, p. 187. * The open right palm is slapped down two or three times on the extended left fist held upright or in oblique position, as if pushing a cork into a bottle. *Lat. Am.* Kany, p. 187. *Russia*. Monahan, pp. 146–47. * Tickling the palm of a woman when shaking hands, usually with the forefinger—proposition. *Lebanon; Syria*. Barakat, no. 82. *Central Africa*. Hochegger, p. 193. * Hitting tightly closed right fist into left palm—proposition. *Lebanon; Syria*. Barakat, no. 8. * When shaking hands with a woman, a man places his right thumb on the back of her right hand and rubs the back slightly with the thumb—proposition. *Lebanon; Syria*. Barakat, no. 15. * Hitting right fist into left palm—obscenity. *Saudi Arabia*. Barakat, no. 106. * Placing palms together and bending two middle fingers while other fingers are still extended in contact, then moving hands in opposite directions so that middle fingers are extended up and down, respectively—obscenity. *Egypt*. Barakat, no. 142. * Fist, front of hand outward, moved from right to left like a pendulum. *Mexico*. Lomas, p. 36. * Flat hand, palm down, repeatedly strikes fist of other hand, held vertically, suggesting the covering of an orifice, which is symbolic of copulation. *Brazil*. Cascudo, *História*, pp. 236–38; "Avec le talon de la main droite, tapoter sur la main gauche repliée en forme de gobelet" ("Tapping left hand in form of a cup with the heel of the right hand"). Very vulgar. *France*. Mitton, no. 75. *See also* ARM, HAND, Copulate.

Creation "describing small circles in the air—in the . . . vicinity of the mover's chest—with the slightly cupped hand . . . The thumb moves minimally and seems to serve as an axis for the movement of the hand . . . The movement observed in connection with expressions suggestive of setting in motion is performed similarly, but the circles described by the hand tend to be larger and the hand less cupped. Madrid, *Spain; Lat. Am.* Green, p. 67.

Cuckoldry   Holding both indexes above the temples ("horns"). *Lat. Am.* Kany, p. 190. * The index and little fingers extended upwards, other fingers closed ("horns"). Southern *Italy.* Efron, no. 59a. *See also* FINGER, FOREHEAD, Cuckoldry; FINGER, HEAD, Cuckoldry; HAND, HEAD, Cuckoldry.

Curse   Beating the ground with the flat hand. Anc. *Greece;* Naples, southern *Italy.* Heiler, p. 103; Sittl, p. 191. Cursing the gods of the underworld and the dead by beating on the ground with the flat hand. Anc. *Rome.* Heiler, p. 103. * Raising or extending the open hand while swearing an oath is a curse upon oneself. *Asia.* Ebert, V, p. 93. * Making the sign of the "horns" toward someone. 19th cent. Naples, southern *Italy.* De Jorio, p. 94. * Holding up open hands in front of shoulders, then moving them forward a few times, palms facing forward. *Jordan; Syria.* Barakat, no. 40. * Clapping hands several times: if one has witnessed the flight of a thief, the curse will follow him. *Central Africa.* Hochegger, p. 112.

Death   Sign of the cross made in the air. Naples, *Italy.* Critchley, p. 89. * Oldest son or nearest relative present closes the eyes of the dead. Hastings, *Dictionary,* I, col. 332.

Deception   Swinging the clenched hand forward, palm down and index extended, away from the chest in a half circle may accompany expressions suggesting "undermining." Madrid, *Spain.* Green, p. 40. * Iniquity gestures behind her back. St. Augustine, *La Cité de Dieu,* Rijksmuseum Meermanno-Westreenianum, The Hague, Ms. 10 A ll, fol. 201v. Ca. 1475–80. See Fig. 16.

Decorum   Unmarried women, whether standing still or walking, are to let their right hand rest upon their left, held in front at the height of the belt. Medieval *Italy. Decor puellarum* (1471); van der Meulen, p. 36. See also the miniatures of König Tyro von Schotten with his son Fridebrant (fol. 8r), Der Winsbeke (fol. 213r), von Monegiur (fol. 247v), Friedrich von Sonnenburg (fol. 407r) in Heidelberg, Univ.-Bibl. cpg 848. 14th cent. *Germany.* Walther, pl. 3, 70, 78, 130 respectively, representing young men or boys in the presence of their elders.

Dedication   Raising hands holding an object. Anc. *Greece.* Sittl, p. 197 and n. 4. In dedicating a sacred building the pontifex held a pillar with his hand, thus, according to Roman law, transferring the building from the *manus* (hand) of man into that of the deity. Sittl, p. 196.

Defiance   "the thief raised his hands with both the figs." 13th–14th cent. *Italy.* Dante, *Inf.,* c. xxv. * Right fist, held vertically, rubbed on the flat palm of the left in a circular motion. 19th cent. *Palestine.* Bauer, p. 222. * "crimson silk pocket handkerchief attached to a walking stick, which was occasionally waved in the air with various gestures indicative

Fig. 16. Iniquity gestures behind her back. St. Augustine, *La Cité de Dieu* (ca. 1475–80). Rijksmuseum Meermanno-Westreenianum, The Hague, Netherlands. 10 A 11, fol. 201v.

of supremacy and defiance." 19th cent. *England*. Dickens, *Pickwick*, II, p. 368. * Throw a cap at someone. *DEP*, 77. "deliberately depositing his hat on the floor." 19th cent. *England*. Dickens, *Pickwick*, II, p. 18. *See also* FINGER, Defiance.

Demonstrate   Open hand in front, palm upwards, finger tips down. *Europe; North Am.* Aubert, p. 91.

Denial   Hand raised, palm forward, or sometimes simply the index extended, shakes rapidly sideways. Equivalent to shaking the head. *France*. Mitton, p. 141.

Depart (Departure)   To an inferior: hand moved downward a few times. St. Jerome, *Vita Pauli Erem.*; 4th–5th cent. *Italy*. Sittl, p. 221. * Palm pushed vertically forward. Schoolchildren. *U.S.* Seton, p. xx. * Wagging hands signify "let's get out of here." *France*. Life Photo by David Scherman, *Life*, Sept. 16, 1946, p. 12. * One hand horizontal at middle of body, palm up, the other hand rapidly moves over it from wrist to beyond fingertips, palm inward, signifies "Let's beat it." *Italy*. Leone, p. XX 11. * Edge of left hand makes chopping motion against the right wrist—"Go away!" *Italy*. Graham, p. 26. * Flat right hand, held with thumb uppermost, flicked slightly upward, while flat left hand, thumb uppermost, is chopped down on right wrist. *France; Italy; southern Europe*. In Italy the gesture is primarily a request to leave, to buzz off; in France it may also refer to the action of going away or having gone away; in *Greece* and *Turkey* it may signify a polite request to pass, move on, move 'this way.' Morris et al., pp. 94–98. * Palm facing body, hand moves back and forth. *Colombia*. Saitz and Cervenka, p. 81. * Right arm extended, elbow close to body, hand vertical, thumb up; "the palm of the left hand is then moved over the wrist of the right hand with a quick jerk; the face shows grave concern; the head is sometimes lowered, as if taking cover; the hands may waggle, indicating trepidation: Tout à coup, voilà le flic qui arrive . . . on se calte! (Suddenly the cop arrives! . . . we scram) I recently observed a French-speaking Belgian woman using a very discreet variant of this gesture. Her hands were held close to the right side of the body, waist high; the left hand was vertical and stationary, crossing the right hand at about the wrist of the latter which was held palm up and which was flipped upward and toward the speaker. General rout . . . left hand bears down on the crook of the right elbow, while the right forearm is raised smartly to the height of the head; . . . There is an American gesture which is analogous . . . to indicate hasty departure . . . a person will sometimes make a rapid, sweeping, and slightly rising motion to the right with the right hand, the fingers and thumb being held together tightly. This gesture is sometimes accompanied by a whistle and . . . the point of departure is frequently the left hand which . . . is held horizontally, palm down, in front of the body, and chest high." *France*. Brault, pp. 377–78. * "Describing a sudden departure needs two hands: the left, fingers held straight, moves upwards from waist level to smack into the palm of the right hand moving downward—a restricted version of the popular and extremely vulgar bicep crunch. (Seen at its best during midsummer traffic jams, when disputing drivers will leave their cars to allow themselves the freedom of movement necessary for a left-arm uppercut stopped short by the right hand clamping on the bicep.)" Provençe, *France*. Mayle, *A Year* *in Provençe*, p. 104. * Right hand placed on shoulder of the person departing, left pointing in direction in which he is going: "Go quickly!" *Central Africa*. Hochegger, p. 5. * Right hand points in the direction in which a person is to be sought. *Central Africa*. Ibid., p. 6. * Hand held with palm downward, fingers flicking away from the body: "Get lost." *U.S.* "Enough already." *Israel*. But *see* Affection. Axtell, *Gestures* p. 93. * Palm downward, hand flicking away from the body: "Leave me in peace." *Netherlands*. Andrea and de Boer, p. 12. * "He waved his hand in signal for Godfrey to be gone." 18th century. *England*. Smollett, ch. ci. * Opening the hand and blowing into it. ("He has disappeared.") *Near East*. Critchley, p. 91.

Despair Holding up hands. Anc. *Greece*. Homer, *Odyss.*, Bk. ix. "And one who had both hands lopped off, lifting the stumps . . ." 13th–14th cent. *Italy*. Dante, *Inf.*, c. xxviii. * Tearing clothing at the breast. Anc. *Greece* and *Rome*. Sittl, p. 22. Tearing one's clothes. Early Christian. Sittl, p. 19. * Wringing hands. 16th–17th cent. *England*. Shakesp., *Two Gentlemen* 2.3.9; *Rom. and Jul.* 3.2.6. *Hamlet* 3.4.34. Wringing hands, beating breast. 16–17th cent. *England*. Shakesp., *Richard III* 2.2.3. "He made me no answer, but, raising his hands clasped together, looked the very image of despair." 18th cent. *England*. Hickey, p. 371. * Elbows against body, hands clasped at the height of the shoulders; from a position touching the chest they are lowered. Feminine and clerical. *France*. Mitton, p. 144. * Wringing hands above one's head. 18th cent. *Switzerland*. Gessner, p. 36. * "Traffic was heavy on the freeway, and the driver threw up his hands in despair as the stream of vehicles slowed to a halt. 'Gets worse all the time,' he said." *U.S.* Lodge, *Paradise News*, p. 115.

Desperation While speaking, trying to be understood, emphasis is added by slightly cupping the hand so that tip of thumb touches index, and moving hand rapidly up and down, palm up. *Italy*. Leone, p. XX 11. * "and beat his hands in perfect desperation." 19th cent. *England*. Dickens, *Oliver Twist*, p. 140.

Destruction Hands chest high, palms down, fingers pushed back and forth vigorously. Verbal context is disintegration. Madrid, *Spain*. Hands successively describe small circles. Verbal context is dissolution. Madrid, *Spain*. Green, p. 42.

Determination Fists clenched. Boys. *England*. Opie, p. 230. "Giving the trousers a hitch shows that a man wants to feel equal to an approaching task." *U.S.* Birdwhistell, "Do Gestures Speak Louder than Words?" p. 56.

Dignity The hand as symbol appears on weapons, insignia of legions, and as symbol of power and dignity. Anc. *Rome*. Seligmann, II, p. 166. *See* Authority above.

Direction Lower arm across waist, left hand points to the right or behind a person. Medieval *Germany*. *Sachsenspiegel*. Amira, "Hand-gebärden," p. 204 and fig. 4c. * Arm raised at elbow, flat hand lowered and pointing in direction of someone or something. Medieval *Germany*. ibid., p. 205 and fig. 4d. The extended hand is the required gesture in Lombard-Beneventan law (Teano, 968), and also in the *Sachsenspiegel*. Medieval *Italy*. Amira, ibid., p. 205. * Point up very high and look up (heaven). Schoolchildren. *U.S.* Seton, p. xx. * Hold out flat left, palm down, and above it hold right in the same way (over or above). School-children. *U.S.* Seton, p. xx. * Hold out flat left, palm down, and under it the right in the same way (under). Schoolchildren. *U.S.* Seton, ibid. * Index extended, pointing down (down). Schoolchildren. *U.S.* Seton, ibid. * Pointing down, hand swung in small circle (here). Schoolchild-ren. *U.S.* Seton, ibid. * Hand pointed toward seat or room in requesting someone to sit or enter. Anc. *Rome*. Sittl, p. 52. * Hand zig-zags. (Push-ing someone around.) Assimilated Jews. Eastern *Europe*. Efron, p. 117. * Hand points down (right here). Assimilated Jews. Eastern *Europe*. Efron, pp. 49, 75. * Hand moves forward, then turns and is moved toward the back (facing the back). Assimilated Jews. Eastern *Europe*. Efron, p. 116. * One hand flat, palm up, the other flat, palm down, glides forward over the former (in between). Trad. Jews. Eastern *Europe*. Efron, p. 72. * Brushing movement of one palm against the other (side-swiping). Assimilated Jews. Eastern *Europe*. Efron, p. 117. * Open hand, palm down, moved up and down: "Come down!" "Sit down!" *Central Africa*. Hochegger, p. 54.

Disagreement Tight fists, palms down, are brought toward each other ("collision," "conflict"). May be repeated. When accompanying verbal expressions suggest confrontation, fingers do not touch, but stop a few inches from one another. Madrid, *Spain; Lat. Am.* Green, p. 47. * Twisting cupped hands away from the speaker at chest level, concluding with palms facing the listener. Madrid, *Spain; Lat. Am.* Expressions of contrast may be accompanied by bent arms at shoulder level or higher, palms facing each other. Madrid, *Spain*. Green, pp. 46–47. * Hands moved up from ca. waist level with palms up. *Lebanon; Saudi Arabia*. Barakat, no. 100.

Disappointment Hand scratches back of head. 19th cent. Naples, southern *Italy*. De Jorio, p. 121. * Palm hits forehead. Intensity of blow determined by intensity of one's displeasure. 19th cent. Naples, southern *Italy*. De Jorio, p. 123. * Fingers of both hands tense, pointing down, are agitated back and forth in a semi-circular fashion in front of body. *Central Africa*. Hochegger, p. 79.

Disapproval Shaking the collar or coat lapel with the right hand. *Near East*. Critchley, p. 91.

Disbelief " 'I couldn't have believed it, sir!' said Mrs. Mann, hold-ing up her hands." 19th cent. *England*. Dickens, *Oliver Twist*, p. 151.

See also Doubt below. * One or both hands, palm outward, raised and pulled back slowly until almost touching toward shoulder(s). Río de la Plata region of *Argentina; Uruguay; Italy.* Meo Zilio, p. 93.

Disclaimer "There is a well-defined silent vocabulary, starting with the hand waggle which had been introduced to us by our builders. They used it only as a disclaimer whenever talking about time or cost, but it is a gesture of almost infinite flexibility. It can describe the state of your health, how you're getting on with your mother-in-law, the progress of your business, your assessment of a restaurant, or your predictions about this year's melon crop. When it is a subject of minor importance, the waggle is perfunctory, and is accompanied by a dismissive raising of the eyebrows. More serious matters—politics, the delicate condition of one's liver, the prospects for a local rider in the Tour de France—are addressed with greater intensity. The waggle is in slow motion, with the upper part of the body swaying slightly as the hand rocks, a frown of concentration on the face." Provence, *France.* Mayle, *A Year in Provence*, p. 103.

Discouragement Fingers close together, palms pressed together, thumbs depressed, hands rhythmically moved up and down. Naples, *Italy.* Critchley, p. 89.

Disgust Rubbing the hands together may accompany verbal expression of repugnance. *Spain; Lat. Am.* Green, p. 75. * "Pnin waved a hand at the raconteur in a Russian disgusted 'oh go-on-with-you' gesture." *Russia.* Nabokov, p. 160. * One hand upright near the face, palm out, or both hands extended forward. *Europe; North Am.* Aubert, p. 86.

Dismay "The gesture known as wringing the hands is one that is seldom seen in real life." *England.* Wodehouse, *Fish Preferred*, pp. 18, 66. "he held up his hands, assured me he could do me no service." 18th cent. *England.* Smollett, ch. xxxiv.

Dismissal "But with an angry wafture of your hand gave sign for me to leave you." 16th–17th cent. *England.* Shakesp., *Jul. Caes.*, 2.1.46–7. * Edge of left hand is brought smartly down on wrist of extended right hand ("Let's get the hell out of here"). WW II. *France.* Alsop, p. 29. *See also* Depart above. * Repeated rapid gesture of discarding something with the flat hand. *France.* Mitton, p. 143. * "He tipped his head back briefly, blew the smoke straight up in the air, and dismissed the driver with a wave of the hand." *Germany.* Mulisch, p. 50.

Distress "The respectable old gentleman wrung his hand fervently, and seemed disposed to address some observations to his son." 19th cent. *England.* Dickens, *Pickwick*, I, p. 455. * " 'Oh!' said the unhappy Bladud, clasping his hands, and mournfully raising his eyes towards the sky." 19th cent. *England.* Dickens, *Pickwick*, II, p. 133. * " 'Oh no, no, Mr. Weller,' said Arabella, clasping her hands." 19th cent. *England.*

Dickens, *Pickwick*, II, p. 183. * "Mr. Snodgrass and Mr. Winkle grasped each other by the hand." 19th cent. *England*. Dickens, *Pickwick*, II, p. 12. * "the two-hand dramatic splash of amazed distress." *Russia*. Nabokov, p. 51.

Divorce   In dissolving a marriage that had been declared invalid, a bishop is depicted as pushing the partners apart with one hand on the shoulder of each. Medieval *France*. Duby, *History of Private Life*, p. 135, from a 13th cent. *Digeste*, in Paris, Bibl. Sainte-Geneviève, Ms. 394.

Doubt   Moving the open extended hand, palm out, back and forth several times and with a wrist movement describing a semi-circle. *Lat. Am.* Kany, p. 107. *See also* Disbelief, Hesitation.

Down   Rapid downward movement of the palm. Assimilated Jews. *Eastern Europe*. Efron, p. 117. * Hands horizontal, arms straight, palms down, hands parting horizontally. *Europe; North Am.* Aubert, p. 89. *See* also Direction.

Drink   Closed fist, thumb extended and moved toward mouth until tip of thumb touches lips. Vulgar. *France*. Mitton, p. 147. " 'You won't go thirsty.' He made the Provençal drinking gesture, fist clenched and thumb pointing towards his mouth.' " Mayle, *A Year in Provence*, p. 164. * Hand moves as though strumming a guitar. *Lat. Am.* Kany, p. 78. * "he turned his glass upside down, by way of reminding his companion that he had nothing left wherewith to slake his thirst." 19th cent. *England*. Dickens, *Pickwick*, I, p. 262. * Thumb extended, fist clenched and moved toward mouth. *Italy*. Efron, p. 46. * " 'Drink?' he asked, making a motion with his hand decanting his thumb downward." Hemingway, p. 141. * Right hand raises an imagined glass to the open mouth: "I want a drink." *Central Africa*. Hochegger, p. 24. * Right hand, placed to mouth, imitates the action of emptying a glass. *Central Africa*. Hochegger, p. 25. * Hands, side to side and palms up, indicate throwing of water to the mouth, or a receptacle for water to drink. *Central Africa*. Hochegger, p. 58.

Drive (automobile)   Fists, thumbs on top, placed ca. 1 ft. apart and 1 ft. in front of chest can indicate: "are we taking the car?" "Did you come by car?" "Shall we leave?" Accompanied by an admonishing expression, it may signify "do you think you can still drive?" *Netherlands*. Andrea and de Boer, p. 60.

Drunkenness   Closed fist, thumb extended, and moved toward mouth until tip of thumb touches lips. *France*. Mitton, p. 147.

Duality   Raising bunched fingers of both hands, palms facing the speaker, to approx. shoulder level (groups of two, two of a kind). Madrid, *Spain; Lat. Am.* Green, p. 50. * "When discussing an issue . . . which has two facets or aspects, each side of the issue may be accompanied by a sweep of the slightly cupped hand, palm inward, beginning at the level of the chest and terminating waist-high at the side of the gesticulator." Madrid, *Spain; Lat. Am.* Green, p. 50.

Eating   Beating the ribs with the flat of the hand. Naples, *Italy.* Critchley, p. 89. * Hand lifted to mouth, imaginary food trickled in as in eating spaghetti by hand, as it was originally done. *Italy.* Efron, p. 148. * Uniting tips of all fingers of one hand, move them repeatedly to the mouth and away again. *Italy.* Efron, p. 148 fig. 43.

Effeminacy   Elbows close to the body, extended open hands are waved to and fro from the wrist as if they were wings. *Lat. Am.* Kany, p. 182.

Ejection   Pushing a person away, from the front or the back, is symbolic of ejection from a property. Medieval *Germany. Sachsenspiegel.* Amira, "Handgebärden," p. 253.

Elation   "Ten minutes later it is over, and Hollands is released to the bracing air of the street, where his elation (fist punching the air, the folds of his stylishly baggy black suit flapping maniacally) might even affect passing motorists." *England. L. A. Times,* Oct. 15, 1992, A1. * "Monica Seles clenches her fist after clinching her 6–3, 6–2 [tennis] victory over Mary Joe Fernandez." [Editors' note: the "Becker-fist," ascribed to Boris Becker.] *Europe; North Am.* AP Photo, *L.A. Times,* Sept. 12, 1992, C1.

Emphasis   Striking chest with fist or open palm, or striking table with fist. 19th cent. *England.* Dickens, *Pickwick,* I, pp. 218, 276; II, pp. 290, 315, 396. * "As the little man concluded, he took an emphatic pinch of snuff, as a tribute to the smartness of Messrs. Dodson and Fogg." 19th cent. *England.* Dickens, *Pickwick,* II, p. 25. * " 'Leave the house,' said Mr. Nupkins, waving his hand emphatically." 19th cent. *England.* Dickens, *Pickwick,* I, p. 433. * " 'Pay it all—stick to business—cash up—every farthing.'—Here Mr. Jingle paused and striking the crown of his hat with great violence." 19th cent. *England.* Dickens, *Pickwick,* II, p. 423. * "Mr. Snodgrass dropped the hand which he had, in the spirit of poesy, raised towards the clouds, as he made the above appeal." 19th cent. *England.* Dickens, *Pickwick,* I, p. 31. * "and then he struck the ground emphatically with his stick." 19th cent. *England.* Dickens, *Pickwick,* I, pp. 315–16. * Accompanying a word by hitting on the table with one's fist. *France.* Mitton, p. 145. * Presenting the hand vertically, palm forward, under the eyes of the other person. Allusion to a written document supporting one's argument. Familiar. *France.* Mitton, pp. 147–49. * "The performance of the gesture [accompanying emphatic verbal behavior] commences at the level of the neck or chest, palm facing the speaker, and consists of a rapid and sweeping motion of one hand. Midway through the downward sweep of the lower arm, the hand rotates at the wrist so that the palm faces away from the speaker at the conclusion of the movement . . . Whereas men tend to return the arm and hand to a neutral position of rest at the conclusion of the movement, women are often observed maintaining the terminal position of the upraised hand." *Spain.* Green, pp. 54–55. * Hand sweeps upward and outward, palm facing away from body. *Colombia.* Saitz and Cervenka, p. 47. * Hammering motion of one fist on the other. Assimilated Jews. Eastern *Europe.* Efron, p. 118. * Open hand in front, palm turned out, hand raised, fingertips up. *Europe; North Am.* Aubert, p. 91. * "Both hands are held in front of the chest, all fingertips touching, and shaken up and down.—I beg you to explain yourself!" *Italy.* Graham, p. 26. * Fist strikes palm (or a surface as of a table) once or several times. *Colombia; U.S.* Saitz and Cervenka, p. 46. *See also* FINGER, HAND, Emphasis. " 'Listen to me,' he said, laying his hand on Denis's sleeve." *England.* Huxley, ch. 6. * The 'hand purse': tips of fingers brought together as if holding a small object, palm upward. As a baton-gesture, i.e. accompanying speech rhythmically, the gesture is usually made when the speaker is making a fine point or requiring more precision; as such it is very common. But the gesture can also be performed independently of speech and it can signify a request for clarity, "a gestural equivalent of a question mark." *Italy.* Morris pp. 45–46. *See also* FINGER, Precision.

Encouragement Clapping of hands. Anc. *Rome.* Sittl, p. 56. *Spain; Lat. Am.* Green, p. 50. * Deity clasps hand of mortal. Anc. *Greece* and *Rome.* Sittl, p. 276. Handshake. Anc. *Greece* and *Rome.* Sittl, p. 30. * "Cracket intimated, by a motion of his hand as he left the room, that there was nothing to fear." 19th cent. *England.* Dickens, *Oliver Twist,* p. 473. * "Matt stroked her hand in encouraging silence." *U.S.* Boucher, p. 207. * "A gesture observed in the theater in association with expressions suggestive of boosting morale or raising spirits is performed by raising both spread hands, palms up, as if actually raising an object with the open hands." *Spain.* Green, pp. 49–50. * "Mr. Barbecue Smith patted his arm several times and went on." *England.* Huxley, ch. vi. * Permission of one parent to a child to follow the other parent is pictorially indicated by one parent pushing the child toward the other parent. Medieval *Germany. Sachsenspiegel.* Amira, "Handgebärden," p. 254. * Both hands hold upper arms of someone standing in front of gesturer and shake him: "Courage!" *Central Africa.* Hochegger, p. 62. *See also* HAND, Recommendation.

Engagement Handshake as sign of formal engagement. Röhrich, *Gebärde-Metapher-Parodie,* p. 32 and plate 30. * Joining hands of bride and groom. 16th–17th cent. *England.* Shakesp., *Twelfth Night* 5.1.159; *Winter's Tale* 1.2.102.

Enmity Edge of extended hand crosses the chest from left shoulder to the right. 19th cent. Naples, southern *Italy.* De Jorio, p. 188. * Drawing back the hand rather than reaching it out to grasp the hand of another. Anc. *Rome*. Livy, XLV, xii; Valerius Maximus, VI, iv, 3. Bulwer, pp. 95–96. * Drawing back the hand with thumb raised. *Life*, Sept. 3, 1945, p. 25.

Enthusiasm   Hands clasped in front of chest. Commonly female. *Colombia; U.S.* Saitz and Cervenka, p. 49.

Equality   Right and left hands raised and lowered alternately, as if balancing something. *France*. Mitton, p. 144. * Hands horizontal, back of hands upwards, moved gradually away from and towards gesturer as if over an imaginary surface. 19th cent. Naples, southern *Italy*. De Jorio, p. 88.

Etiquette   Consul took the hand of the person whom he brought into the senate. Anc. *Rome*. Sittl, p. 81. * After greeting, one led guests to their appointed places by the hand. 13th cent. *Germany*. Gottfried v. Strassburg, 5747–49. *See also* Bergemann, p. 50. * "Whoever wants to observe courtly manners should never put his hand on a superior's head or shoulder." 13th cent. *Germany*. Thomasin von Circlaria, 447–50. * A lady should not extrude her hand from her clothing when riding; squires and knights should take care to hold their hands still while speaking. One should not wave one's hands about so as to endanger the teeth of an honest man. 13th cent. *Germany*. Ibid., 437–40; 441–46. * Invitation to take a seat is accompanied by a lightly smoothing gesture of the right hand. 19th cent. *Palestine*. Bauer, p. 224. * Both hands are used to receive gifts. *Africa*. Ohm, p. 45. * "and the gentleman drew his chair aside to afford the newcomer a sight of the fire." 19th cent. *England*. Dickens, *Pickwick*, II, pp. 167–68. * Coffee, tea or food is always proferred from right hand to right hand of guest. *Saudi Arabia* and other Moslem countries. Barakat, no. 159. * Thanks and politeness are expressed by clapping the hands. *Zimbabwe*. Axtell, *Gestures*, p. 169. * Both wrists are kept above the table while eating; placing one or both hands in the lap while at table is considered impolite. *Yugoslavia*. Axtell, *Gestures*, p. 156. * Business cards should be given and received with both hands, held between index and thumb. *China; Japan*. Axtell, *Gestures*, pp. 172, 181. *See also* BODY, Etiquette; HAND, OBJECT, Etiquette.

Excess   Flat hand, palm down, moved horizontally across forehead: "I've had it up to here"; "I'm in it up to here." *U.S.* Axtell, *Gestures*, p. 93. * Open palm slowly raised several times to level of groin, as if to lift up testicles: "¡Estoy harto de esto!" ("I've had it up to here!") Vulgar. Limited to men. Río de la Plata area of *Argentina; Uruguay*. Meo Zilio, p. 96. * Hand lightly open, palm up, is moved up and down in front of chest. *Netherlands*. Andrea and de Boer, p. 154.

Excitement   Hand placed over heart. Campania, anc. *Rome*. Helbig, 1242. * Hands in front of body, palms facing about 12 inches apart;

hands are then clasped. Women. *Colombia; U.S.* Much more common in Colombia. Saitz and Cervenka, p. 50.

Expectancy (of gift or object) Hand extended, palm up and slightly cupped. Anc. *Greece* and *Rome.* Sittl, p. 110.

Expulsion One or both hands push the expelled person from the front or from the back of the person being expelled. Legal gesture. Symbolizes dispossession, both of real estate and of persons. Medieval *Germany. Sachsenspiegel.* Amira, "Handgebärden," pp. 253–54. For the role of 'the pushing hand' in medieval art, see Barasch, *Giotto,* pp. 145–54.

Exquisiteness Kissing joined fingertips of one hand, then throwing kiss into air. *France; Spain.* Kaulfers, p. 256.

Extreme Shaking loosely hanging hand from the wrist. 19th cent. *Palestine.* Bauer, p. 223. * Both hands suddenly raised simultaneously upward and to the sides. Jews. *Eastern Europe.* Efron, p. 72. * Gesticulating with hands high in the air. Late anc. *Rome.* Sittl, p. 49.

Facility Snapping thumb and middle finger ("just like that!"). Assimilated Jews. *Eastern Europe.* Efron p. 119

Faithfulness Clap hands on sword. Elizabethan *England.* R. H. Bowers, p. 271. * Handclasp. Medieval *Germany. Mainzer Landrecht. DWb,* IV/2, col. 420; 17th cent. *Germany.* Haltaus, p. 814 (1609). 19th cent. *Germany.* Arndt, p. 244. In ancient Germanic law the hand symbolized the commitment of the entire person. Thus the hand symbolized the pledge of the person. Ebert, V, col. 94. * One either clasps the hand of the partner or one's own hand. *Spain.* Flachskampf, p. 224.

Farewell Handshake. Panels of the Apostles. 15th–16th cent. *Germany.* Jörg Ratgeb, *Herrenberg Altar* (Württemb. Staatsgal., Stuttgart), Burkhard, pp. 12–13. * "I hold it fit that we shake hands and part." 16th–17th cent. *England.* Shakesp., *Hamlet* 1.5.127. "He wrung Bassanio's hand, and so they parted." 16th–17th cent. *England.* Shakesp., *Merchant* 2.8.47. "departed for the garrison, after having shook hands with every individual in the house." 18th cent. *England.* Smollett, *Peregrine Pickle,* I, ch. ix. * "lifting the pinched hat a few inches from his head, and carelessly replacing it very much on one side." 19th cent. *England.* Dickens, *Pickwick,* I, p. 16. *Germany. DWb,* IV/2, col. 332. * Flat hand held high, palm down and forward, fingers quickly waved up and down. Schoolchildren. *U.S.* Seton, p. xx. Hand moves up and down at approx. face level, palm down. *U.S.* Saitz and Cervenka, p. 62. * Hand moves more slowly, fingers closed together than in the U.S. goodby wave. *Colombia.* Saitz and Cervenka, p. 61. * Fingers spread apart, sometimes whole arm waves vigorously. *Colombia.* Saitz and Cervenka, p. 62. Arm extended in the direction of someone, hand relaxed but agitated in a lively manner up and down, palm facing down. Familiar. *France.* Mitton, p. 143. * Waving at someone already out of hearing distance. Anc. *Rome*. Sittl, p. 216. * Arm bent, hand approx. shoulder level, fingers cupped, hand and arm moved repeatedly and slightly up and down. *Italy*. Leone, p. XX 11. * Hand waving, palm toward face of gesticulator at arm's length. Southern *Italy*. Efron, p. 156 and fig. 62. * "With palm upward and fingers alternately clenched and outstretched, I bade Gastone farewell." *Italy*. Graham, p. 26. * Hand extended short distance, palm faces gesticulator, tips of fingers repeatedly lowered and raised rapidly, often tapping base of palm. Becoming progressively less common. Principally older madrileños and young children entrusted to the care of middle-aged nannies. More common: open hand, palm out, held at side of head and waved back and forth. *Spain*. Green, pp. 34–36. * The handshake is the customary ritual for closing a prayer meeting of the Quakers. Hayes, p. 258. * Holding up right hand with palm facing backward and moving fingers and hand back. *Jordan; Lebanon; Saudi Arabia; Syria*. Barakat, no. 113. * Europeans wave in one of two ways: palm-out (away from the gesturer) or palm-in (toward the gesturer). The palm-out wave is common in *Britain; Scandinavia; Netherlands; Germany; Austria; Belgium; France; Yugoslavia; Spain; Portugal; Malta; Tunisia; Greece; Turkey*. The palm-in wave is common in *Italy; Sicily; Sardinia*. *Corfu* has no preference for one wave over the other. For the relationship of these two European forms of waving to the two basic European forms of beckoning, *see* Approach, above, and Morris et al., pp. 241–46. "Americans tend to wave goodbye with the hand up, palm out, wrist stiff, and with a [lateral] back-and-forth motion with the whole forearm and hand . . . In much of Europe, that gesture does not mean 'goodbye' but . . . signifies 'no.' In Europe, the customary way to wave 'hello' or 'goodbye' is with the arm up and extended out, . . . palm down, . . . hand bobbing up and down at the wrist. . . . Italians and Greeks will often wave goodbye with the arm extended, *palm up*, curling all the fingers back and forth toward themselves. Most Americans interpret that gesture as meaning 'come here.' " Axtell, *Gestures*, pp. 28–29. "In Europe the correct form for waving hello and goodbye is palm out, hand and arm stationary, fingers wagging up and down. The common American wave with the whole hand in motion means no—except in Greece, where it is an insult." Axtell, *Do's and Taboos*, p. 43. The common European and North American farewell gesture is the handshake. *See* Greeting, below. * Male friends in parting often press the middle finger of one hand participating in the handshake against that of the other participating hand, and, as the grip is released, snap it against the base of the thumb. *West Africa*. Axtell, *Gestures*, p. 23. * Right hand raised, open, palm out, and waved from side to side. *Central Africa*. Hochegger, p. 17.

Fear Holding up both hands, palm forward. Schoolchildren. *U.S.* Seton, p. xxii. * Hands beaten together. *Italy*. Manzoni, ch. xiii. *

Hand(s) upright near the face, palm(s) out. *Europe; North Am.* Aubert, p. 86.

Fervor " 'Indeed, indeed, it was two other boys,' said Oliver, clasping his hands passionately." 19th cent. *England.* Dickens, *Oliver Twist,* p. 85.

Fight The fists menace one another. Schoolchildren. *U.S.* Seton, p. xxiv. * Fists vigorously moved backwards and forwards in front of chest. *Central Africa.* Hochegger, p. 37.

Finish Flat hand slightly extended in front, edge down, makes chopping motion: "Get rid of him/her/it!" "Stop him/her/it!" *Netherlands.* Andrea and de Boer, p. 120.

Finished Turn up hand, palm up. ("It is finished.") *France.* Life Photo by David Scherman, *Life,* Sept. 16, 1946, p. 12. * Palm of one hand brushes the other. *Near East.* Critchley, p. 91. * Palms placed together so that fingers are pointing forward, then twist hands in opposite directions but keep them in contact. *Saudi Arabia.* Barakat, no. 225. * Rubbing hands lightly in front of body. Arab. Barakat, no. 147. * One hand moves upward, the other downward, palms facing each other; as they pass, one hand slaps the other. *Netherlands.* Andrea and de Boer, p. 81. *Russia.* ("I wash my hands of it!") Monahan, pp. 46–47. * Flat hands extended forward, palms down, rapidly move laterally across each other. *Netherlands.* Andrea and de Boer, p. 96. * Open hands, palm outwards, crossed in front of chest, then spread apart, moving left and right respectively. *Central Africa.* Hochegger, p. 73. * Palm of right hand slaps palm of left hand: "Finished! That's it, then!" *Central Africa.* Ibid. * To indicate that the contents of a gourd are finished, i.e. that the gourd is empty, one blows over its orifice, then raises the right hand and snaps the fingers. *Central Africa.* Ibid.

Flattery Passionate handshake without sufficient familiarity or reason. Anc. *Rome.* Sittl, p. 28.

Foolishness "If thou hast done foolishly in lifting thyself up, or if thou hast thought evil, lay thy hand on thy mouth." Biblical. *Middle East. Prov.* 30:32. * Raising and lowering the cupped hand as if trying the weight of an object. *Lat. Am.* Kany, p. 57. * Hand held below the chin, palm up, and moved outward—or something similar. *Lat. Am.* Kany, p. 57. * Fingertips of one hand joined and held at elbow of the other arm, fingertips of the other hand also joined, hand waving back and forth. Southern *Italy.* Efron, p. 157.

Forgiveness Priest raises his absolving hand and pronounces words of forgiveness. Roman Catholics. *Mass,* p. 14.

Forwardness Passionate handshake without sufficient familiarity or reason. Anc. *Rome.* Sittl, p. 28.

Friendship "Give me thy hand." Biblical. *Middle East.* II *Kings* 10:15. "I have called, and ye have refused; I have stretched out my hand,

and no man regarded." Biblical. *Middle East. Prov.* 1:24. The law of hospitality required that host and guest give each other the right hand. Anc. *Greece* and *Rome*. Sittl, p. 135. Right hand of one person grasped by hand(s) of the other. Anc. *Greece* and *Rome*. Stephani, pp. 69–113. Handshake sealing friendship. Anc. *Greece* and *Rome*. Sittl, p. 30. Right hand of one deity clasps right hand of another as symbol of the unity of the cities symbolized by the respective deities. Anc. *Greece* and *Rome*. Sittl, p. 137, n. 5. Handshake while conversing. Anc. *Greece* and *Rome*. Sittl, pp. 28–29. * Hand of one person holding hand of another, walking side by side. Anc. *Greece* and *Rome*. Sittl, p. 31. Men walking hand in hand. William of Newburgh, 12th cent. *England*. Kelly, ch. xvi. Holding hands among men while walking is a sign of friendship and mutual respect in the *Middle East; Korea; China; Vietnam*. Axtell, *Gestures*, p. 83. "In the United States, if two people of the same sex hold hands or place their arms around one another, some people interpret this as a sign of a homosexual relationship. However, in the Middle East, the Balkans, Latin America and Asia, when two men or two women hold hands, it is a sign of friendship. When Arafat and Peres held hands, it demonstrated that enmity had been set aside. [Elsewhere it is common to see] two men or women walking down the street holding hands or with arms around each other's waists, . . . [or for] persons of the same sex [sip] coffee in a cafe while holding hands. But these actions often shock Americans. At the same time, people from the Balkans, Middle East and Asia are amazed when they first observe American men and women engaged in any physical contact in public. From their point of view, it is a sign of great disrespect, especially to women." *Middle East; Balkans; Latin America; Asia*. Dresser, *L.A. Times*, Sept. 16, 1995, B17. * Hand given as pledge of faith and friendship. 16th–17th cent. *England*. Shakesp., *Two Gentlemen* 2.2.8; 5.4.116; *Merry Wives* 2.1.225; *Troil.* 4.5.270; *Hamlet* 2.2.388; etc. 17th cent. *England*. Bulwer, pp. 109, 120. " 'I do assure you, sir,' (says he, taking the gentleman by the hand), 'I am heartily glad to meet with a man of your kidney.' " 18th cent. *England*. Fielding, Bk. II, ch. viii. * "shaking him by the hand, called him his best friend." 18th cent. *England*. Smollett, I, ch. lvii. * Holding up branches of trees, canoe paddles, sticks, poles decorated with feathers, white flags, pieces of cloth in token of friendship. *Polynesia*. Dawson, pp. 96–97. Handclasp in token of friendship not limited to Indoeuropean peoples, but also found among the Papuans of the central mountains of New Guinea and Australian aborigines. *New Guinea; Australia* (Aborigines). Ebert, V, col. 94. Handclasp in token of friendship. *Germany*. DWb, IV/2, col. 367–8. " 'I want your assistance.' 'You shall have it,' . . . clasping his friend's hand." 19th cent. *England*. Dickens, *Pickwick*, I, p. 31. * "When the suppertable was cleared . . . Eckbert took Walter's hand and said: 'My friend, you should have my wife tell you the story of her youth sometime' " 19th cent. *Germany*. Tieck, p. 1. * Passionate handshake is not given to chance acquaintances—only to loved or very much liked people, esp. before or after a long absence. 19th cent. *Italy*. Mantegazza, p. 229. Handshake is an offer of one's friendship and devotion. Became popular in France under the Second Empire. 19th cent. *France*. Mitton, p. 142. * One's right hand shakes one's left hand while one looks in the direction of the other person. In China this takes the place of the European handshake between two persons. *China*. Mitton, p. 142.

Frustration Elbows against body, hands at shoulder height, right palm clasps left, both hands remain joined. From a position touching the chest they are lowered. ("This is lamentable!" "Scandalous!") Feminine and clerical. *France*. Mitton, p. 144. * Sir Benjamin, jarred thoroughly, shook his fist in the air." Carr, *Hag's Nook*, p. 114. * "Mr. Scogan raised his hand and let it limply fall again in a gesture which implied that words failed him." *England*. Huxley, ch. 14.

Future Open hand, at level of face and perpendicular to it, describes a 270 degree arc in the air. Río de la Plata region of *Argentina; Uruguay*. Meo Zilio, p. 94. *See* Past.

"Gently" Flat hand held low, palm down, gently waved up and down. Schoolchildren. *U.S.* Seton, p. xx.

Gossip Thumb and middle finger opening and closing while moving the hand away from the body as if cutting with scissors. Southern *Italy*. Efron, p. 66.

Graft One hand, fingers extended, makes sawing motion on edge of other hand. *Colombia*. Saitz and Cervenka, p. 64.

Gratitude Handshake. Anc. *Greece* and *Rome*. Sittl, p. 30. "Finally he grasped his left with his right hand and shook it in the direction of the committee table in order to thank all of them for permitting him this little escapade." *Germany*. Schwanitz, p. 371; (transl. by eds.) * Lowering the hand as sign of gratitude was part of Roman court etiquette and generally polite expression of gratitude. Anc. *Rome*. Sittl, p. l49. * Folding one's hands. 13th cent. *Germany*. Gottfr. v. Strassburg, 8215-l6. * "Mr. Winkle had fast hold of his friend's hand . . . 'My friend, my benefactor, my honored companion' " 19th cent. *England*. Dickens, *Pickwick*, II, p. 274. * Hands applauding; or open hands, palm toward chest, gently raised and lowered; or joined hands are raised to or above the head: "Merci!" ("Thank you!"). *Central Africa*. Hochegger, pp. 115–16. * "Richard Nixon offered [Billy Graham] the ambassadorship to Israel at a meeting with Golda Meir. 'I said the Mideast would blow up if I went over there,' Graham recalls. 'Golda then reached under the table and squeezed my hand. She was greatly relieved.' " *U.S.* Gibbs and Ostling, p. 46. * Hand open and raised, then given a 90 degree turn. *Mexico*. Cascudo, *História*, p. 130.

Greed Rubbing palms together. 17th cent. *England.* Bulwer, p. 41.
Greeting Shaking hands of people or gods. *Assyria; Babylonia.*
Ohm, p. 243. The handshake originated in the Middle East signifying
an oath or alliance. Biblical. *Middle East. Prov.* 22:26. Anc. *Greece.*
Homer, *Iliad,* vi, 233; x, 541; xxiv, 671. Romans became acquainted
with the gesture in Greece and spread it throughout the *Roman Empire.*
In Renaissance *Italy,* the handshake was customary and spread to the
courts of *Europe.* Too tight a handshake implied love and was considered a violation of good manners. Catherine of Braganza "innocently"
asked her husband, Charles II of England, the meaning of handshakes
given her by Master of the Horse, Edward Montague. Montague was
dismissed and exiled. 17th cent. *England.* Samuel Pepys, *Diary,* May
20, 1664, tells the story somewhat differently, questioning the innocence of the queen. In 1842, in Recife, Father Lopes Gama preached
against shaking hands with women. 19th cent. *Brazil.* Mussolini decreed
the abolition of the handshake, prescribing the Roman raised arm instead. Fascist *Italy.* The handshake was unknown to Africans and indigenous Americans until contact with Europeans. Cascudo, *História,* pp.
147–48. Hand extended to someone in greeting. Anc. *Greece* and *Rome.*
Sittl, pp. 49–50. Hand extended toward someone by someone reporting
good news. Anc. *Greece.* Sittl, p. 50. Grasping the hand of statues standing along the way. Anc. *Rome.* Sittl, p. 181. * Raising right hand, so that
palm remains positioned toward face, hand returned to mouth, kissing
fingertips and then throwing kiss toward divine image. Anc. *Greece* and
Rome. Baumeister, I, p. 592. * Junior official lowered or had the fasces
lowered by his lictors in the presence of a senior or superior official.
Anc. *Rome.* Sittl, p. 154. * Handshake (without kiss) by the emperor
succeeded kiss after Diocletian. Anc. *Rome.* Sittl, p. 80. * Lowering
fasces. Anc. *Rome.* Sittl, p. 155. * In the circus the charioteer lowered
his whip before the patrons. Anc. *Rome.* Sittl, pp. 155–56. * Handshake
was custom of candidates for political office. Anc. *Rome.* Sittl, p. 29. *
Spear was thrust into the ground, the free right hand was raised, the
shield was held with the left against an unexpected thrust. Germanic.
HDV, I, p. 317. * "I give you welcome with a powerless hand."
17th cent. *England.* Shakesp., *King John* 2.1.15. The handshake as a
common greeting may have originated with the Quakers, who saw it as
'more agreeable with Christian simplicity to greet one another by giving
their hand,' than bowing or doffing their hats. 17th–18th cent. *England.*
Sewell, p. 690; see also Roodenburg, p. 176. Roodenburg, however, cau-
tions that Cleland, Bk. V., ch. 5, pp. 176–8, favors "our good olde Scot-
tish shaking of the two right hands togither at meeting with an uncovered head" over the "French" and "apish toies of bowing downe to
everie mans shoe." Fischart, in his 1575 German translation and expansion of Rabelais' *Gargantua and Pantagruel,* mentions handshake as

greeting, though Rabelais did not, suggesting the Germans may have known it as common greeting before the Quakers; also appears to have been used in 16th cent. *Poland*. Roodenburg, p. 178; Bogucka, p. 192. In 1858, Mme la Baronesse de Fresne admits the handshake to her book of manners as a greeting, *De l'usage et de la politesse dans le monde* (Paris, 1858), p. 35, but only among friends. *France*. Roodenburg, p. 176. Roodenburg suggests that the modern handshake as a common greeting probably was first used in England, and spread from there. By 1919 it had reached the imperial court of *China*. Roodenburg, p. 177. "Bows and curtsies were used until 1870, but by 1840 handshaking was seen. In the 1890's a high, exaggerated handshake was fashionable. Ladies shook hands out of doors but continued to curtsy indoors until the crinoline went out of fashion." Rockwood, p. 183. "Hatchway . . . thrust out his hand by way of salutation." 18th cent. *England*. Smollett, I, ch. viii. "He shook him heartily by the hand." Ibid., I, ch. xiii. Handshake. *Germany*. *DWb*, IV/2, cols. 331–368, 385, 414. 19th cent. *England*. Dickens, *Pickwick*, I, pp. 37, 61, 109, 297, 451, etc. "but in the college one shook hands at the most once a year, on one's first appearance each Michaelmas term." Cambridge, *England*. Snow, p. 206. Handshake performed by one person, his right hand shaking his left while he is looking at someone who is generally at too great a distance for the former to shake hands with him. Informal. *France*. Mitton, p. 142. * Right hand grasps left wrist. Muslim. Ohm, p. 276. * Right hand of one grasps right hand of another briefly. Intensity varies with the importance of the act and its emotional content. *Europe*. Revesz, "Die Psychologie," p. 143ff. Handshake in greeting more frequent in *Colombia* than in the *U.S.* Omission may be a discourtesy. In the *U.S.* the handshake is formal, a mark of initial encounter and special occasions. The Colombian handshake is likely to last longer than the handshake as practiced in the U.S. Saitz and Cervenka, pp. 61, 65. * Thumbs brought into contact. Muslim. In modern *Egypt*, at the ceremony of joining hands between the bride's proxy and the bridegroom, the parties sit on the ground face to face, grasp one another's right hands, raising the thumbs and pressing them one against the other. Lane, I, p. 219. Older generation still gives the *salaam* in greeting: right hand raised to the chest, touching the heart, then the forehead, and then sweeps upward and outward, sometimes accompanied with a slight nod of the head. *Middle East*. Axtell, *Gestures*, pp. 21, 84. When the handshake is used in the Middle East, a gentle grip is appropriate. A firm grip suggests aggressiveness. Axtell, ibid., p. 22. "The firm grip used in the American-style handshake can signal aggressiveness—especially if it is accompanied by more arm pumps than are considered normal in the host country." *Middle East; Europe*. Bagott, p. 4. Also *Japan; Korea*, where simultaneous eye contact is avoided as disrespectful. Axtell, ibid. North Americans and many Europeans regard a limp hand as unpleasant, indicating weakness and effeminacy. Some, however, regard Americans as going too far in the direction of firmness of the handshake. Firm, one-pump handshake preferred. Can be initiated by women and children. *Northern Europe*. Women and children do not commonly initiate a handshake. *North America; Asia*. Men not related to a woman are prohibited from touching her; consequently a man should not initiate a handshake. *Muslim*. Axtell, *Gestures*, pp. 22–23. "In Scandinavia and Germany, men women and children all shake hands, but unlike the American-style handshaker, the Northern European will generally offer only one quick pump." Bagott, 1994, p. 4. Among Europeans, the French appear to use the handshake most frequently. "When two unencumbered men meet, the least there will be is the conventional handshake. If the hands are full, you will be offered a little finger to shake. If the hands are wet or dirty, you will be offered a forearm or an elbow. Riding a bicycle or driving a car does not excuse you from the obligation to *toucher les cinq sardines*, and so you will see perilous contortions being performed on busy streets as hands grope through car windows and across handlebars to find each other." Provençe, *France*. Mayle, *A Year in Provençe*, pp. 101–02. "Whenever two friends meet and chat, their greeting usually includes a handshake and a hearty clap on the back." *Bolivia*. Axtell, *Gestures*, p. 23. Handshake commonly warmer and longer than in N. America or N. Europe, "frequently accompanied by the left hand touching the other person's forearm, elbow, or even lapel." *Southern Europe; Lat. Am.* Axtell, ibid., p. 24. Handshake rare as a greeting in face-to-face communities. Between men and women it is less common in smaller towns and villages than in cities. Strangers shake hands briefly, a businessman may shake the hand of another with both hands. Intensity, duration, physical distance determined by social distance: social superior moves less than inferior. *Spain*. Driessen, p. 241. Outside Mexico City, friends greet with conventional handshake followed by grasping each other's thumb. *Mexico*. Axtell, *Gestures*, p. 28. Often grip of handshake covered by left hand. Politicians. *U.S.* Male friends may start the greeting with a firm handshake and continue with a "bear hug," i.e. embrace. *Russia*. No bodily contact other than a handshake. *Finland*. Axtell, ibid. Usually the man initiates a handshake, rather than the woman. Male handshakes are firm, often accompanied by the left hand grasping the shoulder of the other man, and frequently repeated during the course of a day. *Russia*. Monahan, pp. 74–75. * Hands palm to palm vertically in front of chest, accompanied by slight bow. The *namaste* or *wai*. *India; Thailand; Cambodia*. Axtell, *Gestures*, pp. 20–21, 84; Reuters Photo, *L.A. Times*, May 23, 1993, A8. * Conventional handshake is customary greeting, sometimes accompanied by a slight bob of the head. *Taiwan; Hong Kong; Singapore; China*. Axtell, ibid., p. 28. * "He [the chief] first grasped my hand and pressed his thumb against mine as is the custom." East *Africa*. Krapf, p. 138. * Friends shake hands with ligh slap palm against palm, followed by a mutual grasp of cupped fingers. *Kenya*. Axtell, *Gestures*, pp. 28, 162. * Cutting oneself with shark's teeth and wailing as a form of receiving a friend or showing joy at his arrival. *Tahiti*. Ellis, II, p. 337. * Sprinkling water over one's head. *New Hebrides*. Mallery, p. 5. * Sprinkling sand or mud over one's body. *South Africa*. Livingstone, pp. 276, 286, 296. * Spitting (now [1904] falling into disuse). *Uganda*. Johnston, II, p. 833. * After an elaborate exchange of courtesies, the parties slap their sides and pat their stomachs. Uvinza. *Tanganyika*. Cameron, I, p. 226. * Pulling one another's ears in salutation. Gond. *India*. Dawson, p. 94. * Stroking the abdomen. *Marianas*. Mallery, p. 4. * Priest before ancestor's shrine clapped his hands while bending knees, as greeting. Inamwanga. *Tanganyika*. Ohm, p. 283. * Handshake is common in Africa; recorded among men of the Karague, Masai, Wagare, Niamniani, Monbutto tribes. Often accompanied by cracking or snapping of the fingers. *Africa*. Speke, p. 203. * Hand raised above level of the head, turned toward someone, fingers extended and slightly separated, hand agitated slightly in the direction from thumb to little finger, palm inward. Friendly, informal. *France*. Mitton, p. 142. * "She greeted Pnin with a clapping of hands." *Russia*. Nabokov, p. 121. Clapping one's hands as in applause. *China*. Axtell, *Gestures*, p. 15; *Russia*. Axtell, ibid., p. 82; Yoruba, *Nigeria*. Ibid., p. 164. *Central Africa*. Hochegger, p. 172. * Hand, palm up, extended to side, at waist-level or slightly above. Used over distance or with "Que hubo" ("Hi!" "What's new?") Men. *Colombia*. Saitz and Cervenka, p. 66. * "Bad Hands was wearing his gloves. He made no offer to shake hands. Neither did Chee. It was not, after all, a Navajo custom." *U.S.* Hillerman, *Talking God*, p. 95. * Waving the hand back and forth (*see* HAND, Farewell) is appropriate greeting in the *U.S.*, but is rude in *Greece* (the *moutza*). Greenberg, L4. "A quartet of chemical workers . . . lift their thick, white-gloved hands and wave beauty-queen style at the passing train, a gesture that is weirdly genteel." [Editors' note: "beauty-queen style"-hand, palm outward, waved from side to side.] *Daily News*, May 9, 1993, Travel, p. 5. Hand raised to head-level or above and waggled back and forth, left to right, is common for "hello" or "farewell" in *North America*; hand waved up and down is more common in *Europe*, hand held at shoulder height, palm up, fingers waggled inward as if scratching is common in *Italy*. Axtell, *Gestures*, pp. 84–85. * Open hand raised above head, palm out, agitated from left to right. *Central Africa*. Hochegger, p. 172. Among friends: Handshake, left hand placed over right forearm, then the partners raise their hands, holding each other by the thumb, to the height of their heads, then let them drop and separate, then bring them together again, slap each other's palms, and finally raise them, clicking the fingers. *Central Africa.* Hochegger, pp. 174–75. * "Eskimos greet each other by banging the other party with a hand either on the head or shoulders." *North Amerca.* Axtell, *Gestures*, p. 22. * "Men welcome each other by embracing and . . . rubbing each other's back." *Polynesia.* Axtell, ibid. * Hands clasped above head and shaken slightly. Sports greeting. *Brazil.* Cascudo, *História*, p. 167. In China this replaces the European handshake. Cascudo, ibid. * Raising clasped hands above head and alternately raising feet was a greeting for royalty. *Borneo.* Recorded by Antonio Pigafeeta, chronicler of the first circumnavigation of the globe, July 1521; cited by Cascudo, *História*, p. 168. * "He stopped several yards away, pressed his palms together and brought them humbly in toward his body. 'Doctor Prescott, I am Khieu Ngor. Chantou Pran's nephew.' " *Cambodia.* Hendricksen, pp. 62–63.

Guilt " 'What is it she does now? Look, how she rubs her hands.' 'It is an accustomed action with her, to seem thus washing her hands.' " 16th–17th cent. *England.* Shakespeare, *Macbeth* 5.1.30.

Hard times Fist makes firm belt-tightening gesture. *France.* Life Photos, David Scherman, *Life*, Sept. 16, 1946, pp. 12–15.

Harmony Clasped hands. *Etruria;* anc. *Rome.* The Etruscan Concordia is characterized by clasped hands. Pauly-Wissowa, IV, col. 834; XXXI, "Mussidius," p. 900; Babelon, II, p. 42.

Hatred Shaking clenched fist at level of face, fingers inward toward the gesturer. *France.* Mitton, p. 141. * Fingers extended and slightly apart, palm inward, at eye level, in direction of someone. *France.* Mitton, p. 142.

Heat Both hands, palms open and toward chest, move back and forth toward chest as if ventilating it: "What heat!" *Central Africa.* Hochegger, p. 33. * Open hand agitated up and down before mouth: "I'm warm!" *Central Africa.* Hochegger, p. 34.

Helplessness " 'I thought at the time the people we picked out went to a convalescent camp at Birkenau,' Neubert said, turning up his palms in a helpless gesture as a twitter sounded from the spectator gallery. Birkenau housed Auschwitz's gas chambers and ovens." *Germany.* L.A. *Times*, Feb. 4, 1964, p. 2. Cf. the "proof" of "typical Jewish" characteristics of Heinrich Heine's *Loreley* brought by the Hamburg publicist Wilhelm Stapel: "surrender to the words 'Ich weiss nicht, was soll es bedeuten' ['I don't know what it's supposed to mean'] and immediately the words force us to shrug our shoulders, while the open hands extend sideways: a typical Jewish gesture." *Germany.* Nickel, p. 19. "and the 'disjunctive' motion-hands traveling apart to signify helpless passivity." *Russia.* Nabokov, p. 41. * "He looks at him with a pitiful expression. Closes his eyes and wrings his hand in a gesture of helplessness." *Argentina.* Weyland, p. 19. * " 'The racial problem in Israel is a short-term phenomenon. The religious problem, on the other hand, . . .' He lifted his hand palm-up in the Ladino gesture for 'what to do' and abruptly changed the subject." Ladino Jews. *Israel*. Perera, p. 175.

Hesitation   Slow scratching of the head or the nose or playing with the lips or the chin. *France*. Mitton, p. 146. *See also* Doubt.

Hitchhiking   Left hand extended, palm up, right hand repeatedly placed on the palm of the left: "Please pick me up." *Central Africa*. Hochegger, p. 47.

Homage   Palms of hands forward, as if to ward off a blow— submission of a defeated people. Anc. *Egypt*. Meyer, pl. to pp. 242, 266. * Folded hands of vassal before his lord or lower cleric before his bishop. Tomb of Hincmar of Rheims. Medieval *France*. Prutz, I, p. 117. * The receiver of homage spreads his hand out and the one rendering it strokes it softly or gives his hand. Arab. Goldziher, "Über Gebärden," p. 380. * Kneeling, kissing lord's hand. Medieval *Germany*. Stoebe, p. 188. * Hands folded, the lord took them between his own. Medieval *Germany*. *HDV,* I, p. 319; Grimm, *DRA*, I, pp. 191–92. Edward I of England renders homage for Guyenne, Gascogne and Ponthieu to Philippe le Bel, King of France, in 1286, by kneeling before him and placing his hands, palms down, on a gospel placed on the knees of the King of France, who is sitting on his throne, in his right hand the Hand of Justice, in his left the scepter with the Fleur de Lys. Medieval *France*. *Grandes Chroniques de France*, Paris, Bibl. Nat. Franc. 6465, fol. 301. Ca. 1458.

Homosexuality   "Homosexuality has certainly not diminished of late, nor grown more bashful. Two M.P.'s, according to the reported comment of a policeman stationed in the House of Commons, might occasionally be seen going hand-in-hand through the division lobby." *England*. Muggeridge, p. 97. Men led their lovers by the hand or wrist. Anc. *Greece*. Sittl, p. 81. Common in parts of *North America*. Axtell, *Gestures*, p. 83. * One hand rests on top of other, palm to palm, as thumbs flap like wings. ("Pájaro"). *Colombia*. Saitz and Cervenka, p. 120. * Hand, palm down, tipped to one side, then to the other. *Colombia*. Saitz and Cervenka, ibid. * Flat palms rubbed together lightly. Lesbian. *Colombia*. Saitz and Cervenka, p. 121. * Shaking hands with another of the same sex loosely rather than firmly. Usually two men. Sexual or homosexual inference. *Lebanon*. Barakat, no. 57. * Letting hand fall, palm up and open. Executed with delicacy and elegance. *Mexico*. Lomas, p. 36. * Fist, front outward, moved from right to left like a pendulum. If used by a man to a man it is an accusation of homosexuality. *Mexico*. Lomas, p. 36. * Fingers of one hand brushed across back of other hand—someone else is homosexual. *Netherlands*. Axtell, *Gestures*, p. 92. * Fingers of one hand, extended and together, tap on back of other hand. *Netherlands*. Andrea and de Boer, p. 21

Hope   Prayer gesture of both hands flat, palm to palm, held vertically below chin. Feminine gesture—intense hope. *Russia.* Monahan, pp. 102–03.

Horror   Clasping hands together. Arab. Goldziher, "Über Gebärden," p. 382. One hand or both hands covering eyes or face. 15th cent. *Italy.* Giovanni di Paolo (1403?-1482), *Salome presents the Head.* Chicago Art Institute. "she put forth her hands with an involuntary repellent gesture." 19th cent. *U.S.* Hawthorne, ch. xxiii. * Hand(s), either open or loosely closed, placed at side of face. Gesture accompanied by smile when horror disarms itself as grotesque; e.g. children's reaction to Halloween "monster," *L. A. Times,* Oct. 30, 1995, B1.

Humility   "Priest extends his hands and then folds them as a mark of humility." Roman Catholic. *Mass,* p. 23.

Hunger   Tightening the belt. Vulgar. *France.* Mitton, p. 150. * Hand moves to mouth, fingers joined at tips. Vulgar. *France.* Mitton, p. 148. * "The right hand is outstretched, palm down, and the hand is moved back and forth horizontally at waist level—I am extremely hungry." *Italy.* Graham, p. 26. Occasionally in Río de la Plata region of *Argentina; Uruguay.* Meo Zilio, p. 93. * Right hand repeatedly slaps stomach, or both hands rub up and down on stomach. *Central Africa.* Hochegger, p. 69.

Hurry   Palm of one hand gives sharp blow to palm of the other, which simultaneously rises as if to catapult an object resting on it into air. *France.* Mitton, p. 149. * Flat of hand is swung backward and forward repeatedly. ("Pass rapidly." "Leave.") *France.* Mitton, p. 143. * Drawing in flat hand, palm toward gesturer, vigorously and repeatedly several times. Schoolchildren. *U.S.* Seton, p. xx. * Open palm at level of stomach or chest rises very rapidly; may be accompanied by "¡Meta fiero!" ("Get cracking!") Río de la Plata region of *Argentina; Uruguay.* Meo Zilio, p. 97.

Identification   Pointing to oneself. Schoolchildren. *U.S.* Seton, p. xx. * Tapping one's chest. Schoolchildren. *U.S.* Ibid. * Placing one's hand on one's chest. *France.* Mitton, p. 143. * Placing tips of index, middle finger and thumb on table, separated from each other, identifies one as a freemason. *France.* Mitton, p. 150.

Idleness   Hands folded. 17th cent. *England.* Bulwer, pp. 37–39.

Ignorance   Holding coat flaps open, one in each hand. Schoolchildren. *U.S.* Seton, p. xxii. * Hand, palms facing out, held up in front of body, then moved slightly to sides. Slight pursing of lips usually accompanies gesture. *Colombia.* Saitz and Cervenka, p. 92. * One hand raised in front or to side of body, palm out; often mouth tightened, head tilted. *Colombia.* Saitz and Cervenka, p. 92.

Impatience   "Thus to be driven (and I wrung my hands through impatience) by the instigations of a designing, an ambitious brother"

18th cent. *England*. Richardson, I, pp. 145–46. * Rubbing the hand over the wrist or wristwatch. College students. California, *U.S.* McCord, p. 290. * Hand makes gesture of sweeping something behind one. ("Spare us this!") *France*. Mitton, p. 147. * Impatient audience slowly claps hands in rhythm. *North America*. Axtell, *Gestures*, p. 82.

Impulsiveness Seizing someone's hand. 19th cent. *England*. Dickens, *Pickwick*, I, p. 312; II, pp. 269, 336, 441.

Incompetence One hand grasps other, palm turned inward, at or above wrist, both hands either hanging down in front of body or raised to level of chest; in one instance they are held above head. Inability to judge, speak, enfeoff, understand, act. Medieval *Germany*. Illustrations in *Sachsenspiegel*. Amira, "Handgebärden," p. 231. Refusal to judge, answer, enfeoff, accept fief, recognize or act. Ibid., p. 232. Since the 12th cent. connected mainly with incapacity. Barasch, *Giotto*, pp. 90–95.

Indication Flat hand, palm up, extended toward person upon whom the attention is to be focussed. 15th–16th cent. *France*. Anne de Bretagne en prieres, *Grandes Heures d'Anne de Bretagne*. Paris, Bibl. Nat., Lat 9474. Ca. 1500. * "Bülhoff held the new issue of the *Journal* in his left hand and knocked with his right . . . on the open page of the article." *Germany*. Schwanitz, p. 215.

Indifference Fingers of one hand close together, palm towards gesticulator, fingertips under chin, then hand is suddenly flipped outward. Originated with flipping beard. *France*; southern *Italy*. Efron, p. 156. * Twisting open hand back and forth, thumb and fingers spread apart and palm facing away from speaker. *Spain*. Green, p. 90. * Palm facing down, fingers extended, rocking from side to side. ("Más o menos," "more or less"). *Colombia; U.S.* Saitz and Cervenka, p. 91.

Influence Describing small circles in air with slightly cupped hand, gradually increasing height until hand is above head of gesticulator. *Spain; Lat. Am.* Green, p. 74.

Innocence Washing one's hands. Biblical. *Middle East. Deut.* 21:6; *Matth.* 27:24; Otto, p. 210. Simulating the washing of hands. 17th cent. *England*. Bulwer, pp. 40–41. * Hands flat, palms outward and separated. *France*. Mitton, p. 143. * Right hand clasps wrist of left hand behind back, as though in handcuffs: "¡A mí que me registren!" ("Let 'em book me!") Río de la Plata region of *Argentina; Uruguay*. Meo Zilio, p. 111.

Insult Open hand is put against another person's face or held up before other person, accompanied by formula "On your eyes." *Near East*. Critchley, p. 91. * Open palm held up. *India*. Rose, p. 313. * Hand extended, fingers spread. "Hand of Fatima." *North Africa; Spain; Sicily*. Taylor, *Shanghai Gesture*, pp. 53–54 and n. 174. *See* Apotropy. Open hand, fingers stiffly spread, pushed toward the face of another person.

Often accompanied by the formula "Five in your eyes." Greek *moutza*. Crass obscenity of Byzantine origin—the thrusting of feces into faces of chained criminals. (Common Western European or N. American gesture of rejection may be mistaken for it.) Morris et al., pp. 92, 237, 240; Axtell, *Gestures*, pp. 39–40. * Because there is a "half-*moutza*," in which only index and middle fingers are extended, palm-out version of V-for-Victory or its signification of "two" is avoided. *Greece*. Morris et al., p. 240. * Palm pushed toward someone's face with fingers spread means "You could have any one of five fathers!" *West Africa*. Axtell, *Gestures*, p. 40, 164. * "Fig" (thumb protruded between index and middle or middle and ring fingers as symbolic of penis penetrating vagina). Used by Caligula to insult tribune Cassius Chaerea, whom he thought effeminate. *Roman Empire*. Seligmann, II, p. 184. * During Middle Ages, "fig" was outlawed by several statutes, which decreed penalties for its exhibition toward religious images. 1522 Johannes Pauli called exhibition of "fig" a custom of Italians. Seligmann, II, p. 184. When gesture is made at a man—man's desire for sexual intercourse or comment on the sexual desirability of certain woman. Can also be used to mark woman as easy conquest. Use as invitation of a woman by a man or as comment between men about a woman, particularly in *Northern Europe*. Popular as insult in *Greece* and *Turkey*, but unknown in *Tunisia*, where popular as sexual comment. In *Wales* can signify that woman is virgin. Morris et al., pp. 148–60. "Fig" is "good luck" gesture. *Brazil*. Axtell, *Gestures*, p. 87. * Fingers of one hand form a tube. 19th cent. Naples; southern *Italy*. De Jorio, p. 134. * Cupped hand moved up and down approx. 6 in. in front of chest. *Colombia*. Saitz and Cervenka, p. 116. * Thumb placed in each ear, flat hands up. Schoolchildren. *U.S.* Seton, p. xxiii. * Right hand, fingers together and extended, palm down, thumb extended, is placed on top of left hand similarly formed. Thumbs, one on each side of stacked hands, are wiggled, representing movement of swimming turtle. Chinese (San Francisco, *U.S.*). College students, California, *U.S.* King, pp. 263–64. * The "fig" and the "horns" (index and little finger of one hand extended). College students, California, *U.S.* King, ibid. * Flat of one hand placed on inside of bend of other arm, while that forearm is raised with clenched fist. Very vulgar. *France*. Mitton, p. 151. * Jerking clenched fist downward below waist as one says "acá" ("here"). *Lat. Am.* Kany, p. 147. * "Araño": open hand extended with tips of fingers curved inward as in act of scratching. Women. *Lat. Am.* Kany, p. 176. * Tips of thumbs placed into ears or on temple, fingers spread, palms to front, fingers may or may not be waggled back or forth. Childish. Perry, *L.A. Times*, Dec. 15, 1957, Comics. * Holding out left hand, palm up, fingers slightly spread, then quickly and forcefully hitting right wrist into it with clenched fist. Obscenity. *Saudi Arabia*. Barakat, no. 104. * Smacking fist of one hand into palm of the other. Obscenity. *Chile; France.* Axtell, *Gestures*, pp. 41–42, 86. * Holding out right fist, then grasping right wrist with left hand and moving right hand up and down rapidly; wrist may be grasped from beneath or on top. Obscenity. *Lebanon; Saudi Arabia; Syria.* Barakat, no. 94. * Raising closed fist. Rude. *Lebanon.* Axtell, *Gestures*, p. 163. * Holding right fist horizontally at left side, heel of hand facing forward, pumping it vigorously and stiffly on that plane. Obscenity. *Saudi Arabia.* Barakat, no. 171. * Holding out hand with fingers extended, then bending index. Obscenity. *Egypt.* Barakat, no. 143. * Pressing tips of right index and thumb together with other fingers folded into palm, then moving hand up and down with pecking motion from the wrist. Obscenity. *Saudi Arabia.* Barakat, no. 50. * Holding out left hand, palm up, fingers slightly curled, then moving right fist through left hand, grasp right forearm. Obscenity. *Lebanon; Syria.* Barakat, no. 42. * Holding out right hand, turning it slowly, thumb and fingers loosely extended. Obscenity. *Lebanon; Syria.* Barakat, no. 41. * Grasping left wrist or forearm with right hand, then moving left fist up and down rapidly while right hand still grasps wrist or forearm. Obscenity. *Lebanon; Saudi Arabia; Syria.* Barakat, no. 17. * Placing heel of right fist into left open palm and grinding it into palm. Obscenity. *Lebanon.* Barakat, no. 65. * Hitting tightly closed right fist into left palm, extended middle finger just as right hand hits palm. Phallic obscenity. *Lebanon; Syria.* Barakat, no. 68. * Turning right hand over quickly at waist level. *Lebanon; Syria.* Barakat, no. 35. * Hand raised, palm outward, fingers spread, middle finger folded down and held down by thumb. *Lebanon.* Axtell, *Gestures*, p. 163. * Hand knocks off another man's agal. *Syria.* Barakat, no. 207. Index finger of one hand points down at upturned palm of other hand. "Grass will grow on my hand" before speaker's comments come true. *Israel.* Axtell, *Gestures*, p. 161. * Pointing at someone with four fingers extended and thumb folded into palm. *Japan.* Axtell, ibid., p. 182. * Hands raised slightly above head, palms facing each other and indicating swollen head. *Central Africa.* Hochegger, p. 85. * Closed fist, held at level of waist and parallel to it, makes sharp movement(s) outward: "To hell with you." Vulgar. *Río de la Plata region of Argentina; Uruguay.* Meo Zilio, p. 95. *See also* FINGER, Insult; FINGER, HAND, Insult. *See also* de Jorio, p. 156.

Integrity Open hand held out in front, palm flat and level. Also part of iconography of 'Truth.' Anc. *Rome*; 17th cent. *Netherlands.* Van der Meulen, p. 38.

Interrogation Hand cupped behind ear. ("What?") *Colombia; U.S.* Saitz and Cervenka, p. 149. * Hands, palm up, held out to side. Sometimes shoulders hunch and lips purse. *U.S.*, more common in *Colombia.* Saitz and Cervenka, p. 150. * Hand extended in front, palm up, chin and eyebrows may be raised. *Colombia.* Saitz and Cervenka, ibid.

Introduction   Right hand of one person grasps right hand of another briefly. Intensity varies with importance of act and its emotional content. Continental *Western Europe*. Revesz, "Die Psychologie," p. 143. "it was towards him that Mr. Pickwick extended his hand, when he said, 'A friend of our friend's here.' " 19th cent. *England*. Dickens, *Pickwick*, I, p. 39.

Investiture   The vassal extended his folded hands toward his lord, who enclosed these in his own; thereupon the oath of fealty was sworn. 13th cent. *Germany. Kudrun*, st. 190, 1612; *Alphart*, 10; 12th cent. *Germany*. Otto v. Freising, *Gesta Friderici*, II, 5. Medieval *France*. *Elie de St. Gille*, 1202.

Invitation   Grasping someone's hand in offering seat. Anc. *Greece*. Sittl, p. 81. Host takes hand of guest to lead into house or to table. Anc. *Greece*. Sittl, ibid. Host puts hand on coach of arriving guest. Anc. *Greece*. Sittl, ibid. * Hand, palm up, moves toward seat in invitation. *Colombia; U.S.* Saitz and Cervenka, p. 124. Clapping hands is giving erotic invitation. Girl. Alemtejo, *Portugal*. Urtel, pp. 12–13. * The "fig" (thumb protruded between index and middle or middle and ring fingers). Erotic invitation. Anc. *Rome*; 19th cent. Naples; southern *Italy*. De Jorio, p. 157. * Host extends one hand, palm up, toward room guest is to enter; and another, also palm up, is moved in the same direction. *Central Africa*. Hochegger, p. 97. * Man gives his hand to a woman and moves his index finger in hollow of her hand. Invitation to copulate. *Central Africa*. Hochegger, p. 193. * Fingers straight but held tightly together, fingertips pointing down, hand is moved sharply downwards, then hand describes a vertical arc, symbolic of a question mark. Invitation to copulate. *Brazil*. Cascudo, *História*, p. 236.

Jail   One hand grasps wrist of other hand. *Colombia*. Saitz and Cervenka, p. 74.

Jealousy   Woman rubs palms together several times: jealousy [and pleasure?] that her man cannot get another woman. *Syria*. Barakat, no. 218.

Joy   Clapping of hands over discomfiture of someone else. Anc. Jews. *Middle East*. Ohm, p. 284. Clapping hands with joy. Anc. *Egypt*. Ohm, ibid. In general. Ohm, p. 285; Boggs, col. 320; Sittl, p. 11. Clapping of hands in gratitude and in prayer of thanks. *Ps.* 47:2; Ohm, pp. 284–85. See Dodwell, pl. 55 d to p. 163. Clapping of hands during a sermon of Gregorius Nazianzenus. Early medieval *Near East. PG* 36, col. 313. The Church opposed clapping during prayer. Ohm, p. 286. Rapid, vigorous clapping of hands, always hitting the left with the right hand. 19th cent. *Palestine*. Bauer, p. 224. "He was glad, he said, to find himself alive; and his two friends, clapping and rubbing their hands twenty times in an hour, declared, that now, once more, he was all himself" 18th cent. *England*. Richardson, ix, p. 211. Clapping of hands.

Children. *France*. Mitton, p. 146. "He sobbed, and wept, and clapped his hands, and hallooed, and finally ran down the street." 18th cent. *England*. Smollett, *Humphrey Clinker*, Letter of Melford, Sept. 21. "Clinker skipped about, rubbing his hands for joy of this reconciliation" Smollett, ibid., Letter of Melford, May 24. "the children crowded round her, and clapped their hands for joy." 19th cent. *England*. Dickens, *Pickwick*, I, p. 492. * Rubbing of hands. *Germany*. *DWb*, IV/2, col. 331. "and Job, rubbing his hands with delight" 19th cent. *England*. Dickens, *Pickwick*, I, p. 433. "The old man rubbed his hands gleefully together." 19th cent. *England*. Dickens, *Oliver Twist*, p. 164. Imaginary delight: " 'I wish them horses had been three months and better in the Fleet, Sir.' 'Why, Sam?' enquired Mr. Pickwick. 'Vy, Sir,' exclaimed Mr. Weller, rubbing his hands, 'how they would go if they had been!' " 19th cent. *England*. Dickens, *Pickwick*, II, p. 327. * "Her joy with heaved-up hand she doth express." 16th–17th cent. *England*. Shakesp., *Lucrece* 111. * "A tailor pounded the table in joy" *Germany*. Boggs, col. 300. Out of merriment and enthusiasm "the company commenced a . . . thumping of tables." 19th cent. *England*. Dickens, *Pickwick*, I, p. 115. * "was so relieved that he could not restrain his joy, but took off his little straw-hat and threw it up into the air." 19th cent. *England*. Trollope, *Can You Forgive Her?*, II, p. 258. * Breaking pitcher or pot after departure or misfortune of an enemy. 19th cent. *Palestine*. Bauer, p. 221. * Hand(s) rapidly agitated up and down. Children. *France*. Mitton, p. 146. * Hands clasped over right shoulder and vigorously shaken. Support or joy. Arab. Barakat, no. 98. * Hand slapped repeatedly against thigh. Anc. *Rome*. Sittl, p. 12. * Elbow(s) bent, clenched fist(s) held out in front of body, as in reaction of O. J. Simpson on hearing "not guilty" verdict. *Daily News*, Oct. 4, 1995, p. 1. *See also* Applause.

Judgment Nobility swore enmity with raised hands. Medieval *Germany*. Oldest recension of *Herzog Ernst* (orig. ca. 1180). *Herzog Ernst*, 1182–83. Judges and participants in the "Thing" raise hand, palm inwards, and extend one finger in connection with proscription. Medieval *Germany*. Amira, "Handgebärden," p. 217. * Palm of Christ's hand turned towards saved, back of other hand turned toward the damned. Depictions of Last Judgment. Medieval *Germany*. Haseloff, p. 307. * Hands horizontal, backs turned up, on same level but apart from one another. Imitation of scale. 19th cent. Naples, southern *Italy*. De Jorio, p. 171. Both arms extended forward horizontally, both hands in same position. Tips of index and thumb turned down and forming a cone. Imitation of scale. Naples, southern *Italy*. Ibid.

Kill Right hand closed, thumb out, pressed closed as in grasping knife, jerked thumb edge down. *India; Sicily*. Austin, p. 596. * Hand flat, edge down, makes chopping motion. *Netherlands*. Andrea and de Boer, p. 121. "He looked at the sentry as Robert Jordan smiled at him

and, pointing with one finger, drew the other across his throat." *Spain.*
Hemingway, pp. 36–37.

Laziness Scratching limbs. Medieval *France. Mathéolus*, I, 1462. *
Putting hands into one's bosom, into one's lap, or into one's pocket.
Germany. DWb, IV/2, col. 335. * Palms turned upward, fingers slightly
bent as though holding ostrich eggs. Hands move together up and down
as if one were determining their weight. Gesturer is metaphorically
weighing testicles of lazy individual. *Mexico.* Jiménez, 35. * Palm of
one hand up as though to catch a drop of water, fingers bent, hand moving slightly up and down as though weighing something. *Mexico.*
Lomas, p. 33.

Leading Consul took hand of person he brought into senate. Anc.
Rome. Sittl, p. 81. Polite host takes guest by hand or wrist and leads
him to his place. Anc. *Greece* and *Rome.* Sittl, p. 81; Barasch, *Giotto*,
p. 134. Men led woman or lover by hand or wrist. Anc. *Greece.* Sittl, p.
81. Leading someone by hand or wrist indicates possession of led by
leader, normally of woman by man. Legal gesture. Vase in Camposanto
in Pisa features Dionysiac relief of maenad leading companion into
dance by holding wrist. Maenad leading group also grasps next one by
the wrist. For examples, including preservation of motif in medieval art,
see Barasch, *Giotto*, pp. 135–44. Particularly favored in Carolingian and
Ottonian representations of the Ascension. Barasch, ibid., p. 140. *See
also* HAND, Possession.

Legitimation Handshake between god and ruler legitimizes ruler
by transferring part of god's divine nature. Since 1st cent. B.C. Tomb of
Antioch I of Commagene on Namruddagh. *Middle East.* Cumont, II, pp.
187 ff. * Since Commodus Roman emperors appear as equals of gods.
Depicted as standing hand in hand. *Roman Empire.* Sittl, p. 347. *See
also* HAND, Assistance.

Liberty Hand open and fingers spread. Anc. *India.* Rose, p. 312.

Look Flat hand, palm down, placed above eyes. Schoolchildren.
U.S. Seton, p. xxi. * Pointing and looking in same direction. Schoolchildren. *U.S.* Seton, p. xxi.

Luck Knocking on wood. *Spain; Lat. Am.* Green, p. 95. * Hands
clasped, raised to level of face and shaken. "Good Luck!" *Netherlands.*
Andrea and de Boer, p. 172.

Magical Extending hand starts plague. *Exodus* 8:5; 8:17; 9:22; etc.
* When Moses held up hand in battle with Amalekites, Israelites won.
When he let hand fall, enemy was victorious. Biblical. *Middle East.
Exodus* 17:11. * Moses stretched out hand, and Red Sea parted. *Exodus*
Biblical. *Middle East.* 14:16. * Folded hands of evil women hinder birth
and recovery after childbirth. Anc. *Rome.* Sittl, p. 126. Folding of hands,
due to its evil effect, was prohibited at official gatherings, ceremonies,
etc. Anc. *Rom.* Sittl, ibid. * Hands folded around knees or legs hinder

childbirth of another woman. Anc. *Rome*. Sittl, ibid. * Upon ascending throne publicly, emperor makes sign of cross, commending self to God's protection. Late *Roman Empire*. Sittl, p. 128. Making sign of cross over one's open mouth while yawning or when entering public baths. Early Christian. For yawning, see Sittl, pp. 127–28. Old women make sign of cross over open mouth of yawning children, simultaneously saying "Heiligs Kreuz!" 19th cent. Bavaria, *Germany*. Sittl, p. 127. * Rubbing face of god as act of ceremonial greeting appears in funerary inscriptions of pyramid chambers of fifth and sixth dynasties. Supplicant acquired beneficent influence of god. Anc. *Egypt*. Dawson, p. 81. * Hiding thumbs (folding them under fingers of clenched fist) to hold fast incubus so it won't interfere. Part of New Year's wish. *Germany*. *DWb*, II, cols. 848–49; Meschke, col. 331. * Touching one's genitals through holes in pockets. Magically nullifies oath. *Germany*. Meschke, col. 334. * Hand imitates movement of throwing something to rear. Gesture magically causes one to forget something disagreeable. Many popular Brazilian "simpatias" end with this. *Brazil*. Cascudo, *História*, p. 101.

Magnitude   Child raises both hands, palms forward, fingers spread, in answer to question "How much do you love your mother?" Gesture—"this much." *Saudi Arabia*. Barakat, no. 76. * Raising number of fingers to indicate price one will pay for item. Arab. Barakat, no. 123. * Fingers hanging down loosely, hand is moved up and down, swaying. Plenitude of harvest. 19th cent. *Palestine*. Bauer, p. 223. * Thumb and index of one hand holding index of other hand—small measurement. Southern *Italy*. Efron, p. 97. * Flat hand, palm down, held up at arm's length. "So high." Schoolchildren. *U.S.* Seton, p. xx. * Hands horizontally extended and apart, arms straight, palms down—wide expanse. *Europe; North America*. Aubert, p. 89. * Arm extended, fingers cupped, hand brought to rest on desk or table top—figurative limit. Madrid, *Spain; Lat. Am.* Green, p. 63. * Hands, palms down, fingers extended, pushed away from each other at level of gesticulator's waist. Gesture may accompany verbal behavior on topic of mass thought or activity. *Spain; Lat. Am.* Green, p. 69. * Fingers of both hands, held vertically few inches from chest, pushed away from body and returned to original position. Or, raising cupped hand to side of head and twisting wrist and hand outward, so palm faces listener—distance. *Spain*. Green, pp. 61–62. * Both hands raised to level of chest, fingers extended, palms facing one another—simultaneity. Madrid, *Spain*. Green, pp. 69–70. * Palm turned down, indicating height of an animal; palm vertical and thumb thrust up, indicating height of child. *Mexico; Guatemala*. Hayes, p. 259. *Colombia*. Axtell, *Gestures*, p. 90. * Hand, fingers extended, held at certain height with edge of hand down—height of human being. *Colombia*. Saitz and Cervenka, p. 70; Axtell, *Gesture*, p. 90. * Hand, fingers extended, held at certain height with palm down—height of human being or animal. *U.S.* Used only to indicate height of animals. *Colombia* (except for parts of north coast). Saitz and Cervenka, ibid. Length not indicated by extending indices of both hands. Regarded as rude. Flat palm of each hand, held vertically—length of an object. *Colombia.* Axtell, *Gestures,* p. 90. Hand extended, palm down—height of objects. *Mexico.* Cascudo, *História,* p. 131. Hands, palms held flat and facing down, one some distance above other—"a large Pils." Or, right elbow placed in palm of left hand, right arm vertical, right hand at 90 degree angle to arm and turned inward. *Netherlands.* Andrea and de Boer, p. 11. * Hands held some distance one above other, palm of upper hand facing down and held flat, palm of lower hand facing up and held flat—height of an object; hand held at some distance laterally from each other, palms flat and facing each other—length of some object. *Netherlands.* Andrea and de Boer, p. 137. Indicating quantity. *Central Africa.* Hochegger, p. 157. * Open hands, palms inward, moved up and down in front of body: "It rained a lot." *Central Africa.* Hochegger, p. 22. * Open hands at level of head, palms facing one another across width of head and moved backward and forward: "He ate a lot." *Central Africa.* Hochegger, ibid. * Hands joined in front of chest, then swung down and toward back, then right hand grasps left forearm: "I've lost weight all over!" *Central Africa.* Hochegger, p. 108. * One flat hand raised to height of head; gesture of women returning from fishing, indicating: "Beaucoup!" ("Lots!") *Central Africa.* Hochegger, p. 157. * Open right hand, palm down, held out at height of person, object, or plant. Or, open right hand, edge down, held out at height of a quadruped or a flat object. Or, open right hand held vertically, fingertips pointing upward, at height of persons, shrubs, plants. *Central Africa.* Hochegger, pp. 200–01. * Open palm at level of stomach or chest rises rapidly. Abundance. Río de la Plata region of *Argentina; Uruguay.* Meo Zilio, p. 97.

Manumission Servant is taken by hand, then released. Medieval *Spain. Cid,* 1043. Germanic: Grimm, *DRA,* I, p. 459. * Slave freed by a blow. 17th cent. *England.* Butler, II, i, 235. If master wanted to free slave, he led him to praetor, who gave slave blow on head as sign of freedom. Anc. *Rome.* Siuts, p. 109. Owner places hand on slave's head, right hand, or other part of the body, and removes it with "Hunc hominem liberum esse volo" ("I want this man to be free"). Slave then turns around, signifying new station in life. Anc. *Rome;* Medieval Lombardy. Sittl, p. 132. Owner inflicts last stroke with cane. Anc. *Rome.* Sittl, pp. 132–33. Owner turns slave around, to signify slave's entirely new position in life. Anc. *Rome.* Sittl, ibid. Owner strikes slave with hand for last time. Anc. *Rome.* Sittl, p. 133. Pushing a person away, from the front or the back—ejection from a property as well as manumission. Medieval *Germany.* Amira, "Handgebärden," p. 253.

Marriage   Great Being asks Amara by gesture if she is married. He clenches fist. She answered affirmatively by spreading out her hand. Jatakas. *India*. Rose, p. 312. * Religious leader places hands of bride and groom together so that thumbs touch, and holds hands in this position while saying prayer. Muslim. Barakat, no. 222. * In medieval marriage ritual, the priest, satisfied that consent had been given and rules of consanguinity adhered to, watched bride being given to groom by her father or guardian, and concluded ceremony with a prayer. "The joining of right hands concluded the transfer of a gift—with all the artifice and ambiguity implicit in the act. (Later, in the thirteenth century, the Church would interpret it as pledge of faith by both parties, and the priest would join the hands of bride and groom.)" Duby, *A History of Private Life*, p. 130; and the illustrations from the 14th cent. *Credo du sire de Joinville* (Paris, Bibl. Nat., French n.a. 4509 and the 13th cent. *Commentary on the Decretum of Gratian* (Laon Lib., Ms 372) on pp. 129, 130 respectively. Joining of hands at marriage of Tobias and Sara. *La Bible Hystorians ou Les Hystoires Escolastres*. Rijksmuseum Meermanno-Westreenianum, The Hague. Ms. 10 B 23, fol. 249v. 1372. *See* Fig. 17. * It was customary for male relative or friend to slap groom on back as soon as rings had been exchanged with bride. See Duby, ibid., p. 250, the illustration from Sano di Pietro, *Marriage of Nobles: The Exchange of Rings* (Siena, State Archives). After exchange of rings, father (or, if deceased, his eldest son) transferred authority over daughter to son-in-law. Someone would occasionally clap groom vigorously on back as soon as he had spoken "Yes," an act often reproduced on frescoes of Marriage of the Virgin; see Duby, ibid., p. 294.

Masturbation   Loosely clenched fist moved up and down in front of body. *Colombia; U.S.* Saitz and Cervenka, p. 122. *Brazil.* Cascudo, *História*, p. 236.

Medico-magical   Christ healed by touch. Biblical. *Middle East. Matth.* 8:3. Sick recuperated by touching him. *Matth.* 9:20; *Mark* 3:10; *Luke* 6:19; 8:45; *Acts* 19:12. St. Paul healed by laying on of hands. *Acts* 28:8. Bulwer, pp. 113–19. * Slap on ear of demon. 4th cent. Late *Roman Empire*. Palladius, 31, col. 1089a. * King of France touches forehead of scrofulous or epileptic subject by placing index and middle finger side by side. Window of the Eglise abbatiale in the former chapel of Saint-Michel de Circuit of Mont Saint Michel au Péril de la Mer (1488). Bloch, p. 145. * Charles II of England gave regular public notice of receptions in which he would heal by touch. 17th cent. *England*. Baker, p. 54. Charles II performed the "royal touch" at the Court Chapel in The Hague in 1660 under the doubtful eye of the Dutch upper class; William of Orange called it a "silly superstition," but co-regent Mary performed it, as did Queen Anne, the last English sovereign to perform it. Frijhoff, p. 219. Ritual laying on of hand was last carried out by

Fig. 17. Joining hands in marriage. *La Bible Hystorians ou Les Hystoires Escolastres* (1372). Rijksmuseum Meermanno-Westreenianum, The Hague, Netherlands. 10 B 23, fol. 249v.

European royalty by Charles X of France in 1825. Wolff Hurden, p. 1. Hand of King Olaf II of Norway touches chest of patient. Fischer, "Heilgebärden," II, p. 338. Touch of dead hand (not criminal) was used for goiter and other afflictions, stroke being applied nine times from east to west, and nine times from west to east. West Sussex, *England*. Baker, p. 51. In Northamptonshire crowds of sufferers congregated about the gallows on days of public executions to receive the "dead stroke" of the body's hand. Ibid. In Staffordshire it is held that a dead hand rubbed on warts causes them to disappear. Ibid. * Hand of healer laid on head of patient. Fischer, "Heilgebärden," II, p. 338. King Olaf of Sweden laid hand on breast of patient, and King Sancho IV of Castile placed foot on throat of patient. Medieval *Sweden*; medieval *Spain*. Fischer, ibid. Cf. 19th cent. *Palestine*. Bauer, p. 11. "Maud A. Snow, music teacher, testified that as a result of laying on of hands [of evangelist Chas. S. Price], she had been cured of tumors, Bright's disease, and other ailments." Hayes, p. 272. For a cure of a sick cow by a similar process, see Hayes, ibid.

Mediocre Hand, palm down, index and little finger extended, turns repeatedly back and forth so one of the two fingers is up, the other down. 19th cent. Naples, southern *Italy*. de Jorio, p. 127. "So-so"; "Not good, not bad," in reply to "How are you?" *Europe; North America*. "Oh, it's very tricky." *Netherlands*. Axtell, *Gestures*, p. 94. * Hand, palm down, fingers together and extended, moves from side to side. Assimilated Jews, *Eastern Europe*. Efron, p. 117.

Minimization of difficulties "Actress Russell, humped up and hipped out till she resembles a superannuated ostrich, encompasses quite without caricature the standard repertory of Jewish gesture—. . . the vigorous extension of the hands, chest high and palms up, that means: you got problems? I got problems." *Time*, Jan. 19, 1962, Review of "A Majority of One" (Warner), p. 55.

Mockery Wagging the hand. Biblical. *Middle East*. *Zeph.* 2:15. * Striking someone in the face. Biblical. *Middle East*. *Luke* 22:64. Anc. *Rome*. Sittl, p. 108. * The "horns" (clenched fist, index and little finger extended). Mural, amulets. Pompeii, anc. *Rome*. Röhrich, *Gebärde-Metapher-Parodie*, p. 23 and pl. 17, 19. * "Fig" (thumb protruded between index and middle or middle and ring finger). Medieval *Europe*. See Du Cange, "ficus facere." Also 16th–17th cent. *Italy*. Basile, I, p. 103; 19th cent. Naples, southern *Italy*. De Jorio, p. 155. * Sticking out the tongue and making the sign of "fig." 15th–16th cent. *Germany*. Hans Maler, *Christ bearing the Cross*. Chicago Art Institute. "Fig" is common in *France;* esp. southern *France; England; Germany; Spain; Latin America; Portugal; Italy*; esp. Naples. If ridicule is not seriously meant, "fig" is executed under cloak. Liebrecht, p. 186. * "Horns" made by cuckold riding cock. *Germany*. Bolte, "Bilderbogen," pp. 78–79. Cf. Röhrich, *Lexikon*, II, pp. 434–38. * Clapping hands. 19th cent. *Palestine*. Bauer, p. 224. * "Mr. Jingle fluttering in derision a white handkerchief from the coach window." 19th cent. *England*. Dickens, *Pickwick*, I, p. 143. * Shanghai Gesture. *Europe; North America*. Taylor, *Shanghai Gesture*, pp. 9–36, 41–51. * Raising index, then flexing it. *Germany*. Meschke, col. 332. * Crossed extended indexes. Carinthia, *Austria*. Meschke, ibid. * Right fist rubbed around on flat left hand. *Spain; Portugal*. Urtel, p. 28. * Hand put over mouth, accompanied by mocking glances. Little girls. *France*. Mitton, p. 145. * Tips of thumbs placed into ears or on temples, fingers spread, palms to the front, fingers may or may not be wagged back and forth. ("Nuts to you!") Anc. *Rome*; *Europe*. Taylor, *Shanghai Gesture*, pp. 37–39. Childish. *U.S.* Perry, Comics. Flat hands waved near shoulders, palms up—"Jew!" Schoolchildren. *U.S.* Seton, p. xxiii. * "Men shall clap their hands at him." Biblical. *Middle East*. *Job* 27:23. * "The which John Bacon was whistled and clapped out of Rome." Ca. 1555. *OED*, s.v. "clap." * Right hand moved up and down as if playing guitar. Children. *Mexico*. Lomas, p. 35. * Mocking applause by tapping thumbnails together, one on top of other. *Netherlands*. Andrea and de Boer, p. 22. [Editors' note: also *U.S.*] * Right hand scratches back of left hand, indicating scabies. *Central Africa*. Hochegger, p. 80. * Open hands, palms up, held in front of chest—pendulous breasts. *Central Africa*. Hochegger, p. 183. *See also* FINGER, Mockery; FINGER, HAND, Mockery.

Money Putting hand on pocket and tapping on it. 19th cent. Naples, southern *Italy*. de Jorio, p. 126. * Hand extended, palm up. Request for money or "give it to me." *U.S.* Saitz and Cervenka, p. 89. * Hand loosely open, edge of palm down, swept horizontally toward body as if sweeping something off a table: "money" or "pay me." *Peru*. Axtell, *Gestures*, p. 93. *See also* Stealing.

Moot Hands raised, each in outward arc, until both are approx. shoulder high, palms up. Assimilated Jews. *Eastern Europe*. Efron, p. 117. * Hand, palm down, is swung in a semicircle so that palm is up. (Two sides to a question.) Assimilated Jews. *Eastern Europe*. Efron, p. 150.

Mourning Putting ashes on one's head. Biblical. *Middle East*. II *Samuel* 13:19; *Rev*. 18:19. * Laying one's hand upon one's head. Biblical. *Middle East*. II *Rev*. 13:19. * Tearing one's hair and beard. Biblical. *Middle East*. *Ezra* 9:3. * Rending clothes and putting on sackcloth. Biblical. *Middle East*. II *Sam*. 3:31. [Editors' note: Remnant of gesture of rending clothes is Jewish (male) custom of wearing torn black ribbon on lapel.] Tearing of clothes. Anc. *Greece* and *Rome*. Sittl, p. 25. Women tear their clothes. Anc. *Rome*. Sittl, p. 26. Hellenistic *Near East*. Sittl, p. 68. Women tear their clothes. 19th cent. *Palestine*. Bauer, p. 211. * Hand extended toward grave in apostrophe of dead. Anc. *Greece* and *Rome*. Benndorf, pl. 14. 17,1. 21,2. 24,1.3; Sittl, p. 74, n. 2. * Wife takes head of departed husband between both hands. Anc. *Greece*. Sittl, p. 66. * Wife places hand on chest of departed husband. Anc. *Greece*. Sittl, ibid. * Hand extended toward corpse and moving up and down in reproach. Anc. *Greece;* 19th cent. *Corsica*. Sittl, ibid. * Hand extended toward face of corpse during mourning, palm upwards ("Here you lie now!") Sittl, p. 66. Benndorf, pl. 1. * Weapons beaten together four times at burning of the body on funeral pyre with military honors. Anc.

Rome. Sittl, p. 73. * Knight carrying shield upside down signifies mourning for death of his lord. 13th cent. *Germany.* Wolfr. v. Eschenbach, Bk. II, 641–43. * Right hand clasps wrist of left. Medieval *Germany.* Abraham mourning death of Sarah in Wocel, p. 26, pl. 13b. * Slow beating of hands and rubbing of fingers. 19th cent. *Palestine.* Bauer, p. 224. * Light, slow beating of one palm upon other, in which sometimes one and sometimes other palm is uppermost. 19th cent. *Palestine.* Bauer, p. 219. * Wringing hands. *Germany.* Boggs, p. 319. * Casting dust on oneself. Boggs, ibid. A variety of mourning gestures are performed by figures in Giotto's *Lamentation over the Dead Christ* in Arena Chapel, Padua, *Italy.* Barasch, *Giotto*, pp. 40–42. *See also* the illustration from 14th cent. *Decameron* (Paris, Bibl. Nat., Ital. 482, fol. 79v.) in Duby, *A History of Private Life*, p. 251: hands raised above head, hand placed against cheek.

Negation Right hand raised, palm forward, fingers extended. *Spain.* Flachskampf, p. 237. "Anne held up her hand. 'I won't advise,' she said." *England.* Huxley, ch. 7. * Hand raised, palm outward, or simply the index raised, and shaken rapidly from side to side. *France.* Mitton, p. 141. Moving extended index of raised right hand from side to side. *Lat. Am.* Kany, p. 88. Palm open. ("Probably not.") *Italy.* "The High Price of Silent Insults," *Time*, April 9, 1965, p. 67. * Hand in front of body, palm forward, hand shaken vigorously from side to side. *Saudi Arabia; Lebanon; Jordan; Syria.* Barakat, no. 163. *Netherlands.* Andrea and de Boer, p. 113. * Hands, palm down, moved in opposite directions: both moving together in front of body, both moving apart (similar to the baseball "Safe"). *U.S.* Su, <LINGUIST 3.1012>. * Fingers of right hand together and raised, may consist of merely uncurling fingers or may involve raising hand as if to get attention. *Greece.* Su, <LINGUIST 3.1012>. * Right hand passed back and forth across the chest. Ainu. *Japan.* Cascudo, *História*, p. 166.

Nervousness "rubbing the palms of his hands nervously together." 19th cent. *England.* Dickens, *Oliver Twist*, p. 232. * Hands hanging down, opening and closing several times. Aubert, *Europe; North America.* p. 82. * Cracking knuckles. *U.S.* Krout, p. 22. * Jerking hands. *U.S.* Krout, p. 23.

"Never" Right hand, palm down and fingers still, is moved from left to right across the body. *Saudi Arabia; Jordan; Syria; Lebanon.* Barakat, no. 90.

Nonchalance "The camera clearly captured the nonchalant stance, the hand in the pocket" *Israel.* Gur, pp. 1, 3.

Nonsense Open hand is moved from vertical position downward in front of face, closing as it descends, as if one were chasing a fly away. *Netherlands.* Andrea and de Boer, p. 89.

Nothing Hand held out, palm upwards, flat. Anc. *Greece.* Sittl, p.

111. * "Robert Jordan looked up at Primitivo's post and saw him signal, 'Nothing,' crossing his two hands, palms down." *Spain.* Hemingway, p. 283. * The "fig"—a fist, with the thumb protruding between index and middle, or middle and ring finger. Virtually confined to Yugoslavia, where it is common. Morris et al., pp. 152–54, 160, and the map on p. 159.

Oath "I lift up my hand to heaven, and say, I live for ever." Biblical. *Middle East. Deut.* 32:40. Also *Gen.* 14:22; *Rev.* 10:5, 6. * "And he shall put his hand on the head of the burnt offering." Biblical. *Middle East. Lev.* 1:4. * Soldiers, in taking oath, dip hands or swords into shield containing blood of sacrificial animal. Anc. *Greece.* Sittl, p. 143. * In giving oath, both arms are raised (as if to call gods to witness). Anc. *Greece* and *Rome.* Sittl, p. 141. * In giving oath, earth or water is touched (as concrete representation of deities of earth and water). Anc. *Greece* and *Rome.* Sittl, p. 142. * In swearing oath in court of law, altar is touched. Anc. *Greece* and *Rome, Carthage.* Sittl, pp. 142–43. * One whose most valuable property is animals will touch these in swearing. Anc. *Greece.* Sittl, p. 140. * In taking oath, ruler touches scepter, symbol of dominion, as most prized possession. Anc. *Greece* and *Rome.* Sittl, p. 139. * In calling gods to witness oath, swearer raises hand to point at sky. Anc. *Greece* and *Rome.* Sittl, p. 141 and n. 1, fig. 11. * In making covenant, Romans let a pebble be brought from temple of Jupiter Feretrius; swearer held pebble in hand and, in speaking the words "Si sciens fallo, tum me Diespiter salva urbe arceque bonis liciat uti ego hunc lapidem" ["if I knowingly fail to comply, may Jupiter cast me out . . . just as I do to this stone"] let it fall to ground. Anc. *Rome.* Sittl, p. 144. * In swearing oath, one touched bow of Artemis. Anc. *Rome.* Sittl, p. 142. If Olympian gods were witness to an oath, deity's statue or altar is touched. Anc. *Greece.* Sittl, p. 142. Touching of statue was not common unless it stood on altar, so that it and foot of statue could be touched simultaneously. Anc. *Rome.* Sittl, p. 142. In court of law, oaths are given by deity and hand is put upon some insignia representing deity, e.g. the scepter of Jupiter Feretrius. Anc. *Rome.* Sittl, ibid. In taking oath, weapon is touched to signify that weapon is to take life of one who breaks oath. Anc. *Greece; Rome*; pagan Franks. Sittl, p. 134; Grimm, *DRA*, II, pp. 546–47. * Soldiers, in taking oath, hold sacrificial pig by neck and tail, and with right hand point sword to heaven. Anc. *Rome.* Sittl, p. 144. * In taking an oath, two soldiers clasp hands as in handshake, with other hand grasping their swords. Anc. *Rome* (Oscan). Sittl, ibid. * Soldiers, in taking oath, touch sacrificial pig with their hands. Anc. *Rome* (Capua, Atella). Sittl, ibid. * Soldiers touch sacrificial pig with points of swords while servant holds pig. Anc. *Rome.* (Oscan). Friedländer, pl. 9,9.10.12.; 10,19. Sittl, p. 144. * In taking oath, right hand is placed over heart, as most valuable part of body. Medieval *Ger-*

many and modern *Europe*. Sittl, p. 139. * In taking oath, when sacrifice is made to deity, hand is pointed toward sacrificial animal, or laid on it, to identify fate of breaker of oath or perjurer with that of animal. Anc. *Rome; Byzantine Empire*. Sittl, p. 143. * Swearing an oath by touching sacrificial animal. Medieval *Scandinavia*. Grimm, *DRA*, II, p. 552. * Swearing an oath by touching roast peacock. Council of Orléans in 900: king or most honored knight carved peacock and, hand upon bird, swore some brave oath, then passed the dish and everyone who received it did likewise. Medieval *France*. Palaye, I, pp. 184, 187, 244, 246; I, p. 394; Legrand, pp. 365–67; Grimm, *DRA*, II, p. 553. * The *pater familias* swears by heads of his children, children swear by head of their father, wife by head of her husband; in all cases hand of person swearing touches object sworn by. Anc. *Rome*. Sittl, p. 140. * Hand is pointed toward sun, since sun-god is conceived to be omniscient. Anc. *Greece*; Germanic; *Byzantine Empire*. Sittl, p. 141; Grimm, *DRA*, II, p. 545; Simrock, p. 384. * In taking oath, Christians lay hand on, or took hold of Book of Gospels. Ritual legalized by Justinian. *Cod. Justin.*, 4, 1, 12, 5; Sittl, p. 145. "the pope mounted the pulpit of the basilica of the blessed apostle Peter, in the presence of the whole populace. With the Gospel in his hand, he invoked the name of the Holy Trinity and purged himself by oath from the charges." *Annals* (800), p. 80. Jews touch Torah. Sittl, ibid. After Christianization of empire, Christian altar served same purpose. *Roman Empire*. Sittl, ibid. * Touching a reliquary with horizontally extended index or middle finger. Sometimes person swearing is depicted as carrying the reliquary in left hand. Medieval *Germany*. *Sachsenspiegel*. Amira, "Handgebärden," pp. 257–58. Swearing oath by laying each hand on reliquary. Harold swears fealty to William of Normandy. 11th cent. *England*. Bayeux Tapestry. Mus. de Ville de Bayeux. * Handshake. Medieval *Germany*. Grimm, *DRA*, I, pp. 191–92. *Switzerland*. *DWb*, IV/2, col. 403. The swearer of an oath touches the person whom he promises something. Medieval *Europe*. Du Cange, III, 1618. * Defendant holds hand of plaintiff while swearing with the other hand. Medieval *Germany*. Grimm, *DRA*, II, p. 551. * Raising hand. 18th–19th cent. *Germany*. Schiller, *Wallensteins Tod*, v. xi. * Hand on heart. *DWb*, IV/2, col. 331. Women: Grimm, *DRA*, II, p. 548. * Handclasp separated by a blow with the hand of a third person. *See also* Agreement above. *Germany*. *DWb*, IV/2, col. 331. * Each party swearing raises hand and places it palm to palm against that of the other. Medieval *Germany*. Amira, "Handgebärden," p. 239. * Hand raised, first three fingers extended. Prechristian; Cyrenaica, *North Africa*; anc. *Greece*; *Italy*; *Switzerland*; *France; Belgium; England*; Danubian States; Rhineland, *Germany*. Seligmann, II, p. 180. * Open hand extended. Jews, *Middle East*. Seligmann, II, p. 165. * Whenever the word "ego" occurs in an oath, the swearer touches his breast. Anc. *Rome*.

Macrob., *Sat.*, 3, 9, 12; Heiler, p. 102. * Common for swearer to extend index, later index and middle fingers of raised right hand (Saxons). Customary also to offer a staff. (Franks). Medieval *Germany*. Amira, "Handgebärden," p. 239. * Right hand raised, index and middle finger extended. Medieval *Germany*. Grimm, *DRA*, I, p. 195. * Right hand raised, left pointing down with extended index and middle fingers surreptitiously to invalidate the oath. *Germany*. *HDA*, II, col. 667. * Left hand in pocket or behind swearer's back to invalidate oath surreptitiously, while right is raised in oath. Touching one's genitals through hole in pocket in order to invalidate an oath. *Germany*. Meschke, col. 334. * Handshake as treaty of peace. 13th cent. *Germany*. *Kudrun*, st. 833, 4. * Laying hand on judge's staff of office. 13th cent. *Germany*. Wolfr. v. Eschenb., iii, 151. "Sir Gawain, swear to me here between my hands" 13th cent. *Germany*. Wolfr. v. Eschenb., viii, 418. "Taking his hand, Arthur pledged him" Ibid., vi, 331. * Grasping another's hand while raised in giving oath symbolizes existence of proof contradicting the oath being sworn. Medieval *Germany*. *Sachsenspiegel*. Amira, "Handgebärden," p. 249. * Swearing by one's hand. 16th–17th cent. *England*. Shakesp., *Tempest* 3.2.56, 78; *Measure* 2.1.172; *Much Ado* 4.1.327, 337; etc. "And here, to pledge my vow, I give my hand." III *Henry VI*, 3.3.250. Also 19th cent. Naples, southern *Italy*. De Jorio, p. 170. * Right hand pressed to heart. 19th cent. Naples, southern *Italy*. De Jorio, p. 168. * Sign of cross made with index or whole hand on wall or floor or in air indicates resolution not to do something any more. 18th cent. Naples, southern *Italy*. de Jorio, p. 169. Drawing cross over one's heart with fingers or crossing hands over one's breast. Schoolchildren. *U.S.* Seton, p. xxii. * Raising hands with palm toward swearer, making cross with arms, putting up right hand while saying "Here's my Bible, Here's my cross, Here's my right hand up to God." Schoolchildren. *Scotland*. Opie, p. 123. * Hands raised and extended toward Charles V, King of France, who is being anointed by the Archbishop of Rheims, by the French peers swearing oath of loyalty. Medieval *France*. *Rational des Offices de Charles V*, Bibl. Nat., Franc. 437, fol. 44v. * Pulling away hand raised in oath of one suspected of swearing false oath. Traditional legal gesture. Medieval *Germany*? Fischer, "Heilgebärden, p. 342. * If hand is held with palm toward judge, oath is invalid. Röhrich, *Gebärde-Metapher-Parodie*, p. 31. * Right hand of one grasps right hand of another briefly. Intensity varies with importance of act and its emotional content. *Western Europe*. Revesz, "Die Psychologie," p. 143. * " 'I swear,' said Pnin, raising his hand." *Russia*. Nabokov, p. 168. * Holding right hand before right shoulder, palm facing forward. *Libya; Lebanon; Saudi Arabia; Syria*. Barakat, no. 10.

Obedience Right hand clasps closed left. *Sumeria; Babylonia;* anc. Jewish; Muslim (at beginning of Salat and the first Sure of the Koran);

Benedictines (clasp hands under the cuculla). Ohm, p. 276. * Right hand laid into left. Ibid.

Objection Grasping someone by arm or coattail from behind indicates objection to act performed or about to be performed by that person. Medieval *Germany*. *Sachsenspiegel*. Amira, "Handgebärden," p. 252.

Odor Holding palm to nose. Schoolchildren. *U.S.* Seton, p. xxi.

Oppression Wrist of one hand touching wrist of other hand. Hands slightly bent back and either clenched or extended. Head bent, facial expression of sorrow. Representations of Frisian slaves. Anc. *Rome*. 19th cent. Naples, southern *Italy*. De Jorio, p. 272. * Fist raised and turned, as if turning a handle. Little used, vulgar. ("Put on the screws.") *France*. Mitton, p. 150.

Order (arranging in) Pushing both hands, perpendicular, palms facing one another, down and away from gesticulator. Accompanies expressions suggestive of channeling or directing. Madrid, *Spain*. Green, p. 73. * Raising both hands, one in front of other, palms facing inward, directly in front of gesticulator, then moving them back and forth horizontally, accompanying expressions of precedence or order. Madrid, *Spain*. Green, p. 60.

Overburdened Right hand held horizontally at forehead, left horizontally at the chin. *France*. Life Photo by David Scherman, *Life*, Sept. 16, 1946, p. 12.

Pacification "Matt stroked her hand in encouraging silence." *U.S.* Boucher, *Nine times Nine*, p. 207.

Pain Hands beaten together. Anc. *Greece* and *Rome*. Sittl, p. 19. * Hands interlocked. *Medea Ercolanese*. Anc. *Rome*. De Jorio, p. 141. * Thumb touches extended middle finger, ring and little fingers are closed, index extended. Hand is loosely shaken up and down in this position, so that index hits middle finger and produces smacking sound. 19th cent. Naples, southern *Italy*. De Jorio, p. 139.

Pardon Hands extended forward, lowered from above, palms down. *Europe; North America*. Aubert, p. 89. * Joining hands in front, palms touching, fingertips pointing to person addressed. *Europe; North America*. Aubert, p. 89.

Past Open hand, at height of face and perpendicular to it, describes 270 degree (counter-clockwise?) arc in air. Río de la Plata region of *Argentina; Uruguay*. Meo Zilio, p. 94. *See* Future.

Pay Beckon, then write on air. ("Give me my bill"). Schoolchildren. *U.S.* Seton, p. xxiii. *See* Approach.

Peace Laying down of weapons. *Germany*. HDA, I, col. 316. Handclasp. 13th cent. *Germany*. Wolfram v. Eschenbach, 691, 3; *Kudrun*, st. 833, 4; Amira, "Handgebärden," p. 198. * "and they could see a shield lifted up . . . with the point of the shield upward in token of peace."

Medieval *Wales.* "Branwen" in *Mabinogion*, p. 25. * After separating his hands during the beginning of the "Memento etiam . . . ," ["Remember . . . ,"] the priest "joins them at the words 'in somno pacis' ['in peaceful death']," an indication of peace and rest. Roman Catholic. *Mass*, p. 66. * Accompanying expressions indicating peace or truce, bunched fingers of each hand may be brought together. Madrid, *Spain.* Green, p. 47. * "The recently discovered correspondence of Evelyn Waugh and Lady Diana Cooper has provided William F. Buckley with long-sought proof of the continuing efficaciousness of the Holy Ghost. The novelist, since his conversion a joyful and proud Catholic, died on Easter Sunday 1966 after attending mass; shortly thereafter the custom of the greeting of peace was introduced, which requires believers to shake hands with those to the left, right, in front and behind them—the sticky fashion would unquestionably have kept Waugh from attending mass; but at the appropriate time he was summoned." Roman Catholic. Gross, p. 38.

Pederasty   Heel of right hand tapped on cupped left hand. Obscene. *France*. Mitton, p. 151. *See* Insult.

Pensiveness   Picking one's teeth. Latter half of 16th cent. *France*. Lommatzsch, p. 58. * Stroking the beard. *Germany*. *Rhein. Wb.*, I, col. 478. * Palms rubbed together repeatedly as hands are firmly clasped. Fingers may be interlocked. Extreme concern. *U.S.* Saitz and Cervenka, p. 141.

Piety   Upper arms low, arms bent at elbow, forearms raised, palms pressed together. 16th cent. *Germany*. Brant, woodcut, p. 79. *Colombia; U.S.* Saitz and Cervenka, p. 112.

Pity   "She stretches out her hand to the poor." Biblical. *Middle East. Prov.* 31:20. * "folded, sympathetically wringing hands." *Germany. DWb*, IV/2, col. 385. * " 'I am afraid, Sir,' said Mr. Pickwick, laying his hand gently and compassionately on his arm" 19th cent. *England*. Dickens, *Pickwick*, II, p. 235. * Cutting some part of body as symbol of pity and mourning for the dead among many primitive tribes. Frazer, *Golden Bough*, IV, pp. 92–93.

Placation   "Some also, on seeing a little wine left in a glass throw it on the ground or ashes of the fire, crying 'Cottabus,' KOTT + Bus; this is a superstition, but not to be despised. It is said to placate the gods." *Germany*. Belloc, p. 12. "An amusement of young men in ancient Greece, much in vogue at drinking parties, consisting in throwing a portion of wine into some vessel, so as to strike it in a particular manner. 'The simplest mode was when each threw the wine left in his cup so as to strike smartly in a metal basin, at the same time invoking his mistress' name; if the whole fell with a distinct sound into the basin, it was a sign he stood well with her.' Liddell and Scott." Anc. *Greece. OED*, s.v. Cottabus. " 'I know what you're going to say,' said Everthorpe, holding up his pink, fleshy palms, placatingly." *England.* Lodge, *Nice Work*, p. 138.

Plea   Raised hands in supplication to God. Biblical. *Middle East. Ps.* 28:2; 88:9. * Right hand raised while kneeling. Anc. *Greece* and *Rome.* Sittl, p. 157, fig. 13, and p. 158. " 'never think that through terror at Zeus' will I shall become womanish and shall entreat my . . . enemy with hands upturned in a woman's way . . . ' " Anc. *Greece.* Aeschylus, *Prometheus* 1002–06. Bremmer, p. 22, comments that the reason for 'hands upturned' being considered as 'womanish' is probably because, before Aeschylus, to have the hands upturned signified being unarmed, i.e. a man who had relinquished his manhood. Similarly, the passive homosexual, according to Hellenistic physiognomics (see Bremmer, p. 32, n. 21), carried his hands upturned and flabbily, and Chrysostom speaks against those of dubious sexual reputation who converse with upturned palms (*Orationes,* 33.52). This may also be the reason why the Greeks extended their arms toward heaven with palms upturned when praying. It is generally accepted that this is the reason for the modern gesture of raising both arms with hands open in surrender. It may also explain why Spartan and Athenian youths were required to keep their hands in their garments. Anc. *Greece*; also Hellenistic period. Bremmer, p. 22. * Kneeling, both hands grasped by suppliant. Anc. *Rome.* Sittl, p. 166. * Hands sweep dust together while kneeling. Anc. *Greece.* Sittl, p. 158. Hands rub the earth while kneeling, indicating readiness to pick up dust and throw it on oneself. Anc. *Greece.* Sittl, ibid., n. 6. * Both hands extended toward someone. Anc. *Greece* and *Rome.* Sittl, p. 50. * Right hand of someone held or shaken. Anc. *Greece* and *Rome.* Sittl, p. 29. * Hands extended toward judge, women pleaded their case, since they were not permitted to grasp hand of judge. Anc. *Rome.* Sittl, p. 51. Handshake. Anc. *Greece* and *Rome.* Sittl, p. 29. * Clasping knees. "But he, clasping my knees with both hands" Homer, *Odyss.*, Bk. x; Grajew, pp. 25ff. * Raising of the hands or of the right hand does not yet signify submissive attitude during Roman republic. Anc. *Rome.* Sittl, p. 148. * Folding hands, palm to palm. Anc. *India.* Boggs, col. 322. * Putting one's hand to some one's chin. 13th cent. *Germany. Kudrun,* st. 386, 2.3. * Extending both hands. 13th cent. *Italy.* Dante, *Inf.*, c. viii. * Raising hand to heaven. 16th–17th cent. *England.* Shakesp., *Titus Andr.* 3.1.207. "to thee my heaved-up hands appeal" 16th–17th cent. *England.* Shakesp., *Lucr.* 638; *Measure* 1.2.179; etc. * Folded hands placed on someone's feet. Medieval *Germany. DWb,* IV/2, col. 331. * Kneeling at someone's feet and raising hands. Medieval *Germany.* Wirnt von Gravenberg, *Wigalois,* 110, 37. * Extending hand to emperor. *Germany. DWb,* IV/2, col 331. "and clasping his hands together, prayed that they would order him back to the dark room." 19th cent. *England.* Dickens, *Oliver Twist,* p. 25. * "He [the priest] extends [his arms] in an attitude of appeal in memory of our Savior who, with arms extended upon the Cross, interceded with His Heavenly Father for the whole human race." Roman Catholic. *Mass*, p. 23. Beggars throw dust on themselves while standing. 19th cent. *Poland*. Sittl, p. 158. Placing of hands together may be used in pleading or begging; can also mean "Please, I pray you to shut up, I want to talk." Southern *Italy*. Efron, p. 157. * Hands out, palms up and inclined toward protagonist. Jews. Austin, p. 595. * Hands palm to palm, fingers of one hand interlaced with those of other, fingers of both hands bent down toward knuckles. *France*. Mitton, p. 145. * Flat hands, palm to palm, pointing toward a person. Schoolchildren. *U.S.* Seton, p. xxii. * Joining palms of hands in front of the chest. *Spain*. Green, p. 82. * Hands held vertically palm to palm below chin. If used by men or children—a joking accompaniment to a plea or request. *Russia*. Monahan, pp. 102–03. * Right hand taps gently on left side of chest of the person whose pardon is sought. "Pardonne-moi!" *Central Africa*. Hochegger, p. 138.

Pleasure Handshake signifies pleasure in performance of person whose hand is being shaken. Anc. *Rome*. Sittl, p. 30. * "if the tag-rag people did not clap him . . . according as he pleas'd . . . them" 16th–17th cent. *England*. Shakesp., *Jul. Caes.* 1.2.258. * Hands rubbed together over good news or view of pretty girl. *France*. Life Photos by David Scherman, *Life*, Sept. 16, 1946, pp. 11–13. "he smiled to himself and rubbed his large white hands together." *England*. Huxley, ch. vi. One hand rubbing against the other, palm to palm, with a slight turning movement of one hand around the other. Regarded as "typically French" by the English. *France*. Mitton, p. 146. *Netherlands*. Andrea and de Boer, p. 72. *Poland*. Bogucka, pp. 10–11; (1991), p. 196. " 'Ohhhhhh,' breathed Orson Jones, clasping his hands in ecstasy, 'exhibitionists, lots and lots and lots.' " *England*. Robinson, p. 227. " 'Excellent,' murmured Ericson, literally rubbing his hands together." *U.S.* Lathen, p. 114. "The man sitting on the other side of the poet, a prominent publisher, rubbed his hands and exulted: 'A fierce afternoon!' " *Netherlands*. Mulisch, p. 108.

Pointing In speaking of someone, hand is pointed toward him. Anc. *Rome*. Sittl, p. 49. * Fist clenched, thumb pointing horizontally towards rear. Indication of person or object in rear. *France*. Mitton, p. 143. * Thumb used for pointing. *Indonesia; Malaysia*. Axtell, *Gestures*, pp. 180, 188. * Index extended in direction of object or person, other fingers in any other position. *France*. Mitton, ibid. *Central Africa*. Hochegger, p. 6. Considered improper. *Belgium; Zambia; China*. Axtell, *Gestures*, pp. 130, 169, 173. * Hand(s), all fingers together, extended in direction indicated. *Colombia*. Saitz and Cervenka, p. 35. Open hand used for pointing. *China; India*. Axtell, *Gestures*, pp. 173, 176. * " 'Mr. Cook,' said the detective, raising his hands in front of him, outstretched, palms upward, presenting the scene below them for Cook's consideration, 'Mr. Cook, this is a sonofabitch' " *U.S.* Carkeet, p. 49. *See also* FINGER, Pointing.

Possession In dedicating sacred building, pontifex holds pillar with hand, thus, according to Roman law, transferring building from the *manus* of man into that of deity. Anc. *Rome.* Sittl, p. 196. Adopted adult is taken by the hand by the adoptive parent. Anc. *Rome.* Sittl, p. 130. * Laying one's hand on someone. Putting one's hand on slave is followed by slave being led away. Anc. *Rome.* Sittl, p. 130. Accuser lays hand on accused and thus brings him to court. Anc. *Rome.* Sittl, p. 133. Criminal is captured by laying hand on him. Anc. *Rome.* Sittl, ibid. * At marriage ceremony the husband takes hand of wife, which is given to him out of hand of her father. Anc. *Rome.* Vedic *India.* Sittl, p. 131. * An object of which the possession is disputed is grasped by the hands of both claimants before the judge. Anc. *Rome.* Sittl, p. 133. * Father lifts up newborn child. Anc. *Rome.* Sittl, p. 130. Adopted child is lifted up. Anc. *Rome.* Sittl, ibid. *See also* Acceptance and Adoption above. * Hand is laid upon object to indicate possession. Legal symbolism. Anc. *Rome.* Sittl, p. 129. In Giotto's *The Pact of Judas* (Arena Chapel, Padua), the devil places his hand on Judas' shoulder, symbolizing possession. Medieval *Italy.* Barasch, *Giotto,* p. 166. Confiscation of object is indicated by confiscator placing hand on object. Anc. *Rome.* Sittl, p. 133. At marriage ceremony husband takes hand of wife, which is given to him out of hand of her mother. Anc. *Greece.* Sittl, p. 131. (Hellenistic Gks. adopted Roman form, see above.) Mother grasps arm of daughter slightly above wrist to lead her to the bridegroom. Anc. *Greece.* Line drawing of painted vase in Sittl, p. 131. * In repossessing stolen cattle, owner had to grasp right ear of animal with left hand while treading on animal's front leg with right foot. Early medieval *Germany.* Ebert, V, col. 94. * Feudal lord attempts to seize (unsuccessfully) fief from vassal by moving hand up and down, palm turned inward. Medieval *Germany.* *Sachsenspiegel.* Amira, "Handgebärden," p. 223. * Successful plaintiff is conducted into or onto disputed property by being led by lower arm. *Sachsenspiegel.* Similarly at installation of ecclesiastic. Medieval *Germany.* Amira, "Handgebärden," p. 251. Successful plaintiff in dispute about possession of horse is depicted grasping horse's left ear with right hand, left hand raised, index extended. Two consecutively executed gestures conflated: left hand with extended index, requesting attention, refers to plaintiff's request for judge's permission to touch horse as sign of possession. Medieval *Germany.* *Sachsenspiegel.* Amira, "Handgebärden," pp. 254–55. * Grasping hand of malefactor renders him *manufestus,* i.e. arrested. Medieval *Europe.* Du Cange, s.v. arrestare. Grasping a claimed object. Fischer, "Heilgebärden," p. 342. " 'At one point, O. J. [Simpson] grabbed Nicole's crotch and said, 'This is where babies come from and this belongs to me,' Brown said . . . 'And Nicole just sort of wrote it off like it was nothing, like, you know, like she was used to that kind of treatment . . . He wasn't angry when he said it,' she said, 'He wanted it to be known. This was his.' " *U.S.* Denise Brown in testimony against O. J. Simpson; see Gilmore, p. 16. Successful claimant to possession of house grasps door, or ring on door, or doorhinge, with right hand. *Sachsenspiegel* and other Germanic laws. That building is property of a woman is indicated by her touching it. Medieval *Germany*. *Sachsenspiegel.* Amira, "Handgebärden," pp. 255–57. * Fist, thumb covered by fingers, laid against chest denotes jealous possession. 18th–19th cent. Naples, southern *Italy*. Sittl, p. 111 and note 4. * Slapping pocket with flat hand. Schoolchildren. *U.S.* Seton, p. xxiii. *See also* HAND, Leading.

Possibility " 'For instance . . . you ask him whether he can get you a pair of opera tickets. And he answers, 'Forse,' 'Perhaps.' But . . . there are two kinds of perhaps. There is perhaps with the hands spread outward, palms up, which means: 'What you ask is almost impossible; I see no way of helping you, even if I were willing to do so.' And then there is the other perhaps, spoken leaning forward with the forefinger raised in a vertical position . . . And this perhaps means: 'My cousin knows a man whose brother is a scene shifter, and the opera tickets will be yours if I have to go to my grave to get them.' " *Italy*. Graham, pp. 25–26.

Poverty Turning one's pockets inside out. *Lat. Am.* Kany, p. 88. * Tapping empty pockets. *Lat. Am.* Kany, ibid. * Fist clenched and belt-tightening pantomimed, face expresses suffering. "On se la serre!" ("I'm dead broke"). *France*. Brault, p. 380.

Praise Shaking corner of one's clothing (before handkerchiefs became common) while waving with the other hand. Anc. *Rome*. Sittl, p. 62. * Waving handkerchiefs. Anc. *Rome*. Sittl, p. 63. * Clapping of hands at a wedding. 19th cent. *Greece; Sardinia*. Bresciani, *Costumi*, II, p. 153; Sittl, p. 59. * Right fist beating into palm of left hand. Anc. *Greece*. Sittl, p. 57. * Clapping of hands, standing. Anc. *Rome*. Sittl, p. 61. *Germany,* 1839: only men clapped hands, women merely smiled. Sittl, p. 56. Clapping of hands. *Byzantine Empire; Egypt; Macedonia*; Frankish. Sittl, p. 58. Clapping hands. Shakesp., II *Henry VI*, i, i, 160; *Troil.*, II, ii, 87; etc. 17th cent. *Germany*. Nettesheim, p. 236. At the last lecture in a course, students clap loud and long if they enjoyed the course, and softly and politely if they didn't. College students. California, *U.S.* McCord, p. 291. "She is excited now, and draws her thin hands together and separates them again in a gesture of applause, in complete approval of her father's performance." *U.S.* Howard, p. 99. * "matrons flung gloves, Ladies and maids their scarfs and handkerchers, Upon him as he pass'd" 16th–17th cent. *England*. Shakesp., *Coriol*, 2.2.252–55.

* "Having said the last 'Kyrie,' the priest standing in the same place extends his hands, raises them, and intones the 'Gloria in excelsis Deo' ['Glory be to God on high]." Roman Catholic. *Mass*, p. 21. * "There was a busy little man beside him, though, who took off his hat at intervals and motioned to the people to cheer" 19th cent. *England*. Dickens, *Pickwick*, I, p. 195. *See also* Applause above.

Prayer Hands held palm to palm, fingers interlocked. *Sumeria; Turkey*; anc. *Rome;* Protestant; not favored by Catholics. Ohm, pp. 273ff. But also Fernando Gallego (1466–1507), *Calvary.* Prado, Madrid. Cf. Lassaigne, p. 71. * Right hand extended, palm turned inward. *Babylonia;* Buddhist. Ohm, p. 246. In series of hymns, request to raise hand at recitation recurs regularly. *Babylonia.* Heiler, p. 101. * Left hand extended towards deity, right hand held horizontally. *Sumeria.* Jean, p. 220. * Right hand pointed with outstretched index toward deity. *Assyria.* Jeremias, p. 409. * Right hand extended, palm towards deity. Anc. *Greece.* Ohm, p. 246. * Folded hands. *Sumeria.* Heiler, p. 103. * Hands laid one into other, palm of one supporting back of other hand. *Sumeria.* Heiler, p. 103. * Grasping feet of deity. *Assyria.* Heiler, ibid. * Casting oneself down and grasping hands of deity. *Assyria.* Heiler, ibid. * "Assurpanipal opened his hands and stepped before Nebo his lord." Inscription. *Assyria.* Heiler, p. 101. "I raised my hands and prayed to N. N." occurs frequently in inscriptions. *Assyria.* Heiler, ibid. * Right hand, holding symbolic object, raised in prayer of thanks. *Assyria.* King Asarhaddon (680–669 B.C.) on stela in Vorderasiatisches Museum, Berlin. Inv. No. VA 2708. * Worshipper raises one hand, and lets other hang limply. Anc. *Egypt.* Heiler, p. 102. * Hands crossed in front of chest. Anc. *Egypt;* anc. *Rome; Russia;* Buddhist; Dominican friars. Ohm, p. 277. *See also* ARM, Prayer. * Raising of hands to level of head, palms turned outwards. Prayer before Amon-Re. Anc. *Egypt.* British Museum, Stelae V. 43. Brunet, p. 205. * Beating one's breast with fist while rejoicing ecstatically. Anc. *Egypt.* Heiler, p. 102. * "And standing at a distance, the taxcollector would not even lift up his eyes to Heaven. But he beat on his breast, saying O God, be merciful to me, a sinner!" Biblical. *Middle East. Luke* 18:13. * Clapping of hands. Biblical. *Middle East. Ps.* 47:2. * Raising hands toward heaven. Biblical. *Middle East.* I *Tim.* 2:8; also in religious art themes such as Rembrandt's or Lastman's *de Opwekking van Lazarus (1622)*; 17th cent. *Netherlands.* Van der Meulen, p. 17. * Hands laid on sacrificial animal. Jews. Biblical. *Middle East. Levit.* 1:4; 3:2.8.13; 4:4.24.29. Sittl, p. 192. The Jews in Jerusalem raised their hands toward the temple. Biblical. *Middle East. Psalm* 27 (28):2; from which the Muslim Kiblah (facing toward Mecca) is probably descended. Sittl, p. 190. * "but he then called to the lord Poseidon in prayer, reaching both arms up toward the starry heaven." Anc. *Greece.* Homer, *Odyss.*, Bk. ix. * The Vestal Quinta

Claudia precedes her prayer with raising her hands three times in addition to washing her head three times. Anc. *Rome*. Ovid. fast. Sittl, p. 190. Sittl suggests that hands were raised in prayer to attract the attention of the gods before praying. Anc. *Greece* and *Rome*. This is supported by the gesture of stamping or beating upon the ground to attract the attention of the subterranean powers; see below. * Raising the right hand with fingers extended and apart. Anc. *Greece*. Heiler, p. 102. * Callimachus relates that merchants landing on Delos who prayed for success, ran around the altar and then, with hands on their backs, went to nearby olivetree to bite off pieces of its bark. Anc. *Greece*. Callim. *Hymn. Del.* 321; Heiler, p. 103. * The Delians, according to Callimachus (*Hymn.*, 4, 321), beat each other. Anc. *Greece*. Sittl, p. 185. * Raising hands holding an object. Anc. *Greece*. Sittl, p. 197, n. 4. * Touching the altar. Anc. *Greece*. Sittl, p. 192. In raising or extending hands, fingers kept extended and apart. Anc. *Greece*. Heiler, p. 101. * In praying to the chthonic powers, hands directed downwards. "We pray to the gods of the nether world with hands to the ground." Anc. *Greece* and *Rome*. Servius, *Aen.* 4, 205; Macrobius, *Sat.*, 3, 9, 12. * Beating upon earth in calling upon powers of nether world. Anc. *Greece* and *Rome*. Sittl, p. 190. Calling upon dead by beating on ground, and women angrily beat upon the ground in attempting to conjure up evil. Anc. *Greece*. Sittl, p. 191. * Merely stretching hands out toward ground was conceived of as too vague, but perhaps not in Egypt. See Meyer, p. 376; Sittl, p. 191, n. 4. * In making sacrifice, right hand is raised. Anc. *Greece*. Sittl, p. 189, n. 3; but it was more usual to extend the sacrifice with right hand, while the left is raised. Anc. *Greece* and *Rome*; anc. *India*. Sittl, p. 189. * When *supplicatio* (public prayer) was proclaimed in Rome, women tore their hair, scratched their cheeks and beat their shoulders. Anc. *Rome*. Heiler, p. 102. * Touching the altar. Anc. *Rome* from earliest times to the Augustan period. Manner in which the altar was touched appears to have been regulated. Sittl, p. 192. * Touching object to which prayer is directed. Neoptolemos touches sacrifice with his left hand, right hand touches grave mound of his father, upon whom he is calling. Anc. *Rome*. Quintilian, 14, 306f.; Sittl, p. 193. In calling upon Gaia, hand was extended to touch the earth. Anc. *Rome*. Sittl, p. 191. * Raising the right hand in prayer, left hand holds the worshipper's weapons. Anc. *Rome; Near East*. Christian soldiers must free both hands. Lactantius, *De mort. persecut.*, 42, 11; Sittl, pp. 188–89. "Templa deorum immortalium, quae foro imminent, Capitoliumque intuentem et manus nunc in caelum nunc in patentes terrae hiatus ad deos manes porrigentem se devovisse." Anc. *Rome*. Liv. 7, 6, 4. * The Kataphryges (or Quintiliani) put right index to nose while praying. Anc. *Near East*. Heiler, p. 102. * Embracing knees of deity. Anc. *Rome*. Heiler, p. 103. * Germanic tribe of the Semnones do not enter sacred meadow except with hands bound. Primitive Germanic. Tacitus, *Germania* xxxix. Sittl, p. 175; Heiler, p. 103. * Hands folded. 7th cent. Germanic (Franconian). Heiler, p. 103. * In catacombs, worshippers are portrayed with arms outstretched to sides in imitation of crucifixion. Heiler, p. 102. * Extending hand during prayer. Early Christian. Used in worship in contrast to the spreading of the hands—the "orans"-gesture, said to "depict" Jesus on the cross (Suntrup, p. 175 ff.)—more common in prayer of supplication. Today priest holds out hand in prayers before blessing and in absolution. Roman Catholic. Ohm, p. 247. Also Jews. Ohm, p. 246. * Hands palm to palm, fingers intertwined. Origin obscure. Used apotropaically against demons. Anc. *Rome*. Served to invalidate oath and was therefore prohibited in the Roman cult. Pliny, *Hist. nat.* 286. Borrowed from Romans as protection against pagan demons. Early Christian. Ohm, p. 274. * Folding hands. In first centuries A.D. gesture seems to have been unknown or not used. First attested in 9th century, e.g. on the lost sarcophagus of Hincmar of Rheims (d. 882), if Montfaucon's drawing is to be trusted (fig. 30). An abbot of Monte Cassino still disapproved of it in the 9th cent. as deviation from custom. In later Middle Ages it became more common and gradually took the place of the old "orans"-gesture of raising and spreading the hands. For survey of its spread, see Barasch, *Giotto*, pp. 59–71. The folding of hands by putting flat palms together, fingers pointing upwards is favored by Catholicism, but not common among Protestants. Ohm, pp. 269–70. *See above* for principally Protestant interlocking of fingers. Folding of hands and interlacing fingers. *Sumeria; Parthia;* anc. *Asia Minor;* anc. *Rome; East Asia.* First Christian evidence on a sarcophagus of the 5th cent. from Syracusan catacomb on which praying woman is depicted with interlaced fingers. This, rather than facing flat palms, is common Protestant prayer gesture. Ohm, p. 273; but see also John the Baptist in Bloemaert's *Bewening van Christus* (1649), with both hands extended toward the Christ's body, fingers interlaced. 17th cent. *Netherlands.* Van der Meulen, p. 19. Hands extended toward body of Jesus, palms flat and facing each other. School of Cornelisz. Engelbrechtsz., *Voorbereiding to de Kruisiging.* 17th cent. *Netherlands.* Van der Meulen, ibid. Hands folded so that fingers are interlocked and palms together, hands in front of chest. Ritter, p. 375. * Hands partially joined palm to palm in prayer, thumbs crossed. *The Beheading of a female Saint.* Attr. to Starnina, early 15th cent. London, Nat. Gallery, No. 3926. Folded hands symbolize above all composure, concentration, devotion, raised hands symbolize openness, receptiveness. In some circles the latter is sometimes extended by believers clasping each other's raised hands. *GdG*, pp. 33–34. Pope Gregory I, *Dial.* II, 33, speaking of Sta. Scolastica: "insertas digitis manus super mensam posuit, et caput in manibus omnipotentem dominum rogatura declinavit" ("she put her hands with intertwined fingers on the table, and placed herself in the hands of almighty God"). *See also* De Jorio, p. 203. Folding hands, palm to palm, not before eleventh century, according to Sittl, p. 176 and n. 3. Early medieval works of art frequently exhibit an "orans"-like gesture of prayer in which hands are held close to breast and not raised as high as in "orans" gesture proper. Ladner, p. 247. Early panel with image of St. Francis (Pescia, 1235) by Bonaventura Berlinghieri shows transition from extended to joined hands: hands raised, cupped, to receive stigmata. Another is panel of S. Croce in Florence (middle 13th cent.), depicting hands almost but not quite joined. Ladner, p. 273. Second *Vita* of St. Francis by Thomas of Celano states: "When a servant of God at prayer is visited by the Lord with some new consolation, he ought, before coming forth from prayer, to raise his eyes to heaven and, with joined hands [*iunctis manibus*] to say to the Lord . . ." *Vita*, 2, 2, cap. 75, 99; also Ladner, pp. 269–70. The two Franciscan Mass orders of the first half of the 13th century, *Paratus* and *Indutus planeta*, speak of joined hands in connection with pre-consecrational, not post-consecrational elevation of the host. Ladner, p. 267. The *Ordo Paratus* (first version ca. 1230) states, in slightly later version, that priest is to elevate host with joined hands [*iunctis manibus*]. Probably oldest occurrence in liturgical manuscripts. Ladner, p. 265. In *Indutus planeta*, published at the Franciscan General Chapter at Bologna, probably 1243, gesture of joined hands is for the first time mentioned in several of the places in which it is still prescribed in the *Missale Romanum*. Ladner, pp. 265–66. The newer gesture of joining the hands before the breast and kneeling probably introduced during pontificate of Gregory IX (1227–1241), certainly not much later than the death of Innocent IV (1254). Ladner, p. 247. The gesture referred to by Ladner is laying together of the palms with extended fingers, not folding or clasping of hands with interlocking fingers—a gesture which Ladner does not consider to have been common in the Middle Ages before the very end. Ladner, p. 248. "The earliest instance of the feudal gesture [hands palm to palm] as prayer gesture occurs between 1120 and 1130 on the second pillar of the north aisle of Vezelay. First literary evidence is probably Chanson de Roland." 11th cent. *France*. Bertau, I, p. 250. In parallel passage of *Rolandslied*, the old "orans"-gesture of the raised hands (*see* ARM, HAND, Prayer) is substituted. 12th cent. *Germany*. * One hand raised, palm outward. Munich, Cod. lat. 23094, fol. 93b; Stuttg. Bibl. fol. 24, fol. 124b, etc. Medieval *Germany*. Haseloff, p. 303. * Hands, palms outward or toward one another, before or at side of chest. Stuttg. Bibl. fol. 24, fol. 109b; *Breviary of St. Elizabeth*, Cividale, Bibl. del Museo Arch. Nazionale, 25, 313, 318, etc. Medieval *Germany*. Haseloff, pp. 302–03. * Hands raised above head. Medieval *Germany*. *Orendel*, 457–8, 571–2, 1392, 3446; Islamic. Goldziher, "Zauberelemente," p.

322; Kikuyu, *East Africa*. Heiler, p. 101; *Ceylon*. Heiler, p. 102. * Hands raised and spread out toward heaven. 17th cent. *England*. Bulwer, pp. 21–32. * Hands palm to palm, not touching, but slightly cupped; fingertips and thumbtips of one hand touching those of the other. *Germany.* Master Bertram, *Agony* (after 1383); also Perugia, Bibl. augusta Ms. 1238 (15th cent.) in Volpe, p. 14. For prescriptions of prayer-gestures, primarily on the basis of Biblical authority, see *De penitentia et partibus eius*, attributed to Peter the Chanter (1120/30–1197) in Trexler, particularly pp. 38–49, and the illustrations in part 2. * Priest "turns to the faithful, extends and rejoins his hands, while he greets them with the words 'Orate, fratres' " Roman Catholic. *Mass*, p. 39; see also pp. 18, 47. * In invoking Adraseia-nemesis, the Greek Christian crosses himself. *Greece*. Sittl, p. 181. "The priest makes the Sign of the Cross on the book at the beginning of the Gospel, then on his forehead, lips, and breast. This is a prayer that the holy Gospel may be, first, on our mind, . . . secondly, on our lips, . . . thirdly, in our heart." Roman Catholic. *Mass*, p. 29. For gestures used in celebrating Mass, see Knox, pp. 18 and n. 54, pp. 34–35. The Council of Trent eliminated the earlier diversity of ritual; see Knox, p. 18. * With flat right hand, fingers extended, touch forehead, then breast, then left shoulder, then right shoulder. Roman Catholic sign of cross. Ohm, p. 294. Same, but from right to left shoulder. Greek Orthodox. Ohm, ibid. Roman Catholic cross, but with index and middle finger extended. *Netherlands*. Andrea and de Boer, p. 122. * Stroking an idol. Pre-Islamic Arab. Heiler, p. 103. * When you call upon God, show him the inside of your hands and not the outside; when you are finished, put both hands upon your face." Islamic. Cited from commentary on Koran by Seligmann, II, p. 168. In Moslem free prayer the old Arabic gesture of raising and extending the hands has remained customary. Goldziher, "Zauberelemente," p. 321. Moslem prayer: hands extended lightly forward (elbows bent), lightly open palms facing upward; see Bosnian government troops at prayer. AP Photo, *L.A. Times*, Sept. 30, 1995, A14; Crimean Tartars at prayer. Agence France Photo, *L.A. Times*, May 21, 1994, A8. The *Medina Sura* 8 of infidels: "And their prayer at the house of God is nothing but whistling and clapping of hands." Ohm, p. 283, n. 4. * Indians extended their hands forwards palm to palm even before Buddhistic schism. Sittl, p. 175. On Hindu reliefs and statues worshippers extend hands palm to palm. *India*. Heiler, p. 103. * Raising hands. Anc. *Persia*. Heiler, p. 102. * Folding hands. Buddhist; *Tibet*. Heiler, p. 103. * Raising hands and weapons in prayer. Yutu, *Australia*. Heiler, p. 101. * Hand laid to head in passing woods, rivers or fields inhabited by spirits of the dead. Tehuep, Patagonia, *Argentina*. Heiler, p. 102. * Right index laid to nose. Taskodrugites, Galatia, central *Asia Minor*. Heiler, p. 102. * Clapping hands. *Africa; Egypt; China; Japan*. Ohm, p. 283. * Clapping and rubbing of hands. *Peru*. Heiler, p. 102. The new moon is greeted by clapping of hands. Congo, *Central Africa*. Heiler, p. 102. Raised hands, clapping in prayer to the spirits of the sun and the ocean. Kiziba, *Central Africa*. Heiler, ibid. Clapping in prayer of thanks. Anc. Jews, *Middle East;* Ewe, *West Africa*. Heiler, ibid. Clapping in morning prayer. Bantu, southern *Africa*. Heiler, ibid. Clapping upon completing sacrificial prayer. Cameroon, *West Africa*. Heiler, ibid. Hands raised, holding bundles of grass. Massai, *Kenya*. Heiler, p. 101.

In times of distress, when tribal chief or boy in public cult prayed, the oldest man clapped his hands, continually shouting "Pray, sir, pray!" and those present clapped in answer and as gratitude. Safwa, 8th cent. Arab. Ohm, p. 283. Clapping of hands at Paschal feast on Garizim during sacrifice of animals. Samaritan. *Middle East*. Ohm, p. 284. Relative of initiated kneels in front of demi-god Ryangombe, claps three times and prays for initiated. Nyarunda. *East Africa*. Ohm, p. 283. In Christian prayer, hands clap in praise, and are spread to side and raised and lowered rhythmically in asking for fulfilment of wish; or hands are joined palm to palm, or with fingers interlaced, or palm to palm vertically; or hands are raised to height of head and slightly spread to sides, palms up. *Central Africa*. Hochegger, pp. 153–54. Most frequent is clapping of hands at Shinto shrines before and after prayer. *Japan*. Ohm, p. 284. "One does not look at Buddha, one worships him," whereupon the speaker clapped his hands several times and bowed. Buddhist. *Japan*. Ohm, p. 284. * During consecration ceremony after harvest, master of the holy tree has to perform prayer with hands tied behind his back. Mulgoi-Kanuri. *Africa*. Ohm, p. 279. Raising of arms, palms turned toward object being worshipped or addressed, then hands lowered without touching object or person. Sioux. *U.S.* Heiler, p. 101. * Kneeling, turned toward sun, folded hands with fingers extended and apart raised from ground to forehead. *China; Korea*. Ohm, p. 282. * In the 9th cent. Walahfrid Strabo criticizes those who beat breast with fists in prayer. Medieval *Germany*. Heiler, p. 102. * Flat hand, palm down, moved downward, in prayer for continuance or frequency of divine gifts: "Baixai a mão, Mae de Deus!" ("Mother of God, lower your hand!") *Brazil*. Cascudo, *História*, p. 214. * "faces the congregation at Mission Eben-Ezer Pentecostal Church and delivers startling news. 'I just want to stay out of jail from now on and take care of my family,' he says. Immediately, an army of people rises from chairs and mobilizes around him, placing hands on his shoulders and above his head in prayer." *U.S.* Rourke, p. 1.

Pregnancy Lifting skirt over abdomen. Men execute same gesture, lifting skirt of their clothing. 19th cent. Naples, southern *Italy*. De Jorio, p. 173. * Both hands, palms facing inward, in front of stomach, and moving up and down in a semi-circle. *Central Africa*. Hochegger, p. 85.

Preparedness   Both hands slowly swept downward, palms rotating to face away from gesticulator. Madrid, *Spain*. Green, p. 77.

Pride   Hand pressed to side, elbow a little forward, head thrown back, other hand at upper chest and underneath coat. 19th cent. Naples, southern *Italy*. De Jorio, p. 201. * Hands held aloft and clasped. *U.S.* Davidson, p. 4. * "Expressions of pride in craftsmanship accompanied by rapping finished product with knuckles of one hand." *Spain; Lat. Am.* Green, p. 92. * Fist raised, knuckles toward gesturer signifies pride or victory; knuckles turned outward signify threat. *U.S.* Axtell, *Gestures*, p. 40.

Prohibition   " 'Something to do with business,' said Mr. Deane, waving his hands, as if to repel intrusion into that mystery." 19th cent. *England*. Eliot, p. 707.

Promise   Person giving assurance of something gives the other his right hand. Anc. *Greece* and *Rome*. Sittl, p. 135. After promise is fulfilled, person who promised again holds out right hand, which is grasped by receiver of promise as sign that promiser has acquitted himself. Anc. *Greece* and *Rome*; 19th cent. *Greece*; *Japan*. Sittl, p. 136. Emperor's right hand as assurance of life and freedom to one who is punishable. Anc. *Rome*; anc. *Persia* (Persian emperors sent picture of right hand as assurance of forgiveness.) Sittl, p. 138. Emperor's right hand as assurance of goodwill. Anc. *Rome*. Sittl, ibid. Handshake of right hand testifies to a promise to marry. In fiction groom and bride shake hands, in reality groom and father of the bride shake hands. Anc. *Greece* and *Rome*. Sittl, pp. 135–36. The "Handschlag" (handclasp, *manu complosa*) is, according to Sittl, purely Germanic in this sense: *Monumenta Boica*, 24, p. 348. Sittl, p. 136. Medieval *German*. Hartmann v. Aue, 7894; *HDV*, I, col. 319. *Wartburgkrieg*, I, 71 f.: "whom I ever offered my hand, let him benefit from this"; pictorial rendering of these words of the Landgravess Sophia of Thuringia, sparing the life of the defeated (mythical) poet Heinrich v. Ofterdingen, in the miniature of Heidelberg, Univ.-Bibl. cpg. 848 fol. 219b of Landgrave Hermann as judge of the poets' contest, the landgravess at his side, right hand slightly raised at breast while he, with right hand raised, holds sword in the left, extended outward, since contest is for life or death. See Walther, pl. 72. Also Amira, "Handgebärden," p. 197. "The master of the castle was commander of 'his' knights . . . Each 'castle warrior,' upon reaching adulthood, pledged his body to the chief of the castle; the pledge was sealed by the giving and receiving of hands, signifying the gift of oneself, and by a kiss, a sign of peace and token of reciprocal loyalty." Medieval *Europe*. Duby, *A History of Private Life*, p. 20. Handshake as promise in legal context: "Urfehde" (renunciation of combat") of Eckardt Kleinschmidt (1577), Archive of Budingen; "Urfehde" of Jost Pfieler (1580), Budingen; and handshake "instead of a properly sworn oath" (1468) in

Aschbach, II, p. 283. Late medieval *Germany. DWb,* IV/2, col. 389. "Ere I could make thee open thy white hand and clap thyself my love; then didst thou utter 'I am yours for ever.' " 16th-17th cent. *England.* Shakesp., *Winter's Tale* 1.2.102–4. "and so clap hands and a bargain." 16th-17th cent. *England.* Shakesp., *Henry V* 5.2.129. " 'I shall be sure to be with you,' said Mr. Trotter, and wringing Sam's hand with the utmost fervor, he walked away." 19th cent. *England.* Dickens, *Pickwick,* I, p. 392. " 'Here's my right hand upon it.' " 19th cent. *England.* Dickens, *Oliver Twist,* I, p. 328. Right hand of one grasps right hand of another briefly. Intensity varies with importance of the act and its emotional content. *Europe.* Revesz, "Die Psychologie," pp. 143–44.

Proof Hand vertical, palm outward, held up to eyes of someone. Familiar. *France.* Mitton, p. 147. *Brazil.* Cascudo, *História,* p. 137.

Prostitute Hand flat, palm down, moves back and forth in front of body. *Colombia.* Saitz and Cervenka, p. 118.

Protection Generals extend hand to surrendering people. Anc. *Rome.* Sittl, p. 368. Hands horizontal, arms extended straight, palms down. *Europe; North America.* Aubert, p. 88. Thus also the guardian over the ward, the feudal lord over his vassal who is a minor, the father over his children as guardian after the death of their mother, the mother over her children, the cleric over his illegitimate child. In medieval art the gesture is symbolic of the *munt,* i.e. guardianship. *Sachsenspiegel.* Medieval *Germany.* Amira, "Handgebärden," pp. 225–27. * Hand laid on shoulder of another. Medieval *Germany.* Heidelberg, Univ.-Bibl. cpg. 848, fol. 422r. See Walther, pl. 136. As symbolic of spousal or parental relationships, see Garucci, pl. 198, 4, and Kraus, *Geschichte,* I, p. 167. * Hand, palm down, sometimes slightly cupped, held over someone's hand or head. See Giotto's *Pact of Judas.* Barasch, *Giotto,* pp. 167–68; for its use in medieval art and law, see also Amira, "Handgebärden," pp. 225–27.

Punishment A Herr von Ruxleben recants (1576) a lie by declaring that "with this slap he punishes his lying trap publicly." *DWb,* IV/2, 419. * Raising the closed fist to about face-level—one should have beaten the person to whom the gesture is directed. Not a threat, it merely signifies that the other person deserves a beating. *Russia..* Monahan, pp. 162–63.

Quickly Palm of one hand strokes quickly over top of the other. *Portugal.* Flachskampf, p. 222. * Palms of both hands face each other; one rubbed quickly against the other in upward and downward movement. *Spain.* Flachskampf, ibid.

Readiness "As Sam Weller said this, he tucked up his wristbands,—to intimate his readiness to set to work immediately." 19th cent. *England.* Dickens, *Pickwick,* II, p. 184.

Reassurance   Both hands grasp another person's upper arms. *U.S.* AP Photo, *L. A. Times*, Sept. 2, 1992, A1.

Recognition   The handshake is "a masculine ritual of recognition and affirmation" serving "to perpetuate male clubbiness and to exclude women from the club." *U.S.* Henley, p. 10.

Recommendation   Pushing someone from behind toward a person. In medieval Christian art, saints are depicted thus as introducing protégés to Christ; Virtue thus recommends virtuous to God's grace in miniatures of the *Welsche Gast*; in legal symbolism bride is thus depicted as pushed toward groom, or both are pushed towards one another by companions; in the *Sachsenspiegel* a vassal thus requires his lord to represent him before his own lord, and heirs of vassal thus indicate who among them is to receive fief. Medieval *Germany*. Oechelhäuser, *Bilderkreis*, pl. V.; Amira, "Handgebärden," p. 254.

Reconciliation   "I have spread out my hands . . . to a rebellious people" Biblical. *Middle East. Isaiah* 65:2. * Handshake. Anc. *Greece* and *Rome*. Sittl, p. 30. * Taking penitent sinner by right hand. Ecclesiastical forgiveness of sins after penitence. Roman Catholic. Jungmann, pp. 51ff., 93ff; Schmitz, I, 70ff.; Woldhaupter, p. 165. Sinner, in being absolved, knelt before the church portal, reciting the Psalm "Miserere." With each verse he received a blow on the head or shoulder, whose violence accorded with his sin. 13th cent. *Italy*. Henricus Ostiensis, *Summa*, V, de sent. excomm. n. 14. "Let the handclasp heal the wound, which my tongue rashly caused." 19th cent. *Germany*. Schiller, *Jungfrau*, ii, ii. "he . . . extended the hand of reconciliation to that most indignant gentleman." 19th cent. *England*. Dickens, *Pickwick*, II, p. 429. "Mr. Noddy . . . proffered his hand to Mr. Gunter. Mr. Gunter grasped it with affecting fervor." Ibid., II, 49. Grasping the culprit by the hand. 19th cent. *Palestine*. Bauer, p. 6. * The handshake is the sign of formal reconciliation among duellists. *Germany*. Sittl, p. 38. Handshake between Israeli and Egyptian generals on occasion of truce negotiations. UPI Wirephoto, *L. A. Times*, Nov. 15, 1973, p. 1. " 'Hey,' he said, laughing. 'You're the Navajo cop who arrested me.' Chee nodded. Highhawk wanted to shake hands again—a 'no hard feelings' gesture." *U.S.* Hillerman, *Talking God*, p. 89. * Putting headdress back on the head of the culprit. 19th cent. *Palestine*. Bauer, p. 6.

Refusal   Forearm slightly raised, hand turned upward, palm out. Anc. *Rome*. Sittl, p. 85, fig. 6; p. 86, n. 5; medieval *Germany*; *Sachsenspiegel*. Amira, "Handgebärden," pp. 220–22. Assimilated Jews. *Eastern Europe*. Efron, p. 118. * Refusing hand instead of offering it in the feudal *commendatio*—gesture entails either pulling flat hand back, across chest and extending it at side of body with palm facing rear, or holding arm out at side of body. (Not required in feudal law; sufficient if feudal lord did not move hands at all.) Medieval *Germany*. *Sachsens-*

piegel. Amira, "Handgebärden," p. 222, and fig. 9. * Answer to request, indicating that one does not want to give more than minimum, is sign of the "horns" (fist clenched, index and little finger extended). 19th cent. Naples, southern *Italy.* De Jorio, p. 94. * Right hand seizes upper tip of coat and shakes it. *Arab.* Goldziher, "Über Gebärden," p. 370. * Right hand, edge down, moves vertically downward, then, at right angle, horizontally from left to right. *Spain.* Flachskampf, p. 238. * Extended right hand moves energetically from left top to right bottom. *Spain.* Ibid., p. 238. Flat hand moved horizontally. (Gesture for cutting.) *France.* Mitton, 143. One or both hands extended, palm facing forward. ("Stop!" "I don't want it!") *France.* Ibid. *Netherlands.* Andrea and de Boer, p. 78. * "He reached into his inside coat pocket for his silver-plated case. Lofting held up his palm, Indian greeting style, to forestall the offer. Leonard crossed his legs, took out a cigarette" *Britain.* McEwan, p. 1. * Flat hand, palm facing person addressed, describes arc by moving rapidly in front of chest from left to right or right to left. ("I refuse absolutely." "Don't insist upon it.") *France.* Mitton, p. 143. * Shaking one hand, fingers slightly closed and palm outward at level of chest. *Spain; Lat. Am.* Green, pp. 44–45. * Shaking index of one hand at or below the speaker's face. (Denial.) *Spain; Lat. Am.* Green, pp. 44–45. * Holding flat hands to ears. ("I will not listen.") Schoolchildren. *U.S.* Seton, p. xxii. * Open hand, palm facing backwards, is moved backwards past one ear. *Central Africa.* Hochegger, pp. 124, 164. * Eyes covered by hands. (Refusal to look.) Schoolchildren. *U.S.* Seton, ibid. * Open hand, vertical, raised to level of face, then dropped down from wrist: "Oh, never mind." *Netherlands.* Andrea and de Boer, p. 158. * Hands moved up and down, palms brushing each other. ("I wash my hands of it.") *Colombia; U.S.* Saitz and Cervenka, p. 32. * Both hands open, raised to level of head and rotated inversely to each other in semi-circles backward and forward: solemn refusal. *Central Africa.* Hochegger, p. 162. *See also* Incompetence.

Regret Slightly closed palms rubbed together in front of body. *Saudi Arabia.* Barakat, no. 114. * Palm held in front of body, facing it; fingers held loosely and shaken up and down violently; or thumb and middle finger pressed together and arm snapped violently, so index snaps against middle finger. *Colombia.* Saitz and Cervenka, p. 100. * Hands loosely held in front of chest and rapidly agitated. *Central Africa.* Hochegger, p. 166.

Rejection Transverse brushing movement with edge of one hand on palm of other held supine. ("I don't want to hear about it.") Southern *Italy.* Efron, p. 100. * Right palm brushing edge of left palm held vertically. ("I'm through with him.") Assimilated Jews. *Eastern Europe.* Efron, p. 117. * Hands simultaneously moved from middle of body to sides, palms down. ("I'm through with it.") *Italy.* Leone, p. XX 11. *

"With an averted supercilious eye and a rejecting hand, half flourishing—I have no need of help, Sir!—you are in my way." 18th cent. *England*. Richardson, II, p. 142. * Palms horizontal at chest level, fingertips pointing upwards, right arm, nearest to body, left arm crossed in
front of it; both hands then uncrossed smartly, stopping while still in
front of body—"Rien à faire!" ("Nothing doing!") *France*. Brault, p.
379. *See also* Refusal.

Relinquishment　On freeing slave, owner inflicts last stroke with
cane on him. Anc. *Rome*. Not anc. *Greece*. Sittl, pp. 132–33. * On
freeing slave, owner strikes him with hand for last time. Anc. *Rome*. Not
anc. *Greece*. Sittl, p. 133. * On freeing slave, owner turns him around, to
signify slave's new position in life. Anc. *Rome*. Sittl, ibid. * On freeing
slave, owner places hand on slave's head, right hand, or other part of
his body, then removes it, with the words: "Hunc hominem liberum esse
volo" ("I want this man to be free.") Anc. *Rome*. Sittl, p. 132. * "the
one-hand downward loose shake of weary relinquishment" *Russia*. Nabokov, p. 41.

Remain　Left hand taps lightly the shoulder of someone, while the
right hand points downward: "Stay here!" *Central Africa*. Hochegger,
p. 171.

Reminder　Witness in court of law is pulled by the ear to aid his
memory. Anc. *Greece* and *Rome*. Margrave Luitpold of Babenberg. Röhrich, *Gebärde-Metapher-Parodie*, pp. 32–33. For the role of pulling by
the ear or hair, or beating, in German law, see Künssberg, "Rechtsbrauch," para. 17–27. * Future mother-in-law pinched arm of her
daughter's fiancé, and told him not to forget his bride. Children were
taken to witness punishment of criminals, and were beaten so they
would remember. Practice introduced to Brazil from Portugal, where it
was essential part of educative process. Cascudo, *História*, p. 230.

Rendezvous　Hands raised to level of chin, open, pointing forwards,
palm down, and moving from left to right: "La nuit!" ("Tonight!").
Central Africa. Hochegger, p. 168.

Reproach　"Well then, rising (Bella silently with uplifted hands, reproaching my supposed perverseness), I see nothing can prevail with
you to oblige us." 18th cent. *England*. Richardson, II, p. 3. "he was
often observed peeping through the bars of a gate and making minatory
gestures with his small forefinger while he scolded the sheep with an
inarticulate burr" 19th cent. *England*. Eliot, p. 461.

Request　Flat hand opened and directed at someone. To lend emphasis, gesture can be performed with both hands. 19th cent. Naples, southern *Italy*. De Jorio, p. 85. Schoolchildren. *U.S.* Seton, p. xxiv. *Europe;
North America*. Aubert, p. 82. * Hands vertical, palm to palm, under
chin in a version of prayer gesture. Can be used in most banal or most
dramatic circumstances, seriously or ironically. *Netherlands*. Andrea

and de Boer, p. 87. * Both hands open, palm up, extended forward, or both hands open, palm up, extended forward, one hand crossed over the other. *Central Africa.* Hochegger, pp. 45–49. * Open hands raised to height of head in form of prayer gesture, slowly moving up and down while fingers close slightly. *Central Africa.* Ibid. * Hands side by side in front, pointing toward gesturer's chest, then extended forward, palm up and moving up and down: "Please hire me." *Central Africa.* Ibid. * With simultaneous sign of regret, right hand extended toward someone, palm up, while left is placed on head. *Central Africa.* Ibid. * Right hand, palm down, clapped over lightly curled fingers of left hand, which is also held palm down: "Please." *Central Africa.* Ibid. *See also* ARM, HAND, Request.

Resignation "When she folded [her hands and arms] over her bosom in resignation" 19th cent. *England.* Thackeray, *Pendennis*, I, ch. iv.

Respect In the circus the charioteer lowers whip before patrons. Anc. *Rome.* Sittl, pp. 155–56. * Lowering the fasces before the lictors. Anc. *Rome.* Sittl, p. 155. Junior official lowered or caused the fasces to be lowered by his lictors in the presence of a senior or superior official. Anc. *Rome.* Sittl, p. 154. * Hands, hanging down in front of the body, are crossed, palm inward. Medieval *Germany.* *Sachsenspiegel.* Amira, "Handgebärden," p. 233. Hands crossed in front of abdomen; see the miniature of *König Tyro* in Heidelberg, cpg 848, fol. 8r. See Walther, pl. 3. *See also* Attention, above. Van der Meulen, p. 29, interprets holding hands in lap or under vest as medieval iconographical symbol for inactivity. Hands crossed in front of the breast. *Byzantine Empire.* Ibid. * "Her hand, which he gently squeezed . . . in token of regard." 18th cent. *England.* Smollett, *Peregrine Pickle*, I, p. 19. * "He took off his hat as Mr. Pickwick saluted him" 19th cent. *England.* Dickens, *Pickwick*, II, p. 292. * " 'Don't they, Sam?' 'Not they, Sir,' replied Mr. Weller, touching his hat." 19th cent. *England.* Ibid., I, p. 311. "with the touch of the hat which always preceded his entering into conversation with his master." 19th cent. *England.* Ibid., I, p. 368. "They made way for Henry Wimbush, touching their caps as he passed." *England.* Huxley, ch. xviii. * Handshake. 19th cent. *France.* Raim, p. 97.

Retreat Extending one or both hands and moving them alternately and rapidly up and down, palms facing each other, imitating rapid motion of running feet. *Lat. Am.* Kany, p. 111. Sometimes preceded by a clap of the hands. Kany, p. 112. * Placing open right hand on the open, slightly curved left, palm to palm, then drawing right forcibly backward. *Lat. Am.* Kany, p. 112. * Dropping the slightly cupped hand, palm inward, from chest of speaker, twisting lower arm and wrist with extended index, concluding with palm down. Madrid, *Spain.* Green, p. 41.

Reverence Extending hand down to the knee, then raising it. Anc.

Egypt. Ohm, p. 282. * "Lo! The angel of God; fold thy hands." 13th-14th cent. *Italy.* Dante, *Purg.*, c. iv.

Review   Fingers of one hand brush palm of the other repeatedly. Review of written material. *Colombia.* Saitz and Cervenka, p. 112.

Rise   Closed fist, thumb extended upward, raised brusquely. Used in addressing group, not single individual. *France.* Mitton, p. 145. * Raising flat right hand, palm up, from level of hip. Schoolchildren. *U.S.* Seton, p. xxiv. *Europe; North America.* Aubert, p. 88. *Central Africa.* Repetition implies urgency. Hochegger, p. 43.

Robbery   Flat hand, palm down, moved downward—robbing or pillaging. *Brazil.* Cascudo, *História*, p. 214.

Royalty   Raised right hand is symbol of kingship. Wolff-Hurden, *Basler Nachrichten*, Dec. 22, 1957, Supplement. *See also* Authority.

Sacrifice   Jews as well as pagans laid hand on sacrificial animal. Anc. *Rome;* anc. *Near East.* Sittl, p. 192. * In making the sacrifice, it is extended with right hand, while left hand is raised. Altaic, northern *Asia;* anc. *Rome.* Sittl, p. 189. * In making sacrifice, right hand is raised. Rare. Anc. *Rome.* Sittl, p. 189, n. 3.

Salvation   In depictions of the Last Judgment, palm of Jesus' hand is turned towards the saved, back of other hand toward the damned. Medieval *Germany.* Haseloff, p. 307.

Satisfaction   " 'Ah!' observed Mr. Pickwick, rubbing his hands" 19th cent. *England.* Dickens, *Pickwick,* II, 2. " 'Ah!' said Fagin, rubbing his hands with great satisfaction." 19th cent. *England.* Dickens, *Oliver Twist,* p. 358. Rubbing palms against each other, either up and down or in a rotating movement. *France.* Mitton, p. 146. One hand rubbing against the other, palm to palm, with a slight turning movement of one hand around the other. Called "typically French" by the English. *France.* Mitton, ibid. Rubbing hands together, often quite vigorously. *Spain; Lat. Am.* Green, p. 49.

Secrecy   Open hand closes mouth. Usually used in hostile manner. When one has said something insulting about another person one closes one's mouth suddenly in this manner, so that no more will escape. 19th cent. Naples, southern *Italy.* De Jorio, p. 192. * Hands lifted up half way to the head. ("It's strictly between us.") *France.* Life Photo, David Scherman, *Life,* Sept. 16, 1946, p. 12. * Lowering and raising extended fingers of one hand, at level of waist and with palm down, may accompany discussion of clandestine activity. *Spain; Lat. Am.* Green, p. 43.

Seize   Open hand, fingers extended, palm down, thrust forward at level of waist and suddenly closed forcefully. *Europe; North America.* Aubert, p. 83. * "Expressions suggestive of seizing . . . are accompanied by . . . catching an imaginary object in the air and bringing the object to the chest." Madrid, *Spain.* Green, p. 60.

Self-acknowledgment Hand placed upon one's chest. ("It is I.") *France*. Mitton, p. 143.

Self-satisfaction "like a rich merchant, who strolls around happily among the crates . . . rubbing his hands" *Germany*. *DWb*, IV/2, col. 386. *Europe; North America*. Austin, p. 595. *Netherlands*. Andrea and de Boer, p. 72. * Hand moved to sleeve (cuff). *U.S.* Birdwhistell, "Do Gestures Speak Louder than Words?" p. 57.

Separation Moving the two hands apart. Efron, p. 150, fig. 49. Open hands, palms facing each other, lightly slap palms as they move past each other vertically: "Nous nous sommes quittés!" ("We're quits!") *Central Africa*. Hochegger, p. 187.

Series "a succession of stop-and-go movements made with the semi-clenched fingers of one hand, moved progressively further and further away from the speaker. . . . ('fueron dando una serie de batallas')" ("They were involved in a series of battles"). "Another gesture performed under similar circumstances is executed by raising and lowering the fingertips of one hand on the surface of a desk or table top. The fingers are clenched somewhat and the palm of the hand faces the floor" Madrid, *Spain; Lat. Am*. Green, p. 61.

Shame Lowering eyes and covering face with hands. Schoolchildren. *U.S.* Seton, p. xxii.

Shock Raising of hands above head. Illustr. of public reactions to a maid's sudden loss of her skirt. "Wahre Begebenheit am Stuttgarter Markt-Brunnen," 19th cent. *Germany*. Postcard. (Fig. 4).

Shyness Hands folded in lap. Medieval *France*. Lommatzsch, p. 34; also Larivey, p. 62.

Sick Right hand taps the stomach several times, or both hands rub up and down on the stomach. *Central Africa*. Hochegger, p. 69.

Silence Hand extended in front (waving up and down?). Anc. and late *Rome*; 19th cent. *Italy*. Sittl, p. 215. Hand extended in front, waving up and down. Demand for silence while telephoning. *Netherlands*. Andrea and de Boer, p. 35. Hand raised. Anc. *Greece*. Sittl, p. 215, n. 1. * " 'My friends,' said Mr. Humm, holding up his hand in a deprecatory manner, to bespeak the silence of . . . the . . . ladies." 19th cent. *England*. Dickens, *Pickwick*, II, p. 70. * Right hand, fingers extended and apart, palm up, moves gently up and down. *Spain; Portugal*. Flachskampf, p. 238. * "Haggish's hand is high in the air, praying for 'silence.' " 19th cent. *England*. Surtees, 151. "Tom was going to speak, but Mr. Deane put up his hand, and said—'Stop! hear what I've got to say' " 19th cent. *England*. Eliot, p. 566. "He held up his hands to stop the babel of questions and did some more explaining." Provençe, *France*. Mayle, *Hotel Pastis*, p. 45. * "Johnny put both hands out in front of him, fingers spread wide, to signal silence." *U.S.* Schulberg, p. 257. * Hand extended forward, palm down, fingers together. Hand is lowered several times. Used only when addressing a group of people. *France*. Mitton, p. 145. * One or both outstretched hands, palm(s) down, pushed toward the floor. *Spain; Lat. Am.* Green, p. 43. * One or both hands held before body with palms down, then moved slightly up and down several times. *Egypt; Lebanon; Jordan; Saudi Arabia; Syria; Libya.* Barakat, no. 14. * Hand formed like a jaw. ("Shut up.") Very vulgar. *France.* Mitton, p. 150. * Open right palm slapped down two or three times on extended left fist held upright or obliquely, as if pushing cork into bottle. Accompanies expression such as "lo callaron," "lo metieron en tapón" ("they put the lid on it"). *Lat. Am.* Kany, p. 187. * "reached her right hand in under her left arm and squeezed the boy's arm." *U.S.* Birdwhistell, "Background," p. 14. * "placed her right hand firmly across his thighs." *U.S.* Ibid.

Sincerity Hands extended to sides after touching breast. *Europe; North America.* Austin, p. 595. * Hand placed on heart. *Germany.* Seiler, p. 246.

"Sit down" Drop flat hand, palm down. Schoolchildren. *U.S.* Seton, p. xxiv. *Central Africa.* Hochegger, p. 13. * Invitation to sit down: hand extended toward chair. *Central Africa.* Ibid., p. 97.

Solidarity Each partner squeezes back of partner's hand, thus building up a pyramid of hands. *Central Africa.* Hochegger, p. 196.

Sorrow Placing hands over face while weeping. Anc. *Greece.* Homer, *Odyss.*, Bk. xix. * "and the black cloud of sorrow closed on Laertes. In both hands he caught up the grimy dust and poured it over his face and grizzled head, groaning incessantly." Anc. *Greece.* Ibid., Bk. xxiv. * Rubbing of hands. Anc. *Greece.* Sittl, p. 47. * Tearing of clothes. Anc. *Greece* and *Rome.* Sittl, p. 26. * "Silvia prima soror, palmis percussa lacertos, auxilium vocat" ("Silvia . . . beating her upper arms, calls for help"). Anc. *Rome.* Vergil, vii, 503. * Clapping of hands. Anc. *Greece* and *Rome; Ireland.* Neckel, pp. 64–65. Old Saxon. 9th cent. Northern *Germany. Heliand* 2183–84. Old Norse. Medieval *Iceland. Poetic Edda,* first and second song of Gudrun and the shorter song of Sigurd. * Beating breast. Old Saxon. Medieval northern *Germany. Heliand,* 3498–99. * Beating breast or head. 17th cent. *Germany.* Agrippa v. Nettesheim, p. 236. * Hands raised. Anc. *Rome*; 12th cent. *Germany. Orendel* 491. Seligmann, II, p. 166. * Hands extended toward heaven. Master of the Passion, undated. *Christ's Burial.* Bibl. Nat., Paris, Ms. lat. 18014, fol. 94 v. *See also* van der Meulen, p. 19. "and he stood momentarily arrested, one long hand outstretched, warding off realization . . . To see him was like glimpsing a flame, an epitome of grief's impact." *England.* Allingham, p. 81. * Right hand grasps wrist of left. Portal of Baptistry at Parma, murals of Sant' Angelo in Formis. Medieval *Italy.* Haseloff, p. 306. * "began to wring his hands so they cracked like dry twigs." 13th cent. *Germany.* Wolfram v. Eschenb., IV,

219; *Kudrun*, st. 919, 4. *See also* van der Meulen, p. 32. Wringing hands in grief while uttering curse. 15th cent. *Germany*. Johann v. Tepl, ch. i, ii. Anc. *Rome*; early Christian; 17th cent. *England*. Bulwer, pp. 32–33; 17th cent. *Spain*. Cervantes, *La Galatea*, I, 59; see also 17th cent. *Netherlands*. Bloemert's *Bewening* (1649) and several works of Rembrandt; van der Meulen, p. 20. "The governor wrung his hands in the utmost grief and consternation." 18th cent. *England*. Smollett, *Peregrine Pickle*, I, ch. xxxxvi. "Never, never, wringing her hands, should she meet with a mistress she loved so well." 18th cent. *England*. Richardson, I, p. 160; *Germany*. *DWb*, IV/2, col. 385. *

Speech Flat hand and lower arm raised to approx. right angle with upper arm, fingers together, thumb slightly raised. Common in medieval pictures—"speaking-gestures." Two main types: (1) older—flat hand; (2) younger—hollow hand. See Amira, "Handgebärden," pp. 170–203; Garnier, I, pp. 165–70. In digest of clm. 14022 judge appears twelve times with "speaking-gesture," usually raising both hands. 14th cent. *France*. Amira, "Handgebärden," p. 198. Speaking-gestures and other interaction in pictures of saints developed with theme of sacred conversation in late medieval Italy. Fra Filippo, Fra Angelico et al. added other saints to traditional, static representations of enthroned Virgin with Child, providing basis for interaction between figures. Late medieval *Italy*. Van der Meulen, p. 22. For sign of speaking to a crowd and sign for speech of a crowd, see Barasch, *Giotto*, pp. 17–19, who distinguishes two gestural speaking themes in Roman life and art: *adlocutio*, typified by emperor's address to army while standing on raised platform, raising right hand, requesting attention, and *acclamatio*, performed by crowd and can take form of shouting, elevating acclaimed on shield, etc. Visual representation usually as speaking-gesture. E.g., early 5th cent. ivory plaque of Probianus acclaimed by two figures with raised arms, thumb, index and middle fingers extended, other fingers bent so that thumb touches them. Late anc. *Roman*. Delbrück, no. 65. * Latin blessing gesture, *benedictio latina*, also used in narrative scenes, where it is not directed toward anyone, e.g. the Book of Pericopes of Henry II or the Gospel Book of Otto III, where it indicates solemn speech. Medieval *Germany*. Barasch, *Giotto*, p. 19. *See also* FINGER, HAND, Speech.

Speed Hand rapidly describes vertical circle. Jews. *Eastern Europe*. Efron, p. 72. * Swift dorso-ventral motion, palm vertical. Assimilated Jews. *Eastern Europe*. Efron, p. 117.

Stand Fingers together and extended, hand extended and moved up and down several times. *Colombia; U.S.* Saitz and Cervenka, p. 129.

Stealing Hand extended, palm to side, little finger down, fingers spread. As forearm remains in same position, hand is twisted, palm down, back and up again while fingers close. Southern *Italy*. Efron, p.

154. * Right wrist strikes open left palm representlng a diving board, then the right hand is raised over and swung downward like someone diving. *Lat. Am.* Kany, p. 106. * Hand extended open, fingers closed one by one. *Europe; North America.* Aubert, 84. * Hand at thigh-level, palm facing backwards moved as if throwing something backwards. *France.* Mitton, p. 148. * Hand at hip level palm to rear, then turned in circular motion toward hip. *France.* Ibid., also Critchley, p. 91. *Netherlands.* Andrea and de Boer, p. 71. * Hand loosely open, edge of palm down, swept horizontally towards body as if sweeping something off table. In most of *Lat. Am.*—someone getting away with something or stealing something. In *Peru*—"money" or "pay me." Axtell, *Gestures*, p. 93.

Stop   Right hand raised, palm outward, canted toward protagonist or vibrated once or twice in that direction. Native American. Austin, p. 595. Forearm slightly raised, hand pointed upwards, palm out. Anc. *Rome.* Sittl, p. 86. " 'Stop, Mrs. Mann, stop!' saith the beadle, raising his hand with a show of authority." 19th cent. *England.* Dickens, *Oliver Twist*, p. 150. * "but as the Jew, looking back, waved his hand to intimate that he preferred being alone" 19th cent. *England.* Dickens, *Oliver Twist*, p. 227. * " 'Let it be,' said Sikes, thrusting his hand before her." 19th cent. *England.* Dickens, *Oliver Twist*, p. 443. Extending hand, palm forward, toward someone. *France.* Mitton, p. 143. Policeman, indicating he does not want his picture taken. *China. Daily News*, Sept. 4, 1995, p. 1. Schoolchildren. *U.S.* Seton, p. xx. * Hand extended, palm forward, fingers spread, moving quickly from side to side, rotating from wrist. *U.S.* Saitz and Cervenka, p. 130. * Palm down, fingers, hand or arm may be moved up or down. *Colombia.* Saitz and Cervenka, p. 130. * " 'Now then!' said a voice, as my uncle felt a hand on his shoulder, 'You're booked for one inside. You'd better get in.' " 19th cent. *England.* Dickens, *Pickwick*, II, p. 351. * Right hand grasps left wrist from above: "Arrest/stop him!" "He has been arrested/stopped." *Central Africa.* Hochegger, p. 13.

Strike   Moving open hand, palm up, with several lateral strokes from wrist from right to left, slightly downward and inward, usually at chin level. *Lat. Am.* Kany, p. 126. * Raising and extending clenched fist. *Lat. Am.* Kany, ibid. * Striking down with fist. Schoolchildren. *U.S.* Seton, p. xxiv.

Submission (Submissiveness)   "She kissed his feet and anointed them. Biblical. *Middle East. Luke* 7:38. * Kissing the knee of someone. Persian proskynesis. Anc. *Persia.* Sittl, p. 169 and n. 6. * "I gave my back to the strikers and my cheeks to those who plucked off the hair." Biblical. *Middle East. Isaiah* 50:6. * Palms of hands forward, as if to ward off a blow: submission of a defeated people. Anc. *Egypt.* Meyer, pl. to 242, p. 266. * Putting one's own right hand on the shoulder of another. Anc. *Egypt.* Ohm, p. 277. * Lowering the hands. Anc. *Persia.* Sittl, p. 146. * "but she screamed aloud and ran under my guard, and clasping both knees in loud lamentation spoke to me" Anc. *Greece.* Homer, *Odyss.*, Bk. x. * Hands rub the earth while kneeling, indicating readiness to pick up dust and throw it on oneself. Anc. *Greece.* Sittl, p. 158, n. 6. * Hands folded in the manner of the captive awaiting binding and arms extended. *Assyria;* anc. *Greece.* Sittl, p. 149. * Folded hands as sign of submission was part of ancient Germanic formal homage. In commendation, vassal extended folded hands to lord, who took them between his own hands. Medieval *Germany.* Amira, "Handgebärden," pp. 242–46, and Du Cange, s. v. Hominium. Folded hands symbolized tied hands (Amira, ibid.), as well as services which vassal owes his lord (Herwegen, p. 328), as well as his need for protection. "Tassilo, duke of the Bavarians, came there, commended himself into vassalage with his hands, and swore innumerable oaths"; "Hedged in on every side, the duke came in person and putting his hands into the hands of the Lord King Charles he commended himself into vassalage." 8th cent. *Germany. Annals,* pp. 42, 66. By extension the gesture appears in miniatures of Heidelberg, Univ.-Bibl. cpg 848 showing a kneeling knight with folded hands and his lady in the process of either (fol. 82v) putting a helmet or (fol. 151r) a wreath on his head (see Walther, pl. 35, 48), or, conversely, in pictures of a betrothal, in which the bride extends her folded hands toward the groom. Medieval *Germany.* Amira, "Handgebärden," p. 244. * For hands humbly, or in awe, folded in front of abdomen as derivative of the metaphor of the bound hands in late antiquity, early Christianity, the high Middle Ages and the work of Giotto, see Barasch, *Giotto,* pp. 40–55. The commendation ritual has survived in the Catholic church: the newly consecrated priest lays his folded hands into those of the bishop, while giving his oath. Ohm, p. 271, n. 3; Ebert, V, p. 93; Prutz, I, p. 117. * Emperor is received by the people with lowered hands. *Roman Empire; Byzantine Empire.* Sittl, p. 149. * Right hand raised while kneeling. Anc. *Persia.* Sittl, p. 157, fig. 13, and p. 158. * Hands sweep together dust while kneeling. Anc. *Persia.* Sittl, p. 158. * On 17th cent. portraits, women's hands remain on or at side of body; usually they are in lap. On marriage portraits, woman often looks at man, or, if she looks at the viewer, she directs his attention at her husband with some gesture, while husband holds her hand. 17th cent. *Netherlands.* Van der Meulen, p. 36. However, van der Meulen (ibid.) cites an anonymous Roman picture of a marriage ceremony (Palazzo Giustiniani, ca. 1693), in which woman holds man's hand. Similarly symbolic of putting oneself in power of another is the gesture of female plaintiff accepting legal representation by counsellor. *Sachsenspiegel.* Medieval *Germany.* Amira, "Handgebärden," p. 245. Current Christian prayer gesture appears to be an adaptation of this legal gesture. *See also*

Prayer above. * Holding someone's stirrup while he is mounting. 12th cent. *Germany. Orendel*, 2143. * Among the Fellahim, the groom smites his bride on the head so that he shall not be ruled by her. 19th cent. *Egypt.* Bauer, p. 97. * Hands raised to level of head, palms slanted up. ("I submit to your judgment.") Jewish. *U.S.* Austin, p. 595. * Standing with hands behind back, right grasping left hand. 18th cent. *Egypt. 1001 Nights*, III, p. 218. *See also* Wait.

Suffering   Hands extended above head. Ohm, p. 263.

Suicide   Index extended, pointing at temple, thumb pointing upward, suggesting a cocked pistol. *U.S.* Hand makes stabbing motion toward stomach, suggesting *hara kiri. Japan.* One hand grasps throat, suggesting choking. *New Guinea.* Axtell, *Gestures*, p. 91.

Superciliousness   "Maschalla 'ade [oh, habit!]" one says and makes deprecating gesture, hand moving in and outwards from wrist. 19th cent. *Palestine.* Bauer, p. 224.

Superiority   Groom presses bride's hand at wedding to establish his superiority. South Slavic. *Yugoslavia.* Krauss, pp. 391, 396, 406, 417. *See also* FOOT, Submission; FOOT, HAND, Submission.

Surprise   Hands open, raised high above head, or arms bent, raised to an equal height with face. Fingers separated, palms toward person causing surprise. Can be indifferent, comic, pained, joyful, admiring and overdone by hypocrisy or abandon. Anc. *Greece* and *Rome.* Sittl, p. 13. "Mrs. Mann raised her hand in astonishment." 19th cent. *England.* Dickens, *Oliver Twist*, p. 99. "he flung up both his hands and performed other gestures indicating surprise and agitation." 19th cent. *England.* Thackeray, *Virginians*, ch. xxxiv. * Clapping hands. 19th cent. Naples, southern *Italy.* de Jorio, p. 299. Also anc. *Greece.* Homer, *Iliad*, xxiii, 102. Clapping hands, edge of the right against back of the left. Women. Muslim. Ohm, p. 284. * Making sign of the cross. 19th cent. *Greece; Italy.* Sittl, p. 128, and n. 4. Right hand moving up and down violently, palm turned inward, thumb usually touching index and middle finger, other fingers loose, hitting each other. *Spain; Lat. Am.* Flachskampf, p. 220. * Flat hand placed on open mouth. Schoolchildren. *U.S.* Seton, p. xxii.

Surrender   In boxing the defeated indicates surrender by raising both hands. Anc. *Greece.* Sittl, p. 219. * Defeated wrestler signals surrender by hitting winner with his hand. Anc. *Greece.* Sittl, p. 219, n. 4. * Giving the victor one's hand. Anc. *Rome.* Otto, p. 211. * Warriors surrendering or peaceably approaching enemy camp have right hand raised. Anc. *Greece* and *Rome.* Sittl, p. 148.

Sustain   Hand at waist level, palm up, flat and jerked slightly upward. *Europe; North America.* Aubert, p. 88.

Sympathy   "It was as much as she could do to restrain herself from rushing forward to grasp his hand in a gesture of sympathy and solidarity." *England*. Lodge, *Nice Work*, p. 133.

"Teach me" Hand at level of waist close to the body with palm turned up flat. *Europe; North America*. Aubert, p. 88.

Teasing Hands placed together palm to palm, then separated so that palms face forward and hands are next to each other. *Saudi Arabia*. Barakat, no. 214.

Telephone Describing series of small circles in the air in immediate vicinity of the ear. Performed with one hand limp and cupped slightly. *Spain*. Green, pp. 56–57. Right hand circles around right ear. *Italy*. Graham, p. 26.

Thief Left hand closed, right hand, open, moves quickly outward in semi-circle—"Attention, un voleur!" ("Stop, thief!") Or both hands are firmly put into trouser pockets. *Central Africa*. Hochegger, pp. 211–12.

Threat Fists held up to someone's face. Anc. *Rome*. Sittl, p. 43. Hands raised against someone. Anc. *Rome*. Ibid. Raised arm, clenched fist. 16th cent. *Germany*. Brant, woodcut, p. 70. Hand raised to face level and clenched; fingers toward the gesturer. *France*. Mitton, p. 141. " 'I mean to give you a damned good licking'; and he accompanied this threat by putting his clenched fist close to his . . . face." 18th cent. *England*. Hickey, p. 161. Fist raised with knuckles outward is threatening; with the knuckles toward gesturer it denotes pride or victory. *U.S.* Axtell, *Gestures*, p. 40. Fist raised with the knuckles outward and shaken. *Netherlands*. Andrea and de Boer, p. 59. " 'It's time the old queen started acting his age.' Julia brandished a threatening fist in front of her friend's nose. 'You leave him alone. You know that, as far as I'm concerned, César's sacred.' " *Spain*. Pérez-Reverte, p. 149. Death threatens with raised fist. *Germany*. Boggs, p. 321. Fist raised. Schoolchildren. *U.S.* Seton, p. xxii. * Hand turned over indicates total destruction. Anc. *Rome*. Sittl, p. 113. * Index and little finger extended as in "horns," held horizontally towards someone's face. 19th cent. Naples, southern *Italy*. de Jorio, p. 94. * Hand pressed to the side of body. 19th cent. *Italy*. Manzoni, I, p. 158; de Jorio, p. 200. * Fingers of right hand extended and together, then moving hand a few times in chopping movement. 19th cent. *Palestine*. Bauer, p. 219. * Fingertips of the first three fingers together, hand shaken toward someone. 19th cent. *Palestine*. Bauer, p. 219. * Extended arms and hands of mourners on graves of children. Anc. *Rome*. Ebert, V, p. 95. Elbow half bent, right forearm moves from right towards left shoulder. Hand remains there for a moment, then falls back to original position. Vulgar, familiar. *France*. Mitton, p. 145. Fingers extended and slightly apart, hand turned, palm inwards, at eye level, in the direction of someone. *France*. Mitton, p. 142. * Flat hand, palm sideways, at waist level, moving slightly and repeatedly sideways toward the body, the palm turning upward as it moves.

Threat to a child: "Do you want your bottom paddled?" *Netherlands.* Andrea and de Boer, p. 156–57.

Treaty   Handclasp. Ossetes, anc. *India.* Ebert, V, p. 94. *Germany. DWb*, IV/2, col. 331. *See also* Agreement.

Trivia   Hand rapidly agitated, fingers pointing upward, from wrist outward with slack motion. ("It's nothing.") *France.* Mitton, p. 149.

Trust   Handshake, saying "Straight!" Children. *England.* Opie, p. 122. "She took his hand and held it in a clasp warm even through her glove; but there was nothing amorous about the gesture." *U.S.* Boucher, p. 207. Taking another's hand. Arab. Axtell, *Do's and Taboos*, p. 42.

Truth   Hands flat, stretched out toward someone, palms up. ("This is clear, self-evident.") *France.* Mitton, p. 143. Open hand in front, palm turned out, finger tips down. *Europe; North America.* Aubert, p. 90. * Fist clenched, thumb extended vertically. Assimilated Jews. Efron, p. 118. * Chief of tribe places right hand under man's belt so that it barely touches sexual organ: man on whom hand is laid must tell the truth. *Saudi Arabia.* Barakat, no. 202. *See also* HAND, Integrity.

Uncertainty   Right and left hands rising and falling alternately as if balancing two points of view. *France.* Mitton, p. 144. * "When a Provençal looks you in the eye and tells you that he will be hammering on your door ready to start work next Tuesday for certain, the behavior of his hands is all-important. If they are still, or patting you reassuringly on the arm, you can expect him on Tuesday. If one hand is held out at waist height, palm downwards, and begins to rock from side to side, adjust the timetable to Wednesday or Thursday. If the rocking develops into an agitated waggle, he's really talking about next week or God knows when" Provençe, *France.* Mayle, *A Year in Provence*, p. 45. * Hand extended slightly in front, fingers spread, palm down, rocking from side to side: "So-so," "maybe yes, maybe no." *Netherlands.* Andrea and de Boer, p. 112.

Understanding   Hand forward, palm supine. Assimilated Jews. *Eastern Europe.* Efron, p. 119.

Union   In marriage ceremony priest unites hands of bride and groom and ties them together with his stole. 19th cent. *Western Europe; Vedic India.* Sittl, p. 132. * On the wedding portrait of *Casteleyn en zijn vrouw* (1663) by Jan de Bray the man holds the woman's hand as sign of their shared fate. In addition, he raises other hand as sign of his promise to his wife. 17th cent. *Netherlands.* Van der Meulen, p. 38; see also Panofsky, p. 1–20.

Useless   Gesture of throwing something behind one's back. Vulgar. *France.* Mitton, p. 147. * Crossing slightly cupped hand sharply across body. Palm of hand faces shoulder at beginning of movement; at its conclusion, palm faces outward. *Spain; Lat. Am.* Green, p. 85.

Vengeance   Shaking fist or drawing it back toward ear. Men. *Spain.*

Kaulfers, p. 252. * Shaking hand, palm open, thumb and fingers extended but touching, hand cupped. Women. *Spain*. Kaulfers, ibid. * Tip of thumb and index of right hand joined, other fingers lightly bent, hand shaking in threatening manner. 19th cent. *Palestine*. Bauer, p. 218. * Fists twist and slowly pull away from each other. Primarily children. *Colombia; U.S.* Saitz and Cervenka, p. 111.

Verbosity Hand at face level, palm down, fingers move rapidly up and down from tip of thumb. *Colombia; U.S.* Saitz and Cervenka, p. 136.

Victory Raising hand and shaking it. Anc. Jews. Josephus, vii, v, 2; Biblical. *Middle East. Ex.* 14:8; Bulwer, p. 45. * Hands clasped and raised above head. *Colombia; U.S.* Saitz and Cervenka, p. 145. "He let out a great bellow of relief and went into the middle of the road, jigging up and down with both hands clasped above his head in a triumphal salute." Provençe, *France*. Mayle, *Hotel Pastis*, p. 335. * Fist raised with knuckles facing gesturer—victory or pride; with the knuckles outward it is a threatening gesture. *U.S.* Axtell, *Gestures*, p. 40. * Elbow(s) bent, clenched fist(s) extended in front of body. Reaction of O. J. Simpson on hearing the verdict "not guilty." Photo. *Daily News*, Oct. 4, 1995, p. 1.

Virility Amount of force used in slapping friend on back or shoulder in greeting, or violence with which coins are slammed on bar or dominoes on table, or loudness of clap with which drinks are ordered indicates degree of aggressiveness of which gesturer wants to be thought capable. Since virility is associated with testicles, Andalusian men frequently touch their testicles, lifting them with one hand on entering a bar, taking seat at counter or making point in argument. Anything huge or powerful (*cojonudo* = *cojones* + *nudos*) is indicated by open hands, fingers slightly curled, held palm upward in front of the chest and moving them up and down alternately, as if juggling with balls or weighing something. Grabbing friend's testicles from behind is considered amusing male prank. Andalusia, *Spain*. Driessen, p. 244.

Volunteer Hand raised. Anc. *Rome*. Stat., *Theb.*; Sittl, p. 218.

Voting In senate since Tiberius some used the Greek gesture of raising the right arm to vote. Anc. *Rome*. Sittl, p. 218.

Wait Hand raised, palm out, fingers together. *Colombia; U.S.* * Fingers separated, arm moving from side to side. *U.S.* Saitz and Cervenka, p. 146. * Both lower arms raised slightly and parallel to one another, hands hanging down, their backs forward, ministerial kneels before bishop and stands before abbess and waits for pronouncements of his superior; likewise vassal waits for command of feudal lord. Medieval *German. Sachsenspiegel.* Amira, "Handgebärden," p. 223. The gesture also indicates submission. Amira, Ibid., pp. 223–24.

Warning "shaking his hand before him in a warning manner." 19th cent. *England*. Dickens, *Oliver Twist*, p. 179. * Hand(s) extended, palm facing forward. ("Stop!" "I don't want it.") *France*. Mitton, p. 143. * Folding a corner edge of the coat to represent an ear. ("Secret police.") *Guatemala*. Kany, p. 121. * "As we parted, he extended his right hand, palm upward, and shook it a few times horizontally, to tell me 'Be careful! Look after yourself.' " *Italy*. Graham, p. 26.

HAND, GENITALS
Good luck   Touching genitals. *Italy*. Vidossi, note, p. 96. * Wearing horn as talisman, the horn being a phallic symbol. *Italy*. Ibid.

Insult   One or both hands vigorously grab genitals. Male sexual insult. *Argentina*. Axtell, *Gestures*, p. 86.

Shame   Hand(s) cover(s) genitals. *Central Africa*. Hochegger, p. 89.

Virility   *See* HAND, Virility.

HAND, HAIR
Anger   "Captain Gore, looking more wild than usual, raising both hands to his hair, a common motion of his when in a passion, and turning to me hastily said, 'Zounds! sir, did you ever hear anything like this,' and without waiting for my answer, said to Bentley, 'What the devil do you mean? Do you imagine me to be as great an idiot as yourself?' " 18th cent. *England*. Hickey, p. 260.

Mourning   Tearing hair. Anc. *Egypt*. Relief from tomb of a priest, 19th dynasty. Gombrich, p. 74, pl. 56. Idealized: one hand beating breast, the other tearing hair (Sirens). Anc. *Greece*. Schreiber, pp. 86–95. Donatello, "Mourning Woman under the Cross." Detail from pulpit relief, c. 1460–70. San Lorenzo, Florence, *Italy*. Gombrich, p. 76, pl. 59. Also *Middle East*. Gombrich, pp. 74–75.

HAND, HAT
Anger   "he fixed his hat on his head with an indignant knock." 19th cent. *England*. Dickens, *Pickwick*, I, p. 26. * "the cabman dashed his hat upon the ground, with a reckless disregard of his own private property" 19th cent. *England*. Dickens, *Pickwick*, I, p. 9. " 'Now the murder's out and damme, there's an end on it.' With these words, which he repeated with great emphasis and violence, Tom Weller dashed his hat on the ground." 19th cent. *England*. Dickens, *Pickwick*, II, p. 260.

Defiance   *See* HAND, Defiance.

Disbelief   Hat worn askew. *Venezuela*. Kany, p. 70.

Enthusiasm   Deputies to parliament showed their enthusiastic support for a measure by throwing hats and caps into the air. 17th cent. *Poland*. Bogucka, p. 200. [Editors' note: cf. the custom of cadets throwing their caps in the air at graduation at U.S. service academies.]

Etiquette   Hats and caps were removed at table only when drinking to someone's health. Customarily one rose when proposing a toast and when drinking to someone's health, and removed one's hat. Foreigners found this practice annoying and often complained that the constant jumping up and sitting down was a nuisance. 16th and 17th centuries. *Poland*. Bogucka, pp. 196–97. During the Reformation period "men started to take off their hats in the house, although they continued to dance in hats until the end of the eighteenth century." 16th-18th century. *Europe*. Rockwood, p. 179.

Farewell *See* HAND, Farewell.

Good luck Lifting one's hat to a chimney sweep. *England*. Phillips, pp. 191–96.

Greeting Doffing hat to ladies. 16th cent. *Germany*. Emperor Maximilian I, *Freydal*, Cod. vindob. 2831. Louis XIV never passed a woman without removing his hat, including chambermaids. How far he removed his hat depended on the lady's rank. 17th cent. *France*. Hayes, p. 299. * Hand placed to helmet. Military greeting. Anc. *Rome*. Pritzwald, p. 27. * An hidalgo left Castile rather than doff his hat to another person first. 16th cent. *Spain*. *Lazarillo de Tormes*, ch. iii. * "Put off's cap." 16th-17th cent. *England*. Shakesp., *All's Well*, 2.2.10. "Off capp'd to him." 16th-17th cent. *England*. Shakesp., *Othello* 1.1.10. Greetings accentuated by doffing headgear and bowing so that hat swept the floor. It may also just be touched or tipped, depending on social relationship to person being greeted. Taking off hat was sign of special respect, first to do so was the younger person, someone of lower social standing than person being greeted, or someone obliged to those being greeted. Two gentlemen of the same rank would take off hats simultaneously. One also doffed the hat at mention of name of person of superior social standing, or when reading a letter from him. "When Bonifacius Vanozzi described his meeting with . . . the Great Chancellor Jan Zamoyski in 1596, he recorded that Zamoyski doffed his hat while reading Vanozzi's credentials; he also doffed his hat at every mention of the Polish king or of the Pope. Another Italian diplomat, Giovanni Paolo Mucante, wrote in the same year that the Pope's envoy to Poland, whilst attending a royal banquet in Warsaw, doffed his cap every time King Sigismund Vasa drank to somebody's health; this behaviour, however, was criticized by the clergymen present." 16th cent. *Poland*. Bogucka, pp. 193–94. After raising the siege of Vienna in 1683, the Polish King John III Sobieski and his entourage were deeply hurt when Emperor Leopold did not doff his hat before Sobieski's son and his colonels. To make amends, the Emperor not only doffed his hat, but almost threw it before the Polish soldiers at every meeting. Ibid., p. 201. Bogucka, pp. 201–02, observes that "the old Polish army did not have a special military drill for the nobles, who considered it beneath their dignity to be dressed and trained as common soldiers . . . Nevertheless, . . . a particular ritual had developed which was patterned upon general European models. For example, it was obligatory to take off hats before military banners." "Readers of *Madame Bovary* will remember how Emma's father, the old Rouault, urged his future son-in-law [Charles Bovary] to keep his hat on while in his [own] house. By doing so he showed his respect for Charles Bovary as Charles himself, by taking off his hat each time he entered the house [of his future father-in-law], expressed his esteem for the father of his future bride. Such ritual was long-standing. We find it explained as early as the seventeenth century in De Courtin and, having become even more intricate, in Van Laar's *Groot ceremonie-boeck* [Amsterdam, 1735]." *France; Netherlands.* Roodenburg, p. 164. On being received in the house of higher ranking person, one was expected to doff one's hat, take it in left hand and stay on left side of one's host so that his right hand was free. Replacing one's hat without being specifically requested to do so would be discourteous; and even in such a case, if one's host had to sneeze, one was to bare one's head immediately. Both De Courtin and Van Laar regard it as proper to doff the hat a second time, even if invited to keep it on. If invitation was repeated, one was expected to accede. Asking one's superiors to do so was a violation of etiquette. Women, in addition to curtseying, were also expected to remove headdress in presence of their superiors, unless it was merely adornment, such as a fine-meshed cap. Similarly, women were expected to remove masks (worn to protect skin against sun or wind) in presence of someone of superior rank, and not replace it unless specifically requested to do so. Since persons of higher rank required more personal "space" than their inferiors, gestures appropriate to preventing intrusion on their "space" were extended to objects representing them. Thus, at court, it was expected that one remove one's hat when servant passed by, carrying monarch's meal; or when one passed monarch's portrait; or while reading letter from monarch. 17th cent. *France; Netherlands.* Roodenburg, pp. 164–66. "Pipes lifting his hat, as Crabtree passed." 18th cent. *England.* Smollett, *Peregrine Pickle*, ch. c. Lifting hat from one's head, moving one's hand, holding hat in direction of other person, then replacing it on one's head. *France.* Mitton, p. 142. * Tipping hat by grasping crown with fingers and either raising hat a little or removing it completely. Simultaneously head and upper part of body move forward. *Colombia.* Saitz and Cervenka, p. 67. * "In Tibet a respectful salutation is made by removing hat and lolling out the tongue." H. Bayley, II, p. 128. * Tipping hat by grasping brim, sometimes without raising hat. Also before religious shrines and churches. *Colombia.* Saitz and Cervenka, p. 68. *See also* HAND, HEAD, Greeting.

Insult Cocking the hat. Mid-18th cent. London, *England.* T. Burke, p. 94.

Marriage On the evening before marriage, bridal wreath is taken from bride and woman's cap is put on her head. 17th cent. *Germany*. Weise, *Überflüssige Gedanken*, II, p. 220.

Praise "Some followers of mine own at lower end of the hall hurl'd up their caps" 16th-17th cent. *England*. Shakesp., *Richard III* 3.7.35. Applause. Shakesp., *Coriol.* 1.1.216.

Prayer Covering head at prayer. Priests of the Kachin, Hopi, *U.S.*; anc. *Persia*, anc. *Rome*, Jews. Heiler, pp. 104–05. * Baring the head at prayer. Anc. *Greece*; Germanic. Heiler, p. 104. "Any man who offers prayer or explains the will of God with anything on his head disgraces his head, and any woman who offers prayer or explains the will of God bareheaded disgraces her head, for it is just as though she had her head shaved." Biblical. *Middle East*. I *Cor.* 11:4–6.

Respect Removing hat from head. 15th cent. *Spain*. Rojas, ix. "we first went to White-hall gate, where the Lords stood on foot bare-headed, whilst the Herald proclaimed his Majesty's title to the Imperial Crown and succession" 17th cent. *England*. Evelyn, II, p. 219. The Chevalier de la Barre was beheaded on July 1, 1766 partly because he failed to doff his hat to a passing religious procession. 18th cent. *France*. Mornet, p. 52. *See also* HAND, Respect.

Reverence " 'God's will be done!' He took off his hat at these last words." 19th cent. *England*. Gaskell, II, p. 17.

Sorrow "Ne'er pull your hat upon your brows; give sorrow words." 16th-17th cent. *England*. Shakesp., *Macbeth* 4.3.208.

Submission Holding hat in hand. *Germany*. DWb, IV/2, col. 342.

HAND, HEAD

Admiration Both hands grasp head at or above temples. *Russia*. Monahan, p. 28.

Affection Hands laid upon someone's head in blessing. *Germany*. Boggs, p. 321. * "There are twenty washed men at the street door for you to shake hands with; and six children in arms that you're to pat on the head . . . if you could manage to kiss one of 'em, it would produce a very great impression on the crowd." 19th cent. *England*. Dickens, *Pickwick*, I, p. 208. * Head must not be touched by others because it is sacred. Hmong, *Laos*. Dresser, *L.A. Times*, June 8, 1996, B14.

Age Hand, index extended, describes circle on top of head—old age. *Central Africa*. Hochegger, p. 210.

Agreement *See* Obedience below.

Anger Beating the head. Anc. *Greece* and *Rome*. Sittl, p. 21. Slapping back of head in anger and joy. Yuqui Indians. *Bolivia*. Boggs, p. 321.

Annoyance *See* Frustration.

Approach Head held high and protruding forward; hands at waist level, palms up, fingers meeting, hand slightly curled. *U.S.* Birdwhistell,

"Do Gestures Speak Louder than Words?" pp. 56–57. * "Mrs. Tulliver rapped the window sharply, beckoned, and shook her head,—a process which she repeated more than once before she returned to her chair." 19th cent. *England.* Eliot, p. 399.

Approval Nodding and clapping hands. Schoolchildren. *U.S.* Seton, p. xx. " 'You're a clever boy, my dear,' said the playful old gentleman, patting Oliver on the head approvingly." 19th cent. *England.* Dickens, *Oliver Twist,* p. 78.

Attention "Accompanying these words with a gentle rap on the head of the young gentleman before noticed, who, unconscious of his close vicinity to the person in request, was screaming 'Waller' with all his might." 19th cent. *England.* Dickens, *Pickwick,* II, p. 280.

Awareness Hitting one's head at the side with flat right hand—sudden awareness. *Spain.* Flachskampf, p. 223.

Blessing Hand placed on top of someone's head. Ohm, p. 290. *See also* HAND, Blessing.

Clairvoyance Accompanying prognostication of events, fingers of both hands, held at side of head with palms inward, are pushed back and forth to and from the head. Madrid, *Spain.* Green, pp. 76–77.

Cleverness " 'Oh, and Jojo?' He winked and tapped his head. 'Well done.' The little man swaggered as he went off to get his bicycle." Provence, *France.* Mayle, *Hotel Pastis,* p. 123.

Complication Body inclined slightly forward, hands circle around each other in front of stomach, while head wags from side to side: "It's a complicated matter!" *Central Africa.* Hochegger, p. 90.

Concentration " 'You stir up many thoughts,' said Donatello, pressing his hand upon his brow" 19th cent. *U.S.* Hawthorne, ch. xxx. * Head supported by hand, chin cupped in hand. "I sat upon a stone, leg crossed by leg; thereon I put my elbow up and in my hand did cup one cheek, and chin as well." 13th cent. *Germany.* Walther v. d. Vogelweide. *See also* the miniature in Heidelberg cpg 848 fol. 124r; Walther, pl. 45; also *DWb,* IV/2, col. 335. For head supported by hand, cf. the miniature of Reinmar v. Zweter in Heidelberg, Univ.-Bibl. cpg 848 fol. 323r; Walther, pl. 112. 16th cent. *Germany.* Dürer's *Melencolia* I; 17th cent. *Netherlands.* Rembrandt's *Paulus in de gevangenis.* Van der Meulen, pp. 25–26. * Right hand raised to level of cheek with index extended. 3rd-4th cent. sculpture of Bodhisattva Padmapani, anc. Gandhara, present Pakistan and Afghanistan. Los Angeles County Museum of Art, Gift of Henry and Ruth Trubner in honor of the museum's twenty-fifth anniversary and to honor Dr. Pratapaditya Pal. *See* Fig. 18. Posture of executing this gesture while sitting with leg crossed so that right foot rests on left knee first appeared in South Asian art around the 1st cent., and may have had antecedents in West Asian and Greco-Roman art. Significant number of similar pensive bodhisattvas survive

Fig. 18. Bodhisattva Padmapani. (Pakistan, 3rd–4th cent.) Los Angeles County Museum of Art, Gift of Henry and Ruth Trubner in honor of the museum's twenty-fifth anniversary and to honor Dr. Pratapaditya Pal.

from the 2nd cent. trade and cultural centers of Gandhara, whereas few seem to have been produced in northern India, suggesting existence of popular cult surrounding pensive bodhisattvas in Gandhara, but less interest in the theme in India. Markel, p. 12. Cf. this gesture to that of Walther v. d. Vogelweide in Heidelberg, Univ.-Bibl. cpg 848, 124r; Walther, pl. 45.

Confusion   Hiding face in hands. *Portugal.* Basto, p. 24.

Consecration   Touching someone's head. Anc. *Rome.* Sittl, p. 369. *See also* HAND, Consecration.

Contemplation   *See* Concentration above.

Crazy   Flat hand, palm down, extended to the forehead in the form of a military salute can mean "you're *pazzo.*" *Italy.* Axtell, *Gestures*, p. 96.

Cuckoldry   Placing thumbs against temples with indexes extended and other fingers pressed into palms. *Lebanon; Syria.* Barakat, no. 53. * Tips of thumbs placed on temples, other fingers extended, palms forward, fingers wiggling. *Lebanon, Syria.* Barakat, no. 52. *See also* HAND, Cuckoldry.

Curse   Rubbing right palm down over face of another person puts curse on that person. *Libya; Saudi Arabia.* Barakat, no. 124. * Rubbing back of right hand on forehead puts curse on person to whom the gesture is made. Usually made by women. *Jordan.* Barakat, no. 69.

Death   Head back, closed right hand raised to height of head: "He is dead!" *Central Africa.* Hochegger, p. 121.

Despair   Beating one's head. Anc. *Greece* and *Rome.* Sittl, p. 21. 16th-17th cent. *England.* Shakesp., *Lear* 1.4.270–73. Striking one's head with the fist. 18th cent. *Switzerland.* Gessner, p. 145.

Desperation   Elbows close to body, hands raised as high as the shoulders. Right hand hits left palm to palm. Hands remain united and together are raised to touch breast, then lowered. At same time head is shaken. Feminine and clerical. *France.* Mitton, p. 144.

Disappointment   Striking the forehead. Naples, southern *Italy.* Critchley, p. 89. * Scratching head. 19th cent. Naples, southern *Italy*; *Germany.* de Jorio, pp. 121, 123.

Disbelief   Scratching head. 19th cent. *France.* Fail, *Prop. Rustiques*, I, p. 165. * "shows doubt by position of eyes (to side); hand to his mouth." *U.S.* Birdwhistell, "Do Gestures Speak Louder than Words?" p. 56. "they shrugged their shoulders, touched their foreheads." 19th cent. *England.* Dickens, *Pickwick*, I, p. 496.

Disgust   Hand, palm down, put on top of head. *Colombia; U.S.* Reported 1970 as not common among young U.S. adults. Saitz and Cervenka, p. 43.

Distress   Striking one's head. Anc. *Rome.* Ohm, p. 282. Flat hand strikes top of head: "Oh God, I forgot!" *Netherlands*. Andrea and de Boer, p. 163.

Embarrassment Scratching head. 19th cent. *France*. Merimée, p. 146. Medieval *France*. *Ernoul*, p. 136.

Emphasis "bowing his head courteously in the emphasis of his discourse, gently waving his left hand to lend force to his observations" 19th cent. *England*. Dickens, *Pickwick*, II, p. 449.

Fantasy Raising both hands, slightly clenched, spiralling upward above the level of the head. *Spain; Lat. Am.* Green, p. 47.

Farewell Hand placed to temple in military salute. *Colombia; U.S.* Saitz and Cervenka, p. 63.

Fatigue Right hand at waist, head inclined forward. *Central Africa*. Hochegger, p. 70.

Fear Palm placed on back of head. Baumeister, I, p. 588.

Forget Slowly shake head and brush away something in air, near forehead. Schoolchildren. *U.S.* Seton, p. xxii.

Frustration (at having forgotten something or said or done something foolish) Striking forehead with flat hand. *France*. Mitton, p. 146. [Editors' note: *U.S.*, also with heel of hand.] *Netherlands*. Andrea and de Boer, p. 26. * Flat hand, thumb extended outward, strikes forehead, then turned downward so that fingertips are at the brow line, pointing diagonally down: "The brains are upside down." Usually referring to oneself. *Russia*. Monahan, pp. 48–49. * Both hands grasp head at and above the temples. *Russia*. Ibid., pp. 28–29. Right fist raised to side of head and held there for a moment: "Airhead!" Can refer to oneself or someone else. *Russia*. Ibid., pp. 50–51.

Good Wishes (for riches) Hand is moved toward head (hair?). 19th cent. *Greece*. Sittl, p. 115.

Greeting Hand upright, palm inside, held at level of face, arm half bent, moving of the tips of the fingers from forehead outward. *Europe; North America*. Aubert, p. 84. * Modern military salute originated in the 18th cent. Field, pp. 42–49. Salute. *Colombia; U.S.* Saitz and Cervenka, pp. 63, 65. * Hand moving sharply from temple to side and up. Informal. Boyaca, *Colombia*. Ibid., p. 65. * Salute in non-military context is often humorous. *Colombia; U.S.* Ibid., p. 69. *See* Crazy. Hand laid to head while saying: "You are above my head." *Crete*. Siebert, I, p. 284. * Hands joined, raised above the head: "Bonjour!" ("Hello!") *Central Africa*. Hochegger, p. 174.

Hesitation Left arm raised, hand on head, fingers in hair. 16th cent. *Germany*. Brant, woodcut, p. 261. Head is scratched with one or more fingers of one hand—hesitation about what to do or say. *France*. Mitton, p. 146, no. 39.

Identification The bride puts some yeast on her forehead and enters the room with a jug on her head. 19th cent. *Palestine*. Bauer, p. 94.

Ignorance   Scratching head. (Response to "What happened?" "We can't do anything about it.") *Colombia; U.S.* Saitz and Cervenka, p. 93.

Impatience   Raising hand to a position over the head, or bringing it to rest on the back of the head. Men. *Spain.* Green, pp. 89–90. * Raising hand over head, then raising single hair in rear of head. Women. *Spain; Lat. Am.* Green, p. 89.

Indecision   Scratching the head. Schoolchildren. *U.S.* Seton, p. xxi.

Insult   Slap or blow with hand against someone's head or face. Anc. *Greece* and *Rome.* Palladius, *Hist. Lausiaca*, 113, col. 1217; Sittl, p. 109. "If the interviewer dares to express doubts, one slaps him publicly, like the mayoress of the capital. Twenty-one years of military dictatorship have left a primitive style." *Panama.* Karnofsky, p. 34. * "When with dignitaries from Thailand, never raise your hand above their heads. Such a gesture is considered insulting" Lynch, p. 10. * Right hand passes lightly over the hair on top of the head: "Sexe de ta mère!" ("Your mother's pudendum!") *Central Africa.* Hochegger, p. 192.

Intellectual   Hand, fingers extended, palm facing speaker, is brought to side of the head and the rigid fingers are pushed back and forth. Madrid, *Spain; Lat. Am.* Green, p. 75.

Intelligence   Hand gently caresses forehead. *Central Africa.* Hochegger, p. 96.

Joy   Slapping back of head in anger and in joy. Yuqui Indians. *Bolivia.* Key, p. 95.

Manumission   *See* HAND, Manumission.

Memory   " 'They are here,' added the Count, tapping his forehead significantly. 'Large book at home—full of notes, music, . . . all tings.' " 19th cent. *England.* Dickens, *Pickwick*, I, p. 249. * Hitting one's head to arouse the memory or to renounce forgetfulness. Introduced to Brazil from Portugal in the 16th cent., previously unknown to slaves and indigenous peoples. In anc. Rome, the gesture invoked the presence of Mnemosyne, the goddess of reminiscence. Anc. *Rome; Brazil; Portugal.* Cascudo, *História*, p. 240.

Mockery   Hands placed slightly above temples, palms facing, fingertips forward, thumbs pointing up. 15th cent. *France. Grandes Heures of the Duc de Berry* (1409), pl. 16. * Right hand placed on head as if covering a bald spot. *Central Africa.* Hochegger, p. 30. * With index and middle finger extended, hand is held behind the head. Children's gesture without sexual connotation. *Russia.* Monahan, pp. 66–67. *See also* FINGER, HEAD, Cuckoldry.

Mourning   Striking one's head. Boggs, col. 319. Men. Anc. *Greece.* Sittl, p. 25. Striking one's head (cheeks, eyes, temples). Women. Anc. *Rome.* Sittl, p. 26. * Head usually slightly inclined to either side (a "heavy head"), supported by a hand. Anc. *Egypt.* Tomb of a priest. 19th dynasty. Gombrich, p. 74, pl. 56; *Phoenicia.* Sidonian sarcophagus, mid-4th cent. b.c. Gombrich, p. 75, pl. 57; Byzantine ivory, "Crucifixion." 10th cent. Gombrich, pl. 58. *See also* Sorrow; HAND, Mourning.

Need "jerk his clenched fists up and down, vigorously nodding between each inferior-superior movement of his fists." *U.S.* Birdwhistell, "Background," p. 14.

Negation A defensive movement of the hand, a despising movement of the head, in connection with which the eyebrows and eyelashes simultaneously are raised. 19th cent. *Palestine.* Bauer, p. 220.

Oath Someone taking an oath may swear by his head and point to it or the most valuable part of the head, the eyes. Anc. *Greece* and *Rome*; 19th cent. *Greece; India.* Sittl, p. 139. Father of a family swears by heads of children, children by head of father, wife by that of husband; in all cases, hand of person swearing touches object sworn by. Anc. *Greece.* Sittl, p. 140. In swearing by head of accused, accuser touches it. Medieval *Germany. Reineke Fuchs*, 2171; Grimm, *DRA*, II, p. 551. * Hands at sides with palms up, head tilted back. *Jordan; Lebanon; Syria; Saudi Arabia.* Barakat, no. 20. * Palm of right hand placed on top of head. *Jordan; Saudi Arabia.* Barakat, no. 178.

Obedience Flat right hand, palm down, held with tips of fingers against side of head in mock military salute—joking or ironic agreement to carry out a request. *Russia.* Monahan, pp. 120–21.

Passion Right fist moves energetically at level of chest, head thrown back, upper incisors bite lower lip, nose takes air in audibly, eyes squint. *Spain.* Flachskampf, p. 249.

Pensiveness Scratching head. Anc. *Rome.* Horace, *Sat.* I, 10, 70. " 'So they have fired me,' said Pnin, clasping his hands and nodding his head." *Russia.* Nabokov, p. 170. * Head resting in hand. Medieval *Germany.* Haseloff, p. 307; cf. the miniatures in Heidelberg, Univ. Bibl. cpg. 848, fol. 30r (Heinrich v. Veldeke), fol. 124r (Walther v. d. Vogelweide), fol. 323r (Reinmar v. Zweter) in Walther, pl. 16, 45, 112.

Perplexity Scratching head. Medieval *France. Godefroy de Paris* 3587, 5889. Right hand slowly scratches head. *Central Africa.* Hochegger, p. 61.

Plea Grasping head of a person between both hands. Anc. *Greece.* Sittl, p. 33.

Poverty Accompanying the gesture for counting money with a negative head shake. *Lat. Am.* Kany, p. 88. *See also* FINGER, Money.

Praise Right hand taps gently on a child's head. *Central Africa.* Hochegger, p. 103.

Prayer Holding one or both hands over one's head. *India.* Ohm, p. 187. * Putting one hand to the head. Tehuelch, Patagonia, *Argentina.* Ohm, p. 288. * "[The priest] then raises [his hands] to his face, inclines his head, and fixing his eyes upon the Sacred Host prays for the departed." Roman Catholic. *Mass*, p. 66. * The Vestal Quinta Claudia precedes her prayer by washing her head three times and raising her hands three times. Anc. *Rome*. Sittl, p. 190.

Prohibition Palm facing inwards, and shaking head. *India*. Rose, p. 313.

Punishment A blow with hand or fist against some part of someone's head. Anc. *Greece;* anc. *Rome*. Judicial usage; *see also* Insult. Sittl, p. 109. Slap. Anc. *Greece;* 19th cent. *Greece*. Sittl, p. 109.

Refusal Right hand passed over the head from front to back: "Je refuse, va t'en, sexe de ta mère!" ("I refuse, get out of here, you s.o.b.!") *Central Africa*. Hochegger, p. 163.

Regret Hand(s) raised to side of head, palm resting on cheek or side of head. *Colombia; U.S.* Saitz and Cervenka, p. 101.

Reminder Scratching one's head. Anc. *Rome;* 19th cent. Naples, southern *Italy*. De Jorio, p. 123. * Putting right hand on someone's head, turning his ear with the left. Arab. Goldziher, "Über Gebärden," p. 377.

Request Striking one's bare head with the flat hand—signal to someone to take his hat off. *Netherlands*. Andrea and de Boer, p. 95.

Rest Sitting or recumbent person supports laterally inclined head with hand; elbow of supporting arm does not necessarily need to rest on anything. If the person has eyes closed, it may indicate *permission* to rest, or that the person is not informed of surrounding occurrences; if eyes are open—person is guilty of inaction. Arm not serving as support may remain motionless or it may push hand under supporting arm, in which case it is a "speaking"—gesture in medieval art. Medieval *Germany*. *Sachsenspiegel*. Amira, "Handgebärden," pp. 233–34. Laterally inclined head resting on palm of hand indicates desire to take a nap. *Netherlands*. Andrea and de Boer, p. 41. * Both hands flat, palm to palm, held against cheek of laterally inclined head: "I'm sleepy." "It's bedtime." *Russia*. Monahan, pp. 118–19.

Reverence "[The priest] then joins his hands and inclines his head to the Crucifix at the sacred Name with which the blessing ends." Roman Catholic. *Mass*, p. 51. Hands placed palm to palm and held in front of head. Yoga. Ohm, p. 236.

Self-reproach "But on the picket line Bob Busby had pointed out to her that the Shadow Scheme was official University business and that she would be strike-breaking if she kept her appointment. Of course it was and of course she would! *Stupida!* She punched her head with her fist in self-reproach." *England*. Lodge, *Nice Work*, p. 110. "He thumped his head with his own fists as if to knock some sense into it, or the nonsense out of it." *England*. Lodge, *Nice Work*, p. 226.

Sexuality Left hand raised to level of head, palm out, index of right hand inserted between thumb and index of the left. *Central Africa*. Hochegger, p. 193.

Sick Right hand at waist, head inclined forward. *Central Africa.* Hochegger, p. 70.

Silence " 'Hush!' said Mrs. Maylie, laying her hand on Oliver's head." 19th cent. *England.* Dickens, *Oliver Twist*, p. 298.

Snobbishness One hand raised, palm facing away from gesturer, head tilted, eyes half closed, lips pursed. *U.S.* Saitz and Cervenka, p. 128.

Sorcerer Right hand passes over hair on right side of head from front to back, indicating that person referred to is sorcerer. *Central Africa.* Hochegger, p. 197.

Sorrow Hands hitting head. Men. *Anc. Greece.* Sittl, p. 25. * Supporting head by hand. Ritual legal gesture. 12th cent. *Germany.* Hartman v. Aue, *Gregorius* 448–50. Wells, p. 167 and n. 37. * Both hands placed against cheeks, supporting head: "What misery!" *Central Africa.* Hochegger, p. 32. * Both hands placed on head. *Central Africa.* Hochegger, p. 205. * "What dost thou mean by shaking of thy head? Why dost thou look so sadly on my son?" 16th-17th cent. *England.* Shakesp., *King John* 3.1.19. * Applying the hand passionately to the head. Biblical. *Middle East. Jer.* 2:37; Bulwer, p. 71. * Cutting one's hair. Biblical. *Middle East.* Boggs, p. 319. * Strewing face and head with dust and mud. *Middle East.* Boggs, p. 319. Strewing ashes on one's head. Biblical. *Middle East.* Ohm, p. 231. *See* Mourning. * Hands placed on head strewn with dust. Ibid. * Covering head. *Anc. Greece.* Homer, *Odyss.*, Bk. viii. *

Submission Kissing right hand of superior and placing it on one's own head. Arab. Goldziher, "Über Gebärden," p. 370.

Surprise Hitting side of one's face with palm of hand, head tilted slightly to one side and eyes opened wide. *Lebanon; Libya; Jordan; Saudi Arabia; Syria.* Barakat, no. 2. Gesture which keeps sun out of one's eyes, flat hand, palm down, laid against forehead—surprise at seeing someone whom one did not expect to see. *Netherlands.* Andrea and de Boer, p. 28.

Surrender Hands held at shoulder level, palms forward, head turned slightly to one side. *Libya; Lebanon; Saudi Arabia; Jordan.* Barakat, no. 104.

Thief Right hand at shoulder level, fingertips joined, pointing, moving rapidly backward and forward; head is then rapidly turned aside: "Au voleur!" ("Stop, thief!") *Central Africa.* Hochegger, p. 212.

Uncertainty Scratching head. 16th cent. *Netherlands;* 17th cent. *England.* Bulwer, pp. 71–72.

Victory Hands clasped above the head. College students. California, *U.S.* McCord, p. 290. * Victorious warrior who pardons enemy places his agal (ropelike circle of head-piece) over head of person pardoned—vanquished person belongs to victorious warrior together with all he owns. *Iraq; Kuwait; Saudi Arabia.* Barakat, no. 175. *See also* HAND, Victory.

Warning   Flat right hand, palm down, thumb folded under, placed against forehead just above the eyes: "Be careful!" *Russia.* Monahan, pp. 94–95.

HAND, HEAD, KNEE

Prayer   Kneeling, face buried in hands. Late medieval *Austria.* Michael Pacher, *Prayer of St. Wolfgang* (ca. 1483). Lower Belvedere, Vienna.

Sorrow   Head laid upon knees which are held by folded hands, in sitting or squatting position. Anc. *Greece* and *Rome.* Sittl, p. 24. "a girl throws herself upon her knees, tears her clothes and tears out her hair." Boggs, p. 319.

HAND, HEAD, MOUTH

Sick   Head cradled in right hand, mouth slightly open. *Central Africa.* Hochegger, p. 110.

Sorrow   Head raised, hands extended forward and upward, palm to palm, and repeatedly brought back to the mouth and extended forward again: "Ma mère est morte!" ("My mother has died!") *Central Africa.* Hochegger, p. 121.

HAND, HEAD, SHOULDER

Uncertainty   Head is cocked to the right, shoulders shrugged, right hand raised, thumb extended away from the body, lips puckered, eyebrows arched. "Ca . . . [prrrp!] je n'en sais trop rien!" ("Oh that . . . I don't know much about it!") Characteristically French is sudden explosion of air between the lips, causing them to vibrate. Tongue not involved as in American "raspberry." *France.* Brault, p. 380.

HAND, HIP

Authority   Arms akimbo: one or both hands placed on hip(s), chest out, head held high—typical in portrayals of generals and heroes. Anc. *Rome*; 19th cent. Naples, southern *Italy.* De Jorio, p. 199. "In many cultures, this stance signals aggression, resistance, impatience or . . . anger." Axtell, *Gestures*, p. 79. *See* Challenge; ARM, HAND, Defiance; ARM, HEAD, Defiance. On arms akimbo as warrior's gesture, see the illustrations in H. Fischer, "Die kosmurgische Symbolik," and the references in H. Fischer, "Indogermanischer Kriegeryoga," n. 6. For the gesture as indicating boldness and control in Renaissance art, see Spicer, pp. 84–128.

Challenge   Hands on hips (arms akimbo). *Indonesia; Lat. Am.* Axtell, *Gestures*, p. 96. *See* ARM, HAND, Defiance; ARM, HEAD, Defiance.

Defiance *See* ARM, HAND, Defiance; ARM, HEAD, Defiance.

Emphasis One or both hands placed on hips while speaking. Particularly women. 19th cent. *France; Italy.* Sittl, p. 49.

Interrogation "The servant girl, . . . hands on hips, lifted her chin asking what he wanted." *Argentina.* Weyland, p. 24.

Oath Servant swears to his master, son to his father, putting his hand under his thigh. Biblical. *Middle East. Gen.* 24:2–9; 47:29. Also medieval *Germany. Reinke de Vos*, 2171; Grimm, *DRA*, II, p. 551.

Poverty Open hand, palm down, strikes sideways against the belt or waist. *Argentina.* Kany, p. 89.

Readiness Hand on hip. Bogomil grave. 13th-14th cent. *Yugoslavia.* H. Fischer, "Die kosmurgische Symbolik," p. 105.

HAND, JAW, LIP

Cruelty Fists clenched, biting of the upper lip, forcing the lower jaw forward. *Europe; North America.* Aubert, p. 120.

Hatred *See* Cruelty above.

HAND, KNEE

Anger Folded hands pressed around knee, while sitting. Anc. *Greece* and *Rome.* Sittl, p. 23.

Begging "for I was essaying to speak, and had, as soon as she took her dear cheeks from mine, dropt down on my knees, my hands clasped, and lifted up in a supplicating manner." 18th cent. *England.* Richardson, I, p. 100.

Calmness Hands clasped around knee while sitting. Anc. *Rome; Spain;* Grimm, *DRA*, II, p. 375, n. 2.

Commendation Wall painting in the Tour Ferrande at Pernes, *France*, shows Charles of Anjou's enfeoffment with Kingdom of Sicily by Clement IV. King with hands joined kneels before pope. 13th cent. *France.* Ladner, p. 259. *See also* HAND, Commendation.

Despair Folded hands pressed around someone's knee. Anc. *Greece* and *Rome.* Sittl, p. 23.

Emphasis "accompanied this last sentiment with an emphatic slap on each knee." 19th cent. *England.* Dickens, *Pickwick*, II, p. 172.

Farewell Handclasp while person remaining behind kneels. Medieval *France.* Ms. Harl. 43801, fol. 149 in Coulton, p. 98; also fol. 172b in Coulton, p. 109.

Gratitude Touching of knees. Late antiquity. Sittl, p. 164. " 'You have given me life, Madam, said I, clasping my uplifted hands together, and falling on one knee." 18th cent. *England.* Richardson, I, p. 138. *

Falling upon one's knees and clapping hands. Protestant women. *Africa.* Ohm, p. 287.

Greeting Priest before ancestor's shrine clapped his hands while bending knees, as greeting of the god. Inamwanga, *Tanganyika.* Ohm, p. 283. * Grasping a person by the knee. Anc. *Greece.* Ohm, p. 240. Handclasp kneeling. Medieval *France.* Miniature of Meeting of the King of France and the Duke of Brittany at Tours, Ms. Harley 4379, fol. 135b in Coulton, p. 37. See also Ms. Harley 4380, fol. 40 in Coulton, p. 37 and pl. vi. * Right knee bent, left hand placed on left knee, right elbow and shoulder turned toward the tribal chief. *Central Africa.* Hochegger, p. 177. *See also* ARM, KNEE, Gratitude.

Laziness Clasping one's knees with both hands, head between them. 13th-14th cent. *Italy.* Dante, *Purg.*, c. iv.

Luck On seeing three priests or three blacks, a girl will scratch her knee which will bring her luck in finding a husband soon. *Colombia.* Saitz and Cervenka, p. 83.

Oath "The hero knelt before the maiden. . . . Then she took, in her white hand, the oath of loyalty from him." 13th cent. *Germany.* Wolfr. v. Eschenbach, v, 276.

Plea One hand grasps someone's knees; performed kneeling. Anc. *Greece.* Sittl, pp. 163–64. "She clasped his knees and begged for the love of God that he would have compassion, etc." 18th cent. *England.* Smollett, *Peregrine Pickle*, I, ch. vi. Supplicant touches or embraces one or both knees of the person with whom he pleads. If one hand is free, it is raised in supplication. Anc. *Greece.* Sittl, p. 282. Kneeling on both knees or on one (right) knee, hands extended, or one hand extended. Anc. *Greece;* anc. *Persia.* Sittl, p. 157, fig. 13. Kneeling while both hands, palms up, are extended to the front. *Central Africa.* Hochegger, p. 92. A son kneels while both his hands touch his father's knees in asking forgiveness from him. *Central Africa.* Ibid., p. 93. One knee and the back of the left hand touch the ground. *Central Africa.* Ibid. " 'Admit it,' he said, 'you love the Führer.' 'What nonsense,' I cried, 'Hitler is a phenomenon that I admire, not a man to fall in love with.' Now Goebbels lost control. 'You must be my mistress . . .' He actually knelt down in front of me and began to sob . . . I felt quite stunned at the sight of Goebbels on his knees, but then, when he grabbed my ankles, it was too much for me' " *Germany.* Kanfer, p. 48. *See also* BEARD, HAND, Plea; HAND, Plea.

Prayer Genuflecting, upper body resting on heels, hands stretched upward toward deity. Anc. *Egypt.* Ohm, p. 358. Genuflecting, hands raised, palms outward, elbows slightly bent. Anc. *Egypt.* Brunet, pl. 174. * "The knight fell doune upon his kne, vnderneth an olyve tre, and helde up both his handes." 15th cent. *England. Syr Isenbras*, I, p. 79. Portrait of Gregory X (1271–1276) on the scapular which he wore around his neck in the sepulcher shows him kneeling with hands joined. Ladner, pp. 253–54. The Franciscan Pope Nicholas IV (1288–1292) is shown in mosaics in S. Giovanni in Laterano and S. Maria Maggiore in Rome kneeling and praying with joined hands. Ladner, p. 255. "The portraits of Benedict XI and John XXII bring to an end, as far as the Middle Ages are concerned, the series of images of popes who kneel in prayer with hands joined and, almost without exception, wear the tiara, the symbol of their plenitude of power. The combination of the symbolisms of supreme authority and tiara—and of surrender to God—younger prayer gesture—should be noted." Ladner, p. 257. * Kneeling on right knee, hands palm to palm. *Très Riches Heures*, pl. 35. * Right knee on the ground, hands extended toward deity. Buddhist. Ohm, p. 247. * Squatting, elbows supported on knees, raised hands rubbing one another. Advisor to a Safwa king. Ohm, p. 287. *See also* ARM, HAND, Prayer.

Reminder "now and then he knocks upon his knee with his fist" 19th cent. *Palestine*. Bauer, p. 224.

Reverence "She dipped her hand in the font by the entrance, crossed herself, and went on to the main aisle, where she knelt on both knees and was still for a moment. *U.S.* Boucher, p. 206.

Shame "I fell upon my knees and spread my hands." Biblical. *Middle East*. *Ezra* 9:5.

Submission Subject of King Savang Vatthana greets him by kneeling on right knee while holding hands palm to palm before his lowered head. King has hands extended before him palms up, hands close together, as if in request to his subject to rise. *Laos*. UPI Telephoto, *L.A. Times*, Feb. 26, 1963, p. 4. Subject greets King Savang Vatthana by kneeling on one knee while right hand is extended in handclasp with right hand of king. *Laos*. Ibid. Laying joined hands into hands of an overlord while kneeling. Illustr. in 12th cent. Regestum of Tivoli. Ladner, p. 258, n. 34. *See also* HAND, Commendation.

Sympathy "Hagen bent over to his friend and patted him on his knobby knee." *U.S.* Nabokov, p. 168.

HAND, KNEE, LIP

Homage *See* HAND, Homage.

Plea Kneeling while kissing hand and with left hand touching knee of recipient of the supplication. Anc. *Greece* and *Rome*. Sittl, p. 169. Servants and supplicants kneel when kissing hand. Anc. *Greece* and *Rome*. Sittl, ibid. The Romans congratulated Nero upon his discovery of the Pisonian plot by kneeling and kissing his hand. Sittl, ibid.

HAND, LEG

Authority Seal of Pribizlaw von Richenberg, 1249, shows him seated bareheaded with crossed legs, the flat left hand extended, the right holding the sword over the knees; also the seal of Count Egino IV of Urach, 1228, who is also seated bareheaded with crossed legs, the right arm resting on the knee, the left hand raised in front of his chest, palm outwards. Medieval *Germany*. Amira, "Handgebärden," p. 197.

Cold Hands, palm against palm, placed between legs. *Central Africa*. Hochegger, p. 78.

Judgment Judge signifies his function by placing right lower leg horizontally over left knee and left hand to middle of chest. *Germany*. Freiburg Cathedral. Schmidt, I, pl. 70; cf. Grimm, *DRA*, II p. 375.

Plea Supplicant touches (embraces) lower parts (knees, ankles) of someone's leg(s) while he himself is kneeling. Anc. *Greece* and *Rome*. Sittl, pp. 164–65; cf. also the official formula of victory of the kings of *Assyria*. Hommel, pp. 725–26.

Reverence Mosaic at St. Peter's in Rome shows Innocent III (1198-1216) with slightly bent knees, arms and hands extended but not joined. Moderate proskynesis. Common in medieval art. *Italy*. Ladner, p. 249.

Surprise " 'It is him!' exclaimed Sam; and having established Job's identity beyond a doubt, he smote his leg." 19th cent. *England*. Dickens, *Pickwick*, II, p. 293.

HAND, LIP

Admiration Fingertips of right hand united and brought to the lips. To show greater admiration, nails of the three united fingertips are kissed and opened hand is quickly drawn back from the lips. *Spain*. Flachskampf, p. 221.

Adoration Kissing the hand of a woman as modest request—not gallantry! Anc. *Greece*. Sittl, p. 166.

Affection Two lovers kiss one another's hands. Anc. *Greece*. Sittl, p. 104. * Pressing someone's hand to the lips or gently pressing the hand as an expression of affection. 19th cent. *England*. Dickens, *Pickwick*, I, pp. 104, 118, 119; II, pp. 241, 277. Kissing someone's hands and lips. *Germany*. DWb, IV/2, col. 332. "And Joab took Amasa by the beard with the right hand to kiss him." Biblical. *Middle East*. II *Sam*. 20:9. Kissing of the hand, lips and eyes as a sign of affection caused by joy or sorrow. Medieval *Germany*. Hartmann v. Aue, *Gregorius* 7978. * Kissing palm of own hand, then extending hand. Used when gesticulator and referent are at some distance from one another. *Colombia*. Saitz and Cervenka, p. 79. * Joined fingers are kissed, hand is opened, palm upward, at level of mouth, and the imaginary kiss is blown toward the person intended. Limited to women. Río de la Plata region of *Argentina; Uruguay*. Meo Zilio, p. 109. Joined fingers of both hands are kissed, then arms extended to both sides. Observed in actresses and boxers. Río de la Plata region of *Argentina; Uruguay*. Ibid.

Applause Clapping hands together and whistling as sign of approval. *U.S.* Whistling is a sign of derision in a situation in which one would normally applaud in much of Europe. Axtell, *Gestures*, p. 15.

Congratulation   Kissing the hand. Before Alexander this was appropriate only to slaves. Anc. *Greece.* Sittl, p. 166.

Derision   *See* Applause, above.

Despair   "wrung his hands in secret, gnawed his nether lip, and turned yellow with despair." 18th cent. *England.* Smollett, *Roderick Random*, ch. lii.

Disappointment   Arms thrown back, corners of mouth pulled down, lips open as if to curse. *Spain.* Flachskampf, p. 228.

Etiquette   "a compliment which Mr. Pickwick returned by kissing his hand to the lady." 19th cent. *England.* Dickens, *Pickwick*, I, p. 210.

Gratitude   Kissing someone's hand. Anc. *Greece* and *Rome.* Sittl, pp. 167, 168, n. 7, 169. Before Alexander this was appropriate only to slaves. Sittl, p. 166. * Kissing the back of the right hand, then raising it, palm up. *Lebanon; Saudi Arabia; Syria.* Barakat, no. 111. Same gesture, accompanied by raising eyes simultaneously. *Saudi Arabia.* Barakat, no. 84. Servant kisses right hand of master and puts it on his own hand. *Asia.* Petermann, I, p. 172.

Greeting   "You told me you salute not at the court, but you kiss your hands; that courtesy would be uncleanly if courtiers were shepherds." 16th-17th cent. *England.* Shakesp., *As You Like It* 3.2.43–45. "Let them curtsy with their left legs, and not presume to touch a hair of my master's horse-tail till they kiss their hands." 16th-17th cent. *England.* Shakesp., *Shrew* 4.1.80–82. From end of 16th cent. the handkiss became obligatory as greeting of older persons or social superiors. Peasants kissed their lords' hands and those of their lords' relatives, including their children. In 17th and 18th centuries, petty nobles kissed hands of their magnates, which was unheard of before. One also kissed women's hands, whether married or not. The glove was removed first, since it was considered impolite to extend covered hand for a kiss, and hand should be extended sufficiently high for a man to raise it to his lips. Albrycht St. Radziwill recalls that in 1644 King Ladislaus IV Vasa, displeased with citizens of Cracow, extended his hand covered for them to kiss. One of the municipal representatives, confused by the gesture, bent his knee three times before the king. When he decided to kiss the King's gloved hand, the King removed the glove. In 1646, Queen Louise Mary Gonzaga extended gloved hand to Gerhard Denhoff, a Pomeranian dignitary, who, much distressed, kissed her glove. The practice of kissing a lady's hand has survived until well into 20th century, and old men still greet a lady with the expression: "I kiss your hand," or even "I fall at your feet." *Poland.* Bogucka, p. 195. [Editors' note: The expression "I kiss your hand, ma'am" ("Küss' die Hand, gnä' Frau") is still a greeting used by older men, or humorously, in *Austria*.] Man kisses hand of woman. *Hungary*. Revesz, "Die Psychologie," p. 146. * "at last, one day . . . Nathaniel Pipkin had the temerity to kiss his hand to Maria Lobbs." 19th cent. *England*. Dickens, *Pickwick*, I, p. 281. * Kiss and handshake. Anc. *Rome*. Sittl, p. 79.

Hesitation *See* LIP, Hesitation.

Homage Following the Persian example, the Macedonians kissed the hand of their ruler on his deathbed. Anc. *Macedonia*. Sittl, p. 166. Defeated princes kiss the hand of the victor. Anc. *Greece* and *Rome*. Sittl, ibid. Alexandrians kiss Hadrian's hand. *Roman Empire*. Sittl, p. 169. The younger Maximinus extended his hand to be kissed at audiences but was criticized for it. *Roman Empire*. Sittl, p. 167. Clients kiss hand of patron (emperor) at the salutatio. *Roman Empire*. Sittl, p. 168. Gallienus, upon becoming consul, had his hands kissed by matrons. *Anc. Rome*. Sittl, p. 167, n. 6. Caligula and Domitian had their hands and feet kissed by noblemen, for which they were criticized. *Roman Empire*. Sittl, p. 167. At the opening and closing of the Polish General Diet in the 17th cent., the deputies, in procession, kissed the King's hand. To be excluded from this ceremony meant banishment from the community of the Polish gentry. Not to be permitted to kiss the King's hand generally meant banishment, as in the case of the Polish Arians, in 1658. 17th cent. *Poland*. Bogucka, p. 200. *See also* FOOT, HAND, LIP, Homage.

Humility Ecclesiastical officials received handkiss from subordinates. Roman Catholic. 19th cent. *Hungary*. Revesz, "Die Psychologie," p. 147.

Mercy Defeated princes kiss hands of victor in request for mercy. Anc. *Greece* and *Rome*. Sittl, p. 166.

Mourning Hand is kissed, then held out toward grave. Anc. *Greece*. Sittl, p. 74.

Pettiness Thumb and index grasp lips, then are removed from them and simultaneously opened. *Spain*. Flachskampf, p. 233.

Plea Clients kiss hand of patron (emperor) at the salutatio. Anc. *Rome*. Sittl, p. 168. Kissing the hand. Before Alexander this was appropriate only to slaves. Anc. *Greece* and *Rome*. Sittl, p. 166. Supplicant for an office or patronage at the disposal of noblemen or chamberlain kisses their hands. Anc. *Greece* and *Rome*. Sittl, p. 168. Kissing the back of a dignitary's hand in plea for mercy. *Saudi Arabia*. Barakat, no. 122.

Prayer Kissing hand toward astral deities (blowing a kiss), such as Helios, etc. Anc. *Greece* and *Rome*. Heiler, p. 104. Cf. *Job* 31:27; also *Peru*. Heiler, ibid. "Odysseus was gladdened then, rejoicing in the sight of his country, and kissed the graingiving ground, then raised his hands in the air and spoke to the nymphs" Homer, *Odyss.*, xiii. "If my mouth hath kissed my hand." Biblical. *Middle East*. *Job* 31:27. * Blowing a kiss toward crucifixes and sacred images. Rural Swabia, *Germany;* Styria, *Austria*. Heiler, p. 104; R. Fischer, p. 242. *See also* HAND, Prayer.

Regret Flat hand, fingers closed, tips of index and middle finger touching lips—regret at something the signaller said. *Netherlands*. Andrea and de Boer, p. 98.

Request Hand horizontal before face, index and middle finger extended and slightly apart, lips pursed—request for a cigarette. *Netherlands*. Andrea and de Boer, p. 97.

Respect Ecclesiastical officials have their hands kissed by subordinates. 19th cent. *Hungary*. Revesz, "Die Psychologie," p. 147. Soldiers kiss hand of departing general. Anc. *Rome*. Sittl, p. 169. 16th-17th cent. *England*. "Humbly kiss your hand." Shakesp., III *Henry VI* 3.3.61. "I kiss his conquering hand." 16th-17th cent. *England*. Shakesp., *Anth. and Cleo.* 3.13.75. * Kissing nose and then the right hand of a dignitary. *Saudi Arabia*. Barakat, no. 135.

Submission Bowing deeply and kissing someone's hand. *Roman Empire*. Sittl, pp. 166, 167, n. 5.

HAND, MOUSTACHE

Pleasure Twirling moustache. 16th-17th cent. *Poland*. Bogucka, p. 196.

HAND, MOUTH

Apology Suddenly placing a hand over one's mouth is tantamount to an apology for something one has said. *Netherlands*. Andrea and de Boer, p. 168.

Apotropy Making the sign of the cross over one's open mouth while yawning. *Euagrii capita* 66; Sittl, p. 127. *Spain*. Flachskampf, p. 243. Women to children. 19th cent. Bavaria, *Germany*. Sittl, p. 127, n. 6. * Blowing into face of convert and making sign of the cross on his forehead to exorcise evil spirits. Early Christian. Duchesne, p. 296. * Placing thumb side of fist over mouth, then twisting hand a half-turn—threat to jinn. Women. *Saudi Arabia*. Barakat, no. 226. *See also* HAND, Apotropy.

Appreciation (of a meal) Picking teeth with toothpick in public. *Italy; Asia*. In Asia the other hand covers the mouth. Axtell, *Gestures*, p. 75.

Astonishment " 'What made you decide to be a witch, love?' The girl's hand went to her mouth, a completely natural example of a classic gesture." *U.S.* Hill, p. 146. * Open right hand taps lightly on the open mouth. *Central Africa*. Hochegger, p. 67. *See* Surprise.

Boredom   Hands placed at the back of the head while one stretches and yawns. *Central Africa*. Hochegger, p. 63.

Depart   *See* HAND, Depart.

Disagreement   Right hand open, placed on mouth, then brought forward until arm is extended in the direction of person with whom gesturer is speaking: "I'm not going to say anything any more! You're talking nonsense!" *Central Africa*. Hochegger, p. 53.

Disappointment   Right hand makes rapid movement from right to left in front of mouth as if waving something off, or a fanlike folding inward of the fingers. *Spain*. Flachskampf, p. 235.

Discretion   Hand put to mouth, walking on toes. Anc. *Rome*. Baden, p. 450.

Dismay   Hand covers mouth. *Netherlands*. Andrea and de Boer, p. 114.

Drink   Right hand closed, thumb raised and moved to the mouth in the manner of a spigot. *Spain*. Flachskampf, p. 227; Green, pp. 58–59: Fingers either held tightly clenched or extended at right angles to the thumb. Can also indicate drunkenness. Right thumb and small finger extended, other fingers folded into palm, the hand is moved toward the mouth several times. *Lat. Am.* Kany, p. 82. * Hand held to mouth as if grasping a glass or bottle. Southern *Italy*. Efron, p. 149. Schoolchildren. *U.S.* Seton, p. xxiiv. * Putting cupped hand to the mouth. *Germany*. *HDV*, I, col. 321.

Eating   Fingers of right hand curved, tips joined and repeatedly moved to the mouth. *Spain*. Flachskampf, p. 227; also *Lat. Am.* Green, pp. 57–58. Green comments that Kaulfers, failing to distinguish between Spanish and Latin American gestures, writes that "hunger, or the desire for food, is often indicated by a tapping of the lower lip with the tip of the semi-clenched index finger of the right hand." * Right hand, closed, imitates pulling an object from the mouth to the right. "On a de la viande!" ("We have food/meat!") *Central Africa*. Hochegger, p. 209.

Embarrassment   "He continued to blush easily even after he was no longer fearful and tense, covering his blushes with a deprecatory smile and the placing of the fingers of one hand over his mouth, in that universal gesture of embarrassment." Native American, California, *U.S.* T. Kroeber, pp. 124–25.

Enthusiasm   Hands raised, fingers extended, mouth often open. Usually female, often accompanied by intake of breath. *Colombia; U.S.* Saitz and Cervenka, p. 49.

Excitement   Open hand covers mouth. Often in context of impending danger. *Colombia; U.S.* Saitz and Cervenka, p. 50.

Failure   A reaction to failure is the covering of the mouth with the right hand. *Central Africa*. Hochegger, p. 59.

Fatigue   Fingers extended, tapping open mouth lightly and repeatedly. Impolite in formal social context. *Colombia; U.S.* Saitz and Cervenka, p. 125.

Finished Blowing over the back of the hand. 19th cent. Naples, southern *Italy*. de Jorio, p. 231f.

Foolishness "If thou hast done foolishly in lifting up thyself, or if thou hast thought evil, lay thy hand upon thy mouth." Biblical. *Middle East. Prov.* 30:32.

Forgetfulness Left hand placed on mouth, while right hand is agitated in air: "I forgot it!" *Central Africa*. Hochegger, p. 114.

Frustration Biting the palm (ball) of the hand. 19th cent. *Palestine*. Bauer, p. 218.

Greeting Raising right hand, so that palm remains positioned toward face, hand returned to mouth, kissing fingertips and then throwing kiss toward divine image. Anc. *Greece* and *Rome*. Baumeister, I, p. 592. * Grasping one or both hands of someone and occasionally kissing them. 19th cent. *Palestine*. Bauer, p. 171. Between mother and son after long absence: mother rises slightly from seat, extends hands, which are placed together, toward son, who places his hands (also joined) into hers and she kisses the back of his right hand. *Africa*. Ohm, pp. 209–10.

Hot Hand, fingers extended, palm down or facing mouth, moves up and down in front of open mouth. Refers to hot or spicy food. *U.S.* Rare in *Colombia*. Saitz and Cervenka, p. 71.

Incredulity Mouth open, lips pushed forward, right hand forward and rapidly raised from the wrist: "Mensonges!" ("Lies!") *Central Africa*. Hochegger, p. 95. * Both hands, palm down, raised to shoulder height and flipped forward from the wrist, mouth pointed in the direction of the person to whom one is speaking: "Des mensonges, va t'en!" ("Just lies, get on with you!") *Central Africa*. Ibid., p. 95.

Insult Hands joined palm to palm, but slightly opened in the middle, in front of mouth: "Sexe de ta mère!" ("Your mother's pudendum!") *Central Africa*. Hochegger, p. 189.

Magical When a corpse was burned, the priest pretended to catch its soul in his hands, then gave the soul to the dead man's successor by throwing his hands toward him and blowing upon him. Tabilis or Carrier Indians, *British Columbia*. Frazer, *Golden Bough*, IV, p. 199.

Mockery Index of left hand in smiling mouth, right hand vertical with fingers outstretched, palm outward, forearm slightly raised. 16th cent. *Germany*. Brant, woodcut, p. 70. * Hand put over mouth while throwing waggish glances at someone. Little girls. *France*. Mitton, p. 145. Hand placed over mouth, implying a toothless mouth. *Central Africa*. Hochegger, p. 49. * While laughing, gesturer taps his mouth with open right hand. *Central Africa*. Ibid., p. 120.

Negation Blowing between the hands. Arab. Goldziher, "Über Gebärden," p. 379.

Pensiveness Right hand, thumb extended to the side, placed over mouth. *Central Africa.* Hochegger, p. 146.

Prayer Laying hand or finger on mouth. *Sumeria.* Ohm, p. 288.

Regret Hand clapped over mouth quickly. *Colombia; U.S.* Saitz and Cervenka, p. 102.

Respect Kissing someone's hand. Children to fathers, believers to prophet. Anc. *Greece* and *Rome.* Sittl, p. 168. Kissing the hand of Christian priests. Early Christian. Sittl, p. 168. * Placing hand over mouth in maintaining respectful silence. *Brazil.* Probably originated in anc. *Rome*; cf. Pliny the Elder: "In adorando dextram ad osculum" ("Right hand to mouth out of respect"); Samuel Pitiscus: "Ils portaient aussi la main à leur bouche, d'où vient le mot d'adoration" ("They also put their hand to their mouth, from which issued their adoration"). Cascudo, *História*, pp. 39–40.

Secrecy *See* HAND, Secrecy.

Silence Laying hand on mouth. Biblical. *Middle East. Job* 29:9; *Germany. DWb*, IV/2, col. 335. Anc. *Greece* and *Rome.* Sittl, pp. 213–14; Medieval German. *Sachsenspiegel.* Amira, "Handgebärden," p. 235. Gesture imitates action of sewing lips shut. Derives from medieval European magical practice of placing food chewed by person one wants to silence into mouth of toad, which is then sewn shut. Medieval *Europe.* Cascudo, *História*, p. 116.

Sorrow Mourning widow crouches before mummy of husband, her right hand placed over her head, lips pressed against mummy. Mourning widow and daughter, one standing, one kneeling, before a mummy. Both have their right hands raised above their heads, left hands on mummy. Anc. *Egypt.* Dawson, pp. 86–87.

Speech Right hand, palm inward, in front of mouth, moved as if drawing words out of the mouth: "Ils bavardent beaucoup!" ("They chatter a lot!") * Right hand, slightly closed, in front of closed mouth, moved as if turning a key: "Cessez de parler!" ("Shut up!") *Central Africa.* Hochegger, p. 141.

Submission Kissing the back of someone's hand. Anc. *Rome.* Bulwer, pp. 97–104.

Surprise Hand somewhat cupped or straight, placed on mouth. Anc. *Greece* and *Rome.* Sittl, p. 272. * Mouth open, open hands move up and down in front of chest. *Central Africa.* Hochegger, p. 199. *See also* Astonishment above.

Warning Left hand points at a person, right hand taps lightly on the mouth, from which the cry "au voleur!" ("Stop, thief!") escapes. *Central Africa.* Hochegger, p. 211.

HAND, MOUTH, TONGUE

Revulsion Flat hand at the throat, mouth open, tongue sticking out. *Netherlands.* Andrea and de Boer, p. 131.

Secrecy Tongue extruded, moves rapidly from left to right, while one hand hides the gesture from a third party: "Ne rien dire!" ("Not a word about this!") *Central Africa.* Hochegger, p. 182.

HAND, MOUTH, TONGUE, TOOTH

Calmness Flip hand near mouth and simultaneously make a clicking sound with tongue and teeth: to indicate that a person is not to worry. *Saudi Arabia.* Barakat, no. 196.

HAND, NECK

Cold Both hands placed on nape of the neck indicates that the gesturer is either sick or cold. *Central Africa.* Hochegger, p. 111. * Open right hand passes several times up and down the throat: "La boisson est froide!" ("The drink is cold!") *Central Africa.* Hochegger, p. 202.

Compulsion Simulation of being pulled by the neck. Depiction of prisoners led by ropes around necks. Bas relief carved in mountain documenting victory of Darius over the nine rebellious sovereigns. Behistum, *Kurdistan.* Cascudo, *História,* p. 87.

Death Drawing edge of hand across throat, head inclined. *Spain.* Alas, *Las dos cajas,* p. 273. As hand, palm down, is drawn across throat, it is swung inward, so that fingertips point toward throat. *Netherlands.* Andrea and de Boer, p. 37. Gesture is not well known among Flemish speakers, who associate it with the meaning "I've got it up to here!" *Flanders.* Ibid., p. 188. *See* Surfeit. * Drawing swordblade quickly across one's throat and clasping hands to show the execution was completed. Decapitation. Damascus, *Syria.* Goldziher, "Über Gebärden," p. 371. "an elderly Polish man approached one of the cast's Israeli actors in his hotel bar, and asked if he was Jewish. When he was told yes, the old man insultingly drew his finger across his throat, then pulled his fist up behind his neck to indicate a noose." *Poland.* Gritten, p. 70. * The death of an animal is indicated by the right hand grasping the throat and turning slightly to the left. *Central Africa.* Hochegger, p. 122.

Despair Hand grasps throat, eyes closed. ("I'm fed up with everything.") *Italy.* Graham, p. 26. *See* Surfeit. * Hand makes motion of winding rope around neck, then it is raised above head, making a tugging motion. *Russia.* Monahan, p. 30. * Flat hand, palm down, is drawn across neck below chin: "All is lost!" *Russia.* Monahan, pp. 122–23.

Disbelief "You simply half-close the eyes and place your hand on your cravat, or where your cravat would be if you wore a cravat." WW II. *France.* Alsop, p. 26. * Index moves lightly up and down throat several times. Often accompanied by widening of lips. *Colombia.* Saitz and Cervenka, p. 39. * Hand cupped, palm up, at neck ca. 6 in. below chin. Not usually used directly in front of the speaker who is disbelieved. *Colombia.* Saitz and Cervenka, ibid.

Disgust   Hand, palm down, placed across throat. Reported 1970 as not very common among young adults in U.S. *Colombia; U.S.* Saitz and Cervenka, p. 43. *See also* Surfeit.

Drink   Fingertips of right hand, palm inward, scratch Adam's apple—"I'm thirsty." *Central Africa.* Hochegger, p. 25.

Finished   Hitting side of one's neck with right hand. Hadhramaut. *Yemen.* Barakat, no. 184. * The edge of the flat right hand, palm down, strikes the back of one's neck, or, with the edge of the thumb-side, the front of the neck at the side of the Adam's apple: "Heads will roll," or "heads have rolled." *Russia.* Monahan, pp. 90–91.

Homosexuality   Tapping one's neck with the right hand. *Lebanon.* Barakat, no. 56.

Imprisonment   Right hand grasps throat. *Central Africa.* Hochegger, p. 62.

Invitation   Rubbing the back of one's neck with palm of right hand—one would like to meet the woman to whom gesture is made. *Lebanon.* Barakat, no. 51.

Jail   One hand grasps throat. *Colombia.* Saitz and Cervenka, p. 74.

Oath   Both hands flat, extended forward, little fingers together, then folded as if in prayer, then two fingers crossed and one slid across throat. Children. *England.* Opie, p. 124. *See also* FINGER, NECK, Oath.

Sick   Both hands placed on nape of neck. *Central Africa.* Hochegger, p. 109.

Sorrow   Both hands placed on nape of neck. *Central Africa.* Hochegger, p. 205.

Subjection   The so-called combative greeting ("kämpflicher Gruß") in some Germanic laws consisted in grasping opponent by throat, collar or lapels without violence until the judge permits his release. Medieval *Germany. Sachsenspiegel.* Amira, "Handgebärden," pp. 248–49. The *Freiberger Stadtrecht* requires that the "greeting" be carried out by grasping the opponent's "uppermost clothing" with two fingers. Medieval *Germany.* Amira, ibid. p. 249. * In taking possession of, or responsibility for an unfree person, the master strikes him on the neck with the flat hand, sometimes while holding him by the arm or the shoulder. Similarly, acceptance of unfree status is accompanied by being touched on the neck by the new master. Medieval *Germany.* Amira, ibid., p. 249.

Surfeit   Flat right hand, palm down, held against neck under chin for a second or two signifies either physical satiety, as after generous meal, or simply "I'm sick of it!" "I've got it up to here!" *Russia.* Monahan, pp. 112–13. * Flat hand, palm down, moved across neck under chin: "I've got it up to here!" *Flanders.* Andrea and de Boer, pp. 37

and 188 under "Koppie kleiner." Moving flat hand, palm down, across neck from ear to ear. *Russia.* Monahan, pp. 114–15.

Surprise Left hand hooked around neck, left elbow projecting forward and forearm parallel to and touching left side of face. *Spain.* Kaulfers, p. 253.

Threat Stiff right index rubbed across throat, head tilted back slightly. Usually finger is moved from left to right with a squeaking noise accompanying the gesture. Arab. Barakat, no. 91.

Warning Flat hand, palm down, is moved across neck from ear to ear: "They'll have my head for this!" *Russia.* Monahan, pp. 122–23. Hand placed to the side of the neck, fingertips under the collar, to indicate a warning against a lie or deception. Fig. 3. 19th cent. Naples, southern *Italy.* Wundt, I, p. 184, fig. 30 e.

Worry Tapping oneself on the base of the neck with the open hand two or three times: "It's sitting here on my neck." *Russia.* Monahan, pp. 84–85.

HAND, NOSE
Cleverness Tapping one side of the nose ("I am no fool.") Schoolchildren. *U.S.* Seton, p. xxii.

Concentration " 'How old is that horse, my friend?' enquired Mr. Pickwick, rubbing his nose with the shilling he had reserved for the fare" 19th cent. *England.* Dickens, I, p. 7.

Confusion Open right hand is placed vertically in front of face: "What to do?" *Central Africa.* Hochegger, p. 38.

Cunning " 'Mr. Warrington is in his apartment,' said the gentleman; 'but—' and here the gentleman winked at Mr. Draper, and laid his hand on his nose." 19th cent. *England.* Thackeray, *The Virginians*, I, p. 496.

Disbelief Laying right index on right side of nose: "I smell a rat." Schoolchildren. *U.S.* Seton, p. 115.

Disgust The nose is held while an imaginary lavatory chain is pulled. Children. *England.* Opie, p. 319. * "Placing the right hand upon the . . . nose, . . . then a downflinging gesture of the right hand ensues." WW II. *France.* Alsop, p. 28. * Holding the nose (closing nostrils by pressing between thumb and index) is common gesture on medieval representations of the Awakening of Lazarus; occurs rarely after 1590. Gospels of Otto III (10th cent.); van Ouwater, *de Opwekking van Lazarus* (1445–50); Lastman, *Opwekking* (1626–28); Guratzsch, II, pp. 205–08; van der Meulen, p. 24.

Flattery Hand twists tip of nose: "Brownnosing." *U.S.* Saitz and Cervenka, p. 53.

Friendship Touching tip of nose with back of right hand, simulta-

neously moving head back and forth as nose is touched. *Saudi Arabia.*
Barakat, no. 117.

Impatience " 'Just so,' interposed Perker, who had accompanied
this dialogue with sundry twitchings of his watch-chain, indicative rub-
bings of his nose, and other symptoms of impatience" 19th cent. *England.* Dickens, *Pickwick*, II, p. 438.

Insult Rubbing the nose questions the ancestry of the person at
whom the gesture is directed. *Italy. Time*, April 9, 1965, p. 68.

Mockery For Shanghai Gesture *see* FINGER, NOSE, Mockery;
HAND, Mockery. It is "limited to the world of childish mockery . . .
and even there it is scarcely common any longer." Does not exist in
Asia or Africa, except through cultural contact with Europe. Röhrich,
Gebärde-Metapher-Parodie, p. 24 and pl. 39. 16th cent. *France.* Rabelais, *Garg.*, Bk. I, ch. xviii; 16th cent. *Netherlands.* Pieter Breughel, *La
Fête des Fous* (1560), in Röhrich, *Gebärde-Metapher-Parodie*, pl. 40;
18th cent. *Germany.* Goethe, *Lilis Park.* Mitton observes that it is perhaps the remnant of an ancient magic gesture. Hand open, fingers
spread, tip of thumb against tip of nose; tip of thumb of second hand
may be placed against tip of little finger of first hand, and fingers may
be wiggled. Children may add a foot to the hands extending the nose.
Netherlands. Andrea and de Boer, p. 64. *See also* HAND, Mockery. *See
also* "cocksnook." Davidson, p. 4;

Odor Right hand waved in front of nose signifies an unpleasant
odor. *Central Africa.* Hochegger, p. 131.

Prayer Hand laid to nose. Taskodrugites. Ohm, p. 288.

Punishment Those found guilty of slander had to pull themselves
by the nose in retracting. Medieval *Germany;* medieval Normandy,
France. HDV, I, p. 322. * Pulling oneself by the nose, e.g. to indicate
that someone will be scolded by his wife. *Colombia.* Saitz and Cervenka, p. 98.

Rejection "nose rub among Americans is as much a sign of rejection as the word 'No!' " *U.S.* Birdwhistell, "Do Gestures Speak Louder
than Words?" p. 56.

Truth "Hookey, Hookey Walker—and 'with a hook,' usually accompanied by a significant upliftment of the hand and crooking of the
fore-finger, implying that what is said is a lie, or is to be taken contrary-
wise. One tells a long-yarn-story that asks for the disbelief of the audi-
tory; whereupon another cries out 'Hookey Walker!' having previously
shewn the sign above described, or another more elaborate still, which
may be looked upon as a counter-sign, viz. spread the fingers of both
hands wide open, apply one thumb to the tip of the nose, and the other
to the point of the little finger of the other hand—this signifies a
clincher. History: John Walker was an out-door clerk at Longman,
Clementi, and Co.'s in Cheapside, where a great number of Persons

were employed, and 'old Jack,' who had a crooked or hook nose, occupied also the post of spy upon their aberrations (which were manifold). Of course, it was for the interests of the surveillants, to throw discredit upon all Jack's reports to the nobs of the firm, and numbers could attest that those reports were fabrications, however true; Jack was constantly out-voted, his evidence overlaid, and of course disbelieved, when his occupation ceased, but not so the fame of 'Hookey Walker.' " Ca. 1810. *England.* Bee, p. 99.

Understanding " 'It's all right, Sam; quite right'—upon which Mr. Weller struck three distinct blows upon his nose in token of intelligence" 19th cent. *England.* Dickens, *Pickwick*, II, p. 192.

HAND, OBJECT *see also* HAND, STAFF; HAND, WEAPON

Affirmation The *signum manus*, usually a cross, of a person unable to write was often made by the scribe together with the appropriate formula. The actual *firmatio*, affirmation of the content of a charter by its originator and witnesses, consisted in a laying on of hands ("ponere manus in cartula") upon the document. Medieval Lombardy, *Italy*. Redlich, *Urkundenlehre*, pp. 25–26. Anglo-Saxon *England.* Ibid., p. 35. Bavaria, *Germany.* Ibid., p. 48. * In 12th cent. Rheto-Romance charters the formula "tracta est carta et facta (scripta) in N." indicates that charter was thrown by originator to receiver ("tracta" short for "traiecta"), an act completing legal transfer of property. Similarly, a person other than originator, receiver or scribe of charter appeared at beginning of proceedings, "qui pennam levavit," who picked up pen and handed it to scribe; i.e. he authorized production of charter by handing pen to scribe. Redlich, ibid., pp. 43, 51. * Imperial-Roman concept of function of charter was that completed charter completes an agreement. This was changed in Lombard law, which regarded uncompleted charter as piece of parchment which yet had to become a charter subject to an intention. Therefore, particularly in transfers of landownership, the originator, in presence of receiver, witnesses and scribe, declared his intention while holding parchment, which was destined to become a charter, in his hands. Then he handed it to receiver "ad proprium" and then to scribe "ad scribendum." Redlich, ibid., p. 50. Development of charter to symbol continued in Frankish, Burgundian and Alemannic law: in presence of both parties, witnesses and scribe, virgin parchment was placed on ground, originator then picked it up ("pergamentum de terra levare" or "levatio cartae"), holding it in his hands he declared his intention, handed it to receiver and requested scribe to write charter. Bresslau, *Handbuch*, II, p. 83. Thus, act of transferring parchment from originator to receiver paralleled traditional transfer of *festuca* (staff or straw) by handing it over or throwing it to receiver. Throwing parchment from originator to receiver was the practice in 11th and 12th century Burgundian law. It may have developed in analogy to provision for the *stipulatio*, an agreement against renewal of a dispute: one party raised *stipula* (stalk, blade) from ground and threw it down again; other party picked it up and kept it in order to produce it as proof if necessary. Redlich, ibid., pp. 50–51. In 13th cent. Lausanne the phrase "cartam levare" was applied to the *cancellarius* or his representative, in the sense that he pick up charter and hand it to scribe as authorization to write it. This usage was kept by Franks and other German tribes, who added inkpot, knife, twig, or other such object, to charter on ground, which then was to be picked up by originator and handed to receiver. Redlich, ibid., pp. 51–52; see also Bresslau, *Urkundenlehre*, II, 85–86. * In 1027 at Trebur, before Emperor Conrad II, a Count Dietrich renounced properties in favor of the monastery Michelsberg, near Bamberg, by first bending index before Saxon witnesses, then with hand and *festuca* before Frankish witnesses. Ibid., p. 70. For use of knife in transference of real estate, see Künssberg, "Messerbräuche," pp. 7–37.

Anger Beating the ground with a stick. Anc. *Rome*. Sittl, p. 15. * Tearing one's clothes. 8th cent. *England*. OE *Juliana*, 594 ff., Acta S. *Julianae*, cap. 3; Habicht, p. 38. * Hurling one's cap on the floor. 16th-17th cent. *Poland*. Bogucka, p. 196. * "In his anger and frustration, he picked up a long, curved clothes brush and banged it down hard on the surface of the table. It broke in half." *England*. Lodge, *Nice Work*, p. 117.

Apology *See* FINGER, Apology.

Apotropy Vestal of Herero tribe rubs ashes on foreheads of men going on dangerous trip to protect them. Southwest *Africa*. Frazer, *Golden Bough*, II, p. 215. * "Some also, on seeing a little wine left in a glass throw it on the ground or ashes of the fire, crying 'Cottabus', KOTT and BUS; this is a superstition, but not to be despised. It is said to placate the gods." Belloc, p. 12. (Lat. *cottabus* < Gk. *Κότταβος*, a social sport consisting in dashing a liquid upon a brazen vessel. Liddell and Scott, s.v. * Pouring water on floor as sign that a death has occurred and as defense against spirits. Seldom practiced. Jews. Kolatch, p. 51. Covering coffin and filling grave immediately, and throwing sticks, stones, clumps of grass on grave as defense against ghost of deceased. Jews. Kolatch, p. 56. Washing hands after visiting cemetery and before entering home as defense against demons hovering around graves. Jews. Kolatch, p. 62.

Applause Shaking or waving a corner of one's clothing (before handkerchiefs became common), while waving with the other hand. Anc. *Rome*. Sittl, p. 62. * Waving handkerchiefs. Anc. *Rome*. Sittl, p. 63.

Atonement During the ceremony of *Kaparot*, a fowl is waved over the head three times as a formula transferring sins from the believer to the fowl is uttered. Considered barbaric by many, money is substituted for the fowl and later given to the poor. Jews. Kolatch, p. 239; also Kafka, p. 70.

Attention "Snuff-taking . . . was very common [in the Restoration period] and offered gentlemen a fine opportunity to attract attention to themselves . . . The box was carried in the waistcoat pocket and brought out with a flowing, deliberate movement. Before the box was opened, the lid was tapped to make the grains which clung to the top drop back into the box . . . A pinch was taken with the thumb and second finger and either applied directly to the nostrils or placed on the back of the left hand, which was then lifted to each nostril in turn. (And do not sneeze afterward or you will betray your poor breeding.) When the box was returned to the pocket, the cuffs and shirt frills were flicked with a handkerchief, for snuff stains were difficult to remove." 17th cent. *England*. Rockwood, p. 179. * Rising and banging on a water glass with a spoon. College students. California, *U.S.* McCord, p. 292. * Tapping table top with ring or glass, or tapping glass or cup with another object, e.g. a spoon, to get waiter's attention. *Colombia*. Saitz and Cervenka, p. 106. "She taps on the desk with an inverted pencil and clears her throat. A sudden hush falls, and a hundred faces tilt towards her" Lodge, *Nice Work*, p. 72. * " 'Listen.' He lifted up a sharp, claw-nailed finger. Somebody plucked him by the sleeve; he looked down. It was old Mrs. Budge." *England*. Huxley, ch. 27. *See also* HAND, Attention.

Betting Each partner takes one end of a leaf in the right hand and pulls, so that the leaf tears. *Central Africa*. Hochegger, p. 139.

Blessing The major cross made over persons or objects with sacred object. The major Greek cross: thumb and index united, other fingers extended, drawing "IXC" in the air. The major Roman cross: first three fingers extended, last two folded in toward palm, or (since the 13th cent.) all fingers extended as prescribed by Pius V. The latter form was especially favored by the Benedictines since the 8th cent. Roman Catholic. Ohm, p. 295. * Throwing water on someone as a form of wishing him good luck is the customary New Year's (April 13) blessing in *Cambodia*. Dresser, *L.A. Times*, March 31, 1995, B7.

Cancellation "Once the defendants' documentary proof had fallen . . . , the plaintiff had to perform a ritual cancellation of the false documents by a *transpunctio*," i.e. by piercing it, usually with a dagger. 9th cent. *France*. Nelson, p. 58; see also Brunner, 2nd ed., vol. 2, pp. 562–63; Bresslau, *Urkundenlehre*, I, p. 648.

Certification Providing a document with a seal, commanding that it be supplied with a seal, signing it, providing a completion-stroke in a predrawn monogram, or simply placing the hand upon the document constituted the *roboratio* or *(manu) firmatio*. Sources also refer to the *manu firmatio* if no written record of a legal transaction was made at all, so that it might have consisted in a simple handshake. This indicates that the *firmatio* was above all a matter of making a transaction visible to witnesses. If a legal transaction was documented, the *firmatio* also referred to the document as well as to the transaction. If witnesses participated in the completion of a document, it is referred to as a *roboratio*. The *roborare* of witnesses served only to secure the documentary proof; the same can only be said of the *roborare* of the originator of the document if he provided it with some mark of documentary proof, such as a seal, the command that it be sealed, etc. Closely related to the *roboratio* by seal, etc., is the usage of signing *manu propria*, i.e. with the originator's own hand. Medieval *Europe*. Holzhauer, pp. 41–42.

Challenge   Knocking sand from a boy's hand by another boy: challenge or acceptance of a challenge to fight. *Syria; Saudi Arabia.* Barakat, no. 220. * In contesting a document, the contestant perforated the document with a bodkin, which signalled the "solemn challenge" to combat to decide the issue. Gamble, p. 15. * In all seven narratives in twelfth-century Russian chronicles which mention "kissing the cross" (*see* LIP, Agreement) as confirmation of a documentary peace agreement, the same series of events is described: prince sends envoy to rival with *krestnyye gramoty* ("written documents of the cross"); envoy then accuses rival of having broken his oath on the cross, and "casts" document at accused. The chronicles relate only "casting" of document, never their actual composition or issue. "This exclusive concentration on the ceremonial gesture, on the symbolic act of 'casting' the *gramoty*, is crucial: one suspects that in this early period the written document was in fact perceived and treated more as symbol than as text. You cannot 'unkiss' a cross. The physical gesture of 'casting' the *gramoty* provided a neat counterpart to the physical gesture of kissing the cross. The document is less a legal record than a ritual object, and the procedures are symbolic, not bureaucratic . . . The ritual act, the symbolic, physical, public gesture, is the main—the only—function of *krestnyye gramoty* recorded for the period." Franklin, pp. 23–24.

Claim   *See* HAND, Claim.

Commendation   *See* HAND, Commendation.

Contempt   Striking someone with the flat of one's sword. 16th-17th cent. *Poland.* Bogucka, p. 196.

Conveyance   "Before conveyances were made with documents, the witnesses 'heard' the donor utter the words of the grant and 'saw' him make the transfer by a symbolic object, such as a knife or a turf from the land. William the Conqueror went one better and jokingly threatened to make one donee 'feel' the conveyance by dashing the symbolic knife through the recipient abbot's hand saying, 'That's the way land ought to be given.' Such a gesture was intended to impress the event on the memory of all those present." Medieval *England*. Clanchy, p. 203. *

"The Gospel book was used [in conveyancing] because it was customary to reinforce oaths with it (as is still the practice in law courts) . . . To replace a Gospel book by a charter in a conveyancing ceremony was a relatively small change in appearance . . . , but a large one in substance. The charter in its text actually 'represented' . . . in a durable record the terms of the conveyance, whereas the Gospel book merely symbolized the solemnity of the occasion for the witnesses." Medieval *England*. Clanchy, p. 205.

Crazy Snatching at an imaginary fly in front of the gesturer's face indicates that someone is crazy. *Netherlands*. Axtell, *Gestures*, p. 145.

Death A hunter signifies the death of a buffalo by waving its tail in the air. *Central Africa*. Hochegger, p. 122.

Decision Counting beads (odd or even) before taking a trip to decide whether or not to take the trip or embark upon some enterprise. Rwala Bedouin of *Kuwait; Iraq; Syria; Saudi Arabia*. Barakat, no. 132.

Deference "The entry of a guest begins the whole complicated drama which the roles of host and guest impose. The guest, who is penetrating into the host's most vulnerable and intimate space, often makes motions of ritual deference. A man used to leave his hat and stick (vestiges of helmet and sword) with the maid on entering a house; or he would be required to leave his stick at the door, take his hat off, and go into the drawing room holding it." Visser, p. 111. * The giving of gifts, as in *Beowulf* 2144 ff., or symbolically, Beowulf's presentation of a breastplate to Hygelac, by signifying the deference of the giver, signifies also the respect in which the receiver is held. Medieval *England*. Habicht, p. 25.

Despair Tearing one's clothes. 8th cent. *England*. OE *Judith*, 280 ff.; Habicht, p. 50. "So eager were the miserable enthusiasts [Portuguese sailors] to embrace the image of Jesus Christ (which the priest held in his hand) in the instant of their dissolution that they, in their endeavours so to do, actually tore it to pieces." 18th cent. *Portugal*. Hickey, p. 372. *See* HAND, Despair.

Disbelief Right hand fingers tie, eyes half closed, mouth puckered in condescending smile "Oui, bien sur . . . mais, enfin . . ." ("Well, certainly . . . but . . .") *France*. Brault, p. 379. * Hand(s) pull(s) up trouser leg(s) as if one were wading through manure. Usually humorous. Men. *U.S.* Saitz and Cervenka, p. 42.

Dissatisfaction "Anyone not satisfied with his place at the table or with his neighbors would immediately show his dissatisfaction by . . . cutting the tablecloth in front of him." This destroyed the symbolic unity of the table. 16th-17th cent. *Poland*. Bogucka, p. 196. * During sessions of parliament, deputies kept hats on and retained weapons. They frequently showed dissatisfaction by waving swords and banging batons. 17th cent. *Poland*. Ibid.

Drink Lift and tilt glass to indicate that one wants another drink. *Netherlands.* Andrea and de Boer, p. 69. * Spilling part of a beverage on the ground before or after drinking. Gesture is traditional without specific meaning; derived from the *libatio Romana*, in connection with which some of the wine is spilled as an offering to Mercury, Bacchus, and the Lares. Anc. *Rome; Brazil.* Cascudo, *História,* p. 112.

Embarrassment Both hands pull down brim of real or imaginary hat as through to hide one's face. Men. Plebeian. Río de la Plata region of *Argentina; Uruguay.* Meo Zilio, p. 81.

Emphasis *See* HAND, Emphasis.

Etiquette In the Restoration period, ladies used the fan constantly. "There was a whole language of the fan; milady peeked out from behind it, hid behind it, tapped a naughty knuckle with it, gave signals with it." 17th cent. *England.* Rockwood, p. 179. * "the wide cuffs did not permit [men's] hands to hang close to the sides; besides the cuffs were too beautiful to hide, and the hands were kept high . . . to show off the frills at the wrist. Objects were handled deliberately, in a way which brought the lace-trimmed cuffs into focus. . . . Men did not just stand around, they always posed. The extreme fops carried this to a ludicrous degree, with too much waving of the handkerchief, greater flourishes, mincing walks, and even a quick snap of the head to flick their curls away. . . . In the eighteenth century women began to use colored handkerchiefs. These handkerchiefs were, of course, less functional than ornamental. They gave the lady a pretty excuse for waving, and they were superb for accidentally dropping near a gentleman. 17th-18th century. *England.* Rockwood, pp. 179–80. * Keeping hands in pockets while conversing is considered impolite in *Europe; Indonesia; Japan.* Axtell, *Gestures,* p. 96. * Men did not "smoke in front of the ladies until after 1900. Ladies did not smoke in public until about 1912." Rockwood, p. 183. * "Between the thumb and forefinger of her right hand she was holding the drumstick of the dismembered chicken; her little finger, elegantly crooked, stood apart from the rest of her hand." *England.* Huxley, ch. 19. *See* also BODY, Etiquette.

Evasiveness " 'He did seem a bit shifty,' said Robyn. 'All that fiddling with his pipe is an excuse to avoid eye contact.' " *England.* Lodge, *Nice Work,* p. 196.

Familiarity Lighting another's cigarette, esp. if the hand holding the light is steadied by that of the other person. King Hussein of Jordan lighting a cigarette for Yitzhak Rabin. *Middle East.* Reuters photo, *L.A. Times,* Oct. 27, 1994, A9.

Farewell Departing person after divorce takes a piece of a linen cloth, of which the remaining person takes the other piece. *Denmark.* Grimm, *DRA,* I, p. 626. * A piece is cut from the (remaining?) woman's belt or apron. *Montenegro.* Ibid. * "At the close of services in a Baptist

church in Moscow visited by a group of Quakers, the congregation sang
'God be with us till we meet again' . . . and while singing all the women
took out their handkerchiefs and waved them to the visitors." Ca. 1951.
Russia. Lonsdale, p. 26. * Provincial gentry typically indulged in exaggerated ways of delaying a visitor's departure: the host, in addition to
protesting, would sometimes detain the visitor's horses or take the
wheels off his carriage in order to prolong the visit. 16th cent. *Poland.*
Bogucka, p. 193. * Presumably a refusal to say farewell: A Miss Szamowska presented a young man, Tollohub, with a glass of wine as the
customary farewell gesture. Tollohub, already mounted, drank the wine,
placed the glass between the ears of his horse, shattered it with one
shot from his pistol, dismounted, prostrated himself, and asked Miss
Szamowska to marry him. 18th cent. *Poland.* Matuszewicz, I, p. 148;
Bogucka, p. 199. * Waving handkerchief. *Europe.* Mann, ch. xii.

Fear   A king in terror tears everything tearable on his armor. 14th
cent. *England. William of Palerne* 3884. Habicht, p. 51.

Friendship   Both hands hold trouser belt and shake it a little: "We
are united as belt and trousers." *Central Africa.* Hochegger, p. 7. *See
also* HAND, Friendship.

Gratitude   After a man dances he kneels before the musician who
wipes the dancer's cheeks with his head-cloth: expression of gratitude
on part of the participants. *Saudi Arabia.* Barakat, no. 221. "He gave
them each four more [cigarettes], they making a double nod with the
hand holding the cigarettes so that the cigarette dipped its end as a man
salutes with a sword, to thank him." *Spain.* Hemingway, p. 20.

Greeting   Junior official lowered or had the fasces lowered by his
lictors in the presence of a senior or superior official. Anc. *Rome.* Sittl,
p. 154. Lowering fasces by the lictors. Anc. *Rome.* Sittl, p. 155. In the
circus the charioteer lowered his whip before the patrons. Anc. *Rome.*
Sittl, pp. 155–56. * Waving cloth in greeting over a distance. Anc.
Rome. Plutarch, *Pomp.* 73. * In accosting each other peacefully, knights
raised the visor as sign of mutual recognition. Medieval *Europe.* Eichler,
p. 160. * "He that cannot make a leg, put off's cap, kiss his hand, and
say nothing" 16th-17th cent. *England.* Shakesp., *All's Well* 2.2.11–12.
* "Horatio Fizkin, Esquire, touched his hat to the honourable Samuel
Slumkey." 19th cent. *England.* Dickens, *Pickwick,* I, p. 213. * "Being
all on shore, we arose, and took leave with three cheers, which was most
cordially returned by the gentlemen and ladies waving their handkerchiefs" 18th cent. *England.* Hickey, p. 75. * "At slack water Mr. Stephen Bayard, a civil servant of the Company's, came on board to dis-
patch the ship. Upon entering the round house with his hat on, Captain
Gore, with much hauteur, asked him if he knew where he was, to which
Bayard coolly said, 'Yes, on board the *Nassau* East Indiaman.' Gore in
a violent rage observed, 'This is my apartment; and, did you possess the

common civility due from one gentleman to another, you would not have entered it covered'. This speech not producing the desired effect, Captain Gore added, 'I advise your quitting this cabin; otherwise I shall certainly take off your hat for you in a way not the most gentle'; upon which Mr. Bayard made a precipitate retreat to the quarterdeck" 18th cent. *England.* Hickey, p. 260. * "They made way for Henry Wimbush, touching their cap as he passed. He returned their salute." *England.* Huxley, ch. 18. * In greeting a person in mourning, one offers a rod to be grasped; in greeting, one breaks the rod. *Central Africa.* Hochegger, p. 179. *See also* HAND, Greeting.

Independence Hands in trouser pockets signify that one has no superior in the vicinity. *Central Africa.* Hochegger, p. 101.

Insult "One of the most horrible insults a medieval nobleman could endure was to be publicly humiliated and separated from his brethren by having the herald of an angry knight stride up to him at table and slit the table cloth to the left and the right of his place, or across the top of it." Medieval *Europe.* Visser, p. 156. * "It is extremely rude to take away a person's plate before he or she has finished eating. An ancient Roman would interpret this to mean sudden death to the person whose plate or 'portion' it was." Visser, p. 285. * Pulling at upper part of another's garment, such as lapels of a coat or the revers of a cloak with intent to divest its wearer of it, is an attempted degradation of its wearer. Garment is symbol of wearer's dignity, hence *investiture* with an office, and *divestiture* of it. For Giotto's use of the gesture, see Barasch, *Giotto,* pp. 151–54.

Investiture Enfeoffment as a rule is accomplished by symbolic investiture: Frederick I granted Austria to the Dukes of Babenberg by investiture with two flagged lances. The documentary investiture of Archbishop Engelbert of Cologne by Richard in 1261 is explicitly an exception. Bresslau, II, p. 66.

Invitation She "drew in her skirt with a gesture that indicated he was to sit down beside her." *England.* Huxley, ch. 4. * A woman invites someone to sit next to her by repeatedly patting the seat next to her with her hand. *Netherlands.* Andrea and de Boer, p. 150–51. * Dropping handkerchief invites courtship. Women. 18th-19th cent. *Europe; U.S. DEP,* 2nd ed., p. 274.

Joy "was so relieved that he could not restrain his joy, but took off his little straw-hat and threw it up into the air." 18th cent. *England.* Trollope, *Can You Forgive Her?,* II, p. 258. * After departure of an enemy or when one hears of the misfortune of an enemy, one breaks a pitcher or a pot in joy. 19th cent. *Palestine.* Bauer, p. 221. *See also* HAND, Joy.

Judgment Tearing of clothes as sign of excommunication. May have originated at the Synod of Paris (577) called by Chilperic. Medieval Christian. Aimoin., I, iii, c. 26; Wesselski, pp. 140 ff. * Grasping coattail as symbol of conveyance of land or execution of judgment. Medieval northern *Germany*. Schiller-Lübben, IV, p. 243. * Judge ties person's hands together with a head-cloth—person is a felon. *Saudi Arabia*. Barakat, no. 243. * Bedouin spreads out garment before judge and holds one end with left hand, then smoothes it out with the right, indicating that he can obtain sufficient witnesses to substantiate claim in dispute. Rwala Bedouin. *Kuwait; Iraq; Syria; Saudi Arabia*. Barakat, no. 204. * Tearing document of proscription. Since 15th cent. *Germany*. Möller, p. 68, n. 1. Tearing the bull of excommunication. Since beginning of 19th cent. Roman Catholic. Recke, p. 95. * "Then the Peer spoken to, standing up, and laying his right hand upon his breast, said Guilty or Not Guilty, upon my honour, and then sat down, the Lord Steward noting their suffrages . . . upon a paper . . . and then, after proclamation for silence again, the Lord Steward directing his speech to the prisoner, against whom the axe was turned edgeways . . . he then pronounced sentence of death by hanging, drawing, and quartering . . . and then breaking his white staff, the Court was dissolved." 17th cent. *England*. Evelyn, II, p. 162.

Lamentation Rending one's own garment. Weitzmann, pp. 467 ff.; Barasch (1976), pp. 22 (Nonnos), 35 (condemned by Chrysostom), 36, 42 and fig. 18 (Giotto's *Ira*), 67 and fig. 38a, and passim. *See also* Mourning.

Luck When a Hottentot passes a grave of Heitsi-eibeb, the god who died several times, he throws a stone on it for good luck. Frazer, *Golden Bough*, IV, p. 3. * Knocking knuckles on piece of wood indicates that someone has had good luck or that he hopes good luck will continue. *Colombia; U.S.* Saitz and Cervenka, p. 82. *Netherlands*. Andrea and de Boer, p. 67. *Brazil*. Originally anc. *Rome*. Cascudo, *História*, p. 140. * Upon seeing three priests or three blacks, a girl scratches, knots her headscarf, which is to bring her luck in finding a husband. *Colombia*. Saitz and Cervenka, p. 83.

Marriage During prayer at marriage ceremony the newly wedded pair is covered by a precious cloth. 13th cent. *Germany*. Konrad v. Würzburg, *Partonopier* 10807; Schultz, I, p. 629; Zeller, p. 26. *See also* FINGER, Marriage.

Mockery Women raise skirts. Anc. *Persia*; anc. *Egypt*; anc. *Greece* and *Rome*. Sittl, p. 104. * During period of limited literacy in medieval western Europe, the Latin literacy of the clergy was frequently mocked by representations in miniatures of fools, monkeys or dogs, sometimes in monks' cowls, writing or reading. The act of reading, specifically solitary reading, was thus represented as a ridiculous gesture. See Ms 78. D. 40, fol. 124r, Koninklijke Bibl., The Hague; see Camille (1985b), p. 143. *Book of Hours*, Master of Catherine of Cleves. North *Nether-*

lands. 1450/60. Rijksmuseum Meermanno-Westreenianum, The Hague, 10 F 50, 126v, 157v, and ibid., fol. 6r, 133r, for a similar mockery of reading. See also the two marginalized fools in the initial to Psalm 97 of the *Psalter of Stephen of Derby* (Oxford, Bodleian Lib., MS Rawl. G 185, fol. 81v) in Camille, "Seeing and Reading," pl. 12 and pp. 40–41. * "César doffed an imaginary hat, in ironic salute." *Spain.* Pérez-Reverte, p. 276. See also BUTTOCKS, Insult; Mockery.

Money Turning trouser pockets inside out "I have no money." *Russia.* Monahan, pp. 176–77.

Mourning Tearing clothes (men). Hellenistic *Asia Minor.* Sittl, p. 68. Mourners tear garments (*keria*) before funeral service. For parents the left side is torn, for son, daughter, brother, sister, and spouse the tear is on right side. Tear for parents must be made by hand. Tear can be made in a ribbon, instead of garment. Usually officiating rabbi performs *keria* on mourners; among orthodox, women perform it on other women, since a man must not touch a strange woman. For newly married, *keria* is delayed until seven days after weddiing. Orthodox Jews. Kolatch, 59–60. * " 'When someone dies, the body is set up in a tent. . . . They ride around the tent seven times; whenever they come before the entrance of the tent they cut their faces with a knife; crying, their tears flow together with their blood. They do so seven times; afterwards they stop.' " A description of a Türk funeral ceremony cited from the *Chou-shu* by Sinor, p. 7; see also other instances of this Central Asian custom in Sinor, p. 14, n. 23. It is likely that this was the Hunnic custom also. * Mourners put sand or earth into their shoes if they must leave the house while sitting *shiva* to remind them of their duty to return. Jews. Kolatch, p. 66. * Placing stones on tombstones as act of remembrance of the deceased. Jews. Kolatch, p. 77. See also Lamentation.

Oath Swearing by a pebble. Anc. *Rome.* Grimm, *DRA*, II, p. 548. * Oath sworn before the church portal, if missal was not used, was not complete unless swearer touched the doorpost. North Germanic. Grimm, *DRA*, II, p. 557. * The Frisians swore lesser oaths by their clothing or coattails. Medieval *Frisian Islands.* Grimm, *DRA*, II, p. 550. * The swearer touches an object with his right hand. If pagan, the hilt of his sword; if Christian, a relic; if a woman, the left breast and the plait of her hair; if a cleric or prince, right hand is laid on chest and heart. Medieval *Germany.* Grimm, *DRA*, I, p. 194. * "Touching the relics of the saints, he promised fealty to King Pepin and his sons Charles and Carloman, behaving honestly and faithfully, in accordance with the law and as a vassal should to his lords." 8th cent. *Royal Frankish Annals*, p. 42. * "in Edward I's wardrobe there was kept 'a book, which is called *textus*, upon which the magnates were accustomed to swear.' " 13th cent. *England.* Clanchy, p. 205. * Coachmen touched a wheel, horsemen a stirrup or horsecollar, sailors the edge of a boat or ship, warriors a shield or sword, messengers a spear in swearing an oath. Grimm, *DRA*, II, pp. 550–51. * Two persons clasp hands over an altar. Bronze hand from *Cyrenaica* (Leiden, *Netherlands*. Rijksmuseum van Oudheden). Seligmann, II, p. 180. * Touching a tree: "Glagerion (?) swore a full great othe by oake and ashe and thorne." Percy, III, p. 47. * Christians touching an altar. Medieval *Europe*. Du Cange, III, col. 1608-1609. Gregory of Tours, 5, 33: "elevatis manibus super altarium jurare" ("to swear with hands raised above the altar"). * Swearing by a sacred ring. Anc. *Scandinavia*. *Poetic Edda*, 248a; *Eyrbygg*, 10. * Touching the Torah in swearing. Jews. Ohm, p. 244. * Right hand touches the ground, picks up a bit of earth, puts it to the mouth, then the index is drawn across the throat in the gesture for cutting the throat, finishes by pointing toward the sky. *Central Africa*. Hochegger, pp. 187–88.

Ordering (wine) The classic "horns" gesture (index and little finger extended, other fingers folded into palm). When the hand is held vertically rather than horizontally in gesturing toward a glass, it may mean facetiously "dos dedos de vino" ("two fingers of wine"). *Lat. Am.* Kany, p. 191. *See also* HAND, Oath.

Pay Hand holds coattail as if it were a bag. Usually the right hand holds the left coattail, but deviations are numerous. Medieval *Germany*. *Sachsenspiegel*. Amira, "Handgebärden," p. 235.

Pensiveness "As he listened, the [German] general took a flat Egyptian cigarette out of a package and tapped it on the lid" *Germany*. Mulisch, p. 50.

Plea In some medieval German courts of law (Westphalia) it was customary that the defendant, upon pleading guilty or innocent, stuck a knife into the ground, saying "I stick the knife into the ground for mercy," or "I stick it into the ground for justice." Grimm, *DRA*, II, p. 385.

Possession Early German law included the document in its gestural vocabulary, so that, for instance, in cases of transfer of real property the *traditio cartae* could become the essential, executing act. The charter was combined with a gesture, so that a ritual took place in which the parchment page destined for inscription with the appropriate wording was picked up from the ground together with a clump of earth and an inkpot (*levatio cartae*). Holzhauer, p. 23. In transfer of property or investiture in certain rights or privileges, pieces of "turf, a small branch or root, a knife, a ring, a cup, a church key, a glove, a handkerchief" may be transferred, not as representing "abstract qualities or relations, but to validate legal transactions of which later, if attached to a document, they become both record and seal." Pizarro, p. 199; see also Wenzel, pp. 66–72, who cites, among other things, the function of ring and belt in the *Nibelungenlied*. *See also* HAND, Possession.

Poverty Insides of trouser pockets pulled out. Men. *Colombia*;

more common in *U.S.* Saitz and Cervenka, p. 90. Also *Netherlands*. Andrea and de Boer, p. 14. * "gave four distinct slaps on the pocket of his mulberry indescribables with his right as if to intimate that his master might have done the same without alarming anybody much by the clinking of coin." 19th cent. *England.* Dickens, *Pickwick*, I, p. 262.

Prayer   Touching the altar or image of the deity. Anc. *Rome.* Ohm, p. 241.

Punishment   A law of Tomar of 1174 provided that a mugger should pay a fine and let himself be stripped. Forced removal of clothing was the penalty imposed on those convicted of stealing from farms, orchards, etc. 13th and 14th cent. *Portugal.* Cascudo, *História*, p. 35.

Reading   Reading itself can be a gesture. During the period of limited literacy in medieval western Europe charters produced in courts of law were often read, but the content used in arriving at conclusions regarding evidence or for arriving at verdicts. A contemporary of Emperor Henry IV found it remarkable that he could not only read letters, but also understand them. Medieval *Germany.* Ebbo, I, c. 6, p. 826.

Refusal   Shake coffee cup with radial motion to decline another cup of coffee. *Saudi Arabia.* Variation: place palm of right hand over cup and shake a little. Barakat, no. 158.

Relinquishment   Throwing away a straw as symbol for the relinquishment of a plot of land. Salic law. Medieval *Germany. DWb*, IV/2, col. 239.

Remorse   Casting away weapons or armor as symbols of vanity, and trusting, instead, in one's own strength (Beowulf), or submission to God (Launcelot). Medieval *England.* Habicht, pp. 29, 113, 128. *See also* HEAD, Remorse.

Reverence   Touching clerics, relics, sacred images. *Spain.* Ohm, p. 243. *Tibet.* Ohm, p. 241. * Stroking of sacred objects. Semitic. Ohm, p. 244. * Covering hands with cloth or part of one's clothing when approaching sacred person or object. Originally Persian: "On the next day their leaders came sorrowfully to our camp from the city, their hands covered in the manner of supplicants, and pleaded with us" anc. *Rome.* Plautus, *Amphytrio*, 255 ff.; Xenophon, *Hellenica*, II.i.8: "It was in this year that Cyrus put to death Autoboesaces and Mitraeus who were sons of Darius' sister—the daughter of Darius' father Xerxes—because upon meeting him they did not thrust their hands through the *kore* [long sleeve], an honor they showed the king alone"; and the 4th cent. Roman historian Ammianus Marcellinus, XVI.5.11: "When the agents had been summoned by his order on a festal day to his council chamber to receive their gold with the rest, one of the company took it, not (as the custom is) in a fold of his mantle, but in both his open hands. Whereupon the emperor said, 'It is seizing, not accepting, that agents understand.' " Barasch, *Giotto*, p. 103, surmises that "the custom became popular in the Roman Empire at the period when the style and manners of oriental courts became models for Western society and rulership. . . . As in so many respects, . . . the medieval Church inherited ancient patterns and continued their use. The covering of hands, as a symbolic, highly formalized act, is known in the liturgies during the millennium between Ammianus Marcellinus and Giotto." The Synod of Auxerre, c. 578, decreed that women are forbidden to receive the host with bare hands; *PL* 39, col. 2168 requires men merely to wash their hands, whereas women are to carry a linen cloth when approaching the altar. For other examples, see Barasch, *Giotto*, pp. 103–16. The 19th—and, more rarely—the 20th century European custom of wearing white gloves when serving food under formal conditions may be derived from such requirements. *See also* Prayer above.

Royalty "The King ascended the throne, put on his helmet and read the following . . . speech." *Prussia. Volkszeitung* (Berlin), Aug. 6, 1866, p. 1.

Sacrifice Before serving coffee a bit of it is poured onto the ground as sacrifice. Rwala Bedouin, *Kuwait; Iraq; Saudi Arabia; Syria.* Barakat, no. 160.

Sorrow At Passover seder a drop of wine is removed from cup with mention of each of the Ten Plagues. Symbolic of sorrow for Egyptians. Jews. Kolatch, p. 203.

Speed Up One driver signals to another by flicking his cigarette lighter at him: "Step on it, man!" *Netherlands.* Andrea and de Boer, p. 177.

Submission "Dr. John Breton, . . . preached on *John* 1:27, 'whose shoe-latchet I am not worthy to unloose,' &c., describing the various fashions of shoes, or sandals, worn by the Jews, and other nations: . . . how great persons had servants that took them off when they came to their houses, and bare them after them: by which pointing the dignity of our Saviour" 17th cent. *England.* Evelyn, II, p. 48. *See* HAND, Submission.

Surrender Defeated army lowers insignia as sign of surrender. Anc. *Rome.* Sittl, p. 156.

Threat Figure of Death holding a bone horizontally over his head. 16th cent. *Germany.* Brant, woodcut, p. 256. * The act of writing is frequently represented as threatening in western European medieval, and later, art. *Apocalypse*, London, Lambeth Palace Library, Ms 209, fol. 46r; see Camille, "Seeing and Reading," p. 40 and pl. 11. Later examples are the recording devil in Lucas van Leyden's *Last Judgment* (1525) (Lakenhal, Leiden, *Netherlands*), and the secretary in Delaroche's *Joan of Arc in Prison* (19th cent.) (The Wallace Collection, London).

Toast "An ancient Greek libation was a sort of concrete prayer, a sharing of wine with the gods. The Homeric ritual for this act entailed rising to one's feet holding a cup full of wine in the right hand, looking up into the sky, deliberately spilling some of the liquid, praying with both arms and cup raised, then drinking . . . 'Drinking to' people was, and remains, in some respects similar to pouring libations. The toaster rises to his or her feet as a gesture of respect, and everybody else rises too, if the recipient of the honor is important enough; all must certainly raise their glasses. When men wore hats at meals, hats had to be removed. The toast is spoken, and it is very important to look the person being toasted in the eyes. A bow or nod of the head follows, and everyone sips wine. Taking only very little wine at this point is a modern constraint: toasting in the past has often meant draining the whole vessel." Visser, p. 255. * After proposing toast, host would let cup circulate around table. Women were allowed merely to touch it with lips, without drinking. When it had been drunk, empty glass was often thrown on floor and broken, to prevent future use. Occasionally an enthusiastic or drunk noble might break the glass on his own head, and thus show special respect to person toasted. 16th-17th cent. *Poland.* Bogucka, p. 197. " 'Perhaps a small glass of brandy to drink your health, and success to Sammy, Sir, wouldn't be amiss.'. . . and Mr. Weller, after pulling his hair to Mr. Pickwick, and nodding to Sam, jerked it down his capacious throat." 19th cent. *England.* Dickens, *Pickwick,* I, pp. 333–34. * Mary, daughter of Simon the leper, anointed Christ's feet with scent, after which she broke the vessel which had contained it according to ancient usage which consisted in breaking a vessel from which a stranger of distinction had been served. Harou (1898), p. 192. * Girls break vessels from which they have offered their betrothed a drink from the Trevi fountain in Rome before the latter's departure on a journey. Harou (1899), p. 384. * "an old English custom at Christmas was for all the diners to hold up their spoons and wish health to absent friends (spoons were customarily classed with cups and bowls)." Visser, p. 194. * "Chinese generally do not . . . drink at the dinner table without proposing a toast to others at the table, even if only by raising the glass and making eye contact. Only a symbolic sip need be taken in reply." Axtell, *Gestures,* p. 13. * In Asia it is sometimes appropriate to turn the glass upside down after drinking a toast to demonstrate that one has emptied it. In Sweden the traditional toasting motion "begins from the seventh button . . . on the waistcoat upward to the eyes, followed by a nod of the head, a drink, good and direct eye contact," and returning the glass to the level of the seventh button. Axtell, ibid., pp. 91–92. "Modern European toasting rituals are strongest and most formal in Germanic, Scandinavian, and eastern European countries. No one should taste wine or other alcohol in Scandinavia until the host has made a toast. All lift their glasses and look around at everyone present; they toast, taste, then look around at everyone again. Guests in Denmark may give subsequent toasts; the guest of honor is expected to express thanks to the hosts by tapping his or her glass to attract attention, and then proposing a toast ... Today, the custom of toasting includes the clinking of glasses. Drinking wine, people have often remarked, is an action pleasing to four of the senses: taste, smell, touch, and sight. Clinking provides sound as well ... Clinking one glass against another is *making contact*, an action we perform precisely because we are not sharing one cup; in doing it we remind ourselves that the wine, now separated into glassfuls, is still one, and we reach out to each other even though we do not hand our glasses on. Russians go one further and smash their glasses after particularly fervent toasts, vows, or oaths." Visser, pp. 257–58. Clinking full glasses is greeting; may also be final expression of respect at banquet; raising one's cup as gesture of praise can be compared to elevation of chalice in Roman Catholic liturgy. "he leaned over the bowl and dipped the cup full and they all touched cup edges." *Spain.* Hemingway, p. 20. The English do not clink glasses but offer their compliments to each other by raising full glasses to their lips. Harou (1898), p. 192. Cups were raised in dedication to goddess Salus, daughter of Aesculapius, asking for continuing good health. Anc. *Rome.* Cascudo, *História*, p. 218.

Victory   Raising the flag. 19th cent. *Germany.* Schiller, *Tell*, iv, ii. *U.S.* Marines, Iwo Jima. AP Photo, Rosenthal; *Leatherneck* Photo, L. R. Lowery. *Life*, March 26, 1945, pp. 17, 18.

Warning   Hands in trouser pockets is a warning against thieves. *Central Africa.* Hochegger, p. 101.

HAND, SHOULDER

Anger   Pulling shoulders in and extending hand. Anc. *Rome.* Baden, p. 451.

Approval   " 'Quite perfect,' rejoined Fagin, clapping him on the shoulder." 19th cent. *England.* Dickens, *Oliver Twist*, p. 398. Also 16th-17th cent. *England.* Shakesp., *Love's Lab. Lost* 5.2.107; *Much Ado* 1.1.261.

Assurance   " 'I know so little of the gentleman,' said Mr. Pickwick, hesitating, 'that I—' 'I know you do,' interposed Smangle, clasping Mr. Pickwick by the shoulder. 'You shall know him better' " 19th cent. *England.* Dickens, *Pickwick*, II, p. 270.

Attention   "Mr. Pickwick was roused . . . by . . . a touch on his shoulder." 19th cent. *England.* Dickens, *Pickwick*, I, p. 69; II, p. 104. "He grasped my shoulder convulsively" Ibid., I, p. 48.

Consolation   *See* HAND, Consolation.

Counting   Throwing stones of dates over shoulder while eating dates: each stone indicates a camel acquired in a raid. Rwala Bedouin, *Kuwait; Iraq; Syria; Saudi Arabia.* Barakat, no. 134.

Disbelief Shoulders hunched, face shows pain, right hand jiggled vigorously at approx. chin level as if burned, air is sucked in suddenly or quick up and down whistling sound is made. Sometimes only index is jiggled: "Ça, c'est un peu fort!" ("Come on, that's a little strong!") *France.* Brault, p. 381.

Encouragement Clapping someone on the shoulder or patting him on the back of the hand. Bulwer, p. 66. *Colombia; U.S.* Saitz and Cervenka, p. 48.

Familiarity "The newspapers covered [Mark Twain's] every move, and he was perfectly equal to an erroneous report that he had clapped King Edward VII on the shoulder at a Windsor garden party—'an impertinence of which I was not guilty,' Twain retorted. 'I was reared in the most exclusive circles of Missouri and I know how to behave.' " *U.S.* Clemons, p. 73.

Favor Hand brushes shoulder of gesturer—"Apple polishing." *Colombia.* Saitz and Cervenka, p. 53.

Friendship Hands laid on other person's shoulders. Anc. *Greece* and *Rome.* Sittl, pp. 36, 280. * Patting another person's shoulder with right hand—conciliatory. *Lebanon; Syria; Jordan; Saudi Arabia.* Barakat, no. 31.

Greeting In the vemic court the secret jurors' greeting was pronounced while the entering juror placed his right hand first on his left shoulder, then on those of the other jurors. *Germany.* Grimm, *DRA,* I, p. 194. * After handshake, one hand is placed on shoulder of person being greeted while usual courtesies are exchanged. Only among friends. Bahia, Pernambuco, Piauí, *Brazil.* Cascudo, *História,* p. 92.

Helplessness Lifting up shoulders and holding up hands at height of head. *France.* Life Photo, David Scherman, *Life,* Sept. 16, 1946, p. 12. Lifting shoulders, turning palms of both hands up. Physiognomic expression determines meaning. Ghetto Jews. *Eastern Europe.* Efron, p. 146, fig. 34. " 'What you mean is: there's no chance of my being kept on after the three years are up.' Philip Swallow spreads his hands and shrugs. 'No chance at all, as far as I can see.' " *England.* Lodge, *Nice Work,* p. 64. Shoulders lifted, one hand extended, palm up. *Italy.* Farinacci, Mussolini's Minister of State, *Life,* Feb. 10, 1941, p. 26. *See also* Ignorance, Interrogation.

Ignorance Shrugging the shoulders, shaking head, raising right hand, palm up, to level of shoulder, inclining head to one side. *U.S.* Seton, p. 114. Shrugging shoulders and raising one flat hand. *U.S.* Seton, p. 105. Shoulders raised, elbows close to body, hands raised a little to both sides, palms turned up and facing forward from a position slightly in the rear of the body. *France.* Mitton, p. 144. *Netherlands.* Andrea and de Boer, p. 70. Shrugging shoulders, hands extended, palms up, head tilted slightly to one side. Arab. Barakat, no. 99. *See also* Helplessness, Interrogation.

Interrogation Hand extended slightly, palm up, shrugging shoulders. ("What were they supposed to do then?") *France*. Life Photo, David Scherman, *Life*, Sept. 16, 1946, p. 12. *See also* Helplessness, Ignorance.

Kindness Hand clapped on shoulder. 16th-17th cent. *England*. Shakesp., *Much Ado*, 1.1.261; *Love's Lab. Lost* 5.2.107; *Troil.* 3.3.139.

Magnitude Hands touch clavicles. "I've lost weight!" Women. *Central Africa*. Hochegger, p. 109.

Pleasure Right hand rests on left shoulder, left hand taps lightly on right arm: "Quelle joie, nous avons réussi" ("Hurray, we've succeeded!") *Central Africa*. Hochegger, p. 98.

Praise Right hand lightly taps someone on the left shoulder or on the back. *Central Africa*. Hochegger, pp. 102–3.

Pride "I even remember the way he imperceptibly removed his shoulder from under the proud paternal hand, while the proud paternal voice was saying: 'This boy has just got a Five Plus (A +) in the Algebra examination.' " Nabokov, p. 17. * Patting oneself on the shoulder with one hand. *U.S.* Saitz and Cervenka, p. 97.

Resignation "The corporal spread his hands and lifted his shoulders in a gesture of caged resignation." *Mexico*. Steinbeck, p. 100. "Mr. Scoggan shrugged his shoulders and, pipe in hand, made a gesture of resignation." *England*. Huxley, ch. xxiii.

Stop "it may be said of him that Cupid hath clapp'd him o' th' shoulder." 16th-17th cent. *England*. Shakesp., *As You Like It* 4.2.43–44.

Submission Subordinates placed right hand on left shoulder, signifying peaceful intent. An extension of this gesture was the placing of the left hand on the right shoulder also. Anc. *Egypt*. Ohm, p. 277.

Uncertainty Lifting hand to shoulder, palm out, head bent slightly towards hand. *France*. Life Photo, David Scherman, *Life*, Sept. 16, 1946, p. 12.

Urgency In urgent conversation one person puts his hand on the shoulder of the other. Anc. *Greece*. Sittl, p. 280.

HAND, SIDE
Jealousy Hand(s) hit(s) side(s). Anc. *Rome*. Sittl, p. 22.

HAND, STAFF *see also* HAND, OBJECT
Agreement In medieval German law, a symbolic act (*vadium*) of handing over a staff by a debtor to a creditor establishes their relationship. Ebert, II, col. 215.

Anger Beating the ground with a stick. Anc. *Rome;* early Christian.

Sittl, p. 15. * Dashing scepter to the ground. Anc. *Greece*. Homer, *Odyss.*, Bk. ii.

Authority   Holding the staff as symbol for the power of kings, princes, judges. Medieval and post-medieval *Germany*. Grimm, *DRA*, I, p. 186. Court was in session as long as the judge held his staff of office; it was adjourned, as soon as he laid it down. Grimm, *DRA*, II, p. 372; 1503. Rümlang, *Switzerland*. Grimm, *Weistümer*, IV, p. 305. * In pronouncing a ban over someone (*missio in bannum*) a judge had to raise hand and staff. Medieval *Germany*; medieval *Italy*. Amira, "Handgebärden," p. 196. For the symbolic function of the staff, analogous to the sceptre, in Hartmann's *Gregorius* (987 ff.), see Wells, pp. 169–70. *See also* HAND, OBJECT, Judgment.

Emphasis   *See* HAND, Emphasis.

Judgment   Breaking the staff as symbol of proscription. Medieval *Germany*. Siuts, p. 115. Breaking of a staff symbolic of the irrevocability of verdict; for the same reason, when judge and assessor rise for pronouncement of verdict, seats are knocked over. 1511. Augsburg, *Germany*. Grimm, *DRA*, I, p. 187. Breaking of the staff over the head of the condemned, then throwing its pieces before his feet. Ibid. Breaking of the staff is mentioned sparsely in sources of the 9th to the 11th century. Siuts, p. 116. * In accordance with Würzburg-Franconian statute of the late Middle Ages, in pronouncing proscription, the judge, together with jury, is to go into open air, and, after his pronouncement, turn east with bare head, place his staff upon the earth, place his hands upon it crosswise, and pronounce the appropriate formula. Late medieval *Germany*. Siuts, p. 119. * According to the custom of the imperial court of justice at Rottweil, the judge, after pronouncing a ban, hurled his staff away if he did not want to render additional verdicts. Late medieval *Germany*. Siuts, ibid; cf. also Grimm, *Weistümer*, IV, 305. * The judge broke his staff in pronouncing sentence of death. Oldest evidence of this in German territory is the Tiroler Halsgerichtsordnung of 1499 and the *Carolina* (1532) of Charles V, art. 96. Siuts, p. 117.

Manumission   *See* HAND, Manumission.

Marriage   Medieval Italian painters, in depicting marriage of Mary and Joseph represented cessation of Mary's membership in her parents' family by the breaking of a staff. Siuts, p. 116.

Oath   Swearing by placing a hand on the judge's staff. 16th-17th cent. *Germany*. Grimm, *DRA*, II, p. 372. Touching the royal or judge's staff. Grimm, *DRA*, I, p. 187. Kings and judges touched their staves when they swore an oath. Anc. *Greece*. Grimm, *DRA*, II, p. 550; medieval German. Grimm, *DRA*, I, pp. 186–187.

Possession   Transference of ownership of land is symbolized by transference of a staff. Peasants. *Switzerland*. Grimm, *DRA*, I, p. 185; *Germany. Hildesh. Meierd. Stat.*, para. 3; see Grimm, *DRA*, I, p. 182;

late medieval *France*. Ibid., p. 184. This symbolic act was also performed by princes in connection with change in sovereignty over larger lands. Grimm, *DRA*, I, p. 184. In 998 Otto III confirmed to the monastery of St. Ambroglio in Milan all its possessions by investiture "per baculum" ("investiture with staff"). Bresslau, II, p. 74. In 1029 Konrad II had granted the monastery of Obermünster in Regensburg a farm; the charter describes the investiture as having been accomplished by the emperor "baculo nostro" ("with our staff"), and that the emperor had left the staff in the monastery as an eternal memorial. Bresslau, II, p. 72.

Rejection   If someone wished to reject his kinship, he appeared in court and broke three or four staves over his head. Medieval *Germany*. *Lex Salica*. Siuts, p. 116.

Relinquishment   Laying down the staff of office signifies that the office is relinquished and vacant. Medieval *Germany*. Grimm, *DRA*, I, p. 188. * Breaking the staff over the head of the condemned and casting it at his feet is an expression of the fact that he has no longer cause for hope and must relinquish his life. Hence also interdicting the possession of land by casting a staff. medieval *Norway*. *Gulapingslog*, 362–3; Grimm, *DRA*, I, pp. 187–88.

Submission   Convicted rebels had to swear allegiance and to carry a white staff the rest of their lives. 1576. *Germany*; prisoners of war carried white staves. 1711. *Germany*. Grimm, *DRA*, I, p. 185.

Surrender   Carrying a white staff as sign of surrender. 1504. *Germany*. Grimm, *DRA*, I, p. 185.

HAND, STONE
Condemnation   A writ of the Synod of Basel requires that after publication of anathema, clerics and laymen assemble at the church door and cast three stones toward the house of those who have been excommunicated. *Switzerland*. Siuts, p. 101.

HAND, STRAW
Agreement   At the conclusion of an agreement, both parties break a straw between them. *India*. Grimm, *DRA*, II, p. 146.

Authority   Transference to another of the authority to conduct one's case in a court of law by handing him a straw. Grimm, *DRA*, II, p. 146.

Manumission   Casting away a straw in freeing a slave. Anc. *Rome*. Grimm, *DRA*, I, p. 178.

Oath   A master acting for his servant had to swear to his good faith upon a straw. Medieval *Germany*. *Lex Ripuar.*, 31 (30, 1); Grimm, *DRA*, I, p. 169.

Plea   In a supplication to the king (803) that priests be exempted from military service, the people "profitemur omnes, stipulas dextris in manibus tenentes, easque propriis e manibus ejicientes" ("we all declare, holding straws in our right hands, each throwing his separately.") 803. Carolingian Frankish. Grimm, *DRA*, I, p. 170.

Possession   In accordance to a Marculfian formula (1, 13) the testator casts a straw into the lap of the king, who then bestowed the fief upon him for life and to his beneficiary after his death. Medieval *Germany*. Grimm, *DRA*, I, p. 169. In relinquishing real property through sale, gift, or attachment, a straw is handed to the new owner. Medieval *Germany*. Grimm, *DRA*, I, pp. 170–175.

Rejection   A straw is handed, thrown, or grasped by the judge or one of the participants in a case as sign of renunciation or notice of renunciation. First occurrence: *Lex Salica*, 49 (46); Medieval *Germany*. Grimm, *DRA*, I, p. 168. Charles the Simple (879–929) was publicly rejected by throwing straws. Early 10th cent. Medieval *France*. Grimm, *DRA*, I, p. 170.

HAND, TEMPLE *See also* HAND, HEAD
Despair   Hand pressed against temples. Men. Anc. *Rome;* 19th cent. *Italy*. Sittl, p. 22.
Insult   Slap against temple. Anc. *Greece*. Sittl, p. 109.
Punishment   *See* Insult above.

HAND, THIGH
Anger   Beating the thighs with fists. *Lat. Am*. Kany, p. 64.
Horror   Hand slaps thigh. Anc. *Greece* and *Rome*. Sittl, p. 21.
Impatience   One hand slaps lightly against thigh and remains there for a moment. Often indicates imminent castigation for a child. *Colombia*. Saitz and Cervenka, p. 73. * Hands repeatedly slap side of thighs. *Central Africa*. Hochegger, p. 92.
Joy   Hand repeatedly slapped against thigh. Anc. *Greece* and *Rome*. Sittl, p. 12. Vulgar. Taylor, *Shanghai Gesture*, p. 66, n. 35. Kroll, p. 156: "He broke into a laugh, clapping his thigh." Hitting right thigh with palm of right hand. *Lebanon; Jordan; Syria; Saudi Arabia*. Barakat, no. 30. Normandy, *France*. Raim, p. 105.
Mourning   Beating thighs. Anc. *Greece*. Sittl, p. 25.
Oath   "Put thy hand under my thigh." Biblical. *Middle East. Gen*. 24:2.
Prostitute   Hands on slightly spread thighs. *Central Africa*. Hochegger, p. 155.
Shame   "I smote my thigh." Biblical. *Middle East. Jer*. 31:19.
Sorrow   "Smite therefore upon thy thigh." Biblical. *Middle East. Ezek*. 21:12.
Stammer   Flat hands repeatedly hit against sides of thighs until the

mouth succeeds in speaking: "He stammers." *Central Africa*. Hochegger, p. 24.

Surprise   Hitting right thigh with palm of right hand. *Lebanon; Jordan; Syria; Saudi Arabia*. Barakat, no. 30.

HAND, TONGUE

Disapproval   "Pablo made disapproving clucking noises with his tongue. He spread his hands in front of him. 'What is a man to do?' he asked. 'Is there no one to trust?' " *U.S.* Steinbeck, p. 22.

Disbelief   Flip hands up and out in front of body and extend the tongue. *Saudi Arabia*. Barakat, no. 210.

Insult   Sticking out tongue and making sign of the "fig." Hans Maler, *Christ bearing the Cross* (ca. 1488-ca. 1529). Chicago Art Institute.

HAND, TOOTH

Anger   "Mr. Pott, who, stalking majestically towards him, and thrusting aside his proffered hand, ground his teeth, as if to put a sharper edge on what he was about to utter." 19th cent. *England*. Dickens, *Pickwick*, I, p. 289.

Dismay   Biting into one's hand. *Persia*. DWb, IV/2, col. 334.

Pensiveness   Picking one's teeth. Late 16th cent. *France*. Lommatzsch, p. 58.

HAND, TORCH

Judgment   At proscription, the judge swung a burning torch three times. *Netherlands*. Brunner, p. 237. * In pronouncing anathema or excommunication, the bishop is surrounded by twelve priests with burning candles. After completion of the sentencing, the priests cast the candles to the ground and stepped on them. Roman Catholic. Siuts, p. 94. The oldest collection of decretals which mentions this ritual is Regino II, 409. Beginning with the 12th century it is frequently mentioned in decretals and synods. According to Regino and the Heidelberg codex of the *Sachsenspiegel* it was customary to break the burning candles and hurl them away after the sentence was read. See also Grimm, *DRA*, I, p. 269.

Mourning   At the funeral of an unmarried young man, a girl walked on each side of the coffin, carrying upon a pillow a broken candle and a mourning wreath. Teplitz, *Germany*. Siuts, p. 95.

HAND, WEAPON *see also* HAND, OBJECT; HAND, STAFF

Accolade   "As for a knight I will make you, and therewith smote him in the neck with the sword." 15th cent. *England*. Malory, Bk. iii, ch. iii. After sword belt has been put on, there follows blow with sword, the *alapa militaris*. This blow, administered by knight accepting squire into knighthood, is directed against the neck and accompanied by formal admonitions. Medieval *Europe*. Schultz, I, p. 185. Priest blesses the sword, which is then belted on new knight by his lord. Medieval *Germany. Mai u. Beaflor*, 83, 39; *Klage*, 4371.

Agreement As symbol of agreement to repay for damage inflicted, debtor hands over sword to aggrieved party, with understanding that, upon carrying out his part of agreement, he will receive it back. Early medieval *Spain*. Ebert, II, col. 215. " 'Doña Elvira and Doña Sol are in your hands, o king. Give them to whom you please and I shall be content.' 'I thank you and all my court,' said the king. Then arose the Princes of Carrión and kissed the hands of [the Cid] and exchanged swords with him in the presence of King Alfonso." Medieval *Spain. Cid*, ii.

Alarm Beating shield against chest, calling "to arms, to arms!" Anc. *Rome*. Sittl, p. 215.

Belligerence Shaking the spear or raising a weapon toward a perceived enemy. Medieval *Europe*. Habicht, p. 24, who also cites Tacitus, *Germania*, cap. 3, for the Germanic custom of warriors raising their shields to their mouths when chanting their battle-songs, so that they might sound more threatening.

Chastity Placing sword between man and woman in bed. Gottfr. v. Strassburg, 17407–17, 17486, 17510. Medieval *France. Tristrem* 2002 and medieval *England, Tristrem* 3, 20–22. Similarly, when Brunhild has herself burned with the body of Sigurd, she has a sword placed between it and her. Medieval *Iceland. Poet. Edda*, 225b.

Death *See* ARM, NECK, Death.

Defiance Sword laid across knees of sitting person. 13th cent. *Germany. Nibelungenlied*, st. 1783; Wolfr. v. Eschenbach, *Willehalm*, iii, 141, 5; *Alpharts Tod*, 77, 4–78, 2; cf. Wynne, pp. 104–14.

Determination "diu habet er hina geuuorfen den skilt, daz chit tes muotes festi" Throwing down the shield. 10th-11th cent. *Germany*. Notker Labeo, p. 25, lines 9–11.

Faithfulness *See* HAND, Faithfulness.

Greeting Spear was thrust into the ground, the free right hand was raised, the shield was held with the left against an unexpected thrust. Germanic. *HDV,* I, p. 317.

Investiture "We here create thee the first Duke of Suffolk, and girt thee with the sword." 16th-17th cent. *England*. Shakesp., II *Henry VI* 1.1.59–60.

Joy "Those who had been out scouting return and join them, and their joy is so great that they fall to jousting on the banks of the Jalón." Medieval *Spain. Cid*, c. ii; see also c. iii: "[The Cid] heard that they were coming and swiftly spurred to meet them, doing mock battle the while because of his great joy." Also medieval *Germany*. *Nibelungen-lied*, st. 584, 1–3.

Judgment Proscription was announced by the judge with the drawn sword. Geldern, medieval *Germany* Siuts, p. 120. * Public beats weapons together at pronouncement of proscription. Germanic. Tacitus, *Germ.*, ch. xi. A sword on the judge's table or on the knees of a judge symbolized his jurisdiction over capital crimes. Medieval *Europe*. Siuts, p. 120.

Mourning Fasces turned to the ground. Sittl, p. 72. Soldiers turn weapons to the ground in mourning a prince. Anc. *Rome;* 17th cent. *Germany*. Sittl, ibid. * Weapons beaten together four times at burning of the body with military honors. Anc. *Rome*. Sittl, p. 73. Knight carrying his shield upside-down signifies his mourning for the death of his lord. 13th cent. *German*. Wolfr. von Eschenbach, II, 80. *See also* HAND, Mourning.

Negotiation Setting down the shield before one's feet indicates readiness to negotiate. 12th-13th cent. *Germany*. *Nibelungenlied*, st. 2254, 2.

Oath In taking oath, ruler touches scepter, symbolic of his dominion, as most precious possession. Anc. *Greece* and *Rome*. Sittl, p. 139. * Members of family of murdered man and of family of murderer swore upon a weapon that royal peace would be kept. Anglo Saxon. Medieval Germanic. Grimm, *Mythologie*, I, p. 169f.; *HDA*, II, col. 667. * Laying down arms, helmet or hat before kneeling and raising two fingers. Medieval *Germany*. Grimm, *DRA*, II, p. 556. In taking oath, weapon is touched, to signify that this weapon is to take life of one who breaks oath. Anc. *Greece* and *Rome*. Sittl, p. 139. Swearing on a sword. Customary in taking an oath among freemen. Medieval *Germany*. *Wigamur*, 780; Medieval *Iceland*. *Poet. Edda*, 138b; Grimm, *DRA*, I, pp. 228–29. * As late as the end of the 14th cent. the Saxons of Siebenbürgen swore by sticking the bare sword into the earth. Kahle, p. 116. "Come hither, gentlemen, and lay hands again Never to speak of this that you have heard, Swear by my sword." 16th-17th cent. *England*. Shakesp., *Hamlet* 1.5.142. *See also* HAND, Oath.

Peace Messenger takes off his sword on arrival to show that his message is peaceful. Medieval *Germany*. *Nibelungenlied*, st. 1643, 2.

Sincerity Hand clapped on sword to show he meant his word. 17th cent. *England*. Butler, pt. I, c. 2, 681.

Submission In meeting with Hugh Capet, at the time still Duke of the Franks, Emperor Otto II placed his sword on a chair before embracing Hugh. After their conversation the Emperor turned to call for his sword and Hugh bent over to pick it up. At that moment a bishop in Hugh's entourage leapt forward to prevent him from picking it up, pulled it out of his hand and carried it after the Emperor, thereby preventing Hugh from signifying vassalage. Richer, III, p. 85. J.-C. Schmitt, p. 15.

Superiority Bridegroom tries to gain power over his wife by tapping her three or seven times on head or shoulder with sword or dagger, or drinking first from bowl which he then holds for her to drink from. James, p. 61.

Surrender Sword is taken by its point and hilt is extended to the victor. Medieval *France*. *Voeu dy paon*, 108059; Grimm, *DRA*, I, p. 230. * Walk without sword. *Waltharius*, 64. * Sword is handed over as symbolic for transference of land. Grimm, *DRA*, I, p. 230. * Caesarius von Heisterbach, I, 37, tells of the knight Walewan, who joined the monastery of Himmerod by walking through "the church with all his arms and placing them on the altar of Our Lady." This 'new form of conversion,' as Caesarius calls it, is acceptable and even laudable, even though the ideal of taking one's arms into a Cistercian church must have been rather foreign. But the link with Mary and the feudal military ethic made it acceptable in highly aristocratic Himmerod." Medieval *Germany*. McGuire, p. 203. *See also* FINGER, HAND, Surrender.

HAND, WRIST

Capture Captured women are led away by the wrist. Anc. *Rome*.. Sittl, p. 279.

Effeminacy The open right hand clutches the left wrist. *Lat. Am.* Kany, p. 181. * Left wrist seized by right hand and moved with a circular motion. *Lat. Am.* Kany, p. 182.

Jail Right hand may seize the left wrist to suggest handcuffing. *Lat. Am.* Kany, p. 117.

Leading Women and children are led by the wrist. Anc. *Greece* and *Rome*. Sittl, p. 280.

HEAD (see also FACE)

Accompaniment Head slightly inclined to one side, then moved quickly to the other—the person looked at is to come along. *Netherlands*. Andrea and de Boer, p. 83. *See* Depart.

Acknowledgment " 'She!' said the old gentleman, with a knowing shake of the head" 19th cent. *England*. Dickens, *Pickwick*, I, p. 297. * "Mr. Pickwick bent his head very slightly in answer to these salutations" 19th cent. *England*. Dickens, *Pickwick*, II, p. 427. "nodded his head" in acknowledgment of an introduction. *U.S.* Birdwhistell, *Introduction*, p. 34. " 'My name is Slurk,' said the gentleman. The landlord slightly inclined his head." 19th cent. *England*. Dickens, *Pickwick*, II, p. 395. "Again and again he pointed to this creeper or that tree, pronouncing the name of the plant, nodding, as if he wanted to introduce

the plant to the strangers." Yanomami. Southern *Venezuela;* Northeastern *Brazil.* Frevel and Escher, p. 20.
Adoration "The people bow their heads in adoration when the Sacred Host is elevated." Roman Catholic. *Mass*, p. 53. "At the name 'Jesu Christi,' the priest inclines his head toward the Crucifix." Roman Catholic. *Mass*, p. 49. "I, however, crossed my arms upon my breast, and piously inclined my head." 19th cent. *Germany*. Heine, in *DWb*, IV/2, 601.
Affection "Here may his head lie on my throbbing breast." 16th-17th cent. *England*. Shakesp., II *Henry VI* 4.4.5.
Affirmation Head inclined sideways left or right. *Bulgaria;* southern *Yugoslavia*. Röhrich, *Gabärde-Metapher-Parodie*, p. 14 and pl. 6b. *Afghanistan*. Müller, p. 102. Shaking the head back and forth. *Greece; Yugoslavia; Turkey; Iran; Bengal*. Axtell, *Gestures*, p. 60. " 'Too true; too true, indeed,' said Mrs. Weller, murmuring a groan and shaking her head assentingly." 19th cent. *England*. Dickens, *Pickwick*, II, p. 285. * Dropping head downward and forward. Arab. George, p. 320. A nod is favorable, head thrown back has an unfavorable meaning. Onians, pp. 139–40, n. 4. Head tossed backwards—yes. *India;* Maori, *New Zealand;* Tagal, *Philippines;* Dyak, *Borneo*. Axtell, *Gestures*, p. 61. Su, LINGUIST 3.1012. * A nod indicating or emphasizing an affirmative answer. 19th cent. *England*. Dickens, *Pickwick*, II, pp. 302, 316, 338, et passim. * Head inclined in direction of a pleasing object. Anc. *Greece* and *Rome*. Sittl, p. 92. Inclining the head and lifting it again. *France*. Probably signified originally the submission to another person's will, acc. to Mitton, p. 141. *Portugal*. Basto, p. 16. " 'Yes, isn't it lovely?' Jenny replied, giving two rapid little nods." *England*. Huxley, ch. iv. * Shaking of the head from side to side. Arab. Goldziher, "Über Gebärden," p. 370. The statement that Arabs shake their heads in affirmation as we do in negation appears to have been initially made by Petermann, I, p. 172, repeated by Wundt, I, p. 180, and disputed by George, pp. 320–23, see above. * Rocking the head slowly back and forth, side-to-side—yes, I am listening. *India*. Axtell, *Gestures*, p. 62. Su, LINGUIST 3.1012. * Jerking the head to the right shoulder in a sort of modified head shake. *Ethiopia*. Su, <LINGUIST 3.1012>. "The Ceylonese . . . have two ways of saying yes. If one asks a factual question, the answer yes consists of nodding. If . . . agreement to do something is expressed, the Ceylonese sway the head in slow, sideways movements." Eibl-Eibesfeldt, p. 303; Raim, p. 101. * "The most common regulator is the head nod, the equivalent of the verbal mm-hm; other regulators include eye contact, slight movement forward, small postural shift, eyebrow raises, and a whole host of other small nonverbal acts." Ekman and Friesen, p. 83; Raim, p. 102.
Agreement Nodding the head. Anc. *Greece* and *Rome*. Sittl, p. 92.

19th cent. *England.* Dickens, *Pickwick*, I, pp. 452, passim. *Germany.* Boggs, p. 322; *Colombia; U.S.* Saitz and Cervenka, p. 15. *France.* Mitton, p. 141. *Central Africa.* Hochegger, p. 1.

Alarm "backing toward the door, and shaking his head with a kind of sober alarm." 19th cent. *England.* Dickens, *Pickwick*, p. 408.

Amazement Moving the head from side to side horizontally. *HDV,* I, col. 323.

Amusement "Sam said nothing at all. He winked, shook his head, smiled, winked again: and with an expression of countenance which seemed to denote that he was greatly amused with something or other" 19th cent. *England.* Dickens, *Pickwick*, II, p. 118.

Anger Shaking head. *Anc. Greece.* Homer, *Odyss.*, Bk. xix. Moving head from side to side horizontally. *HDV,* I, col. 323. * Running with head against pillar. *Anc. Rome.* Sittl, p. 23. Head inclined forward. 16th cent. *Germany.* Nettesheim, p. 236.

Antipathy Head is thrown back on seeing or hearing something unpleasant. *Greece; Italy.* Sittl, p. 82.

Apology "He looked at her fixedly, shook his head" *U.S.* Birdwhistell, *Introduction*, p. 30.

Appreciation " 'That 'ere young lady,' replied Sam. 'She knows wot's wot, she does . . . Mr. Weller closed one eye and shook his head from side to side in a manner which was highly gratifying to the personal vanity of the gentlemen in blue." 19th cent. *England.* Dickens, *Pickwick*, II, p. 148.

Approach Head tossed up and back in a short jerk. As a beckoning gesture, mainly *Northern Europe.* Morris et al., pp. 166–67.

Approval Nodding the head. *Germany.* *DWb,* IV/2, col. 601. 19th cent. *England.* Dickens, *Pickwick*, I, p. 218; II, pp. 61, 408, 471. "said Mr. Gales, nodding his head, approvingly." 19th cent. *England.* Dickens, *Oliver Twist*, p. 255. A silent nod of approval. *England.* Wodehouse, p. 24. "Mukherjee smiled and waggled his head from side to side in the Hindu gesture of approval. *India.* Mann, pp. 74–75.

Arrogance Head turned and thrown back. *Europe; North America.* Aubert, p. 119. * Head raised with a certain delay. *Portugal.* Basto, p. 27.

Assurance "and nodding his head again, as much as to say, he had not mistaken his man." 19th cent. *England.* Dickens, *Oliver Twist*, p. 338.

Attention "head and neck were cocked one eighth to the right . . . His eyes also were to the right; the brow was furrowed, the mouth somewhat turned down, and the chin tense." *U.S.* Birdwhistell, "Do Gestures Speak Louder than Words?", p. 57. Turning the head. *Europe; North America.* Aubert, p. 99.

Bafflement "There was something in this scene—something in all these sketches now that he was aware of it—that was troubling. A sort of surreal, off-center dislocation from reality. Chee stared at the sketches, trying to understand. He shook his head, baffled." *U.S.* Hillerman, *Talking God*, p. 94.

Carelessness "she tossed her head with affected carelessness." 19th cent. *England.* Dickens, *Oliver Twist*, p. 371.

Challenge Head turned and thrown back. *Europe; North America.* Aubert, p. 119. Head lifted rapidly. *Portugal.* Basto, p. 26.

Clarification Moving head (from side to side?) repeatedly and slowly. *Portugal.* Basto, p. 18.

Command "Fagin nodded to him to take no further notice just then." 19th cent. *England.* Dickens, *Oliver Twist*, p. 418. "The old gentleman nodded; and two ragged boys . . . forthwith commenced climbing up two of the trees." 19th cent. *England.* Dickens, *Pickwick*, I, p. 101.

Concentration Inclining head forward. Medieval *Germany. Graf Rudolf*, p. 42, 8–10. * Stroking beard, head, moustache. *U.S.* Krout, p. 25.

Confidence Raising the head. Biblical. *Middle East. Luke* 21:28. *Germany.* Krukenberg, p. 318.

Confirmation "nodding his head in a confirmatory way" 19th cent. *England.* Dickens, *Oliver Twist*, p. 274.

Confusion Lowering head. *Portugal.* Basto, p. 24. * Turning head aside. *Portugal.* Ibid.

Contempt "he eyed him with a look of ineffable contempt . . . and turned his head another way, in presence of the whole court." 18th cent. *England.* Smollett, *Peregrine Pickle*, ch. cvi. * "she tossed her head in silence with an air of ineffable contempt." 19th cent. *England.* Dickens, *Pickwick*, I, p. 129. * "All they that see me laugh me to scorn . . . they shake the head." Biblical. *Middle East. Ps.* 22:7. * Upward snub of nose executed by throwing head upward and sideward. Women. *Spain.* Kaulfers, p. 254.

Cuckoldry A circular movement of the head may indicate a bull, particularly a meek bull. *Lat. Am.* Kany, p. 190.

Deception Eyelids half-closed, look to side. Brows drawn together, forced smile. Cheeks raised, wrinkling under eyes. *Europe; North America.* Aubert, p. 102.

Defiance "shook her head with an air of defiance." 19th cent. *England.* Dickens, *Oliver Twist*, p. 173.

Denial Shaking the head. 16th-17th cent. *England.* Shakesp., *Much Ado* 2.1.377; *Jul. Caes.* 1.2.286; *Lear* 4.4.122. "shaking her head meanwhile, to intimate that the woman would not die so easily" 19th cent. *England.* Dickens, *Oliver Twist*, p. 212. *India.* Rose, p. 312.

Depart Rapid lifting of the head can be a command: "go away." *Portugal.* Basto, p. 37. * "But suddenly she closed the book . . . shaking her head with a backward movement as if to say 'avaunt' to floating visions." 19th cent. *England*. Eliot, p. 621. * Head inclined to one side and moved quickly to the other while looking angrily at someone indicates 'Scram!' *Netherlands*. Andrea and de Boer, p. 83. *See* Accompany.

Depression Head lowered. Anc. *Rome*. Sittl, p. 155.

Despair Head is moved from side to side around its axis. *France*. Mitton, p. 144. 19th cent. *England*. Dickens, *Pickwick*, II, pp. 111, 271, etc. * Running with the head against a door. Sueton., *Aug.*, 22. * Males hung their heads in shame, despair, or mourning. Anc. *Greece*. Bremmer, p. 23.

Direction " 'She was my daughter,' said the old woman, nodding her head in the direction of the corpse." 19th cent. *England*. Dickens, *Oliver Twist*, p. 44. * " 'And vere is George?' inquired the old gentleman. Mr. Pell jerked his head in the direction of a back parlour" 19th cent. *England*. Dickens, *Pickwick*, II, p. 246. *Portugal*. Basto, p. 37. " 'Come on.' He jerked his head in the direction of the car park." *England*. Lodge, *Paradise News*, p. 148.

Disagreement Shaking of the head. 16th-17th cent. *England*. Shakesp., *King John* 3.1.19; II *Henry IV* 1.1.95. " 'That wouldn't quite fit,' replied Fagin, shaking his head." 19th cent. *England*. Dickens, *Oliver Twist*, p. 407.

Disapproval Shaking the head. Biblical. *Middle East*. *Job* 16:4. 16th-17th cent. *England*. Shakesp., *Much Ado* 2.1.377; *King John* 4.2.231; *Timon* 2.2.211. Anc. *Greece* and *Rome;* 19th cent. *Italy*. Sittl, p. 83; Manzoni, ch. xv. *Spain*. Green, p. 45. " 'Hush!' said Mr. Jingle, in a stage whisper; '—large boy—dumpling face—round eyes—rascal!' Here he shook his head expressively" 19th cent. *England*. Dickens, *Pickwick*, I, p. 127. * "raised one eyebrow, nodded, moved his head slowly from one side to another." *U.S.* Birdwhistell, *Introduction*, p. 34; see also "Do Gestures Speak Louder than Words?" p. 56. * "and soon he was clucking under his breath and shaking his head every time the patriarch, after much dignified meditation, lurched forward to make a wild move [on the chessboard]" *Russia*. Nabokov, p. 48. * Shaking the head with a grimace. Schoolchildren. *U.S.* Seton, p. xx.

Disbelief Shaking the head. Anc. *Greece* and *Rome*. Sittl, pp. 82–83. " 'I doubt it, my dear young lady,' said the doctor, shaking his head." 19th cent. *England*. Dickens, *Oliver Twist*, p. 275. "exchanging a shake of the head with a lady in the opposite shop, in which doubt and mistrust were plainly mingled" 19th cent. *England*. Dickens, *Oliver Twist*, ch. xxvi. Shaking head. *Germany*. Boggs, col. 322; *DWb*, IV/2, col. 601. * Slowly swinging head from side to side. Schoolchildren. *U.S.* Seton, p. xxii. *Portugal*. Basto, p. 29. * Head thrown back repeatedly in excitement. Anc. *Rome*. Sittl, p. 82. * "Wardle measured out a regular circle of nods and winks, addressed to the other members of the company." 19th cent. *England*. Dickens, *Pickwick*, I, p. 301. * Turning head aside ("Don't come to me with a story like that"). *Portugal*. Basto, p. 32. * While someone is speaking, turn head or back to him—disbelief or unwillingness to listen further. *Jordan; Lebanon; Saudi Arabia.*. Barakat, no. 5.

Disgust   Head turned away from something, eyes half closed. Anc. *Greece; Rome;* early Christian. Sittl, p. 84. * Head turned, glance thrown backward, looking at the despised person out of the corner of one's eye. Anc. *Greece*. Sittl, p. 83.

Dislike   Head turned away from something, eyes half closed. Anc. *Greece* and *Rome*; early Christian. Sittl, p. 84. * Head turned, glance thrown backwards, looking at the despised person out of the corner of one's eye. Anc. *Greece*. Sittl, p. 83. Shaking the head. Biblical. *Middle East*. *Job* 16:4; *Mark* 15:29.

Dismay   "Next, they switched to the usual shop talk of European teachers abroad, sighing and shaking heads over the 'typical American college student' who does not know geography" *Europe*. Nabokov, p. 125.

Ecstasy   Head thrown back. Women. Anc. *Greece* and *Rome*. Sittl, p. 27.

Effeminacy   Head inclined toward the left. *Lat. Am.* Kany, p. 181.

Emphasis   " 'What do you want here?' . . . 'Nothing, Ma'am, upon my honor,' said Mr. Pickwick, nodding his head so energetically that the tassel of his night-cap danced again." 19th cent. *England*. Dickens, *Pickwick*, I, p. 380. * "Mr. Weller delivered this scientific opinion with many confirmatory frowns and nods." 19th cent. *England*. Dickens, *Pickwick*, II, p. 288. " 'Nothing will do that, sir,' replied the man, shaking his head." 19th cent. *England*. Dickens, *Oliver Twist*, p. 504.

Etiquette   "he would not . . . give the least nod of civility when they drank to his health." 18th cent. *England*. Smollett, *Peregrine Pickle*, I, ch. ii. "a courteous nod." 19th cent. *England*. Dickens, *Pickwick*, II, p. 202; *Portugal*. Basto, p. 20.

Farewell   Lowering head. 17th cent. *Spain*. Cervantes, *La Galatea*, I, p. 57.

Fear   " 'You were not to be found.' Pickwick looked gloomy. Shook his head. Hoped no violence would be committed." 19th cent. *England*. Dickens, *Pickwick*, II, p. 169. * Head turned away from supposed location of deity encountered or addressed. Christian; Buddhist. Ohm, pp. 177–78.

Flirting   Nods and smiles. 19th cent. *England*. Dickens, *Pickwick*, II, p. 405.

Foolishness   "Sometimes the corner cowboys tapped their heads and laughed, meaning Terry was punchy." *U.S.* Schulberg p. 30.

Friendship   Laying the head on the chest of someone while embracing him indicates particular fondness. Apparently customary at the court of Louis XIV, even among relative strangers. La Bruyère, *Les Charactères;* Cascudo, *História*, p. 102.

Gratitude   Head bowed. Late *Roman Empire; Byzantine Empire.* Sittl, p. 155. *Portugal.* Basto, p. 19.

Gravity   "shaking his head gravely." 19th cent. *England.* Dickens, *Oliver Twist*, p. 112. "Mr. Bumble shook his head with gloomy mystery." Ibid., p. 26.

Greeting   Removal of tip of cloak or cap from head as sign of respect was required in presence of Roman officials. Anc. *Rome.* Sittl, p. 154. "Hat and cowl come off when the priest conducts mass. Everyone knows that one leaves hat and sword before the door if one is to come into the presence of a lord" 14th cent. *Germany.* Teichner, v. 85, 79–85. * Roman officials in office did not greet citizens by baring the head, but greeted vestal virgins all the more assiduously by stepping aside before them and by lowering of fasces on the part of the lictors. Anc. *Rome.* Sittl, p. 154. * Peasants spit on the ground three times when they meet a cleric. *Russia.* Pritzwald, p. 24. * Inclining the head forward. *Germany.* *DWb*, IV/2, col. 601. Nod in greeting. 19th cent. *England.* Dickens, *Pickwick*, I, p. 384. *Portugal.* Basto, p. 20. *Central Africa.* Hochegger, p. 173. * Head is inclined forward, sometimes together with the upper body, in the direction of someone. Greeting for ladies; greeting used by men not wearing a hat. The deeper the bow, the more respectful the greeting. *France.* Mitton, p. 142. * Hat is lifted from the head, and in being lifted the hand tips it in direction of someone, then replaces it on the head. Greeting of men wearing a hat. *France.* Mitton, p. 142. *See also* HAND, HAT, Greeting. * Finishing the ihram on pilgrimage and at the salat by inclining the head to the right and to the left. Muslim. Ohm, pp. 229–30. Inclining the head to the right and left at the end of the Teffila. Perhaps a remnant of the turning of the body which was part of Babylonian prayer ritual. Jews. Ohm, p. 229. * Patting someone on the head when greeting him. Maori, *New Zealand.* Eichler, p. 162.

Helplessness   Shaking the head. Anc. *Greece* and *Rome.* Sittl, p. 83.

Hesitation   Head moves slowly from right to left and back. *France.* Mitton, p. 144.

Homage   Offering oneself in serfdom to the Virgin before the altar with a token offering of money hung around the neck, or with a rope around one's neck. Crusaders entering Jerusalem in 1099 went to the Holy Sepulchre and offered their *capitate tributum* to God thus in the best manuscripts of the *Gesta Franconum.* The editor (p. 206) prefers the reading *debitum* rather than *tributum.* Roman Catholic. Southern, p. 105. For other instances, *see* Southern, ibid., n. 1; also McGuire, p. 202.

Horror   Slow, repeated movement of the head from side to side. *Portugal.* Basto, p. 30.

Humility Bowing the head. 16th–17th cent. *England.* Shakesp., *All's Well* 1.2.3. * Baring the head. 18th cent. *Germany.* Schiller, *Die Räuber*, ii, iii.

Impatience Shaking the head. 19th cent. *England.* Dickens, *Oliver Twist*, p. 229.

Indifference "and shaking her head from side to side, with poor assumption of indifference." 19th cent. *England.* Dickens, *Oliver Twist*, p. 143. Head moves slowly from side to side. *Colombia; U.S.* Saitz and Cervenka, p. 91.

Interrogation Backward nod of the head. *Europe; India.* Rose, p. 312; Basto, p. 25.

Introduction "swept her head from one side to the other. As she said the word 'all' she moved her head in a sweep up and down from one side to the other." *U.S.* Birdwhistell, *Introduction*, p. 30.

Irritation Moving the head from one side to the other, more or less accompanied by movement of torso. *France.* Mitton, p. 144.

Memory Moving head repeatedly and slowly (from side to side?) *Portugal.* Basto, p. 18." 'Bless my dear eyes,' said Mr. Roker, shaking his head slowly from side to side . . . as if he were fondly recalling some peaceful scene of his early youth." 19th cent. *England.* Dickens, *Pickwick*, II, p. 229.

Misery "Thus one will lean his head upon another's, the quicker thereby to excite one's pity." 13th–14th cent. *Italy.* Dante, *Purg.*, c. xiii.

Mockery "But those passing by blasphemed Him, shaking their heads." Biblical. *Middle East. Matth.*, 27:39; *Mark* 15:29.

Modesty "The downcast eyes of youths and maidens also suggest that they did not carry their heads upright and the same applied, apparently, to adult women." Anc. *Greece.* Bremmer, p. 23. Head lowered, blushing. Medieval *France.* Chretien de Troyes, *Erec*, 1751; *Cligès*, 5016; Lommatzsch, p. 68.

Mourning Head covered. Biblical. *Middle East. Esth.*, 6:12. * Uncovering head before the dead but not before the living. Medieval *Frisia.* *HDA*, II, col. 850. * After funeral the relatives of deceased return home with bowed head. Anc. *Rome.* Sittl, p. 73. Hanging one's head. Anc. *Greece.* Bremmer, p. 23.

Negation Head raised. Anc. *Greece* and *Rome.* Sittl, p. 93. * Shaking of the head as reenforcement of voiced disapproval or negation. Anc. *Rome*; 19th cent. *Italy.* Sittl, p. 83. Shaking of the head in weak or strong disapproval. Biblical. *Middle East. Matth.* 27:39; anc. *Greece* and *Rome.* Sittl, pp. 82–83. Shaking head from side to side several times. Arab. Barakat, no. 145. Shaking the head. *U.S.* Ruesch and Kees, p. 33. "Mr. Grummer intimated, by a retrospective shake of the head, that he should never forget it" 19th cent. *England.* Dickens, *Pickwick*, I, p. 405. " 'No, that I wouldn't,' said Mr. Pell; and he pursed up his lips, frowned, and shook his head mysteriously." 19th cent. *England.* Dickens, *Pickwick,* II, p. 246. " 'Commodore!' said the stranger, starting up, . . . 'want change for a five—bad silver—Brummagem buttons—won't do—no go—eh ?' and he shook his head most knowingly." 19th cent. *England.* Dickens, *Pickwick,* II, p. 12. "but God in Heaven shakes his head." 18th cent. *Germany.* Schiller, *Die Räuber,* v, i. Head shaken once or twice around vertical axis. ("This is wrong." "I refuse.") *France.* Mitton, p. 141. *Central Africa.* Hochegger, p. 125. * Head thrown back repeatedly in excitement. Anc. *Greece* and *Rome.* Sittl, p. 82. "He said nothing, only tossed his head back twice abruptly, which was the Greek way of making a silent but emphatic 'no!' " MacInnes, p. 184. Head thrown back in proud negation of something. 19th cent. *Germany.* Sittl, p. 82. * Chin raised in sudden movement, head back, eyelids half closed, eyebrows raised. Sometimes accompanied by click of the tongue. Southern *Italy; Balkans; Greece; Albania;* former southern *Yugoslavia; Bulgaria;* Asiatic *Turkey; Iran; Iraq; Syria; Palestine; Egypt.* Müller, pp. 101–02. * Head raised, restricted movement of face, neck tending to remain stationary. Arab. George, p. 320. * Nodding of the head. Arab; *Africa.* Goldziher, "Über Gebärden," pp. 370, 377ff. Similar to American "Yes." *India.* Su, <LINGUIST 3. 1012>. A nod of the head forward is favorable, the head thrown back has unfavorable meaning. Onians, pp. 139–40, n. 4. Backward jerk of the head accompanied by clicking the tongue. *Near East.* Critchley, pp. 90–91. *Iran.* Su, <LINGUIST 3.1012>. Optional click of the tongue may be added. *Greece.* Su, LINGUIST 3.1012. A click with a toss of the head. *India.* Rose, p. 213. Tossing the head back in negation. *Greece;* southern *Italy; Malta; Tunisia.* Axtell, *Gestures,* p. 61. The head toss as negation is totally absent from N. Europe, the Iberian peninsula and Tunisia; very rare in N. Italy and Sardinia, but generally recognized from Naples to Sicily, and Malta; common in Greece and Turkey. The dividing line between the head toss and the head shake in Italy is N. of Naples, probably the area of the formerly marshy Volturno Basin, which presented an obstance to early Greek settlement; *see* Morris et al., 162–68, 247–59. Chin raised, head back. Southern *Italy;* southern *Balkans.* Röhrich, *Gebärde-Metapher-Parodie,* p. 14, and pl. 6a. * Head tilted back; accompanying "tsk" is optional; several in a row means "too bad!" *Lebanon.* Su, <LINGUIST 3.1012>. A click with a toss of the head. *India.* Rose, p. 213. * Head turned in one direction only. Semitic, *Ethiopia.* Sittl, p. 83. * Negation by gesture, apart from a blank face, does not exist in the Japanese lexicon. Su, LINGUIST 3.1012. * Moving head from side to side rapidly. *Portugal.* Basto, p. 29. *See also* Affirmation.

Nostalgia Expressions of nostalgia may be accompanied by slowly lowering and raising the head. *Spain; Lat. Am.* Green, p. 63. *See* Memory.

Oath Swearing by one's head. 16th–17th cent. *England.* Shakesp., *Troil.* 2.3.95; *Rom. and Jul.* 3.1.38.

Obedience "Mr. Phunky bowed to Mr. Pickwick with the reverence which a first client must ever awaken; and again inclined his head towards his leader." 19th cent. *England.* Dickens, *Pickwick*, II, p. 34.

Pensiveness Eyes closed, head inclined forward, sometimes supported by hand. Medieval *France. Chanson de Roland*, 139. Medieval *Germany.* Walther v. d. Vogelweide, miniature in Heidelberg, Univ.-Bibl. cpg 848, fol. 24r; Walther, pl. 45; Lommatzsch, pp. 45–47. "and bore my head bowed down, like one whose mind is burdened by his thought, looking like half an archway of a bridge." 13th–14th cent. *Italy.* Dante, *Purg.* c. xix. 18th cent. *Germany.* Schiller, *Graf v. Habsburg*, 111.

Piety Continuous inclination of the head forward. 19th cent. *Palestine.* Bauer, p. 192.

Pity Shaking of the head. 16th–17th cent. *England.* Shakesp., *Ven. and Adon.* 223; *Merchant* 3.3.15; *King John* 3.1.19; etc.

Plea Bowing head. Anc. *Greece* and *Rome.* Sittl, pp. 165, 296.

Pleasure Head inclined in direction of pleasing object. Anc. *Rome.* Sittl, p. 92.

Pointing "Mr. Pickwick happened to be looking another way at the moment, so her Ladyship nodded her head towards him, and frowned expressively." 19th cent. *England.* Dickens, *Pickwick*, II, p. 122. Also *Spain;* understood in *Lat. Am.* Green, p. 71. *See* Direction.

Prayer Uncovered head. Anc. *Greece.* Covered head. Anc. *Rome.* Greek custom predominated in *Africa.* Uncovered head. Modern *Greece; Cyprus.* Sittl, p. 177. * Inclining the head forward. Anc. *Rome; Christian.* Sittl, p. 177. Priest bows head in prayer. Roman Catholic. *Mass*, pp. 21, 52. * Beating head against post. Anc. *Rome.* Sittl, p. 185. * Head inclined to the side—once common, no longer favored by Christians. Ohm, p. 229.

Pride Head thrown back in proud negation of something. 19th cent. *Germany.* Sittl, p. 82. Head held high: "But now Truth is victorious and holds her head high." 16th cent. *Germany.* Luther, in *DWb*, IV/2, col. 600.

Recognition "the knowing nod." *U.S.* Birdwhistell, "Do Gestures Speak Louder than Words?" p. 56.

Refusal Head thrown back. Anc. *Greece* and *Rome;* modern *Greece; Italy.* Sittl, p. 82. * Head turned to side to refuse food or to refuse being taken on one's arm. Children. 19th cent. *Germany.* Sittl, ibid. * Shaking the head. 19th cent. *England.* Dickens, *Pickwick*, II, p. 20. Head turns one or two times vertically around its axis. *France.* Inclination of the head indicates negative, the above positive. *China.* Mitton, p. 141. *See also* Affirmation, Negation.

Regret   "The surgeon shook his head, in a manner which intimated that he feared it impossible." 19th cent. *England.* Dickens, *Oliver Twist*, p. 265.

Remorse   Putting ashes on one's head. Biblical. *Middle East.* II *Sam.* 13:19; *Jer.* 6:26; *Job* 42:6.

Repetition   Quick jerk of the head to one side indicates that the person has not understood what has been said and that it is to be repeated. *Lebanon.* Barakat, no. 245.

Reproach   "He shook his head reprovingly." *England.* Wodehouse, p. 73. * Slow swinging movement of the head. *Portugal.* Basto, p. 18. Río de la Plata region of *Argentina; Uruguay.* Meo Zilio, p. 101.

Respect   Bowing the head. Biblical. *Middle East. Gen.* 43:28. Removal of tip of cloak or cap from head as sign of respect was required in the presence of Roman officials. Anc. *Rome.* Sittl, p. 154. Slave lowers his head in the presence of his master. Anc. *Greece;* anc. *Rome;* Arab. Sittl, p. 155. * If a lay dignitary meets a cleric of any rank, he is to bow his head. Early medieval *France.* Synod of Mâcon (585); J.-C. Schmitt, p. 58. If both the layman and the cleric are mounted, the layman is to remove the covering of his head and greet the cleric joyfully. Ibid. "Mr. Pickwick, who, as the spokesman of his friends, stood hat in hand, bowing with the utmost politeness and respect." 19th cent. *England.* Dickens, *Pickwick*, I, p. 414. * Turning head aside when addressing a superior or overlord. Shilluk, *Egypt; China.* Ohm, p. 177.

Rest   Head leaning on one palm, inclined towards one shoulder. To indicate sleep, one closes one's eyes, to indicate rest, one keeps them open. 19th cent. Naples, southern *Italy.* De Jorio, p. 144.

Reverence   Standing with bowed head. Roman Catholic. *Mass*, p. 28. "But I held my head bowed down like one who goes reverently." 13th–14th cent. *Italy.* Dante, *Inf.*, c. xv. * Subjects have to turn their face away when Emperor speaks with them, so he will not be contaminated. Imperial *China.* Moses hid his face when God appeared in the thornbush, for he feared the aspect of God. Biblical. *Middle East.* Ohm, p. 177.

Satisfaction   Nodding the head. 19th cent. *England.* Dickens, *Pickwick*, II, p. 331. Raising the head with anticipation. *Portugal.* Basto, p. 28.

Scorn   "Robyn tossed her head scornfully." *England.* Lodge, *Nice Work*, p. 141.

Secrecy   Looking in both directions before speaking. *Spain.* Green, p. 43.

Self-importance   "Does he not hold up his head, as it were, and strut in his gait?" 16th–17th cent. *England.* Shakesp., *Merry Wives* 1.4.30.

Shame   Hanging one's head. Anc. *Greece.* Bremmer, p. 23. Head lowered. 12th cent. *France*. Chretien de Troyes, *Yvain*, 1785; 13th–14th cent. *Italy*. Dante, *Purg*., c. xxxi; Lommatzsch, p. 72. *Portugal*. Basto, p. 24.

Sorrow "The virgins of Jerusalem hang their heads down to the ground." Biblical. *Middle East. Lament*. 2:10. Hanging head in grief. 16th–17th cent. *England*. Shakesp., *I Henry VI* 3.2.124; *Lucr*., 521. * "And he wept as he went up, and had his head covered, and he went barefoot." Biblical. *Middle East*. II *Sam*. 15:30. * Hiding face in pillow. 18th cent. *Germany*. Stage direction. Schiller, *Die Räuber* ii, ii. * Putting dust on one's head. Biblical. *Middle East. Josh*. 7:6. Ashes on head. Biblical. *Middle East*. II *Sam*. 13:19. * Shaving the head. Biblical. *Middle East. Job* 1:20. * Head shaken in sorrow. Anc. *Greece;* anc. *Rome;* 19th cent. *Italy*. Manzoni, c. xiv. Sittl, p. 83. 16th–17th cent. *England*. Shakesp., *Merchant* 3.3.15; *King John* 3.1.19; etc. * Bowing the head. 19th cent. *England;* 19th cent. *Germany*. Boggs, col. 319. "The tear . . . stole down the old lady's face, as she shook her head with a melancholy smile." 19th cent. *England*. Dickens, *Pickwick*, I, p. 87. " 'My dear young lady,' rejoined the surgeon, mournfully shaking his head." 19th cent. *England*. Dickens, *Oliver Twist*, p. 265.

Strength (of character) Head (of the subject of a portrait) held high, so that he always seems to look down upon the viewer, as in Frans Hals's *Portret van een man* (1622). 17th cent. *Netherlands*. Van der Meulen, p. 35.

Submission Bowing head before demons in a cyclone. 19th cent. *Greece*. Sittl, p. 177. Fearful people passed the Grotta di Posilippo near Naples only with bowed head. Anc. *Rome*. Sittl, p. 177. Lowering head and keeping it lowered. *Portugal*. Basto, p. 20. Bared head. 18th cent. *Germany*. Schiller, *Die Räuber*, ii, ii.

Surprise Slow, repeated movement of head from side to side. *Portugal*. Basto, p. 30.

Surrender Head inclined forward. Anc. *Greece*. Sittl, p. 114.

Sympathy Shaking of the head. 19th cent. *England*. Dickens, *Pickwick*, II, pp. 409, 456.

Threat Head is moved rapidly laterally in threat of punishment, esp. to children. *Portugal*. Basto, p. 35.

Uncertainty Head sways slowly right and left, evoking balance between two viewpoints. *France*. Mitton, p. 144.

Understanding "Sam gave a short nod of intelligence." 19th cent. *England*. Dickens, *Pickwick*, I, p. 438; II, p. 211. * Sudden raising of head, often accompanied by raising hand or index to head. *Portugal*. Basto, p. 28. Head raised very slowly ("Now I see . . .") *Portugal*. Basto, ibid.

Warning Slow swinging movement of the head. *Portugal*. Basto, p. 18.

HEAD, KNEE

Humility Kneeling before altars and images of deities, often on threshold of temple, and bowing head. Anc. *Rome*. Sittl, p. 178.

Prayer *See* Humility above.

Protection Back of head placed on knees of friend in order to rest. Lombardy, early medieval *Italy; Byzantine Empire;* 19th cent. *Greece; Germany*. Sittl, pp. 34–35.

Sorrow Head sinks down between knees, in sitting or squatting position. Anc. *Rome*. Sittl, p. 24. Head sinks down upon knees while sitting or squatting. Anc. *Greece* and *Rome*. Sittl, p. 24.

HEAD, LIP

Apology Kissing the top of another man's head after quarreling. *Saudi Arabia*. Barakat, no. 120.

Contempt "They shoot out the lip, they shake the head." Biblical. *Middle East. Ps.* 22:7.

Disbelief Lips tight, slowly widening; sometimes head nods, accompanied, in English, by "m-hmmm." *Colombia; U.S.* Saitz and Cervenka, p. 40.

Greeting Kiss on the head. Anc. *Greece*. Sittl, p. 41.

Insolence Head thrown back, frown, slight protrusion of lower lip. *Europe; North America*. Aubert, p. 113.

Negation *See* HEAD, Negation.

Pointing "Chepe jerked his head toward the hut and pointed with his lower lip. 'That's where the mosquitoes are.' " *Central America; Kenya*. F. Carr, p. 175; also Hayes, p. 234. Pointing with the finger is tabu in *Central America*. Hayes, ibid.

Pride *See* Insolence above.

Resignation Head inclined slightly and slowly to one side, frequently accompanied by twist of lip and clicking of the tongue. *Portugal*. Basto, p. 36.

Respect Children kiss the top of their mother's head during Moslem holy days. *Saudi Arabia*. Barakat, no. 119.

HEAD, MOUTH

Mockery Head raised, mouth imitates a mute's effort at speaking. *Central Africa*. Hochegger, p. 26.

Psychotherapy Head leaned back, mouth opens and closes in 'speaking' motions, signalling a visit to the psychotherapist. *Netherlands*. Andrea and de Boer, p. 132.

HEAD, OBJECT

Oath The Saxons of Siebenbürgen, in swearing oaths in connection with boundary disputes, swore with bare feet, loosened belt, and a clump of earth on the head. 19th cent. *Hungary*. Kahle, p. 116.

HEAD, SHOULDER

Apotropy Shrugging shoulders and shaking head: "As they sallied forth from Bivar they beheld a bird of happy augury, and as they drew nigh to Burgos, one of evil omen! But my Cid shrugged his shoulders and shook his head." Medieval *Spain. Cid,* c. i. *See also* Indifference.

Fear Head drawn in between shoulders. Anc. *Rome.* Quintil., xi, 3, 90.

Indifference Shrugging shoulders and shaking head. Schoolchildren. *U.S.* Seton, xxiii. *See also* Apotropy.

Joy "and, drawing his head and shoulders into a heap, literally hugged himself for joy." 19th cent. *England.* Dickens, *Oliver Twist*, p. 174.

Pointing Usually considered impolite in Europe and North America to point at someone; therefore one points someone out by dropping one shoulder slightly, raising one eyebrow and jerking head to side in direction of person pointed out. Axtell, *Gestures*, p. 104.

HEAD, THIGH

Disappointment "whereat he strikes his thigh, returns indoors, and grumbles here and there." 13th–14th cent. *Italy.* Dante, *Inf.*, c. xxiv.

HEAD, TONGUE

Negation Clicking the tongue, head simultaneously moved back. 19th cent. *Greece; Italy.* Sittl, p. 96; 19th cent. *Palestine.* Bauer, p. 220.

Resignation Head inclined slightly and slowly to one side, frequently accompanied by twist of lip and clicking of tongue. *Portugal.* Basto, p. 36.

HEAD, TOOTH

Anger Biting lower lip with upper teeth and shaking head from side to side. *Saudi Arabia.* Barakat, no. 154.

Disapproval Shaking head from side to side and clicking teeth simultaneously. Arab. Barakat, no. 146.

Pensiveness *See* HAND, Pensiveness.

Vengeance Grinding the teeth and shaking the head while raising it gradually. 19th cent. *Palestine.* Bauer, p. 218.

HEEL

Contempt Kicking with heels. Anc. *Rome.* Sittl, pp. 106–07.

Displeasure Kicking seats of theater with the heels. Anc. *Greece.* Pollux 2, 4, 4, 19; Sittl, p. 65.

Mockery *See* Contempt.

HIP

Copulation Elbows held on hips, hips moved back and forth rapidly. *Saudi Arabia.* Barakat, no. 236.

JAW
Decisiveness   Protruding lower jaw. *U.S.* Krout, p. 24.

JAW, TOOTH
Pensiveness   With fixed expression, one moves the jaw and grinds teeth. *Central Africa.* Hochegger, p. 147.

KNEE
Accolade   "Iden, kneel down . . . Rise up a knight." 16th–17th cent. *England.* Shakesp., II *Henry VI* 5.2.78.

Adoption   In *Gen.* 30:3 Rachel gives Bilhah to Jacob so that she may "bear on my knees"; and in *Gen.* 50:23 the children of Marchir the son of Manasseh were brought up "upon Joseph's knees." Alluding to custom of placing infants on father's knees as symbol of their adoption. Biblical. *Middle East.* Also Anc. *Greece.* Homer, *Odyss.*, Bk. xix; Fischer, "Heilgebärden," p. 342.

Adoration   According to the Ordinal of Gregory X (1271–76), the pope, assisting at a Mass in his own chapel, first rises just before the consecration, then, his head uncovered, kneels to adore the sacrament. Roman Catholic. Ladner, p. 269. Pious Romans fell on knees on the threshold of the temple and kissed it. Anc. *Rome.* Sittl, p. 184. Stiff, almost military genuflection. Anc. *Rome.* Ohm, p. 47. "[the priest] genuflects once more in adoration of the Precious Blood of Christ now contained under the appearance of wine." *Mass*, p. 57. Women kneel on both knees, men on one. *Portugal.* Basto, p. 9.

Attention   "turned and thrust both knees into the lateral aspect of her left side." Desire for attention while sitting. Women. *U.S.* Birdwhistell, "Background," p. 14.

Confession   "Then I confess, here on my knee, before high heaven and you." 16th–17th cent. *England.* Shakesp., *All's Well* 1.3.182–83.

Determination   "Nathaniel Pipkin went down on his knees on the dewy grass, and declared his resolution to remain there forever" 19th cent. *England.* Dickens, *Pickwick*, I, p. 283.

Distress   "Then down upon her knees she falls, weeps, sobs, beats her heart, tears her hair, prays, curses" 16th–17th cent. *England.* Shakesp. *Much Ado* 2.3.134–5.

Fear   The handwriting upon the wall so frightened Belshazzar that "his knees smote one against the other." Biblical. *Middle East.* Dan. 5:6. * "At the very instant he passed the second door, the son of Mr. Allen entered by the opposite one, and unluckily having a red waistcoat on, one of the soldiers, upon seeing him, presented his firelock and the young man in a fright dropped on his knees; when the soldier fired, killing him upon the spot." 18th cent. *England.* Hickey, p. 72

Gratitude   "I will kneel to him with thanks." 16th–17th cent. *En-*

gland. Shakesp., *Anth. and Cleo.* 5.2.20. "The parson fell on his knees and ejaculated many thanksgivings" 18th cent. *England.* Fielding, Bk. iv, ch. 12. Women kneel on both knees, men on one. *Portugal.* Basto, p. 9.

Homage Kneeling as form of homage was unknown in anc. *Greece* and *Rome.* Euripides regards it as a curiosity in his *Phoen.* Sittl, p. 156.

Humility Kneeling. Biblical. *Middle East. Dan.* 6:10; II *Chron.* 6:13; *Luke* 22:41; etc. *See also* Prayer below. 16th–17th cent. *England.* Shakesp., II *Henry VI* 1.1.

Humility (mocking) "And they struck Him on the head with a reed and spat on Him. And bending their knees, they bowed down to Him." Biblical. *Middle East. Mark* 15:19.

Oath "O Warwick, I do bend my knee with thine; and in this vow do chain my soul to thine!" 16th and 17th cent. *England.* Shakesp., III *Henry VI* 2.3.33–4.

Plea "fell on his knees before Elijah and begged him." Biblical. *Middle East. Matth.* 17:l4; II *Kings* 1:13. "By my advice, all humbled on your knees, you shall ask pardon of his Majesty." 16th–17th cent. *England.* Shakesp., *Tit.* 1.1.472–3. Bending the knee in pleading was frequent during the *Roman Empire.* Sittl, p. 156. Kneeling on one or both knees in prayer or supplication. Anc. *Rome.* Sittl, p. 178. Bending the knee accompanies a request for faithfulness (never a declaration of love). Anc. *Rome.* Tibullus 1, 9, 30. Ambassadors kneel before the senate and defeated kings kneel before victorious generals. Anc. *Rome.* Sittl, p. 156. Doña Elvira and Doña Sol kneel before their father, the Cid. Medieval *Spain. Cid,* c. iii. "Now pay attention: one must kneel humbly before great lords when one requests something of them. And similarly we should kneel before the Lord of Heaven when we pray for His gifts" 14th cent. *Germany.* Teichner, v. 85, 48–53; also Kaufringer, no. 1, 324–30, no. 2, 229. "A conqueror that will pray in aid for kindness where he for grace is kneel'd to." 16th–17th cent. *England.* Shakesp., *Anth. and Cleo.* 5.2.27–28. "I would you had kneel'd, my lord, to ask me mercy." Shakesp., *All's Well* 2.1.66. "Mrs. Grizzle . . . fell upon her knees in the garden entreating her, with tears in her eyes to resist such a pernicious appetite." 18th cent. *England.* Smollett, *Peregrine Pickle,* I, v, vi. "The innkeeper . . . fell upon his knees, protesting in the face of Heaven that he was utterly ignorant." Ibid., I, lviii. "she clasped his knees and begged for the love of God that he would have compassion" Ibid., I, vi. "Mr. Tupman had sunk upon his knees at her feet. 'Oh, Rachel! say you love me.' " 19th cent. *England.* Dickens, *Pickwick,* I, p. 119. "Mr. Jingle fell on his knees, remained thereupon for five minutes thereafter and rose the accepted lover of the spinster aunt." Ibid., I, p. 130. *See also* LIP, Homage.

Possession Bride is placed upon the knee of the groom. 17th cent. *Germany*. Weise, *Comödienprobe*, 333, 334. *See also* Adoption above.

Prayer "The custom of not kneeling on the Lord's day is symbolic of the resurrection." Early Christian. Irenaeus, Fragm. 7. Kneeling in prayer. Anc. *Egypt; Phoenicia*. Sittl, p. 178, n. 8; see also p. 369: the inhabitants of Naukratis knelt in saying grace according to Egyptian custom. Worshipper kneels and holds his hands before him, extended downward, fingers extended. Brunet, p. 207. For St. Paul the expressions "to pray" and "to bend the knee" to God are complementary. Biblical. *Middle East. Phil.* 2:10; *Eph.* 3:14. Adding solemnity to prayer: Solomon dedicated his temple "kneeling down in the presence of all the multitude of Israel and lifting up his hands toward heaven. II *Par.* 6:13; III *Kings* 8:54. For other instances, see Hastings, *Dictionary*, p. 8; Ohm, pp. 346ff. Women fell on their knees before images of deities. Anc. *Greece*. Sittl, p. 186. The anc. Gks., though maintaining the propriety of kneeling only before gods, left this to women and children. Sittl, p. 178. Only women and bigots knelt in prayer. Anc. *Greece*. Sittl, p. 177. Kneeling on one or both knees in prayer or supplication. Sliding forwards on the knees in the temple. Anc. *Rome*. Sittl, p. 178. Kneeling at the threshold of the temple. Anc. *Rome*. Sittl, p. 178. Kneeling before altars and images, often on the threshold of the temple, with bowed head. Anc. *Rome*. Sittl, ibid. In case of danger to the state, the senate ordered a *supplicatio* by the matrons, who fell on their knees in the temples or loosened their hair, threw themselves down and kissed the ground. Others tore their hair on the threshold of the temples, beat their shoulders and scratched their cheeks. Anc. *Rome*. Sittl, p. 185. "The knee is made flexible by which the offence of the Lord is mitigated, wrath appeased, grace called forth." Ambrose, VI, ix; Hraban. II, xli. When forgiveness of some offence is sought, Origen maintains that kneeling is necessary. Roman Catholic. *Cath. Encycl.* I, col. 423–27. "Kneel, and pray your mother's blessing." 16th–17th cent. *England*. Shakesp., *Winter's Tale* 5.3.119. Kneeling in prayer. 16th–17th cent. *England*. Shakesp., *Henry VIII* 4.1.83–85. "The innkeeper . . . fell upon his knees, protesting, in the face of heaven, that he was utterly ignorant." 18th cent. *England*. Smollett, *Peregrine Pickle*, I, ch. lviii.

Respect Bowing the knee to Joseph. Anc. *Egypt. Gen.* 41:43. Women kneel on both knees, men on one. *Portugal*. Basto, p. 9. Common practice to bend the knee to one's parents. "One knee the son, both the daughter / bend down to their mother." 16th–17th cent. *Poland*. J. Kochowski, in Bystron, II, p. 178; Bogucka, p. 198.

Reverence Moving on knees. Roman Catholic. *Brazil*. Ohm, p. 357. "I had knelt down." 13th–14th cent. *Italy*. Dante, *Purg.*, c. xix. See also Ohm, pp. 344ff. Women kneel on both knees, men on one. *Portugal*. Basto, p. 9.

Submission "At this assembly Lothair humbly fell at his father's feet in the presence of all and said: 'I know, Lord Father, that I have sinned before God and you.' " Frankish. 9th cent. *Nithard's Histories*, p. 137. "Mind, mind, thou bend thy knees." 13th–14th cent. *Italy*. Dante, *Purg.*, c. ii. "Then jointly to the ground their knees they bow." 16th–17th cent. *England*. Shakesp., *Lucr*. 1846. Medieval *Germany*. Kaufringer, no. 2, 82–84, 113, 151. Kneeling on one or both knees. Anc. *Greece* and *Rome*. Sittl, p. 158. Bending knee in pleading was frequent during *Roman Empire*. Slave bends knee before master. Sittl, p. 156. Statue of kneeling Roman captive. Early *Roman Empire*. Paris, Bibl. Nat., see Gombrich, p. 70, fig. 52; coin of Trajan, early 2nd cent., Brit. Mus., ibid., fig. 51. Proskynesis (prostration) practiced before miracle workers. Early Christian. Sittl, p. 160. Proskynesis as permanent part of court etiquette was established by Diocletian in 290; not even relatives of the emperor were exempt. It was practiced at the court of Elagabalus, but discontinued by Severus Alexander. It was not officially part of court ceremonial under Caligula, but was performed voluntarily; discontinued under Claudius. *Roman Empire*. Sittl, p. 159. No proskynesis in the early Empire, except for Asiatics, Egyptians, and defeated or won-over barbarians. Sittl, ibid. Alexander the Great insisted on traditional proskynesis; since the Greeks regarded this as an honor due to the gods only, Alexander declared himself a god, which some of his successors imitated. Anc. *Greece* and *Rome*. Sittl, p. 158. * Avar ambassadors knelt thrice before Justinian. This was adopted from Roman imperial court etiquette by the papal court. Sittl, p. 156 and n. 9. [Editors' note: Cf. three bows in Wilhelmine German audiences with the Kaiser.]

Surrender Defeated kings kneel before the emperor. Anc. *Rome*. Sittl, p. 156. Ambassadors kneel before the senate and defeated kings kneel before victorious generals. Anc. *Rome*. Sittl, ibid.

Victory "Parzival brought him down and planted one knee on his chest." Medieval *Germany*. Wolfr. v. Eschenbach, IV, 197.

KNEE, LIP

Respect Combination of throwing a kiss and kneeling on one knee appears to be Semitic. Sittl, p. 152. Kissing someone's knee. Anc. *Greece*. Sittl, p. 169. *See also* LIP, Homage. "As General Hastings Ismay, Churchill's chief of staff, entered the palace he recognized two waiters who used to serve him at Hotel Nationale in Moscow. When they ignored his smile of recognition, he was puzzled, but once alone with him they dropped to their knees, kissed his hand—only to get up quickly and leave without saying a word." *Russia*. Toland, p. 57.

LEG

Attention Kicking legs in desire for attention. Birdwhistell, "Background," *U.S.* p. 14.

Calmness Crossed legs. 15th cent. *France*. Lommatzsch, p. 39. Also 13th cent. *Germany*. Walther v. d. Vogelweide, 8, 5 and the miniature in the Heidelberg, Univ.-Bibl. cpg 848, fol. 124r; see Walther, pl. 45; Oechelhäuser, *Die Miniaturen*, p. 69, no. 103. Prescribed position for judges in deliberation. Medieval *Germany*. Grimm, *DRA*, II, p. 375.

Comfort Crossed legs. Sercambi, pp. 364–65; Weissel, p. 8; Medieval *France*. Lommatzsch, p. 35.

Concentration *See* BODY, Concentration.

Ecstasy " 'Ha! Ha!' roared Mr. Claypole, kicking up his legs in an ecstasy." 19th cent. *England*. Dickens, *Oliver Twist*, p. 406.

Etiquette Well-behaved ladies should not sit with legs crossed; they should not walk with big steps or like men. 13th cent. *Germany*. Thomasin v. Circlaria, 411–12; 417–18. "[Victorian] men only lounged or crossed their legs in the company of other men, never when with ladies." Rockwood, p. 183. A very conservative view of propriety requires women never to cross their legs at the knees while sitting. Keeping the legs parallel or crossing them at the ankles is preferred. *Britain*. *See* Modesty. Axtell, *Gestures*, p. 107. Likewise, it is reprehensible for a knight to ride where a lady walks; also, knights should take care not to show their bare legs when riding. 13th cent. *Germany*. Thomasin v. Circlaria, 419–20; 433–36.

Fear The knees give way. 9th–10th cent. *Germany*. *Waltharius* 1326. Habicht, p. 50.

Greeting Bending one knee, while kneeling on the other, formerly a court gesture, later taken over by the church, shows reverence or homage paid to a nobleman, ecclesiastical superior, statue or fetish. Medieval *Germany*. Stroebe, p. 184. "Let them curtsy with their left legs." 16th–17th cent. *England*. Shakesp., *Shrew* 4.1.80.

Insult "If you find yourself sitting across from an Arab dignitary, don't cross your legs or you risk insulting your guest—pointing a toe at a person is considered rude in the Arab world" Lynch, p. 10. *See also* Greenberg, L4: legs crossed, feet raised and pointing directly at someone, is considered an insult. Arab. Similarly in parts of Southeast Asia. Axtell, *Gestures*, p. 109.

Joy Leaping for joy. Biblical. *Middle East*. *Luke* 6:23; II *Sam.* 6:16. Anc. *Rome*. Sittl, p. 12. * Dancing for joy. Anc. *Greece*. Sittl, ibid. *See also* Boggs, col. 320.

Judgment Crossed legs prescribed for judges during deliberations. Grimm, *DRA*, II, p. 375 (right over left leg). *See also* Lacroix, p. 71.

Magical Women sit cross-legged to procure good luck. Opie, p. 228. Crossing legs prevents birth as well as other processes. Anc. *Rome*. Meschke, ed. 336; Röhrich, *Gebärde-Metapher-Parodie*, p. 29.

Modesty A woman, when sitting down, was to keep her legs close together. Propriety demands that a woman cross her legs at the ankles, if at all, and not at the knees. 17th cent. *Netherlands*. Van Mander, II, p. 471. 19th cent. *England*, still adhered to by Brit. royalty. Axtell, *Gestures*, p. 12. In Spain it is considered inappropriate for women to cross their legs. Axtell, ibid., p. 150. Cf. the verbal gesture: " 'I've a feeling this girl . . . can tell us something. But everyone seems to have shut up tight as a virgin's knees.' " *U.S.* Hill, p. 82.

Oath Oaths are invalidated by the crossing of legs. Agrippa v. Nettesheim therefore says it is prohibited in deliberations of state. 16th cent. *Germany*. Röhrich, *Gebärde-Metapher-Parodie*, p. 29.

Prayer Right leg hangs down to the earth, left leg is extended horizontally in front of body. Manjustri-position. Buddhist. Ohm, p. 333. * Approaching the deity by running. Anc. *Egypt*. Brunet, p. 560. * Pious Japanese show their piousness by walking hundreds of times back and forth from the entrance to the Shinto shrine to the shrine itself. *Japan*. Ohm, p. 307. * At the Trisaghion of Schmone Esre the Jews jump up three times; the same happens at a certain passage in the morning prayer. Probably a remnant of a primitive ritual which was taken over by early Christianity from Judaism. Heiler, p. 101.

Pride "Why, 'a stalks up and down like a peacock." 16th–17th cent. *England*. Shakesp., *Troil*. 3.3.251.

Protest "drew his legs up against the restraint of his mother's hand." Children. *U.S.* Birdwhistell, "Background," p. 14.

Recognition "and knocked gently at the door. It was at once opened by a woman, who dropped a curtsy of recognition." 19th cent. *England*. Dickens, *Pickwick*, I, p. 361.

Respect "Let them curtsy with their left legs." 16th–17th cent. *England*. Shakesp., *Shrew*, 4.1.80.

Sorrow Pacing back and forth. Boggs, p. 319.

Superiority Sitting with legs crossed in company is a sign of superiority. *Central Africa*. Hochegger, p. 199.

Surprise Staggering backwards. Boggs, col. 321. Jumping up from a sitting position. Anc. *Greece* and *Rome*. Sittl, p. 13.

LIP

Acceptance Immediately after baptism, according to Hippolytus and Cyprian, the baptist and the Christians kiss the neophyte. Early Christian. Similarly, a new member of a collegium was kissed by those accepting him. Anc. *Rome*. Also *Russia*. Ohm, p. 220.

Acknowledgment "Many a kiss did Mr. Snodgrass waft in the air, in acknowledgment of something very like a lady's handkerchief." 19th cent. *England*. Dickens, *Pickwick*, I, p. 165.

Admiration Kiss (among men). Anc. *Rome*. Sittl, p. 38.

Adoration Woman kissing Christ's feet. Biblical. *Middle East*. *Luke* 7:38. * Pious fell on their knees on the threshold of the temple and kissed it. Anc. *Rome*; early Christian. Sittl, p. 184. * Deified, beautiful women were addressed with a compliment accompanied by gesture of throwing a kiss. Anc. *Greece* and *Rome*. Sittl, p. 183. * Wounds, bloody garments, reliques, instruments of torture connected with religious martyrdom are kissed. Early Christian. Sittl, p. 184, also n. 7. Greek orthodox kiss saints' images and gospels. Sittl, p. 184. Roman Catholics kiss crucifix. Sittl, ibid. Mementos of saints are kissed. Early Christian. Sittl, ibid. * Priest kisses altar. Roman Catholic. *Mass*, p. 65.

Affection "Dost thou come to kiss this child? I suffer thee not to kiss it." Anc. *Egypt*. Papyrus, Berlin 3027, r. 2, 1–2, containing apotropaic spells. Dawson, p. 85. "Pharaoh perceived him, and . . . folded him into his arms, he placed his mouth on his mouth, and kissed him at length in the manner in which a man salutes his betrothed." Anc. *Egypt*. Maspero, p. 261. "If I kiss her and her lips are open, I am happy" Anc. *Egypt*. Dawson, p. 84. The Ephesians kissed Paul. Biblical. *Middle East. Acts* 20:37. Parents kiss sons and daughters. Biblical. *Middle East. Gen.* 31:28.55; 48:10; *Ruth* 1:9. Brother kisses brother: *Gen.* 33:4; sister kisses brother: *Song of Sol.* 8:1; male cousin has same right as brother, e.g. Jacob kisses Rachel, *Gen.* 29:11; children kiss parents: *Gen.* 27:26; Joseph kisses dead father, *Gen.* 50:1. * Kiss as token of love between sexes seldom mentioned in the Old Testament, plays no role in the New Testament: *Song of Sol.* 1:2; *Prov.* 7:13 (pejorative). Christ and apostles kiss each other: *Matth.* 26:48. * "she laid her left arm about his neck, longing to kiss his tender mouth." Hellenist *Middle East*. Apoll. Rhod., I, 1236, 8. "Hence no Egyptian man or woman will kiss a Greek on the mouth." Anc. *Greece*. Herodot., ii, 41. * Men kiss men. Anc. *Greece* and *Rome*. Sittl, p. 36. Homer's *Odyssey* nowhere mentions the kiss on the mouth explicitly. Sittl, p. 40. Men and women kiss each other. Only in *Roman Empire* and later. Sittl, ibid. Kiss given to slaves. Hellenist *Middle East* and anc. *Rome*; *Byzantine Empire*. Sittl, p. 37. * Kissing while the person being kissed is being held under the hand. Anc. *Greece*. Sittl, p. 39. * Kissing eyes, mouth, etc. *Byzantine Empire*. Sittl, p. 41. Kiss on eyes or forehead as parental affection. Anc. *Greece* and *Rome*. Sittl, p. 40. Sensual. Anc. *Rome*. Sittl, ibid. Kiss on eyes among men. Anc. *Rome*. Sittl, ibid. Kiss on beard. Grandson by grandmother. Hellenistic *Middle East*. Quint. Smyrn. 13, 534. Sittl, ibid. Kiss on forehead in respectful affection. Anc. *Greece*. Sittl, p. 40. Kissing the hair. Sensual. Anc. *Rome*. Sittl, p. 41. Kiss on neck. Sensual. Anc. *Rome*. Sittl, ibid. Kissing a woman in public regarded as indecent. The elder Cato threw Manilius out of the senate, "because, in the presence of his daughter, and in open day, he had kissed his wife." A man kissing his marriageable daughter was punishable by police. Anc. *Rome*. Sittl, p. 39. "He kissed both old men affectionately." 13th cent. *Germany. Kudrun*, st. 474, 1. "And then he put his arms around my neck and kissed my face." 13th–14th cent. *Italy*. Dante, *Inf.*, c. viii. "kindly kissed my cheek." 16th–17th cent. *England*. Shakesp., *Richard III* 2.2.24. * Kissing hand at time of departure can indicate affection. 16th–17th cent. *England*. Shakesp., *Much Ado* 4.1.336. * Affection for parents: Children kiss their father while holding his ears. Anc. *Rome*. Sittl, p. 40. Father kissing children while holding their ears, see Sittl, ibid. * The person being kissed is held by the cheeks. Hellenistic *Middle East*. Sittl, ibid. * Kiss as token of love: 16th–17th cent. *England*. Shakesp., *Venus*, 18, 84, etc. *Two Gent*. 1.2.116; *Measure* 4.1.5; *Much Ado* 2.1.322; etc. "Mrs. Colonel Wugsby kissed her eldest daughter most affectionately." 19th cent. *England*. Dickens, *Pickwick*, II, p. 123. "He [Mr. Tupman] jumped up, and, throwing his arm round the neck of the spinster aunt, imprinted upon her lips numerous kisses." 19th cent. *England*. Dickens, *Pickwick*, I, p. 119. "if you try and kiss me again I shall box your ears." *England*. Huxley, ch. xxix. * Taking someone by the neck or the shoulders, then putting the lips on his forehead, or on his cheeks, or on his lips. *France*. Mitton, p. 141. Kissing considered an intimate sexual act not permissible in public. *Asia*. Axtell, *Gestures*, p. 72. * "I have a faint recollection when between three and four years of age, of my brother Joseph's being highly offended by [my nurse] kissing a certain substantial part of my body, at the same time telling him, that she had much rather kiss my posterior than his face." 18th cent. *England*. Hickey, p. 21. * Pursing the lips, sometimes also making the sound of a kiss, toward someone at some distance indicates affection; similar to throwing a kiss. *Netherlands*. Andrea and de Boer, p. 88. * Kissing the earth of the land which one leaves forever. Anc. *Greece* and *Rome*. Sittl, p. 42. "He kiss'd the ground that he had set his foot on." 17th cent. *England*. Defoe, II, p. 152. Kissing footstep of the beloved. Hellenistic. Sittl, p. 42. Kissing address on a letter to a friend. Hellenistic. Sittl, p. 42. Slave kisses object belonging to his master or mistress in their absence. Anc. *Greece*. Sittl, p. 172. Loyal subject kisses object sent by the emperor, such as a message. Late anc. *Greece*; anc. *Rome*; *Byzantine Empire*. Sittl, p. 172. * Missive of sultan, after being kissed, is held against forehead. 19th cent. *Turkey*. Also message from Greek Orthodox metropolitan. 19th cent. *Greece*. Sittl, p. 172. * Kissing vehicle of departing husband. Anc. *Greece*. Sittl, p. 41. Wife kisses ring with husband's picture. Anc. *Greece* and *Rome*. Sittl, p. 41. Kissing vehicle of Callirhoe. Anc. *Persia*. Sittl, ibid. Ceres kisses spinning wheel of abducted daughter. Anc. *Rome*. Sittl, ibid. Kissing urn. Anc. *Rome*. Sittl, ibid. Kissing door of the beloved. French monk kisses snuffbox that he received as present. 18th cent. *England*. Sterne, c. 11. Anc. *Rome*. Sittl, ibid. Tennis star Bjorn Borg kissed his Wimbledon trophy. Axtell, *Gestures*, p. 72. Emilee Klein kisses Women's Open cup. *U.S.* AP Photo, *Daily News*, Aug. 19, 1996, p. 1. *See* FINGER, LIP, Affection.

Agreement "Alan whistled. 'By Gad, I believe you're right.' " *England.* J. D. Carr, *Constant Suicides*, p. 156. * Peace agreements between Russian princes were confirmed by kissing the cross. 11th and 12th century chronicles record hundreds of such agreements, and from mid-12th century one encounters sporadic references to kissing the cross in connection with a documentary peace agreement. Medieval *Russia.* Franklin, p. 23. *See also* HAND, OBJECT, Challenge.

Anger Lips pressed together. Anc. *Rome.* Sittl, p. 24. * Trembling lips. Anc. *Rome.* Sittl, p. 15. * Biting the lip. 16th–17th cent. *England.* Shakesp., *Shrew* 2.1.241; *Richard III* 4.2.27; *Othello* 5.2.46. " 'Get on!' said Mrs. Proudie, moving her foot uneasily on the hearth-rug, and compressing her lips in a manner that betokened much danger to the subject of their discourse." 19th cent. *England.* Trollope, *Barchester Towers*, ch. xxxiii. "At last, biting her thin lips, and bridling up" 19th cent. *England.* Dickens, *Pickwick*, I, p. 129. Biting one's lips to check the flow of words. *Lat. Am.* Kany, p. 64.

Appreciation Smacking lips: "That tastes good." Schoolchildren. *U.S.* Seton, p. xxiii. * Kissing the tips of one's fingers: "That's great! That's beautiful!" *France; Italy; Spain;* much of *Lat. Am.* Axtell, *Gestures*, p. 73, suggests it is a survival of the anc. Greek and Roman gesture of throwing a kiss to sacred objects. * Whistling at a public performance is usually a sign of approval. *U.S.* Axtell, *Gestures*, p. 73. *See* Disapproval.

Approach Master whistles to summon servant. Anc. *Greece.* Sittl, p. 223.

Attention Pursing lips. Children. *Germany.* Krukenberg, p. 130.

Betrayal The "Judas kiss." Biblical. *Middle East. Luke* 22:48. *See also* Identification, below.

Brotherhood Kiss among men: newly entering robber kisses members of a robberband. Anc. *Rom.* Sittl, p. 38. As token of Christian brotherhood. Biblical. *Middle East. Rom.* 16:16; I *Cor.* 16:20; II *Cor.* 13:12; I *Thess.* 5:26; I *Pet.* 5:14. In time this became the osculum pacis (Tertullian, *de orat.*, 145), which was first given promiscuously, later only by men to men and women to women. Hastings, *Dictionary*, p. 6. The confirmed kiss each other after Eucharist. Ohm, p. 220. Men kiss men, women kiss women, entire congregation kisses priest at Easter. Russian Orthodox. Ohm, p. 222. Baptist kisses neophyte after baptism. Russian Orthodox. *Russia.* Ohm, p. 220.

Calmness Osculum pacis. 12th cent. *Germany.* Eilhart 1646, 1650; Grimm, *DRA*, I, p. 198.

Concentration Pursing lips. *U.S.* Krout, p. 21. " 'It looks like it,' the woman said. She examined whatever had appeared on the screen. Shook her head. Punched again at the keyboard. Leaphorn waited. The woman waited. She pursed her lips. Punched a single key." *U.S.* Hillerman, *Talking God*, p. 115. Lips pressed together. *Brazil*. Cascudo, *História*, p. 220. *See* Attention above. **Condescension** Absalom kisses the people. Biblical. *Middle East*. II *Sam*. 15:5.19.39: David kisses Barzilai. Also 18th cent. *Germany*. Schiller, *Don Carlos*, I, i; *Piccolomini*, II, ii. **Congratulation** Kiss among men. Anc. *Rome*. Sittl, p. 38. The Roman people congratulated Nero upon his discovery of the Pisonic plot by kneeling and kissing his hand. *Roman Empire*. Sittl, p. 169.

Consolation After a funeral, relatives of deceased kiss each other, then other mourners form a lane through which relatives walk in order to be kissed by other mourners. 19th cent. *Palestine*. Bauer, pp. 169–70.

Contempt "All they that see me laugh me to scorn: they shoot out the lip." Biblical. *Middle East*. *Ps*. 22:7. Lips closed, pushed out and up. Hellenistic *Middle East* and anc. *Rome*. Sittl, p. 89. "and lifting up her lip in contempt." 18th cent. *England*. Richardson, I, p. 44. * Spitting. Anc. *Greece*. Sittl, p. 91. Spitting three times into bosom. Anc. *Greece* and *Rome*. Sittl, ibid.

Curse "Valachi said Genovese started talking about apples that are 'touched, not all rotten but touched.' Finally Genovese said good night. 'He grabbed my hand and he gave me a kiss, so I gave him a kiss on the other side.' 'Is that some kind of ritual?' asked McClellan. 'No, that was a suspicious kiss. And Ralph mumbles under his breath 'Hmm, the kiss of death . . . An outsider like Ralph, he even was wise, so ain't I supposed to be smart?' " Kiss of Death. Cosa nostra. UP, "Killer Tells Senators of 'Death Kiss.' Admitted murderer Valachi describes plot in U.S. Prison," *L.A. Times*, Sept. 28, 1963, p. 11.

Debauchery Licking lips as if inebriated; belching as if replete. Anc. *Rome*. Baden, p. 455.

Deception False kiss. Biblical. *Middle East*. *Prov*. 27:6; *Luke* 22:47.48.

Determination Lips pressed together. Voltaire, in describing Francis I exhibiting this gesture, comments: "cet homme n'es pas si doux qu'il est forcé de le paraître" ("That man is not as gentle as he is forced to appear"). *France*. *See* Cascudo, *História*, p. 220.

Direction " 'He's the son of Annie Horseman,' Leaphorn said. 'Used to live back over there across the Kam Bimghi, over on the west slope of the Lukachukais.' He indicated the direction, Navajo fashion, with a twitch of the lips." *U.S.* Hillerman, *The Blessing Way*, p. 35; see also p. 61. " 'They say he was going to preach over between White Rock and Tsaya, over there by the mountains,' the boy said, indicating west in the Navajo fashion by a twist of the lips." Navajo, Native American. Hillerman, *Thief of Time*, p. 132 Lips turned in the direction the gesturer wants to indicate. *Central Africa*. Hochegger, p. 54.

Disagreement   Lips closed, pushed out and up. Hellenistic *Middle East* and anc. *Rome*. Sittl, p. 89.

Disappointment   Biting lower lip. *Europe; North America*. Aubert, p. 105.

Disapproval   *See also* Appreciation. "He hangs the lip at something." 16th–17th cent. *England*. Shakesp., *Troil*. 3.1.132. * Whistling at a public performance is usually a sign of disapproval. *Europe*. It is impolite to whistle in public. *India*. Axtell, *Gestures*, p. 73.

Disgust   Lower lip pushed forward, corners of mouth turned down. *Central Africa*. Hochegger, p. 43.

Dislike   "At this remark [an obscenity], all the ladies retired to another corner of the room, and some of them began to spit." 18th cent. *England*. Smollett, *Humphrey Clinker*, Letter of Melford, Apr. 18. Spitting to the right and left (particularly dislike of an aroma). Anc. *Rome*. Sittl, p. 91. Lips closed, pushed up and out. Anc. *Rome*. Sittl, p. 89. * Hissing. Early Christian. Sittl, p. 64. * Whistling. Anc. *Greece* and *Rome*. Sittl, ibid.

Elation   "[Tennis player] Stefan Edberg expresses his affection [sic] after his shot hit the top of the net and went over for a crucial point against Ivan Lendl [by kissing the net]." AP Photo, *L.A. Times*, Sept. 12, 1992, C1.

Embarrassment   Licking one's lips. *U.S.* Birdwhistell, *Introduction*, p. 34.

Etiquette   Certain ranks of court officials kissed the tip of the emperor's cloak. Probably began with Diocletian. *Roman Empire*. Sittl, p. 170. * Kissing the ground on which the emperor has trodden. *Asia* and late anc. *Rome*. Sittl, p. 171. * "this is he that kiss'd his hand away in courtesy." 16th–17th cent. *England*. Shakesp. *Love's Lab. Lost* 5.2.323. * Women standing under mistletoe may be kissed. 19th cent. *England*. Dickens, *Pickwick*, I, p. 480.

Excitement   Air released through lips so as to produce a whistle. *Central Africa*. Hochegger, p. 68.

Familiarity   Kissing among the sexes was permitted among relatives. Anc. *Rome*. Sittl, p. 38. In Gaul it was still common during the late *Roman Empire*. Sittl, p. 39. Among men. Ibid. Woman kisses man: mother-in-law kisses husband of her daughter. The only anc. Greek evidence Quint. Smyrn. 5, 399. Sittl, p. 38.

Farewell   Laban kisses sons and daughters. Biblical. *Middle East*. *Gen.* 31:55. Naomi and daughters-in-law. *Ruth* 1:9.14. * Brides, upon leaving home, kiss doors, beds, walls. Anc. *Greece* and *Rome*. Sittl, p. 42. * Kissing the earth of the land which one leaves forever. Anc. *Greece* and *Rome*. Sittl, ibid. * "Hagen kissed Hilde and bowed to the king." 13th cent. *Germany*. *Kudrun*, st. 559, 1. "I will kiss thy royal finger, and take leave." 16th–17th cent. *England*. Shakesp., *Love's Lab*.

Lost 5.2.870. "Of many thousand kisses the poor last I lay upon thy lips." 16th–17th cent. *England.* Shakesp., *Anth. and Cleo.* 4.15.20–21. **Flattery** Kissing hem of someone's shawl or kissing cheek. 15th cent. *Spain.* Rojas, ix, 2. * Kissing children of another. Anc. *Greece.* Sittl, p. 37. As dependence of Polish gentry on magnates increased during the 17th century, gestures of adulation became more extreme: hand, chest, stomach, knees, feet of a powerful patron would be kissed at every opportunity. A French visitor to Poland in the second half of the 17th century observes: "Two people of the same social standing would embrace and kiss each other on the shoulders; subordinates are expected to kiss the knees, calves or feet of their superiors." 17th cent. *Poland.* Bogucka, p. 194. * Prostration before one's patron became commonplace, though unheard of in the 16th century. 17th cent. *Poland.* Bogucka, ibid. * Public kissing, regarded as plebeian in the 16th century, likewise became common. Bogucka cites Jan Protasowicz: "Today to kiss is not a Polish habit,/ Only in plebeian Ruthenia / Do they like to greet each other by embraces." 17th cent. *Poland.* Bogucka, p. 194.

Friendship Kiss among men. Anc. *Greece* and *Rome.* Sittl, p. 38. Carried from among brothers to relations outside of immediate family: Biblical. *Middle East. Gen.* 29:13 (Laban and Jacob); I *Sam.*, 20:41 (Jonathan and David).

Gossip Lips pressed together between teeth: "What silly chatter!" "Shut up!" *Central Africa.* Hochegger, p. 21.

Gratitude Actors and musicians threw kisses at the audience at the beginning of a performance and thanked thus for applause. *Roman Empire.* Sittl, p. 171. Reciting author threw kiss to audience when someone called 'bravo!' Anc. *Rome.* Martial 1, 3, 7. * Kissing of statues. Anc. *Rome.* Sittl, pp. 180–81. * Kiss among men. Anc. *Greece.* Sittl, p. 38. * "Still kneeling, [the Cid] kissed the king's hands, and then arose and kissed his mouth." Medieval *Spain. Cid,* ii. "I kissed his Majesty's hand, on his making me one of that new-established Council." 17th cent. *England.* Evelyn, II, p. 60.

Greeting Kissing a superior's hand, then placing it to one's forehead. *Egypt.* Ohm, p. 211. Raquel and Vidas kiss the hands of the Cid. Medieval *Spain. Cid,* i. Cid embraces Minaya Álvar Fañez and kisses his mouth and eyes. Medieval *Spain. Cid,* i. Kiss. Anc. *Egypt; Persia.* Sittl, pp. 78–79; cf. also Biblical. *Middle East. Gen.* 29:11.13; 33:4; *Rom.* 16:16; I *Cor.* 20; I *Pet.* 5:14. Herodotus (i, 133) says of the Persians: "When two of them meet on the street, one can see whether they are of the same rank: instead of greeting they kiss each other on the mouth: if one is a little inferior to the other, then the one kisses him on the cheek; if, however, he is of much inferior rank, he falls to the ground and worships the other." Ohm, p. 210. * Eumaios and Penelope kiss Telemachos' head and eyes. Anc. *Greece.* Homer, *Odyss.* Bk. xvi, xvii.

* Eurykleia kisses Telemachos' head and shoulders. Anc. *Greece.* Homer, *Odyss.* Bk. xviii. "Abengalbón smiles and embraces him, kissing him upon the shoulder, as is the Moorish custom." Medieval *Spain. Cid*, ii. Kings kissed only relatives and those to whom they gave that title. Anc. *Persia.* Sittl, p. 79. Kiss was used without distinction of social class by Caligula, who kissed pantomimics. *Roman Empire.* Sittl, p. 79. * Kissing the ground on return to homeland or on arrival at a new homeland. Anc. *Greece* and *Rome.* Sittl, p. 42. * In entering and leaving a temple a kiss is thrown toward the image of the deity. Anc. *Greece* and *Rome.* Sittl, p. 182. Tacitus, *Hist.* 1, 36, criticizes slavish behavior of Otho, who threw kisses at the cheering crowd at his ascension to the throne. Anc. *Rome.* Sittl, p. 171. * If the regent left the city and entered it again, he had to kiss the senators. Anc. *Rome.* Sittl, p. 80. * In passing the imperial palace, a slave throws a kiss at it. Anc. *Rome.* Sittl, p. 171. Philosophers threw a kiss at buildings named after classical philosophers in passing. Anc. *Rome.* Sittl, pp. 171–72. Beggars threw kisses at passing rich in carriages. Anc. *Rome.* Sittl, p. 171. * In the circus the charioteer kisses the whip before the patrons. Anc. *Rome.* Sittl, p. 165, n. 1. * Kiss among men on returning from journey. Anc. *Rome.* Sittl, p. 38. * Kiss on chest as morning salutation by the gentlemen waiting upon a nobleman. *Roman Empire.* Sittl, p. 166. L. Verus called Fronto into his bedroom for a kiss, in order to avoid insulting the others present. Anc. *Rome.* Sittl, p. 80. * Kissing someone's knee. Late *Roman Empire.* Sittl, p. 169. * The guest kisses only his hostess and those ladies of equal rank with his; sometimes also married women of the house. 12th cent. *Germany. Lanzelet*, 615; Schultz, I, p. 521. Kissing on the mouth. 13th cent. *Germany. Kudrun*, st. 154, 1. 12th cent. *Germany. Orendel*, 3520. * Women permitted to receive equal or higher ranking guests with a kiss: 13th cent. *Germany. Nibelungenlied*, st. 297, 3; 1652, 3. "My lady, the gracious king wishes to receive you here. Whomever I tell you to kiss let this be done: you are not to greet all Etzel's men equally." 13th cent. *Germany. Nibelungenlied*, st. 1348, 2–4. * Men embracing and kissing. Medieval *England. Beowulf* 1870–71; see also Habicht, pp. 17, 26. Layamon deems it important, that only relatives of the same sex greet each other with a kiss (1380, 3631). Late 12th cent. *England.* Habicht, pp. 26, 54–55. Wace is more liberal. Mid-12th cent. *England.* Ibid., p. 55. "I kissed the Duke's hand" 17th cent. *England.* Evelyn, II, p. 142. * "Mr. Pickwick kissed the young ladies—we were going to say, as if they were his own daughter, only as he might possibly have infused a little more warmth into the salutation, the comparison would not be quite appropriate." 19th cent. *England.* Dickens, *Pickwick*, I, p. 165. * The kiss at the altar [priest kissing altarstone] is expressive also of a greeting to Christ, the Bridegroom who is represented by the altar, on the part of His Bride, the Church." Roman Catholic. *Mass*, p. 19. The

kissing of liturgical objects is no longer in use in the postconciliar Roman liturgy. Roman Catholic. *GdG*, p. 36. The Early Christian fraternal kiss on the cheeks (clergy) was replaced in the East by the kiss of peace on the hands or (in both East and West) by a stylized embrace. * The kiss of greeting received positive comment from Erasmus in 1499 in a letter from England to his friend Faustus Andrelinus: "Nevertheless, did you but know the blessings of Britain, you would clap your wings to your feet, and run hither . . . To take one attraction out of many; there are nymphs here with divine features, so gentle and kind that you may well prefer them to your Camenae. Besides, there is a fashion which cannot be commended enough. Wherever you go, you are received on all hands with kisses; when you take leave, you are dismissed with kisses. If you go back, your salutes are returned to you. When a visit is paid, the first act of hospitality is a kiss, and when guests depart, the same entertainment is repeated; wherever a meeting takes place, there is kissing in abundance; in fact, whatever way you turn, you are never without it. Oh Faustus, if you had once tasted how sweet and fragrant those kisses are, you would indeed wish to be a traveller, not for ten years, like Solon, but for your whole life in England." 15th cent. *England*. Frijhoff, p. 225. In contemporaneous Holland the kiss was virtually confined to the context of love. Public kissing was characteristic outside of marriage, in courtship or love-games with codified rules. The wedding kiss itself appears as a rite of separation, closing the period of permissible public kissing, and transferring the kiss of love to the private realm. Kisses other than the kiss of love were gender-specific: during the Batavian Revolution (1795) women kissed each other on the streets in the name of liberty and equality, whereas men shook hands. 15th–18th cent. *Netherlands*. Frijhoff, pp. 226–28. Kissing both cheeks in greeting after long absence. 19th cent. *Palestine*. Bauer, p. 169. * "kissing ritual among Spanish women of all ages. One of the two women permits herself—by design or by accident—to be kissed by the other woman . . . The gesture often consists simply of brushing the other woman's cheek—almost always both—with the lips . . . American women are rarely observed kissing both cheeks of their women friends . . . Throwing kisses and pointing to the area to be kissed are movements common to both cultures" *Spain; Lat. Am.* Green, p. 39. In kissing the cheeks in greeting, the lips do not actually touch the cheek, except in *Russia* and perhaps in the *Middle East*. In kissing cheeks, in *Latin America* only one cheek is kissed, in *France* both cheeks, and in *Belgium* and *Russia* three kisses are usual, alternating sides, beginning on the left. In cheek-kissing, the initial kiss is always bestowed on the left side of the person kissing. Axtell, *Gestures*, p. 71, who cites a "seasoned world traveler" on the propriety of kissing a woman's cheek: " 'You'll quickly learn when a woman acquaintance expects you to kiss her cheek—she just reels you in with her hand.' " "In my early days of . . . discovery, I would plant a single kiss, only to find that the other cheek was being proffered as I was drawing back. Only snobs kiss once, I was told, or those unfortunates who suffer from congenital *froideur*. I then saw what I assumed to be the correct procedure—the triple kiss, left-right-left, so I tried it on a Parisian friend. Wrong again. She told me that triple-kissing was a low Provençal habit, and that two kisses were enough among civilized people. The next time I saw my [Provençal] neighbor's wife, I kissed her twice. '*Non*,' she said, '*trois fois*.' I now pay close attention to the movement of the female head. If it stops swiveling after two kisses, I am almost sure I've filled my quota, but I stay poised for a third lunge just in case the head should keep moving." Provençe, *France*. Mayle, *A Year in Provençe*, p. 102. [Editors' note: three kisses by a man on the cheeks of a woman friend, left-right-left, are also customary as a greeting in the *Netherlands*.] In Flanders, one kiss on the cheek could suffice, whereas the Walloons distinguished themselves from other Belgians by embracing three times. Goosse, XLVI–XLVIII, pp. 205–10; L, pp. 235–6. * "the gesture of embracing each other by means of holding the shoulders and kissing the cheeks seems to be—at least in France—an example of an original peasant custom adopted by urban culture, probably through migration, but with one important change: in the countryside, the affection shown by the gesture could be measured by the sound of the kisses on the cheeks; in urban culture, body sounds are reprehensible. Hence, perhaps, the reinvestment of affection in the number of the kisses." *France*. Frijhoff, p. 224, who also quotes van Gennep, I, p. 376: "Embracing in the sense of 'giving one or more kisses' [*baisers*] is rather new. In the countryside, this kiss is given on the cheeks, never on the mouth as in Russia. In most cases it is simulated. A person with rural *savoir-vivre* touches another man's cheeks only very slightly, although a real kiss is given between mother and daughter, and between sisters or close cousins. The more such a kiss sounds, the stronger is its manifestation of friendship. This friendly kiss is given two times, rarely three." A kiss at Christmas is a customary greeting. 17th cent. *England*. Swift, p. 175. Women (friends or related) kiss one another when meeting and departing. *Western Europe*. Révész, "Die Psychologie," p. 146. * Men kiss woman's hand in greeting and farewell. Common in Europe [Editors' note: particularly in Austria, where the phrase "Küss' die Hand, gnä' Frau" ("I kiss your hand, ma'am,") survives the custom until the early 20th cent. among the upper and middle classes. Actually the hand is not kissed; the man simply holds the woman's right hand in his and bows low over it, at most touching it with his lip. In a more flirtatious style and with the woman's cooperation, the man may raise the woman's hand to his lips.] * Men (friends or related) kiss one another on both cheeks in greeting. Pre-20th cent. *Russia*. Révész, "Die Psychologie," p. 146. Two men kiss quickly on the lips in greeting. *Lebanon; Saudi Arabia; Syria*. Barakat, no. 140. Woman kisses man on the cheek in public without being married to him. Punishable in *Saudi Arabia*. Axtell, *Gestures*, p. 11. "She smiled at him, lips pulled back from clenched teeth. . . . She smiled toothily again . . . pointed to the guest with her lips . . . pursed her lips." *U.S.* Birdwhistell, *Introduction*, p. 30. "Upon entering the small room where Cabrera sat on his throne, guests touched the floor and then kissed their fingers and held them out in greeting to Chango and the novice." Afro-Cuban Santeria. *Cuba*. M. Miller, p. A9. * In the Orient, kissing is considered an intimate sexual act and not permissible in public. Axtell, *Gestures*, p. 72.

Hesitation To pull or stroke lip or lips. *France*. Mitton, p. 146.

Homage Falling to ground and kissing earth before person of importance. Anc. *Egypt*. Eichler, p. 95. "Minaya and Pedro Bermudez rise forward and dismount and kneel before King Alfonso. They kiss the earth and his feet." Medieval *Spain*. *Cid*, c. ii. * "Then [the Cid] casts himself upon the ground and plucks a mouthful of grass, weeping in his great joy. Thus he pays homage to King Alfonso, his lord, and falls at his feet." Medieval *Spain*. *Cid*, c. ii. * "Sub-sheiks . . . kiss the hand and dagger, the latter in a holster, of the Chief Sheik." *Middle East*. Hayes, p. 262. * Kissing the foot. 16th–17th cent. *England*. Shakesp., *Temp.* 2.2.142. Soldiers and common people voluntarily kiss Otho's hand at his election as well as after his death. Anc. *Rome*. Tacit. *Hist.*; Sittl, p. 167. *See* KNEE, Plea.

Honor "And here my bluest veins to kiss—a hand that kings have lipp'd, and trembled kissing." 16th–17th cent. *England*. Shakesp., *Anth. and Cleo.* 2.5.28–30.

Humility Since the beginning of Christian sculpture, the feet of saints' statues were kissed. Early Christian. Sittl, p. 181. The only occurrence of kissing feet of a deity in literature is Chariton 1, 1, 7. 8, 8, 15. Anc. *Greece*. Sittl, p. 181. Kissing feet of statues in the temple. Anc. *Rome*. Sittl, ibid. * Pope John Paul II's prostration and kiss of the earth of the countries he is visiting symbolizes humility; on the other hand, he takes possession of the community, an act symbolized by the aggregation rite of kissing the soil. Roman Catholic. Frijhoff, p. 212.

Identification Judas' betrayal of Christ. Biblical. *Middle East*. *Matth.* 26:49; *Mark* 4:45.

Indifference Lower lips move forward, expulsion of air results in noise made with upper lip. *Spain; Portugal*. Flachskampf, p. 228. Lower lip thrust forward over upper lip. Implies hostility or scorn. Río de la Plata region of *Argentina; Uruguay*. Meo Zilio, p. 104.

Insult Air is forced through pursed lips to make a noise. "Raspberry." Children. *England*. Opie, p. 319. * Lips thrust forward in form of a pig's snout. *Central Africa*. Hochegger, p. 27.

Investiture Lord kisses vassal in investing him with fief. Medieval *Germany*. Grimm, *DRA*, I, p. 197.

Irony " 'Sorry,' he said, with a smirk that showed he wasn't." *England*. Lodge, *Nice Work*, p. 183. "Up to this point Tomasito had been candid, loyal and revolutionary, critical only in constructive ways. My question, however, drew a silent and sideways smile. It meant that the answer was so clearly fraught with the basic flaws in the system that any response would acknowledge the illusion. The sideways smile is a vital element in Cuba's facial vocabulary, a reply that by saying nothing says everything. Tomasito's face slowly returned to normal. 'It's not that the government doesn't allow the people to leave,' he said, 'it's that the finances are simply not available. Besides, everything Cubans need is here.' " *Cuba*. Tom Miller, *L.A. Times Magazine*, Dec. 20, 1992.

Joy Smiling. Boggs, p. 320. In Christianity the smile is outer expression of happiness which fills believer at thought of salvation and God's beauty. In Buddhism the smile on the face of Buddha indicates that he has overcome the world and has achieved inner peace. Christian; Buddhist. Ohm, pp. 195–96. For symbolic function of smile, and its contrast to laughter, in Hartmann's *Gregorius* (12th cent. *Germany*) see Wells, pp. 170–71. * Japanese do not smile for official photographs. "In general, people in Japan smile when they are sad, happy, apologetic, angry or confused." To smile for a driver's license photograph would mean that one does not take one's driving responsibility seriously. Equating smiling with frivolous behavior may also be the reason why so few Japanese government officials are photographed with smiles, except when they are coached to do so for photos with American dignitaries. Koreans have a similar attitude about smiling. "Americans smile primarily as an expression of friendliness." Dresser, *L.A. Times*, May 9, 1994, B11.

Luck Tossing a kiss or lifting one's hat to a chimney sweep, or having the bride kissed by a sweep at the wedding means good luck. *England*. G. L. Phillips, pp. 191–96.

Medico-magical St. Martin is said to have healed a Parisian leper with a kiss, showing that kiss of a saint has curative power; similarly that of some nobles: the counts of Habsburg were said to heal stammering children with a mouth kiss. *France; Germany*. Frijhoff, p. 211.

Mourning Kissing the departed. Biblical. *Middle East. Gen.* 50:1. Anc. *Greece* and *Rome*. Sittl, p. 72. Kissing the urn containing the ashes of the deceased. Anc. *Rome*. Sittl, p. 74. Kissing forehead and hand of the departed by relatives in church. Greek Orthodox. Goar, pp. 435–36.

Nervousness Biting lips. *U.S.* Krout, p. 22.

Nothing Lower lip thrust forward and down: "I didn't have anything." *Central Africa.* Hochegger, p. 27.

Oath Kissing "the book" in swearing an oath. 16th–17th cent. *England.* Shakesp., *Temp.* 2.2.132. "When the oath was given, Mr. Lincoln bent, as by ancient custom, and kissed the open pages of the Bible." 19th cent. *U.S.* Catton, p. 410. Kissing the Bible is required in many states of the United States before testimony in court can be legal. In the South some communities had two Bibles in court: one for whites and the other for blacks. *U.S.* Hayes, p. 268.

Peace Kiss of peace. *Osculum pacis.* Early Christian. Sittl, p. 39. *See also* Brotherhood above, Union below. Kisses exchanged only between males as sign of peace among the Tapuya of *South America.* Axtell, *Gestures*, p. 73.

Plea Daughter of the king pleads with her father and kisses the ground before him. Anc. *Greece.* Sittl, p. 171, n. 1. Doña Ximena kneels before her husband, the Cid, and attempts to kiss his hands. Medieval *Spain. Cid*, c. i. Kissing someone's knee. Anc. *Greece.* Homer, *Iliad., Odyssey.* Sittl, p. 169. Noblemen kiss the chest of their benefactor. Anc. *Rome.* Sittl, p. 166.

Pleasure " 'Good stuff that,' observed Mr. Claypole, smacking his lips." 19th cent. *England.* Dickens, *Oliver Twist*, p. 397.

Pointing Lips protruded. Movimas do not accompany this with quick thrust of the head as the Tacana and Ayorco do, but instead thrust their hand straight out with palm held sideways. Bolivian Indians. Key, "Gestures," p. 94. Extending lower lip to point at another person. *Portugal.* Basto, p. 38. Lips pursed and moved in direction of object intended to be pointed at. For nearby people and objects. *Colombia.* Saitz and Cervenka, p. 33. Use of the chin or "lip pout" to point. Native American. *U.S.* Axtell, *Gestures*, p. 79. *See* Direction and HEAD, LIP, Pointing.

Prayer Before beginning and after concluding a journey one kisses the Mezuzah over or at side of one's door. During worship one kisses the Torah when it is taken from the Ark and carried by the community. While praying the third paragraph of the Schema in morning prayer, one kisses the Tsitzith on the Tallis. Jews. Ohm, p. 213. Kissing thresholds of churches. Early Christian. Sittl, p. 184. Canaanites kissed the idols of the ba'alim. Biblical. *Middle East.* I *Kings* 19:18; *Hos.* 13:2; Heiler, p. 103; Hastings, *Dictionary*, p. 9 suggests comparison to kissing the black stone in the Ka'ba at Mecca. Muslim. Kissing the sacred oak of Zeus at Aegina. Anc. *Greece.* Ovid, *Metam.*, vii, 631. Kissing sacred trees, cup and healing potion, threshold of house. Anc. *Greece* and *Rome.* Sittl, 180–81. Kissing feet of statues in temples. Anc. *Rome.* Sittl, p. 181. Sulla kissed his statuette of Apollo which he carried with him. Sittl, ibid.; for kissing statues, cf. Cicero, *Verr.*, 4, 94; Sittl, p. 180–81. Kissing graves of martyrs. Early Christian. Heiler, p. 104. Kissing crucifix. Roman Catholic. Sittl, p. 184. Since the beginning of Christian sculpture the feet of saints' statues have been kissed. Sittl, p. 181. The only occurrence of kissing feet of a deity in Greek literature occurs in Chariton 1,1,7.8,8,15; Sittl, p. 181. Kissing mementos of saints. Early Christian. Sittl, p. 184. Wounds, bloody garments, reliques, instruments of torture connected with religious martyrdom are kissed. Early Christian. Sittl, p. 184 and n. 7. Kissing altar as liturgical act. Roman Catholic. *GdG*, p. 36. Kissing images of domestic deities when entering or leaving one's house as well as the black stone in the Ka'ba at Mecca. Muslim. Heiler, p. 103. "The priest bends and kisses the altar as if to salute Jesus Christ" Roman Catholic. *Mass*, p. 39. Kissing the threshold of churches, and kissing saints' images and Gospels. Greek Orthodox. Sittl, p. 184 * Semitic adoration of unreachable heavenly bodies by throwing kiss. Biblical. *Middle East. Job* 31:26–27. To honor Ge without throwing oneself on the ground one could throw her a kiss. Anc. *Greece*. Sittl, p. 182. A kiss was part of the adoration of Helios and Silene as well as the gods of the wind and the Adrasteia-Nemesis. Anc. *Greece*. Sittl, p. 181. Throwing kiss at saints' images. 19th cent. Naples, southern *Italy*. De Jorio, p. 67. Throwing kiss. 4th–5th cent. St. Jerome, *Rufinus* 2, 19. Sittl, p. 183. Christian page throws kiss toward crucifix. Sittl, p. 182. * Combination of throwing a kiss with kneeling on one knee seems to be Semitic. Sittl, ibid. 184.

Reconciliation   Kiss. Biblical. *Middle East. Gen.* 45:15; II *Sam.* 14:33; *Luke* 15:20. Also anc. *Rome*. Sittl, p. 38, and as formal reconciliation of prizefighters after bout. Sittl, ibid. "Louis kindly raised and kissed [Lothair] and thanked God for the lost son with whom he had been reconciled." Frankish. 9th cent. Nithard, pp. 138. 13th cent. *German. Kudrun*, st. 159, 1. The treacherous *baiser Lamourette* that deputies of the French Legislative Assembly gave each other on 7 July 1792 was intended as a gesture of reconciliation. 18th cent. *France*. Frijhoff, p. 211.

Respect   Moses kisses his father-in-law. Biblical. *Middle East. Ex.* 18:7; *see also* I *Sam.* 10:1; *Prov.* 24:26; *Luke* 7:38.45. * Vitellius kissed the shoe of the empress. *Roman Empire*. Sittl, p. 172, n. 4. The slave kisses objects belonging to his master or mistress in their absence. Anc. *Greece*. Sittl, p. 172. Throwing kiss at sacred objects, such as altars, sacred stones, graves, statues. *See* Prayer above. Anc. *Greece*. and *Rome*. Sittl, p. 182. Early Christians kissed the threshold of the church— presumably in imitation of Romans who kissed the thresholds of temples, altars, dying people and dead people. Kissing the dead was prohibited by the Council of Auxerre (585). Ohm, p. 215. Kissing a priest's stole at departure after mass. Rojas, ix. Respect and love for parents is shown by a kiss. Kissing one's hand in token of respect to another: "it

had been better you had not kiss'd your three fingers so oft, which now
again you are most apt to play the sir in." 16th–17th cent. *England.*
Shakesp., *Othello* 2.1.171–72. "To see him walk before a lady and to
bear her fan! To see him kiss his hand, and how most sweetly 'a will
swear!" 16th–17th cent. *England.* Shakesp., *Love's Lab. Lost*
4.1.138–9; I *Henry VI* 5.3.47–49: "For I will touch thee but with rever-
ent hands; I kiss these fingers for eternal peace, and lay them gently on
thy tender side." Kissing someone's hand. 18th cent. *Germany.* Schiller,
Fiesko IV, xii, 14. Bride kisses groom's hand, which she then puts
against her forehead. *See* Greeting above. 19th cent. *Palestine.* Bauer,
p. 94. Kissing hand of superior and then putting it against one's forehead. When friends meet they first shake hands and then kiss their own
hand or bring their hand to the lips or forehead or at least lift it close to
the forehead. *See also* Greeting. 19th cent. *Egypt.* Ohm, p. 211.

Reverence "Let the men that sacrifice kiss the calves." Biblical.
Middle East. Hos. 33:2. Egyptian priests kissed the earth before the
image of a deity. Kissing of idols' hands, feet, clothing or earth on
which they stood was common in anc. *Egypt; Sumeria; Babylonia; Assyria; Syria; Persia.* In the cult of Baal the statue of the god was kissed.
Arabs kissed stone fetish in the Ka'aba at Mecca. Sacred kiss. Anc.
Greece and *Rome.* Kissing hands, feet of idols, threshold of temples,
sacred trees and other objects. Anc. *Rome.* Shiites kiss Koran when they
take it in their hands. Muslim. Ohm, p. 213. Throwing kisses to the sun.
Anc. *Peru.* Throwing kisses to sun and moon. Semitic. Biblical. *Middle
East. Job* 31:27. Worshipping rising sun and other astral deities by
throwing kisses. Anc. *Greece*; Hittite; *Babylonia.* Throwing kisses to
deities when passing their statues and temples or on entering a temple.
Anc. *Rome.* Similarly, Roman Catholics to statues, crosses, pictures. In
passing the imperial palace, a slave throws a kiss at it. *Roman Empire.*
Sittl, p. 171. Ohm, pp. 217–18. Kissing the foot of pharaoh or emperor.
Anc. *Egypt; Rome; Byzantine Empire.* Ohm, p. 216. Kissing the foot of
pope or bishop. Roman Catholic. Ohm, ibid. Deacon kisses knee of
bishop before reading gospel. Early Christian. Ohm, 216–17. Worshipper of the Sungod kisses the legs of the latter's horses. Anc. *Rome.* Sittl,
p. 184. Sulla kissed the statuette of Apollo which he carried about with
him. Anc. *Rome.* Sittl, p. 184. In joining the mourning community
around a coffin, making sign of the cross, then kissing icons standing
on coffin or on grave. Today one kisses the icons which replace these,
i.e. those in church. Russian Orthodox. Kissing ground before iconosta-
sis, then the icons. Russian Orthodox. Pilgrims to Santiago de Compost-
ela in the late 17th cent. kissed image of saint on main altar three times
and put on its head the hat they were wearing. Roman Catholic. d'Aulnoy, p. 76. French monk kisses snuffbox he received as gift. 18th cent.
France. Sterne, ch. xi. "The priest . . . inclines a little, and kisses [the

Missal] where he signed it at the beginning to show his love and veneration for the Divine Word." Roman Catholic. *Mass*, p. 30. Kissing a letter, which is then touched to the forehead, indicates reverence for its sender and obedience to its contents. Originally a Middle Eastern gesture, it passed to Portugal and, eventually, Brazil. Most common in the 16th and 17th centuries in the Iberian peninsula and Brazil. When Sancho Panza returns from supposedly delivering a letter from Don Quixote to Dulcinea, Don Quixote asks him: "Cuando le diste mi carta, ¿besóla? ¿Púsosela sobre la cabeza?" ("When you gave her my letter, did she kiss it? Did she put it on her head?") *Quijote* I, xxxi; *Spain.* Cascudo, *História*, p. 111. Kissing the ground: Luigi of Savoy, returning from voyage to Arctic Ocean, kissed Italian soil upon returning in 1900. *Italy.* In 1909, Dr. Jean Charcot kissed French soil upon return from polar exploration. *France.* Cascudo, *História*, p. 216. Ulysses kisses the sacred ground of the Phaeacians, and repeats the gesture on his return to Ithaca. Anc. *Greece.* Homer, *Odyss.* v, 464; xiii, 354. Touching ground with face was a propitiatory gesture to gods of underworld and telluric forces. Anc. *Greece* and *Rome.* Cascudo, *História*, p. 216.

Silence Pressing lips together. Anc. *Rome.* Sittl, p. 214. Pressing lips together between teeth. *Central Africa.* Hochegger, p. 21. * Biting lips, lowered eyes (emphatic). Anc. *Greece.* Sittl, p. 54.

Submission Kissing someone's feet. Asian in origin. *See* Reverence above. Ohm, p. 215f. * Samuel anointed Saul and kissed him. Biblical. *Middle East.* I *Sam.* 10:1. Moses kisses his father-in-law. Biblical. *Middle East. Ex.* 18:7. * "went out into the way of the king and up to his chariot and kissed his knees and clasped them." Anc. *Greece.* Homer, *Odyss.*, Bk. xiv. * Kissing someone's shoulder. Anc. *Greece.* Homer, *Odyss. See also* Greeting. * Kissing the knee was part of Persian proskynesis and was absorbed by Roman *salutatio.* Heliodorus applies this to the Ethiopian king. Anc. *Rome.* Sittl, p. 169 and n. 6. * Defeated army kisses ground before emperor. *Roman Empire.* Sittl, p. 171, n. 1. * At coronation of Emperor Henry VI, April 15, 1191, emperor elect, empress and barons and clerics kiss pope's feet and swear allegiance to him. Thereafter the pope asks him whether he desires peace with the Church, which Henry affirms thrice and pope agrees to "give you peace as the Lord gave it to his disciples." He kisses his forehead, chin, both cheeks, then the mouth. Then pope rises and asks him thrice whether he wants to be son of Church, which Henry affirms thrice whereupon pope, replying "and I accept you as son," takes him under his cloak and Henry kisses chest of pope, taking his right hand, while his chamberlain supports pope on the left. 12th cent. Papacy. Schultz, II, p. 659. * Kissing the rod. 16th–17th cent. *England.* Shakesp., *Gentlemen* 1.2.59. Kissing the earth. 16th–17th cent. *England.* Shakesp., *Macb.* 5.8.28. Kissing the foot of the sultan. *Book of Accomplishments*, Topkapi Palace Mus., Istanbul. *Turkey. See* Respect above. Penitent Syrian woman kisses ground before bishop. 5th cent. *Syria.* Sittl, p. 171, n. 1. At Fatima, all those "who participate in the ritual form a single undifferentiated crowd, held together by an initial rite: kissing the earth of the holy place on arrival at the shrine. That kiss, ritual mark of deference, is the sign of recognition which effects the reception of the individual into the society of pilgrims. It is a rite of aggregation." Roman Catholic. Frijhoff, p. 215.

Surprise   Biting lower lip. *Europe; North America.* Aubert, p. 105. "Alan whistled. 'By gad, I believe you're right!' " *England.* J. D. Carr, *Constant Suicides*, p. 156.

Threat   "having picked up the pieces and put them into three separate pockets, folded his arms, bit his lips, and looked in a threatening manner at the bland features of Mr. Pickwick." 19th cent. *England.* Dickens, *Pickwick*, II, p. 337.

Union   *Osculum sanctum* or *osculum pacis.* Early Christian Church took the kiss over from paganism. Achelis, p. 229. In Roman liturgy kiss of peace became common before communion, as provided by Innocent I. Originally all Christians kissed each other, later priests kissed bishop, men other men, women other women. In the 13th century the osculum pacis as popular custom disappeared under influence of Franciscans and was replaced by kiss of osculatorium, which in turn has disappeared. Ohm, pp. 220–21. In Russian Orthodox churches kiss of peace is common at Easter, when men kiss men, women kiss women. Swedish Protestants use *osculum sanctum* at consecration of bishop, Hungarians at ordination of pastor. It is also used at reception of novices into the Zentraldiakonissenhaus Bethanien, Berlin. Ohm, p. 222.

Warning   Puckering lips and blowing: "Secret police." *Lat. Am.* Kany, p. 121.

LIP, NECK
Affection   Kiss on neck (sensuous as well as paternal). Anc. *Rome.* Sittl, p. 41.

LIP, NOSE
Disgust   Sneering. *Universal.* Krukenberg, p. 318.

LIP, OBJECT *See also* LIP.
Affection   Lucius kisses the magic box (Apul. *met.* 3, 24), Pantheia kisses the chariot of the departing husband (Xen. *Cyr.* 6, 4, 10), the wife kisses the ring with the cameo image of her husband (Chariton 1, 14, 9), Ceres kisses the loom of her abducted daughter (Claud. *Rapt. Pros.*). Anc. *Rome.* Sittl, p. 41, n. 8. French monk kisses a snuffbox received as token of friendship. 18th cent. *England.* Sterne, xi. Tennis champion Stefan Edberg expressed his affection for the net after his shot hit the

top of the net and went over for a crucial point against Ivan Lendl. AP Photo, *L.A. Times*, Sept. 12, 1992, C1.

Submission The expression "to kiss the rod," meaning submission to punishment willingly (Brewer, p. 926), probably originated in the performance of the act. A robber kisses the sword with which he kills himself. Anc. *Rome*. Apul. *met.* 4, 11. Sittl, p. 41, n. 8.

LIP, SHOULDER

Greeting During the Hadj (pilgrimage) one may kiss only on the shoulders in greeting. *Saudi Arabia*. Barakat, no. 179. Parents of a recently deceased son or daughter may kiss only on the shoulders in greeting. *Bahrain; Saudi Arabia*. Barakat, no. 180. Two social equals greeted each other by a kiss on the shoulder. 17th cent. *Poland*. Bogucka, p. 195. *See* LIP, Greeting, Submission.

Homage Kissing right shoulder of a dignitary as sign of respect or show of homage. *Kuwait; Saudi Arabia*. Barakat, no. 238.

LIP, TONGUE

Affection Kiss and simultaneous projection of tongue into the other's mouth. Anc. *Rome*. Sittl, p. 43. * Tongue protrudes slightly and moves slowly along lips. Primarily male adolescents. Request for a kiss. *Colombia; U.S.* Saitz and Cervenka, p. 79.

Apology Kissing the nose of a person with whom one has fought. *Saudi Arabia*. Barakat, no. 242.

Contempt Whistling and clicking the tongue. Anc. *Greece*. Sittl, p. 96.

Pleasure Licking one's lips in anticipation (or remembrance) of food, or in anticipation of erotic pleasure. *Netherlands*. Andrea and de Boer, p. 116.

Speech Tongue extruded and agitated from left to right: "Tu parles beaucoup!" ("You talk a lot!") *Central Africa*. Hochegger, p. 140.

LIP, TOOTH

Affection Kiss and simultaneous bite. Anc. *Greece* and *Rome*. Sittl, p. 42.

Anger Biting lower lip indicates more intense rage than that manifested by gnashing teeth. Anc. *Greece*. Homer, *Odyss.* xx; anc. *Rome*; 19th cent. *Italy*. Sittl, p. 16; de Jorio, p. 265. "The king is angry; see, he gnaws his lip." 16th–17th cent. *England*. Shakesp., *Richard III* 4.2.27. * Biting the moustache. 19th cent. *Greece*. Sittl, p. 16, n. 4. * Biting both lips folded inward. Río de la Plata region of *Argentina; Uruguay*. Meo Zilio, p. 108.

Embarrassment Biting lip. Anc. *Greece*. Sittl, p. 17. Biting the lower lip in regret for saying something one should not have said. Río de la Plata region of *Argentina; Uruguay.* Meo Zilio, p. 108.

Envy Biting lip. Anc. *Greece.* Sittl, p. 17.

Excitement Biting lips. *Universal.* Krukenberg, p. 257.

Mockery Upper lip lifted to bare canine. Anc. *Greece* and *Rome*; 19th cent. *Italy.* Sittl, p. 89.

Pain Biting lip to suppress pain. Early Christian. Sittl, p. 17.

Regret Tongue protrudes over upper lip; often accompanied by a finger flap. *Colombia.* Saitz and Cervenka, p. 101.

Self-discipline "his hollow eyes flashing fire, and biting his underlip, to show he could be manly." 18th cent. *England.* Richardson, II, p. 235. Also *U.S.* Krout, p. 21.

Sorrow Biting lip. 19th cent. *Greece.* Sittl, p. 17.

Threat Pulling back one's lips so that teeth show. 16th cent. *Portugal.* Cascudo, *História*, p. 77.

MOUTH

Admiration " 'What do you think of the skirt?' She made a little turn for him. She was pleased and excited. The Frenchmen were watching her. Someone right at the back made a wolf whistle." *Germany.* McEwan, p. 225.

Adoration Spitting in the direction of a deity. Zulu, *South Africa;* Ovambo, *Southwest Africa;* Shinto, *Japan;* Buddhist. Ohm, pp. 224–25.

Affection A high whistle produced between the teeth. Used between lovers to attract the affection of the other. 19th cent. Naples; southern *Italy.* De Jorio, p. 161. * Spitting. 3rd cent. B.C. *Rome*; 17th and 18th cent. *Portugal; Spain.* Cascudo, *História*, p. 118.

Amazement "Hitler was so impressed that his mouth fell open." *Germany.* Toland.

Anger Chewing on one's moustache. *Germany.* Boggs, p. 321.

Apotropy To protect oneself against evil eye or evil glance of insane person or epileptic one spits once or thrice into folds of one's garment. Anc. *Greece* and *Rome;* old women, 19th cent. *Greece.* Sittl, p. 120. Patients suffering from illness thought to come from the gods are spat on, e.g. epileptics or the insane. Anc. *Rome.* Sittl, p. 119. Those watching over children spit on them to protect them against evil eye, particularly if child is asleep and a stranger present. Anc. *Rome.* Sittl, p. 118. Spitting on someone or oneself as protection against evil eye. Only *Roman Empire.* Sittl, p. 120. Murderer spits victim's blood out three times to protect himself against avenging spirits. Anc. *Greece.* Sittl, p. 117. Spitting three times as part of incantation. Anc. *Rome.* Sittl, ibid. Nurse spits three times on child entrusted to her in order to protect it against evil eye and envy. Anc. *Rome.* Seligmann, p. 207. For other instances of apotropaic spitting in anc. *Greece* and *Rome, see* Cascudo,

História, p. 52. *Brazil*. Ibid., p. 118. "A child is never to be praised or admired. If one looks at a child for a while in admiration, he should then spit on it three times." *Hungary*. Temesvary, p. 75. Owner of a horse spits on it after it is praised. 19th cent. *Sardinia*. Sittl, p. 118. Mothers spit on children whose beauty is praised. 19th cent. *Sardinia*. Sittl, p. 118. Mother spits after one who has praised her child. 19th cent. *Sardinia*. Bresciani, *Costumi*, II, pp. 200–01; Sittl, p. 118. Mother must spit thrice upon spot where her child has fallen, so that no adverse consequences may result from the fall. 19th cent. *Palestine*. Bauer, p. 195. Spitting three times as protection against spirits when dog howls or cat meows. 19th cent. *Germany*. Sittl, p. 118. Spitting once or three times while urinating, so that the insulted spirit of the place does not persecute offender. Thrace, 19th cent. *Greece*. Sittl, pp. 117–18. Slaves spat over their shoulder as protection against magic. Anc. *Rome*. Sittl, p. 118, n. 1; Ohm, p. 227. Spitting over one's shoulder (three times?) to protect oneself against magic. Slavic. Sittl, p. 118. Spitting three times over one's left shoulder to ward off bad luck. *Russia*. Monahan, pp. 134–35. Someone handing medicine to sick person spits on floor or out of window as protection of patient against demons. 19th cent. *Sardinia*. Sittl, p. 118. Visitor of sick person spits on threshold to protect the patient against demons. 19th cent. *Sardinia*. Sittl, ibid. Shepherds spit on newborn lambs and their mothers. 19th cent. *Sardinia*. Bresciani, *Costumi*, II, p. 201; Sittl, p. 119. Mother spits on and makes sign of the cross over a child who has cramps. 19th cent. *Sardinia*. Bresciani, ibid., II, p. 200; Sittl, p. 128. When one yawns evil spirits enter the body; therefore one makes sign of cross in name of Holy Trinity when one opens the mouth. Tirol, *Austria*. HDA, III, col. 254; *see* also the references in col. 335. Spitting into one's bosom after praising something to protect it against the evil eye—for whoever has the evil eye harms by means of praise. Old women. 19th cent. *Greece*. Sittl, p. 120. Spitting into one's bosom lest one has aroused jealousy through self praise. Anc. *Rome*. Lucian, *Navig*. 15; anc. *Greece*. Theocrit., vi, 39; anc. *Rome*. Juvenal, viiii, 153. One also spat at one's breast if one praised someone else, in order to protect him from harm. Seligmann, II, pp. 208–09. A friend may spit in a baby's face to prove he has no 'evil eye' intentions. *Hungary*. Benedekfalva, pp. 108–14. A close relative spits in the face of an adult to protect him against the evil eye. Anc. and 19th cent. *Greece*. Sittl, p. 118. Tribes in southern Africa spit to avert the evil omen when they see a shooting star. Frazer, *Golden Bough*, IV, p. 61. Use of saliva in healing. Anc. *Rome*. Lucian, *Navig*., 7, 33; 8, 23. Early Christians spat against the devil at baptism. The neophyte spits out the devil toward the West or other direction deemed to be toward the devil. Greek Orthodox and Armenian rite. Ohm, p. 227. Women spit three times to frighten a demon when they see a falling star. *India*. Frazer, *Golden Bough*, IV, p. 62.

Spitting over the left shoulder at the devil. Muslim. Ohm, p. 227. The face of a believer in a magical process is spit at once or three times. Anc. Rome. Sittl, p. 119. In a case of love magic the girl must spit three times into the lap of her nurse. Anc. Rome. Sittl, p. 119. Priest applies saliva to ears and nose of neophyte at baptism (Chrism). Roman Catholic. Saliva removes a rash, particularly if one says at the same time "garlic," since the smell of garlic is supposed to be disliked by spirits. 19th cent. Greece. Sittl, p. 119. Ohm, p. 227. Breathing on a cat. 19th cent. Germany. Meschke, col. 333; Sittl, p. 121. Blowing as a means of driving evil spirits away is probably a consequence of the description of the devil as malus spiritus in the New Testament. Early Christian. Sittl, p. 121. Old women spit on and blow on their charges. Sittl, ibid. A finished piece of work is spat on to protect it from harm. 19th cent. Germany. Sittl, p. 119. Blowing is a magic gesture in Catimbó, Pajelança, Muamba, Bruxaria as a transmission of the powers of Mestre, Feiticeiro, Babalorixá. Brazil. Cascudo, História, p. 53. Blowing on checkers-piece after wrong move. Brazil. Ibid., p. 54. Blowing on a child's bruise. Ibid. See also Magical.

Approach Hissing as form of beckoning. Biblical. Middle East. Isaiah 5:26; 7:18; Zech. 10:8. (Variants in textual transmission and translations: whistling, signalling.)

Approval Belching as a sign that one has enjoyed a meal. Jordan; Lebanon; Kuwait; Syria; Saudi Arabia; Egypt. Barakat, no. 244.

Attention "and announced her presence by a slight cough: the which being disregarded, was followed by a louder one." 19th cent. England. Dickens, Pickwick, II, p. 409; see also I, p. 127; II, p. 388. * Short hiss to call waiter. Colombia. Saitz and Cervenka, p. 107. See also Approach.

Blessing In blessing one's son, one spits on his head and strokes his head with his hand into which he has spit before. Dinka, nilotic Sudan. Ohm, p. 226. The Lama spits on the soles of his feet at the morning worship, while saying the mantras, thus assuring rebirth of creatures he treads on as gods. Hindu. Ohm, p. 226.

Boredom Yawn, deliberate or involuntary. If deliberate, it is a signal that one wants to leave. Colombia; U.S. Saitz and Cervenka, p. 25. Tiredness or boredom; impolite in public in most of Europe; U.S., esp. if one does not place a hand over the mouth. Universal. Axtell, Gestures, p. 75.

Contempt Spitting into someone's face. Biblical. Middle East. Num. 12:14; Job 30:10. Frequent in medieval and post-medieval pictorial representations of the Mocking of Christ. Jörg Ratgeb, Herrenberg Altar (1518), panel 2. Württemb. Staatsgal., Stuttgart, Germany. Burkhard, p. 8. "Wouldst thou not spit at me and spurn at me." 16th–17th cent. England. Shakesp., Com. of Errors 2:2:133. "This amendment drew bitter invective from an ultra-Orthodox Knesset member, Rabbi Manahem Porush, who at one point spat on a prayer book of the Reform movement and hurled it to the floor." *Israel*. AP Report, "Israel Adopts New Definition of Jew," *L. A. Times*, March 12, 1970, pp. 1, 18. "and spit upon my Jewish gaberdine" 16th–17th cent. *England*. Shakesp., *Merchant* 1.3.110 Spitting at someone or in someone's face. Anc. *Greece; Rome;* 19th cent. *Italy; Spain*. Sittl, p. 105. Spitting at someone or in someone's face as judicial punishment. Biblical. *Middle East*. *Deut*. 25:9; Sittl, p. 106. Spitting prohibited in a temple. Anc. *Rome*. Arrian, *Epict*. 4, 11, 32. Spitting on the threshold of one who has broken the laws of hospitality. 19th cent. *Sardinia*. Bresciani, *Costumi*, II, p. 202. 19th cent. *Corsica*. Sittl, p. 106. Mouth in the act of spitting, directed at the face of the other person. Highest expression of contempt. 19th cent. Naples; southern *Italy*. De Jorio, p. 131. Mouth in the act of spitting, directed towards the ground. Intense degree of contempt. "The quirky American chess master [Bobby Fischer] spits on a U. S. government letter warning against the event." *U.S.* Williams, p. 1. * A sudden puff of air, with a little upward movement of the head and expression of contempt. Mild contempt. 19th cent. Naples; southern *Italy*. De Jorio, p. 130. Mouth open, air suddenly exhaled, or blowing air out. Anc. *Rome*. Sittl, p. 97. * Hissing. Biblical. *Middle East*. I *Kings* 9:8; *Job* 27:23; *Jer*. 18:16, etc. * Whistling. 19th cent. Naples; southern *Italy*. De Jorio, p. 164. * One corner of the mouth as if smiling, the other drawn down, eyelids slightly drooping. *Europe; North America*. Aubert, p. 108. Corner of mouth pulled back. Anc. *Rome*. Plaut., *Mil*. 94. * An intentional belch is a sign of scorn for a speaker or an argument. *Brazil*. Cascudo, *História*, p. 240. " 'Would anyone have dreamed of recording an event like a departmental seminar for posterity unles Shaul Tirosh's name was connected with it?' And he let out a snort of contempt." *Israel*. Gur, p. 2.

Copulation   Gently blowing smoke into a woman's face indicates desire for her. Northern *Syria*. Barakat, no. 4.

Debauchery   Belch. Anc. *Rome*. Baden, p. 455.

Decisiveness   Tightly closed mouth. *Germany*. Krukenberg, p. 212.

Defiance   "but as she spit in his face, so she defied him." 16th–17th cent. *England*. Shakesp., *Measure* 2.1.80–81; "I do defy him, and I spit at him" Shakesp., *Richard II* 1.1.60.

Difficulty   Head tipped backward slightly, air is sucked in audibly between the teeth, indicating that the matter under discussion is "very difficult," thus avoiding an outright "no." *China; Japan; Korea*. Axtell, *Gestures*, pp. 173, 185.

Disagreement   One corner of mouth smiling, the other drawn down, eyelids drooping. *Europe; North America*. Aubert, p. 108.

Disapproval   Hissing. *U.S.* Krout, p. 23.

Dislike One corner of mouth pulled back. Anc. *Rome.* Sittl, p. 89.
* Both corners of mouth pulled down. Anc. *Rome;* children, 19th cent.
Italy. Sittl, p. 89.
Disregard " 'Don't mind him,' Clinton said. 'We'll only have to
put up with him a few more days if we do our jobs. Blow it off.' "
Verbal conversion of the gesture of blowing a brief gust of air out be-
tween slack or rounded lips to signify a lack of importance of a subject
matter. *U.S. L.A. Times,* Oct. 21, 1992, A 12.
Dissatisfaction Grunting. *U.S.* Krout, p. 23. * "Letting the mouth
hang," i.e. corners of the mouth hang down. 17th cent. *Germany. DWb,*
IV/2, col. 450. * Exhale very slowly. *Saudi Arabia; Syria.* Barakat, no.
205.
Embarrassment "and several of the beholders tried to cough down
their emotions." 19th cent. *England.* Dickens, *Pickwick,* II, p. 79.
Enmity Spitting. 19th cent. *Palestine.* Bauer, p. 200.
Etiquette When coffee is ready, host tastes a little of it in order to
show that all is as it should be. 19th cent. *Palestine.* Bauer, p. 183. A
little wine is poured first into glass of host so that he may make sure
that wine is not "corked," before guests are served. Only in restaurants.
At home, host does not serve himself first, since he has opened wine
first and therefore knows that cork has not deteriorated and affected the
wine. Lichine, p. 13. * Smile is not necessarily spontaneous expression
of amusement, but law of etiquette. *Japan.* Ruesch and Kees, p. 22. *
Displaying open mouth, whether yawn or laugh, is considered very rude
in much of Asia, esp. *Japan; Korea.* Axtell, *Gestures,* p. 75. * Difference in etiquette of speaking betweeen proper behavior of men and
women throughout the history of European literature; e.g. "A young
lady is to speak softly and not loudly." 13th cent. *Germany.* Thomasin
v. Circlaria, 405–06. And McConeghy observes in reference to Hartmann von Aue: "Men are allowed to seek social status by performing
deeds of physical might: they 'speak.' Women rise in status by passive
means, being saved or espoused by exemplary men: they remain silent."
But moderation in speaking is also demanded of men: "I wish that
young nobles abide by the demands of courtly manners: let them abstain
from noisiness and bluster; let them leave that to the ale-house keeper;
it's their business to kick up a row." 13th cent. *Germany.* Thomasin v.
Circlaria, 337–42. Women are not to "drink like slaves," throwing their
head back and baring their throat, but gracefully, keeping their lips
closed over the alabaster drinking vessels." 3rd cent. Christian. *Greece.*
Clemens Alexandrinos, p. 70; J.-C. Schmitt, p. 66. *See also* EYE, Etiquette. Maintenance of silence is norm of monastic rules: the tongue is
"a restless evil, full of deadly poison" (Biblical. *Middle East. James*
3:8). The same holds for laughter (*Eccl.* 2:2; 7:3; and the *Regula Bene-*

dicti, Cap. IV, 53 f., VI, 8); similarly, Der Teichner (14th cent. *Germany*) comments that one seldom sees an intelligent person laugh (391, 2 ff.). **Exasperation** "The face expresses annoyance and exhaustion, the shoulders sag, the knees buckle, and air is audibly forced out of the lungs; occasionally the right hand appears to be limply tossing something over the right shoulder, or the thumb is jerked in that general direction: 'J'en ai marre.' " ("I've had it") *France.* Brault, p. 377.

Expectancy "licking his chops." *India. Panchatantra,* V, 12.

Fatigue Yawning. *U.S.* Krout, p. 26.

Flirting Men make chirping sound in flirting with woman. *Lebanon.* Barakat, no. 247.

Foolishness Mouth open. *Germany.* Krukenberg, p. 163.

Friendship South African tribe spits at seeing shooting star as sign of friendliness toward dead chief, whom the shooting star is felt to represent. *South Africa.* Frazer, *Golden Bough,* IV, p. 65.

Greeting Spitting upon the other person. Dyurs, *Sudan.* Ohm, p. 226. Members of some tribes greet by spitting at each other's feet. *East Africa.* Axtell, *Gestures,* p. 22. With saliva one gives part of one's strength to the other. Ohm, p. 226.

Humility In early and medieval Christianity carefree laughter was thought of as unbecoming. Biblical. *Middle East:* "Be afflicted, and mourn, and weep; let your laughter be turned to mourning, and your joy to heaviness." *James,* 4:9. St. Chrysostom justifies this by the example of Christ, who never laughed nor smiled. For a more balanced medieval view, see Bernhard of Clairvaux, col. 1193, and the discussion in J.-C. Schmitt, pp. 145–46.

Hunger Mouth open as far as possible, eyes animated. Head moving repeatedly from left to right. 19th cent. Naples, southern *Italy.* De Jorio, p. 149.

Hygiene Spitting regarded as an act of hygiene. *China.* Axtell, *Gestures,* pp. 74–75.

Impatience Blowing on one's fingers. *Brazil.* Cascudo, *História,* p. 54.

Insult Spitting in someone's face. Biblical. *Middle East. Deut.* 25:9; *Job* 30:10. Spitting at someone. *Matth.* 27:30. anc. *Rome.* Persius, *Sat.,* iv, 35. Catull. 50, 19. Delinquent sailor was punished by having his comrades spit in his face. Anc. *Rome.* Cascudo, *História,* p. 95. Students at the University of Alcalá de Henares hazed new arrivals by spitting in their faces. 17th cent. *Spain.* Quevedo, *Buscón,* V; see also Cascudo, *História,* p. 95. Spitting at some other person's feet or in his face. *Lebanon; Bahrein; Saudi Arabia.* Barakat, no. 185. "if you had but look'd big and spit at him, he'd have run." 16th–17th cent. *England.* Shakesp., *Winter's Tale* 4.3.101–02. "Went to London, to visit my Lady Gerrard, where I saw that cursed woman called the Lady Norton, of whom it was reported that she spit in our King's face as he went to the scaffold." 17th cent. *England.* Evelyn, I, p. 299 (Oct. 28, 1652). "When his correspondent [Lady] Diana [Cooper] was planning a trip to Rome in Spring 1965, [Evelyn] Waugh, depressed over the reforms of the Church, asked her to spit in the face of Cardinal Augustine Bea if she got a chance. On March 7, 1965, Lady Cooper answered that she had the unbelievable good fortune to find herself in a tiny elevator with Bea, 'and so I could spit in his eye for you.' " *England.* Gross, p. 38. "when Dreyer began mocking two women who were speaking to each other in Armenian. . . . He then spit [sic] on one of the women" *U.S.* "Metro Briefs," *L.A. Times*, Aug. 10, 1995, B12. * Drawing the mouth to the side before a superior. *Central Africa.* Hochegger, p. 161.

Magical The saliva of the good destroys evil. Anc. *Greece; Rome; Egypt.* Sittl, p. 119. The face of a believer in a magical process is spat at once or three times. Anc. *Rome.* Sittl, ibid. One who praises a child or its beauty is requested to spit on it. Anc. *Rome;* 19th cent. *Greece.* Sittl, p. 118. The dug-up vampire spits burning saliva at his supposed betrayer. Anc. *Greece.* Sittl, pp. 119–20. Egyptian magician spits Greeks in the face, causing them to look like the dead during the day. Anc. *Greece.* Sittl, p. 119. Spitting back at someone destroys the power of prophecy. Anc. *Greece* and *Rome.* Sittl, ibid. Whoever wants to see devils must let his mouth be spat into. *Byzantine Empire.* Sittl, ibid. Murderer spits the victim's blood out three times to protect himself against avenging spirits. Anc. *Greece.* Sittl, p. 117. Spitting out three times as part of an incantation. Anc. *Rome.* Sittl, ibid. Old women spit on and blow on their charges. *Byzantine Empire.* Sittl, p. 121. Blowing as a means of driving evil spirits away—a consequence of the description of the devil as *malus spiritus* in the New Testament. Early Christian. Sittl, ibid. Mother spits after someone who has praised her child. 19th cent. *Sardinia.* Sittl, p. 118. Owner of a horse spits on it after it has been praised. 19th cent. *Sardinia.* Sittl, ibid. A finished piece of work is spat on. 19th cent. *German.* Sittl, p. 118. Visitor of a sick person spits on his threshold to protect the patient against demons. 19th cent. *Sardinia.* Sittl, ibid. Spitting once or thrice while urinating so that the insulted spirit of the place does not persecute the offender. 19th cent. Thrace, *Greece.* Sittl, pp. 117–18. Spitting over one's shoulder (thrice?) to protect oneself against magic. Slavic. Sittl, p. 118. Spitting into someone's mouth gives him magical wish-power. 19th cent. *Greece.* Sittl, p. 119. Shepherds spit on newborn lambs and their mothers. 19th cent. *Sardinia.* Sittl, ibid. A dervish, in transferring his duties to another, moistens a piece of sugar with saliva and gives it to his successor, who takes it with closed eyes, then blows his breath into his mouth. 19th cent. *Palestine.* Bauer, p. 11. Exhaling at cats. 19th cent. *German.* Sittl, p. 121; Meschke, col. 333. * In the religious festival of Maranguape,

Ceará, *Brazil*, whistling was a public performance, aiding the lift-off of large paper balloons, "carried by the wind, called by the whistle of almost everyone there present. If one did not whistle, the wind did not arrive." Cascudo, *História*, p. 189, who also cites Count José Tuckner as remarking that one did not whistle up the wind on large sailing ships. *See also* Apotropy above.

Medico-magical Vespasian is said to have cured a blind man by placing his saliva on the blind man's eyes. *Roman Empire*. Tacitus. Axtell, *Gestures*, p. 74. Also Biblical. *Middle East*. *Mark* 8:23; *John* 9:6. Mother spits on and makes sign of cross over child who has cramps. 19th cent. *Sardinia*. Sittl, p. 128. Breathing into mouth of sick people. 19th cent. *Palestine*. Bauer, p. 11.

Mockery Spitting at someone or into someone's face. Anc. *Greece* and *Rome*; 19th cent. *Italy*; 19th cent. *Spain*. Sittl, p. 105. Also Biblical. *Middle East*. *Matth*. 26:67; 27:30; *Mark* 10:34; 14:65; 15:19. * Mockery in the theater was expressed by whistling. *Roman Empire*. Suetonius, *Aug.*, xlv. [Editors' note: similarly *Germany; Austria*.] * The most common and vulgar manifestation of plebeian scorn is produced by extending the tongue and simultaneously blowing. "The raspberry." *Brazil*. Cascudo, *História*, p. 123 maintains it is an imitation of flatulence.

Nervousness Twitching mouth. *U.S.* Krout, p. 26.

Oath Spitting to the side to emphasize the solemnity of an oath. Peasants. 19th cent. Normandy, *France*. Raim, pp. 104–05.

Prayer Ritual laughter while ascending the stake. Women. Hindu. During sacrifice of old people. Anc. *Sardinia*. During sacrifice of children. *Phoenicia*. At the death of fellow Thracian. Anc. Thrace, *Greece*; at celebration of Hera, priestess had to tear veil of idol and break into laughter. Anc. *Greece*. At the festival of the Lupercalia the priest, after sacrificing goats, touched the forehead of two young men with the bloody knife, wiping the blood off with wool, whereupon the two men (the "laughers") broke into laughter. Anc. *Rome*. Ohm, pp. 191–92. * Hiding mouth behind cloth while praying. *Parthia*. Heiler, p. 105. * While praying, chewing the leaves of Spaneba tree, then spitting them out. Safwa. *Africa*. Ohm, p. 224. Looking at the sky, asking for blessing, spitting three times. Dschajga. *Kenya*. Ohm, ibid. Pious Shintoists and Buddhists spit at statues and images of certain gods in an effort of having prayers heard. Limited to apply to those deities which grant health. If worshipper's concern is for his eyes, he spits at eyes of deity, thus facilitating the deity's taking over his illness. Worshipper is healed if a piece of paper, spat out, hits the eye of the deity. *Japan*. Ohm, p. 225. The Ni-o are spit at in belief that one receives strength from upper arm of deities if a paper, spat at the deity's arm, sticks there. *Japan*. Ohm, ibid.

Reconciliation Spitting into a vessel is a symbol of reconciliation. Medieval *Iceland. Prose Edda.* Ohm, p. 226.

Refusal Mouth drawn to the side. *Central Africa.* Hochegger, p. 161.

Rejection "All my fond love thus do I blow to heaven. 'Tis gone." 16th–17th cent. *England.* Shakesp., *Othello* 3.4.449–50.

Relief Sighing. *U.S.* Krout, p. 25.

Reverence Spitting was common in the Sabazius-cult. Anc. *Greece.* Ohm, p. 225.

Sarcasm One corner of mouth as if smiling, the other drawn down, eyelids slightly drooping. *Europe; North America.* Aubert, p. 108.

Scorn (see also Mockery) St. Eulalia spat upon her executioners. Anc. *Rome.* Cascudo, *História,* p. 108.

Sorrow Screaming, sobbing, sighing, groaning. *Europe.* Boggs, p. 319.

Submission " 'How does thy honor? Let me lick thy shoe.' " 16th–17th cent. *England.* Shakesp., *Tempest* 3.2.22.

Surprise Opening the mouth. *Europe.* Boggs, p. 321; *U.S.* Krout, p. 23.

Warning Ulysses whistles, warning Diomedes. Anc. *Greece.* Homer, *Iliad,* x, 503.

MOUTH, TONGUE

Disbelief Moving tongue in and out of mouth rapidly. *Saudi Arabia.* Barakat, no. 156.

Pain "He twisted up his mouth, and like an ox that licks his nose, stuck out his loathsome tongue." 13th–14th cent. *Italy.* Dante, *Inf.,* c. xvii.

MOUTH, TOOTH

Anger Gnashing teeth. Biblical. *Middle East. Acts* 7:54. *See also* TOOTH, Anger.

Contempt Hissing and gnashing teeth. Biblical. *Middle East. Lament.* 2:16.

Incomprehension Mouth is snapped shut so one hears click of teeth. May be accompanied by backward jerk of head. Río de la Plata region of *Argentina; Uruguay.* Meo Zilio, p. 82.

Mockery Gnashing teeth. Biblical. *Middle East. Ps.* 35:16. *See also* TOOTH, Anger.

Regret Mouth exhales between clenched teeth: "Je regrette beaucoup!" ("I'm very sorry!") *Central Africa.* Hochegger, p. 165.

MUSTACHE *see* BEARD

NECK

Affection Falling on someone's neck. Biblical. *Middle East. Gen.* 45:14; *Acts* 20:37.

Curiosity   Stretching one's neck. "Ye other few who lifted up your heads betimes." 13th cent. *Italy.* Dante, *Par.*, c. ii.

Flirting   "A woman will tilt her head to the side and expose her neck" when flirting. *U.S.* Moody, p. 9.

Greeting   Falling on someone's neck. Biblical. *Middle East. Gen.* 33:4; *Luke* 15:20.

Obstinacy   Making a stiff neck. Biblical. *Middle East. Jer.* 17:23.

Plea   Falling about someone's neck. "With his strong arms he fastened on my neck." 16th–17th cent. *England.* Shakesp., *Lear* 5.3.212; *Othello* 4.1.140.

Shame   "bending down his corrigible neck, his face subdu'd to penetrative shame." 16th–17th cent. *England.* Shakesp., *Anth. and Cleo.* 4.14.73–75.

Submission   Marinus, brother of Peter Damian, offered himslf as serf at the altar of the Virgin with a rope round his neck. Petrus Damiani, col. 566. St. Odilo offered himself as a serf to the Virgin, with the token offering of serfdom hung round his neck. *Vita Sti. Odilonis,* cols. 915–916. St. Gerard of Brogne went to Rome every other year with 10 shillings hanging from his neck to offer himself as a serf to his Lord. Odo of Cluny, col. 680. Walter of Birbech, when still a layman and knight, tried to express his submission to Mary, and once "went into a church dedicated to her and placed his neck in a rope." 13th cent. *Germany.* Caesarius von Heisterbach, II, 51. McGuire, p. 202.

Superciliousness   Walking with stretched-forth necks. Biblical. *Middle East. Isaiah* 3:16.

NOSE

Affection   Father of the house "kissed" the newborn infant or the child returned from journey three times by sniffing it. Anc. *India;* anc. *Egypt.* Ohm, p. 212. * Rubbing of nose on nose. Maori, *New Zealand; Lapland.* Krukenberg, p. 111; 19th cent. *Malaya.* Mantegazza, p. 227.

Amusement   Wrinkled nose, air drawn in through nose and expelled, accompanied by a dull sound. (Hidden amusement.) Anc. *Greece.* Sittl, p. 88.

Anger   Distended nose. Anc. *Greece.* Sittl, p. 15. * Wrinkled nose. Anc. *Rome.* Sittl, p. 14. * Desire to pull the nose as outlet for frustrated anger. 19th cent. *England.* Dickens, *Pickwick,* I, p. 52; II, p. 44.

Contempt   Turning up one's nose. *Britain. ODP,* p. 677.

Curiosity   Nostrils drawing in air abruptly and repeatedly. Head forward, moving from right to left, eyes lively, lips pursed. Imitating sniffing dog. 19th cent. Naples, southern *Italy.* De Jorio, p. 124. * Wiggling nose—"What's going on?" *Puerto Rico.* Axtell, *Gestures,* p. 68.

Defiance   "There was a general nose-in-the-air, defiant kind of aspect." *Britain. OED,* s.v. Nose, 6a.

Disapproval "Lady Constance had a high, arched nose, admirably adapted for sniffing. She used it now to the limits of its power." *England.* Wodehouse, p. 24. * Wrinkling nose. Anc. *Rome.* Sittl, p. 87. *Colombia; U.S.* Saitz and Cervenka, p. 38.

Disgust "Heaven stops the nose at it." 16th–17th cent. *England.* Shakesp., *Othello* 4.2.79; also *Anth. and Cleo.* 3.13.39. * Wrinkling nose. Anc. *Rome.* Sittl, p. 87; *U.S.* Axtell, *Gestures*, p. 68.

Dislike Wrinkling nose. *U.S.* Krout, p. 26. Nose wrinkled, air drawn in through nose and forcefully expelled. Hellenistic *Near East*; anc. *Rome.* Sittl, p. 88.

Etiquette Sneezing and blowing one's nose in public. Impolite. *Japan.* Axtell, *Gestures.* p. 75.

Farewell "One or two of them then took my hand and smelt it, making rather a noise about it, which is here a very courteous and respectful method of salutation and farewell." *Fiji.* Johnson, p. 302. * Salutation by nose contact. *Malaya;* southern *India; Mongolia; Lapland;* some tribes in *Africa.* Dawson, p. 89.

Friendship Joining noses. 18th cent. *Hawaii.* J. Cook, Bk. v, ch. iii.

Greeting "Geb rejoices at thy approach; he extends his hand to thee; he kisses thee, he fondles thee." Term for "kiss" is anc. Egyptian "sn," i.e. "smell" and has as determinative two noses, tip to tip. Pyramid text from the pyramid of Teti. Anc. *Egypt.* Dawson, p. 83. Cf. also the pillar from Karnak, depicting Sesostris I touching noses with the god Ptah. Anc. *Egypt.* Cairo Museum. Ibid. Sniffing without joining noses as salute. *Fiji Islands; Malaya; Burma; Nicobar Islands; Melanesia.* Dawson, pp. 88–89. Applied principally to children. *Melanesia.* Rubbing noses. *Polynesia.* Dawson, p. 88. Nose-pressing as kiss of welcome, of mourning and sympathy. Maori, *New Zealand.* Dawson, p. 87; Axtell, *Gestures*, rubbing noses, still current, pp. 22, 190. Rubbing noses as sign of affection and greeting. *Polynesia; Lapland;* Eskimos. Eichler, p. 161. Rubbing noses, nose to knee, or nose to foot in case of most eminent member of community. Acknowledged by recipient holding head of gesturer. *Tikopia.* Jalink, rec. radio interview. Two men touch noses three times, then smack lips in greeting. Bedouin, *Saudi Arabia.* Barakat, no. 136. Bedouin touch noses three times in greeting. *Saudi Arabia.* Barakat, no. 116.

Hesitation Nose is scratched with one or more fingers. *France.* Mitton, p. 146.

Laziness "A jailer stood reclining against the dock-rail, tapping his nose listlessly with a large key." 19th cent. *England.* Dickens, *Oliver Twist*, p. 410.

Odor Open hand, palm toward face, is put in front of nose: "Cela sent bon!" ("That smells good!") Or nose raised and breathing in:

"Quel parfum!" ("What a perfume!") *Central Africa.* Hochegger, p. 130.

Penitence   "had been for some seconds scratching his nose with the brim of his hat in a penitent manner." 19th cent. *England.* Dickens, *Pickwick*, II, p. 322.

Superciliousness   Nostrils somewhat distended. Appears in *Roman Empire* under Augustus. Sittl, pp. 87–88. * "She tossed her nose in disdain. 18th cent. *England.* Smollett, *Humphrey Clinker*, letter of Melford, May 24. "she observed, with a toss of her nose, that Brown was a civil fellow enough, considering the lowness of his origin." Smollett, ibid., letter of Melford, Sept. 21.

SHOULDER

Contempt   Rapid shrugging of shoulders once or twice, often accompanied by sighs and raising of eyes to sky. Feminine. Regarded by English as typically French. *France.* Mitton, p. 144.

Copulation   Shrug of the shoulders. *Lat. Am.* Kany, p. 187. *See also* ARM, HAND, Copulate.

Disengagement   "And by the time Marilyn had hobbled into the elevator, apparently without offering any clear explanation of what had been done to her, there were shrugs, raised eyebrows, other signs of disengagement." *U.S.* Logan, p. 53.

Dog   Raise shoulders several times in imitation of a small jump. *Central Africa.* Hochegger, p. 35.

Doubt   Shrug of the shoulders. Boggs, p. 322. "having misplaced their confidence once . . . so they looked wise as they could, shrugged their shoulders." 19th cent. *England.* Dickens, *Pickwick*, I, p. 496. "Lieutenant Tappleton turned round to his friend Doctor Slammer, with scarcely perceptible shrug of the shoulder, as if implying some doubt of the accuracy of his recollection." 19th cent. *England.* Dickens, *Pickwick*, I, p. 50.

Fear   " 'Don't,' said Tess, clutching her arms, and hunching her shoulders, 'I don't like to think of Daddy dying.' " *England.* Lodge, *Paradise News*, p. 316.

Frustration   Shoulders raised and lowered rapidly once or twice. Often reenforced by sigh, eyes directed upward. Mainly feminine. Called "typically French" by the English. *France.* Mitton, p. 144.

Helplessness   Shrugging shoulders. 15th–16th cent. *Italy.* Ariosto, 42, 27.

Ignorance   Shoulders slightly raised, lips pursed. *Colombia; U.S.* Saitz and Cervenka, p. 93.

Impatience   "Mrs. Colonel Wugsby would shrug up her shoulders, and cough, as much as to say she wondered whether he ever would begin." 19th cent. *England.* Dickens, *Pickwick*, II, p. 124. "Sikes shrugged his shoulders impatiently." 19th cent. *England.* Dickens, *Oliver Twist,* p. 173.

Indifference Shrugging shoulders. *U.S.* Krout, p. 25. *Spain.* Flachskampf, p. 229. " 'and suppose the verdict is against me?' said Mr. Pickwick. Mr. Perker smiled . . . shrugged his shoulders and remained expressively silent." 19th cent. *England.* Dickens, *Pickwick,* II, p. 27. " 'Has Mr. Pickwick a strong case?' The attorney shrugged his shoulders." 19th cent. *England.* Dickens, *Pickwick,* p. 31. "I must have shrugged or shown some sign that I didn't think it would make any difference who got the story." *England.* Marrin, p. 91. *U.S.* McCord, p. 292; Seton, p. xxiii; Saitz and Cervenka, p. 43. Very impolite if used by a child to an older person. *Colombia.* Saitz and Cervenka, p. 43. "It doesn't concern me." *Central Africa.* Hochegger, p. 53.

Insult Right shoulder drawn up in imitation of a hunchback. *Central Africa.* Hochegger, p. 26.

Mockery Right shoulder drawn up in imitation of a hunchback. *Central Africa.* Hochegger, p. 26.

Negation " 'Eh! I am selfish: but am I more selfish than the rest of the world?' asks my Lord, with a French shrug of his shoulders, and a pinch out of his box." Thackeray, *Virginians,* II, ch. xxiv, p. 262. * Quick jerk of left shoulder. *Africa.* Ohm, p. 44.

Resignation Shrugging shoulders. 14th cent. *Italy.* Boccaccio, 2, 8. "he shrugged up his shoulders, and, with a peculiar grimace in his countenance, said, he was sorry for my misfortunes; but there was no remedy like patience." 18th cent. *England.* Smollett, *Roderick Random,* ch. xliii. Also 16th cent. *Italy.* Folengo, 3, 33. "Mr. Scogan shrugged his shoulders and, pipe in hand, made a gesture of resignation." *England.* Huxley, ch. 22.

Submission Shoulders raised in acceptance of an unpleasant situation. *Roman Empire*; early Christian. Sittl, p. 113.

Truth "Actress Russell, humped up and hipped out till she resembles a super-annuated ostrich, encompasses . . . the standard repertory of Jewish gesture—the delicately deprecating shrug that says: I don't mean to offend, but a fact is a fact" Review of "A Majority of One" (Warner), *Time,* Jan. 19, 1962, p. 55.

TOE

Apotropy "The sound of the ambulance siren recedes. 'Cross my fingers, cross my toes, Hope I don't go in one of those,' Amanda chants under her breath, crossing her toes inside her sandals, as she lopes along, taking care at the same time not to tread on the cracks between the paving-stones" *England.* Lodge, *Paradise News,* p. 107.

Rudeness "pointing a toe at a person is considered rude in the Arab world" Lynch, p. 10.

TONGUE

Admiration Erotic admiration is expressed by quickly extruding and withdrawing the tongue. *Netherlands*. Andrea and de Boer, p. 159. * " 'He's got the gift of the gab and he has class. Moreover, he's got no scruples and he can smell a deal thirty miles away.' She clicked her tongue in admiration." *Spain*. Pérez-Reverte, p. 39.

Affection Sticking out one's tongue at someone. Anc. *Rome*. Plaut., *Asin*. 795.

Anticipation Tongue extended ca. 1/4 in., moving slowly along lips. Eyes widen. *Colombia; U.S*. Saitz and Cervenka, p. 18.

Apotropy Sticking out tongue against evil spirits and enemies; hence the gargoyles of medieval cathedrals, of gate towers of medieval castles, and gorgonheads at the eaves of temples in antiquity. Also late medieval depictions of the Passion of Christ. *Europe*. Röhrich, *Gebärde-Metapher-Parodie*, p. 26. Sticking out the tongue is an imitation of a phallus. Anc. *Greece*: Gorgons' heads with protruding tongues; similar gestures on portals and elsewhere on Romanesque and Gothic churches. *See also* Insult. Mellinkoff, *Outcasts*, I, p. 198. Old women lick children's forehead with tongue to protect them against the evil eye. *Byzantine Empire*. Sittl, p. 120. Sticking tongue out against cats (demons) at night. 19th cent. *Italy*. Children. Sittl, p. 117.

Applause Smacking the tongue. Anc. *Greece*; *Australia* (aborigines); Eskimos. Sittl, p. 61.

Approach Master clicks tongue to summon servant, muledriver to hurry mules. Anc. *Greece*. Sittl, p. 223.

Approval " 'They've come about the painting,' Belmonte explained. Alfonso clicked his tongue. 'Of course, the painting. Your famous painting.' " *Spain*. Pérez-Reverte, p. 45.

Copulation Tongue protruded slowly. Invitation to a prostitute. *Colombia*. Saitz and Cervenka, p. 117. * Wagging tongue from one side of mouth to the other without extending the tongue fully from the mouth: proposition by man to woman. *Lebanon*. Barakat, no. 107. Erotic suggestion. *Netherlands*. Andrea and de Boer, p. 55.

Defiance Tongue is stuck out in the direction of someone. Childish. *France*. Mitton, p. 150. Primarily women and children. *Netherlands*. Andrea and de Boer, p. 55. Adults. *U.S*. Woodyard, p. A3.

Direction Tongue extended in direction the gesturer wants to indicate. *Central Africa*. Hochegger, p. 55.

Disbelief "Duncan clucked his tongue thoughtfully." *England*. J. D. Carr, *Constant Suicides*, p. 102.

Disdain Sticking out the tongue. *Germany*. Meschke, col. 337.

Doubt Clicking the tongue. *Brazil*. Cascudo, *História*, pp. 123–24. *See also* Scorn below.

Drink Tongue protrudes over lower lip. Often comic. *U.S.* Saitz and Cervenka, p. 44.

Gossip Protruded tongue moves rapidly from left to right: "You are a gossip." *Central Africa.* Hochegger, p. 21.

Greeting Sticking out the tongue. *Polynesia.* Röhrich, *Gebärde-Metapher-Parodie* p. 13. *Tibet.* Axtell, *Gestures*, pp. 22, 75. *See also* FINGER, TONGUE and HAND, HAT, Greeting.

Indifference Clicking the tongue. *Brazil.* Cascudo, *História*, pp. 123–24. *See also* Scorn below.

Insult Sticking out tongue at someone. Children and, joking, adults. *Colombia.* Saitz and Cervenka, p. 76. *Europe.* Ohm, p. 45. Biblical. *Middle East. Isaiah* 57:4. For the gesture in medieval art, see Mellinkoff, *Outcasts*, I, pp. 198–200. In 362 B.C., during an attack on the Romans, a Gallic warrior stuck out his tongue at them before being killed by Titus Manlius. *Anc. Rome.* Livy, vii, 9, 10; Val. Max., vi, 9, 1–2; Aul. Gellius, ix, 13, 3. 13th cent. *Italy.* Dante, *Inf.* xvii, 74–75: "Di fuor trasse la lingua, come bue che il naso lecchi" ("stuck out his tongue, like an ox that licks its nose"). 16th cent. *Germany.* Lucas Cranach the Elder, *Mocking of Christ* (1538). *Germany. HDA*, I, col. 323. *U.S.* Krout, p. 24. As Russian revolutionaries were being entrained for Siberia in 1906, a Russian woman stuck out her tongue at the photographer. Originally limited to the Middle East and Western Europe. It was unknown to Africans and native Americans before contact with Arabic and Iberian cultures. Cascudo, *História*, p. 146. Childish. *France.* Mitton, p. 150. Schoolchildren. *U.S.* Seton, p. xxi. Gesture may be ironic in its significance as unacceptable behavior by being "planted" on a face with which it is unlikely to be associated. See the photomontage in an advertisement of the Arbeitsamt in *Die Zeit*, May 22, 1992, p. 4. *See* Mockery below. * Protruded tongue moving rapidly from left to right is an insult to young women. *Central Africa.* Hochegger, p. 21. Tongue extruded in front of a woman. *Central Africa.* Hochegger, p. 191. *See* Apotropy, Mockery.

Mockery Sticking out the tongue. Meschke, col. 337. The "Lallekönig" of Basle, who mocked the German Empire across the Rhine. Late medieval *Switzerland.* Röhrich, *Gebärde-Metapher-Parodie*, pl. 21 and p. 26. Childish. *France.* Mitton, p. 150. "The Prentice speaks his Disrespect by an extended finger, and the Porter by sticking out his Tongue. 18th cent. *England. Spectator*, no. 354 (Apr. 16, 1712). Sticking out the tongue, according to Sittl, pp. 90–91, was known to the ancient Greeks only as signifying bloodthirstiness, and he deems it probable that the Romans borrowed it as signifying mockery from Gaul. *Anc. Greece* and *Rome. See also* Taylor, *Shanghai Gesture*, p. 17; Mellinkoff, *Outcasts*, I, p. 198, who points to anc. Gk. Gorgons' heads sticking out the tongue and *Isaiah*, 57, 4 as evidence from Biblical antiquity.

Jan Polack, *Ecce Homo* (1492)—in combination with the "Schabab"-gesture of crossing one index with the other and rubbing it along the lower index. *See also* FINGER, Mockery ("Rübenschaben"). Frequent in representations of the mocking of Christ; *see* van der Meulen, pp. 23–24. Tongue stuck out of the corner of the mouth. 19th cent. *Italy*. Bresciani, *Edmondo*, vii, 144. Tongue stuck out frontally. Children. 19th cent. *Germany*. Sittl, p. 90. *See* Apotropy; Insult.

Negation Clicking the tongue. 19th cent. *Italy*; 19th cent. *Greece*. Sittl, p. 96.

Respect Sticking out the tongue. *Tibet*. Ohm, p. 45.

Reverence "lick up the dust off your feet." Biblical. *Middle East*. *Isaiah* 49:23.

Satisfaction "He gave a satisfied click of his tongue, as if savouring some delicious morsel." *Spain*. Pérez-Reverte, p. 176.

Scorn Clicking the tongue. *Brazil*. Almost entirely a woman's gesture, imported from Angola with the black slaves. Still common among certain Bantu groups. *South Africa*. Cascudo, *História*, pp. 123–24.

Secrecy Tongue is repeatedly and rapidly extruded: "On le dira!" ("It'll come out!") *Central Africa*. Hochegger, p. 183.

Submission "They shall lick the dust like a snake." Biblical. *Middle East*. *Micah* 7:17; *Ps.* 72:9.

Teasing Tongue extended from open mouth. *Jordan; Lebanon; Kuwait; Syria; Saudi Arabia; Iraq*. Barakat, no. 70.

TONGUE, TOOTH

Anger "So York must sit and fret and bite his tongue." 16th–17th cent. *England*. Shakesp., II *Henry VI* 1.2.225.

Disbelief Snicking teeth with tongue, simultaneously lifting head quickly: "No, never," "perhaps," "I don't believe you." Arab. Barakat, no. 144.

Embarrassment Biting tongue. Anc. *Greece*. Sittl, p. 17. *France*. Rousseau, *Émile*, v.

Pain "and they gnawed their tongues for pain." Biblical. *Middle East*. *Rev.* 16:10.

TOOTH

Admiration Putting a coin between one's teeth, which is then taken between the teeth of a drummer, expresses admiration for the drummer. Or: a boy offers a banknote in his teeth to a dancer, who takes it between her teeth. *Central Africa*. Hochegger, pp. 56, 57.

Anger Gnashing of teeth. Anc. *Greece* and *Rome*; predominantly Roman. Sittl, p. 44, cf. also p. 16. Boggs, p. 321. 9th cent. *England*. *Juliana*, 594 ff., *Acta S. Julianae*, cap. 3; Habicht, pp. 38–40, 50. In Old and Middle English such extreme displays of anger are associated with diabolical nature or possession by the devil. Habicht, p. 40. 16th–17th cent. *Poland*. Bogucka, p. 196. *U.S.* Krout, p. 23. Gritting one's teeth as indication of extreme anger or rage. *U.S.* Ruesch and Kees, p. 36. * Biting into moustache. 19th cent. *Greece*. Sittl, p. 17.

Apotropy Gnashing teeth against cats (demons) at night. Children. 19th cent. *Italy*. Sittl, p. 117; Meschke, col. 337. * Showing teeth to a person suspected of having the evil eye. *Italy*. Seligmann, II, p. 287. * Biting a child in the finger to make it weep, for someone who weeps is not envied and is therefore safe from the evil eye. Bengal, *India*. Seligmann, II, p. 207.

Chagrin "grinding his teeth together, with a look that baffles all description." 18th cent. *England*. Smollett, *Peregrine Pickle*, ch. lxix.

Despair "There shall be weeping and gnashing of teeth." Biblical. *Middle East*. *Matth*. 8:12; 13:42.50; etc.

Determination Gritting teeth. Boys. *England*. Opie, p. 230.

Ecstasy Gnashing of teeth in orgiastic ecstasy. Anc. *Greece*. Sittl, p. 27.

Etiquette One is not to show one's teeth at table. 14th cent. *England*. Books of table manners; *see* Habicht, p. 60.

Greeting Cutting oneself with shark's teeth and wailing as a form of receiving a friend or showing joy at his arrival. *Tahiti*. Ellis, II, p. 337.

Hatred Gnashing of teeth. Anc. *Rome*. Pausanias 10, 28, 7. 13th–14 cent. *Italy*. Dante, *Inf.*, c. v; 19th cent. Naples, southern *Italy*. De Jorio, p. 265. Early Christian. Sittl, p. 44.

Mockery Gnashing of teeth and laughing. Anc. *Rome*. Sittl, p. 98. * Hissing and gnashing of teeth. Biblical. *Middle East*. *Lam*. 2:16; *Ps*. 35:16.

Submission Biting the grass. Medieval *Spain*. *Cid*, 2022.

Threat Gnashing teeth. Anc. *Rome*. Pausanias 10. 28, 7; Devil in the Tomba dell' Orco of Tarquinius. *Etruria*; 13th–14th cent. *Italy*. Dante, *Inf.*, c. v. "Our Eastern Shore Virginians are again beginning to growl and to show their teeth." 19th cent. *U.S.* Simms, 30.

Index of Significances

Absence: Hand.

Acceptance: Finger; Hand; Lip.

Acclamation: Arm, finger, hand.

Accolade: Hand; Hand, weapon; Knee.

Accompaniment (Accompany): Hand; Head.

Accusation: Arm, finger; Arm, hand; Finger; Finger, hand.

Acknowledgment: Arm, hand; Hand; Head; Lip.

Acquiescence: Body.

Address (Passionate): Hand.

Admiration: Arm, hand; Beard, hand; Cheek, eyebrow, head, mouth; Cheek, finger; Cheek, forehead, mouth; Chin, finger, head, nose; Chin, hand; Eye, finger; Eye, hand; Eyebrow; Finger; Finger, lip; Finger, mouth; Fingernail, tooth; Hair, hand; Hand; Hand, head; Hand, lip; Lip; Tongue. Tooth.

Admonition: Finger; Hand.

Adoption: Beard, hand; Hair, hand; Hand; Knee.

Adoration: Arm; Arm, breast; Body; Body, face; Ear, hand, leg; Eye, hand, leg; Face, hand, knee; Finger, lip; Foot; Foot, lip; Hand; Hand, lip; Head; Knee; Lip; Mouth.

Affection: Arm; Arm, breast; Arm, hand; Arm, lip; Arm, neck; Arm, shoulder; Back, hand; Beard, hand;

Beard, lip; Breast, hand; Breast, hand, head; Breast, lip, shoulder; Cheek, eyebrow, head, mouth; Cheek, finger; Cheek, hand; Cheek, hand, lip; Cheek, nose; Chin, hand; Ear, eye, hand, lip; Ear, hand, lip; Eye, hand; Eye, mouth; Face; Face, hand, knee; Finger; Finger, lip; Finger, mouth; Forehead, hand; Forehead, lip; Hair, hand; Hair, lip; Hand; Hand, head; Hand, lip; Head; Lip; Lip, neck; Lip, object; Lip, tongue; Lip, tooth; Mouth; Neck; Nose; Tongue.

Affirmation: Arm, finger, hand; Breast, hand; Chin; Eye, Eyebrow; Eyebrow; Eyebrow, head; Finger; Hand; Hand, object; Head.

Affluence: Buttocks, hand.

Age: Chin, hand; Hair, hand; Hand; Hand, head.

Aggressiveness: Hand.

Agreement: Body; Breast, hand; Eyebrow; Eyebrow, head, shoulder; Finger; Glove; Hand; Hand, head; Hand, staff; Hand, straw; Hand, weapon; Head; Lip.

Ahead: Finger; Hand.

Alarm: Arm, breast; Breast, hand; Hand; Hand, weapon; Head.

Alertness: Eye, finger.

Amazement: Cheek, hand; Ear, hand; Eye; Eye, hand; Eyebrow, mouth, shoulder; Finger, nose; Hand; Head; Mouth.

Amusement: Arm; Eye; Finger, lip; Head; Nose.

Anger: Abdomen; Arm; Arm, body, hand; Arm, finger, hand; Arm, hand; Beard, hand; Breast, hand; Cheek; Cheek, hand; Ear, hand; Eye; Eye, eyebrow, fist; Eye, finger; Eye, hand; Eye, mouth; Eyebrow; Face; Face, hand; Finger; Finger, hand; Finger, tooth; Fingernail, tooth; Foot; Forehead, hand; Forehead, lip; Hand; Hand, hair; Hand, hat; Hand, head; Hand, knee; Hand, object; Hand, shoulder; Hand, staff; Hand, thigh; Hand, tooth; Head; Head, tooth; Lip; Lip, tooth; Mouth; Mouth, tooth; Nose; Tongue, tooth; Tooth.

Annoyance: Eye, eyebrow, head; Hand, head.

Anticipation: Elbow, hand; Eyebrow; Hand; Tongue.

Antipathy: Hand; Head.

Anxiety: Finger, lip; Fingernail, tooth; Hand.

Apology: Arm, hand; Body; Finger; Finger, tooth; Hand; Hand, mouth; Hand, object; Head; Head, lip; Lip, tongue.

Apotropy: Arm; Arm, hand; Arm, mouth; Body; Breast, forehead, hand, mouth; Breast, hand; Buttocks; Cheek, finger; Eye; Eye, finger; Face; Face, hand; Finger; Finger, hand; Finger, hand, mouth; Finger, head; Finger, object; Finger, testicles; Foot; Genitals; Hand; Hand, mouth; Hand, object; Head, shoulder; Mouth; Toe; Tongue; Tooth.

Appeasement: Hand.

Appetite: Eyebrow, head, lip.

Applause: Body; Breast, foot, hand,

lip; Finger; Hand; Hand, lip; Hand, object; Tongue.

Appreciation: Abdomen, hand; Hand; Hand, mouth; Head; Lip.

Approach: Arm; Arm, finger, hand; Cheek, nose; Finger; Finger, hand; Hand; Hand, head; Head; Lip; Mouth; Tongue.

Approval: Cheek, finger; Ear, finger; Eye; Eye, finger; Finger; Finger, hand; Finger, head; Finger, lip; Foot; Hair, hand; Hand; Hand, head; Hand, shoulder; Head; Lip; Mouth; Tongue.

Approximation: Hand.

Arrest: Hand.

Arrogance: Arm; Body, head, lip; Eyebrow; Finger, hand; Hand; Head; Nose.

Assistance: Arm; Arm, finger; Arm, hand; Breast, hand; Chin, finger; Finger; Hand.

Assurance: Eye, finger; Finger, hand; Finger, tooth; Forehead, head; Hand; Hand, shoulder; Head.

Astonishment: Arm, finger, hand; Arm, hand; Chin; Finger, lip; Hand; Hand, mouth.

Asylum: Arm, knee.

Atonement: Hand, object.

Attention: Arm; Arm, breast; Arm, finger; Arm, hand; Body; Cheek, finger; Ear, finger; Elbow; Elbow, rib; Eye; Eye, eyebrow, head; Eye, finger; Eye, head; Eye, head, mouth; Eyebrow, head; Eyebrow, head, lip; Finger; Finger, hand; Finger, lip; Finger, nose; Foot; Hand; Hand, head; Hand, leg; Hand, object; Hand, shoulder; Head; Knee; Leg; Lip; Mouth.

Authority: Arm; Arm, hand; Body; Elbow; Glove; Hand; Hand, hip;

Hand, leg; Hand, staff; Hand,
straw.
Avarice: Arm, elbow; Arm, hand;
Elbow; Elbow, hand; Finger;
Hand.
Aversion: Buttocks, hand; Hand.
Awaken: Eye.
Awareness: Eye, finger; Forehead,
hand; Hand, head.
Awe: Hand.

Babble: Hand.
Baby: Arm; Arm, hand.
Bafflement: Head.
Bargain: Hair, hand.
Beckoning: Eye, finger.
Begging: Finger; Hand; Hand, knee.
Begin: Arm, finger, hand.
Behind: Finger; Hand.
Belligerence: Hand, weapon.
Betrayal: Lip.
Betting: Finger; Finger, tongue; Hand;
Hand, object.
Blessing: Arm; Arm, finger, hand;
Arm, hand, mouth; Body; Eye,
hand; Finger; Finger, hand; Fin-
gernail, hand; Fingernail, lip; Foot;
Foot, hand; Hand; Hand, head;
Hand, object; Mouth.
Body distance: Body.
Book (request for): Finger, hand.
Boredom: Beard, hand; Cheek, finger;
Cheek, hand; Chin, finger; Chin,
hand; Eyebrow, jaw; Finger; Fin-
ger, hand; Hand; Hand, mouth;
Mouth.
Bravery: Finger; Finger, hand.
Breastfeeding: Breast, hand.
Brevity: Body.
Bribery: Finger; Hand.
Bring: Arm, finger, hand.
Brooding: Eye, eyebrow, lip.
Brotherhood: Lip.
Buxom: Breast, hand.

Calmness: Arm, hand; Beard, hand;
Finger, hand; Glove; Hand; Hand,
knee; Hand, mouth, tongue, tooth;
Leg; Lip.
Cancellation: Hand, object.
Capture: Hand, wrist.
Carelessness: Hand; Head.
Cat: Finger, hand.
Caution: Finger.
Censure: Eye, finger; Eye, hand;
Finger.
Certification: Hand, object.
Chagrin: Finger, tooth; Fingernail,
tooth; Tooth.
Challenge: Beard, hand; Cheek, hand;
Chin, finger; Finger; Finger, hand;
Glove (gauntlet); Hand; Hand, hip;
Hand, object; Head.
Change: Hand.
Chastity: Hand, weapon.
Cheap: Finger, nose.
Cheating: Finger, hand.
Childishness: Finger, mouth.
Chinese: Eye, finger.
Choice: Finger, hand.
Christ: Finger.
Cigarette: Finger, hand; Finger, lip.
Claim: Hand; Hand, object.
Clairvoyance: Hand, head.
Clarification: Finger; Head.
Cleansing: Finger; Hand.
Cleverness: Eye, finger; Finger, fore-
head; Finger, nose; Genitals, hand;
Hand, head; Hand, nose.
Climb: Arm, hand.
Cold: Arm, breast; Arm, hand; Hand;
Hand, leg; Hand, neck.
Collect: Hand.
Comfort: Leg.
Command: Arm; Arm, finger, hand;
Eyebrow, finger; Eyelid; Finger;
Finger, hand; Hand; Head.
Commendation: Hand; Hand, knee;
Hand, object.

Complaint: Cheek, head, lip.
Complication: Arm, hand; Hand; Hand, head.
Complicity: Eye; Eye, finger; Eye, finger, lip; Finger, nose.
Compliment: Buttocks, hand; Hand.
Compulsion: Hand, neck.
Concentration: Body; Cheek, tongue; Chin, hand; Ear, hand; Eye; Eye, eyebrow, jaw; Eye, hand; Eye, head; Eyebrow; Eyebrow, jaw; Face, hand; Finger; Finger, head; Finger, nose; Fingernail, tooth; Forehead; Forehead, hand; Hand; Hand, head; Hand, nose; Head; Leg; Lip.
Condemnation: Hand, stone.
Condescension: Lip.
Confession: Arm; Knee.
Confidence: Body; Eye, hand; Finger; Hand; Head.
Confirmation: Cheek, hand; Hand; Head.
Confusion: Arm, head; Eyebrow, foot, head, mouth; Face, hand; Forehead, hand; Hand; Hand, head; Hand, nose; Head.
Congratulation: Arm; Back, hand; Breast, hand; Hand; Hand, lip; Lip.
Consecration: Hand; Hand, head.
Consolation: Arm, hand; Arm, hand, shoulder; Back, hand; Finger; Hand; Hand, shoulder; Lip.
Contemplation: Cheek, finger; Chin, hand; Hand, head.
Contempt: Arm, wrist; Back; Buttocks, hand; Cheek, tongue; Chin, finger; Chin, foot, hand; Eye; Eye, tongue; Face; Finger; Finger, hand; Finger, nose; Finger, tooth; Fingernail, tooth; Foot; Foot, hand; Genitals; Hand; Hand, object; Head; Head, lip; Heel; Lip; Lip, tongue;

Mouth; Mouth, tooth; Nose; Shoulder.
Contentment: Hand.
Conveyance: Hand, object.
Conviviality: Eye.
Copulation: Arm, hand; Body; Breast, hand; Finger; Finger, hand; Finger, mouth; Finger, nose; Hand; Hip; Mouth; Shoulder; Tongue.
Corpulence: Arm, hand.
Counting: Finger; Finger, hand; Hand, shoulder.
Crazy: Forehead, hand; Hand, head; Hand, object.
Creation: Hand.
Criticize: Finger, hand.
Crowd: Arm, hand.
Cruelty: Hand, jaw, lip.
Cuckoldry: Ear, finger; Finger; Finger, forehead; Finger, hand; Finger, head; Finger, temple; Hand; Hand, head; Head.
Cunning: Cheek, finger; Eye, mouth; Finger; Finger, nose; Hand, nose.
Curiosity: Eye, hand, head; Eye, head; Neck; Nose.
Curse: Arm, hand; Breast, hand; Buttocks; Face, hand; Finger; Hand; Hand, head; Lip.
Cut: Finger.

Dance: Finger.
Danger: Finger, hand; Finger, neck; Finger, shoulder.
Dead: Body.
Deafness: Finger.
Death: Arm; Arm, body, hand; Arm, neck; Finger; Finger, neck; Hand; Hand, head; Hand, neck; Hand, object; Hand, weapon.
Debauchery: Ear, finger, mouth; Lip; Mouth.
Deception: Eye, eyebrow, jaw; Fin-

Discouragement: Eye, head, mouth, nose; Eyebrow, head, lip; Finger; Hand.

Discretion: Eye; Hand, mouth.

Disdain: Eyebrow; Finger; Tongue.

Disengagement: Eyebrow; Shoulder.

Disgust: Body; Breast, hand; Eye, head, mouth, nose; Eye, lip, nose; Face, hand; Finger, hand, tongue; Finger, tongue; Hand; Hand, head; Hand, neck; Hand, nose; Head; Lip; Lip, nose; Nose.

Dishonest gain: Finger.

Dishonor: Face, hand.

Disinterest: Chin, finger.

Dislike: Ear, hand; Eye; Face, hand; Finger; Forehead, mouth; Head; Lip; Mouth; Nose.

Dismay: Eyebrow, hand, mouth; Forehead, hand; Hand; Hand, mouth; Hand, tooth; Head.

Dismissal: Hand.

Displeasure: Ear, hand; Eye, hand; Eyebrow; Fingernail; Foot; Heel.

Disregard: Face, hand; Mouth.

Dissatisfaction: Finger, head; Finger, nose; Hand, object; Mouth.

Dissociation: Finger.

Distress: Breast, hand; Eye, hand; Hand; Hand, head; Knee.

Distrust: Eye, finger; Eye, head, mouth, nose.

Divorce: Hand.

Dog: Shoulder.

Doubt: Cheek, hand; Hand; Shoulder; Tongue.

Down: Hand.

Drink: Finger; Finger, hand; Finger, hand, mouth; Finger, lip; Finger, mouth; Finger, neck; Finger, nose; Hand; Hand, mouth; Hand, neck; Hand, object; Tongue.

Drive: Hand.

Dropping: Finger.

Drunkenness: Finger, hand; Finger, lip; Finger, nose; Hand.

Duality: Hand.

Ease: Arm, hand.

Eating: Abdomen, hand; Breast, hand; Finger, hand, mouth; Finger, lip; Finger, mouth; Hand; Hand, mouth.

Ecstasy: Eye, eyebrow, head, jaw; Head; Leg; Tooth.

Effeminacy: Arm, hand; Body; Buttocks; Cheek, finger; Chin, finger; Ear, finger; Hand; Hand, wrist; Head.

Egotism: Arm, finger.

Ejection: Hand.

Elation (see also Joy): Hand; Lip.

Embarrassment: Beard, hand; Cheek, eye; Cheek, finger; Cheek, hand; Eye; Eye, finger; Face, hand; Finger; Finger, head; Finger, lip; Finger, mouth; Finger, tooth; Fingernail, tooth; Foot; Hand, head; Hand, mouth; Hand, object; Lip; Lip, tooth; Mouth; Tongue, tooth.

Emphasis: Arm; Breast, hand; Elbow, hand; Elbow, rib; Eye; Finger; Finger, hand; Finger, nose; Foot; Forehead, hand; Hair, hand; Hand; Hand, head; Hand, hip; Hand, knee; Hand, object; Hand, staff; Head.

Encouragement: Arm; Arm, elbow; Arm, finger, hand; Arm, hand; Breast; Breast, hand; Buttocks, hand; Finger; Finger, hand; Finger, mouth; Hand; Hand, shoulder.

Enforce: Finger, hand.

Engagement: Foot; Glove; Hand.

Enjoyment: Ear, hand.

Enlightenment: Finger, forehead.

Enmity: Arm, finger; Breast, hand; Eye; Finger; Hand; Mouth.

Enthusiasm: Arm; Arm, hand; Body; Ear, finger; Finger; Hand; Hand, hat; Hand, mouth.

Envy: Lip, tooth.

Equality: Finger; Hand.

Etiquette: Arm; Arm, hand; Body; Body, hand; Eye; Finger; Finger, hand; Finger, lip; Finger, nose; Foot; Glove; Hand; Hand, hat; Hand, lip; Hand, mouth; Hand, object; Head; Leg; Lip; Mouth; Nose; Tooth.

Evasiveness: Fingernail; Hand, object.

Exasperation: Mouth.

Excess: Hand.

Exchange: Finger.

Excitement: Breast, hand; Hand; Hand, mouth; Lip; Lip, tooth.

Exclamation: Eye, jaw.

Expansiveness: Arm.

Expectancy: Hand; Mouth.

Expulsion (see also Ejection): Hand.

Exquisiteness: Finger, lip; Hand.

Extraordinary: Ear, finger.

Extreme: Hand.

Eye contact: Eye.

Facetiousness: Eye; Finger, nose.

Facility: Finger; Hand.

Failure: Finger, hand; Hand, mouth.

Fairness: Finger, hand.

Faithfulness: Hand; Hand, weapon.

Falseness: Finger, hand.

Familiarity: Body, object; Finger, nose; Hand, object; Hand, shoulder; Lip.

Fantasy: Hand, head.

Farewell: Arm; Arm, hand; Arm, head; Body; Cheek, hand; Finger; Finger, lip; Hand; Hand, hat; Hand, head; Hand, knee; Hand, object; Head; Lip; Nose.

Fasting: Finger, mouth.

Father: Chin, hand.

Fatigue: Cheek, eye, hand; Cheek, hand; Chin, hand; Eye; Eye, finger; Eye, hand; Eye, hand, head; Face, hand; Finger; Finger, forehead; Foot; Hand, head; Hand, mouth; Mouth.

Favor: Hand, shoulder.

Fear: Arm; Arm, hand; Beard, hand; Body; Body, face; Cheek, hand; Chin; Chin, hand; Eye, forehead; Eyebrow; Face, hand; Finger; Finger, hand; Foot; Hand; Hand, head; Hand, object; Head; Head, shoulder; Knee; Leg; Shoulder.

Femininity: Foot.

Fervor: Hand.

Fever: Cheek, hand; Forehead, hand.

Fight: Hand.

Film: Ear, hand.

Finish: Finger, hand; Hand.

Finished: Arm, finger, hand; Arm, hand; Body, hand; Chin, finger; Elbow; Finger; Finger, throat; Foot; Hand; Hand, mouth; Hand, neck.

Flat: Arm, hand.

Flattery: Arm; Ear, finger; Finger; Hand; Hand, nose; Lip.

Flirting: Eye; Eyebrow; Eyebrow, head, lip; Finger, tooth; Foot, leg; Head; Mouth; Neck.

Foolishness: Ear, hand; Elbow, finger; Elbow, hand; Finger, forehead; Finger, head; Finger, lip; Hand; Hand, mouth; Head; Mouth.

Forget: Hand, head.

Forgetfulness: Fingernail, tooth; Foot, hand; Hand, mouth.

Forgiveness: Hand.

Forwardness: Hand.

Freedom: Body.

Friendship: Arm; Arm, hand; Arm, hand, shoulder; Finger; Finger, hand; Hand; Hand, nose; Hand, object; Hand, shoulder; Head; Lip; Mouth; Nose.

Frustration: Abdomen, hand; Arm, hand, shoulder; Eye, lip, tooth; Finger; Finger, nose; Finger, tooth; Fingernail, tooth; Hair, hand; Hand; Hand, head; Hand, mouth; Shoulder.

Future: Finger; Hand.

"Gently": Hand.

Gift: Glove.

Goad: Arm, hand.

Gone: Hand.

Good luck: Hand, genitals; Hand, hat.

Good wishes: Hand, head.

Gossip: Ear, hand; Finger; Finger, hand; Finger, tongue; Hand; Lip; Tongue.

Graft: Hand.

Gratitude: Arm; Arm, knee; Body; Body, face; Body, hand; Breast, hand; Breast, hand, head; Eye; Finger, forehead; Finger, hand, mouth; Finger, head; Foot, lip; Hair, hand; Hand; Hand, knee; Hand, lip; Hand, object; Head; Knee; Lip.

Gravity: Head.

Greed: Arm, finger; Hand.

Greeting: Abdomen, hand; Arm; Arm, body; Arm, body, hand; Arm, hand; Arm, lip; Back, hand; Body; Body, face; Body, hand; Breast, forehead, hand, mouth; Breast, forehead, lip; Breast, hand; Breast, hand, head; Breast, lip; Buttocks; Cheek, hand; Cheek, hand, lip; Chin; Chin, hand, lip; Ear, hand; Eye; Eye, finger; Eye, hand; Eye, head; Eyebrow; Eyebrow, head; Eyebrow, head, lip; Finger; Finger, hand; Finger, hand, mouth; Finger, head; Finger, lip; Finger, nose;

Finger, tongue; Finger, wrist; Foot; Foot, hand, head; Foot, lip; Forehead, hand; Forehead, lip; Glove; Hand; Hand, hat; Hand, head; Hand, knee; Hand, lip; Hand, mouth; Hand, object; Hand, shoulder; Hand, weapon; Head; Head, lip; Leg; Lip; Lip, shoulder; Mouth; Neck; Nose; Tongue; Tooth.

Guilt: Arm, finger; Body, head; Breast, hand; Hand.

Gunshot: Finger.

Hanging: Body, hand, neck; Finger, neck.

Hard times: Hand.

Harmony: Hand.

Hatred: Hand; Hand, jaw, lip; Tooth.

Health: Finger.

Hearing: Ear, finger.

Heat: Hand.

Helplessness: Eye, hand; Hand; Hand, shoulder; Head; Shoulder.

Hesitation: Arm, finger; Chin; Chin, hand; Finger, head; Hand; Hand, head; Hand, lip; Head; Lip; Nose.

Hitchhiking: Finger, hand; Hand.

Homage: Body; Finger, hand; Foot, lip; Foot, hand, lip; Forehead; Hand; Hand, knee, lip; Hand, lip; Head; Knee; Lip; Lip, shoulder.

Homosexuality: Arm, finger, hand; Arm, hand; Buttocks; Cheek, finger; Ear, finger; Eye; Eyebrow, finger; Finger; Finger, hand; Finger, hand, lip; Finger, neck; Finger, nose; Hand; Hand, neck.

Honesty: Back.

Honor: Lip.

Hope: Hand.

Horror: Eye, hand; Eye, jaw; Face, hand; Hand; Hand, thigh; Head.

Hot: Finger; Forehead, hand; Hand, mouth.

Humiliation: Finger, nose.

Humility: Arm, breast; Body; Body, hand, head; Breast, hand; Breast, hand, head; Cheek, head, mouth; Eye; Finger; Hand; Hand, lip; Head; Head, knee; Knee; Lip; Mouth.

Humility (mocking): Hand, lip; Head, knee; Knee.

Hunger: Abdomen, hand; Finger, hand; Hand; Mouth.

Hunt: Finger, hand.

Hurry: Finger; Finger, nose, tongue; Hand.

Hygiene: Mouth.

Hypocrisy: Eyelid.

Idea: Finger; Finger, hand.

Idealism: Finger; Finger, head.

Identification: Breast, hand; Finger; Hand; Hand, head; Lip.

Idleness: Finger; Hand.

Ignorance: Arm, hand, shoulder; Chin, finger; Eyebrow; Eyebrow, mouth, shoulder; Face, hand; Finger; Finger, nose; Fingernail, hand; Hand; Hand, head; Hand, shoulder; Shoulder.

Illness: Cheek, finger.

Impatience: Arm, hand; Cheek, hand; Chin, hand; Eyebrow; Finger; Finger, knee; Foot; Foot, hand; Hand; Hand, head; Hand, nose; Hand, thigh; Head; Mouth; Shoulder.

Impossibility: Finger, hand.

Impotence: Finger; Finger, hand.

Impressiveness: Body.

Imprisonment: Hand, neck.

Impulsiveness: Hand.

Incompetence: Hand.

Incomprehension: Ear, hand; Mouth, tooth.

Incredulity: Eye; Hand, mouth.

Indecision: Cheek; Ear, hand; Finger; Finger, tongue; Hand, head.

Independence: Hand, object.

Indication (see also Direction, Pointing): Hand.

Indifference: Arm, hand, shoulder; Chin, finger; Chin, hand; Finger; Fingernail, hand; Hand; Head; Head, shoulder; Lip; Shoulder; Tongue.

Inferiority: Body; Finger, hand.

Infidel: Finger.

Influence: Ear, finger; Hand.

Innocence: Abdomen, chest, hand; Arm; Arm, hand; Hand.

Insolence: Head, lip.

Insult: Abdomen, finger; Arm, elbow; Arm, hand; Beard, hand; Body; Breast, hand; Buttocks; Buttocks, hand; Cheek, hand; Cheek, hand, lip; Cheek, mouth; Chin, hand; Ear, finger; Ear, hand; Eye, finger; Eye, hand; Face, hand; Finger; Finger, hand; Finger, hand, tongue; Finger, head; Finger, mouth; Finger, neck; Finger, nose; Finger, shoulder; Finger, tooth; Fingernail; Fingernail, tooth; Foot; Forehead, hand, neck, nose; Genitals; Glove; Hand; Hand, genitals; Hand, hat; Hand, head; Hand, mouth; Hand, nose; Hand, object; Hand, temple; Hand, tongue; Leg; Lip; Mouth; Shoulder; Tongue.

Integrity: Hand.

Intellectual: Hand, head.

Intelligence: Finger, head; Forehead, hand; Finger, temple; Hand, head.

Interest: Eyebrow, head, jaw.

Interrogation: Arm; Arm, hand; Chin; Ear, finger; Eye, head; Eyebrow; Eyebrow, head; Finger, hand;

Mercy: Finger; Hand, lip.

Minimization of difficulties: Finger; Hand.

Misery: Head.

Mistake: Eye, eyebrow; Finger, head; Finger, neck.

Mockery: Abdomen; Abdomen, hand; Arm; Arm, finger; Arm, finger, hand; Arm, hand; Arm, hand, mouth; Beard, hand; Body; Breast, hand; Buttocks; Buttocks, hand, tongue; Cheek, finger; Cheek, hand; Chin, finger; Chin, hand, mouth; Ear, hand; Ear, hand, tongue; Eye; Eye, finger, mouth, tongue; Eye, head; Face; Face, hand; Finger; Finger, forehead; Finger, hand; Finger, hand, nose; Finger, lip; Finger, mouth; Finger, mouth, tongue; Finger, navel; Finger, neck; Finger, nose; Finger, nose, tongue; Finger, shoulder; Genitals; Hand; Hand, head; Hand, mouth; Hand, nose; Hand, object; Head; Head, mouth; Heel; Lip, tooth; Mouth; Mouth, tooth; Shoulder; Tongue; Tooth.

Modesty: Arm, head, shoulder; Body; Eye; Eye, head; Head; Leg.

Money: Arm, finger; Arm, finger, hand; Arm, hand; Eyebrow; Finger; Finger, hand; Hand; Hand, object.

Moot: Hand.

Mother: Breast, hand.

Mourning: Arm; Arm, hand; Arm, shoulder; Beard, hand; Body; Body, hand; Body, object; Breast, cheek, hair, hand; Breast, eye, hair, hand; Breast, hair, hand; Breast, hand; Breast, hand, head; Cheek, finger; Cheek, hand; Eye; Eye, hand; Face; Face, hand; Finger; Finger, hand; Finger, neck; Finger,

tooth; Foot; Hair, hand; Hand; Hand, hair; Hand, head; Hand, lip; Hand, object; Hand, thigh; Hand, torch; Hand, weapon; Head; Lip.

Mysterious: Finger, lip.

Nagging: Finger.

Need: Hand, head.

Negation: Arm; Arm, finger, hand; Arm, shoulder; Chin, finger; Chin, hand; Eyebrow; Eyebrow, hand, head; Eyelid; Finger; Finger, hand; Finger, mouth; Finger, neck; Finger, tooth; Fingernail, tooth; Hand; Hand, head; Hand, mouth; Head; Head, lip; Head, tongue; Shoulder; Tongue.

Negotiation: Hand, weapon.

Negro: Finger, hand; Finger, head.

Nervousness: Beard, hand; Face, hand; Finger; Foot, leg; Hand; Lip; Mouth.

"Never": Hand.

Nonchalance: Hand.

Nonsense: Hand.

Nostalgia: Head.

Nothing: Arm, hand; Chin, finger; Chin, hand; Eye, finger; Finger; Finger, hand; Finger, tooth; Fingernail; Fingernail, tooth; Hand; Lip.

Oath: Animal, hand; Arm; Arm, breast; Arm, breast, shoulder; Arm, hand; Arm, hand, shoulder; Arm, knee; Beard, hand; Breast, hand; Cheek, hand; Chin, hand; Eye, hand; Eyelid, finger; Finger; Finger, hand; Finger, head; Finger, knee; Finger, lip; Finger, mouth; Finger, neck; Finger, tooth; Fingernail, tooth; Foot; Hair, hand; Hand; Hand, head; Hand, hip; Hand, knee; Hand, neck; Hand, object; Hand, staff; Hand, straw; Hand, thigh; Hand, weapon; Head; Head, object; Knee; Leg; Lip; Mouth.

Obedience: Arm, hand; Breast, hand; Finger; Finger, hand; Hand; Hand, head; Head.

Objection: Hand.

Obstinacy: Fingernail; Neck.

Obviousness: Elbow, hand.

Odor: Finger, nose; Hand; Hand, nose; Nose.

Often: Arm, finger, hand.

Oppression: Finger; Hand.

Order (arranging in): Hand.

Ordering (wine): Finger; Hand, object.

Ostracism: Body.

Overburdened: Hand.

Overcoming obstacles: Finger, hand.

Pacification: Arm; Hand.

Pain: Cheek, hand; Eye, eyebrow, head, lip; Finger; Finger, tooth; Foot; Forehead, hand; Hand; Lip, tooth; Mouth, tongue; Tongue, tooth.

Pardon: Hand.

Passion: Arm, breast; Arm, hand; Eye; Hand, head.

Past: Finger; Finger, hand; Hand.

Patience: Arm, hand; Finger, hand.

Pay: Finger; Finger, hand; Hand; Hand, object.

Peace: Arm finger; Finger; Hand; Hand, weapon; Lip.

Pederasty: Ear, hand; Hand.

Penitence: Breast, hand; Head; Nose.

Pensiveness: Arm, hand; Arm, hand, head; Beard, hand; Body, finger, hand; Cheek, hand; Chin, finger; Chin, finger, head, nose; Chin, forehead, hand, leg; Chin, hand; Chin, hand, knee; Ear, hand; Fin-

ger; Finger, hand; Finger, hand, mouth; Finger, lip; Finger, mouth; Finger, nose; Finger, tooth; Hand; Hand, head; Hand, mouth; Hand, object; Hand, tooth; Head; Head, tooth; Jaw, tooth.

Perfection: Finger; Finger, lip.

Permission: Glove.

Perplexity: Arm, hand, head; Chin, hand; Eyebrow, hand, head; Eyebrow, head, lip; Finger, forehead; Finger, head; Finger, neck; Hand, head.

Pettiness: Hand, lip.

Photograph: Finger, hand.

Piety: Hand; Head.

Pity: Hand; Head.

Placation: Hand.

Plea: Arm; Arm, breast; Arm, hand; Arm, knee; Beard, hand; Body; Body, face; Body, hand; Breast, hand; Breast, lip; Cheek, finger; Cheek, hand, knee; Cheek, head, lip; Chin, hand; Chin, hand, knee; Elbow; Eye; Finger, forehead; Finger, hand; Finger, hand, mouth; Foot, lip; Forehead, hand; Hand; Hand, head; Hand, knee; Hand, knee, lip; Hand, leg; Hand, lip; Hand, object; Hand, straw; Head; Knee; Lip; Neck.

Pleasure: Arm, mouth; Body; Chin; Ear, finger; Eye, head, lip, tooth; Finger; Hand; Hand, moustache; Hand, shoulder; Head; Lip; Lip, tongue.

Pledge: Glove.

Plenty: Finger; Finger, hand.

Pointing: Arm; Arm, finger; Arm, finger, hand; Arm, hand; Chin; Eye, head; Finger; Finger, head, mouth; Finger, shoulder; Hand; Head; Head, lip; Head, shoulder; Lip.

Possession: Arm, hand; Body; Body, hand; Foot; Glove; Hand, Hand, object; Hand, staff; Hand, straw; Knee; Ring.

Possibility: Hand.

Poverty: Ear, hand; Eye; Finger; Finger, mouth; Finger, neck; Finger, nose; Finger, throat; Finger, tooth; Fingernail, tooth; Hand; Hand, head; Hand, hip; Hand, object.

Praise: Arm; Ear, finger; Finger; Finger, hand; Hand; Hand, hat; Hand, head; Hand, shoulder.

Prayer: Arm; Arm, breast; Arm, breast, knee; Arm, face; Arm, finger, hand; Arm, hand; Arm, knee; Back, hand; Body; Body, face; Body, foot; Body, hair; Body, hand; Breast, forehead, hand mouth; Breast, forehead, hand, shoulder; Breast, hand; Buttocks, hand; Chin, hand; Eye; Eye, hand; Eye, navel; Eye, nose; Face, hand; Finger; Finger, hand; Finger, nose; Foot; Foot, leg; Forehead, knee; Hair, hand; Hand; Hand, hat; Hand, head; Hand, head, knee; Hand, knee; Hand, lip; Hand, mouth; Hand, nose; Hand, object; Head; Head, knee; Knee; Leg; Lip; Mouth.

Precision: Finger.

Pregnancy: Abdomen, hand; Arm; Arm, hand; Hand.

Preparedness: Hand.

Pride: Arm; Arm, finger; Arm, finger, hand; Arm, hand; Body, finger, mouth; Body, head; Breast, hand; Hand; Hand, shoulder; Head; Head, lip; Leg.

"Probably": Finger.

Proceed: Arm, hand.

Prohibition: Eye; Eyebrow; Eyelid; Glove; Hand; Hand, head.

Promise: Body, head, lip; Breast, finger; Chin, hand; Finger; Finger, forehead; Finger, nose; Hand.

Proof: Hand.

Prophecy: Finger.

Prosperity: Cheek, eyebrow, head, mouth.

Prostitute: Finger; Hand; Hand, thigh.

Protection: Arm; Hand; Head, knee.

Protest: Breast, hand; Leg.

Proxy: Eyelid, finger.

Psychotherapy: Head, mouth.

Punishment: Cheek, hand; Ear, hand; Hand; Hand, head; Hand, nose; Hand, object; Hand, temple.

Quantity: Finger.

Quarrel: Body, hand.

Question: Eyebrow, finger; Finger; Finger, hand.

Quickly: Finger; Hand.

Readiness: Eye, finger; Hand; Hand, hip.

Reading: Hand, object.

Reassurance: Hand.

Recognition: Body; Eye; Eye, hand; Hand; Head; Leg.

Recommendation: Hand.

Reconciliation: Elbow; Finger; Finger, hand; Forehead, hand; Hand; Lip; Mouth.

Redemption: Finger.

Reflection: Finger, hand.

Refusal: Arm; Arm, breast; Arm, hand; Body, hand; Body, hand, neck; Buttocks, hand; Cheek, mouth; Ear, finger; Ear, hand; Eye, finger; Eye, hand; Finger; Finger, mouth; Finger, nose; Foot; Genitals, hand; Hand; Hand, head; Hand, object; Head; Mouth.

Regret: Arm; Breast, hand; Cheek, hand; Eyebrow, jaw; Finger, hand;

Finger, lip; Finger, tooth; Hand; Hand, head; Hand, lip; Hand, mouth; Head; Lip, tooth; Mouth, tooth.

Rejection: Arm; Arm, finger, hand; Arm, hand; Chin, hand; Eye, hand; Face; Finger, hand; Foot; Genitals, hand; Hand; Hand, nose; Hand, staff; Hand, straw; Mouth.

Relax: Finger, hand.

Reliability: Eye, finger.

Relief: Breast, hand; Eye, lip; Forehead, hand; Mouth.

Relinquishment: Hand; Hand, object; Hand, staff.

Remain: Hand.

Remembering: Finger, hand.

Reminder: Elbow, rib; Finger; Finger, forehead; Finger, mouth; Finger, tooth; Forehead, hand; Hand; Hand, head; Hand, knee.

Remorse: Breast, hand; Eyebrow, hand, head; Hand, object; Head.

Rendezvous: Arm, hand; Finger, hand; Hand.

Renunciation: Finger, hand.

Repetition: Finger; Head.

Reproach: Cheek, head, lip; Eye; Eye, head; Finger; Hand; Head.

Request: Arm, hand; Finger, hand; Hand; Hand, head; Hand, lip.

Resignation: Arm; Breast, hand; Finger, hand; Fingernail, lip; Hand; Hand, shoulder; Head, lip; Head, shoulder; Head, tongue; Shoulder.

Respect: Abdomen, hand; Back, breast, hand, head; Body; Body, face; Body, finger, hand; Breast, hand, lip; Chin, finger; Eye; Finger, head; Finger, lip; Foot; Foot, lip; Forehead, lip; Hair, hand; Hand; Hand, hat; Hand, lip; Hand, mouth; Head; Head, lip; Knee; Knee, lip; Leg; Lip; Tongue.

Rest: Arm; Hand, head; Head.

Result: Finger; Finger, hand.

Retraction: Finger, nose.

Retreat: Finger; Hand.

Reverence: Arm, hand; Body, eye, hand; Body, face; Body, hand, head; Hand; Hand, hat; Hand, head; Hand, knee; Hand, leg; Hand, object; Head; Knee; Lip; Mouth; Tongue.

Review: Hand.

Revulsion: Body; Finger, nose; Hand, mouth, tongue.

Ride: Arm, body, hand.

Rise: Arm, hand; Finger, hand; Hand.

Robbery: Hand.

Royalty: Finger; Hand; Hand, object.

Rudeness: Eye; Finger; Toe; Tongue.

Sacrifice: Animal, hand; Breast, hand; Hand; Hand, object.

Sadism: Finger.

Salvation: Hand.

Sanctimoniousness: Eye, eyebrow.

Sanctuary: Finger.

Sarcasm: Mouth.

Satisfaction: Abdomen, hand; Arm; Beard, hand; Breast, hand; Cheek, eyebrow, head, mouth; Hand; Head; Tongue.

Saturation: Abdomen, hand.

Scorn: Finger; Head; Mouth; Tongue.

Secrecy: Eye; Finger, nose; Finger, tooth; Hand; Hand, mouth; Hand, mouth, tongue; Head; Tongue.

Seduction: Arm, lip.

Seeking: Finger.

Seize: Hand.

Self-acknowledgment: Hand.

Self-discipline: Body; Lip, tooth.

Self-gratitude: Eye, hand.

Self-identification: Breast, hand.

Self-importance: Body; Breast; Cheek, head, mouth; Head.

head; Hand, knee; Hand, lip; Hand, mouth; Hand, object; Hand, shoulder; Hand, staff; Hand, weapon; Head; Knee; Lip; Lip, object; Mouth; Neck; Shoulder; Tongue; Tooth.

Success: Cheek, finger; Finger, tongue.

Suffering: Eye, eyebrow, head, lip; Hand.

Suicide: Finger; Hand.

Superciliousness: Hand; Neck; Nose.

Superiority: Arm, hip; Body; Finger; Hand; Hand, weapon; Leg.

Superlative: Finger; Finger, lip.

Surfeit: Hand, neck.

Surprise: Arm; Arm, eye; Cheek, eyebrow; Cheek, finger; Cheek, hand; Eye; Eye, eyebrow, mouth; Eye, finger; Eye, hand; Eye, head; Eyebrow; Eyebrow, hand, mouth; Eyebrow, head; Eyebrow, mouth; Finger; Finger, lip; Forehead, hand; Hand; Hand, head; Hand, leg; Hand, mouth; Hand, neck; Hand, thigh; Head; Leg; Lip; Mouth.

Surrender: Arm; Arm, hand; Arm, neck; Elbow; Finger; Finger, hand; Finger, mouth; Glove; Hair, hand; Hand; Hand, head; Hand, object; Hand, staff; Hand, weapon; Head; Knee.

Suspicion: Eye, finger; Finger, nose.

Sustain: Hand.

Sympathy: Eye; Hand; Hand, knee; Head.

Sympathy (false): Arm, hand.

Talk: Finger

Taste: Finger; Finger, tongue.

"Teach me": Hand.

Teasing: Arm, hand; Breast, hand; Ear, finger; Eyebrow; Finger; Finger, hand; Finger, lip; Finger, nose, tongue; Hand; Tongue.

Telephone: Ear, finger; Ear, hand; Hand.

Tension: Fingernail, tooth.

Thief: Cheek, hand; Hand; Hand, head.

Thin: Finger; Finger, hand.

Thirst: Finger, hand.

Threat: Arm, clothing; Arm, finger; Arm, hand; Arm, hand, shoulder; Body, finger; Body, head; Cheek, finger; Chin, finger; Chin, hand; Ear, finger; Elbow, hand; Eyebrow; Finger; Finger, forehead; Finger, hand; Finger, nose; Finger, tooth; Genitals; Hand; Hand, neck; Hand, object; Head; Lip; Lip, tooth; Tooth.

Time: Arm; Eye, hand; Finger; Finger, hand.

Toast: Hand, object.

Tomorrow: Finger.

Tortuousness: Finger.

Treachery: Eye.

Treaty: Hand.

Trivia: Hand.

Trust: Hand.

Truth: Breast, hand; Finger; Finger, hand; Hand; Hand, nose; Shoulder.

Uncertainty: Cheek, eye, mouth; Eye, head; Eyebrow, mouth, shoulder; Hand; Hand, head; Hand, head, shoulder; Hand, shoulder; Head.

Understanding: Arm; Eye; Eye, hand; Eye, head; Finger; Finger, forehead; Finger, nose; Finger, temple; Hand; Hand, nose; Head.

Undetermined (future): Finger.

Union: Finger; Finger, hand; Hand; Lip.

Unreliability: Elbow, hand.

Urgency: Hand, shoulder.

Useless: Body, hand; Finger; Finger, mouth; Finger, nose; Hand.

Vanity: Foot.

Vengeance: Arm, mouth; Finger; Finger, hand; Fingernail; Hand; Head, tooth.

Verbosity: Hand.

Victory: Arm; Arm, hand; Beard, hand; Finger; Finger, hand; Foot; Hand; Hand, head; Hand, object; Knee.

Virility: Arm; Body, hand; Elbow, hip; Finger; Hand; Hand, genitals.

Volunteer: Arm, hand; Hand.

Voting: Arm; Arm, hand; Hand.

Wait: Hand.

Walking: Body.

Warning: Arm, elbow; Arm, hand; Cheek, finger; Ear, hand; Eye, finger; Eye, hand; Eye, mouth; Finger; Finger, head; Finger, nose; Finger, object; Finger, tooth; Hand; Hand, head; Hand, mouth; Hand, neck; Hand, object; Head; Lip; Mouth.

Weakmindedness: Eyebrow, jaw.

Welcome: Arm; Arm, hand.

Wisdom: Chin, finger.

Wish: Finger; Finger, hand.

Withdraw: Finger, hand.

Woman: Breast, hand.

Work: Arm, hand; Finger; Finger, forehead.

Worry: Hand, neck.

Bibliography

A. "The Evil Eye and Red Hand." *Notes and Queries*, Series 5 (Aug. 9, 1879), XII, 118.

Achelis, H. *Das Christentum in den ersten drei Jahrhunderten*. Leipzig, Germany: Quelle & Meyer, 1912.

"Acta Juliana. Acta auctore anonymo ex xi veteribus MSS." *Acta Sanctorum*. vol. 2, 875–79. Antwerp, Belgium: Meurs, 1643.

Ades, Raphael. "My First Encounter with the Spanish of Medellín." *Hispania* 36 (1953): 325–27.

Aeschylus. *Persae*. Edited by H. D. Broadhead. Cambridge, England: Cambridge University Press, 1960.

Aimoinus. *Aimoini monachi . . . historiae Francorum libri V.* Paris: A. Wechel, 1567.

Alas, Leopoldo. *Las dos cajas*. Alicante, Spain: Aguaclara, 1886.

——— *Pipá*. Madrid, Spain: F. Fé, 1886.

Alföldi, A. "Die Ausgestaltung des monarchischen Zeremoniells am römischen Kaiserhof." *Mitteilungen des deutschen archäologischen Instituts* 50 (1935): 1–171.

Allen, John Romilly. *Early Christian Symbolism in Great Britain and Ireland before the 13th century*. London: Whiting & Co., 1887.

Allingham, Margery. *The Tiger in the Smoke*. London: Chatto & Windus, 1952.

Alós, Concha. *Los enanos*. Barcelona: Planeta, 1963.

Alpharts Tod. Deutsches Heldenbuch. Edited by E. Martin. Vol. 2. Berlin: Weidmann, 1866–73.

Alsop, Stewart. "How to Speak French without Saying a Word." *Saturday Evening Post*, 24–31 December 1960, 26–29.

Altdeutsche Gedichte. Edited by A. Keller. Tübingen, Germany: Litterarischer Verein Stuttgart, 1846–80.

Amades, Joan. *El gest a Catalunya*. Anales del Instituto de Lingüística. Vol. 6, 88–148. Mendoza, Argentina: 1957.

Ambrosius. *Hexaemeron; De officiis*. Patrologiae cursus completus . . . series Latina. Edited by J.-P. Migne. Vols. 13–17. Paris: Garnier et Migne successores, 1884.

Amira, Karl von. "Die Handgebärden in den Bilderhandschriften des Sachsenspiegels." *Abhandlungen der bayerischen Akademie der Wissenschaften*, philos.-philol. Kl., 23 (1909): 161–264.

——— *Nordgermanisches Obligationenrecht.* Berlin and New York: de Gruyter, 1973.

Amis, Kingsley. *That Uncertain Feeling.* New York: Gollancz, 1971.

Ammianus Marcellinus. With an English translation by John C. Rolfe. Cambridge, Mass.: Harvard University Press, 1982–86.

Anderson, J. D. "The Language of Gesture." *Folk-Lore* 31 (1920): 70–71.

Andersson, Charles John. *Lake Ngami, or, Explorations and Discoveries during Four Years' Wanderings in the Wilds of South Western Africa.* London: Hurst & Blackett, 1856.

Andrea, Pat, and Herman Pieter de Boer. *Het Gebarenboekje.* Baarn, Netherlands: Fontein, 1993.

Anrich, G. *Das antike Mysterienwesen in seinem Einfluss auf das Christentum.* Göttingen, Germany: Vandenhoeck & Ruprecht, 1894.

Apollonius Rhodius. *Argonautica.* Edited by R. C. Seaton. Cambridge, Mass.: Harvard University Press, 1912.

Apuleius, Lucius. *Metamorphoses.* Edited by R. Helm and P. Thomas. Leipzig: Teubner, 1905–09.

Arce, Manuel. *Oficio de muchachos.* Barcelona: Seix Barral, 1963.

Archer, Dane. "A World of Gestures: Culture and Nonverbal Communication." *Harvard Graduate Society Newsletter,* Spring 1992: pp. 4–7.

Argyle, Michael. *Körpersprache und Kommunikation.* Paderborn, Germany: Junfermann, 1979.

Ariosto, Ludovico. *Orlando Furioso.* Turin, Italy: Unione tipografico-editrice, 1923–29.

Armstrong, Karen. *A History of God.* New York: Ballantine, 1994.

Arndt, Ernst Moritz. *Gedichte.* Leipzig, Germany: Stiller, 1840.

Arnobius. *Adversus nationes.* Edited by A. Reifferscheid. Corpus scriptorum ecclesiasticorum latinorum. Vol. 4. Vienna: Gerold, 1875.

Arrianus, Flavius. *Discourses of Epictetus. Arrian.* Cambridge, Mass.: Harvard University Press, 1946–49.

Aschbach, Josef. *Geschichte der Grafen von Wertheim.* Frankfurt/M., Germany: Andreaeische Buchhandlung, 1843.

Ashby, R. E. "The Evil Eye in Italy." *Notes and Queries,* Series 10 (Feb. 22, 1908), IX, 145–46.

Athanasius. *Apologia ad imperatorem Constantium.* Patrologiae cursus completus . . . series Graeca. Edited by J.-P. Migne. Paris: Garnier et Migne successores, 1884. Vol. 25.

Aubert, Charles. *The Art of Pantomime.* New York: Arno, 1976.

Augustinus, Aurelius (St. Augustine). *De Doctrina Christiana.* Patrologiae cursus completus . . . series Latina. Edited by J. P. Migne. Paris: Garnier et Migne successores, 1887. Vol. 34.

——— *Confessionum, libri tredecim.* Edited by F. v. Raumer. Stuttgart, Germany: Liesching, 1856.

Austin, Mary. "Gesture in Primitive Drama." *Theatre Arts Magazine* 11 (1927): 594–605.

Axtell, R. E. *Gestures. The Do's and Taboos of Body Language around the World.* New York: Wiley & Sons, 1991.

—— *Do's and Taboos around the World.* New York: Wiley & Sons, 1993.

Babelon, Ernest. *Description historique et chronologique des monnaies de la République Romaine vulgairement appelées monnaies consulaires.* Paris: Rollin & Feuardent, 1885–86.

Badcock, John. *Sportsman's Slang: A New Dictionary of Terms used in the Affairs of the Turf, the Ring, the Chase, and the Cock-Pit; with those of Bonton, and the Varieties of Life.* London: W. Lewis, 1825.

Baden, T. "Bemerkungen über das komische Gebärdenspiel der Alten nach den Originalen," *Neue Jahrbücher für Philologie*, Supplementband I (1832): 447–56.

Bäumer, S. "Kreuzzeichen." *Lexikon für Theologie und Kirche.* Edited by J. Höfer and K. Rahner. Freiburg/Br., Germany: Herder, 1957–67.

Bagott, Jeremy. "Taking matters in hand can be dangerous." *Daily News* Woodland Hills, California. 10 April, 1994, pp. 1 and 4.

Baker, Frank. "Anthropological Notes on the Human Hand." *American Anthropologist* 1 (1888): 51–75.

Ball, C. J. *Light from the East.* London: Eyre & Spottiswoode, 1899.

Balzac, Honoré de. *Traité de la vie élégante; suivi de la Théorie de la démarche.* Paris: Bossard, 1922.

—— *Théorie de la démarche et autres textes.* Paris: Pandora, 1978.

Barakat, Robert A. "Arabic Gestures." *Journal of Popular Culture* 6 (1973): 749–87.

Barasch, Mosche. *Gestures of Despair in Medieval and Early Renaissance Art.* New York: New York University Press, 1976.

—— *Giotto and the Language of Gesture.* Cambridge, England: Cambridge University Press, 1987.

Barbazan, E. de, and D. M. Méon. *Fabliaux et Contes.* Paris: B. Warée oncle, 1808.

Bartholomae, Chr. *Die Gathas des Awesta.* Strassburg, France: Trübner, 1905.

Basile, Giambattista. *Pentamerone.* Edited by N. M. Penzer. London: Lane, 1932.

Basto, Cláudio. "A linguagem dos gestos em Portugal," *Revista Lusitana* 36 (1938): 5–72.

Bastow, A. "Peasant Customs and Superstitions in 13th-century Germany," *Folk-Lore* 47 (1936): 313–28.

Batchelor, J. *The Ainu of Japan.* London: Religious Tract Society, 1892.

Baudoin de Sébourc. *Li Romans de Baudoin de Sébourc, IIIe roy de Jherusalem.* Valenciennes: B. Henry, 1841.

Bauer, L. *Das Volksleben im Lande der Bibel.* Leipzig, Germany: Wallmann, 1903.

Baumeister, A. *Denkmäler des klassischen Altertums zur Erläuterung des Lebens der Griechen und Römer in Religion, Kunst und Sitte.* Munich and Leipzig, Germany: Oldenbourg, 1885–88.

Baxandall, Michael. *Painting and Experience in Fifteenth-Century Italy.* Oxford: Oxford University Press, 1972.

Bayley, Harold. *The Lost Language of Symbolism.* London: E. Benn, 1957.

Bee, Jon. *Sportsman's Slang: a new dictionary of terms used in the affairs of the turf, the ring, the chase, and the cock-pit; with those of Bon-ton, and the varieties of life.* London: for the author, n.d. [1825].

Behrens, David. "Jews, Gems Share History." *Los Angeles* (California) *Times.* 7 October 1977, part 7, pp. 1 and 3.

Beitl, Richard. *Deutsche Volkskunde.* Berlin: Deutsche Buchgemeinschaft, 1933.

Belloc, Hilaire. "Advice on Wine, Food, and Other Matters." *Gourmet* 22 (Jan. 1962): 12–13.

Bélon, Pierre. *Les observations des plusiers singularitez et choses mémorables, trouvées en Grèce, Asie, Iudée, Egypte.* Paris: Corrozet, 1553.

Benedekfalva, M. L. de. "Treatment of Hungarian Peasant Children," *Folklore* 52 (1941): 101–19.

Benndorf, O. *Griechische und sicilische Vasenbilder.* Berlin: Guttentag, 1869–83.

Beowulf. Edited by F. Klaeber. Boston and New York: Heath, 1922.

Berceo, G. de. *La vida de Santo Domingo de Silos.* Edited by J. D. Fitzgerald. Bibl. de l'École des hautes études. Vol. 149. Paris: Bouillon, 1904.

Bergemann, Bernhard. *Das höfische Leben nach Gottfried von Strassburg.* Cothen, Germany: Schettler, 1876.

Bergmann, J. "Folkloristische Beiträge." *Monatsschrift für Geschichte und Wissenschaft des Judentums* 79 (1935): 329–32.

Bernheimer, Martin. "Love Fest With a Korean Coloratura." *Los Angeles* (California) *Times,*8 November 1995, F1.

Bertau, Karl. *Deutsche Literatur im Europäischen Mittelalter.* Munich: Beck, 1972.

Bieber, M. *Ancient Copies: Contributions to the History of Greek and Roman Art.* New York: University of New York Press, 1977.

Biederman, Patricia Ward. "French Teen-Agers Say It With Their Bodies," *Los Angeles* (California) *Times,* 9 August 1987, E10–11.

Birdwhistell, R. L. *Introduction to Kinesics.* Louisville, Ky.: Louisville University Press, 1952.

——— "Background to Kinesics," *ETC.* 13 (1955): 10–18.

——— "Do Gestures Speak Louder than Words?" *Collier's* (4 March 1955): 56–57.

——— *Time,* 70 (15 July 1957): 68.

——— *Kinesics and Context.* Philadelphia: University of Pennsylvania Press, 1970.

Bischoff, Erich. *Die Elemente der Kabbalah.* Berlin: Barsdorf, 1913.

Biterolf und Dietleib. Edited by O. Jänicke. Deutsches Heldenbuch. Vol. 1. Berlin: Weidmann, 1866.

Blasco Ibáñez, Vicente. *En la boca del horno.* In: *Veinte Cuentos Españoles del Siglo XX,* ed. E. Anderson-Imbert and L. B. Kiddle. New York: Appleton-Century-Crofts, 1961.

Bloch, Marc. *Les rois thaumaturges.* Strasbourg, France: Librarie Istra, 1924.

Blumenthal, Sidney. "The Handshake." *The New Yorker* 4 October 1993: 74–76.

Boccaccio, Giovanni. *Decamerone.* Milan: Ulrico Hoepli, 1951.

Boehm, F. *De symbolis Pythagoreis.* Berlin: Driesner, 1905.

Boggs, R. S. "Gebärde." *Handwörterbuch des deutschen Märchens.* Vol. II. Berlin: de Gruyter, 1934. Pp. 318–22.

Bogucka, Maria. "Gesture, ritual, and social order in sixteenth- to eighteenth-century Poland." In *A Cultural History of Gesture.* Edited by J. Bremmer and H. Roodenburg, 190–209. Cambridge, England: Polity, 1991. Pp. 190–209.

Boileau-Despréaux, Nicolas. *Satires.* Paris: Droz, 1932.

Boissonade, J. F. *Marini vita Procli.* Amsterdam: Hakkert, 1966.

Bolte, J. L. K. "Bilderbogen des 16. und 17. Jahrhunderts." *Zeitschrift für Volkskunde* 19 (1909): 51–82.

——— and G. Polivka. *Anmerkungen zu den Kinder- und Hausmärchen der Brüder Grimm.* Leipzig, Germany: Dieterich, 1913–32.

Bonnanini, Philippe. *Musaum Kircherianum, sive Musaum a p. Athanasio Kirchero in Collegio romano Societatis Jesu, jam pridem incoptum nuper restitutum, auctum, descriptum, et iconibus illustratum.* Rome: G. Plachi, 1709.

Bonne, Jean-Claude. "Depicted Gesture, Named Gesture: Postures of the Christ on the Autun Tympanum." *History and Anthropology* 1 (1984): 77–95.

Bonnet, H. *Reallexikon der aegyptischen Religionsgeschichte.* Berlin: de Gruyter, 1952.

Borchard, W., and G. Wustmann. *Die sprichwörtlichen Redensarten im deutschen Volksmund.* Leipzig, Germany: Brockhaus, 1925.

Booth, Edwin. *Promptbook.* New York: Magonigle, 1878–90.

Borrow, George. *The Bible in Spain.* London: Oxford UP, 1920.

Boswell, James. *Boswell's London Journal 1762–1763.* Edited by F. A. Pottle. New York, London, Toronto: McGraw-Hill, 1950.

Boucher, Anthony. *Nine times Nine.* New York: Holmes, 1962.

Bouissac, Paul A. R. *La mesure des gestes. Prolégomènes à la sémiotique gestuelle.* Approaches to Semiotics. Vol. 3. The Hague: Mouton, 1973.

Bouquet, Alan Coates. *Everyday Life in New Testament Times.* London: Batsford, 1953.

Bowers, F. "Encounters in Moscow." *The New Yorker* 33, 15 February 1958: 102–14.

Bowers, R. H. "Gesticulation and Elizabethan Acting." *Southern Folklore Quarterly* 12 (1948): 267–77.

Bracton, Henry de. *De legibus et consuetudinibus Anglia.* London: Kraus Repr., 1964.

Brant, Sebastian. *Das Narrenschiff.* Edited by F. Bobertag. In *Deutsche National-Litteratur.*vol. 16. Berlin and Stuttgart: Kürschner, n.d.

Branwen, Daughter of Llyr. In: *Mabinogion,* transl. by G. and T. Jones. London: Dent, 1950. Pp. 25–40.

Brault, Gerard J. "Kinesics and the Classroom: Some Typical French Gestures." *The French Review* 36 (1963): 374–82.

Braun, Stephen. "Wary Circling by Buchanan, Dole Points to Risks for GOP." *Los Angeles* (California) *Times.* 17 March 1996, A1, A18.

Bredero, G. A. *The Spanish Brabanter: A Seventeenth-Century Dutch Social Satire in Five Acts.* Edited by H. D. Brumble. Binghamton, N.Y.: Center for Medieval and Early Renaissance Studies, 1982.

Bremen und Verden. Die Herzogtümer. Bremen, Germany: Pratje, 1757–62.

Bremmer, Jan. "Walking, standing, and sitting in ancient Greek culture." In *A Cultural History of Gesture.* Edited by J. Bremmer and H. Roodenburg. Pp. 15–35. Cambridge, England: Polity, 1991. Pp. 15–35.

———— and Herman Roodenburg. Eds. *A Cultural History of Gesture.* Cambridge: Polity, 1991.

Bresciani, A. *Dei costumi dell'isola di Sardegna.* Milan: Muggiani, 1872.

———— *L'ebreo di Verona.* Milan: Ditta Boniardi-Pogliani di E. Besotti, 1858.

———— *Don Giovanni.* Milan: Ditta Boniardi-Pogliani di E. Besotti, 1857.

———— *Edmondo.* Milan: Ditta Boniardi-Pogliani di E. Besotti, 1872.

Bresslau, Harry. *Handbuch der Urkundenlehre für Deutschland und Italien.* Vol. 1. 2nd ed. Leipzig, Germany: Veit, 1912.

———— *Handbuch der Urkundenlehre für Deutschland und Italien.* Vol. 2. 2nd ed. Berlin and Leipzig, Germany: de Gruyter, 1931.

Brewer, Ebenezer Cobham. *Dictionary of Phrase and Fable,* Revised by I. H. Evans. New York: Harper & Row, 1970.

Brilliant, R. *Gesture and Rank in Roman Art.* In *Memoirs of the Connecticut Academy of Arts and Sciences.* Vol. 14. New Haven: The Academy, 1963.

Brissonius, B. *De formulis et sollemnibus populi romani verbis Libri VIII.* Paris: S. Nivelle, 1583.

Brown, Peter. *The Body and Society.* New York: Columbia University Press, 1988.

Brownstein, Ronald. "Gramm's Relentless Crusade." *Los Angeles* (California) *Times,* 14 February 1995: A1.

Bruckheim, Allan. *Daily News* (Woodland Hills, California) "L.A. Life," 2 January 1995: 18.

Brunner, H. *Deutsche Rechtsgeschichte.* Leipzig, Germany: Duncker & Humblot, 1887–92.

———— 2nd ed., Leipzig, Germany: Duncker & Humblot, 1906–28.

Buchwald, Art. "Purple Prose for Bush." *International Herald Tribune* (The Hague, Netherlands). 6 August 1992: 20.

Buck, M. R. *Medizinischer Volksglauben und Volksaberglauben aus Schwaben.* Ravensburg, Germany: Dorn, 1865.

Bulwer, John. *Chirologia or the Natural Language of the Hand and Chironomia: or the Art of Manual Rhetoric.* Reprinted from the edition of 1644 and edited by T. Cleary. Carbondale, Ill.: Southern Illinois University Press, 1974.

Burke, Peter. "The language of gesture in early modern Italy." In: *A Cultural History of Gesture.* Edited by J. Bremmer and H. Roodenburg. Pp. 71–83. Cambridge, England: Polity, 1991.

Burke, Thomas. *The Streets of London.* London: B. T. Batsford, 1949.

Burke, T. A. *Polly Peablossom's Wedding and Other Tales.* Philadelphia: T. B. Peterson, 1851.

Burkhard, Arthur. *The Herrenberg Altar of Jörg Ratgeb.* Munich, Germany: Bruckmann, 1965.

Buschan, G. *Über Medizinzauber und Heilkunst im Leben der Völker.* Berlin: Arnold, 1941.

Butler, Samuel. *Hudibras.* Edited by A. R. Waller. Cambridge, England: Cambridge University Press, 1905.

Byatt, A. S. *Possession.* New York: Random House, 1990.

Bystron, J. *Dzieje obyczajów w dawnej Polsce.* Warsaw, Poland: Trzaski, 1933–34.

Caballero Bonald, J. M. *Dos Días de Setiembre.* Barcelona: Seix Barral, 1962.

Cabrol, F. and Leclerq, H. M. *Dictionnaire d'archéologie chrétienne et de liturgie.* Paris: Letouzey et Ane, 1913–53.

Cadalso, José. *Cartas Marruecas.* Madrid: Espasa-Calpe, 1956. Reprint of the edition of 1789.

Caesarius von Heisterbach. *Dialogus miraculorum.* Edited by J. Strange. Cologne, Bonn, Brussels: H. Lempertz, 1851. Reprinted in Ridgewood, N.J: Gregg, 1966.

Calbris, Geneviève. *The Semiotics of French Gestures.* Translated by O. Doyle. Bloomington and Indianapolis, Indiana: Indiana University Press, 1990.

Cameron, V. L. *Across Africa.* London: Daldy & Isbister, 1877.

Callimachus. Edited by R. Pfeiffer. New York: Oxford University Press, 1987.

Camille, Michael. "Seeing and Reading: Some Visual Implications of Medieval Literacy and Illiteracy." *Art History* 8 (1985): 26–49.

———— "The Book of Signs: Writing and visual difference in Gothic manuscript illumination." *Word and Image* 1/2 (1985): 133–48.

Caminha, V. B. "Gestos (mímica)." *Boletín da Comissão catarinense do folclore* (Florianópolis, Brazil) 8 (1957–58): 26–31.

Canisius, Henricus. *Thesaurus monumentorum ecclesiasticorum et historicum, sive Henric Canisii lectiones antiquae: . . .* Amsterdam: Wetsten, 1725.

Cantar de Mío Cid. Edited by R. Menéndez Pidal. Translated by L. B. Simpson. Berkeley and Los Angeles: University of California Press, 1957.

Cardim, Fernao. *Do principio e Origem dos Indios do Brasil e de seus Costumes, Adoração, Cerimônias.* Rio de Janeiro: Typographia das Gazeta de notícias, 1925. Reprint of the edition of 1584.

Cardona, Miguel. "Gestos o ademanes habituales en Venezuela." *Archivos venezolanos de folklore* 2 (1953–54): 159–66.

Carkeet, David. *Double Negative.* New York: Dial, 1980.

Caroli Ogerii Ephemerides sive iter Danicum, Suecium, Polonicum . . . In: Karola Ogiera Dziennik podrózy do Polski 1635–36. Edited by W. Czaplinski. Gdansk, Poland: Bibl. Miejska, 1950.

Carr, Elston. "The Last Days of Rancho de Los Diablos." *Los Angeles* (California) *Times Magazine.* 27 November 1994: pp. 20–56.

Carr, F. *The Windward Road.* New York: Knopf, 1956.

Carr, John Dickson. *The Case of the Constant Suicides.* London: Hamilton, 1941.

————— *Hag's Nook.* New York: Harper, 1963.

————— *To Wake the Dead.* New York: Books, Inc., 1965.

Carr, Philippa. *Will You Love Me in September?* New York: Fawcett, 1981.

Cascudo, Luis da Câmara. *Locuções tradicionais no Brasil.* Recife: Universidade Federal de Pernambuco, 1970.

————— *História dos nossos gestos.* São Paulo: Ediçoes Melhoramentos, 1976.

————— *Dicionário do Folclore Brasileiro.* Rio de Janeiro. Ministério da Educação e Cultura, 1962.

————— *História dos nossos Gestos.* São Paulo, 1976.

The Catholic Encyclopaedia. New York: Appleton, 1907–12.

Catton, Bruce. *Never Call Retreat.* New York: Pocket Books, 1967.

Catullus. Edited by E. Baehrens. Leipzig, Germany: Teubner, 1885.

Cela, Camilo José. *Viaje a la Alcarria.* Barcelona: Ediciones Destino, 1958.

Cervantes, Miguel de. *Don Quijote.* Edited by F. Rodríguez Marín. Madrid: Espasa-Calpe, 1943.

————— *Novelas ejemplares.* Edited by F. Rodríguez Marin. Vol. 2. Madrid: Espasa-Calpe, 1943.

————— *La Galatea.* Edited by J. D. Avalle-Arce. Madrid: Espasa-Calpe, 1961.

Chanson de Roland. Edited by J. Bédier. Paris: Piazza, 1927.

Charitonis Aphrodisiensis. *Chaereas and Callirhoe.* Edited by W. E. Blake. Oxford: Clarendon, 1938.

Chauvé, P. R. G. In: *North Indian Notes and Queries* 5 (1895): 125.

Chevalerie Vivien. Edited by A.-L. Teracher. Paris: Champion, 1923.

Chevalier, Abbé L. *Naples, le Vésuve et Pompei.* Tours, France: A. Mame et fils, 1871.

Li Chevaliers as deus espées. Edited by W. Foerster. Halle/Saale, Germany: Niemeyer, 1877.

Chrétien de Troyes. *Sämtliche Werke.* Edited by W. Foerster. Halle/Saale, Germany: Niemeyer, 1884–1932.

Chriss, Nicholas C. "Single Digit Inflation Sweeps the Country." *Los Angeles* (California) *Times.* 17 February 1977, part 2, p. 7.

Chronicon Petershusanum see *Petershusanum Chronicon*

Clanchy, M. T. *From Memory to Written Record. England, 1066–1307.* Cambridge, Mass.: Harvard University Press, 1979.

Clarke, Hyde. "Evil Eye." *Notes and Queries,* Series 3 (Nov. 2, 1867), XII, 365.

Claudianus, Claudius. *In Eutropium; De raptu Proserpinae.* Edited by C. Gruzelier. New York: Oxford University Press, 1993.

Cleland, James. *The Institution of a Young Noble Man.* Oxford: 1607.

Clemens Alexandrinos. *Paidagogos.* Edited and translated by Cl. Montdésert and H. I. Marrou. In: Sources chrétiennes. Vol. 108. Paris: Editions du Cerf, 1985.

Clemons, Walter. Review of Stanley Weintraub, *The London Yankees,* in *Newsweek,* August 5, 1979, p. 73.

Clèomadès. *Li roumans de Cléomadès, par Adenés li Rois.* Brussels, Belgium: V. Devaux, 1865.

Codex Justinianus. Edited by P. Krüger. Berlin: Weidmann, 1877.

Codrington, R. H. *The Melanesians: Studies in Their Anthropology and Folk-Lore.* Oxford: Clarendon, 1891.

Collection des Documents inédits. Paris: Imprimerie royale, 1836 ff.

Comrie, P. "Anthropological Notes on New Guinea." *Journal of the Anthropological Institute* 6 (1877): 102 ff.

Concilia Galliae. Edited by Ch. de Clercq. Corpus Christianorum, series latina 148. Turnholt, Belgium: Brepols, 1963.

Concilium IV aurelianense. In: *Mansi sacrorum conciliorum nova et amplissima collectio.* Paris: Welter, 1901–1927.

Conrad, Joseph. *The Rover.* Garden City, N.Y.: Doubleday, Page, 1923.

Conybeare, F. C. *Rituale Armenorum.* Oxford: Clarendon, 1905.

Cook, Arthur. "CYKOØANTHC," *Classical Review* 21 (1907): 133–36.

Cook, James. *Voyages round the World.* London: J. Robins, 1819.

Cortese, Paolo. *De cardinalatu.* Castro Cortesio: S. N. Nardi senensis, alias Rufus Calchographus, 1510. Microform.

Coulton, G. G. *The Chronicler of European Chivalry.* In *Creative Art,* Winter 1930.

Critchley, MacDonald. *The Language of Gesture.* London, New York: E. Arnold, 1939.

Cumont, F. *Textes et monuments figurés relatifs aux Mystères de Mithra.* Brussels, Belgium: Lamertin, 1896.

Cuvelier, Jean. *Chronique de Bertrand du Guesclin.* Paris: Firmin Didot frères, 1839.

d'Abreu Bras, Luis. *Portugal Medica.* Coimbra, Portugal: J. Antunes da Silva, 1726.

Dante Alighieri. *The Divine Comedy.* Translated by L. G. White. New York: Pantheon, 1948.

Danzel, Th. W. *Kultur und Religion des primitiven Menschen.* Stuttgart, Germany: Strecker & Schroeder, 1924.

d'Artois, Comte. *Le livre du très chevalereux.* Paris: Techener, 1837.

Darwin, Charles R. *The Expression of the Emotions in Man and Animals.* New York: Philosophical Library, 1955.

d'Aulnoy, Condesa. *Un Viaje por España en 1679.* Madrid: Ediciones "La Nave," 1942.

David-Neel, A. *Meister und Schüler.* Leipzig, Germany: Brockhaus, 1934.

Davidson, Levette J. "Some Current Folk Gestures and Sign Languages." *American Speech* 25 (1950): 3–9.

Dawson, W. R. *The Bridle of Pegasus.* London: Methuen, 1930.

de Coincy, Gautier. *Du riche homme à cui le Diable servi por vii ans. Les Miracles de la Sante Vierge.* Paris: Comrie, 1857.

de Courtin, Antoine. *Nouveau traité de la civilité qui se pratique en France parmi les honnestes gens.* 3rd edition. Amsterdam: Jaques Le Jeune, 1679.

de Custine, Stolphe Marquis. *L'Espagne sous Ferdinand VII.* Paris: L'advocat, 1838.

de Deguileville, Guillaume. *The Pilgrimage of human Life. Pélerinage de vie humaine.* Translated by E. Clasby. New York: Garland, 1992.

Defoe, Daniel. *Moll Flanders.* Oxford: Blackwell, 1927.

de Jong, Mayke. "Het gebaar als spiegel van de middeleeuwse ziel." *NRC Handelsblad* (Netherlands), Zaterdags Bijvoegsel. 21 March 1992: 4–5.

de Jorio, Andrea. *La mimica degli antichi investigata nel gestire Napoletano.* Naples: Fibreno, 1832.

Delbrück, R. *Die Consulardiptychen und verwandte Denkmäler.* In *Studien zur spätantiken Kirchengeschichte.* Vol. 2. Berlin, Leipzig: de Gruyter, 1926–29.

Della Casa, Giovanni. *Il Galateo.* Riprodotto secondo l'edizione veneziana del 1558. Milan, Italy: F. Vallardi, 1933.

Demosthenes. *Reden.* Edited by C. Fuhr. Leipzig: Teubner, 1914–27.

de Nie, Giselle. "Trampling the Invisible Enemy Underfoot: A Sixth-Century Miracle Story as Ritual in Narrative Form. In *Talks on Text.* Papers read at the closing session of the NIAS theme group *Orality and Literacy* on May 27th, 1992. Ed. W. P. Gerritsen and C. Vellekoop. Wassenaar, Netherlands: NIAS, 1992. Pp. 27–46.

Denkmäler alter Sprache und Kunst. Bonn, Germany: E. Weber, 1823–27.

Despériers, Bonaventure. *Oevres Françaises.* Paris: P. Jannet, 1856.

Deutsches Wörterbuch. Edited by J. and W. Grimm. Leipzig, Germany: Hirzel, 1854–1983.

Diamant, Anita. *The New Jewish Wedding.* New York: Simon & Schuster, 1995.

Dickens, Charles. *Oliver Twist.* New York: Scribner's Sons, 1910.

——— *Little Dorrit.* London: Macmillan, 1911.

——— *Posthumous Papers of the Pickwick Club.* Lombard St. ed., London: Piccadilly Fountain, 1932.

Dictionary of English Proverbs. Edited by W. G. Smith. Oxford: Clarendon, 1948.

Didron, A. N. *Christian Iconography*. Translated by E. I. Millington. London: G. Bell, 1886.

Dietrichs Flucht. Edited by E. Martin. In *Deutsches Heldenbuch*. Vol. 2. Berlin: Weidmann, 1866–73.

Dodwell, C. R. *The Saint Albans Psalter*. Vol. 2: *The Initials*. London: Warburg Institute, 1960.

Donaldson, D. J. *New Orleans Requiem*. New York: St. Martin's Press, 1994.

Dotter, Franz and Daniel Holzanger. "Typologie und Gebärdensprache: Sequenzialität und Simultanität," *Sprachtypologie und Universalienforschung* 48 (1995): 349.

Dracontius, Blossius Aemilius. [*Poems*]. In *Christian Latin Poetry*. Edited by F. J. E. Raby. Oxford: Clarendon, 1953.

Dresser, Norine. "Multicultural Manners," *Los Angeles* (California) *Times*, 9 May 1994, B11; 31 March 1995, B7; 17 May 1995, B7; 8 June 1995, B19; 21 October 1995, B7; 4 May 1996, B15.

Driessen, Henk. "Gestured masculinity: body and sociability in rural Andalusia." In: *A Cultural History of Gesture*. Edited by J. Bremmer and H. Roodenburg. Cambridge, England: Polity, 1991. Pp. 237–52.

Duby, Georges. *Foundations of a New Humanism 1200–1440*. Translated by P. Price. Geneva, Switzerland: Skira, 1966.

———— *A History of Private Life. II. Revelations of the Medieval World*. Edited by Georges Duby; translated by A. Goldhammer. Cambridge, Mass.: Harvard University Press, 1988.

Du Cange, Charles du Fresne. *Glossarium mediae et infimae latinitatis*. Graz: Akad. Druck- u.- Verlagsanstalt, 1954.

Duchenne, G. B. *Mécanisme de la physionomie humaine*. Paris: Bailliere, 1876.

Duchesne, L. M. O. *Christian Worship*. London: Society for Promoting Christian Knowledge, 1903.

Dürer, Albrecht. *Maximilian's Triumphal Arch. Woodcuts by Albrecht Dürer and Others*. New York: Dover, 1972.

Ebbonis Vita Ottonis episcopi Babenbergensis. In *Monumenta Germaniae Historica, Scriptores XII*, sect. 13, pp. 822–883. Hanover, Germany: Hahn, 1856.

Ebert, M. *Reallexikon der Vorgeschichte*. Edited by M. Ebert. Berlin: de Gruyter, 1924–32.

Efron, David. *Gesture and Environment. A tentative study of some of the spatiotemporal and linguistic aspects of the gestural behavior of Eastern Jews and Southern Italians in New York City*. New York: King's Crown, 1941.

Eibl-Eibesfeldt, Irenäus. "Similarities and Differences between Cultures in Expressive Movements." *Non-Verbal Communication*. Edited by R. Hinde. Cambridge, England: Cambridge University Press, 1972. Pp. 297–314.

———— *Ethology: The Biology of Behavior*. New York: Holt, Rinehart, Winston, 1975.

Eichler, Lillian. *The Customs of Mankind*. Garden City, N.Y.: Garden City Publishing Co., 1924.

Eike von Repgow. *Sachsenspiegel*. Edited by K. A. Eckhardt. Göttingen, Germany: Vandenhoeck & Ruprecht, 1956.

Eilhart von Oberge. *Tristrant*. Edited by F. Lichtenstein. Strassburg, Germany: Trübner, 1877.

Eitrem, S. *Opferritus und Voropfer der Griechen und Römer*. Hildesheim and New York: Olms, 1915.

Ekman, Paul and Wallace Friesen. "The Repertoire of Nonverbal Behavior: Categories, Origins, Usage and Coding," *Semiotica: Journal of the International Association for Semiotic Studies* 1 (1969): 49–98.

Elie de St. Gille. Edited by G. Raynaud. Paris: Firmin Didot, 1879.

Eliot, George. *The Mill on the Floss*. New York: Harper and Bros., n.d.

Ellis, W. *Polynesian Researches*. London: P. Jackson, 1832.

Elworthy, F. T. *The Evil Eye*. London: Murray, 1895.

——— *Horns of Honour*. London: Murray, 1900.

Encyclopaedia Judaica. Das Judentum in Geschichte und Gegenwart. Berlin: Eschkol, 1928–34.

Encyclopedie Mensuelle d'Outre-Mer. Paris: Encyclopedie, 1954.

Endres, J. A. and A. Ebner. "Ein Königsgebetbuch des 11. Jahrhunderts." *St. Elises-Festschrift zum elfhundertjährigen Jubiläum des deutschen Campo Santo in Rom*. Freiburg, Germany: Herder, 1897.

Erasmus, Desiderius. *De civilitate morum puerilium libellus*. In: *La civilité puerile / Erasme; precedé d'une notice sur les livres de civilité depuis le XVIe siècle par A. Bonneau; presenté par Ph. Ariès*. Paris: Ramsay, 1977.

——— *Het boeckje van Erasmus aengaende de beleeftheidt der kinderlijcke zeden*, ed. H. de la Fontaine Verwey. Reprint of the edition of 1678. Amsterdam, Netherlands: Universiteits-Bibliotheek, 1969.

Ermisch, Hubert. *Das sächsische Bergrecht des Mittelalters*. Leipzig, Germany: Giesecke & Devrient, 1887.

Ernoul. La Chronique d'Ernoul et de Bernard le Trésorier. Edited by L. de Mas-Latrie. Paris: Renouard, 1871.

Eschenbach, see Wolfram von Eschenbach.

Esquire, January 1968. "Esquire's Seventh Annual Dubious Achievement Awards for 1967. 'Gotcha,' " pp. 49–55.

Euripides. *Hecuba; Iphigeneia in Tauris*. In: *Tragoediae*. Edited by A. Nauck. Leipzig, Germany: Teubner, 1869–81.

Evagrius Scholasticus. *Historia ecclesiastica*. Edited by J. Bidez and L. Parmentier. London: Methuen, 1898.

Evelyn, John. *Diary and Correspondence of John Evelyn, F.R.S.* London: Bohn, 1862.

Eyrbyggja Saga og Laksdola Saga. Edited by N. M. Petersen. Copenhagen, Denmark: Gyldendal, 1925.

F. S. "Gloucestershire Superstitions: The Evil Eye." *Notes and Queries*, Series 5 (Apr. 25, 1874), I, 324–25.

Fail, Noël du. *Propos Rustiques, Baliverneries, Contes et discours d' Entrapel.* Paris: Gosselin, 1842.

———— *Oevres Facétieuses.* Paris: Daffis, 1874.

Feijóo, P. "Sabiduría aparente." In *Antología mayor de la literatura española.* Edited by G. Díaz-Playa. Vol. 4. Barcelona, Madrid, Buenos Aires, Rio de Janeiro, México, Montevideo: Editorial Labor, 1962: 12–16.

Feilberg, H. F. "Der böse Blick in nordischer Überlieferung." *Zeitschrift für Volkskunde* 11 (1901): 420–30.

Ferres, Antonio. *Los Vencidos.* Paris: Librairie du Globe, 1965.

Ficker, Julius. *Forschungen zur Reichs- und Rechtsgeschichte Italiens.* Aalen, Germany: Scientia, 1961.

Field, C. "Salutes and Saluting, Naval and Military." *Journal of the Royal United Service Institute* 63 (1918): 42–49.

Fielding, Henry. *Joseph Andrews.* London: Millar, 1742.

Fierabras. Paris: Vieweg, 1860.

Fischart, Johann. *Geschichtklitterung (Gargantua). Text der Ausgabe letzter Hand von 1590* . . . Edited by U. Nyssen. Düsseldorf, Germany: K. Rauch, 1963–64.

Fischer, Herbert. "Heilgebärden." *Antaios* 2 (1960): 318–47.

———— "Leben und Tod in alter Mittelfingersymbolik." *Basler Nachrichten. Sonntagsblatt* 30 October 1960: 1.

———— "Das Wort im Nacken." *Zeitschrift für Ganzheitsforschung* 5 (1961): 125–33.

———— "Die kosmurgische Symbolik der Sonnen-Erde-Stellung." *Symbolon* 3 (1962): 89–107.

———— "Indogermanischer Kriegeryoga." In: *Festschrift Walter Heinrich.* Graz, Austria: Akad. Druck- u. Verlagsanstalt, 1963: 65–97.

———— "Wehrhaltungen." *Der Soldat* (Austrian Army Newspaper). 8 October 1961: 2 pp. unnumbered.

Fischer, R. *Österreichisches Bauernleben.* Vienna: J. Deubler, 1903.

Flachskampf, Ludwig. "Spanische Gebärdensprache." *Romanische Forschungen* 52 (1938): 205–58.

Flaubert, Gustave. *Bouvard et Pécuchet.* Paris: Lemerre, 1881.

Folengo, Teofilo. *Orlandino.* Bari, Italy: Laterza & Figli, 1911.

Formaggio, Dino and Carlo Basso, eds. *A Book of Miniatures.* Translated by P. Craig. London: Nevill, 1962.

Foz, Braulio. *La vida de Pedro Saputo.* Saragossa, Spain: Rivera, 1955.

Franklin, Simon. "Literacy and Documentation in Early Medieval Russia." *Speculum* 60 (1985): 1–38.

Frayn, Michael. "Japan Waits for Next Holocaust." *Los Angeles* (California) *Times,* 5 September 1973: pt. 1, pp. 47.

Frazer, James G. *The Golden Bough.* London: Macmillan, 1911.

———— *The New Golden Bough.* New York: Criterion, 1972.

Frenzen, Wilhelm. "Klagebilder und Klagegebärden in der deutschen Dichtung des höfischen Mittelalters." *Bonner Beiträge zur deutschen Philologie*, 1 (1936): 22–24.

Fresne, Baronesse de. *De l'usage et de la politesse dans le monde*. Paris: s. n., 1858.

Frevel, Chr. and Jürgen Escher, "Kinder des Mondes," *Zeitmagazin*, 22 May 1992: 10–20.

Freyberg, Herrmann. *Afrika erzählt*. 2nd ed. of *Afrika ruft*. Berlin, 1936. Kempen: Thomas, 1942.

Frezzi, Federigo. *Il Quadriregio o poema de' quattro regni*. Foligno, Italy: Campana, 1725.

Frijhoff, Willem. "The kiss sacred and profane: reflections on a cross-cultural confrontation." In *A Cultural History of Gesture*, ed. J. Bremmer and H. Roodenburg. Cambridge, England: Polity, 1991. Pp. 210–36.

Frobenius, L. *Kulturgeschichte Afrikas*. Zürich: Phaidon, 1935.

Fruin, J. A., ed. *De oudste Rechten der Stad Dordrecht en van het baljuwschap van Zuidholland*. s'Gravenhage, Netherlands: Nijhoff, 1882.

Galtier, Paul. "Imposition des mains et bénédictions au baptême," *Recherches de science religieuse*, 25 (1937): 464–66.

Gamble, W. T. M. *The Monumenta Germaniae Historica: Its Inheritance in Source-Valuation and Criticism*. Diss. Washington D.C.: Catholic University of America, 1927.

Ganzinger, K. *Apothekenaltertümer in Österreich*. Stuttgart, Germany: Deutscher Apotheker-Verlag, 1951.

García de Pruneda, Salvador. *La encrucijada de Carabanchel*. Las Cruces, Spain: Espantajo, 1965.

Gardiner, A. H. *The Tomb of Huy*. London: Egypt Exploration Soc., 1926.

Garnier, François. *Le langage de l'image au moyen âge*. Paris: Le Léopard d'or, 1982–89.

Garrucci, Raffaele. *Storia dell' arte cristiana nei primi otto secoli della chiesa*. Prato, Italy: Guasti, 1872–81.

Gaskell, Mrs. *Cranford and Other Tales*. In *Works*. Vol. 2. London: J. Murray, 1906.

Gaudentius. *S. Gaudentii Episcopi Brixiensis Tractatus. De evangelii lectione*. In: *Corpus scriptorum ecclesiasticorum latinorum*. Edited by A. Glueck. Vol. 68. Vienna, Austria: Hoelder-Pichler-Tempsky, 1936. Pp. 60–92.

Gennep, Arnold van. *Manuel de folklore français contemporain*. Paris: A. Picard, 1943.

George, S. S. "Gesture of Affirmation among the Arabs." *American Journal of Psychology* 27 (1916): 320–23.

Gerhard, E. *Etruskische und Kampanische Vasenbilder des kgl. Museums zu Berlin*. Berlin: Reimer, 1843.

Gerritsen, W. P. and C. Vellekoop, eds. *Talks on Text*. Papers read at the closing session of the NIAS theme group *Orality and Literacy* on May 27th, 1992. Wassenaar, Netherlands: NIAS, 1992.

Gessner, Salomon. *Der Tod Abels in fünf Gesängen.* Zürich, Switzerland: Gessner, 1758.

Gesta Franconum et aliorum Hierosolymitanorum. Edited by L. Brehier. Paris: Champion, 1924.

Gestalt des Gottesdienstes. In *Gottesdienst der Kirche. Handbuch der Liturgiewissenschaft.* Edited by H. B. Meyer et al. Part 2. Regensburg, Germany: F. Pustet, 1987.

Gibbs, Nancy and Richard N. Ostling. "A Christian in Winter," *Time* (Atlantic Edition) November 15, 1993, pp. 46 ff.

Gifford, Edward. *The Evil Eye. Studies in the Folklore of Vision.* New York: Macmillan, 1958.

Gilmore, Janet. "Tearful Brown tells of abuse by Simpson." *Daily News* (Woodland Hills, California) February 4, 1995, pp. 1, 16.

Glionna, John M. "Turning East for the Answers to Medical Mysteries." *Los Angeles* (California) *Times*, 17 September 1996, E1–6.

Goar, Jacques. *Euchologion, sive rituale Graecorum complectens ritus et ordines divinae liturgiae, ...* Venice: Barthol. Javarina, 1730.

Godefroy de Paris. In *The Memoirs of Philip de Comines, Lord of Argenton, containing the history of Louis XI and Charles VIII, Kings of France, with the most remarkable occurrances . . . from the year 1464 to 1498 . . .* London: printed for John Starky at the Miter in Fleet Street within Temple-Bar, 1674.

Gödecke, August. *Die Darstellung der Gemütsbewegungen in der isländischen Familiensaga.* Hamburg, 1933.

Goethe, Johann Wolfgang von. *Werke.* Edited by E. Trunz. Munich: Beck, 1981.

Gogol, Nikolai. *Betrachtungen über die göttliche Liturgie.* Translated by R. v. Walter. Freiburg: Herder, 1954.

Gold, Jonathan. "Laptops and Sprouts." *Los Angeles* (California) *Times Magazine*, Sept. 24, 1995: 8.

Goldziher, I. "Über Gebärden und Zeichensprache bei den Arabern." *Zeitschrift für Völkerpsychologie und Sprachwissenschaft* 16 (1886): 369–86.

——— "Zauberelemente im islamischen Gebet." In *Orientalische Studien. Festschrift Nöldeke.* Giessen: Töpelmann, 1906. Pp. 303–29.

——— "Die Entblössung des Hauptes." *Der Islam* 4 (1915–16): 304 ff.

Gombrich, Ernst H. *The Image and the Eye.* Ithaca, N. Y.: Cornell University Press, 1982.

Goosse, W. "Geographie du baiser." *Enquêtes du Musée de la vie Wallonne,* 46–48 (1969–71): 205–10; 50 (1973): 235–36.

Gottfried von Strassburg. *Tristan,* ed. F. Ranke. Zürich, Switzerland: Weidmann, 1965.

Gougaud, L. *Dévotions et pratiques ascétiques du moyen âge.* Paris: Desclée de Brouwer, 1925.

Gould, J. "Hikateia." *Journal of Hellenic Studies* 93 (1973): 74–103.

Gowing, Lawrence. "Brueghel's World." *Art News Annual* 36 (1970): 12.

Graf, Heinz J. *Untersuchungen zur Gebärde in der Islendinga Saga*. Diss., Bonn, Germany: 1938.

Graf Rudolf. Edited by P. Ganz. Berlin: E. Schmidt, 1964.

Graham, Janet. "A Handful of Italian," *Gourmet*, (May 1969), 24 ff.

Grajew, Felix. *Untersuchungen über die Bedeutung der Gebärden in der griechischen Epik*. Diss., Freiburg/Br., Germany: 1934.

The Grandes Heures of Jean, Duke of Berry. New York: Braziller, 1971.

Green, J. R. *A Gesture Inventory for the Teaching of Spanish*. Philadelphia: Chilton, 1968.

Greenberg, Peter S. "Learning the Language of Customs." *Los Angeles* (California) *Times*, 26 November 1989: L4.

Gregorii Magni Dialogi. Edited by U. Moricca. Rome: Tip. del Senato, 1924.

Gregorius of Nazianzus (Gregorius Naziazenus). In *Patriologiae cursus completus . . . series Graeca*. Edited by J.-P. Migne. Vols. 35–38. Paris: Garnier et Migne successores, 1886.

Gregory of Tours. *Vitae Patrum*. In *Patrologiae cursus completus . . . series prima*. Edited by J.-P. Migne. Vol. 71. Paris: d'Amboise, la Barrière d'Enfer, 1849.

Grimes, Martha. *The Horse You Came In On*. New York: Knopf, 1993.

Grimm, Jakob. *Deutsche Mythologie*. Edited by E. H. Meyer. Darmstadt, Germany: Wissenschaftliche Buchgesellschaft, 1965.

——— *Deutsche Rechtsaltertümer*. Reprint of the edition of 1899. Darmstadt, Germany: Wissenschaftliche Buchgesellschaft, 1955.

——— *Weistümer*. Reprint of the edition of 1840–1878. Darmstadt, Germany: Wissenschaftliche Buchgesellschaft, 1957.

——— und Wilhelm Grimm. *Kinder- und Hausmärchen*. Wiesbaden, Germany: Vollmer, n.d.

Grimmelshausen, H. J. Chr. von. *Der abenteuerliche Simplicissimus Teutsch*. Stuttgart, Germany: Reclam, 1961.

Gritten, David. "Grim, Black and White . . . Spielberg?" *Los Angeles* (California) *Times*, 9 May, 1993. Calendar, p. 70.

Grönbech, V. P. *Mystikere in Europa og Indien*. Copenhagen: Branner, 1932.

Gross, Johannes. "Notizbuch." *Frankfurter Allgemeine Magazin*, 14 February 1992: 38.

Günther, J. "Kultur der Geste-Geste des Kultus." *Gestalt* 3 (1930–31): 41–48.

Gula ingslog. In: *Norges gamle love indtil 1387*. 5 vols. Edited by R. Keyser, P. A. Munch, G. Storm, E. Herzberg. Christiania: Gröndahl, 1846–95.

Gulliveriana. Edited by J. K. Welcher and G. E. Bush, Jr. Gainesville, Fla.: Scholars' Facsimiles, 1970.

Gur, Batya. *A Literary Murder*. New York: HarperCollins, 1994.

Guratzsch, H. *Die Auferweckung des Lazarus in der niederländischen Kunst von 1400 bis 1700. Ikonographie und Ikonologie*. Kortrijk, Netherlands: van Ghemmert, 1980.

Guys, P. A. *Voyage littéraire de la Grèce*. Paris: Veuve Duchesne, 1783.

Habicht, Werner. *Die Gebärde in englischen Dichtungen des Mittelalters*. In: *Bayerische Akademie der Wissenschaften. Phil.-Hist. Kl. Abhandlungen*. N. F. Heft 46. Munich: in Komm. bei Beck, 1959.

Hahn, J. G. von. *Griechische und albanesische Märchen*. Leipzig, Germany: Engelmann, 1864.

Hall, Edward T. *The Hidden Dimension*. Garden City, N. Y.: Doubleday, 1969.

——— *The Silent Language*. New York: Doubleday, 1990.

Handbuch der deutschen Volkskunde. Edited by W. Pessler and A. Bach et al. Potsdam, Germany: Athenaion, 1934 ff.

Handwörterbuch des deutschen Aberglaubens. Edited by H. Bächtold-Stäubli. Berlin and Leipzig, Germany: de Gruyter, 1927–42.

Handwörterbuch des deutschen Märchens. Edited by Lutz Mackensen. Berlin and Leipzig, Germany: de Gruyter, 1933–40.

Harou, Alfred. In: *Revue des traditions populaires* 13 (1898): 192.

——— In: *Revue des traditions populaires* 14 (1899): 384.

Harris, Ann Sutherland, and Linda Nochlin. *Women Artists: 1550–1950*. Exhibition Catalog. New York: Los Angeles County Museum of Art and Alfred A. Knopf, 1976.

Hartmann von Aue, *Iwein*. Edited by G. F. Benecke and K. Lachmann. Berlin: de Gruyter, 1965.

——— *Gregorius*. Edited by L. Wolff. Tübingen: Niemeyer, 1966.

Haseloff, Arthur. *Eine thüringisch-sächsische Malerschule des 13. Jahrhunderts*. Strassburg, Germany: Heitz, 1897.

Hastings, James, ed., *Dictionary of the Bible*. New York: Scribner, 1927.

——— *Encyclopaedia of Religion and Ethics*. Vols. 5 and 6. New York: Scribner, 1926.

Hawthorne, N. *The Marble Faun*. New York: Sears, 1925.

Hayes, Francis. "Gestures: A Working Bibliography." *Southern Folklore Quarterly*, 21 (1957): 219–317.

Heiler, Friedrich. *Das Gebet. Eine religionsgeschichtliche und religionspsychologische Untersuchung*. Munich, Germany: E. Reinhardt, 1920.

Heinrich der Löwe. *Urkunden*. Edited by K. Jordan. In: *Monumenta Germaniae Historica*. C3, 1.1. Stuttgart: Hiersemann, 1949–57.

Heinrich der Teichner. *Die Gedichte Heinrichs des Teichners*. Edited by H. Niewöhner. Deutsche Texte des Mittelalters 44, 46, 48. Berlin: Akademie, 1953–1956.

Heinrich von Freiberg. *Tristan*. Edited by R. Bechstein. Leipzig, Germany: Brockhaus, 1877.

Helbig, W. *Untersuchungen über die campanische Wandmalerei*. Leipzig, Germany: Breitkopf u. Hartel, 1873.

Heliand. Edited by O. Behaghel. Tübingen: Niemeyer, 1965.

Heliodorus of Emesa. *Opera (Les Ethiopiques)*. Edited by R. M. Rattenbury, T. W. Lumb, J. Maillon. Paris: Soc. d'édition "Les Belles Lettres," 1935–43.

Hellwig, A. "Mystische Meineidzeremonien." *Archiv für Religionswissenschaft* 12 (1909): 46–66.

Hemingway, Ernest. *For Whom the Bell Tolls*. New York: Scribner, 1940.

Hendricksen, Louise. *Lethal Legacy*. New York: Zebra, 1995.

Henley, Nancy. *Body Politics. Power, Sex, and Nonverbal Communication*. Englewood Cliffs, N. J.: Prentice-Hall, 1977.

Herodotus. *Historiae*. Edited by H. B. Rosén. Leipzig, Germany: Teubner, 1987 ff.

Herwegen, J. "Germanische Rechtssymbolik in der römischen Liturgie" *Deutschrechtliche Beiträge* 8 (1913): Heft 4.

Herzog Ernst. Edited by K. Bartsch. Vienna: Braumüller, 1869.

Hickey, William. *The Prodigal Rake. Memoirs of William Hickey [1749–1783]*. Edited by Peter Quennell. New York: Dutton, 1962.

Hildburgh, W. L. "Notes on Spanish Amulets." *Folk-Lore* 17 (1906): 454–61.

——— "Notes on some Contemporary Portuguese Amulets." *Folk-Lore* 19 (1908): 214–22.

——— "Notes on Spanish Amulets." *Folk-Lore* 24 (1913): 63–66.

——— "Notes on Spanish Amulets. Series III." *Folk-Lore* 25 (1914): 206–10.

——— "Psychology Underlying the Employment of Amulets in Europe." *Folk-Lore* 62 (1951): 231–51.

Hill, Reginald. *An Advancement of Learning*. Woodstock, Vt.: Foul Play, 1971.

Hillerman, Tony. *The Blessing Way*. New York: HarperCollins, 1970.

——— *A Thief of Time*. New York: HarperCollins, 1988.

——— *Talking God*. New York: Harper & Row, 1989.

Hindman, Sandra. Review of Meyer Schapiro, *Words and Pictures. On the Literal and the Symbolic in the Illustration of a Text*. In: *Speculum* 51 (1976): 789–92.

His, R. *Das Strafrecht der Friesen im Mittelalter*. Leipzig, Germany: Dieterich, 1901.

Hochegger, Hermann. *Le langage gestuel en Afrique Centrale. Publication du Centre d'Etudes Ethnologiques*. Série II, vol. 47. Bandudu, Zaire: CEEBA, 1978.

Hofmeister, Philipp. *Die christlichen Eidesformen. Eine liturgie- und rechtsgeschichtliche Untersuchung*. Munich, Germany: Zink, 1957.

Holzhauer, Heinz. *Die eigenhändige Unterschrift*. Frankfurt/M.: Athenäum, 1973.

Holzwarth, J. *Die Bartholomäusnacht*. Münster, Germany: Russell, 1872.

Hommel, Fritz. *Geschichte Babyloniens und Assyriens*. Berlin: Grote, 1885–88.

Hone, William. *Year Book of Daily Recreation and Information*. London: T. Tegg, 1832.

Horace (Horatius Flaccus, Quintus). *Works*. London: G. Pickering, 1826.

Hovorka, O. von and A. Kronfeld. *Vergleichende Volksmedizin*. Stuttgart, Germany: Strecker & Schroeder, 1908–09.

Howard, Maureen. *Not a Word about Nightingales*. New York: Atheneum, 1962.

Hrabanus Maurus. *De institutione clericorum.* In: *Patrologiae cursus completus . . . series Latina.* Edited by J.-P. Migne. Vol. 107. Paris: Garnier et Migne successores, 1887.

Hugo von Trimberg. *Der Renner.* Edited by G. Ehrismann. Vol. I. Tübingen: 1908; repr. Berlin: de Gruyter, 1970.

Hupel, A. W. *Topographische Nachrichten von Lief- und Ehstland.* Riga, Latvia: Hartknoch, 1777.

Huxley, Aldous. *Chrome Yellow.* New York: G. H. Doran, 1922.

Immermann, K. *Münchhausen.* Düsseldorf, Germany: Schaub, 1841.

Irenaeus. *Quaestiones et Responsiones ad Orthodoxos, Fragm. 7.* Edited by A. Stieren. Leipzig, Germany: Weigel, 1848–53.

Isidorus Hispalensis (Isidor of Seville). *Etymologiae.* Edited by W. M. Lindsay. Oxford: Oxford University Press, 1957.

s'Jacob, Henriette Eugenie. *Idealism and Realism: A Study of Sepulchral Symbolism.* Leiden, Netherlands: Brill, 1954.

Jacobus de Cessolis. *De ludo scaccorum.* Translated by W. Caxton. Bruges, Belgium: Caxton, 1476? Photocopy.

Jahn, O. "Über den Aberglauben des bösen Blicks bei den Alten." *Berichte über die Verhandlungen der sächsischen Akademie der Wissenschaften 7* (1855): 28 ff.

Jalink, Marijke. "Proskynese." Humanistisch Verbond. Recorded interview. Radio 5, August 4, 1986. Netherlands.

James, E. O. *Primitive Ritual and Belief.* London: Methuen, 1917.

Japenga, Ann. "Hidden Dangers." *Los Angeles* (California) *Times.* 21 May 1992, E1, E10.

Jean, Charles-F. *La religion sumerienne.* Paris: Geuthner, 1931.

Jean de Joinville, *La vie de Saint Louis: le temoignage de Jehan, seigneur de Joinville. Texte du XIVe siècle.* Edited by N. L. Corbett. Québec, Canada: Sherbrooke, 1977.

Jeremias, A. *Handbuch der altorientalischen Geisteskultur.* Berlin and Leipzig: de Gruyter, 1929.

Jeremias, Joachim. *Infant Baptism in the First Four Centuries.* Philadelphia: Westminster, 1962.

Jerome, St. (Hieronymus). *Vita S. Pauli primi eremitae.* In *Patrologiae cursus completus . . . series Latina.* Edited by J.-P. Migne. Vol. 23. Paris: Garnier et Migne successores, 1884.

Jiménez, A. *Picardía Mexicana.* Mexico: Libro Mex, 1962.

Johannes Damascenus. In *Patrologiae cursus completus . . . series Graeca.* Edited by J.-P. Migne. vol. 94. Paris: J.-P. Migne, 1864.

Johnson, S. *Camping among Cannibals.* London: Macmillan, 1883.

Johnston, H. H. *The Uganda Protectorate.* London: Hutchinson, 1904.

Josephus, Flavius. *De bello Judaico.* Edited by O. Michel and O. Bauernfeind. Darmstadt, Germany: Wissenschaftliche Buchgesellschaft, 1959–69.

Judith. In *The Anglo-Saxon Poetic Records.* Vol. 4. New York: Columbia University Press, 1931–53. Pp. 99–109.

Juliana. In *The Anglo-Saxon Poetic Records.* Vol. 3. New York: Columbia UP, 1931–53. Pp. 113–33.

Jungmann, J. A. *Die Frohbotschaft und unsere Glaubensverkündigung.* Regensburg, Germany: Pustet, 1936.

Justinger, C. (Diebold Schilling). *Berner Chronik.* Edited by H. Bloesch and P. Hilber. Bern, Switzerland: Aare, 1943–45.

Juvenal, Decimus Iunius. *Saturae.* Edited by A. E. Housman. Cambridge, England: Cambridge University Press, 1931.

K. P. D. E. "The Evil Eye." *Notes and Queries,* Series 5 (May 9, 1874), I, 374.

Kafka, Barbara. "Festive Jewish Fare." *Gourmet* (September 1996): 70.

Kahle, Bernhard. Review of R. F. Kaindl, *Geschichte der Deutschen in den Karpathenländern. Zeitschrift für Volkskunde* 18 (1908): 116.

Kampeas, Ron. "Wife uses ancient law to fight male barrier to Jewish Divorce." AP Report. *Daily News* (Woodland Hills, Calif.). 27 April 1996: 18.

Kamrisch (Kramrisch), Stella. *The Art of India.* London: Phaidon, 1955.

Kanfer, Stefan. "Leni Riefenstahl sees no Evil." *Civilization* 1 (Nov.–Dec. 1994): 47–51.

Kany, Charles E. *American-Spanish Euphemisms.* Berkeley and Los Angeles: University of California Press, 1960.

Kapp, Volker, ed. *Die Sprache der Zeichen und Bilder. Rhetorik und nonverbale Kommunikation in der frühen Neuzeit.* Ars Rhetorica 1. Marburg, Germany: Hitzeroth, 1990.

Karnata ragini: deux courtisans saluant Krishna-chasseur. Inde centrale, Malwa ou Rajastan, Mewar; vers 1590–1600. Postcard. Fondation Custodia. Collection F. Lugt. Paris: Union, n.d.

Karnofsky, Eva. "Wie Kinder stehen wir da. Panama und die Macht der Amerikaner." *Frankfurter Allgemeine Magazin,* 14 February 1992: 34.

Kaufringer, Heinrich. *Gedichte.* Edited by K. Euling. Tübingen, Germany: Litterarischer Verein Stuttgart, 1888.

Kaulfers, W. V. "Curiosities of Colloquial Gestures." *Hispania* 14 (1931): 249–64.

Kelleher, Kathleen. "In the World of Psychology, the Eyebrows Surely Have It." *Los Angeles* (California) *Times,* 19 August 1996, E2.

Kellerman, Jonathan. *The Butcher's Theater.* New York: Bantam, 1989.

Kelly, Amy. *Eleanor of Aquitaine.* New York: Vintage, 1957.

Kelly, Jonathan F. *The Humors of Falconbridge: A Collection of Humorous and Every-Day Scenes.* Philadelphia: T. B. Peterson and Bros., 1856.

Kemelman, Harry. *Friday the Rabbi Slept Late.* New York: Fawcett Crest, 1966.

Kendon, Adam. "The Study of Gesture: Some Observations on its History." *Recherches Sémiotiques / Semiotic Inquiry* 2 (1982): 45–62.

Kenyatta, Jomo. "Kikuyu Religion, Ancestor-worship and Sacrificial Practices." *Africa,* 10 (1937): 310 ff.

Key, Mary Ritchie. "Gestures and Responses: A Preliminary Study among Some Indian Tribes of Bolivia." *Studies in Linguistics* [University of Buffalo], 16, no. 3–4.

——— *Paralanguage and Kinesics [Nonverbal Communication].* Metuchen, N.J.: Scarecrow, 1975.

——— *Nonverbal Communication: A Research Guide and Bibliography.* Metuchen, N.J.: Scarecrow, 1977.

Kindlinger, V. N. *Geschichte der ältern Grafen bis zum 13. Jahrhundert.* Münster, Germany: Koppenrath, 1793.

King, W. S. "Hand Gestures." *Western Folklore*, 8 (1949): 263–64.

Diu Klage. Edited by K. Bartsch. Darmstadt, Germany: Wissenschaftliche Buchgesellschaft, 1964.

Klauser, T. "Studien zur Entstehungsgeschichte der christlichen Kunst." *Jahrbuch für Antike und Christentum* 2 (1959), 3 (1960).

Kleinpaul, Rudolf. *Das Leben der Sprache und ihre Weltstellung.* Leipzig, Germany: W. Friedrich, 1888–93.

Klitgaard, C. "Skaelsord og foragtelig gestus." *Danske Studier* 31 (1934): 88–89.

Knox, Dilwyn. "Late medieval and renaissance ideas on gesture." In *Die Sprache der Zeichen und Bilder: Rhetorik und nonverbale Kommunikation in der frühen Neuzeit.* Edited by Volker Kapp. (Ars Rhetorica 1). Marburg, Germany: Hitzeroth, 1990. Pp. 11–39.

Kolatch, Alfred J. *The Jewish Book of Why.* Middle Village, N.Y.: Jonathan David, 1995.

Konrad von Haslau. *Der Jüngling. Nach der Heidelberger Hs. Cpg. 341 mit den Lesarten der Leipziger Hs. 946 und der Kalocsaer Hs. (Cod. Bodmer 72).* Edited by W. Tauber. Tübingen, Germany: Niemeyer, 1984.

Konrad von Würzburg. *Otte mit dem Barte* In: *Erzählungen und Schwänke.* Edited by H. Lambel. Leipzig, Germany: Brockhaus, 1883.

——— *Partonopier und Meliur.* Edited by K. Bartsch. Berlin: de Gruyter, 1970.

Korte, Barbara. *Körpersprache in der Literatur. Theorie und Geschichte am Beispiel englischer Erzählprosa.* Tübingen, Germany: A. Francke, 1993.

Kramrisch see Kamrisch

Krapf, J. L. *Travels, Researches and Missionary Labours during an Eighteen Years Residence in Eastern Africa.* London: Trubner, 1860.

Kraus, F. X., ed. *Realenzyclopädie der christlichen Altertümer.* Freiburg, Germany: Herder, 1882–86.

——— *Geschichte der christlichen Kunst.* Freiburg, Germany: Herder, 1896–1908.

Krauss, F. S. *Sitte und Brauch der Südslaven.* Vienna: Holder, 1885.

Kriss-Rettenbeck, Lenz. "Probleme der volkstümlichen Gebärdenforschung." *Bayrisches Jahrbuch für Volkskunde* (1964–65): 14–47.

Kroeber, A. L. "Sign Language Inquiry." *International Journal of American Linguistics* 24 (1958): 1–19.

Kroeber, Theodora. *Ishi in Two Worlds: A Biography of the last Wild Indian in North America*. Berkeley and Los Angeles: University of California Press, 1961.

Kroll, H. H. *Rogues' Company*. Indianapolis: Bobbs-Merrill, 1943.

Krout, M. H. *Autistic Gestures*. In *Psychological Monographs*, 46 (1935), 1–126.

Krukenberg, Eberhard von. *Der Gesichtsausdruck des Menschen*. 2nd ed. Stuttgart, Germany: F. Enke, 1920.

Krumrey, Horst-Volker. *Entwicklungsstrukturen von Verhaltensstandarden. Eine soziologische Prozeßanalyse auf der Grundlage deutscher Anstands- und Manierenbücher von 1870–1970*. Frankfurt a. M., Germany: Suhrkamp, 1984

Kudrun. Edited by B. Boesch. Tübingen: Niemeyer, 1954.

Künssberg, Eberhard Freiherr von. "Rechtsbrauch und Kinderspiel." *Sitzungsberichte der Heidelberger Akademie der Wissenschaften. Phil.-Hist. Kl.*, Heidelberg: Winter, 1920.

———— *Der Sachsenspiegel: Bilder aus der Heidelberger Handschrift*. Leipzig, Germany: Insel, 1934.

———— *Rechtliche Volkskunde*. Halle/Saale, Germany: Niemeyer, 1936.

———— "Messerbräuche. Studien zur Rechtsgeschichte und Volkskunde" *Sitzungsberichte der Heidelberger Akademie der Wissenschaften. Phil.-Hist. Kl.*, Heidelberg: Winter, 1940/41.

———— *Schwurgebärde und Schwurfingerdeutung*. Freiburg/Br., Germany: 1941.

Kunz, George. *The Magic of Jewels and Charms*. Philadelphia: Lippincott, 1915.

L. L. K. "The Hand in Islam." *Notes and Queries*, Series 6 (July 11, 1885), XII, 32.

Laar, C. van. *Het Groot Ceremonie-Boek*. Amsterdam: B. Mourik, 1753.

La Bruyère, Jean de. *Les Charactères ou les moeurs de ce siècle*. Paris: J. Tallandier, 1966.

Lacroix, Paul. *Moers, usages et costumes au moyen âge et à l'époque de la renaissance*. Paris: Firmin Didot, 1874.

Lactantius. *De passione domini*, and *De mortibus persecutorum*. Edited by S. Brandt and G. Laubmann. In: *Corpus Scriptorum Ecclesiasticorum Latinorum*. Vol. 27. Vienna: Gerold, 1866 ff.

Ladner, Gerhart B. "The Gestures of Prayer in Papal Iconography of the Thirteenth and Early Fourteenth Centuries." In *Didascaliae. Studies in Honor of Anselm M. Albareda*. New York: Rosenthal, 1961. Pp. 247–75.

Laiglesia, A. de. *La Rueda: farsa en dos actos*. Madrid: Alfil, 1955.

Les lamentations de Mathéolus. Paris: C. Bouillon, 1892–1905.

Lammens, H. *L'Islam*. Beirut, Lebanon: Imprimerie catholique, 1926.

Lampedusa, Giuseppe di. *The Leopard*. Translated by A. Colquhoun. New York: New American Library, 1961.

Landers, Ann. "Advice." *Daily News* (Woodland Hills, Calif.) "L.A. Life," 11 September 1996, p. 9.

Lane, E. W. *An Account of the Manners and Customs of the Modern Egyptians.* London: C. Knight, 1846.

Larivey, Pierre. *Les Laquais.* Paris: Nizet, 1987.

Larsson, Lars Olof. "Der Maler als Erzähler: Gebärdensprache und Mimik in der französischen Malerei und Kunsttheorie des 17. Jahrhunderts am Beispiel Charles Le Bruns." *Die Sprache der Zeichen und Bilder. Rhetorik und nonverbale Kommunikation in der frühen Neuzeit.* Edited by V. Kapp. Ars Rheorica 1. Marburg, Germany: Hitzeroth, 1990. Pp. 173–189.

Lathen, Emma. *Ashes to Ashes.* New York: Simon & Schuster, 1971.

——— *East Is East.* New York: Simon & Schuster, 1991.

Lauter, David. "Clinton Fires Back at Bush on Trust Issue." *Los Angeles* (California) *Times.* 21 October 1992: A12.

Lazarillo de Tormes. Edited by José Miguel Caso González. Barcelona: Grupo Zeta, 1989.

Leach, Maria. Ed., *Standard Dictionary of Folklore, Mythology and Legend.* New York: Harper & Row, 1949.

Le Bas, Philippe. *France: Dictionnaire encyclopaedique.* Paris: Firmin Didot, 1840–45.

Leclercq, Jean. *L'amour des lettres et le désir de Dieu.* Paris: Cerf, 1957.

Legrand d' Aussy, P. J. B. *Histoire de la vie privée des Français.* Paris: P. D. Pierres, 1815.

Lehmann, Chr. *Chronica der freyen Reichsstadt Speyer.* Frankfurt/M.: Oehrling, 1711.

Leone, Joseph. "A Guide to Some Italian Hand Gestures," *New York Times,* 1 March 1959. XX 11.

Leuzinger, E. *Afrika. Kunst der Negervölker.* Baden-Baden, Germany: Holle, 1959.

Levi, Carlo. *Words Are Stones.* Translated by T. A. Davidson. New York: Farrar, Straus & Cudahy, 1958.

Lex Alamannorum. In *Monumenta Germaniae Historica.* Legum, I. Hannover, Germany: Hahn, 1888.

Lex Bajuvariorum. In *Monumenta Germaniae Historica.* Legum, III. Hannover, Germany: Hahn, 1926.

Lex Ribuaria. In *Corpus juris germanici antiqui.* Edited by P. Georgisch. Halle/Saale, Germany: Waisenhaus, 1738.

Lexikon für Theologie und Kirche. Edited by J. Höfer and K. Rahner. Freiburg/Br., Germany: Herder, 1957–67.

Lichine, Alexis. *Encyclopedia of Wines and Spirits.* London: Cassell, 1979.

Liddell and Scott. *A Greek-English Lexicon.* Oxford: Clarendon, 1968.

Liebrecht, Felix. "Über den Ursprung und die Bedeutung der Redensart: die Feige weisen." *Germania. Neues Jahrbuch der Berlinischen Gesellschaft für deutsche Sprache und Alterthumskunde* 7 (1846): 182–190.

———— *Zur Volkskunde. Alte und neue Aufsätze.* Heilbronn, Germany: Henninger, 1879.

Liell, H. F. J. *Die Darstellungen der allerseligsten Jungfrau und Gottesgebärerin Maria.* Freiburg, Germany: Herder, 1887.

LINGUIST. Electronic publication: *The Linguist List* <linguist@TAMSUN.TAMU.EDU>.

Liutprandi Relatio de legatione Constantinopolitana. Edited by J. Becker. In *Monumenta Germaniae Historica.* Scriptores Hanover and Leipzig, Germany: Hahn, 1915. Pp. 175–212.

Livingstone, D. *Missionary Travels and Researches in South Africa.* London: J. Murray, 1857.

Livy. *Ab urbe condita.* With a translation by B. O. Foster. Cambridge, Mass.: Harvard University Press, 1988.

Llewellyn, Caroline. *Life Blood.* New York: Macmillan, 1993.

Lodge, David. *Nice Work.* Harmondsworth: Penguin, 1988.

———— *Paradise News.* Harmondsworth: Penguin, 1988.

Löfgren, O. "Die beiden äthiopischen Anaphoren des heiligen Cyrillus." Translated by S. Euringer, *Orientalia Christiana*, 30 (1933): 44–86.

Logan, Margaret. *The C.A.T. Caper.* New York: Walker, 1990.

Lomas, Juan. *Teoría y práctica del insulto mexicano.* Mexico, D. F.: Posada, 1974.

Lommatzsch, Eduard. *System der Gebärden, dargestellt auf Grund der mittelalterlichen Literatur Frankreichs.* Diss., Berlin: Reimer, 1910.

Lonsdale, Kathleen. *Quakers visit Russia.* London: East-West Relations Group of the Friends' Peace Committee, 1952.

Louis d'Orléans et Bragance. *A travers l'Hindu-Kush.* Paris: Beauchesne, 1906.

Lucian of Samosata. *Sämtliche Werke.* Translated by C. M. Wieland. Munich: G. Müller, 1911.

Lynch, Rene. "Protocol." *Daily News* (Woodland Hills, Calif.) 13 September 1992: 4, 10.

Mabillon, J. *De re diplomatica.* Supplementum. Paris: C. Robustel, 1704.

The Mabinogion. Translated by G. Jones and T. Jones. London: Dent, 1949.

MacDonald, Philip. *The List of Adrian Messenger.* Garden City, N.Y.: P. MacDonald, 1959.

MacInnes, Helen. *Decision at Delphi.* New York: Harcourt Brace, 1965.

Macrobius, Ambrosius Theodosius. *Saturnalia.* Edited by J. Willis. Leipzig, Germany: Teubner, 1963.

Maguire, Henry. *Eloquence and Gestures in Byzantium.* Princeton: Princeton University Press, 1981.

Mahabharata. Bhagavadgita. Transl. and notes by S. Rhadakrishnan. New York: Harper & Bros., 1948.

Mai und Beaflor. Edited by F. Pfeiffer. Leipzig, Germany: G. J. Goschen, 1848.

Maimon, Solomon. *Autobiography.* New York: Schocken, 1947.

Mallery, Garrick. "Greetings by Gesture." *Popular Science Monthly* 38 (1891), 477–490, 629–644.

Malory, Sir Thomas. *Le morte d'Arthur*. London: Dent, 1897.

Man, E. H. "On the Aboriginal Inhabitants of the Andaman Islands." *Journal of the Anthropological Institute* 12 (1883): 69 ff., 117 ff., 327 ff.

Mander, Carel van. *Den Grondt der edel vrij schilderconst*. Edited by H. Miedema. Utrecht, Netherlands: Haentjens Dekker & Gumbert, 1973; orig. 1604.

Mann, Paul. *The Ganja Coast*. New York: Ballantine, 1996.

Mann, Thomas. *Buddenbrooks*. Frankfurt/M., Germany: Fischer, 1981.

Mantegazza, Paolo. *Physiognomik und Mimik*. Translated by R. Löwenfeld. Leipzig, Germany: Elischer Nachf., 1890.

Manzoni, A. *I promessi sposi*. Florence: Sansoni, 1922.

Markel, Stephen. "Bodhisattva." *The Magazine of the Los Angeles County Museum of Art*. September 1994, p. 12.

Marques-Rivière, Jean. *Amulettes, talismans, et pantacles. Les traditions orientales et occidentales*. Paris: Payot, 1972.

Marrin, Minette. *The Eye of the Beholder*. New York: Penguin, 1989.

Marsh, Ngaio. *Died in the Wool*. London: Collins, 1947.

——— *Spinsters in Jeopardy*. Mattituck, N. Y.: Aemian Press, 1953.

——— *Death of a Fool*. Boston and Toronto: Little, Brown, 1956.

Marshall, F. H. *Catalogue of the Jewelry, Greek, Etruscan and Roman in the Department of Antiquity*. London: British Museum, 1911.

Martial d'Auvergne. *Aresta amorum*. Lyon, France: Gryphius, 1538.

Martialis, Marcus Valerius. *Epigrammaton libri*. Edited by L. Friedländer. Leipzig, Germany: Hirzel, 1886.

Martianus Capella. *De nuptiis Philologiae et Mercurii*. Edited by A. Dick. Stuttgart, Germany: Teubner, 1969.

Martinez, Al. "Ira Reiner—Graying Lone Ranger." *Los Angeles* (California) *Times*, 6 February 1978: pt. 2, pp. 1, 3.

——— "It didn't happen that way," *Los Angeles* (California) *Times*, 29 March 1996: B10.

Maspero, G. *Popular Stories of Ancient Egypt*. London: Grevel, 1915.

Masters, John. "Bugles and a Tiger." *Atlantic Monthly*, December 1955, pp. 33–41.

Matuszewicz, M. *Diariusz zycia mego*. Edited by B. Królikowski. Warsaw: 1986.

Maximilian's Triumphal Arch. Woodcuts by Albrecht Dürer. New York: Dover, 1972.

Mayle, Peter. *A Year in Provence*. New York: Knopf, 1991.

——— *Toujours Provence*. New York: Knopf, 1992.

——— *Hotel Pastis*. New York: Knopf, 1993.

Mazaris. *Vizantiiskii satiricheskii*. Edited by S. V. Poliakova and I. V. Felenkovskaia. Leningrad: Nauka, 1986.

McConeghy, Patrick M. "Women's Speech and Silence in Hartmann von Aue's *Erec*," *PMLA* 102 (1987): 772–83.

McCord, Charlotte. "Gestures [at the University of California, Berkeley]." In: *Western Folklore* 7 (1948): 290–92.

McEwan, Ian. *The Innocent or The Special Relationship*. London: Pan Books, 1990.

McGuire, Brian Patrick. "Friends and Tales in the Cloister: Oral Sources in Caesarius of Heisterbach's *Dialogus Miraculorum*." *Analecta Cisterciensia*, 34 (1980), 167–247.

McHale, Tom. *Farragan's Retreat*. New York: Viking, 1971.

Medieval Frescoes from Yugoslavia. An exhibition organized by the Gallery of Frescoes, Belgrade. Washington D.C.: Smithsonian Institution, Publ. 4594, 1966.

Medio, Dolores. *Diario de una maestra*. Barcelona: Ediciones Destino, 1961.

Meichelbeck, C. *Historia Frisingensis*. Augsburg, Germany: Hermann, 1724.

Meier, John. "Alter Rechtsbrauch im Bremischen Kinderlied." In: *Festschrift zur 400–Jahrfeier des Alten Gymnasiums zu Bremen 1520–1928*. Bremen: G. Winter, 1928. Pp. 219–44.

——— "Der blaue Stein zu Köln," *Zeitschrift für Volkskunde*. 40 (1931): 29–40.

Meier, Jonas. *De gladiatura romana*. Bonn, Germany: C. Georg, 1881.

Mellinkoff, Ruth. *The Devil at Isenheim*. California Studies in the History of Art. Discovery Series I. Berkeley, Los Angeles, London: University of California Press, 1988.

——— *Outcasts: Signs of Otherness in Northern European Art of the Late Middle Ages*. Berkeley and Los Angeles: University of California Press, 1993.

Mencken, J. B. *The Charlatanry of the Learned*. Edited by H. L. Mencken. New York: Knopf, 1937.

Meo Zilio, Giovanni. *El lenguaje de los gestos en el Río de la Plata*. Montevideo, Uruguay: s.n., 1960.

Mérimée, Prosper. *Colomba*. Paris: Charpentier, 1854.

Meschke, Kurt. "Gebärde." In: *Handwörterbuch des deutschen Aberglaubens*. Vol. 3. Berlin: de Gruyter, 1927–42. Cols. 329–37.

Meyer, E. *Geschichte des alten Ägyptens*. Berlin: G. Grote, 1887.

Michel, Francisque. *Histoire des races maudites*. Paris: A. Franck, 1847.

Miller, Jonathan. *The Body in Question*. New York: Random House, 1978.

Miller, Marjorie. "For Cuba, a Blend of Religions." *Los Angeles* (California) *Times*, 5 April 1993: A1, 8, 9.

Miller, Tom. "Fade-Out in Havana." *Los Angeles* (California) *Times Magazine*, 20 December 1992: 44–60.

Mitton, A. "Le langage par gestes." *Nouvelle Revue des Traditions Populaires*, 1 (1949): 138–51.

Möller, E. v. *Die Rechtssitte des Stabbrechens*. Weimar, Germany: H. Böhlau, 1900.

Monahan, Barbara. *A Dictionary of Russian Gesture*. Ann Arbor, Mich.: Hermitage, 1983.

Mone, F. J. *Anzeiger für Kunde der deutschen Vorzeit*. Vol. 4. Nürnberg, German. Mus., 1835.

Montaiglon, M. Anatole. *Recueil général et complet des fabliaux des XIIIe et XIVe siècles imprimés ou inédits*. Paris: Librairie des Bibliophiles, 1872–90.

Montandon, Alain. *Über die deutsche Höflichkeit*. Berne, Switzerland; Berlin, Frankfurt/M., New York, Paris, Vienna: P. Lang, 1991.

Montesquieu, Charles de Secondat. *Lettres persanes*. Paris: Hachette, 1913.

Montfaucon, B. de. *Les monuments de la monarchie françoise*. Paris: J. M. Gandouin, 1729–33.

Monumenta Boica. Munich: Akademie d. Wissenschaften, 1763–1916.

Monumenta Germaniae Historica. Hanover, Germany: Hahn, 1877 ff.

Moody, Lori. "Sending Signals." *Daily News* (Woodland Hills, California). 14 February 1995. "L.A. Life," p. 9.

Moore, Clement. "A Visit from St. Nicholas." *The Christmas Book*. Philadelphia: Thomas and Cowperthwait, 1846.

Morais, Antonio de Silva Grande. *Dicionário da lingua portuguesa*. Lisbon, Portugal: Editorial Confluência, 1949–59.

Mornet, D. *French Thought in the 18th Century*. New York: 1929.

Morris, Desmond, Peter Collett, Peter Marsh, Marie O'Shaughnessy. *Gestures, their origins and distribution*. New York: Stein & Day, 1979.

Moser, O. "Zur Geschichte und Kenntnis der volkstümlichen Gebärden." *Carinthia*, 1 (1954): 735–74.

Muchembled, Robert. "The order of gestures: a social history of sensibilities under the Ancien Régime in France." In *A Cultural History of Gesture*, ed. J. Bremmer and H. Roodenburg. Cambridge: Polity, 1991. Pp. 129–51.

Müllenhoff, K. and W. Scherer, eds. *Denkmäler deutscher Poesie und Prosa aus dem VIII.-XII. Jahrhundert*. Berlin: Weidmann, 1892.

Müller, G. "Über die geographische Verbreitung einiger Gebärden im östlichen Mittelmeergebiet und dem nahen Osten." *Zeitschrift für Ethnologie*, 71 (1939): 99 ff.

Müller, W. *Der schauspielerische Stil im Passionsspiel des Mittelalters*. Diss., Greifswald. Leipzig, Germany: H. Eichblatt, 1927.

Muggeridge, Malcolm. "Dolce Vita in a Colder Climate." *Esquire*, 60 (Nov. 1963): 97.

Mulisch, Harry. *The Assault*. Translated by C. N. White. New York: Pantheon, 1985.

Murdock, George P. *Our Primitive Contemporaries*. New York: Macmillan, 1934.

Mystères inédits du XVe siècle, ed. A. Jubinal. Paris: Techener, 1837.

Nabokov, Vladimir. *Pnin*. Garden City, N. Y.: Doubleday, 1957.

"National School Celebration of Columbus." *The Youth's Companion*, 65 (Sept. 8, 1892): 446.

Neckel, G. "Über eine allgemeine Geste des Schmerzes." *Archiv für das Studium der neueren Sprachen* 167 (1935): 64 ff.

Nelson, J. L. "Dispute settlement in Carolingian West Francia." In *The Settlement of Disputes in Early Medieval Europe*. Edited by W. Davies and P. Fouracre. Cambridge, England: Cambridge University Press, 1986.

Nettesheim, H. C. Agrippa von. *Magische Werke*. Berlin: H. Barsdorf, 1916.

Neumann, G. *Gesten und Gebärden in der griechischen Kunst*. Berlin: De Gruyter, 1962.

Newman, J. H. *Essays on Various Subjects*. London: Bell, 1853.

Das Nibelungenlied. Edited by K. Bartsch and H. de Boor. Wiesbaden, Germany: Brockhaus, 1956.

Nickel, Gunther. "Seismograph seiner Zeit." *Der Tagesspiegel* (Berlin, Germany). 17 July 1996: p. 19.

Niebuhr, Carsten. *Reisebeschreibung nach Arabien und andern umliegenden Ländern*. Copenhagen: Moller, 1778.

Nietzsche, Friedrich von. *Sämtliche Werke: Kritische Studienausgabe*, ed. G. Colli and M. Montinari. Munich: Deutscher Taschenbuchverlag; Berlin, Germany, and New York: de Gruyter, 1980.

Nithard's Histories. In *Carolingian Chronicles*. Translated by B. W. Scholz. Ann Arbor: University of Michigan Press, 1970.

Nitschke, August. *Bewegungen in Mittelalter und Renaissance*. Düsseldorf, Germany: Schwann, 1987.

Nonnos (5th cent. A.D.) *Dionysiaka*. Leipzig, Germany: Teubner, 1926–33.

Notker Labeo. *De Consolatione Philosophiae*, ed. W. Sehrt and T. Starck. Halle/Saale, Germany: Niemeyer, 1933 ff.

Notscher, F. *Biblische Altertumskunde*. Bonn, Germany: Hanstein, 1940.

Nykl, A. R. *Hispano-Arabic Poetry and its Relations with the Old Provençal Troubadours*. Baltimore: J. H. Furst, 1946.

Odo of Cluny. *Vita Sancti Geraldi*. In: *Patrologiae cursus completus . . . series Latina*. Edited by J.-P. Migne. Paris: Garnier et Migne successores, 1887. Vol. 133.

Oechelhäuser, Adolf von. *Die Miniaturen der Universitätsbibliothek zu Heidelberg*. Heidelberg: Koester, 1887–95.

——— *Der Bilderkreis zum Wälschen Gaste des Thomasin von Zerclaere*. Heidelberg: Koester, 1890.

Ogier, Charles. *Caroli Ogierii Ephemerides* (1636). In *Dziennik podrozy do Polski, 1635–1636*. Tlum. E. Jedrkiewicz. Wstepem historycznym i objasnieniami opatrzyl W. Czaplinski. Gdansk, Poland: Bibl. Miejska, 1950–53.

Ohm, Thomas. *Die Gebetsgebärden der Völker und das Christentum*. Leiden, Netherlands: Brill, 1948.

Ombredane, A. "Le langage, gesticulation significative mimique et conventionelle." *Nouveau traité de psychologie* 3 (1933): 363–458.

"On with the Show." *The New Yorker*. 11 January 1993: 23–26.

Onians, R. B. *The Origins of European Thought about the Body*. Cambridge, England: Cambridge University Press, 1951.

Opie, Iona and Peter. *The Lore and Language of Schoolchildren*. Oxford: Clarendon, 1959.

Orendel. Edited by A. E. Berger. Bonn, Germany: Weber, 1888.

Ortnit. Edited by A. Holtzmann. Heidelberg: Winter, 1865.

Ostrow, Ronald J. "Engineer Recalls Payoff in Office of Vice President." *Los Angeles* (California) *Times*, 11 October 1973, pt. 1, p. 1.

Ostrup, D. J. *Orientalische Höflichkeit. Formen und Formeln im Islam*. Leipzig, Germany: Harrassowitz, 1929.

Otfrid von Weissenburg. *Liber Evangeliorum*, ed. O. Erdmann. Tübingen, Germany: Niemeyer, 1957.

Otto, A. *Die Sprichwörter und sprichwörtlichen Redensarten der Römer*. Leipzig, Germany: Teubner, 1890.

Otto, W. G. A. *Handbuch der Archaeologie*. Munich: Beck, 1939–54.

Otto von Freising. *Gesta Frederici*. Edited by G. Waitz et al. Berlin: Deutscher Verlag d. Wissenschaften, 1965.

Ovid. *Metamorphoses*. Edited by A. Miller. Cambridge, Mass.: Harvard University Press, 1957–60.

The Oxford Dictionary of English Proverbs, see *Dictionary of English Proverbs*.

Palaye, S. *Mémoires sur l'ancienne chevalerie*. Paris: Girard, 1759.

Palladius. *Historia Lausiaca*. Edited by P. R. Coleman-Norton. London: Society Promoting Christian Knowledge, 1958.

Palol, Pedrode and Max Hirmer. *Early Medieval Art in Spain*. New York: Abrams, n.d.

Panchatantra. Translated by A. W. Ryder. Chicago: Univ. of Chicago Press, 1956.

Panofsky, E. "Jan van Eyck's Arnolfini Portrait." In *Renaissance Art*. Edited by C. Gilbert. New York: Harper & Row, 1970.

Pardo Bazán, Emilia. *La madre naturaleza*. In: *Obras completas* 4. Madrid: Editorial Fuego, n.d.

Paris, Godefroy de. *Chronique métrique de Philippe-Bel*. Paris: Les Belles Lettres, 1856.

Paris, Matthew. *Chronicles of Matthew Paris: Monastic Life in the Thirteenth Century*. Edited by R. Vaughan. New York: St. Martin's Press, 1984.

Paso, Alfonso. *Cosas de Mamá y Papá*. In *Teatro Español*. Madrid: Ediciones Alfil, 1962–63.

Das Passional. Edited by F. K. Koepke. Amsterdam: Rodopi, 1966.

Paulinus of Petricordia. *Vita Sancti Martini episcopi libri vi*. Ed. E. F. Corpet. Paris: Panckoucke, 1852.

Pauly, A. F. von and A. Wissowa, eds., *Realenzyclopaedie der klassischen Altertumswissenschaft*. Stuttgart, Germany: Metzler, 1894–1963.

Pederson, Rena. "Take these Conventions, please." *Daily News* (Woodland Hills, Calif.) 4 September 1996: 13.

Peer, Elizabeth. Review of Morris, et al., *Gestures*, in *Newsweek*, 6 August 1979: 71–73.

Peil, Dietmar. *Die Gebärde bei Chrétien, Hartmann und Wolfram. Erec— Iwein—Parzival.* In *Medium Aevum. Philologische Studien.* Vol. 28, Munich: Fink, 1975.

Pélerinage de vie humaine. see Deguileville, Guillaume de.

Percy, Thomas. *Reliques of Ancient English Poetry.* Edinburgh: Nommo, 1927.

Pereda, José María de. *La Puchera.* Madrid: Tello, 1889.

———— *Peñas arriba.* Mexico, D. F.: Editorial Porrúa, 1966.

Perera, Victor. *The Cross and the Pear Tree.* New York: Knopf, 1995.

Pérez Galdós, Benito. *Fortunata y Jacinta.* Madrid: Aguilar, 1950.

Pérez-Reverte, Arturo. *The Flanders.* Translated by M. J. Costa. New York, 1990.

Perry, Bill. "Gasoline Alley." *Los Angeles* (California) *Times*, 15 December 1957: Comics.

Persius Flaccus, Aulus. *Saturae.* Edited by F. Villeneuve. Paris: Hachette, 1918.

Peter the Chanter. *De penitentia et partibus eius.* In *The Christian at Prayer: An illustrated Prayer Manual attributed to Peter the Chanter.* Edited by R. C. Trexler. Binghamton, N.Y.: Medieval & Renaissance Texts and Studies, 1987.

Petermann, H. *Reisen im Orient.* Leipzig, Germany: Veit, 1860.

Petershusanum Chronicon see *Chronicon Petershusanum.* In *Germaniae Sacrae Prodromus.* Edited by K. Ussermann. Sankt Blasien, Germany: Typis Sanblasianis, 1790.

Petrus Damiani. *De bono suffragorum.* In *Patrologiae cursus completus . . . series Latina.* Vol.145. Edited by P.-J. Migne. Paris: Garnier et Migne successores, 1887.

Phillips, George L. "Toss a kiss to the sweep for luck." *Journal of American Folklore* 64 (1951): 191–96.

Philostratus, Verus. *Vita Apollonii.* Edited by F. C. Conybeare. Cambridge, Mass.: Harvard University Press, 1969.

Pitiscus, Samuel. *Lexicon antiquitatum romanorum: . . .* Leuven, Belgium: F. Halma, 1713.

Pitrè, Giuseppe. *Usi e costumi del populo siciliano.* Palermo: Luigi Pedone Lauriel, 1889.

Pizarro, Joaquín Martínez. *A Rhetoric of the Scene. Dramatic Narrative in the Early Middle Ages.* Toronto: University of Toronto Press, 1989.

Plautus, Titus Maccius. *Asinaria*, ed. Havet and Freté. Paris: "Les Belles Lettres," 1925.

Pliny the Elder. *Natural History.* Cambridge, Mass.: Harvard University Press, 1938–63.

Plutarch, L. Mestrius. *Lives*, tr. Dryden. New York: Random House, n.d.

Pollock, F. and F. W. Maitland. *The History of English Law before the Time of Edward I.* Cambridge, England: Cambridge University Press, 1923.

Pollux, Julius. *Onomasticon.* Edited by A. Bethe. Leipzig, Germany: Teubner, 1900–37.

Possart, P. A. F. K. *Die russischen Ostseeprovinzen. Kurland, Livland und Esthland.* Teil 2. Stuttgart, Germany: Literatur-Comptoir, 1846.

Potter, Charles. "Gesture." In *Standard Dictionary of Folklore.* Edited by M. Leach. New York: Funk & Wagnalls, 1949.

Pound, Ezra. *Lustra.* New York: Knopf, 1917.

Powers, Charles T. "A Ph.D. for Would-Be Cabbies. *Los Angeles* (California) *Times*, 15 October 1992, A2.

Prelutsky, Burt. "West View. Gestures." *Los Angeles* (California) *Times*, 26 March 1972. "West Magazine," p. 7.

Pritzwald, Stegmann von. "Der Sinn einiger Grussformeln im Lichte kulturhistorischer Parallelen." *Wörter und Sachen* 10 (1927): 23 ff.

Prutz, H. *Staatengeschichte des Abendlandes im Mittelalter.* Berlin: Grote, 1885–87.

Quasten, J. *Musik und Gesang in den Kulten der Heiden. Antike und christliche Frühzeit.* Münster, Germany: Aschendorff, 1930.

Quevedo, Francisco de. *Obras completas.* Edited by F. Buendía. Madrid, Spain: Aguilar, 1961.

Quintilianus, Marcus Fabius. *Institutio oratoria.* Edited by M. Niedermann. Cambridge, Mass.: Harvard University Press, 1958–60.

Quintus Smyrnaeus. *Quinti Smyrnaei Posthomericorum libri XIV.* Edited by A. Zimmermann. Stuttgart, Germany: Teubner, 1969.

Rabelais, F. *Oeuvres.* Edited by A. Lefranc. Paris: Nilsson, 1928 ff.

Rabener, G. W. *Satiren.* Leipzig, Germany: G. J. Dyck, 1759.

Raim, Anne Marmot. *La Communication non-verbale chez Maupassant.* Paris: Nizet, 1986.

Rajna, Pio. *Le fonti dell'Orlando Furioso.* Florence: Sansoni, 1900.

Ramage, C. T. "Superstitious Notions in Italy." *Notes and Queries*, Series 3 (Oct. 5, 1867), XII, 261.

Randolph, Vance. *We Always Lie to Strangers.* New York: Columbia University Press, 1951.

Read, A. W. "The first stage in the history of 'O.K.' " *American Speech* 38 (1963): 5–27.

Recke, E. v. d. *Tagebuch einer Reise durch einen Teil Deutschlands und durch Italien in den Jahren 1804–06.* Edited by K. Böttiger. Berlin: Vieweg, 1815–17.

Recueil Géneral see Montaiglon, M. Anatole.

Redlich, Oswald. *Urkundenlehre.* Part III. In *Handbuch der Mittelalterlichen und Neueren Geschichte.* Edited by G. v. Below and F. Meinecke. Munich and Berlin: Oldenbourg, 1911.

Reinecke Fuchs. In K. Simrock, *Die deutschen Volksbücher.* I. Basel, Switzerland: Schwabe, 1887.

Reinke de Vos. Edited by F. Prien. Halle/Saale, Germany: Niemeyer, 1925.

Renart le Nouvel. Edited by H. Roussel. Paris: Picard, 1961.

Révész, G. *Ursprung und Vorgeschichte der Sprache.* Bern, Switzerland: Francke, 1946.

—— "Die Psychologie des Händedrucks und der Weltsprache der Hände." *Universitas* 11 (1956): 143–48.

Reyes, A. "Ademanes." In *Norte y Sur.* Mexico, D. F.: Editorial Legenda, 1944.

Rheinisches Wörterbuch. Edited by J. Müller. Bonn, Germany: F. Klopp, 1928.

Richardson, Samuel. *Clarissa Harlowe.* London: Chapman & Hall, 1902.

Richer of St. Rémi. *Histoire de France.* Paris: Les Belles Lettres, 1964–67.

Riefenstahl, Leni. *Leni Riefenstahl. A Memoir.* New York: St. Martin's Press, 1993.

Ripa, Cesare. *Baroque and Rococo Pictorial Imagery.* New York: Dover, 1971; orig. *Iconologia,* 1758–60.

Ritter, K. B. "Das liturgische Gebet. Die liturgische Gebärdensprache." *Christentum und Leben* 11 (1936): 373–76.

Robertson, D. W. *Preface to Chaucer.* Princeton: Princeton University Press, 1962.

Robinson, Robert. *Landscape with Dead Dons.* New York: Rinehart, 1956.

Rockwood, J. 1966. *The Craftsmen of Dionysus. An Approach to Acting.* Glenview, Ill.: Scott, Foresman, 1966.

Röhrich, Lutz. "Gebärdensprache und Sprachgebärde." In: *Humaniora. Essays in Literature, Folklore, Bibliography Honoring Archer Taylor.* Locust Valley, N. Y.: J. J. Augustin, 1960. Pp. 121–49.

—— *Gebärde-Metapher-Parodie.* Düsseldorf: Schwann, 1967.

Rojas, Fernando de. *La Celestina.* Translated by L. B. Simpson. Berkeley and Los Angeles: University of California Press, 1959.

Das Rolandslied. Edited by K. Bartsch. Leipzig, Germany: Brockhaus, 1874.

Le Roman de Renart. Edited by M. Roques. Paris: H. Champion, 1951–60.

Roodenburg, Herman. "The 'hand of friendship': shaking hands and other gestures in the Dutch Republic." In *A Cultural History of Gesture,* ed. J. Bremmer and H. Roodenburg. Cambridge, England: Polity, 1991. Pp. 152–189.

Rose, H. A. "The Language of Gesture." *Folk-Lore* 30 (1919): 312–15.

Rosenberg, A. "Die Kreuzmeditation." In *Meditation in Religion und Psychotherapie.* Edited by W. Bitter. Munich: Kindler, 1967.

Roth, H. Ling. "On Salutations." *Journal of the Anthropological Institute* 19 (1890): 164.

Rother. Edited by J. de Vries. Heidelberg: Winter, 1922.

Rourke, Mary. "Finding Their Religion." *Los Angeles* (California) *Times,* 1 August 1996: E1–8.

Rousseau, J.-J. *Confessions.* Paris: L. Giraud-Badin, 1928.

—— *Emile.* Paris: Garnier, 1957.

Royal Frankish Annals. Translated by B. W. Scholz. In *Carolingian Chronicles.* Ann Arbor: Michigan University Press, 1970.

Ruesch, Jürgen and Weldon Kees. *Nonverbal Communication.* Berkeley and Los Angeles: University of California Press, 1956.

Ruíz, Juan. *Libro de Buen Amor.* Edited by J. Cejador y Frauca. Madrid: Espasa-Calpe, 1955.

Sabouroff, P. A. *Sammlung Sabouroff der Kunstdenkmäler aus Griechenland.* Edited by C. Furtwängler. Berlin: A. Asher, 1883–87.

Sachau, E. *Reise in Syrien und Mesopotamien.* Leipzig, Germany: Brockhaus, 1883.

Der Sachsenspiegel. Edited by C. Schott. Zürich: Manesse, 1984.

Sacks, Oliver. *Seeing Voices.* New York: HarperCollins, 1990.

Saitz, Robert L. and Edward J. Cervenka. *Handbook of Gestures: Colombia and the United States.* Approaches to Semiotics 31. The Hague and Paris: Mouton, 1972.

Sartori, Donato and Bruno Lanata, in collaboration with Paola Piizzi. *Maschera e Maschere: storia, morfologia, tecnica: Centro Maschere e Strutture Gestuali.* Florence, Italy: Usher, 1984.

Schaefer, Ursula. *Vokalität. Altenglische Dichtung zwischen Mündlichkeit und Schriftlichkeit.* ScriptOralia 39. Tübingen, Germany: Narr, 1992.

Scheflen, A. E. "The Significance of Posture in Communication Systems." *Psychiatry,* 5 (1961): 316–31.

Schiller, Friedrich von. *Wilhelm Tell; Die Räuber; Die Jungfrau von Orleans; Die Piccolomini; Wallensteins Tod.* In *Werke.* Nationalausgabe. Edited by L. Blumenthal and B. v. Wiese. Weimar, Germany: Böhlau, 1943 ff.

Schiller, Karl, and August Lübben. *Mittelniederdeutsches Wörterbuch.* Bremen, Germany: J. Kuhtmann, 1875–81.

Schjelderup, Kr. *Die Askese.* Berlin and Leipzig, Germany: De Gruyter, 1928.

Schmid, Reinhold, ed. *Die Gesetze der Angelsachsen.* Leipzig, Germany: Brockhaus, 1858.

Schmidt, Leopold. "Die volkstümlichen Grundlagen der Gebärdensprache." *Beiträge zur sprachlichen Volksüberlieferung* 2 (1953): 233–49.

——— *Volksglaube und Volksbrauch.* Berlin: Schmidt, 1966.

Schmidt, O. *Die gotischen Skulpturen des Freiburger Münsters.* Frankfurt/M.: Frankfurter Verlags-Anstalt, 1926.

Schmidt-Pauli, Elisabeth von. *Kolumbus und Isabella.* Aschaffenburg, Germany: P. Pattloch, 1953.

Schmidt-Wiegand, Ruth. "Gebärdensprache im mittelalterlichen Recht." *Frühmittelalterliche Studien* 16 (1982): 363–79.

——— "Die Bilderhandschriften des Sachsenspiegels als Zeugen pragmatischer Schriftlichkeit." *Frühmittelalterliche Studien* 22 (1988): 357–87.

——— "Mit Hand und Mund. Sprachgebärden aus dem mittelalterlichen Rechtsleben." *Frühmittelalterliche Studien* 25 (1991): 283–299.

Schmitt, Jean-Claude. *Die Logik der Gesten im europäischen Mittelalter.* Stuttgart: Klett-Cotta, 1992. Translated by R. Schubert and B. Schulze from *La raison des gestes dans l'Occident médiéval*. Paris: Gallimard, 1990.

Schmitz, H. J. *Die Bussbücher und die Bussdisziplin der Kirche*. Mainz, Germany: Kirchheim, 1883.

Schrader, Hermann. *Der Bilderschmuck der deutschen Sprache*. Berlin: Felber, 1886.

Schreiber, Th. *Die Sirenen*. Berlin: Engelmann, 1868.

Schreiber, W. L. and Paul Heitz. *Die deutschen 'Accipies' und 'Magister cum Discipulis' Holzschnitte*. Studien zur deutschen Kunstgeschichte 100. Kehl, Germany: Heitz, 1957.

Schroeder, H. R. P. *Geschichte des Lebensmagnetismus und des Hypnotismus*. Leipzig, Germany: A. Strauch, 1899.

Schubert, Martin J. *Zur Theorie des Gebarens im Mittelalter: Analyse von nichtsprachlicher Äusserung in mittelhochdeutscher Epik: Rolandslied, Eneasroman, Tristan*. Koelner Germanistische Studien. Vol. 31. Cologne, Germany: Boehlau, 1991.

Schulberg, Budd. *On the Waterfront*. Carbondale, Ill.: Southern Illinois University Press, 1955.

Schultz, Alwin. *Das höfische Leben zur Zeit der Minnesänger*. Leipzig, Germany: Hirzel, 1889.

Schulze, F. *Bilderatlas zur deutschen Kulturgeschichte*. Leipzig, Germany: Bibliographisches Institut, 1936.

Schwäbisches Wörterbuch. Edited by H. v. Fischer. Tübingen, Germany: H. Laupp, 1904–36.

Schwanitz, Dietrich. *Der Campus*. Frankfurt/M.: Eichborn, 1994.

Schweizerisches Idiotikon. Edited by F. Staub and L. Tobler. Frauenfeld, Switzerland: J. Huber, 1881–1961.

Schwineköper, Berent. *Der Handschuh im Recht, Ämterwesen, Brauch und Volksglauben*. Sigmaringen, Germany: Thorbecke, 1981.

Sébourc, Baudoin de, see Baudoin de Sébourc.

Seemann, Otto. *Die gottesdienstlichen Gebräuche der Griechen und Römer*. Leipzig, Germany: A. Seemann, 1888.

Seiler, Friedrich. *Deutsche Sprichwörterkunde*. Munich: Beck, 1922.

Seligmann, Siegfried. *Der böse Blick und Verwandtes*. Berlin: H. Barsdorf, 1910.

Sercambi, Giovanni. *Novelle inédite*. Turin, Italy: E. Loescher, 1889.

Séroux d'Agincourt, J. B. L. G. *Histoire de l'art par les monuments depuis sa décadence au IVe siècle jusqu'à son renouvellement au XVIe*. Paris: Treuttel & Wurtz, 1823.

Servius. *Servii Grammatici qui feruntur in Vergilii carmina commentari*. Edited by G. Thilo and H. Hagen. Leipzig, Germany: Teubner, 1881–87.

Seton, Ernest Thompson. *Sign Talk*. Garden City, N. Y.: Doubleday, Page, 1918.

Sewell, William. *The History of the Rise, Increase and Progress of the Christian People called Quakers, . . .* London: Sowle, 1722.

Siccama, S. T. *Lex Frisionum*. Leipzig, Germany: Gärtner, 1730.

Sidonius Apollinaris. *Epistolae et carmina*. Edited by C. Luetjohann. In *Monumenta Germaniae Historica*. Auct. antiqu. 8. Berlin: Weidmann, 1887.

Simenon, Georges. *Maigret Abroad*. New York: Harcourt, Brace, 1940.

Simms, W. G. *Southward Ho!* New York: Redfield, 1882.

Simon Sugg's Adventures. Philadelphia: T. B. Peterson, 1848.

Simrock, K. *Handbuch der deutschen Mythologie*. Bonn, Germany: A. Marcus, 1874.

Sinor, Denis. "The Historical Attila." In *Attila. The Man and His Image*. Edited by F.H. Bäuml and M. Birnbaum. Budapest, Hungary: Corvina, 1993. Pp. 3–15.

Sittl, Carl. *Die Gebärden der Griechen und Römer*. Leipzig, Germany: Teubner, 1890.

Siuts, Heinrich. *Bann und Acht und ihre Grundlagen im Totenglauben*. Berlin: de Gruyter, 1959.

Slick, Jonathan (Mrs. Ann S. Stephens). *High Life in New York*. New York: Bunce, 1954.

Smith, Margaret. *Studies in the Early Mysticism in the Near and Middle East*. London: Sheldon, 1901.

Smollett, Tobias. *Peregrine Pickle*. London: D. Wilson, 1751.

——— *Roderick Random*. Edinburgh: A. Donaldson, 1778.

——— *The Expedition of Humphrey Clinker*. London: Rivington, 1810.

Snethlage, Emilia. *Travessia entre o Xingu e o Tapajós*. Pará, Brazil: Museo Goeldi, 1913.

Snow, C. P. *The Affair*. London: Macmillan, 1962.

Soester Gerichtsordnung. Westphalen monumenta inedita. Leipzig, Germany: Hannemann, 1730–45.

Southern, R. W. *The Making of the Middle Ages*. New Haven: Yale University Press, 1961.

The Spectator. London, 1711–15. Repr. Philadelphia: Crissy, 1840.

Speke, J. H. *Journal of Discovery of the Source of the Nile*. London: W. Blackwood, 1863.

Spicer, Joaneath. "The Renaissance Elbow." In *A Cultural History of Gesture*. Edited by J. Bremmer and H. Roodenburg. Cambridge, England: Polity, 1991. Pp. 84–128.

Spinola, A. *Scritti scelti*. Edited by C. Bitossi. Genoa, Italy: Sagep, 1981.

Starowolski, S. see Bystron, J.

Statius, Publius Papinius. *Thebais*. Edited by A. Klotz. Leipzig, Germany: Teubner, 1973.

Steinbeck, John. *Tortilla Flat*. New York: Viking, 1973.

Steinen, Karl von den. *O Brasil Central*. São Paulo: Comp. Edit. Nacional, 1942.

Steiner, George. "Franco's Games," *The New Yorker*, 17 October 1994: 116–20.

Stephani, L. *Compte rendu de la commission archéologique de l'académie de St. Petersbourg*. St. Petersburg, Russia: Comm. arch., 1861.

Sterne, Laurence. *The Life and Opinions of Tristram Shandy, Gentleman*. London: Hinxman, Dodsley, Cooper, 1760–67.

Stroebe, Klara. "Altgermanische Grussformen." *Beiträge zur Geschichte der deutschen Sprache und Literatur* 37 (1911–12): 173–212.

Su, Vincent. 23. Dec. 1992 "Markedness and Exception." LINGUIST 3.1012. <linguist@TAMSUN.TAMU.EDU>.

Suetonius, Gaius Tranquillus. *Opera*. Edited by M. Ihm. Leipzig, Germany: Teubner, 1908.

Suntrup, R. *Die Bedeutung der liturgischen Gebärden und Bewegungen in lateinischen und deutschen Auslegungen des 9. bis 13. Jahrhunderts*. Münsterische Mittelalter-Schriften, 37. Munich: Fink, 1978.

Surtees, R. S. *Plain or Ringlets*. London: Bradbury and Evans, 1860.

Swete, H. B. *Church Services and Service Books*. London: Society for Promoting Christian Knowledge, 1905.

Swift, Jonathan. *Polite Conversation*, ed. Partridge. London: A. Deutsch, 1963.

Sybel, Ludwig von. *Katalog der Sculpturen zu Athen*. Marburg, Germany: N. G. Elwert, 1881.

Syr Isenbras. In *Select Pieces of Early Popular Poetry*. London: Longman, Hurst, Rees, Orme, and Brown, 1817.

Tacitus, Cornelius. *Annales*; *Germania*. Heidelberg, 1988.

—— *Historia*. Edited by A. M. Hakkert. Amsterdam, 1966.

Taylor, Archer. *The Shanghai Gesture*. In *Folklore Fellows Communications (FFC)*, 166 (1956).

—— Note in *Western Folklore* 23 (1964): 114.

Temesvary, R. *Volksbräuche und Aberglauben in der Geburtshilfe und der Pflege des Neugebornen in Ungarn*. Leipzig, Germany: T. Grieben, 1900.

Tepl, Johann von (Johann von Saaz). *Der Ackermann aus Böhmen*. Edited by L. L. Hammerich and G. Jungbluth. Copenhagen, Denmark: Munksgaard, 1951.

Terence, Publius Terentius Afer. *Andria*. Oxford: Oxford University Press, 1960.

Tertullianus, Quintus Septimus Florens. *De oratore*. *Opera*. Turnholt, Belgium: Brepols, 1954.

Tey, Josephine. *The Singing Sands*. New York: Macmillan, 1960.

Thackeray, William M. *The Virginians*. London: Dent, 1911.

—— *The History of Pendennis*. New York: Garland, 1991.

Theocritus. *Works*. Edited by J. M. Edmonds. London: Heinemann, 1912.

Thomas, P. *Hindu Religion, Customs and Manners*. Bombay: D. B. Taraporevala, 1956.

Thomasin von Circlaria. *Der Welsche Gast*. Repr. of the ed. of 1852 with intro. by F. Neumann, Berlin: de Gruyter, 1965.

Thompson, James Maurice. *A Banker of Bankersville*. New York: Cassell, 1886.

A Thousand Nights and a Night. Translated by R. F. Burton. London: H. S. Nichols, 1897.

Thümmel, M. A. von. *Reise in die mittäglichen Provinzen von Frankreich im Jahre 1785–86.* Leipzig, Germany: G. J. Goschen, 1791–1805.

Tibullus, Albius. *Works.* Edited by F. W. Lenz. Leipzig, Germany: Teubner, 1937.

Tieck, Ludwig. *Der blonde Eckbert.* In: *Schriften,* vol. 4. Repr. of the ed. of 1828–54, Berlin: De Gruyter, 1966.

Time. Review of the film "A Majority of One" (Warner). 19 January 1962: 55.

—— Review of Christopher Hibbert, *Il Duce.* 4 May 1962: 94, 96.

—— "The High Price of Silent Insults." 9 April 1965: pp. 67–68. Photo Pais & Sartarelli.

Toland, John. *The Last Hundred Days.* New York: Random House, 1965.

Treasures of the Mass. Clyde, Miss.: Benedictine Convent of Perpetual Adoration, 1949.

Treitinger, O. *Die oströmische Kaiser- und Reichsidee nach ihrer Gestaltung im höfischen Zeremoniell.* Darmstadt, Germany: H. Gentner, 1956.

The Très Riches Heures of Jean, Duke of Berry. New York: Braziller, 1969.

Trexler, Richard C. *The Christian at Prayer. An illustrated Prayer Manual attributed to Peter the Chanter (d. 1197).* Medieval and Renaissance Texts and Studies 44. Binghamton, N. Y.: 1987.

Trissino, G. G. *L'Italia liberata.* Orléans, France: Bibl. de meilleurs poètes ital.: 1787.

Trollope, Anthony. *Can You Forgive Her?* London: Oxford University Press, 1948.

—— *Barchester Towers.* Edited by M. Sadleir, F. Page. Oxford: Oxford University Press, 1980.

Ulloa, Alfonso. *Delle lettere dell'ill.re signore Don Antonio de Guevara.* Venice: La Comp. de gli uniti, 1585.

Ulrich von Zatzikhoven. *Lanzelet.* Edited by K. A. Hahn. Berlin: De Gruyter, 1965.

Urkundenbuch der Stadt Freiberg. Edited by K. Ermisch. Leipzig, Germany: Giesecke, 1891.

Urtel, Hermann. *Beiträge zur portugiesischen Volkskunde.* Hamburg: L. Friedrichsen, 1928.

Valerius Maximus. *Factorum et dictorum memorabilium.* Stuttgart, Germany: Teubner, 1966.

van der Meulen, Jelle. *Gebaren in de Hollandse Schilderkunst van de 17e eeuw.* Diss. Utrecht, Netherlands: Typescript, 1987.

Vasconcellos, Pereira de Mello Leite de, J. *A Figa.* Porto, Portugal: Araugo & Sobrinho, 1925.

Venantius Honorius Clementianus Fortunatus. *Opera pedestria.* Edited by B. Krusch. In: *Monumenta Germaniae Historica,* AA, 4. Berlin: Weidmann, 1885.

Vergilius Maro, Publius. *Aeneid.* Translated by J. Conington. London: Longmans, Green, 1870.

Versuch eines schwäbischen Idiotikons. Edited by K. Schmid. Berlin, Stettin, Germany: Veit, 1795.

Vetus disciplina monastica. Paris: C. Osmont, 1726.

Vidossi, Giuseppe. Note in *Archivio Glottologico Italiano* 29 (1937): 96–97.

——— "La più antica testimonianza finora nota dell'Albanese *mjekre* 'barba,' " *Saggi e Scritti Minori di folklore.* Turin, Italy: Bottega d'Erasmo, 1960. Pp. 270–81.

Vielhauer, A. "Heidentum und Evangelium im Grasland Kameruns." *Evangelische Missions-Zeitschrift* 3 (1942): 150.

Vierordt, C. F. *De iunctarum in precando manum origine Indo-Germanico.* Karlsruhe, Germany: Braun, 1851.

Vinogradoff, P. *Outlines of Historical Jurisprudence.* London: Oxford University Press, Milford, 1920.

Visser, Margaret. *The Rituals of Dinner. The Origins, Evolution, Eccentricities, and Meaning of Table Manners.* New York: Penguin, 1991.

Vita Sancti Odilonis abbatis. In *Patrologiae cursus completus . . . series secunda.* Edited by J.-P. Migne. Vol. 142. Paris: Garnier, 1880.

Völgyesi, F. A. *Die Seele ist alles. Von der Dämonologie bis zur Heilhypnose.* Zürich: Orell, Füßli, 1948.

Vogt, M. In: *Geschichte des Sports aller Völker und Zeiten.* Edited by G. A. E. Bogeng. Leipzig, Germany: Seemann, 1926.

Volsungasaga. Translated with introduction by Jesse L. Byock in *The Saga of the Volsungs.* Berkeley, Los Angeles, Oxford: University of California Press, 1990.

Voullième, E. *Quomodo veteres adoraverint.* Diss., Halle/Saale, Germany: E. Karras, 1887.

Wächter, Theodor. *Reinheitsvorschriften im griechischen Kult.* Giessen, Germany: A. Topelmann, 1910.

Wainwright, G. A. "The Earliest Use of the Mano Cornuta." *Folk Lore*, 72 (1961): 492–95.

Walahfrid Strabo. *De rebus ecclesiasticis.* In *Patrologiae cursus completus . . . series Latina.* Edited by J.-P. Migne. Vol. 114. Paris: Garnier et Migne successores, 1886.

Wallnöfer, H. and A. v. Rottauscher. *Der goldene Schatz der chinesischen Medizin.* Stuttgart, Germany: Schuler, 1959.

Waltharius. Edited and translated by K. Langosch. Darmstadt, Germany: Wissenschaftliche Buchgesellschaft, 1956.

Walther, Ingo F., ed. (with Gisela Siebert). *Codex Manesse. Die Miniaturen der Großen Heidelberger Liederhandschrift.* Frankfurt/M.: Insel, 1988.

Walther von der Vogelweide. *Die Gedichte.* Edited by H. Kuhn. Berlin: de Gruyter, 1965.

Ward, Ian. "Maori plans obscene Royal Insult." *Daily Telegraph* (London), 24 February 1986: 3.

Wehrhan, Karl. *Frankfurter Kinderleben in Sitte und Brauch, Kinderlied und Kinderspiel*. Wiesbaden, Germany: H. Staadt, 1929.

Weinert, H. *Der geistige Aufstieg der Menschheit*. Stuttgart, Germany: F. Enke, 1940.

Weisbach, Werner. *Ausdrucksgestaltung in mittelalterlicher Kunst*. Einsiedeln, Switzerland: Benziger, 1948.

Weise, Christian. *Überflüssige Gedanken*. Leipzig, Germany: Fritzsche, 1701.

———— *Die drey ärgsten Ertznarren in der gantzen Welt*. Halle/Saale, Germany: Niemeyer, 1878.

———— *Comödienprobe*. Leipzig, Germany: J. Gerdesius, 1696.

Weise, G. and G. Otto. *Die religiösen Ausdrucksgebärden des Barock und ihre Verbreitung durch die italienische Kunst der Renaissance*. Stuttgart, Germany: W. Kohlhammer, 1938.

Weissel, L. *Der Mönch von Montaudon*. Basel, Switzerland: B. Schwabe, 1882.

Weitzmann, K. "The Origins of the Threnos." In *De Artibus opuscula XL: Essays in Honor of Erwin Panofsky*. Edited by M. Meiss, New York: University of New York Press, 1961.

Wells, D. A. "Gesture in Hartmann's *Gregorius*." In *Hartmann von Aue: Changing Perspectives. London Hartmann Symposium 1985*. Edited by T. McFarland and S. Ranawake. Göppinger Arbeiten zur Germanistik. Vol. 486. Göppingen, Germany: Kümmerle, 1988. Pp. 159–86.

Wensinck, A. J. "Über das Gebetsweinen in den monotheistischen Religionen Vorderasiens." In *Enzyklopädie des Islams*. Vol. 4. Leipzig, Germany: Harrassowitz, 1910–1938.

Wentworth, H. and S. B. Flexner. *Dictionary of American Slang*. New York: Crowell, 1960.

Wenzel, Horst. *Hören und Sehen. Schrift und Bild. Kultur und Gedächtnis im Mittelalter*. Munich: C. H. Beck, 1995.

Wesselski, Albert. *Der Sinn der Sinne. Ein Kapitel der ältesten Menschheitsgeschichte*. In *Ceskoslovenskú ústav orientální v Praze. Archiv orientální*. Monografie, vol. 4. Prague: Czechoslovakia, Orientální ústav, 1934.

Weyland, W. G. *Aspero intermedio*. Buenos Aires: Botella al Mar, 1949.

Widukind of Corvey. *The Three Books of the Deeds of the Saxons*. Diss. Typescript. Los Angeles: University of California, 1949.

Wigamur. Edited by D. Büschinger. Göppinger Arbeiten zur Germanistik. Vol. 320. Göppingen, Germany: Kümmerle, 1987.

Wigand, P. *Das Fehmgericht Westfalens*. Halle/Saale: H. W. Schmidt, 1893.

Williams, Carol J. "Fischer Gambits Familiar as 'Revenge Match' Starts Up," *Los Angeles* (California) *Times*, 2 September 1992: A1.

Wilson, Edmund. *A Window on Russia*. New York: Farrar, Straus & Giroux, 1972.

Winckelmann, J. J. *Herkulaneische Entdeckungen*. In *Sämtliche Werke*. Vol. 2. Donaueschingen, Germany: Verlag deutscher Classiker, 1825–29.

Winkler, H. "Der alte Orient und die Geschichtsforschung." *Mitteilungen der vorderasiatischen Gesellschaft* 11 (1906): 124 ff.

Winsbecke. In *König Tirol, Winsbeke und Winsbekin.* Edited by A. Leitzmann. Halle/Saale: Niemeyer, 1888.

Wirnt von Gravenberg. *Wigalois.* Edited by J. M. N. Kapteyn. Bonn, Germany: F. Klopp, 1926.

Wise and Aldrich. Cartoon. "Real Life Adventures." *Daily News* (Woodland Hills, Calif.), 14 December 1995: "L.A. Life," p. 18.

Wittenweiler, Heinrich. *Der Ring.* Edited by E. Wiessner. Leipzig, Germany: 1931.

Wocel, Johann Erasmus. *Welislaws Bilderbibel aus dem 13. Jahrhundert.* Prague, Czech Republic: Tempsky-Rziwnatz, 1871.

Wodehouse, P. G. *Fish Preferred.* Mattituck, N. Y.: Rivercity Press, 1929.

Wolff-Hurden, Philipp. "Die Lichtgebärde und die grosse Hand." In *Basler Nachrichten.* Sonntagsblatt. Dec. 22, 1957.

Wolfram, Herwig. "The Huns and the Germanic Peoples." In *Attila. The Man and His Image.* Edited by F. H. Bäuml and M. Birnbaum. Budapest, Hungary: Corvina, 1993. Pp. 16–25.

Wolfram von Eschenbach. *Parzival.* Edited by K. Bartsch. Leipzig, Germany: Brockhaus, 1875.

Woodyard, Chris. "McMartin Kin Enter Pleas of Innocence." *Los Angeles* (California) *Herald Examiner,* 21 April 1984: A3.

Wundt, Wilhelm. *Völkerpsychologie. Eine Untersuchung der Entwicklungsgesetze von Sprache, Mythus und Sitte.* Leipzig, Germany: W. Engelmann, 1904.

Wuttke, A. *Der deutsche Volksaberglaube der Gegenwart.* Berlin: Wiegandt & Grieben, 1900.

Wynne, Marianne. "Hagen's Defiance of Kriemhild." In *Mediaeval German Studies Presented to Frederick Norman.* London: University of London, Institute of Germanic Studies, 1965. Pp. 104–14.

Xenophon. *Cyropaedia.* Loeb Classical Library. Cambridge, Mass.: Harvard University Press, 1960–61.

——— *Hellenika.* Edited by C. Hyde. Stuttgart, Germany: Teubner, 1969.

Zappert, G. "Über den Ausdruck des geistigen Schmerzes im Mittelalter." *Denkschriften der Akademie der Wissenschaften zu Wien* 5 (1854): 73.

Zeller, Paul. *Die täglichen Lebensgewohnheiten im altfranzösischen Karlsepos.* Marburg, Germany: N. G. Elwert, 1885.

Zigler und Klipphausen, H. A. von. *Die asiatische Banise.* In *Deutsche National-Litteratur* vol. 36. Berlin and Stuttgart: Kürschner, n.d.

Zimmerische Chronik, 2nd ed., ed. by K. A. Barack. Tübingen, Germany: Litterarischer Verein Stuttgart, 1932.

Zingerle, I. V. *Sagen aus Tirol.* Innsbruck, Austria: Wagner, 1891.

Zoega, G. *Abhandlungen.* Göttingen: Dieterich, 1817.

Zola, Emile. "Le Forgeron." In *French Short Stories.* Edited by D. L. Buffum. New York: H. Holt, 1933.

Index of Countries and Peoples

261, 265, 266, 267, 270, 273, 275,
277, 278, 279, 280, 281, 283, 284,
285, 286, 287, 289, 290, 292, 295,
296, 297, 298, 299, 302, 303, 304,
305, 306, 307, 308, 309, 310, 312,
313, 317, 319, 320, 321, 322, 324,
325, 326, 327, 328, 329, 331, 333,
335, 336, 338, 339, 340, 343, 345,
346, 347, 350, 351, 352, 354, 355,
356, 357, 358, 360, 362, 363, 370,
371, 373, 374, 375, 377, 378, 379,
380, 381, 383, 384, 385, 386, 387,
388, 389, 390, 392, 394, 395, 396,
397, 401, 402, 403, 404, 405, 406,
408, 410, 412, 415, 416, 418, 419,
423, 424, 425, 426, 427, 428, 429,
430, 432, 436, 437, 438
Ghana, 113
Gond *(India),* 105, 288
Great Britain, 90, 113, 213
Greece, 25, 26, 27, 28, 29, 30, 31, 32,
33, 35, 36, 37, 38, 39, 41, 44, 45,
46, 48, 49, 51, 54, 55, 56, 57, 59,
63, 66, 68, 69, 70, 71, 73, 74, 75,
76, 78, 79, 81, 82, 83, 84, 85, 86,
88, 89, 91, 93, 95, 96, 100, 102,
103, 105, 106, 107, 111, 112, 114,
115, 117, 122, 123, 125, 126, 127,
129, 130, 133, 134, 135, 136, 137,
139, 140, 144, 145, 150, 151, 153,
58, 161, 169, 171, 172, 173, 176,
177, 178, 185, 199, 200, 201, 202,
204, 205, 207, 208, 211, 214, 222,
224, 225, 228, 229, 230, 231, 232,
235, 236, 237, 238, 240, 246, 247,
248, 249, 250, 251, 252, 255, 257,
258, 259, 267, 268, 269, 270, 272,
273, 278, 281, 282, 283, 284, 285,
290, 292, 293, 295, 297, 303, 304,
305, 306, 308, 309, 310, 312, 313,
314, 315, 318, 320, 322, 323, 324,
327, 328, 330, 332, 336, 338, 339,
342, 343, 344, 345, 346, 347, 348,
349, 350, 351, 352, 353, 357, 358,

371, 375, 378, 379, 380, 382, 385,
386, 387, 388, 389, 390, 391, 392,
393, 394, 395, 396, 397, 398, 399,
400, 402, 403, 404, 405, 406, 407,
410, 411, 412, 415, 416, 417, 418,
419, 420, 422, 423, 424, 425, 426,
429, 430, 431, 432, 436, 437, 438,
439
Greek Orthodox, 73, 82, 84, 143, 146,
236, 262, 263, 318, 365, 405, 407,
416, 418, 424
Guam, 97, 129
Guatemala, 219, 258, 298, 335

Hadhramaut *(Yemen),* 87, 359
Hawaii, 198, 433
Hellenistic, 68, 246, 303, 406, 433
Herero *(Southwest Africa),* 364
Hesychasts, 111, 127
Hindu, 58, 111, 127, 228, 234, 318,
425, 430
Hindustan, 83
Hispanic, 113
Hittites, 134, 419
Hmong *(Laos),* 339
Honduras, 122
Hong Kong, 116, 140, 287
Hottentots *(South Africa),* 371
Hungary, 232, 353, 354, 355, 398,
423, 424
Huns, 372

Iceland, 89, 172, 328, 384, 385, 430
Inamwanga *(Tanganyika),* 288, 349
India, 37, 46, 52, 69, 70, 79, 83, 105,
107, 111, 114, 115, 132, 137, 139,
146, 154, 157, 174, 184, 185, 221,
232, 234, 237, 246, 258, 267, 287,
288, 292, 296, 297, 299, 310, 311,
312, 315, 318, 333, 334, 340, 344,
345, 381, 387, 388, 389, 392, 394,
410, 424, 428, 432, 433, 439
Indonesia, 140, 185, 257, 311, 348,
368

About the Authors

Betty J. Bäuml (B.A., M.A. in Spanish, Ohio State University; Ph.D. in Romance Languages and Literatures, University of California, Berkeley) is professor emerita of Spanish at California State University, Northridge. In addition to her research on gestures, she has been concerned principally with the work of Benito Pérez Galdos and the grotesque.

Franz H. Bäuml (Ph.D. in German, University of California, Berkeley) is professor emeritus of German at the University of California, Los Angeles, and has published widely on medieval German literature and the development of literacy in the Middle Ages.